I0748948

MILITARY PLAZA — SAN ANTONIO, TEXAS.

34th Congress, 1st Session. } HOUSE OF REPRESENTATIVES. { Ex. Doc. No. 135.

# REPORT

ON THE

# UNITED STATES AND MEXICAN BOUNDARY SURVEY,

MADE UNDER

THE DIRECTION OF THE SECRETARY OF THE INTERIOR,

BY

WILLIAM H. EMORY.

MAJOR FIRST CAVALRY AND UNITED STATES COMMISSIONER.

VOLUME I.

WASHINGTON:
CORNELIUS WENDELL, PRINTER.
1857.

## IN THE HOUSE OF REPRESENTATIVES.

AUGUST 15, 1856.

*Resolved*, That there be printed, for distribution by the members of this House, ten thousand extra copies of Major Emory's Report on the Survey of the Boundary between the United States and Mexico.

Attest: WM. CULLOM, *Clerk.*

# PART I.

# MESSAGE

FROM

# THE PRESIDENT OF THE UNITED STATES,

TRANSMITTING

*A report of the survey of the boundary between the United States and the republic of Mexico.*

---

AUGUST 4, 1856.—Laid upon the table and ordered to be printed.

---

WASHINGTON, *August* 1, 1856.

*To the Senate and House of Representatives of the United States:*

I communicate to Congress, herewith, the report of Major W. H. Emory, United States Commissioner, on the survey of the boundary between the United States and the republic of Mexico, referred to in the accompanying letter of this date from the Secretary of the Interior.

FRANKLIN PIERCE.

---

DEPARTMENT OF THE INTERIOR,
*Washington, August* 1, 1856.

SIR: I have the honor to submit to you, herewith, to be laid before Congress, a report of Major W. H. Emory, United States Commissioner, on the survey of the boundary between the United States and the republic of Mexico.

I am, sir, very respectfully, your obedient servant,

R. McCLELLAND.
*Secretary.*

The PRESIDENT OF THE UNITED STATES.

OFFICE UNITED STATES BOUNDARY COMMISSION,
*Washington, July* 29, 1856.

SIR: I have the honor to send herewith my report on the boundary between the United States and Mexico, together with proofs of such maps and illustrations as have been completed, numbered from 1 to 63. The plates and blocks from which these proofs are struck are held by me subject to your order, or that of Congress.

The general map cannot be completed until next winter, and the map of the new Territory is not quite completed, but when finished, no delay will ensue in the publication. By consultation with the printer, I find these maps will be done quite as soon as the printing of the report, should it be concluded to print that report.

Besides the volume now sent in, there will be an appendix, containing reports upon the botany and natural history of the country adjacent to the boundary, with from two to three hundred illustrations, many of which are already engraved and the plates deposited in this office. These reports are in the hands of Drs. Torrey, Engelmann, and Professor Baird, and other savans of the country. They promise to have them all finished in the course of the year. These reports not being of the same general interest, I concluded it was proper not to delay sending in the general report until their completion.

Should it be deemed proper to publish the general report and a limited number of copies of the appendix, I beg to call attention to my letter to you of April 23, 1856, by which it will be seen there is a large surplus of funds which may be made available for the purpose, and which has been saved from the appropriations made by Congress for the prosecution of the work. That surplus is at present more than $100,000.

I have the honor to be, your obedient servant,

W. H. EMORY,
*United States Commissioner.*

Hon. ROBERT MCCLELLAND,
*Secretary of the Interior.*

# CONTENTS.—PART I.

## CHAPTER I.

### PERSONAL ACCOUNT.



## CHAPTER II.

### PERSONAL ACCOUNT CONTINUED.



## CHAPTER III.

### GENERAL DESCRIPTION OF THE COUNTRY.



## CHAPTER IV.

### LOWER RIO BRAVO.

CHAPTER V.

FROM MOUTH OF DEVIL'S RIVER TO EL PASO DEL NORTE.



CHAPTER VI.

SKETCH OF TERRITORY ACQUIRED BY TREATY OF DECEMBER 30, 1853.

## CHAPTER VII.

FROM THE 111TH MERIDIAN OF LONGITUDE TO THE PACIFIC OCEAN.—REPORT OF LIEUTENANT MICHLER.

## CHAPTER VIII.

### ASTRONOMICAL AND GEODETIC WORK.



## CHAPTER IX.

### METEOROLOGY.



---

# LIST OF MAPS AND ILLUSTRATIONS OF PART I, VOLUME I, FROM ORIGINAL SURVEYS AND SKETCHES IN THE FIELD.

## ENGRAVINGS ON STEEL.

### GENERAL MAP OF THE COUNTRY WEST OF THE MISSISSIPPI, ON A SCALE OF $\frac{1}{6000000}$.

## ENGRAVINGS ON COPPER.

FOUR MAPS OF THE BOUNDARY LINE ON A SCALE OF $\frac{1}{600000}$, (NOT BOUND WITH THE REPORT.)



## ENGRAVINGS ON STONE.



## WOOD CUTS.



* The peak represented in the wood cut as "Gomez Peak," is incorrectly named in the report—it is properly called "Mitre Peak."

# ERRATA.

Page 4, line 37, for "steppes" read steps.

Page 24, line 17, for "Chas. Weiss" read John E. Weiss.

Page 24. The name C. B. R. Kennerly, surgeon, omitted, should come after J. E. Weiss.

Page 41, line 17, for "4, 000" read 5, 000.

Page 66, line 3, for "Los Adjuntas" read Las Adjuntas.

Page 70, line 21, for "Zocate" read Zoqueté.

Page 85, line 1, for "Beyonp" read Beyond.

Page 115, line 34, for "laid" read lay.

Page 120, line 19, for "present" read presents.

Page 121, line 30, for "Fonquiera" read Fouquiera.

Page 127, line 29, for "fluviatic" read fluviatile.

Page 128, line 41, for "Yumas" read Yuma.

Page 134, line 31, for "Pelatado" read Palotal.

Page 134, line 37, for "Samalurca" read Samalayurca.

Page 125, line 4, for "1, 727. 32" read 1, 730. 50.

Page 125, line 6, for "1, 695. 22" read 1, 698. 40.

Page 113, line 39, for "Manual" read Manuel.

Page 68, line 12, for "Islitas" read Islétas.

Page 123, line 17, for "Babuquivari" read Baboquivari.

Page 131. The distances from New San Diego to Fort Yuma were measured by Major N. W. Brown, paymaster U. S. A. Those from the Pacific ocean to the Gulf of Mexico, not otherwise designated, were measured under the direction of Lieut. N. Michler.

# PREFATORY REMARKS.

The instructions given to me August 15, 1854, by the Hon. Robert McClelland, Secretary of the Interior, direct that, "in all cases where they do not conflict with the stipulations of the treaty, or the specific directions contained in these instructions, you will be guided by the instructions issued by the Department of State, and those of this department, to the Commissioner, for running and marking the boundary line under the treaty of Guadalupe Hidalgo."

The instructions referred to, given to one of my predecessors, and not repealed, directed an examination of the country contiguous to the line to ascertain its practicability for a railway route to the Pacific; and also directed information to be collected in reference to the agricultural and mineral resources, and such other subjects as would give a correct knowledge of the physical character of the country and its present occupants.

A compliance with these instructions has necessarily extended this report very much beyond the limits of the record necessary to show the official acts of the joint commission.

Fifteen thousand extra copies of this report have been ordered by Congress. It consists of two volumes, divided into four parts. The first part comprises the personal narrative; general description of the country; journal of the joint commission; the astronomical work; barometrical levels; meteorological record, and magnetic observations. The second part consists of the geological researches, with annotations, and a review of the whole by Professor James Hall. The third part comprises the general botanical features of the country, by Dr. John Torrey, described from memoirs of the assistants, and from the plants themselves, and a separte description of the cactaceæ, by Dr. George Engelmann, of St. Louis. The fourth part embraces the natural history of the country, by Spencer F. Baird, based upon the notes and memoirs by the assistants, and upon the specimens themselves.

The first two parts, forming volume I, are now presented to the government; the third and fourth parts, forming volume II, are delayed in consequence of the difficulty of getting the illustrations engraved.

Accompanying the first volume are five maps: first, a general map on a scale of $\frac{1}{6000000}$, and maps numbered from 1 to 4, on a scale of $\frac{1}{60000}$, showing the boundary line and topography of the country contiguous, as far as information has been obtained from actual survey or reconnoissance. If these maps were placed in the hands of department commanders, with directions to fill up the intervals not covered by actual survey, from the best information within their reach, which, from the numerous expeditions sent out under intelligent officers of the army, is very great, the government would be in possession of delineations of our whole southern frontier, more authentic in character than the maps of many of the old States.

I have confined myself in all these maps, except the general map, to actual information, derived from instrumental survey, and in doing so, have sacrificed considerable general interest which might have been given them had I incorporated all the loose information which exists upon the subject; but I have considered that the time has come when hypothetical geography should cease, particularly when the graphic representation of a country is confided to the hands of officers of the United States army.

In all cases where I have used surveys other than those made under my orders, I have endeavored to give full credit to the officers by whom the labor was performed; and in cases where the work has been done under my own supervision, the name of each assistant has been given.

The system of borrowing, without acknowledgment, hitherto adopted, has tended very much to obscure and distort the history of the explorations and surveys of the western portion of the American continent, and has led Baron Humboldt into grave errors, and to commit personal injustice, when, in his Aspects of Nature, he attempts to present the progress of discovery in this region.

Besides the maps named in the preceding part of these remarks, fifty-four maps have been constructed, and are nearly completed, on a scale of $\frac{1}{60000}$, showing the boundary line in detail from the mouth of the Rio Bravo across the continent to where the line terminates on the Pacific ocean. These maps, to be signed jointly by the Mexican commissioner and myself, are to be deposited in the Department of the Interior, to form the official record of the boundary. They are too voluminous to admit of publication, and it is believed all the information which they contain is condensed in the five maps which are published.

Since the orders first given for this work, which contemplated, in addition, an exploration of a route for a railroad, a series of surveys have, by act of Congress, been organized under the War Department for the purpose of ascertaining the best railroad route to the Pacific ocean. All the information derived by the survey of the boundary line, including astronomical determinations, topography, and barometrical levels, have been placed at the disposal of the War Department in reference to its researches as to the routes for the railway. The thoroughness, completeness, and fairness, with which all these investigations have been conducted by the War Department, and the able manner in which all the reports and reconnoissances have been collated, have rendered it necessary for me to say but little of the practicability of the southern route, and have necessarily relieved me of the duties expected of me in this respect.

The reports from that department clearly demonstrate the practibility of a railroad route through the newly acquired territory, and go to confirm the opinion heretofore expressed by me, that it is the most practicable, if it is not the only feasible route, by which a railway can be carried across the "Sierra Nevada" and its equivalent ranges to the south.

In my report of the proceedings of the joint commission, I have omitted the correspondence which passed between the Mexican commissioner and myself, and our respective governments, upon the subject of paying the three millions of dollars, the balance of the indemnity due Mexico, and claimed by her representatives when the field-work of running and marking the boundary line was completed. That correspondence has already been printed by Congress, and will be found in Senate Ex. Doc. No. 57, 34th Congress, 1st session. It is sufficient for me to state here that I considered the claim of Mexico premature, and that the money should not be paid until the plans delineating the boundary were completed.

I conclude these remarks by appending extracts from the treaties defining the boundary between the United States and the republic of Mexico, and a copy of the commission conferring upon me the authority to run and mark the line.

*Extract from treaty, dated Guadalupe Hidalgo, February* 2, 1848.

ARTICLE V.

The boundary line between the two republics shall commence in the Gulf of Mexico, three leagues from land, opposite the mouth of the Rio Grande, otherwise called Rio Bravo del Norte, or opposite the mouth of its deepest branch, if it should have more than one branch emptying directly into the sea; from thence up the middle of that river, following the deepest channel, where it has more than one, to the point where it strikes the southern boundary of New Mexico; thence, westwardly, along the whole southern boundary of New Mexico (which runs north of the town called *Paso*) to its western termination; thence, northward, along the western line of New Mexico, until it intersects the first branch of the river Gila; (or if it should not intersect any branch of that river, then to the point on the said line nearest to such branch, and thence in a direct line to the same;) thence down the middle of the said branch and of the said river, until it empties into the Rio Colorado; thence across the Rio Colorado, following the division line between Upper and Lower California, to the Pacific ocean.

The southern and western limits of New Mexico, mentioned in this article, are those laid down in the map entitled "*Map of the United Mexican States, as organized and defined by various acts of the Congress of said republic, and constructed according to the best authorities. Revised edition. Published at New York, in* 1847, *by J. Disturnell.*" Of which map a copy is added to this treaty, bearing the signatures and seals of the undersigned plenipotentiaries. And, in order to preclude all difficulty in tracing upon the ground the limit separating Upper from Lower California, it is agreed that the said limit shall consist of a straight line drawn from the middle of the Rio Gila, where it unites with the Colorado, to a point on the coast of the Pacific ocean distant one marine league due south of the southernmost point of the port of San Diego, according to the plan of said port made in the year 1782 by Don Juan Pantoja, second sailingmaster of the Spanish fleet, and published at Madrid in the year 1802, in the Atlas to the voyage of the schooners *Sutil* and *Mexicana*, of which plan a copy is hereunto added, signed and sealed by the respective plenipotentiaries.

In order to designate the boundary line with due precision, upon authoritative maps, and to establish upon the ground landmarks which shall show the limits of both republics, as described in the present article, the two governments shall each appoint a commissioner and a surveyor, who, before the expiration of one year from the date of the exchange of ratifications of this treaty, shall meet at the port of San Diego, and proceed to run and mark the said boundary in its whole course to the mouth of the Rio Bravo del Norte. They shall keep journals and make out plans of their operations; and the result agreed upon by them shall be deemed a part of this treaty, and shall have the same force as if it were inserted therein. The two governments will amicably agree regarding what may be necessary to these persons, and also as to their respective escorts, should such be necessary.

The boundary line established by this article shall be religiously respected by each of the two republics, and no change shall ever be made therein, except by the express and free consent of both nations, lawfully given by the general government of each, in conformity with its own constitution.

---

*Extract from treaty, dated City of Mexico, December* 30, 1853.

ARTICLE I.

The Mexican republic agrees to designate the following as her true limits with the United States for the future: retaining the same dividing line between the two Californias as already defined and established, according to the 5th article of the treaty of Guadalupe Hidalgo, the limits between the two republics shall be as follows: Beginning in the Gulf of Mexico, three leagues from land, opposite the mouth of the Rio Grande, as provided in the 5th article of the treaty of Guadalupe Hidalgo; thence, as defined in the said article, up the middle of that river to the point where the parallel of * 31° 47′ north latitude crosses the same; thence due west one hundred miles; thence south to the parallel of 31° 20′ north latitude; thence along the said parallel of 31° 20′ to the 111th meridian of longitude west of Greenwich; thence in a straight line to a point on the Colorado river twenty English miles below the junction of the Gila and Colorado rivers; thence up the middle of the said river Colorado until it intersects the present line between the United States and Mexico.

* In the copy of the 4th article of this treaty, filed in the Department of State and published, this parallel is described as the parallel of 31° 47′ 30″; but it was so clearly an error of transcribing that the Mexican commissioner, with that good sense which characterized all his proceedings, agreed to ignore it. W. H. E.

For the performance of this portion of the treaty, each of the two governments shall nominate one commissioner, to the end that, by common consent, the two thus nominated, having met in the city of Paso del Norte, three months after the exchange of the ratifications of this treaty, may proceed to survey and mark out upon the land the dividing line stipulated by this article, where it shall not have already been surveyed and established by the mixed commission, according to the treaty of Guadalupe, keeping a journal and making proper plans of their operations. For this purpose, if they should judge it necessary, the contracting parties shall be at liberty each to unite to its respective commissioner, scientific or other assistants, such as astronomers and surveyors, whose concurrence shall not be considered necessary for the settlement and ratification of a true line of division between the two republics ; that line shall be alone established upon which the commissioners may fix, their consent in this particular being considered decisive and an integral part of this treaty, without necessity of ulterior ratification or approval, and without room for interpretation of any kind by either of the parties contracting.

The dividing line thus established shall, in all time, be faithfully respected by the two governments, without any variation therein, unless of the express and free consent of the two, given in conformity to the principles of the law of nations, and in accordance with the constitution of each country, respectively.

In consequence, the stipulation in the 5th article of the treaty of Guadalupe upon the boundary line therein described is no longer of any force, wherein it may conflict with that here established, the said line being considered annulled and abolished wherever it may not coincide with the present, and in the same manner remaining in full force where in accordance with the same.

ARTICLE II.

The government of Mexico hereby releases the United States from all liability on account of the obligations contained in the eleventh article of the treaty of Guadalupe Hidalgo ; and the said article and the thirty-third article of the treaty of amity, commerce, and navigation between the United States of America and the United Mexican States concluded at Mexico, on the fifth day of April, 1831, are hereby abrogated.

---

FRANKLIN PIERCE, *President of the United States of America:*

To all who shall see these presents, greeting: Know ye, that, reposing special trust and confidence in the integrity, ability, and diligence of William H. Emory, of the District of Columbia, I do appoint him to be commissioner, on the part of the United States of America, to run the boundary line between the United States and the Mexican republic according to the treaty between the two nations entered into the 30th day of December, 1853, and do authorize and empower him to execute and fulfil the duties of that office according to law; and to have and to hold the said office, with all the powers, privileges, and emoluments thereunto legally appertaining unto him, the said William H. Emory, during the pleasure of the President of the United States for the time being.

In testimony whereof, I have caused these letters to be made patent, and the seal of the Department of the Interior of the United States to be hereunto affixed. Given under my hand, at the city of Washington, the fourth [SEAL.] day of August, in the year of our Lord one thousand eight hundred and fifty-four, and of the independence of the United States of America the seventy-ninth.

FRANKLIN PIERCE.

By the President:

ROBERT McCLELLAND,
*Secretary of the Interior.*

# CHAPTER I.

## PERSONAL ACCOUNT.

ORGANIZATION OF THE COMMISSION FOR RUNNING THE BOUNDARY LINE BETWEEN THE UNITED STATES AND THE REPUBLIC OF MEXICO, UNDER THE TREATY OF AUGUST, 1848.—CHANGES IN THE HEAD OF THE COMMISSION.—GOLD MANIA IN CALIFORNIA.—FAILURE OF THE GOVERNMENT TO KEEP ITS ENGAGEMENTS.—MISAPPLICATION OF THE PUBLIC MONEY.—GENERAL MISMANAGEMENT OF THE AFFAIRS OF THE COMMISSION.—FINAL REORGANIZATION.—CORRECTION OF STATEMENTS IN MR. BARTLETT'S NARRATIVE.

The narrative of the connexion which different individuals have had with the Boundary Commission would no doubt be instructive, but the commission organized under the treaty of Guadalupe Hidalgo was changed so frequently, and the controversies between different members of the commission were so acrimonious, as to make the task both complicated and unpleasant, and the execution of it might, perhaps, be attended with injustice.

I will, therefore, confine myself to such accounts as will enable the government, should occasion require it, to trace the history of the work, or any particular portion of it, and to the correction of some erroneous impressions which have gone abroad, not under authority of the government, but of books published as a private venture.

There have been two boundaries agreed upon with Mexico—that provided for in the treaty of Guadalupe Hidalgo, August, 1848, and that which now exists as the boundary, agreed upon in the city of Mexico, December 30, 1853, and usually known as the Gadsden treaty.

The treaty under which the first commission was organized required the appointment of a commissioner and surveyor, to run and mark the boundary from the Pacific to the Atlantic, a distance following the sinuosities of the boundary of several thousand miles, extending over a portion of the Continent but little known, and diversified with much variety of climate and topography, and infested throughout its whole extent with formidable and hostile bands of Indians.

I traversed a considerable portion of the line, in the campaign of 1846 and 1847, and made a reconnoissance of the country adjacent. The information obtained formed the basis of Mr. Buchanan's specific instructions to our minister in Mexico, in reference to the boundary, which instructions, unfortunately for the country, were not carried out.

It was, no doubt, from my supposed knowledge of the country that President Polk tendered me the office of commissioner, but attached the condition that I should resign from the army. This I respectfully declined. Colonel Weller was then appointed commissioner, and I was attached to the commission as chief astronomer and commander of the escort of United States troops, which was to accompany it.

The commission was organized on a moderate plan, and proceeded, according to the terms of the treaty, to commence at a point south of San Diego, on the Pacific side. The only way to get there was by Cape Horn or by the Isthmus of Panama. Most of the commission took the latter route, and reached Panama in March, 1849, expecting to meet one of the line of mail steamers just established by the government. In this we were disappointed, and were kept in Panama, at great expense, until the middle of May.

Soon after the organization of the commission in Washington, and on the eve of departure, the news came of the discovery of fields of gold in California. This report set all "the wide awake" and unemployed men in the country in motion towards the new Eldorado, and it was with the greatest difficulty that passage to Chagres could be procured in the meanest craft. Every steamer and sailing vessel, without regard to sea-going qualities, that could be drawn from the regular channels of commerce, were put in requisition, and it was with considerable trouble that I procured a passage in the steamer Northerner, which sailed from New York.

Simultaneously with our arrival on the Isthmus, there was a precipitation upon it of all the odds and ends of the inhabitants of the Atlantic coast of North America and Europe. The state of Panama, with its mongrel race of Indians, negroes and Spaniards, with their intellects obfuscated by bigotry, and their bodies enervated by a tropical climate, was wholly unequal to the task of receiving and entertaining, in an orderly manner, such an influx of strangers. Fortunately, the mass of them was of the self-governing race of the whites of North America, and when disorder and confusion seemed inevitable, propriety resumed the sway, and a germ of civil liberty and self-government was planted for the first time in that mis-called republic, the fruits of which are now beginning to be made apparent in the new code of laws, and the extended and liberal views of some of her citizens; among whom stands conspicuously Señor Arosemena, to whose good offices we were indebted for a roof over our heads during our long delay in Panama.

It was estimated that as many as four thousand people were collected in Panama, awaiting transportation to California. The price of passage-tickets in the expected steamers rose to an exorbitant sum. Each person seemed to think that there was a limited supply of gold, and that his hopes of getting any portion of it depended upon his early arrival in the field. Panama, at that time fallen into decay, and her name, in fact, stricken from the list of commercial cities, was out of the highway of ships. Boats, something in shape and awkwardness like the "dug-outs" of the Mississippi, in use among the natives to transport fruit from the neighboring island of Toboga, were the only description of vessels that could then be obtained. The largest of them did not exceed ten or fifteen tons in capacity. Yet many were put in requisition to navigate the ocean over a space of three thousand miles, extending along a rock-bound coast, swept for a considerable portion of the way by adverse north winds. Many of the bold adventurers were wrecked, and few, if any, reached their destination in their frail barks, but were obliged to put in at Acapulco and other ports along the coast.

Seeing that there was little probability of our obtaining passage to San Diego before the middle of May, I unpacked the instruments, and set them up for the double purpose of practising my assistants and making observations at Panama for latitude and longitude, magnetic dip and intensity, and other phenomena, the results of which will be found elsewhere. The result of these observations threw much light on the geographical position and the climate of those tropical regions; but as the observations upon which they were founded were published in the fifth volume of the proceedings of the American Academy of Arts and Sciences, at Boston, it has not been considered necessary to reproduce them in this work.

When we arrived, in March, the summer or dry season was not ended, and the country was very healthy; but towards the latter end of April the rainy season set in, and with it came fever and cholera. Rejecting the sanitary precautions of abstemiousness usually resorted to in such cases, I employed a good cook, and purchased light wines, and, by a generous diet, myself and companions escaped all disease, although we were out every clear night observing—at a time when it was thought certain death to the foreigner to expose himself. I learned this agreeable preventive treatment in Vera Cruz, which I twice visited when the vomito was raging—the last time under aggravating circumstances. Being engaged in embarking my regiment, which was encamped two miles from the city, I was obliged to make frequent visits to the latter both night and day, exposed alternately to the scorching sun and the evening dews; and although frequently passing through infected districts since, it was not until the autumn of 1853 that I suffered from this disease. I attribute the attack at that time to the fact of being kept on board a ship, where, by an unexpectedly long voyage of eighteen days from Brazos Santiago to Pensacola, we were reduced to salt junk and whiskey. With the system suffering under this diet, I incautiously visited Mobile, where the epidemic was very violent. In all places where this malady has prevailed, it is undoubtedly the case that those addicted to the use of salt meats, brandy, whiskey, and the stronger wines, Madeira and Sherry, are the most likely to suffer. And we may not see any important changes in the health of the southern coast of the United States until its inhabitants shall conform to the habits of tropical nations—discard rich, unctuous food, and all alcoholic drinks, and substitute pilaus and the light wines which can be produced in the mountains of the Carolinas and Georgia, but more particularly in the champagne country of Texas.

It was not until after the middle of May that a steamer appeared in the harbor, which proved to be the "Panama," one of the line of United States Pacific mail steamers, upon which I had shipped from New York the heaviest of the astronomical instruments intended for the boundary survey, in charge of Captain Hardcastle, corps Topographical Engineers.

The "Panama" was built before the discovery of gold in California, when it was supposed but very little would be carried by her except the United States mails and the government officers passing to California and Oregon. Her tonnage was, I think, something under 1,000 tons; yet such was the irresistible press for passage to California, that when she weighed anchor to proceed on her voyage, no less than seven hundred souls, exclusive of her crew, were found to be on board. Every reasonable effort was made by Capt. Bailey and other officers of the ship to administer to our comforts, yet the voyage was of the most disagreeable and unsatisfactory character.

The treaty with Mexico required that we should be in San Diego on or before the 31st of May. We arrived there on the 1st of June, but finding the Mexican commissioner had not come, we were at once satisfied that no evil would result from the unavoidable delay. On reaching San Diego we found the escort of troops awaiting us. It was composed of company "A," 1st dragoons, commanded by Lieut. Coutts, and company "H," 2d infantry, commanded by Capt. Hayden.

San Diego appeared to me not to have changed since 1846–'47. The news of the discovery of gold in the northern part of California, produced less commotion in that quiet town than in New York or Panama. Fortunately for us, it did not feel the effect until the reaction came from the Atlantic side, some months after our arrival. Had it been otherwise, all attempts to keep together the enlisted men and laborers of the survey would have been idle, and the commission would have been disorganized before doing anything.

The Mexican commissioner arrived July 3, at San Diego, accompanied by one hundred and fifty troops. The joint commission was organized on the 6th, and on the 9th I established my observatory at the Punta, and called it Camp Riley, after the general then commanding in California, to whom we were much indebted for affording many facilities in conducting the survey. The infantry company was encamped in the valley near me, and the dragoons were sent up the valley of the Tia Juana, to a point where the grazing was good, to get in condition for the hard service upon which they were soon to be employed.

The following distribution was made of that portion of the officers and employés of the boundary commission under my direction: Aided by James Nooney and George C. Gardner, I took the personal charge of the determination of the latitude and longitude of Camp Riley, and the triangulation by which that determination was to be carried to the initial point on the Pacific; no convenient place for wood and water, which was at the same time protected from winds and the drifting sands, being nearer to the initial point than Camp Riley.

Lieut. A. W. Whipple, corps Topographical Engineers, assisted by Messrs. Parry and Ingraham, were assigned to the charge of the party to determine the other extremity of the straight line forming the boundary at the junction of the Gila and Colorado. In addition to his duties as asssistant, Dr. Parry was charged with the geological and botanical investigations to illustrate the physical geography of the country.

Capt. E. L. F. Hardcastle, corps Topographical Engineers, assisted by Mr. George C. Gardner, and escorted by Lieut. Slaughter, with a detachment on foot, was placed in charge of the party to reconnoitre the country, gain a knowledge of the topography, and select elevated points by which the extremities of the line, or the two observatories in charge of Lieut. Whipple and myself, could be connected in longitude by flashes of gunpowder.

A party under the charge of the United States surveyor, assisted by Messrs. Whiting, Taylor, and Foster, were employed in surveying the shore-line of the head of the bay, for the purpose of showing on paper the initial point of the boundary on the coast of the Pacific, described in the treaty as being one marine league south of the port of San Diego.

The portion of the boundary which the commissioner designed to run first, consisted of a straight line from a point on the Pacific ocean, one marine league south of the port of San Diego, to the junction of the Gila and Colorado. The most obvious way of determining the direction of this line was to connect the two points by triangulation, and in this way ascertain their relative positions on the face of the earth, and compute the azimuth of the line joining them. But the character of the intervening country made it impossible to pursue this mode of operating, when the time and means at our disposal were considered. Triangulation is the most accurate, but the slowest and most expensive method of surveying, even in old settled countries, where the stations to be selected are easily accessible in wagons.

The peculiarities of this country presented obstacles almost insurmountable to such an operation. The whole distance, about 148 miles, may be divided into two nearly equal parts, differing in character, but both unfavorable to geodetic operations. The first, rising in steppes from the sea, devoid of water, and covered with spinous vegetation, attains in abrupt ascents the height of five or six thousand feet above the sea in the short distance of thirty miles. From this point, for about thirty miles more, the country is occupied by a succession of parallel ridges, striking the boundary nearly at right-angles, and separated by deep and sometimes impassable chasms. It then falls abruptly to near the level of the sea. The remainder of the line stretches across the desert of shifting sand at the head of the Gulf of California, destitute for the most part of both water and vegetation, rendering it impossible to mark the boundary in the usual manner on the ground.

At the various conferences of the joint commission, the mode of conducting the survey was discussed; and it was agreed to determine the line by astronomical methods, as the only mode by which we could do so correctly and within our means. Although not then a member of the joint commission, I was invited to their consultations; and my knowledge of the country, derived from a previous exploration, was brought into requisition.

I would here be doing injustice to Colonel Weller, the United States commissioner, and General Conde, the Mexican commissioner, if I did not place their conduct in contrast with what subsequently happened, by commending the just and enlarged views which guided their early conferences, and the intelligence and liberality with which all suggestions for the guidance of the scientific operations of the commission were received and adopted by those two gentlemen.

It will be seen by those conversant with geodetic matters, that the determination I had undertaken was of no ordinary kind, and required for its success the most accurate and elaborate observations, and a skilful application of those observations by analytic formulae, involving the figure of the earth and other elements, a perfect knowledge of which has not yet been attained, although researches upon the subject have occupied the minds of the great astronomers; and the last half century has seen their labors embodied, and our knowledge brought very near perfection, by the beautiful analysis of Bessel, and the successful application of that analysis by Professor A. D. Bache.

An error in the latitude or longitude of either extremity, of a few seconds, would produce a great departure of the line from the point it was intended to strike; the utmost precision was, therefore, necessary to be observed in all determinations connected with the line.

In this operation I looked for little or no aid from the Mexican commission, for although composed of well educated and scientific men, their instruments were radically defective. Our determinations, after being re-observed and re-computed by the Mexican commission, were received by them without correction; and the actual tracing of the line on the ground by the two parties, operating in different directions from the two extremities of the line, showed their correctness. When the parties met on the desert, they were found to be so nearly on the same line, that the difference might as properly be attributed to the inaccuracy of prolonging straight lines over such vast and almost impassable tracts, as to error in the original direction.

The elaborate observations and computations by which the result was arrived at, will be found in their proper place.

It was in the month of September, while engaged in this dreary and thankless work, that intelligence was received that Colonel Weller was removed, and Mr. J. C. Fremont was substituted. This official, although he accepted the appointment, afterwards declined it, and never joined the commission. At this time Colonel Weller was absent at the north, engaged in the fruitless task of raising funds. About the same time, intelligence reached our hitherto quiet and secluded camp, of the successful accumulation of wealth by many who had gone to the gold region without a dollar in their pockets. News came, too, that was afterwards confirmed, that Colonel Weller's drafts had been protested, his disbursements repudiated, and himself denounced as a defaulter; when, at that very time, as the settlement of his accounts afterwards showed, he was in advance to the government.

The wages of common laborers employed at the port of San Diego suddenly rose to $150 per month, and of carpenters to $10 per day. Subsistence of every kind rose in proportion; the soldiers' rations from 20 cents to $1 50 per day. Our people had not been paid for some time, and we were without a dollar. This seemed more than poor human nature could bear, and one by one our force dropped off, until but four or five of the civil employés remained, and among them three persons in subordinate positions, whose fidelity, I think, deserves to be remembered—Francis Holley, Frank Stone, and my servant Robert, a slave.

I find no fault with any gentleman in civil life who left the commission at this time.

Had I not been an officer of the army in command of troops, and in charge of an important work co-operating with a foreign commission, I should have undoubtedly exercised the privilege of withdrawing. The government failed to comply with its obligations to pay the civil officers and employés their salaries, and even to supply them with the necessary subsistence. On the other hand, the field of gold was spread before them, and almost within their reach. I cannot say that any of the commission would have yielded to the temptation had those in authority been supplied with the means to pay them, or had they been invited to remain. As it was, I am not prepared to say that one left the commission without receiving and deserving an honorable discharge, and not a single member ever deserted the commission. I was at this time in a position of extreme embarrassment. It was a critical period in the progress of the work. All the preliminary steps had been taken ; the observations nearly completed at one end of the line, and the party designed for the mouth of the Gila ready to start ; the commissioner absent ; without a dollar in my pocket ; the commission dishonored at home, and without credit in the field. In this dilemma I did not hesitate to take the responsibility of using the military power in my hands to keep the work from being abandoned.

I directed the quartermaster and commissary of the army attached to the escort to furnish supplies and transportation, and I engaged to give each soldier, with the assent of his captain, when not on military duty, two dollars for each day's work done in running the boundary.

This arrangement, which was cordially approved by the commissioner, and subsequently, on a change of administration, by the government, worked well in more ways than one. While it supplied me with the manual labor necessary to carry on the work, it prevented desertion from the escort, which, in other branches of the army in California, occurred to an alarming extent; in some cases entire guards going off with their arms. Throughout the whole campaign we had but three desertions, and when I was relieved from the command I was complimented in orders from the commanding general of California for the successful manner in which the troops had been held together.

The outrage inflicted on the commission by withholding funds, and attempting to place at its head persons under influences avowedly hostile, so far from shaking my interest in the great scientific work which I had commenced, only increased my determination to complete it. At the same time I felt it my duty to resent the indignity, by tendering my resignation, to take effect on the completion of the line I had commenced, which was the only one indeed in the boundary, as then agreed upon, involving any very great degree of scientific skill. I accordingly wrote to the honorable Secretary of State the following letter :

CAMP RILEY, *September* 15, 1849.

SIR : * * * * * * * * * *

It is questionable in my mind whether the Department of State has followed up its intention, conveyed in the preliminary instructions of February 15. But if it has done so, and I am considered as occupying the position of chief astronomer and topographical engineer (of the boundary commission,) I now desire, for reasons which, in my judgment, form an insurmountable obstacle to the proper performance of these duties, to be relieved from all duty on the commission.

I request the person may be designated to whom the instruments in my custody shall be turned over. They are at present distributed between Captain Hardcastle, Lieut. Whipple, Mr. A. B. Gray, and myself. In due season an account will be rendered of my astronomical determinations on this work, and the commission will be furnished with the result.

By the time of receiving my recall, I hope to have finished the determination of the astronomical line forming the boundary between the Pacific and the mouth of the Gila river, and it will be a convenient point for the transfer of the work to other hands.

* * * * * * * * * * *

I am, sir, very respectfully, your obedient servant,

W. H. EMORY.

In reply to this letter I received, almost simultaneously, the two following letters:

WASHINGTON, *November* 21, 1849.

SIR: Your letter of the 15th of September has been received. I learn from it with regret that you wish to be relieved from your duties as astronomer and topographical engineer, in connexion with the commission, on the part of the United States, for marking the boundary pursuant to the treaty of Guadalupe Hidalgo. Your claims and peculiar aptitude for that service were so generously acknowledged, that there was every reason to hope you might not be severed from the commission until the close of the business confided to it. Entertaining no doubt, however, that the reasons to which you allude are sound, and that the public will derive advantage from your employment in any other professional duty which may be assigned to you, your request is acceded to, and in a letter of this date I have requested the Secretary of War to designate your successor. In regard to the civil assistants to whom you refer, it is presumed that it would be best for them to remain, with a view to aid your successor in the discharge of his duties.

I am, sir, very respectfully, your obedient servant,

J. M. CLAYTON.

WASHINGTON, *November* 28, 1849.

SIR: The letter addressed to you by this department under date of 21st has been detained for the purpose of being sent by the officer whom the Secretary of War might appoint as your successor. It appears, however, from the communication of Mr. Crawford of this date, a copy of which is enclosed, that the order for your relief, which had been requested of him, would be so greatly inconvenient to the military service that he deems himself constrained to deny the request.

Under these circumstances, it is hoped that you will continue to discharge the duties of commander to the escort and chief astronomer to the commission, with the same fidelity and ability by which you have attained your high professional and personal character.

I am, sir, very respectfully, your obedient servant,

J. M. CLAYTON.

Major W. H. EMORY, *Astronomer, &c., &c.*

It might be supposed, after the receipt of these letters, that the desperate condition in which the affairs of the boundary commission had been left, by the neglect to supply it with funds, had at last received the attention of the authorities at Washington, and that a brighter day was dawning on our work. Unfortunately for us, just after these letters were written, the work was transferred from the Department of State to the Department of the Interior, and these promising hopes were doomed to disappointment.

With the organization above described depending chiefly upon the military officers and escort attached to the commission, I completed the determination of the latitude and longitude of the two observatories near the extremities of the line, and proceeded to transfer, by triangulation, the determination of Camp Riley to the initial point on the Pacific. Although this was accomplished by a single triangle, the longest side of which was not five miles, such was the peculiarity of the atmosphere rendering objects near the coast indistinct, that I was nearly two months in completing this work satisfactorily. I had now lost nearly all my assistants, and the computation of the azimuth of the line and the tracing of the line on the face of the earth were done with no other aid than that of Captain Hardcastle and assistant Gardner and the infantry soldiers of the escort. Lieutenant Whipple, with the cavalry escort, was still at the junction of the Gila and Colorado, faithfully aided by the escort and assistants Parry and Ingraham.

In the mean time Colonel Weller had received official information that he was removed, and a successor, as before stated, was named who was to relieve him. His successor, however, never appeared, and things remained in a state of suspense until the receipt of the following letter:

DEPARTMENT OF THE INTERIOR,
*Washington, January* 8, 1850.

SIR: Mr. John B. Weller having been relieved from duty, as head of the commission to survey the boundary line between the United States and Mexico, and the direction of said commission having, therefore, fallen temporarily upon you, I have to request that the persons employed on the work may be reduced to the lowest number consistent with the proper though economical management of the business confided to you, by the discharge of all such as are not indispensable to the proper performance of the work, and whose services can therefore be dispensed with without detriment.

The number of surveyors ought not to exceed three; and in reducing the force you will have a view to the suggestions of Col. Abert to Lieut. Col. McClelland, a copy of which is enclosed.

I am, sir, very respectfully, your obedient servant,

T. EWING, *Secretary.*

Major W. H. EMORY, *San Diego, California.*

Upon the faith of these instructions, emanating, as they did, from the fountain-head of the authority of the government of the United States, I proceeded to reorganize the commission and make arrangements for the continuation of the survey of the line, and placed one efficient party in the field, under the charge of Capt. E. L. F. Hardcastle, and organized another to send by the most expeditious route to the Paso del Norte, on the Rio Grande, at which point it was agreed by the joint commission to meet in November of the same year, (1850.) A schedule of the reorganization and an application for funds, with an urgent letter showing our necessities, were sent and received by the Department of the Interior, and the following answer was returned:

Department of the Interior,
*Washington, April* 10, 1850.

Sir: Your letter from San Diego, (without date,) enclosing papers marked 1 to 4, has been received.

The bill to supply deficiencies of appropriation for the present fiscal year, containing an appropriation for the boundary service, has passed the House and is now before the Senate, but will not probably be disposed of by that body in time to enable me to forward a remittance to you by the steamer which sails on the 13th instant. Funds will be sent to you, however, by the next departure from New York.

Your views as to the further prosecution of the work are generally approved, but you will receive more specific instructions by the next steamer; and you will in the mean time go on as you propose.

The monuments are in course of preparation, and will be sent as soon as practicable.

I am, sir, very respectfully, your obedient servant,

T. EWING, *Secretary.*

Major W. H. Emory, *U. S. A., San Diego, California.*

Here is not only a distinct approval of my proceedings, but a promise that funds should be sent by the next steamer. Yet it will challenge belief when I state no money was sent, and the reorganization was practically repudiated by the appointment, for the second time, of a commissioner (Mr. J. R. Bartlett) to succeed Col. Weller, and new assistants were appointed, omitting all those appointed by me, under the authority and with the approbation of the Secretary himself.

To understand fully this extraordinary and inexplicable proceeding, and to give a comprehensive view of the gross injustice done not only to the individuals, but to the government, it must be borne in mind that we were co-operating with a foreign government in a great public undertaking, and that the few assistants who remained, faithfully performing their duties, did so at the sacrifice of going to the mines of California, where certain wealth awaited all who went at that time.

Congress also, with a just liberality which always characterizes it when legislating for those who are faithfully performing their duty, had voted $50,000 to pay the deficiencies due this very party. Not one cent of it was paid, as Congress designed, but it was improperly, if not illegally, diverted from its channel and given to the new commissioner, who expended it before he got on the ground, and incurred debts in addition far exceeding this sum. The persons for whom this money was intended, who had honorably sacrificed the certainty of private fortune to a sense of duty, were left in the field without pay and without subsistence.

It was hard to believe, and still harder to comprehend, that such an act of injustice could be perpetrated in a republican government. But when the fact became undoubted, and there was no longer hope, I called the small party together, and informed them that I should leave them to finish the line, as my instructions authorized me to do, in charge of a tried and faithful officer, Captain Hardcastle, and I would go to Washington in the first boat, to represent in person their situation. It was all that could be done in the case, and nothing else could be satisfactory after the clear breach of faith perpetrated twice, and in both instances, apparently, without the shadow of excuse.

On reaching Washington, I found a change had taken place in the office of Secretary of the Interior, and that the new Secretary, the Hon. A. H. H. Stuart, among the first acts of his administration, had sent relief to my party. By the aid of the means then furnished, the work was completed on the Pacific side, and the party returned to Washington in September, 1851.

Before leaving the Pacific coast, orders were sent me to turn over all the instruments, and the persons to whom they were turned over were directed to take them to El Paso, overland, by way of the junction of the Gila and Colorado.

The country to be traversed, as far as then known, was of the most difficult character, and almost impassable for wagons. The wages of teamsters and other laborers was $150 per month ; mules, and all the means of subsistence, at a proportional price ; and not a wagon was in the possession of the boundary commission. I reported all these facts, and showed the difficulty of complying with the order if we had funds ; and, in addition to the natural obstacles interposed, it was well known there was not a cent in my hands ; yet in the face of my remonstrances, the orders were reiterated, and, so far as my efforts went, were faithfully executed ; but, as might be supposed, the persons who were charged with the performance of this duty utterly failed to accomplish it.

Foreseeing this result, and thinking it all-important that we should have a party on the ground in time to meet the commission at El Paso on the first Monday in November, the day on which they agreed to meet, and also that all the topographical information might be gained necessary to enable the commission to come to a proper decision on the point to be selected as the initial point of the boundary on the Rio Grande, I took the responsibility of ordering Lieutenant Whipple, with a suitable supply of instruments, to proceed to El Paso, by the way of Panama to New Orleans, and thence take the smooth road through Texas in wagons. But for this, the commission would have been at El Paso without an astronomical instrument, and without persons capable of using them, and wholly dependent upon the Mexican commission. A couple of weeks preceding my arrival from the Pacific, intelligence reached the department that the affairs of the new commission had fallen into great disorder at El Paso, and the Secretary of the Interior applied to the Department of War for me, by name, to be reassigned to the duty of astronomer, &c., to the boundary ; but the intervention of the Bureau of Topographical Engineers caused another officer to be named in my place. I was quite satisfied to have nothing more to do with a mixed commission, governed by persons wholly unused to public affairs, and ignorant of the first principles of the scientific knowledge involved in the questions to be determined by them ; but in little less than a year from this time, (September 13, 1851,) I was directed to proceed to El Paso and resume my duties, by taking charge of the survey of the boundary.

On the 15th I left Washington, and, after a dreary march across the prairies and uplands of Texas, reached El Paso in November, and resumed my duties in the field on the 25th of that month.

Having in view the difficulties of transportation over such a vast extent of country, uninhabited by civilized races, and infested by nomadic tribes of savages, I recommended, when in temporary charge of the commission, that the number of civil employés and assistants on the footing of officers should be reduced to fifteen. This recommendation was seemingly approved, yet on reaching the boundary commission I found that this number had been increased at one time to as many as one hundred and upwards ; and although it had been greatly reduced, when I reached the scene of operations there were still a great many, the most of whom were unemployed, and, with the exception of one or two, none were fitted for the service on which they were engaged; most of them ignorant of the first principles of surveying, and embroiled in feuds with each other, and arrayed in hostility either to the commissioner or to the head of the scientific corps.

The commissioner was absent on an expedition into Sonora, the commission was in debt, and not one cent was at my disposal to prosecute the survey. Beyond running an erroneous line a degree and a half west of the del Norte, and starting a party, with limited means, under Lieutenant Whipple, to survey the Gila, and another to survey the Rio del Norte from the point established by the commissioner, nothing had been done.

The situation was one of extreme embarrassment; but finding officers and men sufficient who were willing to undertake the work upon credit, I immediately established an observatory at Frontera, one at San Elceario, and another at Eagle Pass, and placed two surveying parties in the field in addition to those already out. In carrying out this design I was much aided by Mr. Magoffin, an influential and wealthy citizen residing near El Paso, with whom I had made the campaign in 1846, which resulted in the conquest of that country.

Clear and distinct representations were made of the condition of things to the Department of the Interior, and recommendations made to reduce and re-organize the commission which had been formed by the preceding administration on a scale preposterous in magnitude and absurd in principle. It was oppressed with a multitude of officers, quartermasters, commissaries, paymasters, agents, secretaries, sub-secretaries—all officers wholly unknown to any well regulated surveying corps, and worse than useless by the conflict of authority which these officers engendered, and the enormous expense which the payment of their salaries and personal expenses entailed on the commission.

The sum of five hundred thousand dollars had been expended, and I can safely say that not more than one hundred thousand had been appropriately used in running and marking the boundary up to that time, and all the work that could be said to be fairly accomplished was that done by the first commission—the completion of the line from the initial point on the Pacific to the junction of the Gila and Colorado rivers.

At the same time that I wrote a full account to the Department of the Interior of the condition of affairs in the field, and urged the necessity of immediate re-organization and relief in money, I despatched a special messenger, Mr. Edward Ingraham, with thirteen rifles, through the Indian country, in the direction of the Pimo villages on the Gila, to see if any intelligence could be had of the commissioner, with a letter to him representing in urgent terms the necessity for immediate aid. I entertained the reasonable expectation that from one or the other of these sources help would be obtained; and so believing, I did not hesitate to make all the necessary purchases to prosecute the work.

Although the Rio Bravo, from El Paso to its mouth, has been frequently mapped, it will surprise many to know, that up to the time when I commenced the survey, by far the largest portion of it had never been traversed by civilized man. This surprise will, however, cease when the reader reaches that part of the report which treats of the physical geography of the country, and his eye rests on the sketches by which it is illustrated. He will then see the impassable character of the river; walled in at places by stupendous rocky barriers, and escaping through chasms blocked up by huge rocks that have fallen from impending heights, where, if the traveller should chance to be caught in a freshet, inevitable destruction would be the consequence.

The plan adopted for the survey was to touch the river at convenient intervals, accessible to wagons, determine those points astronomically, establish depots for the surveying parties, and connect the intervening spaces by lineal survey. I attended in person to the astronomical work and the establishment of the depots. Lieutenant Michler, and assistants Von Hippel and Chandler, were placed in charge of the three surveying parties, and to their able assistance I am much indebted for the successful execution of the plan.

It would subserve no useful purpose to recite the difficulties which we encountered in the prosecution of this work. Superadded to the physical obstacles to be overcome, the men became almost insubordinate from the long absence of the commissioner from the work, and his unpardonable neglect to furnish money for their payment. Some of them had not received any pay for eighteen months, and the commissioner was at that moment, with an equipage and corps of attendants, visiting the States of Chihuahua and Sonora, and the Geysers of California—places sufficiently distant from the line.

When at Presidio del Norte, about one-third of the way down the river, the men, disgusted with long-deferred "promises to pay," became very mutinous; and on one occasion, I was obliged to put down a riot in my camp, single-handed, and at the risk of being shot by an insubordinate fellow, insane from the effects of the intoxicating mezcal. Shortly after, a whole party rebelled and refused to proceed further. Fortunately, at this moment I received, by an express sent out to intercept the mail from San Antonio to El Paso, an order from the Secretary of the Interior, authorizing me to draw on the department for a limited amount of funds. At this time, there was passing from Chihuahua to San Antonio a return merchant train with $5,000 in specie, which I obtained and turned over to the person acting as disbursing agent. With this sum I was enabled to pay off a portion of the men, and discharge the disaffected.

It was not until late in the fall of 1852 that we reached Eagle Pass (Fort Duncan) with the survey, having encountered no disaster, except the suspension of the work of Mr. Chandler's party, which was wrecked in the Cañon of the Rio Bravo, one hundred and twenty miles above the mouth of the Pecos. In the mean time, Mr. Michler's party had carried the survey from the mouth of the Pecos to Loredo.

At this stage of the work, just one year after my return to it, I received the first letter or notice of the commissioner, who sent me a check for twelve thousand dollars, which was handed over to Mr. Tansill, the disbursing agent, who, before he completed the negotiation of the note, received notice that it was dishonored. The work was, at the same time, inconvenienced by our receiving intelligence that the check for five thousand dollars was repudiated at Washington, which I had drawn upon the faith of the written order of the Secretary of the Interior, and which had been cashed by an unsuspecting and honest American merchant.

I considered that any attempt to push the work further, under the circumstances, was not called for on my part. The following letters were addressed to the commissioner, and all work was suspended except that of myself and personal assistants:

CAMP NEAR FORT DUNCAN, *October* 30, 1852.

SIR: I received your two checks—one for $12,000, the other for $8,000. The merchants here refused to cash them, alleging that similar drafts had been protested in Washington.

Unfortunately, a few days afterwards, notification was served on me, through one of the leading houses here, that a small draft drawn by me, under the authority of the Secretary of the

Interior, at Presidio del Norte, and without which the work would have been suspended at that point, had also been protested.

The protest was dated after the deficiency bill and the appropriation bill had become laws of the land. This settled the business. I had before this sent an agent to San Antonio to see what could be done, and unofficial advices are this day received, informing me the largest draft has fallen into hands of persons having, I know, large and just claims against the commission; so the whole object of my requisition, which was to have twenty thousand dollars here in cash to discharge and reorganize parties concentrating on this point, is defeated.

I made the requisition for that limited amount, supposing you, of course, would follow on immediately and join me here. Under these circumstances, seeing the work about to be suspended and myself placed in so false a position, I immediately, on the receipt of the notification that my draft was repudiated in Washington, despatched Lieutenant Michler to ascertain the cause, and correct, if possible, the delinquencies.

I have now been one year on this work without receiving a dollar from you, and have been obliged to sustain it by a system of credits, promises and threats, wholly unknown to our government. Considering the munificent appropriations made by Congress, I cannot think the survey has received anything like its just proportion of the funds.

I received by mail your letter informing me you could not keep your engagement to meet me at this place; in consequence of which I have this day made a requisition for funds directly on the Department of the Interior, to prevent, if possible, a suspension of the work, and the scenes of disorder that must ensue if the parties collecting here are detained for want of means to send them on or discharge them.

I regret to learn by your letter that you have taken Mr. Radziminski and assistants with you, as two opportunities presented themselves since your arrival, and that of Mr. Whipple, at El Paso, by either of which he and his party could have joined us with ease and safety.

I regret to learn, also, from Lieutenant Whipple, that you have not seen proper to furnish him with funds. I understood your letter as agreeing to my proposition that it was necessary to furnish with funds each chief of party.

So many and so complicated have become the difficulties growing out of the long continued absence of yourself, in whom rest all the moneyed powers of the commission, that I would, to obviate them and other difficulties, leave my work and go to any point to meet you; but your letter is indefinite both as to time and place of meeting, and, for the present, I content myself with sending this to the place you name as the most probable to meet you—Camargo, or rather Ringgold barracks, the American post opposite.

My estimate for the year 1852 was $90,000; not a cent too much, though many of the items in that estimate would, from my increased experience, now be changed. This estimate was made at El Paso in duplicate, accompanied by letter. One copy was directed to you at, I think, San Diego, and the other copy was directed to you through the Department of the Interior. If you were not in place to receive it, that is no fault of mine, and surely can never be used as a reason for the distressing and unusual condition in which I am placed, both personally and officially, by the total failure to keep the working people of this commission supplied with a portion of the munificent funds voted by Congress for this work.*

* For a statement of all the money voted by Congress for this survey, see statement at the end of this chapter.

At El Paso, to avoid stopping the work, and to relieve the immediate necessities of individuals, I certified to the correctness of accounts, and the individuals sold them to shavers and brokers.

This necessity should never occur in government work, as it leads to speculation, and is injurious to the credit of the government.

Should this meet you, I desire you will send me, with as little delay as possible, twenty thousand dollars in cash, and cause thirty thousand to be placed to my credit either in New Orleans or at Fort Brown. Should you do so, the requisition on the government, if complied with, will not be used.

I am, sir, very respectfully, your obedient servant,

W. H. EMORY.

JOHN R. BARTLETT, Esq.,
*United States Commissioner.*

RINGGOLD BARRACKS, *December* 20, 1852.

SIR: The drafts drawn by me, under authority of the Secretary of the Interior, and the drafts sent me by you from El Paso, were all protested. Notice of this, and other circumstances beyond my control, caused me, in effect, to stop operations about the 5th of November, since which time I have been, as directed by the Secretary, awaiting your arrival; so that we have, in fact, been at work one year, without receiving a dollar from the government; and many of the employés have not been paid for a much longer time. As stated to you in conversation, at Presidio del Norte, a panic seized a large number of the men—first, with the idea that they never were to be paid, and, second, with a fear of the Indians.

Being in a country wholly remote from any aid, I found it absolutely necessary to keep the men in service; and upon the faith of orders from the department, and the expectation of soon meeting you, I promised they should be paid and discharged at Fort Duncan. I desire now to take the only remaining step left to enable me to redeem that pledge, and to request, if there is a dollar left, it may be distributed among these men.

Enclosed is a list of officers and men in the service, and the amounts due to each up to November 20, 1852. Subsequent revision of the accounts may show a slight alteration.

| | |
|---|---|
| The total amount of this list is | $16,439 |
| The pay, &c., up to this time will be, in addition | 7,000 |
| To which is to be added a check for $12,000 drawn by you in my favor, and turned over to T. W. Tansill, quartermaster of the boundary commission, accepted by Messrs. Lewis & Groesbeck, expended in drafts by Mr. Tansill, and subsequently repudiated by Messrs. Lewis & Groesbeck | 12,000 |
| There is also due, chiefly in San Antonio, about $8,000, the amount of the drafts drawn by me, under the authority of the Secretary, not accepted | 8,000 |
| | 43,439 |

I think it unnecessary to make a requisition on you for a further prosecution of the work until the above demands are satisfied.

I am, sir, very respectfully, your obedient servant,

W. H. EMORY,
*Bt. Maj. U. S. A., Chief Astronomer Survey B. C.*

J. R. BARTLETT, Esq., *U. S. Commissioner.*

After making the best arrangements I could to satisfy the various demands of the men and other creditors of the commission, I repaired to Ringgold barracks, where it was reported the commissioner would strike the boundary on his return trip from Mexico. There I awaited his arrival, occupying my time by establishing an observatory, to be used in the event of the resumption of the work.

On the 20th of December the commissioner arrived; and finding that no security could be given for the payment of the debts already contracted, or for those necessary to be contracted in the future prosecution of the work, I did not hesitate to avail myself of the authority granted by the Secretary to suspend the work of the survey of the river. A resolution of Congress had already suspended the survey west of the river.

After turning over all the property and papers of the commission, except the instruments and notes of the survey, I repaired to Washington city, and commenced the computation of the field-work as far as it had been completed.

In the month of March, 1853, Congress appropriated a sum of money to complete the survey of so much of the Rio Bravo as constituted the boundary, and to prosecute the office-work of the survey. The commission was immediately reduced and reorganized. A new commissioner (being the fourth) was appointed.

The parties were organized by me, and placed in the field in less than a month; and by the middle of December, 1853, all the field-work was completed within the time and for a less amount than had been estimated.

The following is the organization under which the work of the old boundary was concluded:

Robt. B. Campbell, U. S. commissioner.
Lucius Campbell, secretary.
W. H. Emory, chief astronomer and surveyor.
G. C. Gardner, assistant.
J. H. Clark, do.
Lieut. Michler, corps Topographical Engineers, in charge of surveying party.
E. A. Phillips, assistant.
Ed. Ingraham, do.
Chas. Radziminski, in charge of surveying party.
Thos. W. Jones, assistant.
Jas. H. Houston, do.
Arthur Schott, in charge of surveying party.
M. Seaton, assistant.
J. E. Weiss, do.

Capt. George Thom, corps Topographical Engineers, was left in charge of the office-work, assisted by assistants Chandler, Herbst, Thom, Wheaton, and O'Donoghue.

The collation of the geological work was left in charge of Drs. Hall and Parry; that of the zoological, in charge of Prof. Baird; and the botanical, in charge of Prof. Torrey.

Lieut. Michler was assigned to the unfinished work above Eagle Pass, Schott to the survey from Laredo to Ringgold barracks, and assistant Radziminski to the survey from Ringgold barracks to the mouth of the Rio Bravo; whilst I, with assistants Gardner and Clark, determined astronomically the points along the boundary, intended as checks upon the accuracy of the surveys.

Before the completion of the work, the yellow fever made its appearance, and myself and several of the assistants were attacked—some on the line, and others after leaving it and reaching the northern shores of the Gulf of Mexico, where this disease raged with unusual violence.

No serious inconvenience was experienced, however, in the prosecution of the work, from this cause, and nothing happened to interrupt the harmonious and rapid execution of the field work, but the melancholy loss of assistant Thomas Walter Jones, who was drowned in the Rio Bravo by the upsetting of a skiff, in which he was returning to camp from his labors in the field, on the evening of 23d July, 1853. His body was found two days after, a few miles down the stream, and was buried by his afflicted companions at the rancheria of Dr. Merryman, on the banks of the Rio Bravo.

This ends the narrative of the operations in the field of the various commissions organized under the treaty of Guadalupe Hidalgo.

It is proper for me, however, before closing this chapter, to refer to a publication issued by Mr. J. R. Bartlett, one of the late commissioners on the part of the United States, which professes to give an accurate account of the affairs of the commission. It is not my purpose to review that work, and expose its errors, but simply to correct some statements affecting myself.

Mr. Bartlett's principal achievement on the boundary was the agreement with General Conde, the Mexican commissioner, fixing the initial point on the Rio Bravo, in the parallel of 32° 22′, instead of a point as laid down on the treaty map about eight miles above El Paso, which would have brought it to the parallel of 31° 52′. That agreement is no less remarkable than the adroitness and success with which Mr. Bartlett convinced the authorities at Washington of its correctness.

The question has been so thoroughly discussed, that a reproduction of it here is not called for. It is sufficient to say, that it was disapproved by the astronomer and surveyor on the commission at the time, and was finally repudiated by the government. Mr. Bartlett, in his account of the matter, states I was ordered to sign the map of his initial point, and that I did sign it. But he does not state what was the purport or meaning of my signature, nor does he give my letter which reported the circumstances to the government; but only an extract of that letter, selecting paragraphs of it to suit his own views. I here supply the deficiency by giving the letter in full, and the agreement signed by myself and Mr. Salazar, the Mexican commissioner, who succeeded General Conde. It will be seen that the Secretary of the Interior took the responsibility of making the action of the two commissioners final, thereby rendering the joint commission authorized by the treaty, as I understood it, a nullity. In view of such an interpretation, my signature as surveyor was only required, as alleged, to perfect the *official documents;* the words of the order were, "*You will sign the map of the initial point agreed upon by the two commissioners.*"

By reference to the treaty it will be seen that any agreement of the kind required the action of the joint commission, and that the joint commission was to be composed, not only of the *two* commissioners, but of the two surveyors also.

I refused to recognise the act as that of the joint commission, and signed the map as the order directed, carefully and studiously attaching a certificate that it was the initial point of the two *commissioners;* and to prevent the possibility of misconstruction, an agreement in writing was entered into with Mr. Salazar, and our signatures attested by witnesses, showing that the map was only that of the boundary agreed upon by the two commissioners, and nothing else.

This course, while it permitted me to obey a specific order in writing from a superior, left the government free to act, and repudiate the agreement by the two commissioners, as it subsequently did.

It is evident that any other course would have resulted in committing the government, irretrievably, to an erroneous determination of our southern boundary. It is but just, however, to Mr. Bartlett, to state, that so far as the facility for a route for a railway to the Pacific was considered, the line agreed to by him was no worse than that claimed by his adversaries. My own reports, based upon previous explorations, had presented the whole case very clearly to view. Yet these reports were overlooked, and it was ignorantly represented that while Mr. Bartlett's line lost the route for the railway, the other line secured it. I will not here fatigue the reader by a topographical description of the country, showing where the obstacles to a railway route exist; but he will see by a glance at the map, that the practicable route so adjudged by myself, and by other officers who retraced my steps and re-surveyed this country, is to the south of both these lines of boundary claimed under the treaty of Guadalupe Hidalgo.

In this same book, Mr. Bartlett claims to have produced the first correct map of the Gila. He labors to place himself on the footing of an explorer of a new country, and only mentions previous explorers of that river to repudiate them.

On page 192, volume II, Mr. Bartlett, in his personal narrative, says: "It is also proper to state, that Lieutenant Whipple and Mr. Gray found the bend of the river to be much greater than is laid down by Major Emory on his map." It would have been no more than truth required, for Mr. Bartlett to have stated, what I expressly state in my printed memoir accompanying this map, that I did not explore this bend, but laid it down from conjecture. It is a small affair, subtended by a chord of thirty or forty miles. I passed over the chord, and not the bend, and so stated.

The survey of that bend is given in the map of this report, and it will be seen it differs from that laid down by Mr. Bartlett as the first correct map of the Gila. A comparison of his map with that published by me in 1846 will show that, with the exception of this bend, which he has laid down erroneously, he has copied literally my map of 1846, even those parts laid down conjecturally.

The reconnoissance of the Gila made by me in 1846 was under adverse circumstances, made, I may say, in the face of the enemy; yet it has stood the test of re-survey, and Mr. Bartlett has added to the injustice of attempting to depreciate my labors, the meanness of appropriating them.

On the same page, and in the same spirit, Mr. Bartlett says: "Mr. Gray, in his official letter to the Secretary of the Interior, from San Diego, says that many errors of others who have been along this river, in astronomical observations, were corrected by Lieutenant Whipple."

As I am the only person who ever made an astronomical observation on the Gila, previous to my sending Lieutenant Whipple there, who was one of my assistants on the boundary, I am the person referred to.

The points selected by him, and those selected by me in 1846, are not identical, and no survey connected them; they therefore, as a general rule, cannot be compared directly with each other. Fortunately, however, the only point determined elaborately by Mr. Whipple can be placed in direct comparison with my reconnoissance in 1846. By reference to my journal, published by Congress in 1847, it will be seen I observed with the sextant, in 1846, at a camp about one mile and a half south of the junction of the Gila and Colorado, and obtained for the—

Latitude of the camp.............................................................. 32° 44′ 09″
Longitude west of Greenwich.................................................... $7^h$ $38^m$ $28^s.6$

Lieutenant Whipple, under my orders, determined the junction with a 36-inch transit, and a 46-inch zenith telescope, to be in—

Latitude.............................................................................. 32° 43′ 32″.3
Longitude............................................................................ $7^h$ $38^m$ $11^s.8$

Upon this determination of Lieutenant Whipple's being recomputed by Professor Hubbard and myself, introducing the new element of the corresponding observations at Greenwich, furnished by Professor Airy, we obtained—

For latitude.......................................................................... 32° 43′ 23″.3
For longitude........................................................................ $7^h$ $38^m$ $24^s.27$

Now, if we make allowance for this mile and a half, which was not accurately measured, we find a coincidence in the two results truly remarkable, considering that I used, in 1846, only a reconnoitring instrument, a small Gambey sextant.

The above will show that Mr. Bartlett had no authority, in fact, for what he states; and to show, further, that he has given currency to an insinuation neither justified by facts nor by reliable information within his reach, I give the following letter of Lieutenant Whipple, who made the re-survey of the Gila, and who is the only person from whom Mr. Bartlett could derive his information:

WASHINGTON, *June* 13, 1853.

DEAR SIR: Your note of this date communicates a paragraph from "Bartlett's Personal Narrative," stating that Mr. Gray, in his official letter to the Secretary of the Interior, from San Diego, relating to the survey of the Gila, says, "that many errors of others who have been along this river, in astronomical observations, were corrected by Lieut. Whipple."

If the above was intended, as you infer, to throw discredit on your astronomical labors in 1846, I do not hesitate to pronounce it unjust. *During the progress of the survey and afterwards*, I freely expressed my admiration of the general precision with which the Gila had been laid down upon the map from your astronomical observations.

I am, very respectfully, your obedient servant,

A. W. WHIPPLE.

CAMP NEAR FORT DUNCAN, *October* 1, 1852.

SIR: I have the honor to acknowledge this day the receipt of your letter enclosing me the commission of United States surveyor, for running and marking the line between the United States and the republic of Mexico.

Your letter enclosing the appointment was handed me on the 30th of January at Samalurca, in Mexico, together with a letter of instructions, and a copy of instructions to the commissioner, dated November 4, defining the duties of the surveyor, and directing me to be governed accordingly.

I have been hoping from that day to this to have an interview with the United States commissioner, but have not, in consequence of his absence, nor have I received any communication from him whatever, until the day on which I broke up my camp at the Presidio del Norte, August 20. I received by express a letter from him, a copy of which is herewith enclosed, by which it will be seen he arrived at El Paso on the 16th of August, and proposed to meet me at this place.

There are several points in these instructions, based, as I have reason to believe, upon erroneous information conveyed to the Secretary; and as I believe the commissioner to whom they refer as directly as to myself will concur with me in the recommendation I design making, I have, for obvious reasons, deferred making them until his arrival, and shall defer doing so with the hope of at length meeting him. In the mean time I have pushed the survey with unceasing diligence and economy; and many subjects now press so closely, that it is necessary for me to communicate directly with the Secretary, and no longer await the arrival of the commissioner.

I have carried the survey down as far as Laredo, with the exception of a small space still to be covered between the great Chizo Cañon and the Rio San Pedro. On this portion two parties are now operating. One was disbanded and reorganized by me in consequence of a panic which seized it in regard to the Indians; and the other has within these last few days been surrounded by Indians, forced to abandon the survey, retire to the hills, and send in for aid.

To the first I was obliged to give the entire escort, and pass through the infested country myself without a soldier; to the last I gave all the spare men I had; and it was also furnished, at my request, by Major Lamotte, commanding at Las Moras, with five infantry soldiers. This region is the thoroughfare for all the bad Indians on the frontiers. I have passed through it myself without damage, and I hope the two parties will do the same; but enough has happened to justify me in having in previous communications so often urged the necessity of additional escort, and I have now respectfully to request that the Secretary will apply to the War Department to furnish a company of soldiers to escort either of these parties should they be again driven back; below here no escort will be required.

The parties have each been so well reinforced, I do not believe either of them will have any further trouble, for all work bravely and cheerfully; but if they should, it would cause much delay unless a company of soldiers is held in hand to send them.

On my reaching the ground to take charge of the survey, November, 1851, I found that Mr. Bartlett and the acting surveyor had agreed upon the initial point, 32° 22', and that a great stone monument had been erected marking the point, and having the usual inscriptions, and the names of the American and Mexican conmissioners, astronomers, and surveyors; and Mr. Salazar informed me this had been hastened at the urgent request of the American astronomer and surveyor.

I also found that articles of agreement, based upon the letters of instruction from the commissioner to Col. Graham, my successor and predecessor as chief astronomer, had been entered into with Mr. Salazar for the survey of the boundary, and the survey had been commenced at the initial point, 32° 22', by Col. Graham.

On the 30th January, 1852, while on my route west of El Paso, in pursuit of the commissioner, I received unexpectedly, and certainly unsolicited, the letter of appointment as United States surveyor, and your letters of instructions, one to myself and a copy of the letter of instructions to Mr. Bartlett, dated November 4, 1851, in which it is directed that "should the surveyor at any time differ with you [the commissioner] on any question connected with the survey, he [the surveyor] will defer to your [the commissioner's] opinion until the case is submitted and decided by the department.

The surveyor came out long after the initial point was agreed upon, and the monument erected and the line begun, relieved the acting surveyor, and protested against the point. With the protest and the views of the commissioner before him, both sides it is presumed fairly stated, the honorable Secretary instructed the surveyor to sign the maps; but before the instructions reached him, he was relieved, and I was appointed in his place, with the same instructions.

I therefore considered the matter as settled, and the action of the government as final. "The official documents which have been prepared for the purpose," referred to in my letter of appointment and instructions, never having been presented, no action has been taken in the matter definitely and finally to "settle this important point." I quote from my instructions, for, as I shall presently show, it has, by the views taken of the subject by both sides, ceased to be an important point.

But I have done this in compliance with the letter and spirit of my instructions. Mr. Salazar, the Mexican commissioner and surveyor, met me at the Presidio del Norte, August 1st, to sign the maps of the Rio Grande forming the boundary. Neither party had the maps properly prepared, nor was Mr. Salazar at all prepared in money or means to go on with the work at the rate I was progressing. I had already signed, conjointly with him as astronomer and surveyor, the only maps fit for signature, but he remained pressing me to sign other maps which involve incidentally the initial point agreed upon by Mr. Bartlett, Mr. Conde, Mr. Salazar, and Mr. Whipple, from which Colonel Graham had started his survey of the river. I therefore, on the 28th August, signed the maps according to my instructions, with the reservation contained in the paper, a copy of which is herewith sent, marked "A," signed conjointly by Mr. Salazar and myself, and the statement therein referred to setting forth on the face of the maps that it was the "*boundary-line agreed upon by the two commissioners, April* 20, 1851."

I presume it was never intended I should give my certificate, as astronomer and surveyor, to the correctness of the determination of a point which had been determined by the observations of others, and without consultation or advice of mine. On the other hand, I do not for a moment doubt the power of the government to instruct me on the subject, or hesitate as to my duty to obey its mandates, which I understand as requiring me only to authenticate the initial point agreed upon by the commissioners of the two governments.

In reference to the importance of the point, I think it as well to state that the line agreed upon by the commission, April, 1851, is about 33′ north* of the line contended for, as that laid down by Disturnell's map, but it reaches about 16′ of arc further west; and as both lines run 3° of longitude west, the difference of territory is 3° of longitude multiplied by about 40′ of latitude, each having a middle latitude that may, for the purpose of computation, be assumed at 30°. Neither line gives us the road to California, and the country embraced in the area of the difference, with the exception of a strip along the Rio Grande about nine miles long and from one to two wide, is barren, and will not produce wheat, corn, grapes, trees, or anything useful as food for man, or for clothing.

Neither line will give us a channel of communication for posts along the frontier, without which it is impracticable to comply with the XIth article of the treaty, which enjoins the United States to keep the Indians out of Mexico.

When originally on the work, before the point was determined, having a knowledge of the country from previous reconnoissance, I had the honor of asking the attention of your predecessor to this very subject, in a communication dated April, 1849, San Diego, California, which was subsequently printed by the Senate. I then pointed out what I believed to be the only view taken of the treaty, which would have given us the road, it being, in truth, the only important matter involved in the question. No notice was taken of this, and I was superseded in my command until restored by you, although Mr. Clayton, the Secretary of State, had declined, on my application, to relieve me, on the ground of my knowledge of the particular duties to which I was assigned.

On my return to the work, both governments having been committed in the matter by the commission, the time was passed when anything could be effected with the Mexican commission.

It is not pretended that the view there taken of the treaty is as close a legal construction as that taken since; but it is the only one which could have given us a wagon road from the Del Norte to the Pacific by way of the Gila river. And it is believed that, if this point had been urged before discussion took place, or before either party had committed itself, the obvious advantages to both would have secured its adoption.

I have the honor to be your obedient servant,

W. H. EMORY.

The Hon. SECRETARY OF THE INTERIOR.

I give here a copy of my letter of April 2, 1849, which, had it received attention, would have been the means of saving much controversy and expenditure of time and money:

BOUNDARY COMMISSION, SAN DIEGO, *April* 2, 1849.

SIR: Paper marked "A" will exhibit to you the adoption of my determination of the astronomical line forming the boundary between the United States and Mexico, from the initial point on the Pacific to the junction of the Gila and Colorado rivers, by the Mexican astronomer and surveyor, Señor Don José Salazar y Larregui. The line passing through the five points stated in that paper, as determined by me, is in view of the Tecaté mountain, thirty miles distant, and Señor Salazar undertook to establish on the Tecaté a signal in the prolongation of this line, and has succeeded in doing so; and the same has been verified under my orders.

Knowing the long time that must elapse before the monuments arrive, I have, in conjunction with Mr. Salazar, to secure this line beyond all cavil, and for the convenience of property holders on either side, caused monuments of a pyramidal shape, twelve feet at the base, and twelve feet high, composed of stones and earth, to be erected at the points established. These extend over a space of thirty miles, and embrace all the settled portions. I have bound the government for the payment of one-half the cost of the monuments, the Mexican commission paying the other half.

You were apprized in my last despatch that this commission, when I received the charge of it, was without one cent of money, without a mouthful to eat, and without a hoof or wheel for transportation; and that I was deprived of the only means of doing anything, by being deprived at the same time of military command.

I have not been instructed to estimate funds for the past or future. I have no means of estimating the debts of the commission, but presume this has been done by the late commissioner. I think it proper, however, to send an estimate herewith of funds required by Brevet Captain Hardcastle, to enable him to carry out his instructions. I think it also proper to inform the Department, for the benefit of the operators from the "Paso del Norte," that authentic information has reached here, that the Mexican frontier towns of Fronteras and Santa Cruz, which have always been counted on by the officers of the commission to furnish supplies, have been ravaged by the wild Indians, and deserted by the inhabitants, and the means of subsistence of the Pimos Indians have been eaten out by the emigrants. In addition to the American emigration, a dense stream of "Sonoreans," and other Mexicans, is now pouring over a portion of the same route into California, desolating the herbage and means of subsistence as they pass. Five thousand and upwards have already penetrated the country this season, and it is estimated by intelligent men that fifteen thousand more are in movement in the same direction.

In connexion with this same subject, and reverting to my despatch No. 2, I presume enough was then said to satisfy you that the expedition should not move from the "Gila eastward." The fact alone, that all it may accomplish, if it can accomplish anything, between the mouth of the Gila and the "Paso del Norte," beyond that of overcoming space, will be by the movement of the Mexican commission, growing out of the action of the joint commission of an ex parte character, and therefore of no value. But, in addition to this, we may lose a great advantage by pushing the survey in that direction—no less than the only practicable route for a railway over the Sierra Madre; which route is near the 32d parallel of latitude. That supposed to have been recently discovered by Lieutenant Simpson I believe impracticable. Had that intelligent officer come further "westward," he would have found an insurmountable barrier.

By pushing the survey eastward, and looking for a branch of the Gila which shall fulfil the conditions of the treaty—the first to intersect the boundary of New Mexico—you will inevitably be made to strike that boundary far north of the parallel of the copper mines; because all the streams south of that parallel, having their sources in the Sierra Madre, running towards the Gila, disappear in the sands before they reach Gila, except in cases of unusual freshets. Working eastward, their almost trackless beds must escape the notice of the keenest explorer. Working from the "Paso del Norte" northward and westward, you strike the sources of the streams themselves; and although they may disappear many leagues before reaching the Gila, they may nevertheless be affluents of that river, and fulfil the condition of the treaty.

Another view of the case may also be taken. The inaccuracy of the map upon which the treaty was made, and which thereby became a part of the treaty, is notorious. It is also known to all who have been much in the frontier States of Mexico, that the boundaries of those States have never been defined on the ground, and are unknown. This is particularly the case of the boundary betwixt New Mexico and Chihuahua. In this condition of things the commissioners must negotiate, and they may adopt the 32d parallel of latitude, until it strikes the San Pedro, or even a more southern parallel of latitude. This would give what good authority, combined with my own observations, authorizes me to say is a practicable route for a railroad—I believe the only one from ocean to ocean within our territory.

Another consideration is, the treaty makes the Gila for a certain extent the boundary. The Gila does not always run in the same bed; whenever it changes the boundary must change, and no survey nor anything else can keep it from changing. The survey of that river, therefore, as it fixes nothing, determines nothing, is of minor importance. It forms of itself a more apparent and enduring monument of the boundary than any that can be made by art; and on the principle that that which is of the greatest necessity should be done first, the line from the Paso del Norte, until it strikes a branch of the Gila, would seem to demand the first attention.

It is but just to say these are not views recently adopted by me; they were entertained and expressed before leaving Washington and since, and I urged that none but the astronomical party, and just as much of the commission, should be sent to the Pacific side as was necessary to fulfil the conditions required by the letter of the treaty.

Very respectfully, your obedient servant,

W. H. EMORY.

Hon. T. Ewing, *Secretary of the Interior.*

[*Letter referred to in the note on page* 14.]

Office United States Boundary Commission,
*Washington, April* 23, 1856.

Sir: In answer to your instructions of April 22, predicated on a resolution of Congress, received this day, I have the honor to submit the following table, showing the several appropriations made by Congress for the survey of the boundary line between the United States and Mexico, as established under the treaty of Guadalupe Hidalgo:

| U. S. Statutes. | | Date of law. | Object of appropriation. | Amount appropriated. |
|---|---|---|---|---|
| Vol. | Page. | | | |
| 9 | 301 | Aug. 12, 1848 | Running and marking boundary line under treaty of Guadalupe Hidalgo | $50,000 00 |
| 9 | 426 | May 15, 1850 | Do.............do..............do.............do.............do.. | 50,000 00 |
| 9 | 541 | Sept. 30, 1850 | Do.............do..............do.............do.............do.. | 135,000 00 |
| 9 | 614 | March 3, 1851 | Do.............do..............do.............do.............do.. | 100,000 00 |
| 10 | 17 | July 21, 1852 | Do.............do..............do.............do.............do.. | 80,000 00 |
| 10 | 95 | Aug. 31, 1852 | Arrearages of boundary commission.......... | 25,000 00 |
| 10 | 140 | Dec. 23, 1852 | Running and marking boundary line below El Paso, including expenses already incurred.......... | 120,000 00 |
| 10 | 209 | March 3, 1853 | Arrears due Major Emory's party.......... | 20,000 00 |
| 10 | 209 | March 3, 1853 | Expenses of Lieut. Whipple's party.......... | 6,000 00 |
| 10 | 209 | March 3, 1853 | Running and marking boundary line under treaty of Guadalupe Hidalgo | 93,012 00 |
| 10 | 296 | May 31, 1854 | Arrearages prior to July 1, 1853.......... | 50,000 00 |
| 10 | 296 | May 31, 1854 | Engraving maps, views, &c., of boundary survey.......... | 10,000 00 |
| 10 | 570 | Aug. 4, 1854 | Compensation of officers, office-work, &c.......... | 38,100 00 |
| 10 | 664 | March 3, 1855 | Engraving maps, views, &c., of boundary survey.......... | 10,000 00 |
| | | | Total.......... | 787,112 00 |

Of the above amount, the disbursement of only a very small portion came under my direction or within my knowledge. The item of $38,100 for office-work and the two items of $10,000, each were disbursed by Captain Thom under my immediate direction. Of the first sum, there was, January 1, 1856, a balance untouched of $24,445 54; and of the two last sums a balance of $12,900. As far as my authority has extended, there have been no defalcations.

I have also to submit a table showing the appropriations made by Congress for the survey of the boundary between the United States and Mexico, as established under the treaty of December 30, 1853.

| U. S. Statutes. | | Date of law. | Object of appropriation. | Amount appropriated. |
|---|---|---|---|---|
| Vol. | Page. | | | |
| 10 | 568 | Aug. 14, 1854 | Running and marking boundary under treaty of December 30, 1853. | $168, 130 00 |
| 10 | 661 | March 3, 1855 | Do.............do.............do.............do | 71, 450 00 |
| | | | Total | 239, 580 00 |

Of the amount appropriated for the survey, &c., of the boundary under the treaty of December 30, 1853, most of it was disbursed by myself, and a portion by Lieut. Michler; and there remained, on the 1st of January, 1856, in the hands of the assistant treasurer of the United States at New York, to my credit ........ $42, 004 59
In the hands of Lieut. Michler ........ 5, 000 00
In the treasury of the United States at Washington, not drawn........ 51, 450 00

Total........ 98, 454 59
Total from above ........ 37, 345 54

Grand total........ 135, 800 13

And I have further to report that no defalcations have occurred in those under my orders.

I have the honor to be your obedient servant,

W. H. EMORY, *U. S. Commissioner.*

Hon. ROBERT McCLELLAND, *Secretary of the Interior.*

The field-work of the boundary survey under the treaty of 1850, confided to my charge, was finished within the time estimated by the government. It will be seen from the above statement that the whole work will be completed at an expense much within the appropriation made by Congress.

# CHAPTER II.

## PERSONAL ACCOUNT CONTINUED.

ORGANIZATION OF COMMISSION UNDER TREATY OF DECEMBER 30, 1853.—TRIP TO EL PASO DEL NORTE.—JOURNAL OF JOINT COMMISSION.

On the 15th August, 1854, I received from the President of the United States, through the Hon. Robt. McClelland, Secretary of the Interior, the appointment of commissioner "to survey and mark out upon the land the dividing line between the United States and the republic of Mexico, concluded on the 30th of December, 1853, the ratifications of which were exchanged in the city of Washington on the 30th day of June, 1854." At the same time I received special instructions from the Secretary of the Interior, and a copy of the treaty, which will be found in the appendix.

The terms of the treaty required that each of the two governments should nominate one commissioner, and that "the two thus nominated should meet in the city of El Paso del Norte three months after the exchange of ratifications of the treaty, and proceed to survey and mark out the line," &c.

To reach El Paso del Norte in the time required by the treaty, (October 1st,) it would have been necessary to leave my outfit to take care of itself, and travel post-haste. Knowing well the character of the country in which that service was to be performed, I concluded to send forward a special messenger to meet the Mexican commissioner, and to remain and give my personal attention to the outfit. Everything in the way of astronomical and surveying instruments, transportation, arms, provisions, and medicines required for the campaign, was to be provided in advance, and shipped from New York.

By employing men to work night and day, and shipping my wagons, at great expense, on board the passenger steamers, I was enabled to land the whole outfit at Indianola, Texas, by the 25th of September.

On the night of the 18th September, while crossing the Gulf, a terrific tornado swept the coast, and every wharf in Matagorda bay, except that upon which a portion of our outfit was landed, was carried away, and the town of Matagorda itself levelled with the ground. We found at Indianola a number of mules belonging to the old commission; but they were in such miserable condition, I determined to send them up to San Antonio with the empty wagons, and hire transportation for the supplies which had been purchased in New Orleans and safely landed at Indianola. The low country between Indianola and Kilpatrick's, a distance of twenty miles, was inundated, and the roads so bad, that the contractor for the transportation of our supplies was twenty days passing as many miles. The yellow fever was then prevalent, and added much to our embarrassments, several of our party having been stricken down at the moment of entering upon a distant and arduous service. I was, however, so thankful to have escaped without damage the tornado of the 17th–19th of September, which proved so disastrous around us, that every other adverse circumstance seemed trifling.

On the 25th of October I had succeeded in enlisting and equipping sixty or seventy men for the service, and in purchasing the necessary number of animals.

The escort, consisting of a company of the 7th infantry, commanded by Brevet Capt. E. K. Smith, reported itself in readiness on the same day, and on the next we took up the line of march for El Paso.

Before leaving Washington I organized, with the assent of the Secretary, a party, under Lieut. Michler, to proceed to California and work from the Pacific side to meet me.

When the commission took the field the following was its organization; and this organization was continued with scarcely a change until the successful conclusion of the field-work, in the fall of 1855:

W. H. Emory, U. S. commissioner, chief astronomer and surveyor.
Chas. Radziminski, secretary.
Lieut. Chas. N. Turnbull, corps Topographical Engineers, general assistant.
M. T. W. Chandler, do.
J. H. Clark, principal assistant astronomer.
Hugh Campbell, assistant.
Winder Emory, clerk.
Maurice Von Hippel, principal assistant surveyor.
Chas. Weiss, assistant surveyor.
F. Wheaton, reconnoitring assistant.
Wm. Likens, assistant in charge of commissary stores.
Jas. Houston, assistant.
David Hinkle, do.
Benj. Burns, assistant in charge of instruments.
Lieut. N. Michler, corps Topographical Engineers, in charge of party operating from the Pacific side.
Arthur Schott, assistant to Lieut. Michler.
E. A. Phillips, do. do.
John O'Donoghue, do. do.

Capt. George Thom, corps Topographical Engineers, with a few civil assistants, was left in Washington in charge of the office, to reduce the observations and project the work done under the old commission.

Besides the above, there were employed in the different parties about one hundred men, in the various capacities of teamsters, laborers, cooks, servants, and arrieros.

The infantry escort accompanied the commission from the time of leaving San Antonio until our return to El Paso. From that point to San Antonio it was commanded by Lieutenant Cummins. At El Paso, on the outward journey, we received an accession to the escort of thirty dragoons, commanded by Lieutenant Hastings. Lieutenant Michler was escorted by a detachment of artillery soldiers, commanded by Lieutenant (now Captain) Patterson. In addition to his military duties, Captain Smith aided me materially in the business of the boundary survey.

The first part of the journey from San Antonio to El Paso was very slow, in consequence of the heavy rains, which made the roads in many places almost impassable for our heavily laden wagons. Beyond Devil's river we found the roads good, water and grass plenty, and succeeded at last in reaching El Paso in time for the Mexican commission.

We did not see an Indian on the route, although in front and in rear of us they were committing depredations along the whole road.

At Cantonment Blake, on the Devil's river, they waylaid and killed a couple of soldiers; at Live Oak they drove off, in open day-light, all the animals of the military post temporarily established at that point. At Fort Davis, we found they had attacked a party and killed a sergeant and musician; just beyond, at Dead Man's Hole, they attacked the mail party, and would probably have handled them severely, had not another party coming in the opposite direction, joined them at the critical moment.

On arriving at the cañon about seventy miles below El Paso, I left my escort and train, with directions to proceed slowly up the river, while I went to make such arrangements with the Mexican commissioner as would enable me to move the parties directly on the new line, and commence operations.

I accomplished this with the Mexican commissioner satisfactorily; although winter had now set in with severity, and the small-pox showed itself in our camp, and we had just accomplished a journey of sixteen hundred miles, every assistant and man took the field as cheerfully as if he had just left his barracks.

Each one of the principal assistants was selected upon the estimate of his professional abilities, derived from personal knowledge, and I had no reason to make any changes of importance from the beginning to the end of the work. My own expectations, and I hope those of the government, were entirely fulfilled in the manner in which the work was accomplished. Under all circumstances—during the cold winter exposed upon the bare ground of the bleak plains, and in the summer to the hot sun blazing over the arid desert—every order was executed with fidelity, and the work was completed within the time, and largely within the amount appropriated by Congress. We passed the entire width of the continent and returned with the loss only of two men, and without losing a single animal, (except those worn out by service,) or suffering a stampede by the Indians; at the same time that our co-operators on the Mexican commission were twice robbed of every hoof by the Apaches, and extensive losses were sustained by other detachments of United States troops, and by our citizens traversing this region.

I close this short personal account by giving the journal of the joint commission, composed of Señor Salazar and myself. It will be seen, that throughout the whole expedition the utmost harmony prevailed, and I take this occasion to express, not only for myself, but for the whole American commission, the pleasant recollection of the agreeable intercourse which existed between ourselves and the Mexican commissioner, and the officers under his command. Señor Salazar failed to receive from his government means to carry on the work with the rapidity contemplated in the agreement with myself, and he was twice crippled in his operations by the depredations of the Indians.

# JOURNAL OF THE JOINT COMMISSION.

Paso del Norte, *December* 4, 1854.

The undersigned, commissioners respectively on the part of the United States of America and of the Mexican republic to run and mark the boundary line between the two countries, according the treaty concluded in the city of Mexico on the 30th day of December, 1853, met informally in the town of El Paso del Norte on the 2d instant, and on the 4th, the date of this joint record of their proceedings, they had another meeting in the same town, when, having exchanged credentials, they proceeded to discuss and arrange the business upon which they were called together by their respective governments.

Both parties being ready to commence operations, and there being no difference of opinion upon the scientific and practical manner of determining the boundary between the two countries, it was agreed that each should proceed, with all the means at his disposal, to determine the initial point of said boundary on the Rio Grande, which the treaty stipulated to be at the parallel of 31° 47′ north latitude. It was further agreed that as soon as each party ascertained the precise point, both parties should compare notes and eliminate any differences or errors, by the methods best known to science, and conclude the final result, giving to each set of observations the weight due to them.

There being no other business before the commission, it adjourned, to meet when either commissioner should signify to the other that he had concluded the observations necessary to determine where the parallel of 31° 47′ north latitude intersects the Rio Grande.

W. H. EMORY.
JOSÉ SALAZAR Y LARREGUI.

Rio Grande, Latitude 31° 47′, *January* 10, 1855.

On the 9th of January, both commissioners having finished the observations necessary to determine the initial point of the boundary on the Rio Grande, met this day to compare results. The necessary measurements being made to connect the two observatories, and also the observatory established at Frontera in 1851–'52, it was ascertained that the difference between the determinations of the parallel of 31° 47′, made by the two commissions, was eighty-four hundredths of one second. It was then mutually agreed to take the mean between the two results; and the point thus ascertained was marked on the ground in presence of both commissioners, as the point where the parallel of 31° 47′ strikes the river; that is to say, the point where the boundary under the treaty of December 30, 1853, leaves the river to run westward.

The commission adjourned, to meet to-morrow at 10 o'clock a. m.

JOSÉ SALAZAR Y LARREGUI.
W. H. EMORY.

Rio Grande, Latitude 31° 47′, *January* 11, 1855.

The commission met and laid off the tangent to the parallel of 31° 47′, and having agreed upon the elements assumed for the figure of the earth, (Bessel's,) and compared the results of their computations for the length and azimuth of the ordinates connecting the tangent with the parallel, found them to correspond.

The commission adjourned, to meet to-morrow at 10 o'clock a. m.

JOSÉ SALAZAR Y LARREGUI.
W. H. EMORY.

PASO DEL NORTE, *January* 12, 1855.

The commission met agreeably to adjournment, and agreed to place one monument as near the river as the nature of the ground will admit, to be of dressed stone, having on the north face:

U. S.
BOUNDARY,
Under the treaty of December 30, 1853.

On the south face:

R. M.
Limite conforme al tratado de 30 de Diciembre de 1853.

On the west:

JOSE SALAZAR Y LARREGUI, *Comisionado Mexicano.*

On the east:

W. H. EMORY, *U. S. Commissioner.*

The commission further agreed:

1st. To erect a pyramid of rough stone, cemented with mortar, where the line strikes the crest of the first range of hills, and one of the same description in sight of the road leading from El Paso to the north.

2d. To put up a monument at the extremity of the line of 31° 47′ of the same kind, and with the same inscription, as that first named; to put up pyramids along the line wherever the facilities of water and stone will admit.

3d. To lay the foundation of the monument nearest the river on the 24th January.

There being no further business before the commission, it adjourned, to meet at 12 m. on the 24th instant.

W. H. EMORY.
JOSÉ SALAZAR Y LARREGUI.

PASO DEL NORTE, *January* 26, 1855.

The commission met on this day.

The Mexican commissioner having notified the American commissioner, by letter, on the 16th, that, in consequence of his absence in making a reconnoissance, he could not attend the placing of the corner-stone of the monument until the 31st, the American commissioner agreed with him to postpone the establishment of the foundation of the monument to that day at meridian, and we have this day met to give validity to that agreement. The American commissioner stated that, in consequence of not getting a sufficient supply of water immediately on the line, he had somewhat changed his plans, and had adopted, as the base of his operations, the north and south line between the parallels of 31° 47′ and 31° 20′. The first division of his party (the astronomical) had completed all their work here, and was ready to move on that line, escorted by the dragoons, and would so move to-morrow; that he, the commissioner, would follow with the balance of his party, the surveyors and the supplies, immediately after the completion of their joint labors on the 31st instant. He further stated, he had established points on the line beyond the road, and by the 31st his parties would have progressed with the line as far on the Mesa as was convenient to operate from this side. He proposed to the Mexican commissioner to concur in these plans, and to start also westward. The Mexican commissioner stated he fully concurred in those plans and adopted them, but that in consequence of having no escort, he could not move at the time proposed, but would follow as soon as his escort arrived; the Mexican commissioner further stated, that whilst here he would take the charge of the three monuments, agreed upon at our meeting of the 12th to be erected at this end, and see them completed.

The American commissioner assented, and further stated that he would leave Jean Ball, the stone-mason, to assist in the work under the direction of the Mexican commissioner.

The American commissioner stated, that the treaty required, for the establishment of the line, the concurrence of the two commissioners; that when he establishes the points west in the absence of the Mexican commissioner, if any accident should prevent a subsequent visitation and verification of the points by the Mexican commissioner, the validity of the point might be questioned, and the work of himself, the American commissioner, achieved at great cost, might go for nothing.

The Mexican commissioner stated, in reply, that to avoid that difficulty, he would now adopt all those points which the American commissioner, in his absence, might establish, in his own name, on the line which the treaty stipulates.

JOSE SALAZAR Y LARREGUI.
W. H. EMORY.

INITIAL POINT ON THE RIO GRANDE, LAT. 31° 47′,
*January* 31, 1855.

The commission met, according to agreement, at meridian.

The chief officers of the vicinity, military and civil, from both sides of the line, being present, the foundation of the monument was laid. The following paper—one copy in English, the other in Spanish—was signed by the two commissioners and by the persons aforesaid, placed in a glass bottle, and deposited, at the depth of five feet, under the centre of the monument:

COPY OF THE PAPER.

"We, the undersigned, have this day assembled to witness the laying of the foundation of the monument which is to mark the initial point of the boundary between the United States and the Republic of Mexico, agreed upon, under the treaty of Mexico, on the part of the United States by William Hemsley Emory, and on the part of the Republic of Mexico by José Salazar y Larregui, latitude 31° 47′.

"W. H. EMORY, *U. S. Commissioner.*
"JOSÉ SALAZAR Y LARREGUI.
"C. RADZIMINSKI, *Sec'y U. S. B. C.*
"JOEL S. ANKRIM.
"E. B. ALEXANDER.
"CALEB SHERMAN.
"E. K. SMITH.
"JUAN JOSE SANCHEZ.
"ANTONIO ZEPEDA.
"GUADALUPE MIRANDA.
"VINCENTE AGUIRRE."

The American commissioner stated that he had already sent the whole of his astronomical force to the western end of the 100-mile line, and that it was his intention to follow in the coming week with the balance of his force.

The question of the time and place of the next meeting having been raised, the Mexican commissioner stated it was not in his power to say when he would be able to join the American commissioner, but that he would endeavor to do so as soon as possible.

The commission adjourned, to meet when the Mexican commissioner shall join the American commission.

JOSÉ SALAZAR Y LARREGUI.
W. H. EMORY.

FORT BLISS, *August* 14, 1855.

In pursuance of notification from the Mexican commissioner of his arrival, made in conformity with the last article agreed upon January 31, 1855, the commissioners met this day.

The United States commissioner stated that he had concluded the running and marking of the line up to the 111th meridian of longitude, at which point he met the United States and Mexican parties working eastward from the Colorado, and that in the unavoidable absence of the Mexican commissioner he had concluded an agreement with Señor Jimenez, first engineer of the Mexican commission, which he now presented to the Mexican commissioner, and asked his approval of the same.

The agreement is in the words following, to wit:

Señor Don Francisco Jimenez, first engineer of the boundary commission, on the part of Mexico, being duly empowered by the Mexican commissioner to run the line between the Colorado and the 111th meridian of longitude, having arrived at the camp of the American commissioner, the latter invited him, in the absence of the Mexican commissioner, to a conference, having for its object the more speedy completion of the unfinished portion of the line; and accordingly the two have met this day, and the following is the report of that conference and its results:

The American commissioner stated that he had separated from the Mexican commissioner on the 6th of February; that the Mexican commissioner being unable to proceed with the line at that time, had empowered the American commissioner to proceed with it, and had agreed to adopt the line established by him in conformity with the treaty.

The journal of the joint commission, duly signed and sealed, was exhibited to Señor Jimenez, and a copy of the record of the 26th January, duly authenticated, furnished him. The American commissioner stated that he had caused the line to be run and the monuments to be erected as far as the 111th meridian of longitude. That meridian had been established from observations at Los Nogales by principal assistant Clark; and Señor Jimenez was invited to inspect the instruments, still in position, with which these observations were made, the observations themselves, and the computations by which the results were obtained. The result of that inspection being satisfactory, the American commissioner proposed, that in view of the urgent demands of both governments, to complete the line, Señor Jimenez should unite with the American party, and direct the whole force of both parties to complete the tracing and marking of the line on the face of the earth from the 111th meridian, already established, to the point where Señor Jimenez and Lieutenant Michler left off in their attempt to run the line eastward.

Señor Jimenez assented to this proposition, and it was, therefore, agreed as follows:

That the plan of triangulation is impracticable; that the American and Mexican surveying party shall proceed forthwith to run the unfinished portion of the line; take the topography near the line; erect monuments at points where the line crosses a mine, a settlement, a road, or water.

It is agreed if either party break down, the other is not to suspend or delay operations in consequence of it.

It is agreed the Mexican party is to determine the latitude and longitude of some central point of the line as a check upon the tracing of the line, and the result is to be furnished the American commissioner, who agrees to accept that determination.

It is further agreed that the convention entered into between Señor Jimenez and Lieutenant Michler, April 26, and the additional article agreed upon May 1, 1855, are approved in all the articles not in conflict with this convention.

W. H. EMORY,
*United States Commissioner.*
FRANO. JIMENEZ,
*First Engineer de la Como. de Limites Mexicano.*

LOS NOGALES, *June* 21, 1855.

The Mexican commissioner having approved this step on the part of the first engineer of his commission, the United States commissioner gave a brief legend of operations up to the 111th meridian of longitude, and invited Mr. Salazar to inspect the notes, astronomical and geodetic, upon which the line was based, and the rough draughts of the maps made in the field.

The following is the substance of the legend:

After concluding all operations in the vicinity of the Rio Bravo, and pushing the line as far as was convenient, from that place, an astronomical station was established at Carrizalillo, which proved, from 72 observations with 46-inch zenith telescope, to be in latitude 31° 50′ 55″.23 north; and longitude 107° 56′ 03″.90, the result of observations during one lunation.

Carrizalillo was the nearest water to the terminal point of the 100-mile line near to parallel 31° 47′. A monument was established on the road due south of the observatory, and the parallel extended in both directions—east, until it met, in the sand-hills, the line produced from the Rio Bravo; west, it was extended to the end of the 100 miles, and the parallel was obtained by measuring ordinates from the tangent. The 100 miles was obtained by combining the observed longitude at Carrizalillo, and the distance actually measured.

From the end of the 100 miles a line was produced due south to meet the parallel of 31° 20′. The reconnoissance to find water at the junction of the meridian and 31° 20′ failed, and the observatory was established at the Espia, on the Rio Janos, ten or twelve miles east of the meridian. An elaborate set of observations (81) with zenith telescope, gave us the latitude of this observatory 31° 20′ 56″.45; the tangent of 31° 20′ was determined from this by direct measurements and produced to intersect meridian, and ordinates laid off to ascertain parallel. After producing parallel about seven miles, it was ascertained, as will be seen by the map, that the Ojo del Perro was near the line. The zenith telescope was reset, and a new tangent obtained; which result corresponding well with the last, this tangent was produced to the San Luis range of mountains. At the San Luis springs, about thirty miles west of the initial point of the parallel 31° 20′, a new observatory was erected, the latitude of which (31° 20′ 31″.51) was ascertained by more than 97 observations. The tangent to the parallel 31° 20′ was ascertained and produced in both directions, east and west, and the ordinates to the curve of the parallel established. The coincidence between the new tangent and the old one, produced from Ojo del Perro, was satisfactory ; after making the necessary allowance for the difference of ordinates, the error was found to be only a few feet. The tangent west was produced across the level of the San Luis valley and the Guadalupe Pass. In the mean time, a new observatory was erected at San Bernardino springs, and the latitude obtained with the same instrument, and nearly the same set of stars, was ascertained to be 31° 19′ 40″.38 by 57 observations. A third tangent was produced east and west, that east being found to correspond and verify the second tangent. This last tangent, being the third, was, on account of the absence of water, produced as far as the hills west of the San Pedro. While this was progressing, the astronomical party established itself to the north of Santa Cruz, on the river of the same name, and the latitude of the point was ascertained to be 31° 17′ 56″.33, from 73 observations. From this, a point on the parallel 31° 20′, due north, was ascertained by direct measurement, and a fourth tangent obtained, as in all the preceding cases, by elaborate measurements of the elongations of Polaris. An apprehension was entertained that the third tangent, by reason of its great prolongation, sometimes, as in passing the Guadalupe mountains, running over rough country, might prove crooked ; but the verification by means of the fourth tangent was complete, showing the greatest probable error of either tangent, a distance of only 15 or 20 feet.

A chronometric reconnoissance was then made to the westward, and it was ascertained that the nearest durable water to the intersection of the meridian of 111 degrees west of Greenwich, and the parallel of 31° 20′, was at Los Nogales. At this point was established an observatory. The transit and zenith instruments were both mounted ; and the result of 120 observations with the latter, and observations during two lunations with the first, gave for the latitude 31° 21′ 00″.48, and longitude 110° 51′ 02″.10 west of Greenwich. From observations at this observatory a fifth tangent was deduced, and extended by a separate party in both directions, running westward until the 111th meridian of longitude was reached. Owing to the difficulties of the country, the longitude was transferred by direct measurement and by triangulation.

Before this was concluded, a despatch was received giving the joint result of the Mexican and United States parties, of the latitude and longitude of the initial point on the Colorado river. With these data the azimuth of the line westward was computed to be 69° 19′ 45″.9, and laid off by measurements from the elongation of Polaris.

This left nothing to be done but to trace the line and complete the topography between the 111th and the Colorado, and the dispositions made for that are all embraced in the convention between Senor Jimenez and myself, and Señor Jimenez and Lieutenant Michler, to which your approval has been given.

Major Emory, the American commissioner, further stated, that in reference to the instruments used, and the methods employed in obtaining results, Mr. Salazar, the Mexican commissioner, from long experience, was familiar with the mode adopted by both commissions, and it was therefore not necessary to enter into particulars—the notes would show for themselves ; but he begged to remind Mr. Salazar that they had discussed before, the subject of longitude, and it was agreed between them, that in all determinations of longitude by the moon and moon-culminating stars they should take the Greenwich ephemeris, and not await the publication of the corresponding observations made at Greenwich, as at this distance it would necessarily involve a delay of eighteen months or two years—a result clearly not contemplated by either government. The correction due from corresponding observations cannot be foretold, but is small, and as likely to be to the advantage of one as the other.

The monuments erected on the line were of two classes—first, of dressed stone, laid without mortar; second, of round stones undressed, forming simply mounds.

Of the first, one was erected at the point south of the Carrizalillo; another at the intersection of meridian 108° 09′ 41″.85 and parallel 31° 20′; one at San Luis springs; two at San Bernardino; one at San Pedro; one north of Santa Cruz; one where the line crosses (second time) Santa Cruz river; one at Los Nogales; and one at intersection of 111° and 31° 20′. Many mounds of the second class were erected, always at points where the line crosses a road or trail. Mr. Salazar stated that he had erected, of dressed stone, in a permanent and durable manner, a monument at the initial point on the Rio Bravo, and two monuments west of that point.

To give the Mexican commissioner time to make a thorough and critical examination of the data upon which the determinations are based, and to inspect the maps and take copies of such portions of them as he might desire, they were placed in his hands, and the commission adjourned, to meet in El Paso at 10 o'clock on the 16th.

W. H. EMORY, *U. S. Comm'r.*
JOSÉ SALAZAR Y LARREGUI, *Com'o Mex'o.*

EL PASO, *August* 16, 1855.

The commission met, agreeably to adjournment.

Mr. Salazar, the Mexican commissioner, stated he had fully examined all the documents, observations, notes, and maps, and the result of his examination was an entire conviction that the line had been run correctly throughout, including those parts during the running of which he was necessarily absent. But since the subject had been called to his notice by Mr. Emory, the U. S. commissioner, to the effect that, in consequence of the absence of water at the time, only a mound had been established at the junction of the meridian and parallel of 31° 47′, he thought, now that the rainy season had commenced, and water was everywhere to be found, a monument of dressed stone should be erected at that point; and he stated he would himself undertake to place it at that point. He stated, also, in consequence of the absence of water he had not been able to place a monument, as he had intended to do, to the south of the Potrillo mountains, on the parallel of 31° 47′, and that he would do both at the same time.

Mr. Emory, the American commissioner, stated his assent to this proposition, and further stated, that although he believed he had erected monuments or mounds along the whole line wherever the line crossed or passed near permanent water, a road, a mine, or town, or, in fact, any habitable point, yet he desired Mr. Salazar, if, in the course of his visitation of those parts of the line not before examined by him he should see any point omitted where a monument should be placed or substituted for a mound, not to hesitate to do so.

Mr. Emory said he would now state what he had informally stated before, that he had directed Lieut. Michler to send him an express to San Antonio the moment Señor Jimenez and himself finished the topography of the line between the 111th meridian and the Colorado.

The examination of the notes, maps, &c., being completed, and all discussion of the different subjects connected with the line being closed, the results of the foregoing conferences were embodied in the following articles of agreement:

1. Mr. Emory, the American commissioner, agrees to adopt, unconditionally, all monuments, mounds, lines, and points now established by Mr. Salazar, the Mexican commissioner, and by Don Francisco Jimenez, first engineer of the Mexican commission.

2. Mr. Salazar, the Mexican commissioner, agrees to adopt unconditionally all the monuments, mounds, lines, and points now established by Mr. Emory, the American commissioner, and by his assistants, reserving the right to substitute a monument for a mound at the intersection of the meridian with the parallel of 31° 47′, and to erect a mound or monument on the same parallel to the south of the Potrillo, and at any point along the line already established where it may appear to him necessary, and where heretofore it was impracticable, owing to the absence of water.

3. The two commissioners agree to declare, and do declare, the line surveyed, marked, and established as far as the 111th meridian of longitude, as the true line of boundary between the two republics, and they agree also to declare, and do declare, the line established from the 111th to its intersection with the Colorado, the true line between the two republics. They further agree to declare the line fully surveyed, marked, and established through its whole extent as soon as notification is received from Señor Jimenez and Lieutenant Michler that the topography of the last named line is completed between the 111th meridian and the Colorado river, and it shall be the duty of each to inform the other when such notification is received, and also to report to their respective governments that all the field-work of the boundary is concluded.

4. To carry out the stipulations in the first article of the treaty of December 30th, 1853, requiring the commissioners to make proper plans of their operations. It is agreed that the two commissioners, with their assistants, shall meet in the city of Washington on the first day of April, 1856.

W. H. EMORY, *U. S. Commissioner.*
JOSÉ SALAZAR Y LARREGUI, *Comm'o Mex'a.*

There being no further business before the commission, it adjourned, to meet in Washington, April 1, 1856.

W. H. EMORY, *U. S. Commissioner.*
JOSÉ SALAZAR Y LARREGUI, *Comm'o Mex'a.*

---

AGREEMENT BETWEEN LIEUTENANT MICHLER AND SEÑOR JIMENEZ, REFERRED TO AT THE MEETING OF THE JOINT COMMISSION, AUGUST 14, MADE AT CAMP NEAR THE INITIAL POINT ON THE RIO COLORADO, ON THE TWENTY-SIXTH OF APRIL, 1855.

According to article first of the treaty of December 30, 1853, between the republics of the United States and Mexico, we, the undersigned, duly authorized to fix the initial point on the Rio Colorado, twenty English miles below the junction of this river with the Gila, and to trace and mark the line from this point to the intersection of the parallel of 31° 20′ north latitude, with the 111th meridian of longitude west from Greenwich—all the operations necessary to determine this point and the direction of the line having been completed—agree as follows:

1. That the latitude of said initial point, by a mean of the results obtained by each party, is 32° 29′ 44″.45 north, and that the longitude is 114° 48′ 44″.53 west from Greenwich, determined from a triangulation by N. Michler, lieutenant Topographical Engineers, United States army, who has transferred the position of the monument on the old boundary line near the junc-

tion to the new initial point. This longitude has been adopted by Mr. Francisco Jimenez, first engineer Mexican boundary commission, although he proposed to refer it by flashes between the two points.*

2. That with the above data the computed azimuth of the line running eastward is found to be 71° 20′ 43″.8 southeast at the initial point, and 69° 19′ 45″.9 northwest at the end of the line, and the distance between the two points is 382,844.87 metres, equal to 237.63565 English miles. Having commenced to trace said line on the bank of the river, distant from the initial point 964.62 metres, equal to 3,164.84 English feet, the azimuth at this point, newly computed, was found to be 71° 20′ 25″ southeast.

3. That the line be traced by both parties at the same time, each alternating with the other at the successive stations; that the distance of the line be measured by triangulation, one party operating from the initial point to the environs of Sonoyta, the other thence to the termination of the line; and that the results be mutually exchanged.

4. That at all prominent points of the line which are deemed proper, suitable monuments, from such materials as are at hand, be erected to mark it.

5. That the point where the line has commenced to be traced be called by the Roman number (1;) that all succeeding stations shall be in the order (II,) (III,) (IV,) &c., &c.

6. That as it is impossible to place a permanent monument at the starting point (I) of the line, an iron monument has been placed at station (II) in the direction of the line, and distant from station (I) 3171.12 metres, equal to 10404.12 English feet; computed latitude of said monument, 32° 29′ 01″.48 north, and longitude 114° 46′ 14″.43 west of Greenwich.

7. That the above be submitted to the consideration of the commissioners of the respective countries for their approval.

N. MICHLER, *Lieut. Topl. Engrs. U. S. A.,*
*U. S. Boundary Commission.*
FRANCISCO JIMENEZ,
1*st Ingo. de la Com. del Limite Mex'o.*

After having signed the above agreement the tracing of the line was continued, in accordance with the same, from station II to station III, a distance of 829.81 metres. From station III a party was sent to a point of the mountain range, about twenty-five miles distant, to endeavor to establish station IV. This party having made a reconnoissance of the country for the purpose of finding water, was unsuccessful in discovering sufficient for the wants of even the small number of men necessary to execute the work; the nature of the country forbid the practicability of furnishing by any means of transportation what was deemed necessary, as it is a continuous desert of heavy sand, entirely destitute of vegetation. A party previously sent to reconnoitre the country for water also brought the intelligence that not a drop was to be had from the Colorado to Quitobaquita, a distance of one hundred and twenty-five miles in the direction of the line. In consequence, therefore, of the utter impracticability of prosecuting the work from the west end of the line, we, the undersigned, on this the first day of May, 1855, agree to add the following article to the above agreement:

8. That both parties cease operations at the west end and proceed to the east end of the line, by the road along the Gila, the only one available at this season of the year, there to fix the

* NOTE.—Captain Jimenez subsequently caused the monument on the old boundary, and the new initial point on the Colorado, to be connected by triangulation, and obtained the same result as Lieutenant Michler.

point of intersection of the parallel of 31° 20′ north latitude with the 111th meridian west of Greenwich, and afterwards to proceed to trace the line from that point westward as far as practicable.

N. MICHLER, *Lieut. Topl. Engrs. U. S. A.,*
*U. S. Boundary Commission.*
FRANCISCO JIMENEZ,
*1st Ingo. de la Com. del Limite Mex'o.*

WASHINGTON, *December* 18, 1855.

SIR: I communicated to you, a few days ago, a telegraphic despatch reporting the completion of the survey of the boundary.

I have now the honor to inform you that I have received official information of the arrival of the last surveying party of the commission in San Antonio, and the completion of the work assigned to it.

I have also to communicate to you the copy of a letter from Señor Salazar, the Mexican commissioner, informing me of the complete fulfilment of the 3d article of the convention with him, signed August 16.

The field-work of the boundary commission is therefore at an end.

I have the honor to be, your obedient servant,

W. H. EMORY, *U. S. Commissioner.*

Hon. ROBERT MCCLELLAND, *Secretary of the Interior.*

[Translation.]

JANOS, *October* 15, 1855.

SIR: Lieut. Michler has just delivered to me, personally, an official note, whereby I am informed that the survey of the line between the meridian of 111° and the Colorado has been completed.

This I have communicated to my government; and I advise you of the same, hoping that you will be pleased to communicate it to that of the United States, conformably to the resolution of article 3d of the convention held on the 16th of August of the present year.

I have the pleasure again to subscribe myself, with the greatest respect, your obedient servant,

JOSÉ SALAZAR Y LARREGUI,
*Mexican Commissioner, &c., &c.*

Col. W. H. EMORY,
*United States Commissioner.*

[Translation of official document sent by Mr. Salazar to the government of Mexico.]

EXCELLENT SIR: With my note under date of the 20th August, I enclosed to you copies of the last meeting held by the commissioner of the United States and myself on the 14th, 16th, and 20th of that month. By the 3d article of the agreement of the 16th, your excellency will have seen that we agreed on declaring, and do declare, in effect, that the line was completely *surveyed, marked,* and *fixed* in all its length, so soon as notice was received from Señor Jimenez and Lieut. Michler that the topography of the last-mentioned line had been completed between the 111th meridian and the Colorado; and the same 3d article imposes upon us the mutual obligation to advise each other, and our respective governments, that all the field-work of the line was concluded.

In complying with the 3d article of this convention, celebrated on the 16th August, between the American commissioner (Major W. H. Emory) and myself, I now notify your excellency that the topography of the line between the 111th meridian and the Colorado is now complete, by the acknowledgment of Messrs. Jimenez and Lieut. Michler, as your excellency will see by the original letter, which is herewith enclosed, and which was handed to me in person by Lieut. Michler, who to-day takes his departure for the United States; and Lieut. Michler also informed me that Señor Jimenez had started on the 1st instant for the city of Mexico, after they had, together, concluded and officially agreed upon the line which had been placed under their charge.

All the work, therefore, necessary for the surveying, marking, and establishing of the boundary line between Mexico and the United States, in conformity with the treaty of the 30th of December, 1853, is now terminated.

In carrying out still further the requirements of the said 3d article of the convention with the commissioner of the United States, I have to-day written him as follows:

"JANOS, *October* 15, 1855.

"SIR: Lieut. Michler has just handed to me, in person, an official note, by which I am informed that the topography of the line between the meridian 111° and the Colorado is completed, the which I have communicated to my government; and I advise you of the same, trusting that you will also communicate the fact to the United States, in conformity with the 3d article of the convention made between us the 16th August.

"With great respect, I have the honor to be, &c.,

"JOSÉ SALAZAR Y LARREGUI.

"Sr. Don W. H. EMORY,
"*Commissioner of the United States.*"

And now, most excellent sir, the treaty indicates who should declare surveyed, marked, and established (or fixed) the boundary line, and gives to the commissioners ample powers; and thus no doubt can exist that the commissioners, and not the governments, can, and must, make this declaration. This was accordingly done by Major Emory and myself, as such commissioners, by our convention on the 16th of August, as shown by its terms, with the sole condition that it shall be valid whenever either of us received the advice which I have just communicated to your excellency and to the American commissioner. It now only remains for the government of the United States to fulfil its part of the obligations imposed by the 3d article of the treaty.

God and liberty. Janos, October 15, 1855.

JOSÉ SALAZAR Y LARREGUI.

His Excellency the MINISTER OF FOREIGN RELATIONS, *Mexico.*

WASHINGTON CITY, *June* 24, 1856.

In pursuance of previous adjournment, the two commissioners met this day at the office of the joint commission. Señor Salazar stated that after he separated from Mr. Emory on the 20th August, 1855, he reviewed with his parties the different lines of the boundary; that is to say, the parallel 31° 47′, the meridian, and the parallel 31° 20′, on which lines the Mexican commission executed the following work:

From the point south of El Carrizalillo, on which was erected a monument, he observed minutely on Polaris to determine the prime vertical on both sides, east and west. The prime vertical and the parallel 31° 47′ were connected by a triangulation—on the east side with that which had been made at the initial point, and on the west side with the intersection of meridian. By this triangulation five points to the east were fixed, at which points he caused to be erected monuments of stone, with mortar, because he found not one established by the United States commission in said direction.

The monument at the road was reconstructed of stone, with mortar. Upon all of them was inscribed the abridged inscription agreed upon. This line was then marked with ten monuments. That at the west end he caused to be erected of dressed stone with mortar, and inscribed with the complete inscription agreed upon, similar to that which was erected at the initial point cn the Rio Bravo.

Mr. Salazar stated that he observed at the south end of the meridian for latitude and longitude, his results differing very little from those of the United States commission; that from this point was carried north a triangulation which was connected at the north end with that made on the parallel 31° 47′, and was used to determine the position of said end on the parallel and on the meridian; that these two extreme points were left where the United States commission established them; that having found no monument between them, he caused one to be erected intermediate, in sight of the Ojo de los Mosquitos, of dressed stone laid in mortar, with the usual inscriptions; that the monument at the south end was erected of dressed stone and mortar with inscriptions similar in all respects to those at the north end and at the initial point. On the parallel 31° 20′, besides the observations he made at the intersection, he observed for latitude at San Luis springs, at San Bernardino, and San Pedro river; he found monuments at the two first named points, but none at the last; that his observations proved that the points were on the parallel 31° 20′, and he caused monuments to be erected at these points with mortar, having the usual inscriptions upon them, and that he thought it proper to erect a monument of the same kind in Guadalupe Pass.

Mr. Emory stated his entire satisfaction with what had been done by Mr. Salazar, and gave his assent thereto, except with regard to the monument at San Pedro river. He desired to call in Mr. Weyss, who was with Mr. Von Hippel when the monument was erected on the San Pedro. His own recollection was, that a very substantial monument had been erected at the San Pedro by the United States commission.

Mr. Weyss was brought before the commissioners, and stated that a monument of dressed stone, with the usual inscription, was erected on the parallel 31° 20′, three thousand eight hundred and twenty-five feet west of the San Pedro river. The maps and views were exhibited showing the exact locality of this monument. Mr. Emory stated, if the Indians had destroyed that monument it was all very well; but if it was still standing, there might be some discrepancy, amounting, possibly, to 1″ of arc, or one hundred feet between the latitude of the monument erected by Mr. Salazar and that erected under his orders. If so, it might hereafter, when the country was settled, produce confusion.

Mr. Salazar stated, that in case both existed he would take the monument erected by Mr. Von Hippel as the true boundary. Assented to by Major Emory.

The commission then adjourned, to meet at 9h 30m to-morrow morning.

WASHINGTON CITY, *June* 25, 1856.

Commission met at 9h 30m a. m., and the following preamble and resolution were adopted:

Whereas Señor Salazar has stated it to be within his personal knowledge that some of the monuments erected by Mr. Emory were destroyed and others mutilated by the Indians, in the short space of time elapsing between the construction of these monuments and the final inspection of them by Mr. Salazar; and whereas it appears, from the maps and views which have been drawn, that the topographical features of the country, based upon astronomical determinations, are represented in sufficient detail to enable any intelligent person to identify the line at any required point; therefore, be it

*Resolved,* and agreed upon in joint commission, that these maps and views, duplicate copies of which will be made—one to be deposited with the United States, the other with the Mexican government—shall be the evidence of the location of the true line, and shall be the record to which all disputes between the inhabitants on either side of the line, as to the location of that line, shall be referred; and it is further agreed that the line shown by these maps and views shall be regarded as the true line, from which there shall be no appeal or departure.

Mr. Salazar proposed, with the view of carrying out the labors to the end in the soonest time, that the detailed maps be made, one copy by each commission, on a scale of $\frac{1}{60000}$, and a general map of the whole boundary on a scale of $\frac{1}{600000}$. That at the end, when the total work was done, the maps should be signed, to be given to the respective governments, and the two commissions should exchange the topographical and astronomical data by which each commission has arrived at its results in the field.

Mr. Emory stated that he had constructed the maps of the country from San Diego to the Colorado on the scale of $\frac{1}{30000}$; the projections for the maps of all the other portion were on a scale of $\frac{1}{60000}$. It would be exceedingly inconvenient, if not impracticable, to reconstruct them; he therefore proposed that Mr. Salazar's proposition should be so far modified as to leave the California section of the work to stand as it is, on a scale of $\frac{1}{30000}$. This was assented to by Mr. Salazar, and it was agreed as follows, viz:

That the detailed maps of the California section of the work shall be received on a scale of $\frac{1}{30000}$, the detailed maps for all the other portion of the boundary shall be completed on a scale of $\frac{1}{60000}$, and that a general map of the boundary shall be constructed on a scale of $\frac{1}{600000}$, which maps, when completed, shall form the evidence of the true line referred to in the agreement made this day.

W. H. EMORY.
JOSÉ SALAZAR Y LARREGUI.

Lith of SARONY MAJOR & KNAPP New York.

PRAIRIE OF THE ANTELOPE.

# CHAPTER III.

## GENERAL DESCRIPTION OF THE COUNTRY.

SUITABLENESS AS A BOUNDARY.—GREAT PLATEAU OF AMERICA AND MOUNTAIN RANGES.—DEPRESSION OF MOUNTAINS NEAR THE PARALLEL OF THIRTY-TWO DEGREES NORTH LATITUDE.—GEOGRAPHICAL ERRORS.—METALLIFEROUS REGIONS.—LAKES.—SAND DESERTS.—VEGETATION AND AGRICULTURAL CAPACITY.—CHARACTER OF THE RIO BRAVO.—RAILWAY.—ASTRONOMICAL DETERMINATIONS.

The boundary between the United States and Mexico, extends entirely across the continent from ocean to ocean. That portion of it which is formed by the Rio Bravo, below the mouth of the San Pedro, or Devil's river of Texas, makes a boundary, which, in the absence of extradition laws, must always be a source of controversy between the United States and Mexico.

In other respects, the boundary is a good one; and if the United States is determined to resist what appears to me the inevitable expansive force of her institutions and people, and set limits to her territory before reaching the Isthmus of Darien, no line traversing the continent could probably be found which is better suited to the purpose.

In this respect it is fortunate that two nations, which differ so much in laws, religion, customs, and physical wants, should be separated by lines, marking great features in physical geography.

The boundary is embraced in the zone separating the tropical from the temperate and more northern regions. Here, waters unite, some of which are furnished by the melting of northern snows, whilst those from the south are supplied from mountains watered by the tropical rains. To the north of this zone, the showers from the tropics cease to refresh the earth, and within it, all the flora and fauna which characterize the northern and temperate regions almost disappear, and are not entirely supplanted by those of the tropics.

It is indeed a neutral region, having peculiar characteristics, so different as to stamp upon vegetable and animal life features of its own.

The most remarkable and apparent difference between this region and those of the States of the Union generally, and that which, perhaps, creates, as much as any other one cause, the difference in its botanical and zoological productions, is the hygrometric state of the atmosphere; for, while the plants and animals assume new forms in life, the crust of the earth, the soil, and the rocks, are everywhere familiar, and have many types, indeed fac similes, over the rest of the American continent.

It is very arid; but this is also the character of all the country north of the tropics, and west of the 100th meridian of longitude, until you reach the last slope to the Pacific—a narrow belt, seldom exceeding 200 miles in width, and sometimes not more than ten. The zone extending from the Gulf of Mexico to the Pacific, embracing the boundary, contains a large proportion of arid lands; yet this dry region is, perhaps, narrower on the line of boundary than on any portion of the continent north of it, within the limits of the United States, and is occasionally refreshed by showers in the summer season, and so far presents an advantage over the arid belt to the north.

A general description of the topographical features of the country along the boundary between the United States and Mexico, (traversing the whole breadth of the continent,) cannot be made comprehensive, without presenting in the same view the great outline of the continent itself.

It is now well known that the most extensive feature in the continent is the plateau, or table-land, which traverses this country from the unexplored region of the north to its southernmost extremity, varying in width from five miles to one thousand, attaining its greatest elevation in the Andes of South America, its least elevation and breadth on the Isthmus of Panama and in Central America, and its greatest breadth about the parallel of 38° north latitude. On the northern portion of the continent, this plateau attains its greatest height in Mexico, where it is ten thousand feet above the level of the sea. Its lowest depression is along the line of boundary, about the parallel of 32° north latitude, where it is about four thousand feet above the sea. Thence it ascends again, and preserves an elevation varying from seven to eight thousand feet, to near the 49th parallel, where it is again depressed. This plateau, both in North and South America, occupies the western side of the continent and is traversed by ranges of mountains, the highest peak of which, in North America, is Mount Elias, 17,000 feet above the sea, and in South America is Mount Aconcagua, 21,500 feet above the sea. The climatic features in this plateau, within the United States, are excessive dryness and great changes of temperature between night and day, often as much as 65°.

The principal ranges of these mountains in North America, naming them in the order of their proximity to the coast of the Pacific ocean, are, first, the Cordilleras of California and Oregon, or the Coast Range of mountains; second, the Sierra Nevada, (which, as its name denotes, is a ridge of mountains and craggy rocks, covered with snow;) third, the Sierra Madre, another range of mountains, which was supposed to separate the waters flowing into the two oceans; and, fourth, the Rocky mountains.

The idea conveyed by the name Sierra Madre is very generally adopted by the Mexicans, yet I doubt very much if any continuous ridge or chain of mountains can be found which separates the waters flowing into the Pacific from those flowing into the Atlantic. I am also quite well satisfied that the mountains known as Sierra Madre, in New Mexico, are not the same range as those known by that name in Chihuahua and Sonora, and that both are distinct from the range west and south of Monterey of the same name; but the Coast Range, the Sierra Nevada, and the Rocky mountains, preserve a very considerable continuity throughout the limits of the United States. The Coast Range follows the generally northwest direction of the beach of the Pacific coast, and, for a very considerable distance, rises abruptly from the sea. Along the whole coast it is in view of the navigator, presenting an imposing and ever-changing panorama. It may be said to terminate at Cape San Lucas, the southern extremity of Lower California.

It is the slope towards the sea of this range of mountains which forms the western border of the arid region, and is, in my judgment, the only continuous agricultural country west of the 100th meridian. There are many detached valleys and basins affording facilities for irrigation, where the cereals, the vine, and all the plants which conduce to the comfort of man, are produced luxuriantly; but they form the exception rather than the general rule, and are separated by arid plains or mountains.

The Sierra Nevada, the Cascade Range, and the Rocky mountains, preserve a general parallelism to each other and to that of the Coast Range. Commencing at the north, they can be traced continuously until we reach to within a few degrees of latitude of the region

VIEW TOWARDS THE EASTERN SLOPE OF THE CALIFORNIAN CORDILLERAS TAKEN FROM NEAR CARRIZO CREEK

UPHEAVINGS BORDERING THE COLORADO DESERT ON THE FOOT OF THE CALIFORNIAN CORDILLERAS
TAKEN FROM CARRIZO CREEK-LOOKING SOUTH EAST

of the boundary, where occurs, in all the ranges except the Coast Range, the remarkable depression in the continent, or rather absence in the continuity of the ranges of mountains, hereafter to be described.

The Sierra Nevada, in latitude 33° N., branches; one great division unites with the Coast Range, forming the elevated promontory of Lower California, and presenting, when figured on the map, the appearance of the letter Y, (Tulare valley resting in the fork of the letter;) other branches or spurs are thrown off in a southeast direction, crossing the Gila at the mouth, and many miles above, and traversing the newly-acquired territory in the meridian of Santa Cruz and Tucson.

That range, as well as the Sierra Madre and the Rocky mountains, about the parallel of 32°, lose their continuous character, and assume the forms that are graphically described in the western country as *lost* mountains—that is to say, mountains which have no apparent connexion with each other. They preserve, however, their general direction N. W. and S. E., showing that the upheaving power which produced them was the same, but in diminished and irregular force. They rise abruptly from the plateau, and disappear as suddenly, and, by winding around the bases of these mountains, it is possible to pass through the mountain system, in this region, near the parallel of 32°, almost on the level of the plateau; so that if the sea were to rise 4,000 feet above its present level, the navigator could cross the continent near the 32d parallel of latitude. He would be on soundings of uniform depth, from the Gulf of California to the Pecos river. He would see to the north and to the south prominent peaks and sierras, and at times his passage would be narrow and intricate. At El Paso he would be within gun-shot of both shores.

I noticed this remarkable depression in the continent, in an exploration made by me in 1846, and called to it the attention of Mr. Buchanan, then Secretary of State; and it was upon this information that he instructed our minister, then negotiating the treaty of Guadalupe Hidalgo, not to take a line north of the 32d parallel of latitude, in the boundary between the United States and Mexico.

Passing to the south of this parallel, in about that of 31°, we find the plateau rising rapidly to the table-lands of Mexico, the ranges above described are no longer traceable, and the plateau gives evidence of having been disturbed by tremendous plutonic forces, and the mountains assume a loftier and more rugged and diversified appearance. As I have said before, the Sierra Madre range of mountains cannot be traced distinctly with our present information.

The Rocky mountains, near the head-waters of the Rio Bravo, throw off spurs, which add to the confusion and make it difficult to separate the range from that called in New Mexico the Sierra Madre.

It may be a question whether the Rocky mountain range is not divided by the Rio Bravo; and if so, that which I have designated as the Sierra Madre of New Mexico will, in that case, become a spur of the Rocky mountains. The geological formations to which I shall presently refer, seem to favor this hypothesis. If this hypothesis be true, the Sierra Madre of New Mexico and the Rocky mountain system are the same, and are only divided by the Rio Bravo. But this is a question which does not affect the general topographical description of the country, and may be disregarded here. What I have described refers more particularly to the country west of the Rio Bravo.

The Rocky mountain system, commencing in the north, beyond the source of this river, and beyond the limits of the 49th degree of north latitude, is the distinguishing feature of the country east of that river until we reach the great plains lying between the base of those mountains and the valley of the Mississippi. The axis of maximum elevation preserves a general parallelism to the Sierra Nevada range. Its principal chain, after passing the 36th parallel of latitude, becomes less elevated, and finally terminates in the Organ mountains near El Paso, re-appearing again to the south and east, and becoming at last merged in the great mountain masses in Mexico.

Another branch of these mountains diverges about the head of the Pecos, and running south with unequal elevation, crosses the Rio Bravo between the 102d and 106th meridian of longitude, forming the great bend in that river, and producing one of the most remarkable features on the face of the globe—that of a river traversing at an oblique angle a chain of lofty mountains, and making through these on a gigantic scale, what is called in Spanish America a cañon—that is, a river hemmed in by vertical walls.

Entrance to Cañon of Sierra Carmel, Rio Bravo del Norte.

These mountains to the south of the river expand in width and height, attaining a great elevation in the neighborhood of Monterey, Saltillo, and Buena Vista, and forming one side of the Bolson Mapimi, and it is my impression that these mountains are identical with what is called in Nuevo Leon the Sierra Madre.

A third, but subordinate range, branches from the main chain about the same parallel as that last described, and terminates in the Llano Estacado or the Staked Plains, from which issue the Red river and other rivers of Texas. From the foot of the Llano Estacado the country falls, sometimes by steps, but most generally by gentle slopes, to the shores of the Gulf of Mexico, the crust only broken by the washing of water, and in a few places by the protrusion of igneous rocks. The view of the bed of Devil's river will give a very good idea of the manner in which the general level of the surface forming this great cretaceous plane is broken by the action of water.

A. de Vaudricourt. J. D. Sm. sc.

RIO SAN PEDRO _ ABOVE SECOND CROSSING.

The igneous protrusions which occur are composed of greenstone or basalt, and are traced from the San Saba mountain, by the head of the Leona, to Santa Rosa, in Mexico, where it unites with the main ridge, at an angle of about forty-five degrees. The point where they unite is rich in silver mines. At Santa Rosa the Spaniards had sunk extensive shafts and made a tunnel a mile and a half in length, which was not completed when the revolution of 1825 broke out; since then all extensive operations have been suspended, and the country, rich in minerals and in the production of the cereals and of tropical plants, has been a prey to the incursions of banditti and Indians, and at this time Wild Cat and his band of Florida Indians are settled near there, to add to the disorder and misrule of this beautiful region.

It has been observed that these metalliferous rocks generally occur at the junction of two systems, or where some unusual disturbance or change in the geological structure takes place. Hence we may expect to find these silver-bearing rocks along the boundary line, where the upheaving force, after subsiding near the bed of the Gila river, begins again to re-appear to the south.

The remaining mountain feature of North America, the Appalachian, is referred to here, only to illustrate by comparison the mountain system of the western part of the continent. That chain, grand as it is, sinks into insignificance when compared to those I have attempted to describe. It is nearly at right-angles to the western chain of mountains, is less elevated, and sheds its waters, as is well known, clear on both sides; on the one side into the Atlantic, and on the other side into the Mississippi and the Gulf of Mexico. On both sides, the slopes are comparatively gentle, and the soil fertile, and, refreshed by frequent showers, yields in abundance all that contributes to the wants of man; on the western side of this slope, between it and the desert border of the Rocky mountains, such an expanse of fertile country exists as can be found, in one body, nowhere else on the face of the globe, producing all the fruits of the earth, including those found in every zone, from the boreal regions to the tropics. Persons familiar with its character, as most who read this memoir are, will scarcely be able to comprehend, still less to believe, the character given to the more western and less favored regions described in this report.

In the fanciful and exaggerated description given by many of the character of the western half of the continent, some have no doubt been influenced by a desire to favor particular routes of travel for the emigrants to follow; others by a desire to commend themselves to the political favor of those interested in the settlement and sale of the lands; but much the greater portion by estimating the soil alone, which is generally good, without giving due weight to the infrequency of rains, or the absence of the necessary humidity in the atmosphere to produce a profitable vegetation. But be the motive what it may, the influence has been equally unfortunate by directing legislation and the military occupation of the country, as if it were susceptible of continuous settlement, from the peaks of the Alleghanies to the shores of the Pacific.

Between the two most distinctly-marked ranges of mountains, before described, (the Rocky mountains and the Sierra Nevada,) a succession of minor ranges occur, some of which are many hundred miles in extent, while others appear like isolated mountains, rising above the general level of the plateau. Most of them preserve a general system of parallelism; others present their lines of maximum elevation, forming very considerable angles with the general direction, and all, when traced upon a map, exhibit lines varying from right lines to every degree of curvature.

The whole system, plateau and mountain, seems to have been produced by a succession of forces analogous to each other in direction, but differing in intensity and occurring at long intervals. The prevalence of granite and other unstratified rocks throughout the Sierra Nevada suggests the probability of its being the oldest of the western range of mountains. The identity of its rocks, generally, with those of the Alleghany mountains, marks these two distinct and detached chains as probably contemporaneous. The rocks marking these mountains are of the description commonly traversed by gold and copper veins, as is the case in Oregon, California, Virginia, and North Carolina. Travelling eastward from the Pacific along the bed of the Gila, we encountered similar rocks in a chain of mountains as far east as the Pimo village. This chain, characterized also by the presence of gneiss, mica, and talcose slate, has been traced as far south as the present boundary, where it crosses the Santa Cruz river, between longitude 110 and 111; and in that neighborhood we saw everywhere the remains of gold mines, from which the operators had been driven by the Apaches.

Pursuing our course eastward along the boundary from the meridian of 110°, we cross the San Pedro, the Guadalupe, and the San Luis range of mountains in the order in which they are named, the middle range being chiefly characterized by sienitic aggregates, granitic lava, and immense masses of conglomerate, or breccia. Precisely the same formation is found in the cañon of the Gila, some distance to the north, about the meridian of what is called, in my reconnoissance of 1846, Disappointment creek. And no doubt, when future surveys shall develop a more minute knowledge of the physical geography of the country, each of these ranges of mountains will find its equivalent to the north and to the south. With the present information, I shall not even attempt to connect them conjecturally.

Hypothetical geography has proceeded far enough in the United States. In no country has it been carried to such an extent, or been attended with more diastrous consequences. This pernicious system was commenced under the eminent auspices of Baron Humboldt, who, from a few excursions into Mexico, attempted to figure the whole North American continent. It has been followed by individuals to carry out objects of their own. In this way it has come to pass, that, with no other evidence than that furnished by a party of persons travelling on mule-back, at the top of their speed, across the continent, the opinion of the country has been held in suspense upon the subject of the proper route for a railway, and even a preference created in the public mind in favor of a route which actual survey has demonstrated to be the most impracticable of all the routes between the 49th and 32d parallels of latitude. On the same kind of unsubstantial information maps of the whole continent have been produced and engraved in the highest style of art, and sent forth to receive the patronage of Congress, and the applause of geographical societies at home and abroad, while the substantial contributors to accurate geography have seen their works pilfered and distorted, and themselves overlooked and forgotten.

The San Luis mountains, a distant view of which is given from the Alamo Hueco springs looking west, rise abruptly from the plains about three leagues north of the parallel 31°.20, and, as they run south, assume by far the most formidable appearance of any range, on that parallel, west of the Rio Grande. They are called, in Sonora and part of Chihuahua, the Sierra Madre mountains, yet they do not fulfil entirely the conditions implied by that term, for I am credibly informed that the waters flowing from their base towards the Pacific coast often take their rise to the east of these mountains, and flow through chasms impassable for men, and fall down the western slope in rapid descent, producing sublime and picturesque cascades.

OJOS DE LOS ALAMOS VIEJOS

It was not in my power to explore this range to the south, but I was informed by persons worthy of confidence, that throughout its whole extent, as far south as the parallel of Mazatlan, it was utterly impassable for wagons, and there was no possibility of finding, south of 31° 20′, a line for a railway. The report of its impracticability for wagons was confirmed by the fact that the Camino real, (highway,) established by the Spaniards to connect Chihuahua and Guymas, makes a great circuit, and passes to the north of 31°.20, and within what is now the territory of the United States.

This stupendous range of mountains, which drops so abruptly a few miles north of the boundary, as if to make room for the highway which is to connect the Pacific and Atlantic States, no doubt, reappears to the north, in the neighborhood of the Gila, but our information is not yet sufficient to establish the connexion. I am quite satisfied of one thing, however; its equivalent is not to be found in what is called the Sierra Madre, in New Mexico.

Pursuing our course still eastward, we pass over wide plains bounded by detached ranges of mountains of metamorphic and other limestones, associated with igneous rocks, rich in silver and lead, and at El Paso we encounter the western flank of the third great mountain chain, the Rocky mountains, known in that particular locality as the Organ mountains; and at intervals of about eighty miles we cross two other ranges, the Eagle Spring mountains and the Limpia range of mountains.

The view will give a very good idea of the appearance of the Organ mountains in the distance, and of the Great Mesa, which reaches far away to the west. It is from the bed of the Rio Bravo, just above the gorge, where the river breaks through the range at El Paso.

These three chains of mountains appear to be spurs of the Rocky mountains, and are characterized by the presence of carboniferous limestone, greatly disturbed by igneous protrusions of what Professor Hall characterizes as of "comparatively modern origin."

And throughout this whole region, the carboniferous and metamorphic limestone is not unfrequently traversed by rich seams of argentiferous lead ore. Between the San Luis range and the Organ mountains, the first of the Rocky mountain range, the metamorphism of the rocks is so complete and the irruptive lines so frequent, and protrusion above the crust of the earth so detached, it is impossible to say, with our present information, where the one begins or the other ends, or whether they do not all belong to the same system.

It is between these two ranges, upon the banks of the Janos river, that we discover the first evidences from the west of that vast cretaceous formation which has been traced from the 108th to the 101st meridian of longitude, and as far north as the Great Salt Lake, and south to the 25th parallel of latitude.

The western limit of this formation, discovered by the boundary survey, is the basin of the Janos river in Chihuahua, and its easternmost limit San Antonio, in Texas. How far it extends north and south has never been ascertained, but it has been traced in one direction as far as the Big Salt Lake of Utah Territory.

Granite, and its associated gold-bearing rocks, occur sporadically throughout the Rocky mountain chain, and its spurs; but the distinguishing feature, in an economical point of view, is the prevalence of carboniferous limestone, with which is found associated argentiferous galena.

Silver mines of richness have been discovered, and some of them worked to a limited extent, in the mountains about Tucson, at Barrancas, Presidio del Norte, Wild Rose Pass, in the Organ mountains, and other localities, accounts of which will be found elsewhere.

Gold mines have been worked at the Calabasas, on the Santa Cruz river, and in the mountains of New Mexico, on both sides of the Rio Bravo.

It will not be extravagant to predict the discovery of many localities where silver mines can be worked to advantage throughout the whole region where carboniferous limestone exists, extending on the line of boundary from the great bend of the Rio Bravo, in Texas, to the meridian of the San Luis range. Should this conjecture prove true, we shall have then, in abundance, the only commodity in which we are now deficient, and for which we are at all dependent upon any other country.

Another argentiferous region of exceeding richness, and, I think, one wholly disconnected from the other, is in the basin west of the Santa Cruz river, between that river and the Gulf of California. Veins of metal were discovered traversing a coarse sandstone, which will be more particularly referred to in Chapter VI on that section of the boundary.

I have stated that the eastern portion of the continent, with which we are familiar, is entirely different in its physical geography from the western, and among the distinguishing features of the first is the Appalachian chain of mountains, which sheds its waters clear from the summit to the ocean; that is to say, water once above the surface at any point, continues to flow in that position until it reaches tide-water.

Between the two great chains, which I have attempted to describe, occupying the western portion of the continent, there are other chains of mountains, so numerous that it is impossible to describe them by words; some are continuous, some are detached ridges, others isolated peaks, rising from the plateau almost with the uniformity and symmetrical proportions of artificial structures. Between them are found basins, which have no outlets to the ocean, but are the receptacles of the drainage of the surrounding water-sheds. Of these, the most extensive is the Great Salt Lake in Utah Territory, and the most remarkable for its historical associations and present importance is the valley of the city of Mexico.

These successions of basins form a prominent feature in the geography of North America, extending two-thirds its length, and quite one-third its breadth. They belong to what has been appropriately designated as the Basin system of North America.

Those found near the boundary are Santa Maria, Guzman, and Jaqui—all to the south of the boundary, and within the limits of Mexico. The first is fed by the waters of the river Santa Maria, which runs in a northern direction, and Guzman by the river bearing the several names of Casas Grandes, San Miguel, and Janos, the general course of which is also from the south to the north; and the waters of Lake Guzman and Lake Santa Maria are said to unite in seasons of unusual freshets.

The waters of the Rio Mimbres, near the same meridian as Lake Guzman, which take their rise near the Santa Rita del Cobre, run towards that lake, but they disappear in the plain to the north of the boundary, before reaching it.

The waters of these lakes, or inland seas, are brackish at all times, but in seasons of drought, which last two-thirds of the year, they become salt, and wholly unpalatable. Their shores are covered with lacustrine deposites, and are usually unsuited to cultivation. The waters of these vast basins are not all locked up, however, by the mountains. Three great rivers, with their tributaries, have made their way in different directions to the ocean, cutting, in their passage, gigantic chasms in the mountains. These rivers are the Columbia, the Colorado of the West, and the Rio Bravo. Another river, the Gila, drains this plateau, cutting the mountains nearly at right angles, which, although a tributary of the Colorado, joins it near its

Pl. 45.

Engraved by James D. Smillie.

RIO GRANDE _ NEAR FRONTERA.

mouth, and at an elevation so little above the sea, that it may, in a general description, be considered a separate and independent drainage.

Another feature of this basin system remains to be described, which is also common to all the rest of the mountain regions occupying the plateau, and the region lying east of the Rocky mountains. Between the ridges of mountains the traveller occasionally encounters vast plains, which, when the sun is above the horizon, producing the phenomenon of the mirage, present to him all the appearance of the sea. The plain bounds the view, and the line of the horizon is broken into waves, resembling, in appearance, the edge of the Gulf Stream, when seen from the deck of a vessel ten or fifteen miles distant. The plains are clothed with vegetation of a scrubby growth, incapable of affording subsistence to any but a class of small animals, such as antelope, prairie-dogs, and rabbits. Most generally, however, in the southern part of the United States, these plains are clothed with a luxuriant growth of "grama," the most nutritious of all the grasses. Sometimes they are destitute of all vegetation, except the larrea Mexicana, the yucca, the cactus, and other spinous plants, and are paved with minute fragments of chalcedony, basalt, agate, and other hard rocks. Occasionally in these plains we encounter sand-dunes, called by the Spaniards *medanos*, extending over a large area of country, and encircling what might at first sight be supposed the shores of dried-up lakes. But an examination of the sand with a microscope of sufficient power, dispels this idea. The grains seem to be angular, and are not rounded by the attrition of water. An extensive formation of this kind occurs between the Rio Colorado of the West and the base of the Sierra Madre, and extends many miles along almost the whole extent of the western coast of the Gulf of California. Another very extensive waste of sand lies to the south of the Arkansas river; a third is traversed by the Platte river; and a fourth, which has come under my notice, less in extent, lies to the south of the Rio Bravo, on the road from El Paso to the city of Chihuahua.

The plains or basins which I have described as occurring in the mountain system, are not the great plains of North America which are referred to so often in the newspaper literature of the day, in the expressions, "News from the plains," "Indian depredations on the plains," &c.

The term "plains" is applied to the extensive inclined surface reaching from the base of the Rocky mountains to the shores of the Gulf of Mexico and the valley of the Mississippi, and form a feature in the geography of the western country as notable as any other. Except on the borders of the streams which traverse the plains in their course to the valley of the Mississippi, scarcely anything exists deserving the name of vegetation. The soil is composed of disintegrated rocks, covered by a loam an inch or two in thickness, which is composed of the exuviæ of animals and decayed vegetable matter. The growth on them is principally a short but nutritious grass called buffalo-grass, (Sysleria dyctaloides.) A narrow strip of alluvial soil, supporting a coarse grass and a few cotton-wood trees, marks the line of the water-courses, which are themselves sufficiently few and far between.

Whatever may be said to the contrary, these plains west of the 100th meridian are wholly unsusceptible of sustaining an agricultural population, until you reach sufficiently far south to encounter the rains from the tropics.

The precise limit of these rains I am not prepared to give, but think the Red river is, perhaps, as far north as they extend. South of that river, the plains are covered with grass of larger and more vigorous growth. That which is most widely spread over the face of the country is the grama or mezquite grass, of which there are many varieties. This is incomparably the most nutritious grass known.

South of the Red river, also, the plains are not unfrequently covered with a growth of mezquite trees, (algaroba,) of which there are many varieties. This tree varies in size according to the character of the soil and quantity of rain. It is usually from fifteen to thirty feet in height, crooked, gnarled, and armed with thorns. The wood is hard and full of knots, and is unfit for purposes of carpentry, but in other respects it fulfils many of the economical uses of life. It is excellent firewood, and makes good posts, being very durable. It exudes a gum which is equal to gum-arabic, but to the traveller its most important quality is the fruit which it bears—a nutritious bean, much relished by animals, and not wholly unsuited to the tastes of man.

The vegetation of the mountain and basin region, while it differs materially in the genera and species of plants according to the locality, possesses, nevertheless, a general similarity which is striking and peculiar. I have described that of the plateau or levels as consisting of a diminutive growth of shrubs; but as we ascend from these to the heights of the surrounding mountains we pass through a succession of floral products, varying in character according to the elevation to which we ascend, until we reach a sub-Alpine flora. North of the parallel of 32° this appears at the height of about six thousand feet above the sea.

In situations protected from the winds we usually find, at this height, pines and cedars, and at a less elevation different varieties of oak. Wherever this region is traversed by water-courses, cotton-wood and occasionally sycamore grow on the edges of the streams. There are throughout this region, on the sides of the mountains, growths of pine, oak, and cedar, which are quite extended and present a forest-like appearance, but nowhere, until we begin to descend the Pacific slope and get within the influence of the humidity from the ocean, do we encounter timber at all approximating in size or luxuriance of growth the forests with which we are familiar in the basin of the Mississippi and the eastern slope of the Alleghanies. The Pacific slope, including the water of the Sacramento and its tributaries below the Cascade range, and Puget sound and its tributaries, it is not my intention to describe in this general sketch, or the memoirs which follow, further than to say that, refreshed by frequent showers and fogs from the ocean, it presents a different and more inviting picture than the country to the east of it. It is on this slope that we find that stupendous growth of red-wood, the accounts of which appear almost fabulous. We find here, too, in all that region north of Monterey, considerable adaptation, both in soil and climate, to the production of the cereal plants. About Santa Barbara, in parallel 34° north latitude, the mountains run to the sea; thence the coast deflects sharply to the east; and below, or south of this point, the trade-winds, which sweep along the Pacific coast, charged with humidity for nine months in the year, from as far north as the Aleutian islands, seem to diminish in force, and finally die away, at the lowest extremity of California. The mountain range at Santa Barbara cuts off these humid winds from the land to the south of them; and it is my opinion, that on the Pacific slope beyond this point, and until we reach the region of the tropical rains, no crops can be raised with anything like certainty without irrigation. South of this range, the agricultural character of the country is much the same as that of the mountain and basin systems, and this character is retained along the coast until we reach the parallel of Mazatlan, where the tropical rains begin to be felt in great force. For the four months (July, August, September, and October) during which I kept a meteorological record at Camp Riley, no rain fell in sufficient quantity to be measured. The mean height of the barometer for that period was 29.853, the thermometer 68.37, and the mean dew-point 58.13.

There are considerable portions of the extensive mountain system which I have attempted to describe, where wheat and rye can be raised without irrigation; but these portions are exceptions to the general rule; and I think I am safe in stating, that as a general rule throughout this vast region, corn, cotton, and vegetables cannot be produced without irrigation; and furthermore, the limits of the ground which can be brought under the effects of irrigation are very circumscribed. The town of El Paso, in latitude 31° 44′ 15″.7, and longitude 106° 29′ 05″.4, is considered, and justly so, one of the garden-spots of the interior of the continent. A meteorological record was kept at Frontera, a few miles north of this point, for two years, by assistant Chandler, the results of which are embodied in the diagram herewith presented.

From this it will be seen how very dry the climate is, and how unsuited for agricultural purposes, according to the notion entertained of farming in the eastern States. The settlements about El Paso are irrigated by the Rio Bravo, and are happily not dependent on rains for their fertility.

Whatever population may now, or hereafter, occupy the mountain system, and the plains to the east, must be dependent on mining, or grazing, or the cultivation of the grape. The country must be settled by a mining and pastoral or wine-making population; and the whole legislation of Congress, directed heretofore so successfully towards the settlement of lands east of the 100th meridian of longitude, must be remodeled and reorganized to suit the new phase which life must assume under conditions so different from those to which we are accustomed.

Southern California, the whole of the upper valley of the Gila, and the upper valley of the del Norte, as far down as the Presidio del Norte, are eminently adapted to the cultivation of the grape. In no part of the world does this luscious fruit flourish with greater luxuriance than in these regions, when properly cultivated. Those versed in the cultivation of the vine represent that all the conditions of soil, humidity and temperature, are united in these regions to produce the grape in the greatest perfection. The soil, composed of the disintegrated matter of the older rocks and volcanic ashes, is light, porous, and rich. The frosts in winter are just sufficiently severe to destroy the insects without injuring the plant, and the rain seldom falls in the season when the plant is flowering, or when the fruit is coming to maturity, and liable to rot from exposure to humidity. As a consequence of this condition of things, the fruit, when ripe, has a thin skin, scarcely any pulp, and is devoid of the musky taste usual with American grapes.

The manufacture of wine from this grape is still in a crude state. Although wine has been made for upwards of a century in El Paso, and is a very considerable article of commerce, no one of sufficient intelligence and capital, to do justice to the magnificent fruit of the country, has yet undertaken its manufacture. As at present made, there is no system followed, no ingenuity in mechanical contrivance practised, and none of those facilities exist which are usual and necessary in the manufacture of wine on a large scale; indeed, there seems to be no great desire beyond that of producing as much alcoholic matter as possible. The demand for strong alcoholic drinks has much increased with the advent of the Americans; and in proportion as this demand has increased, the wine has decreased in quality. On one occasion I drank wine in El Paso which compared favorably with the richest Burgundy. The production of this wine must have been purely accidental, for other wine made of the same grape, and grown in the same year, was scarcely fit to drink. Cotton and corn grow with luxuriance, where water can be brought to irrigate the soil, throughout the valleys of the Gila and Rio Bravo, and upon the lower Rio Bravo; and upon the Rio Colorado, below its junction with the Gila, sugar-cane flourishes.

It sometimes happens that the irrigation is produced by natural causes—the overflow of the river. This is the case in the basin of the Presidio del Norte, and on most of the country susceptible of tillage in the valley of the lower Rio Bravo. Crops depending upon this mode of irrigation are very uncertain, the overflows of the river being very unequal as to time and extent. In some portions, however, of the Rio Bravo there are two overflows. This is the case at the Presidio del Norte, below the junction of the Conchos river. The first overflow occurs in June, from the melting of the snows near the head of the Rio Bravo, in latitude 36° 37′; the second occurs in August, from the tropical rains which fall on the mountains near the sources of the Conchos, in latitude 26° 28′.

This occurs to a limited extent on the lower Rio Bravo, which is principally supplied in the summer months by its tributaries—the Salado, the San Juan, &c. These take their rise in the mountains to the south, within the regions of tropical rains. How far the lower Rio Bravo is supplied by the melting of the snows at the head of the river, I am not prepared to say; but I am inclined to the opinion that, before reaching the tertiary region near the mouth of the river, most of the waters from that source are expended either by evaporation or absorption. In the intermediate portion of the Rio Bravo, that lying between Valverde, north of which the river is kept running by the melting of the snows throughout the summer, and the Presidio del Norte, where the Conchos joins it, and supplies it with water from the tropics, great inconvenience is felt for water in years of unusual drought. I was informed, on good authority, that in the summer of 1851 a man drove a gang of mules along the bed of the river from the Presidio del Norte to El Paso. The bed was dry for nearly the whole distance, occasional pools of water standing in places where the river-bed was formed of rock or clay, impervious to water. It was always possible, however, to procure water in sufficient quantities for drinking or watering animals by digging in the river-bed a few feet below the surface.

It might be expected in this report that I should say something of the practicability of a railway route to the Pacific through the newly-acquired territory; and it was my intention to do so, but the subject has been so ably and thoroughly examined and discussed by the Secretary of War, and the officers of the Topographical Engineers acting under his orders, as to leave nothing more to be said. All the topographical and other knowledge bearing on the subject which has been acquired by the boundary survey has been freely placed at the disposal of the War Department. The signal ability with which that information and the information acquired by the surveys specially ordered for the purpose have been collated, leaves nothing for me to say, except that our information fully sustains the conclusions of the War Office report; and it is decided, beyond all question, that a practicable, and, indeed, a highly advantageous route, from the upper basin of the Rio Bravo to the valley of the Gila, exists through the new territory.

It has already been stated, as one of the facts elicited by this and previous surveys, that if the sea were to rise four thousand feet, a vessel could pass from the Gulf of California to the Gulf of Mexico, near the parallel of 32°, and that north of that parallel no good road even for wagons could be found, uniting the valleys of the Bravo and Colorado rivers. This remarkable fact was noticed by me in a reconnoissance made in 1846–'47, and was first brought to the notice of the government through Mr. Buchanan, then Secretary of State, who immediately sent a despatch to our minister in Mexico, indicating that no boundary north of that parallel of latitude should be accepted. The treaty of Guadalupe Hidalgo, however, fixed a line north of that parallel, which cut off entirely the communication by wagons between the two rivers;

and leaving out of view the consideration involved in securing a railway route to the Pacific, it was a line which must sooner or later have been abandoned. No traveller could pass, nor could a despatch be sent, from a military post on the Rio Bravo to one on the Gila without passing through Mexican territory.

I again called the subject to the attention of the government in a letter dated San Diego, April, 1850, which has been already given, in the hope that the United States commissioner might succeed in torturing the treaty of Guadalupe Hidalgo to embrace a practicable route. That letter, however, received no attention, and I am now of the opinion that the Mexican commissioner was so impressed with the importance of the advantage to his government of making a boundary which would not only exclude the railway route, but which would cut off the communication between our military posts in New Mexico, on the Rio Bravo, and those we might establish on the Gila, that any attempt to construe the words of the treaty so as to embrace the railway and wagon route would have been abortive.

It was a great mistake to suppose, as was urged at the time, that the line projected and claimed by the United States surveyor, in opposition to that agreed to by Mr. Bartlett, gave the United States this route. Subsequent surveys have entirely sustained what I have stated on this subject in the letter to the Secretary of the Interior, dated Fort Duncan, which will be found in the first chapter of this report.

The report of Lieut. Parke, who made the recent survey for the railway route over this portion of the country, fully confirms the opinions expressed by me of the practicability of the route; and he has further reported, as the result of his examinations, that the San Pedro river offers the best route by which to descend to the Gila from the table-lands west of the Rio Bravo. I went so far only as to indicate it as a practicable route. Lieut. Parke gives it the preference above all others; and the most prominent of the reasons he assigns, is the important fact that this route affords water in abundance, and traverses valleys capable of continuous settlement.

It is no part of my business to criticise the blunders made in the treaty of Guadalupe Hidalgo, or to defend the provisions of the treaty of December, 1850; but it is undeniable that the last treaty has secured to us what before did not exist—a means of communication between the military establishments on the Rio Bravo and those on the Gila; and what is more important, it has secured what the surveys made under the orders of the War Department demonstrate to be the most feasible if not the only practicable route for a railway to the Pacific. But the importance of these considerations is very little when compared to the important pecuniary consideration secured by the same treaty, in the revocation of the 11th article of the treaty of Guadalupe Hidalgo. That article made it incumbent on the United States to keep the Indians living within our own territory from committing depredations on the Mexicans, and, by implication, imposed on the United States the obligation of indemnity for all losses resulting from failure to carry out the provisions of the treaty.

No amount of force could have kept the Indians from crossing the line to commit depredations, and I think that one hundred millions of dollars would not repay the damages they have inflicted. Whole sections of country have been depopulated, and the stock driven off and killed; and in entire States the ranches have been deserted and the people driven into the towns.

It is true, all this has not been done since the war, and would form no just claim against the United States; but those conversant with the history of Mexican claims against the United States will at once admit that the United States would have been fortunate if she could have escaped with paying real claims for depredations, whether committed before or after the war. I should not be true to history if I did not state what is within my own personal knowledge—that companies were formed, and others forming, composed of persons of wealth, influence, and adroitness, who projected extensive schemes for the purchase of these claims, with the view of extorting them from the Congress of the United States.

I have said nothing in this sketch of the races of men which inhabit this vast western region. I have attempted only to present such a general view of the country as will prepare the reader for the more detailed description of each portion of the boundary line, and the memoirs of the assistants on the separate branches of geology, botany, and zoology, and the ethnographic information which will be found in the local geographical descriptions.

I give in its proper place a table of latitudes and longitudes determined by myself and assistants, and also those determined by others, which have been used in the projection of the general map which accompanies this memoir.

The mode in which these determinations have been made will form the subject of a separate chapter. It will be sufficient to state here, that the important points in the boundary have all been determined by the largest and most improved portable instruments—the latitudes with forty-six inch zenith telescopes, by Troughton & Simms, of London, and the longitudes by moon culminations, observed with telescopes of equal power. As the occasion for taking these large instruments into the interior of the continent, thousands of miles from navigable streams, will perhaps not again soon occur, I have aimed to produce results which would inspire sufficient confidence to make the determinations on the boundary the base of future and minor surveys in the interior of the continent. It has been suggested to me that all the astronomical, magnetic, and hygrometric observations should be published, particularly the observations on the moon and the moon culminating stars; but these alone would form a volume as large as the volume of observations made at the royal observatory at Greenwich, published annually.

The results of the observations made by me and under my orders, as fast as attained, have been given freely to all who asked for them; but I regret they have been used in several notable instances by officers of the government, and others, without due acknowledgment to myself or my assistants.

The best excuse that can be offered for such plagiarists is their ignorance of the labor, privation, self-denial and exposure incurred in the accurate determination of a single point in those far distant regions.

At none of the cardinal points have less than three lunations been used in the determination of longitude, and six nights for that of latitude.

Arthur Schott del.

Lith. of Sarony & Co. New York.

NOCO-SHIMATT-TASH-TANAKI.
GRIZZLY BEAR.
SEMINOLE CHIEF.

# CHAPTER IV.

## LOWER RIO BRAVO.

BRAZOS SANTIAGO AND MOUTH OF RIO BRAVO AS PORTS OF ENTRY.—POINT ISABEL.—PALO ALTO.—RESACA DE LA PALMA.—COAST.—HURRICANES.—TIMBERED BELT.—COUNTRY WEST OF RIO NUECES.—MUSTANGS.—BURRITA.—BROWNSVILLE.—FILLIBUSTERING.—REYNOSA.—RINGGOLD BARRACKS.—ROMA.—POPULATION.—ISLANDS.—RIO SALADO AND BELLEVILLE.—LOREDO.—RAPIDS.—FORT DUNCAN.—SPANISH RULE AND MISSIONS.—AMALGAMATION OF RACES.—DEVIL'S RIVER.—NAVIGATION.—CAÑONS.—MEXICAN SIDE.—STATISTICS.—DISTANCES.

The general view which I have attempted to sketch of the region traversed by the boundary, will prepare the reader for the more minute description of the different sections of the country, and the individual reports of the assistants. It will not be convenient to arrange these sections in the order in which the work was pursued, nor to follow the order in which the general view was presented, commencing on the Pacific, and ending on the Gulf of Mexico. The order has been reversed. The first section embraces the lower Rio Bravo, from its mouth up to its junction with Devil's river; the second, the Rio Bravo, from the mouth of Devil's river to the initial point of the treaty of 1853, in the parallel of 31° 47′; the third, the line west to the intersection of the 111th meridian; the fourth, the line thence to the Pacific.

It will be remembered that I stated in the Personal Account, that in the year 1852, while engaged under the old commission, I found it necessary to suspend the work after bringing it as far down the river as Loredo. The following year, under a new appropriation by Congress, and a new organization, I sailed from New Orleans in the month of May, in a miserable steamer, for the mouth of the Rio Bravo, accompanied by a well organized party, with a complete set of instruments, camp equipage, &c. In crossing the Gulf, the sea was happily smooth, and it was not until we neared the coast and encountered the trade winds, which blow there almost ceaselessly from the southeast, that it became very rough. The steamer did not enter the mouth of the Rio Bravo, but steered her course towards the Brazos Santiago, eight miles up the coast. It was a long time before a pilot could be got on board, and then we were informed the sea was running so high on the bar, it was impossible to cross, and we were reduced to the necessity of lying "off and on" until the sea ran down. The captain gave orders to the mate to put the vessel's head to sea and stand out until day-break, under easy steam, and, with the pilot, went to sleep. The mate, a silly young man, addicted to intemperance, had made several remarks which destroyed my confidence in him, and having much at stake in the safety of the vessel, I did not go to bed. It was fortunate I did not, for, while dozing on the upper deck, I was gradually aroused by a roaring, seething sound, and on looking forward, saw that we were going head on to the breakers. There was no time to wake the captain, and I gave the alarm to the man at the wheel, and ran to the engineer to make him put on all steam. For many moments it was doubtful if the vessel could be got round. By great exertion, however, the steam was raised, and she barely escaped what appeared to be inevitable destruction.

The next day the sea continued to run high, and being thoroughly disgusted with my sojourn aboard the steamer, I went ashore in the pilot-boat.

The steamer was stranded a few trips subsequently, in attempting to make the entrance of the Brazos Santiago.

The bar has but eight feet of water, and is very shifting. That at the mouth of the Rio Bravo has still less. Yet it was at these two points that the troops were landed, and all the supplies for the army which invaded Mexico, under the orders of General Taylor. Most of the merchandise intended for the lower Rio Bravo is landed at the Brazos, and thence reshipped in a strong river steamer, which passes out to sea and thence into the Rio Bravo. The channel of the mouth of the Rio Bravo varies a little in depth, but is seldom more than six feet or less than four; it is of soft mud, and of the numberless vessels grounded there during the war, not more than one or two were lost. The bar of Brazos Santiago is of hard sand, and a vessel grounded there is certain to be stranded. The mouths of both these harbors open towards the prevailing wind, and I can suggest no method by which they can be improved at any reasonable cost. The town of Brazos stands on a sand-spit immediately within the bar, and is little more than a collection of wooden shanties, left there by the army, which may be washed away some day by a norther forcing the water from the lagoon, or bay, above, faster than it can escape over the beach and through the narrow inlet into the sea.

Three miles within the lagoon, or bay, and standing upon the first firm ground, a bluff of alluvial soil, about six or ten feet high, is Point Isabel. Here is the custom-house, where the goods intended for the river, as high up as Roma, are entered. Those for the towns above that point are supplied usually by the way of Indianola and San Antonio. Point Isabel is a small settlement, the principal buildings being those erected by the army of occupation in 1846. It was from this point the army made its march to fight the battles of Palo Alto, Resaca de la Palma, Fort Brown, &c.

It is well known that the Mexicans selected their own ground for the two first named battles; but if General Taylor had had in his hand the correct map now presented of that country, as will be seen by a glance, he could not have selected, in the neighborhood, a better field than Palo Alto to fight a small force against a larger one. This fact may have been known to others, but was not developed to my mind until the completion of this map. It will be seen that both flanks of the American army were protected, and the Mexicans were prevented by the ground from using the advantage due a much superior force to extend their flanks and envelope the American forces. The country is almost a dead level, and presents to the view of a horseman one unbounded plain, relieved by clusters of mezquite trees, (chapparal,) and the existence of the morasses to the right and left of the American position was probably not known to the Mexicans until they attempted to outflank their adversaries.

It was not my good fortune to have been present at either of those engagements; but I trust some of those who were will take advantage of the map now furnished, to figure for the military student the position and manœuvres of the troops on both sides, in those battles, so unique in their execution and results. Those two battles gave the prestige to our arms in the Mexican war, and saved the United States Military Academy from destruction.

The Mexican army was well organized, well disciplined, and well equipped, inured to war by contests with the Indians, and in suppressing internal revolution. The American army was perfectly disciplined, but, with the exception of its chief, and a few other gallant old officers, had never been under fire, and numbered only one-third of the opposing force. Yet on their first encounter, the subordinate officers, chiefly from West Point, executed their orders with the precision of a field day exercise, showing beyond all question the utility of military education and discipline, and putting to rest at once the attacks on the Military Academy, which had become so formidable that few believed it possible to sustain the institution a year longer.

The general description of this part of the country will apply equally to all the coast of Texas, from the mouth of the Rio Bravo to the bay of Corpus Christi—indeed to Matagorda bay. It is well known to be a low, flat coast, with soundings diminishing regularly in depth as you approach the shore. The first shore-line is that of an island varying from some hundred yards to several miles in width, and penetrated at various points by inlets with shifting bars, few of which are practicable for the entrance of even the smallest sea-going craft. Separating this from the main land are shallow lagoons, as variable in breadth as the island which separates them from the ocean.

When the army marched from Corpus Christi to Point Isabel, General Taylor attempted to transport his supplies by the lagoon separating the two places, but found it impracticable even with small boats. These lagoons abound in delicious fish and fowl.

Proceeding inward, the land bordering the lagoons is, in the first ten or twenty miles, usually a flat prairie, composed of alluvial soil and sedimentary deposites of the ocean in alternate layers, showing how gradual and well contested have been the encroachments

Laguna below Lomita, fifteen miles above mouth of Rio Bravo del Norte.

of the land upon the sea. The rivers taking their rise in the cretaceous formations, both the sedimentary and alluvial deposites are heavily charged with lime, making the soil rich, black, and fiery—often so surcharged as to destroy some descriptions of vegetation. Within this belt, salt lakes of value are not unfrequently found, and throughout its whole extent spots occur devoid of vegetation, and encrusted with a white saline deposite. Most generally, however, the vegetation is a luxuriant coarse grass which grows nearly waist-high, with an occasional clump of live oak bordering the wet places. I think it likely this whole belt of country has been formed in the following manner: the trade-winds from the southeast are felt here with considerable force, and, blowing inward for nine-tenths of the time, fill the lagoons with salt water. Suddenly the wind will shift in a contrary direction, and blow with violence for two or three days, called there a norther, forcing the salt water out to sea, and leaving the dry places to be covered by fresh water, thus forming alternate layers of salt and fresh water deposites.

This coast, as well as the whole coast of Texas, is sometimes swept by terrific tornadoes, which produce marked changes in its topographical and hydrographic features. In the latter part of the month of September, 1854, on my passage in the steamship Louisiana from New Orleans to Indianola, we encountered a violent hurricane. A few days afterwards we entered the mouth of Matagorda bay, and found the channel had been improved by the storm. It was deepened two feet, and instead of finding only nine, we found eleven feet of water on the bar, and the channel straightened. This beneficial effect remains, I am told, to this day. This hurricane, which swept the town of Matagorda level with the ground, and destroyed every wharf in the bay of Matagorda, except that upon which our instruments were placed, forced the water out of the bay at such a rapid rate, that it could only escape by deepening and widening the channel.

After passing the belt of prairie, we find a ridge of low sand-hills which seem to have marked the former limits of the coast, and here for the first time going towards the interior, we meet with clumps of post-oak called *mots*. The trees are usually crooked and wind-shaken, and unfit for timber.

Throughout this second belt or steppe, which extends many miles into the interior, wherever sand occurs to give consistency to the limestone soil, we find this growth in great abundance.

This admixture of soil produces the richest cotton and corn-growing soil in the world; but west of the Nueces, and between that river and the Rio Bravo, the want of rain makes agriculture a very uncertain business, and as we approach the last named river, this aridity becomes more marked, and the vegetation assumes a spinose stunted character—indeed, so marked is the change, that when we get within a few miles of the river the vegetation is a complete chapparal.

West and south of the Nueces the country is sometimes exposed to excessive and long continued droughts, and it is doubtful if agriculture can be made profitable without irrigation; all the region between that river and the Rio Bravo is, however, a fine grazing country, and the numbers of horses and cattle that ranged it, belonging to the settlers on the Rio Bravo under the Spanish rule prior to 1825, are incredible. To this day the remnants of this immense stock are running wild on the prairies between the two rivers. Hunting the wild horses and cattle is the regular business of the inhabitants of Loredo and other towns along the river, and the practice adds much to the difficulty of maintaining a proper police on the frontier to guard against the depredations of Indians and the organization of fillibustering parties. In times of agitation and civil war on the Mexican side, parties assemble on the American side ostensibly to hunt, but in reality to take part on one side or the other in the affairs of our neighbors. I had heard a great deal of these wild horses, but on an examination of many hundred that had been caught, I never saw one good one. They are usually heavy in the forehand, cat-hammed, and knock-kneed. Their habits are very peculiar; they move in squads, single file, and seem to obey implicitly the direction of the leader. They evince much curiosity, always reconnoitring the camp of the traveller at full speed, and when there chances to be a loose animal, be he ever so poor and jaded, he is sure to run off with the crowd and disappear entirely. Many a luckless horseman passing through this country has been left on foot by the "stampede" caused by the visits of these wild animals.

Passing through that region in 1852, after a long journey of several thousand miles, my animals so jaded and worn down that I considered nothing could stimulate them to a gallop, my line was charged by one hundred and fifty of these animals, and six mules with a heavy wagon, containing all the astronomical and other instruments of the boundary commission, followed them across the prairie at full speed for nearly two miles. The coolness of the driver, and the boldness of the wagon-master, who threw himself in front of the lead-mules, stopped their further progress.

The section of country, particularly that part under consideration, is traversed by deep gullies called arroyos, sometimes difficult to pass in wagons. The sketch here presented shows one of these arroyos crossed by the road leading to Loredo.

Arroyo Secate, two miles below Loredo.

These arroyos are natural consequences of the unequal manner in which the rain falls throughout the year. Sometimes not a drop falls for several months; again, it pours down in a perfect deluge, washing deep beds in the unresisting soil, leaving behind the appearance of the deserted bed of a great river.

The streams which are found in this country have their rise in limestone regions, and the water is very unwholesome even when the stream is flowing, but usually the beds of the streams are partly dry, and the water is found standing in holes. Superadded to its noxious mineral ingredients, it holds in solution offensive vegetable matter, and is disgusting to drink; yet it is upon this water that our soldiers are kept nine-tenths of the time while watching and pursuing the Indians who are constantly making incursions from the Mexican side into the settlements of Texas. While the country was in the military occupancy of the Spaniards previous to the revolution of 1825, they provided against this inconvenience by making at certain stations great reservoirs of solid masonry to catch the rain-water. The remains of many of these wells were found, and they form one of the many external objects to be seen throughout the extent of the frontier which convey the impression that the country has steadily gone backwards since the days of the Spanish rule.

Having now given the general view of the country on the American side of the first section of the boundary, I will ask the reader to ascend with me the Rio Bravo along the boundary, where I will describe in detail all that is worth noting as high as the mouth of the Rio San Pedro, or Devil's river, from which point we will take a general view of the country on the Mexican side, comprising the States of Coahuila, Tamaulipas, and New Leon.

Before ascending the Rio Bravo, it may be as well to state that the appointments for the survey of the river consisted mostly of light boats unsuited to hydrographic work in the open Gulf; and not wishing to incur the expense of an outfit for the limited surveys required by the treaty, outside the river, I proposed, with the concurrence of the Secretary of the Interior, to obtain the co-operation of the Superintendent of the Coast Survey, who had several well equipped parties in the Gulf, and whose operations I knew would eventually be extended to that locality. Under this arrangement, by which the boundary commission paid the expenses incidental to changes in its original plan of operations, and by which it was agreed that the hydrography should be done by the Coast Survey, and the astronomy and topography by the boundary commission, Lieut. Wilkinson, in command of the brig Morris, repaired at the appointed time to the mouth of the river and made soundings, marked on sheet No. 1, by which we were enabled to trace the boundary, as the treaty required, "three leagues out to sea."

This survey was conducted in the summer of 1853, that in which the yellow fever scourged the whole Gulf coast; yet up to the time of leaving the station, late in the summer, no case of the disease had occurred on board the vessel, and but a single one among the land parties. In conformity with a promise made, I took passage in the "Morris," which was not entirely sea-worthy, and went with the party to Pensacola, where the yellow fever was raging, and we had to lament the loss of the surgeon, Dr. Bryan, whose high professional skill and many social virtues endeared him to all who were honored with his friendship. Several others of the party, myself among the number, were taken down and narrowly escaped the fate of Dr. Bryan.

The voyage across the Gulf, which should have occupied five days, was, owing to adverse winds, gales, and the condition of the ship, extended to eighteen days. I had an opportunity on this voyage to watch narrowly the effect of the storms on the barometer, and observed for the first time a fact which, I believe, has since been well established, that in the Gulf the fluctuations of the barometer fail to give the usual indications of the approach or subsidence of storms.

The entrance to the mouth of the Rio Bravo is over a bar of soft mud, varying from four to six feet deep, and the river within a few hundred yards of its mouth is not more than one thousand feet wide. The shore-line of the coast, scarcely broken by the action of the river, is formed of a series of low shifting sand-hills, with a scanty herbage. Inside these hills are numerous salt marshes and lagoons, separated by low belts of calcareous clay but a few feet above the level of the sea, and subject to overflow. The first high ground is Burrita, ten miles from the mouth, where there is a small settlement of Mexicans engaged in agriculture upon a very limited scale.

Mouth of the Rio Bravo del Norte.

At the mouth of the river there are a few frame houses erected by the army in 1846, now owned by the steamboat company engaged in the navigation of the river. Opposite is a small Mexican settlement called Bagdad, where the Mexicans from the interior, as far as Monterey, resort for sea bathing. The sites on either side of the river are very unsafe. A few years before the Mexican war, the whole population was swept off except the pilot, an American, who, with his family, took refuge on the top of the sand-hill upon which my observatory was afterwards erected.

Beyond Burrita, the river still pursues its serpentine course through alluvial soil, with an occasional patch of arable ground occupied by Mexican rancheros engaged in the cultivation of maize and the rearing of goats and chickens.

At the Rancheria de San Martin, a mouth of the Rio Bravo, forty feet wide, opens on the American side into the Laguna Madre, allowing some of the water of the river to escape to the sea by the Boca Chica and the Brazos St. Iago. On the American side the road leading from the mouth of the river to Brownsville crosses this outlet at San Martin, over a substantial wooden bridge erected by the army.

From this point upward to Brownsville the river makes a great bend to the South, and is so winding in its course that frequently the curves almost touch. The land on each side is level, and covered with a dense growth of heavy mezquite, (Algaroba.) It is generally too high for irrigation, and the climate is too arid to depend with certainty upon rain for the purposes of agriculture. The vegetation is of a semi-tropical character, and the margin of the river, which is exposed to overflow, abounds in reed, canebrake, palmetto, willow, and water-plants, and would no doubt produce the sugar-cane in great luxuriance.

Brownsville, situated on the American side of the river fifty miles from its mouth by the course of the river, is only twenty-two miles distant by the road. It contains about three thousand inhabitants. The houses are mostly of wood and well built. The town has sprung up since the Mexican war, and owes its prosperity chiefly to the contraband trade with Mexico.

Opposite Brownsville is the ancient town of Matamoras, with a population about the same in number as Brownsville.

Old Fort Brown, Texas.

Below Brownsville, and adjoining it, is the military post, with old Fort Brown at the farthest extremity of the public grounds. In the middle of the parade ground, unmarked by any monument, lie the remains of the gallant officer who fell in defence of the fort which now bears his name. The height of Fort Brown above the sea is, by barometrical measurement, fifty feet. The mean temperature for the years beginning 1850, and ending 1855, was 73° Fahrenheit; the mean quantity of rain in the same years was annually 33.65 inches. These quantities are taken from the Army Meteorological Register, and are used in preference to my own, as they cover a much longer space of time. They would seem to indicate an abundance of rain for all the purposes of agriculture, and we should be at a loss to understand the arid character of the country on both sides of the river, were it not that the tables give us the solution ; we there find that more than one-half the rain falls in the autumn, which is followed by a winter during which the thermometer frequently falls below the freezing-point. One-fourth the whole quantity of rain falls in a single month, and it very often happens that no rain whatever falls in the months of May, June, and July. Consequently, throughout the whole valley of the Rio Bravo and its tributaries, we seldom see corn growing except in the bottoms, subject to over-

flow, or upon lands which are below the water-level and can be irrigated by artificial channels. Somewhat of this barrenness is due undoubtedly to the excess of lime and saline matter with which the soil is charged.

As we ascend above Brownsville, lands within the water-level become more frequent and extended, and at many places cultivated fields form a prominent feature in the landscape. Up as high as Reynosa, the belt of alluvial soil subject to the influence of the moisture from the river is very considerable in width, and in addition to corn, the sugar-cane has been planted with success. The foliage on this portion of the river indicates a richer soil, and the trees assume very much the dimensions of those on the alluvial bottoms of the Mississippi.

It is within this region, embracing a river coast of one hundred miles, that the sugar-cane can be cultivated to advantage; and in situations sheltered from the northers, I have no doubt oranges and lemons could be raised with facility.

Property, however, is very insecure all along the boundary, and unless extradition laws with Mexico are passed, this fertile tract will never have its capacities developed.

The boundary between the United States and Mexico is here only an imaginary line running down the centre of the river, and an offence can be committed on either side with impunity. A few minutes served to place the offender over the line, when the jealousies of the law on either side step in to protect him; and where national prejudices are involved, the criminal is not unfrequently extolled for his exploits.

It was in the summer of 1853 that this portion of the boundary was surveyed, and a revolution headed by Caravajal was in its last throes. This chief had retired to the American side of the river, and was occupied in making occasional forays into Mexico, aided by some American volunteers, mostly composed of young men, whose tastes for civil pursuits had been destroyed by the Mexican war. These efforts were attended with no other effect than that of irritating the peaceable inhabitants on both sides, and were of great inconvenience to us in the prosecution of the survey. Attempts were made several times to stop the parties under my command engaged in the survey of the river, and on one occasion nothing but the forbearance of the officer in command prevented his party from firing upon a detachment of Mexican cavalry which threatened to charge them. In the absence of the Mexican commissioner, I was at length compelled to make a direct appeal to General Cruz, then in command on the Mexican side, who promptly gave orders along the line which had the effect to lessen, in some degree, the interruptions to which the surveying parties were exposed.

We were scarcely more in favor on the American side of the line; for some months previously the United States troops had interfered with a strong hand to break up the enlistment of men and the concentration of fillibustering forces on our side of the river. Although most of the hired men employed by me were disbanded fillibusteros, the parties escorted by a detachment of United States soldiers were usually mistaken for military scouts in search of the violators of the law, who at that time composed the majority of persons on the frontier.

Some idea of the reckless character of the persons then infesting that frontier may be formed from the following circumstance, the truth of which is vouched for by several respectable eye-witnesses. My own camp was but a short distance from the place where the scene occurred:

One mild summer's evening several gentlemen, among them a retired officer of the fillibusteros, were enjoying the delicious twilight of that climate on the bank of the river opposite a point where was usually posted a picket-guard, detached from a Mexican military station four miles distant. The guard of ten men were seen to approach the jacal, dismount, tie their horses, and stretch themselves on their blankets, some to sleep, others to smoke, but none particularly to watch.

The conversation of the first-named party was rather of a jocose character, directed at the expense of the young American fillibuster who had joined in the Caravajal revolution, which had just been ended with such signal advantage to the regular Mexican troops. A little nettled, probably, at what had passed, he offered a wager of one hundred dollars that he would cross in a boat and take the guard, single-handed. His wager not being accepted, he offered to bet "drinks for the party." Some person, not dreaming he was in earnest, indiscreetly took the bet.

The absence of the fillibuster was scarcely noticed, and the conversation about other subjects had continued for nearly an hour, when it was interrupted by the sharp reports of a revolver, and a yell which reverberated from shore to shore, giving the impression of many voices; these were quickly followed by the rolling fire of a platoon of musketry, and then all was silent. "Could that be S——?" asked one. "Impossible!" was the reply. "It would be just like him," said a third. Shortly after a boat containing two or three men was seen to dart across the rapid current from the shadow of the high bluff on the American side. As it approached the opposite side, its occupants, not wishing to violate the usages of the guard, called out in Spanish they were friends, going over to see what was the matter. "*Matter? Hell!*" answered a voice in English, "Come here and help me to drive these mustangs in the river." They found the guard dispersed, and S—— with one arm shattered by a musket-ball; with the other he was trying to lead all the ten horses to the river-shore.

Reynosa is a small Mexican town of about 1,500 inhabitants, opposite an American settlement called Edinburgh, with one or two substantial warehouses. The last-named town, like all the others on the American side, except Loredo, has been built since the war, and owes its existence chiefly to the contraband trade with Mexico. Reynosa is built on a low cretaceous ridge, and it is here the first rocks above the surface are seen; yet none appear on the immediate banks of the river until we reach Las Cuevas, some distance above, where we find a stratum of cretaceous sandstone 10 or 15 feet thick. At the last named point, and thence up the river, there is also a marked diminution in the quantity of bottom-land susceptible of cultivation, and vegetation changes its character, becoming more dwarfed and spinose. The uplands on either side impinge close upon the river, and the vegetation is principally mezquite and cactus. On the Texas side, as we recede from the river, the chapparal gives place to the open prairie, covered with luxuriant grass. This character of the river lands extends with little variation up to Ringgold Barracks.

This military post consists of a few comfortless frame houses, situated half a mile below Rio Grande city. Opposite, and four miles from the Rio Bravo, is the town of Camargo, of about one hundred inhabitants. It is situated on the San Juan river, the first unfailing tributary to the Rio Bravo from the Mexican side. It is one of a series of rivers which rise in the so-called Sierra Madre, and go to supply the Rio Bravo in summer, the season of tropical rains, when that river most requires replenishing, as then the supply of water from the melting of the snows at its northern sources is nearly exhausted.

Ringgold Barracks was one of the points selected for the close determination of latitude and longitude to check the lineal surveys, and a point from which excursions could be made with facility, to determine secondary points by reflecting instruments and by the transmission of chronometers.

The result of the astronomical observations, and some of the observations themselves, will be found in the Astronomical Appendix.

Ringgold Barracks and Rio Grande City.

Through the courtesy of Major Paul, the commanding officer at Ringgold Barracks, the observatory was placed within the enclosure of the military grounds, and west of the officers' quarters. The height of this point above the sea, by the barometer, is 521 feet; the magnetic dip 52° 27′, and the declination 9° 15′ east. The observatory was 70 feet above the bed of the river, so that the river-bed is 451 feet above the sea at this point. The distance to the sea, measured by the sinuosities of the river, is 241 miles; the direct measurement only 75 miles. If the river had a direct run to the level of the sea, it would have a fall of six feet to the mile, and would probably empty itself in dry seasons, so that the tortuous course of the river, so vexatious to the traveller, is of importance in an economical point of view. My observations embraced three summer months at Ringgold Barracks, during which time the excessive heat was tempered by the sea-breeze, which was felt here daily with great force. Dr. Brown, assistant surgeon United States army, stationed at this post, has kindly furnished me with the meteorological journal kept by him for several years, and I give it in place of my own, as it extends over a much greater space of time, and will, therefore, afford a much more comprehensive view of the climate. It may, also, be taken as a fair type of the climate of that region of country which extends from Brownsville to Eagle Pass. It will be seen from this and subsequent records how dry the country becomes as we go towards the centre of the continent.

The beautiful town of Roma, 16½ miles above Ringgold Barracks, is the present head of steamboat navigation; it is built upon a high bluff of yellowish sandstone, containing ferruginous nodules. When I visited this small town, I was at a loss to know how such fine residences and warehouses, all recently built, could be sustained by its trade; but being the guest of the owner of one of these large establishments, I did not think proper to be very inquisitive. At night, when I went out to take my observations for the determination of the latitude and longitude of the place, I found that the mercury of the artificial horizon was very tremulous, notwithstanding the calmness of the night. Not being able to overcome the difficulty, or ascertain its cause, I

Roma, Texas.

put up my instruments and returned to my quarters. On the way I encountered a long train of mules, heavily laden, directed towards the Mexican side of the river. The motion of the animals caused the disturbance of the mercury, and their rich burden of contraband goods, intended for the Mexican market, explained the commercial prosperity of the town. As might reasonably be expected in any country where the duties on foreign goods amount almost to prohibition, smuggling ceases to be a crime, but is identified with the best part of the population, and connects itself with the romance and legends of the frontier.

Between Roma and Ringgold Barracks there is much excellent land susceptible of irrigation, and both banks of the river are thickly settled with Mexicans. There are many Americans in this part of the country engaged in trade, but I cannot, at this moment, recall to mind a single one engaged in agricultural pursuits. Sugar cane will grow on this part of the river, but the land is rather too elevated for that plant to be grown with profit. Indian corn is the staple product, and when extradition laws are enacted and enforced, and the Indians who periodically plunder the country are exterminated, the rearing of cattle will be followed with advantage.

After studying the character and habits of that class of Indians called wild Indians, and bearing in mind the mild and humane government extended over them by the missionaries of the Church of Rome, without producing any results, I have come to the deliberate conclusion that civilization must consent to halt when in view of the Indian camp, or the wild Indians must be exterminated. Nothing could exceed the judgment, perseverance, and humanity with which the various orders of the Catholic Church have pursued, for three hundred years, the work of redemption among these savages; but at the very moment when Christianity appeared most likely to triumph, the savages turned upon their benefactors and swept them from the face of the earth. There are distinct races among the Indians as among the white men, and before the advent of Christianity they were divided into semi-civilized and wild races. The semi-civilized then, as now, cultivated the soil, lived in houses, some three stories high, and kept faith with each other, and it is among these that Christianity has made any permanent impression. The wild Indians were then, as they are now, at perpetual war with them, leading a nomadic life, defying all restraint, and faithless in the performance of their promises. They have but two settled principles of action—to kill the defenceless and avoid collision with a superior or equal force. In the early stages of my experience with these Indians, I was inclined to believe them maltreated, and to consider their present reckless condition the result of the encroachments of the white people upon their rights ; but such is not the case—experience proved to me that no amount of forbearance or kindness could eradicate or essentially modify the predominant savage element of character. The semi-civilized Indians form, however, much the larger class of Indians on the Mexican frontier. Indeed, nine-tenths of the population of all Mexico are Indians, or have the blood of Indians coursing in their veins. A pure white, of unadulterated Spanish blood, is rather the exception than the rule. I do not know how far the effects of the sun can be considered to have bronzed the complexion, but it seemed to me the proportion of pure white in the northern States of Mexico bordering on the boundary, was greater than in southern Mexico, always excepting the cities of Jalapa, Puebla, and Mexico.

One of the most important duties of our survey was to determine to which side the islands in the Rio Bravo belonged. For this purpose it was agreed between the Mexican commissioner and myself to sound the river on each side of every island, and the centre of the deepest channel should be the boundary line. From the mouth of the river to Ringgold Barracks there are eleven islands, marked on the map from 1 to 11, commencing at the mouth, and this order of numbering the islands is observed until we reach the parallel of 31° 47′, where the boundary leaves the river. The sheets of the boundary, on a scale of $\frac{1}{60000}$, are numbered from 1 to 54, No. 1 being the mouth of the Rio Grande, and the numbers progressing regularly from the Gulf of Mexico to the Pacific. The islands are numbered on these sheets to indicate their geographical position, but they are represented also on separate sheets on a scale of $\frac{1}{6000}$, to show their topographical and hydrographic details, and to exhibit upon what data they have been allotted to the United States or to Mexico.

Up to Ringgold Barracks these islands are of little value, but above that they are of more importance. Islands Nos. 12 and 13, between Ringgold Barracks and Roma, both fall to the United States. No. 13, called on the maps Beaver island, divides the waters of the river into three parts, and the channel which lies nearest to the Mexican shore is so narrow that steamers can with difficulty pass through it, yet the branches are, by reason of their shallowness, wholly impassable for them. An attempt was made by the Mexican local authorities to arrest the steamboat in its passage through this channel, but not only the survey, but the actual experience of the navigator, proved the narrow one to be the true channel, and consequently the boundary between the two countries. The allotment of all the islands was made upon the condition of things as they existed when the boundary was agreed upon. The channel of the river may change and throw an island once on the Mexican side to the American, and vice versa, but neither the Mexican commissioner nor myself could provide against such a contingency, none having been anticipated in the treaty.

We however agreed, as far as that agreement may be worth anything, that in case the channel of the river changed, the right of navigation through the new channel should remain unimpaired to both countries, but the jurisdiction of the land must remain as we had arranged.

Five miles above Roma, and opposite Mier, there is a large island called Los Adjuntas, which was awarded to the Mexican side. At present the channel is between the island and the American shore. Formerly the channel was very nearly equally divided on either side of the island, but during the occupation of Mier by the American troops a temporary causeway was constructed of loose stone, to enable the cavalry to cross their horses to the island for the purpose of grazing. This causeway, now nearly washed away, has given a permanent direction to the channel which rules the island out of our territory. At the lower end of the Los Adjuntas and on the Mexican side are tepid baths, luxurious for the robust, and valuable for a certain class of diseases. The springs which supply these natural baths are near them, and are supposed to possess medicinal virtues of a high order. They were supposed to be sulphur springs, but analyses of the water which I placed in the hands of Dr. Easter detected no trace of sulphuretted hydrogen.* The zoological character of the rocks from Reynosa, where the cretaceous formation was first noticed, up to Las Moras, a distance measured on the parallel of latitude of 144 miles, is much the same, while they differ in their lithological character. If any difference is to be noted in the zoological character of these rocks it is in the exposure, just above Roma, at the foot of the island of Las Adjuntas, and at several other localities in the neighborhood, of banks of fossil oyster-shells of great size, some of them measuring 18 inches in length.

I have noted at Roma the occurrence of sandstone studded with nodules of ferruginous iron. Throughout the section between the San Juan river and Loredo, septaria and strata of yellowish and green sandstone frequently cocur. Often the nodules of more durable substance project beyond the weather-worn surface of the softer sandstone, producing picturesque appearances.

The town of Mier, famed in the history of the war of independence of Texas, stands upon the Alamo river, four miles back from the Rio Grande, contains about 700 inhabitants, and is now chiefly noted for the superior quality of the blanket manufactured there. It was an important point during the war with Mexico, being the point where the road to Monterey diverges from the Rio Bravo, and where the supplies for the invading army were transferred from water to land transportation. From Mier upwards, the course of the river is more nearly north and south, and less winding in its course. The banks on either side become more abrupt and rocky, and for the first time in ascending we find a rocky bottom.

Forty-six miles above Roma, measured by the river, is Bellville, the trading establishment of a hospitable and enterprising gentleman who has built himself a warehouse something after the fashion of old feudal castles—not for the purpose of ornament, but for defence against the Indians

---

*The following is the result of the quantitative analyses by John D. Easter. The whole quantity of solid matter was 0.6763 per cent., consisting of—

| | | |
|---|---|---|
| Silica | 0.016586 | per cent. |
| Botoreide iron | 0.000754 | " |
| Alumina | traces. | |
| Lime | 0.009389 | " |
| Magnesia | 0.009580 | " |
| Sodium | 0.243323 | " |
| Chlorine | 0.340470 | " |
| Sulphuric acid | 0.010180 | " |
| Phosphoric acid | traces. | |
| Iodine acid | traces. | |
| | 0.630282 | |

Drawn by J. E. Weyss.

Lith of SARONY & Co. New York.

FALLS OF THE RIO SALADO.

and banditti of that country. Opposite, on the banks of the Salado, and four miles from the Rio Bravo, is the town of Guerrero. The Salado, like the San Juan, and the Alamo which comes in at Mier, is a clear stream, having its rise in the sierras of igneous and metamorphic rock to the west, and forms a true oasis in the wilderness of rotten limestone which is found on either side of the lower Rio Bravo, and which causes the waters of most of its tributaries to be brackish and unwholesome.

The falls of the Salado are seven miles above its junction with the Rio Bravo. A floral phenomenon exhibits itself on the Rio Bravo, which finds its explanation at these falls. Just above Roma, and thence to the mouth of the Salado, the cypress is found growing in the bed of the Rio Bravo, and it was a matter of conjecture why it should grow there and not elsewhere. On ascending the Salado to the falls, it was ascertained the principal growth on that river was cypress, and the trees in the Rio Bravo were evidently emigrants from this colony. It is to be hoped that this useful tree will continue its emigration downwards, where the country is now destitute of all building wood.

The land from Bellville to Loredo is not altogether barren; there are many flats on which the water of the river could be brought for the purposes of irrigation; but, until recently, the Indians have had entire possession of the country, and now they make continual forays, crossing and recrossing the river to elude pursuit, at some of the many fords which occur in the river. I was myself very near falling into the hands of a party of these savages. Passing in a wagon from Bellville to Ringgold Barracks, in one of our excursions to determine the astronomical position of the former place, accompanied only by assistant Clark and the driver of the instrument wagon, we struck the trail of a band of Indians, where two roads united, so close that the dust was still flying. We supposed at the time we were following on the heels of a gang of wild mustangs going to water. These Indians were pursued by Captain Granger of the rifles, and brought to bay just as they were crossing the river and making good their escape to Mexico. That energetic officer succeeded in killing the chief and several others, and capturing all their horses and arms.

In many instances, along this portion of the river, American capital has associated with it Mexican labor, in the attempt to open farms for the produce of grain and the rearing stock, but the incursions of the wild Indians, and the depredations of the semi-civilized and half-breed Indians, render such enterprises uncertain and unprofitable. After we ascend about thirty miles above Loredo, all settlements on the Texas side cease until we get in the immediate neighborhood of Eagle Pass.

At Loredo there is a very considerable Mexican settlement, which dates back to the times when the Spaniards occupied the country. It has at present fallen into decay, and derives its support principally from the United States garrison, (Fort McIntosh,) one mile above the town. Loredo was once the residence of proprietors of countless horses and cattle, which have been run off by the Indians. Some of them, escaping from their captors, have formed the source of the numerous herds of wild horses and cattle that are now roaming the prairies to the east and north, the pursuit of which affords the chief occupation of many of the inhabitants of the Rio Bravo.

The country around Loredo is much the same as that described about Ringgold Barracks, but is more elevated and more frequently intersected by dry arroyos, which give evidence of more frequent and copious falls of rain.

Here, too, the geological character of the country is a little changed by the frequent occurrence of strata of compact blue limestone, useful in building. The public buildings at Fort Duncan (Eagle Pass) are of this material. Other strata also alternate with the main stratum of cretaceous sandstone, composed of blue clay, more or less hard, and marls of various colors, and oyster breccia of solid consistence. In the neighborhood of the arroyo Sombreretillo, ten or fifteen miles above Loredo, three miles below Eagle Pass, and also at Eagle Pass, strata of lignite coal occur three or four feet thick. This coal is of great prospective value, considering the scarcity of wood in this country, and the probable demand for fuel when the rich silver mines of the mountains to the south are in full operation.

Between Loredo and Eagle Pass, or Fort Duncan, a distance of 120 miles, measured by the sinuosities of the river, the river, its banks and adjacent country, retain very much the same character; the obstructions in the bed of the river become more rocky, and the fall more precipitous. At one place, called the falls of Rio Grande, or the Islitas, the rapids are impassable, even in small boats, except in the summer months, when the river is swollen by the tropical rains which fall on the mountains to the south and west. These falls, or more properly rapids, are forty miles below Eagle Pass; just above, the old Mexican trail crosses by which the army under General Wöll invaded Texas in the war of Independence, and is the same by which the column of United States troops under General Wool invaded Mexico, to effect a junction with General Taylor, in the war of 1846.

Fort Duncan, five hundred miles from the Gulf, measured by the sinuosities of the river, is only 208 miles measured in a direct line. It is the westernmost of the military posts placed at intervals along the lower Rio Bravo. The town of Eagle Pass adjoins the fort, and is a place of some trade, having a few large warehouses, built of the bluestone obtained in the neighborhood. Opposite is the military colony of the Mexicans, called Piedras Negras (black rocks,) after the coal layers which crop out here. The view of this military colony here presented is not strictly true. The artist has taken the liberty of placing on the houses roofs of carpentry work. The houses are, in truth, only jacals; that is to say, poles placed vertically, with the interstices stopped with mud, and the tops covered in by thatched roofs. The garrison on the Mexican side, below this place, is composed of regular troops. This military colony is an establishment peculiar to Mexico, and similar establishments are to be found at several points higher up the river. The idea attempted to be carried out is to combine colonization and military defence. Each soldier is allowed a certain quantity of land, and is permitted to live with his wife and children, and not required to live in barracks. A certain quantity of land is cultivated for the benefit of the whole colony; beyond the labor required for this, and military service of rather irregular character, the time of each soldier is his own, and he is permitted to cultivate as much land as he pleases.

Under the Spanish rule, prior to 1825, this system was combined with the missionary power of the Catholic Church; and all those Indians now running wild from the Gulf of Mexico to the Gulf of California were brought under the benign influence of the church; and about the beginning of the present century had attained a state of semi-civilization which may truly be called the golden age of this, now, vast deserted country. Under the Spanish dominion, a cordon of military and ecclesiastical stations extended from sea to sea, over a distance of fifteen hundred miles. Military patrols passed regularly from station to station, and at each station great structures were erected for the accommodation of troops, for religious worship, and for the storing of provisions, the remains of which are still to be seen. Among them some of the most beautiful specimens of architecture on the American continent are still to be seen. The

A. Schott del. R. Metzeroth sc.

LAS ISLETAS—FALLS OF PRESIDIO DE RIO GRANDE.

two in most perfect state of preservation are the Mission of San José, a church on the San Antonio river, a few miles below the town of that name, a sketch of which is here given, and the Mission of San Xavier, on the Santa Cruz river, in the newly acquired territory, the view

Mission of San José, near San Antonio, Texas.

of which, I regret to say, has been lost. Most of the buildings at these stations, however, were erected of perishable materials, adobe walls, and thatched roofs. As soon as the thatches were destroyed, the walls were washed down nearly to their bases by the rains. The Indians were required to cultivate the soil, and their families were domiciled in the immediate vicinity of the station. The most active and intelligent warriors were incorporated into the ranks of the military.

The downfall of this magnificent cordon of military and ecclesiastical establishments, and the return of the Indians to a savage life tenfold more ferocious than ever, is directly traceable to two causes. First, the revolution, where both the Monarchists and Republicans courted the co-operation of the Indians, and thus invited them to insubordination. Second, and more prominently, the attempts at amalgamation, by intermarriage of the whites and Indians.

This last cause, which is now operating so banefully over the whole of Spanish America, I do not think has been sufficiently estimated, in the attempts to account for the decline and retrograde march of the population of that entire region.

Wherever practical amalgamation of races of different color is carried to any extent, it is from the absence of the women of the cleaner colored race. The white makes his alliance with his darker partner for no other purpose than to satisfy a law of nature, or to acquire property, and when that is accomplished all affection ceases. Faithless to his vows, he passes from object to object with no other impulse than the gratification arising from novelty, ending at last in emasculation and disease, leaving no progeny at all; or if any, a very inferior and syphilitic race. Such are the favors extended to the white man by the lower and darker colored races, that this must always be the course of events, and the process of absorption can never work any beneficial change. One of the inevitable results of intermarriage between races of different color is infidelity. The offspring have a constant tendency to go back to one or the other of the original stock; so that in a large family of children, where the parents are of a mixed race but yet of the same color, the children will be of every color, from dusky cinnamon to chalky white. This phenomenon, so easily explained without involving the fidelity of either party, nevertheless produces suspicion, followed by unhappiness, and ending in open adultery.

The only mode by which a country can be benefited by the introduction of the white race is by the introduction of both sexes, which, with proper guards upon morals, results in exterminating or crushing out the inferior races, or placing them in slavery.

Throughout Mexico, wherever the white race has preserved its integrity, there will be found a race of people very superior in both mental and physical ability; a condition due to the excellence of the climate, which combines all the qualities requisite for the development of the human being in the highest degree.

From Eagle Pass upwards there are no settlements on the American side, and but a single one on the Mexican side. In places are found the remains of settlements from which the inhabitants have been driven or carried off by the savages. This district of country, extending along the river seventy miles, until within five or ten miles of the mouth of the San Pedro, or Devil's river, is nevertheless the most fertile and desirable portion of the whole Rio Bravo for settlement. On the Texas side it is watered by the beautiful, limpid streams of Las Moras, Piedras Pintas, Zocaté, and San Felipe, which come into the Rio Bravo at right angles, and at equal intervals.

A very extensive region of land is here within the water-level, and can be successfully irrigated; and if we may judge from the products of the settlement at Santa Rosa, in nearly the same parallel, all the sub-tropical fruits and cereals can be raised in these bottom lands to advantage; while the uplands are clothed with a luxuriant growth of the most nutritious grasses. This country is unsurpassed in salubrity, and when the Indians are exterminated, and the adjacent mines shall receive their full development, it will be the paradise of Western Texas. Two causes will operate to postpone this to a very distant day: the proximity to the boundary, which affords so many facilities for the operations of banditti and horse-thieves; and the character of the country beyond, which will be seen, as you ascend the river, to be incapable of continuous settlement, and which must for a long time remain the hiding-place of the wild Indians.

One source of wealth in these table lands, and which is common to all the table lands contiguous to the Rio Bravo as far down as Reynosa, I have not yet pointed out; that is, the extensive growth of certain indigenous plants, the virtues and properties of which are well known to the Mexican and Indian population, and will be found elaborated and specifically noticed in the botanical memoirs appended.

On the mesas, or table lands, which are unsuited to the purposes of cultivation, many plants are found growing useful in medicine and dyeing; and various yuccas, dasylirions, and agaves, genera well known for their useful fibres, which we now import from foreign countries. There are also extensive growths of shrubs and trees of the leguminous order, furnishing gums, tannin, and nutritious pods, highly relished by the herbiferous animals, wild and domestic.

I have before stated that the present head of steam navigation is Roma. At some distant day, no doubt, the navigation will be extended up as high as the mouth of Devil's river, a distance, measured by the sinuosities of the river, of 567 miles; and with this in view, the assistants in charge of the lineal surveys have been directed to make special notes of the obstructions in the river. The large maps designating the boundary, and deposited in the Department of the Interior, will form the basis upon which estimates for this purpose can be made, but they are too voluminous to accompany this printed report. The ideas now suggested are from the notes of assistant Arthur Schott, who was charged with the lineal surveys of the river from Devil's river to Ringgold Barracks, and from my own observations.

The navigation of the river between Edinburgh and Roma is not free from obstructions, but they are mostly of shifting sand-bars, except the one formed by Island 13 on the boundary map, which may be improved by damming two of the three channels. Between Roma and Bellville the obstructions are principally occasioned by Islands 15, 16, 17, and 20, dividing the channel of the river; and the navigation may be improved in the same way by damming all the channels but one, and dredging the bottom of the one left open. It is above Bellville that obstructions become of rocky character, difficult to remove, such as are to be found at Islands 25, 30, 31, 33, 35, 39; and above Loredo, at the Heron islands, Las Islitas, Cazneau island, and Chess-Board island.

The worst of these are Islands 25, 30, and the Islitas; 25 is sometimes called Major Brown's island, from the circumstance of the steamer Major Brown being detained there a whole season waiting for a rise of water; No. 30 is a couple of small islands, at the foot of which the channel is only eleven or twelve feet wide. Of the three last-named obstructions, the Islitas is the most formidable. Here, in fact, there is no channel, and the rocky islands obstructing the passage of the water can only be passed at high water from June to September.

Other obstructions besides islands are caused by numerous reefs and spurs of rock. Just above Bellville there is a formidable obstruction of this kind, marked by the wreck of the steamer "Exchange;" this obstruction is formed by two reefs running in from the opposite sides, and overreaching each other, thus leaving but a crooked channel, through which the river passes at the rate of five miles per hour. A similar obstacle occurs about fifteen miles below Eagle Pass.

Other reefs occur running entirely across the river, and are disposed in steps, one above the other. In seasons of excessive dryness they are bare of water. Of such character are the obstructions noted in the field-notes of Mr. Schott as "the snares," "the meshes," "the stone turtles," and the "Devil's pen," all situated between the Islitas and Eagle Pass.

In most cases the rocks forming the obstructions are sedimentary rocks of the upper cretaceous age, lying in horizontal strata; these would yield easily to the pick. How far it would be prudent to resort to cutting away these natural dams, as a mode of improving the navigation, which would necessarily lower the pools above, would be a subject of investigation for each locality. My object in this report is only to present a general view of the character of the difficulties in the way, and to present such maps as would render unnecessary any general survey of the river hereafter.

Except where interrupted by arroyos, the country is uniformly level, no hill breaking the general view until we reach Eagle Pass; and it may be that in time the resources of the country will be sufficient to justify its connexion by railroad with San Antonio or Brownsville, in which event the improvement of the navigation of the river will become of minor importance.

Ascending beyond the mouth of the San Pedro or Devil's river, the whole character of the country changes. The bed of the river becomes hemmed in by rocky mural banks, the tops of which are beyond the reach of irrigation, and, from the aridity of the climate, they can never be made subservient to the purposes of agriculture. The general formation of the country is limestone, deposited in strata perfectly horizontal, and where the river has washed its way through the banks, presents the appearance of gigantic walls of dry-laid masonry. The course of the river from this point up to Fort Leaton, near the Presidio del Norte, a distance of 387 miles, is almost one continuous cañon, utterly unsuited to navigation, and, with a few exceptions, unsuited for settlement. Occasionally this limestone formation, over 1,000 feet in depth, is broken through and upturned by igneous irruptions from below, forming stupendous mountains and gorges of frightful sublimity. I leave to the officers under my command, who so bravely surveyed these chasms heretofore untrodden by white men, and probably by Indians, the task of describing in detail this section of the work, which was only visited by me at certain places to determine the latitude and longitude.

My notices have been principally confined to the Texas side of the boundary. Before leaving the mouth of the Rio San Pedro to ascend the Rio Bravo, I will take a rapid view of the country on the Mexican side between this point and the Gulf. The most prominent topographical feature is a chain of lofty mountains of unequal elevation which cross the Rio Bravo about 250 miles above Rio San Pedro, and run in a southeasterly direction towards the Gulf. It is composed of a variety of ridges, preserving towards each other, and towards the river and the Gulf coast, a general parallelism. The principal range is called the Sierra Madre. The eastern slope of these mountains forms portions of the States of Coahuila, Nuevo Leon, and Tamaulipas. The area between the Rio Bravo and the bases of these slopes is an arid, cretaceous plain, covered with a spinose growth similar to that on the Texas side. Passing from this plain into the mountains, we encounter a soil made up of the debris of the older rocks, and watered profusely by limpid streams having their sources in the crystalline rocks. And here, in the valleys formed by these mountains, we find large tracts of country within the influence of some irrigating stream, sheltered from the northers of the winter, and at an elevation above the sea sufficient to overcome the excessive heat of the summer due this parallel of latitude, producing all the fruits of the tropics and the cereals of the more northern climates. The climate is unsurpassed in salubrity, and nothing is requisite to make this region the garden-spot of the valley of the Rio Bravo but a stable form of government and security from the bands of roaming savages that plunder it at intervals.

In the more northern portions, as at Parras, the vine is grown with success, and a luscious wine is made, which, however, will not bear transportation. On the seacoast and southern portion, commencing at Santa Rosa, oranges, limes, &c., are cultivated successfully. Some of the mountains are rich in silver, and at Santa Rosa, as has been elsewhere noticed, the mines were once extensively worked by the Spaniards, and have now passed into the hands of an American company.

In no civilized country are statistics more difficult to obtain than in Mexico, and several attempts to obtain the population of this region, composing the largest portion of the States of Nuevo Leon, Coahuila, and Tamaulipas, have resulted in such discrepancies as to induce me to give credit to none. I have, however, made an estimate of the resident population of the Rio Bravo on both sides, from the Devil's river down, which I here present. This estimate is rather under than over the number, which has heretofore been registered too high:

Drawn by Arthur Schott. Pl. Engraved by J.D. Smillie.

MILITARY COLONY, OPPOSITE FORT DUNCAN_TEXAS.

| | |
|---|---:|
| Eagle Pass | 300 |
| Piedras Negras | 600 |
| Loredo | 700 |
| Colonia Militar | 50 |
| Loredo Nuevo | 700? |
| Mier | 700 |
| Roma | 400 |
| Guerero | 600 |
| Camargo | 500 |
| Rio Grande city | 500 |
| Reynosa | 600 |
| Brownsville | 3,000 |
| Matamoras | 4,500 |
| Burrita | 300 |
| Lomita | 200 |
| Rancherias at different points on the river | 6,060 |
| Total | 20,210 |

*Table of distances along the course of the river.*

| Names of places. | Distance between places. | Distance of each place from mouth of Rio Grande. |
|---|---|---|
| | *Miles.* | *Miles.* |
| Mouth of Rio Bravo | | |
| Brownsville | 49. 81 | 49. 81 |
| Edinburgh | 120. 36 | 170. 17 |
| Ringgold Barracks | 71. 21 | 241. 38 |
| Roma | 16. 67 | 258. 05 |
| Bellville | 45. 93 | 303. 98 |
| Fort McIntosh | 61. 46 | 365. 44 |
| Falls of Presidio de Rio Grande | 90. 44 | 455. 88 |
| Fort Duncan | 39. 77 | 495. 65 |
| Mouth of Rio San Pedro | 71. 12 | 566. 77 |
| Mouth of Rio Pecos | 41. 48 | 608. 25 |
| Point where Lieut. Michler came to the Rio Bravo from San Antonio road | 96. 88 | 705. 13 |
| Point of beginning of Lieut. Michler's survey in 1853 | 49. 05 | 754. 18 |
| Presidio de San Vincente | 67. 61 | 821. 79 |
| Presidio del Norte | 132. 00 | 953. 79 |
| Cañon on San Antonio road | 222. 78 | 1, 175. 57 |
| San Ignacio | 60. 89 | 1, 236. 46 |
| San Elceario | 40. 25 | 1, 276. 71 |
| El Paso del Norte | 25. 38 | 1, 302. 09 |
| Initial point of boundary where it leaves the Rio Bravo, running west | 3. 41 | 1, 305. 50 |
| Frontera observatory | 2. 70 | 1, 308. 20 |

# CHAPTER V.

## FROM MOUTH OF DEVIL'S RIVER TO EL PASO DEL NORTE.

PECOS SPRINGS.—KING'S SPRINGS.—INDEPENDENCE CREEK.—RIO BRAVO INACCESSIBLE.—LIPANS.—CAÑONS AND RAPIDS.—MOUTH OF THE PECOS.—DEVIL'S RIVER.—DIFFICULTY OF NAVIGATION.—CAÑON OF BOFECILLOS.—COMANCHE PASS.—SAN CARLOS.—MOUNT CARMEL AND LOS CHISOS.—SAN VINCENTE.—PRESIDIO DEL NORTE.—VADO DE PIEDRAS.—TOWNS NEAR EL PASO.

The description of the boundary, up the river, is continued by the following reports of Lieutenant Michler and assistant Chandler:

WASHINGTON CITY, D. C., *March* 10, 1856.

SIR: The following is an extract of your orders to me, dated Washington City, D. C., April 4, 1853: "You are charged with the responsible duty of completing the unfinished portion of the survey of the Rio Grande, which forms the boundary between the United States and Mexico, between Fort Vincente and the mouth of the Rio Pecos."

Soon after their receipt the survey was commenced, and in the following August completed. Since then the maps have been finished, and several views of the scenery in the immediate locality of the work engraved.

I now have the honor of submitting a report of the manner in which the survey was conducted, and a description of that portion of the river, and the country adjacent.

Having organized a party, and made all preparations at San Antonio, Texas, we proceeded on the road to El Paso, and followed it as far as the Pecos Springs. At this place I determined to leave the road and strike for the Rio Grande, as directly as the nature of the country would permit. Owing to its character, and the necessity of taking wagons along, our route, as shown by the map, became somewhat circuitous. For the first fifty miles, from the Rio Pecos to King's Springs, the course was nearly due west, enabling us to avoid the many impassable arroyos setting in towards the former river. The road ran the greater part of this distance in small narrow valleys, gradually ascending towards their heads, passing from one into another, over high ridges, by precipitous ascents and descents. These valleys are bounded by chains of hills, either of a conical or oblong shape, the tops of which are on the same level and capped by horizontal layers of cretaceous limestone; the slopes are regular, well rounded, and steep. From the ridges, or high plains, which are generally very narrow, valleys ramify in every possible direction towards the Pecos. The grass is rich and luxuriant; low, scrubby bushes are found, but no growth of timber. No water, except what collects in the gullies during heavy rains, until you reach King's Springs. This is a large spring of water, deep and clear, with a fine gravel-bottom, and well protected from the sun by shelving rocks, but without bush or tree to mark its place. Whilst the main party encamped there, a reconnoissance was made in a so thwesterly direction for nearly sixty miles, when it was found impracticable to proceed further. The course lay towards the "Los Chisos" mountains. The country is cut up by immense chasms, closed in by steep cliffs, unseen until standing upon the very edge of their fearful depths; rugged hills, covered with sharp igneous stones, make it difficult for animals to travel. The same volcanic formation as found along the Limpia extends over this section of country. The San Carmel range appears in the distance—high mountains, with their turreted peaks, could be seen, presenting a magnificent prospect like the spires of some distant city. Our efforts to travel in a southwesterly direction having proved unsuccessful, on leaving King's Springs we changed our route to a southeasterly one, and arrived at Independence creek. Along this distance of forty miles the country is of the same character as that first passed over. Whilst the train remained on the creek, a small party made examinations in advance. This is a beautiful stream, running boldly among the hills, and is fed by innumerable springs bursting out from its banks. It is a rich treat for the eye in that arid country. Besides a copious supply of fresh, clear water, there is more timber than is ordinarily found upon streams draining these high plains; mezquite trees grow in large numbers for miles around, and the valley furnishes luxuriant grazing for animals. This place is much frequented by Indians; an oasis in a desert country.

Numerous trails from the Pecos and the Escondido here unite and form a large broad one, running south to the Rio Grande; there are unmistakable signs of their constant use. Leaving the creek, we ascended the contiguous hills and rose upon a high plain, over which we travelled forty miles, following the guidance of the Indian trail; this was deeply marked, although it

Lipan Crossing—Eighty-five miles above the mouth of the Pecos.

is difficult to make an impression on the surface. It was a dreary sight to look upon the dull, wide waste around us; its parched barrenness, combined with the influence of a scorching July sun, was enough to madden the brain. The nearer we approached the river, the more rough the country became; deep ravines and gullies constantly impeded the progress of the wagons, and the whole surface was covered with sharp angular stones and a growth of underbrush armed with thorns. Along this portion of the route, we found plenty of water in tanks at the heads of the ravines. There were, also, many fine springs. One in particular is noticeable for its beauty; falling over a precipice of forty feet, its waters were emptied into a large basin worn out of the solid rock. This was a favorite camping place of the Indians; the many paintings of men and animals found covering the rocks, testify to their rude attempts in the artistic line. The last ten miles kept gradually descending towards the river; occasionally the wagons had to be let down steep descents by means of ropes. Our road finally emerged upon a low flat plain about twenty feet above the level of the Rio Grande. We had, fortunately, struck the only place, as our examinations afterwards proved, where we could possibly reach the river with our wagons; the route was a circuitous one, in all 140 miles from the Pecos springs. The initial point of our work was found to be a little over forty miles above; the surveying party of the previous year had there suspended operations in consequence of the rugged character of the country, and had returned to Eagle Pass through Santa Rosa and San Fernando, Mexico. It was next to an impossibility to approach the river for the first twenty miles of the survey, this section being literally cut up by deep arroyos; steep hills, covered with rocks of igneous origin, intervene and jut into the water's edge. The river here is very tortuous. From the end of this section, the country undergoes a great change; the formation is limestone, and the river forces its way through a deep cañon nearly twenty miles in length, its banks being composed of

Lipan Crossing—View down the river.

high perpendicular masses of solid rock, resembling more the work of art than of nature. Arroyos of the same structure, at many places, open into the river; in following its course, we had frequently to make detours of twenty-five and thirty miles, in order to advance our work a few hundred feet. The plain where the main party encamped, and where we first struck the river, made a gradual descent to the water. Here was the first break in the cañon, and the crossing being fordable, formed an accessible pass for the Indians into Mexico. This ford, known as the Lipan crossing, is represented by the preceding sketches.

The Lipans often visited us here, and made themselves useful as guides. As it proved to be impracticable to conduct the survey on land without taking an interminable length of time, it was decided to make the attempt in the bed of the river; anticipating such an emergency, boats had been built at San Antonio and brought along in wagons. After they had been put together and launched, and everything in readiness, the train was sent back by the road to Eagle Pass, there to meet the small party selected to descend the river to the same point. Upon trial, we found the boats, which were our only resource, would float—the only thing that could be said in their favor. The wood of which they were made was only partially seasoned, and the hot sun had so warped them, that they presented anything but a ship-shape appearance. The two skiffs were frail—a moderate blow would have knocked a hole in them—and the flat-boat was unwieldy and unmanageable. The current was so strong that two good oarsmen could not stem it in a light skiff. At the point of embarkation was a short break in the cañon of a few hundred feet on both sides of the river; the water then again rushed between rocky banks ten or twelve feet high, which increased in height as we proceeded. It would seem incredible that the bed of the stream could have been formed through ledges of solid rock, as shown in the accompanying sketch.

Cañon—One hundred and five miles above mouth of the Pecos.

The occurrence of a freshet whilst encamped on its banks, however, convinced me of the impetuosity of its waters, which appeared to force everything before them. The bed is narrow, and hemmed in by continuous and perfect walls of natural masonry, varying from 50 to 300 feet in height; the breadth of the river being extremely contracted, these structures, seen from our boats, look stupendous as they rise perpendicularly from the water. It is not unfrequently the case that we travel for miles without being able to find a spot on which to land. The limestone formation is capped by an infinite number of hills, about 150 feet in height, and of every imaginable shape. The whole adjacent country is traversed by deep arroyos or cañons, intended by nature to drain the high plains bordering on the river; they are, in their appearance, but miniature creations of the same power which forced a passage for the Rio Grande. Their junctions with the river form large rapids or falls, caused by the rocks and earthy matter washed down them. These rapids are numerous, many of them dangerous, and will always prove insurmountable obstructions to future navigation. The force of the current is very great, and for thirty miles above the mouth of the Pecos is one continued rapid; its average rate is nearly six miles an hour. The width of the river varies from 80 to 300 feet, and at a few points narrows down to 25 and 30; when confined between its rocky walls the channel is very deep. There are no tributaries along this section of the work, but several fine springs contrast their clear blue with the muddy waters of the river. There is but little growth until the approach to the mouth of the Pecos; a narrow strip of soil is then occasionally found at the base of the rocks, and gives growth to some fine live-oak and mezquite trees; grape-vines flourish in abundance, yielding a very palatable fruit. Catfish were the only kind of fish caught, some of them very large and heavy. Soft-shell turtle

Junction of the Rio Bravo del Norte and the Pecos.

abound. But few varieties of game were seen; the wild turkey in large numbers, and some few deer—the latter of the black-tail species. The only practicable way of making the survey through the cañon was by allowing the boats to drop down the channel, taking the direction of the courses and timing the passage from bend to bend; when opportunity offered, the speed of each boat was ascertained by distances accurately measured on land, making allowances for change of current and other causes of error. Observations for time and latitude were taken every night to check the work. On arriving at the mouth of the Pecos, a view of which is given above, the survey, 125 miles in extent, was completed. The Pecos is more deserving of its other Mexican name, "Puerco," for it is truly a rolling mass of red mud, the water tasting like a mixture of

A. Schott. del. Lith. of SARONY, MAJOR & KNAPP, N.Y.

LIPAN — WARRIOR.

every saline ingredient; its banks are like those of the Rio Grande for some distance above its mouth, and then become low and flat. As we continue to float down stream, we find the country below the junction undergoes some very considerable changes; these become still more apparent on reaching the San Pedro or Devil's river, whose waters form a dividing line between two distinct portions of country. The banks of the Rio Grande here present an entirely new appearance—they become low, and prairie land, covered with mezquite, extends as far as the eye can see; numerous well timbered and beautiful streams unite their waters with the river along this portion. Within a few hours of each other, both the party in charge of the train and the boat party reached Fort Duncan, near Eagle Pass, 110 miles by the river below the mouth of the Pecos.

View of Fort Duncan, near Eagle Pass.

To add to the interest of the expedition, a constant excitement was experienced in the descent of numerous falls. Ignorant of what unforeseen dangers awaited us, our frail boats were dashed blindly ahead by the force of a swift current over rocks and rapids, hemmed in on both sides by insurmountable walls which seemed mountain high, and at times not a spot upon which to rest a foot; there was but little chance of escape from destruction, letting alone the immediate peril of drowning in case of any accidents to the boats. Nor were these dangers imaginary—a serious accident, and one almost fatal to the success of the expedition and to the lives of most of the party, occurred the very first day after taking to the boats; notwithstanding every precaution had been taken, we were unable to avoid it, and our minds were most forcibly impressed with the truth that real dangers did exist. After having descended the river for a few miles an immense rapid presented itself to our view. The river here narrowed from nearly three hundred feet to the width of twenty-five; both shores could be touched with the ends of the oars; an immense bowlder divided the main into two smaller channels, leaving but a narrow chûte for the boats to descend. The bottom was covered with large rocks, and over these the whole mass of water rushed, foaming and tumbling in a furious manner; a dangerous rapid was thus formed of several hundred feet in length, extending from bank to bank. The two skiffs made the descent in safety, although the waves rolled so high that each plunge filled them almost to overflowing. The flat-boat was not so fortunate; totally unmanageable, she ran square against the rocky walls, splintering and tearing away her entire front; such was the force of the blow that the crew were knocked flat on their backs, and the boat-hooks left firmly imbedded in the crevices of the rocks. Thrown back by the great swell, she commenced floating stern foremost down the rapid, gradually sinking. The men stuck to her faithfully, and the skiffs were put into immediate requisition; but by the expert swimming of two of the men, both Mexicans, who had dashed into the current ere the sound of the crash had died away, and seized her lines, she was landed on the end of a sand-bar which most providentially lay at the foot of the rapid; a few feet further, both men and boat would have been destroyed, and our all—provisions and ammunition—irrecoverably lost, the perpendicular banks offering no foothold where to land. With means at hand to repair the wreck, we were again afloat the following day, our craft bereft of all her fair proportions.

Before closing this report, I cannot refrain from informing you of the very able and willing assistance rendered me by my assistants, Messrs. E. A. Phillips and E. Ingraham, and Prof. Conrad Stremme; and of the patience and perseverance displayed by them and the men composing the party, under circumstances most peculiarly trying.

I am, sir, very respectfully, you obedient servant,

N. MICHLER,

*Lieut. Corps Topographical Engineers, U. S. A.*

Major W. H. Emory, U. S. A.,
*U. S. Commissioner.*

---

## SAN VINCENTE TO PRESIDIO DEL NORTE.

Fort Duncan, *December* 1, 1852.

Sir: In accordance with your directions, I have the honor to make the following report on the topographical survey of that portion of the Rio Grande intrusted to my charge. The survey commenced a few miles above Fort Leaton, in the neighborhood of the Presidio del Norte, and extended to a point about one hundred and twenty-five miles above the mouth of the Rio Pecos, embracing a section of country which for ruggedness and wildness of scenery is perhaps unparalleled.

The appearance of the valley in the vicinity of Fort Leaton, with its succession of plains and arable bottoms, forms a contrast to the rugged country beyond. From this valley, which is from one to three miles wide on each side of the river, we suddenly enter the range of the Bofecillos mountains, through which the river has found or forced a passage, forming extensive rapids at its entrance.

A narrow path along the river on the American side is the only means of passage in the immediate vicinity of the stream; and numerous rocks and branches of trees obstruct even this narrow trail.

The cañon of the Bofecillos mountains is less rugged in its character than those met with subsequently. Although the passage of a mule train on the immediate borders of the river is utterly impossible, there is on the American side a valley extending nearly parallel to the course of the stream, at a distance varying from two thousand to three thousand feet; along this passes an extensive Indian trail, but to all appearances not recently used. Dangerous and long

Entrance to Cañon Bofecillos, Rio Bravo del Norte.

rapids occur where the river leaves the cañon, and the country loses entirely the features which characterize the north side of the Bofecillos range. The hills approach and recede from the river in varied succession; nearly always, however, admitting of the possibility of carrying the line of survey along the river bottom, at least as far as the Comanche Pass. Scarcely a tree or branch of the smallest size marks the hill-sides or summits, and it is only on the immediate border of the river that the eye, wearied by the continued succession of sterile plains, is relieved by the sight of verdure; and this only when the rocky barriers recede sufficiently for a narrow strip of soil to form.

Comanche Pass, on the Rio Bravo, the most celebrated and frequently used crossing place of the Indians, was found to be just below this Bofecillos range; here broad, well-beaten trails lead to the river from both sides. A band of Indians, under the well known chief Mano, (hand,) crossed the river at the time of our visit; they had come, by their own account, from the head-waters of Red river, and were on their way to Durango, in Mexico—no doubt on a thieving expedition.

At this pass the hills on either side are less elevated, and to the northwest the depression seems to extend many miles. Below the crossing the river passes through a country varying but little from that which was met with above. The San Carlos mountains rise in front to a considerable height. The strips of bottom land now become narrow, and occur at longer intervals.

The passage of the river through these mountains is grand and imposing. The entrance is shown in the accompanying sketch; dashing with a roaring sound over the rocks, the stream, when it reaches the cañon, suddenly becomes noiseless, and is diminished to a sixth of its former width; it enters the side of this vast mountain, which seems cut to its very base to afford a

Entrance to Cañon of San Carlos, Rio Bravo del Norte.

passage to the waters. On the right of the entrance, the rock is rounded and smoothed by the action of the water into an artificial appearance; on the opposite side the mountain receives the river in its full force. It is impossible to keep along the edge of the stream in its course through the mountain, and just as impossible to navigate it. The rapids and falls which occur in quick succession, make the descent in boats entirely impracticable.

A detour by San Carlos was rendered necessary, and the river was again reached at a point some twenty miles below the lower termination of the cañon. It is in the passage through these mountains that the well defined "rapids of the Rio Grande occur," which from their extent, and their near approach to a perpendicular line in their descent, merit the name of "falls." From the edge of the cañon the river may be seen far below, at a distance so great as to reduce it in appearance to a mere thread; and from this height the roar of the rapids and falls is scarcely perceptible.

It was impossible to approach them in consequence of the rugged nature of the country; the fall of the river at this point, however, may be estimated at twelve feet, without including the rapids above and below. The stream is hemmed in by the cañon for ten miles, and then leaves it with the same abruptness that marks its entrance.

It was here found necessary to cross the mule train from the Mexican side, where it had travelled since the commencement of the survey. This was effected, though with considerable difficulty, at one of the usual crossings of the Indians. Near this point, for some distance above and below, the country is more open, the valleys broader, and are susceptible of cultivation; the bottom land is, however, limited by an elevated bank of gravel. There is also an abundance of cottonwood and mezquite timber.

Whenever the spectator was elevated sufficiently to see beyond the valley of the river, two prominent peaks were always presented to his view: one of these marks a summit in the range of the Mexican Sierra Carmel; and the other, from its peculiar shape and great height, was long and anxiously watched during the progress of our survey. From many places on the line it was taken as a prominent point on which to direct the instrument; and, though the face of the country might change during our progress down the river, still, unmistakable and unchangeable, far above the surrounding mountains, this peak reared its well known head. The windings of the river, and the progress of our survey, led us gradually nearer to this point of interest, and it was found to be a part of a cluster, rather than range, of mountains on the American side, known as "Los Chisos." For this peak, a view of which is here given, we have proposed the name of Mount Emory.

Mount Emory—Los Chisos mountains—Rio Bravo del Norte.

After passing this range of mountains, the survey was carried on with less labor than was previously encountered until we reached the Sierra San Vincente. Through these mountains the river forces its way, forming a cañon that equals the San Carlos in many places both in ruggedness and grandeur. A small party only could attempt the survey of this part of the line; and the command was divided, one party accompanying the mule train, and the other, under my personal charge, crossed the mountains. Here we experienced another series of falls or sharp rapids far down in the abyss along which the river finds its difficult course; the roaring of the waters announced a more than usual disturbance, and the boats soon encountered difficulties which, for one of them at least, were insurmountable. In this, as in other cañons, it was impossible to carry the line nearer the bed of the river than the summits of the adjoining hills. Two days were necessary to overcome the obstructions of the passage through this cañon, from the top of which we thought we saw a comparatively smooth country extending nearly to the Sierra Carmel, the highest range of mountains seen on the Mexican side of the river. On a high mesa of gravel, some sixty feet above the level of the river bottom, is situated the old presidio of San Vincente, one of the ancient military posts that marked the Spanish rule in this country, long since abandoned; the adobe walls are crumbling to decay, and scarcely a stick of timber remains in the whole enclosure, except in that part devoted to the chapel. The line of survey was connected with this place at a point distinguished by a survey flag, and distinctly pointed out in a note left, in accordance with your orders, for Señor Salazar, of the Mexican Commission.

Continuing the survey from the Sierra de San Vincente, it was soon found that what in the distance seemed to be a smooth and open country was really rough and broken.

It proved to be a country cut up with deep arroyos, presenting to the survey almost insurmountable obstacles. Passing these arroyos, a wild valley, nearly at right angles with the course of the river, preceded the approach to the cañon of Sierra Carmel, another of those rocky dungeons in which the Rio Grande is for a time imprisoned. No description can give an idea of

Cañon below Sierra de Carmel.

the grandeur of the scenery through these mountains. There is no verdure to soften the bare and rugged view; no overhanging trees or green bushes to vary the scene from one of perfect desolation. Rocks are here piled one above another, over which it was with the greatest labor that we could work our way. The long detours necessarily made to gain but a short distance for the pack-train on the river were rapidly exhausting the strength of the animals, and the spirit of the whole party began to flag. The loss of the boats, with provisions and clothing, had reduced the men to the shortest rations, and their scanty wardrobes scarcely afforded enough covering for decency. The sharp rocks of the mountains had cut the shoes from their

J. Serz sc.

LIMPIA — WILD ROSE PASS.

feet, and blood, in many instances, marked their progress through the day's work. Beyonp the Sierra Carmel the river seemed to pass through an almost interminable succession of mountains: cañon succeeded cañon; the valleys, which alone had afforded some slight chances foɪ rest and refreshment, had become so narrow and devoid of vegetation that it was quite a task to find grass sufficient for the mules. At a point some few miles below Sierra Carmel, it was supposed that a better pathway could be found on the Mexican side of the river. Just above the entrance of the river into a small cañon a place was chosen, which seemed to afford the most feasible opportunity for fording the river. With great difficulty the whole train was passed over without loss. With this slight interruption, the line of survey was carried on until it reached a point since shown to be about one hundred and twenty-five miles above the mouth of the Pecos. Here the work was suspended, owing to the failure of provisions and the means of transportation on the river. With the whole party we passed down on the Mexican side through the town of Santa Rosa, and arrived at Fort Duncan after a long and tedious journey. It is but proper, in justice to Messrs. Thompson and Phillips, the gentlemen associated with me as assistants, to mention their names as an expression of my appreciation of their exertions. To Mr. Phillips, for his able assistance and unvarying industry, I feel especially indebted.

I have forborne any but an incidental allusion to the difficulties of the survey under my charge, leaving it for yourself, so well acquainted with the character of the country gone over, to appreciate these difficulties, and thus excuse any deficiencies that may have occurred in the work.

I have the honor to be, very respectfully, your obedient servant,

M. T. W. CHANDLER,

*Assistant in charge of party U. S. and Mexican Boundary Commission.*

Major WM. H. EMORY,

*Chief Astronomer and Surveyor U. S. and Mexican Boundary Commission.*

---

## PRESIDIO DEL NORTE.

We arrived in front of the Presidio del Norte July 8, 1852, and found watermelons ripe and the corn in tassel. The town, isolated and very remote from any other settlement, had been suffering from famine. The Indians had run off most of the cattle, and the drought for the three preceding years had caused a failure in the corn.

The Presidio is a miserably built mud town, situated upon a gravelly hill overlooking the junction of the Conchos and the Rio Bravo—the latter called here the Rio Puerco, no doubt from the contrast of its muddy waters with those of the Conchos, which, except during freshets, is limpid. The town, which contains about eight hundred souls, is one of the oldest Spanish settlements in northern Mexico; but from the barrenness of the soil, an attempt is making to settle a military colony forty miles higher up the Rio Bravo, where the land is supposed to be better adapted to agriculture.

The church is within the walls of the Presidio, or fort, and contains one or two paintings of a better class than are usually found disfiguring the walls of frontier churches. In almost every house is found, in addition to the cross, a figure of our Saviour, which is sometimes so very grotesque that piety itself cannot divest it of its ridiculous appearance.

These customs, however, are a source of comfort and happiness in prosperity and in adversity, in youth and in old age. They fill the imagination and give occupation to the idle, as the light literature of the day serves the more cultivated races. The padre who presides over the church in this district was by nature intended for the military profession. Brave, frank, handsome, and energetic, he is the leading spirit in every foray against the Indians, and is by no means an insignificant person in the trade of the place. He bears on his person more than one wound received in battle. In the present isolated and defenceless state of the Presidio, this gentleman is nevertheless as good a spiritual and temporal adviser as could be desired.

The relations between the Indians of this region and several of the Mexican towns, particularly San Carlos, a small town twenty miles below, are peculiar, and well worth the attention of both the United States and Mexican governments. The Apaches are usually at war with the people of both countries, but have friendly leagues with certain towns, where they trade and receive supplies of arms, ammunition, &c., for stolen mules. This is undoubtedly the case with the people of San Carlos, who also have amicable relations with the Comanches, who make San Carlos a depôt of arms in their annual excursions into Mexico. While at the Presidio we had authentic accounts of the unmolested march through Chihuahua, towards Durango, of four hundred Comanches under Bajo Sol. It seems that Chihuahua, not receiving the protection it was entitled to from the central government of Mexico, made an independent treaty with the Comanches, the practical effect of which was to aid and abet the Indians in their war upon Durango.

In the fall of 1851 I had the honor of entertaining at my camp the excellent and reverend Bishop Leamy, who was then on his return from a visit to the Bishop of Durango, to adjust the territorial limits of their respective dioceses to make them conform to the altered boundaries of New Mexico and Texas. He stated as his opinion, that the wealthy State of Durango must soon be depopulated by the Indians. Haciendas within a few leagues of the city, that once numbered one hundred thousand animals, are now abandoned.

This condition of things, together with the three years' drought, had overwhelmed the inhabitants of that State, and had driven them to unmanly despair. On the occasion of a great fiesta in the city of Durango, where no less than ten thousand people were assembled in and around the plaza, the cry was heard of Los Indios! Bajo Sol! and in a very short time every one had retreated to his house, leaving no one to face the enemy. The enemy, however, did not appear on the occasion, for it turned out to be a false alarm.

"Bajo Sol" is the title assumed by a bold Comanche, who, as his name signifies, claims to be master of everything under the sun. His name, which strikes dismay into every heart throughout Durango, is mentioned only in a whisper. I have never seen the villain or heard his name on the American side, where he probably takes another soubriquet; but I did meet one of his lieutenants, who, I have no doubt, was in all respects a worthy disciple. I give here a sketch of this rascal, by Mr. Schott: He called himself "Mucho Toro," and represented himself as a Comanche, but he was evidently an escaped Mexican peon. It was in the fall of 1851, in making a rapid march across the continent, escorted by only fifteen soldiers under Lieut. Washington, as we approached the Comanche springs after a long journey without water, that we discovered grazing near the spring quite one thousand animals, divided into three different squads. As we approached we could see with the naked eye a party of thirty or forty warriors drawn up on the hill overlooking the spring. I considered it inevitable to fight, or die with thirst; so, without making a halt, the men were deployed to the right and left of the wagons as light infantry, and the whole moved rapidly towards the water. A flag was raised by the Indians, which was answered by Lieut. Washington and two others riding forward; but believing it a ruse to divide our forces, or give time to deliberate, I quickened the speed of the column, so as to keep Lieut. Washington under cover of our fire; so that we reached the ground and got within pistol-shot of the water before we halted to talk. A man was sent to the top of the hill with a spy-glass to look back, as if additional force was expected. We promptly corraled our wagons near the water, and put ourselves, without appearing to do so, in a good position to fight. We succeeded, without so stating, in producing the impression that we were only the advanced guard of a large force which would come on the next day, and possibly that night. We assumed all the air of the superior party, staid eighteen hours on the ground, and moved off the next day, as if we had a regiment to back us.

The party were Kioways and Comanches, returning from a foray into Mexico with nearly one thousand animals. "Mucho Toro," the chief of this party, who spoke Spanish well, stated he had purchased his animals in Mexico, and that he was but the advanced party of several hundred warriors, who were close behind him. We desired very much to attack the party, but our force was too small, and we were three hundred miles from support. The next day, when crossing the dividing ridge between the Comanche and Leon springs, we discovered the dust rising from the trail which crossed our road as far as the eye could reach, leaving no doubt of the truth of "Mucho Toro's" statement, that his was but the advanced party of "Bajo Sol's" four hundred men. The following summer we found that such a party had passed out of Mexico over this road.

View of Gomez Peak, from near Fort Davis.

"Mucho Toro" paid me a visit in full dress, on which occasion he displayed great humility, exhibiting conspicuously on his person an immense silver cross, which he stated had been given him by the Bishop of Durango when he was converted to Christianity. He had, no doubt, robbed some church of it. His features showed the profile of the Mexican Indian peon, but the warriors he commanded had the bold aquiline profile of the Kioways and Comanches. I present him as a type of that class of Mexicans who, by affiliation with the wild Indians, have produced such irreparable ruin to the northern States of Mexico.

We heard of many such parties, and encountered many adventures similar to that just narrated, but I shall not trouble the reader with any reference to these rascals, or our adventures with them, except to say that I never trusted them; and during the last year of my experience with them I gave orders to permit none to come into any camp under my orders, and to kill them at sight. By taking this harsh but necessary step, I was the only person passing through this country who did not incur difficulty and loss. The Mexican commission was robbed repeatedly, and on more than one occasion was, in consequence, obliged to suspend its operations.

The Rio Bravo, accommodating itself to the geological formation of the country, makes, between the 100th and the 104th meridian of longitude, two great bends nearly symmetrical, one to the south and the other to the north. The area included in the southern bend is one vast cretaceous bed, upheaved by igneous protrusions, sometimes forming ranges of mountains, as the Limpia range, and at others isolated peaks, like Gomez Peak and San Jacinto. To the east and north of the Leon springs the limestone beds are in repose, and do not appear disturbed until we get to Las Moras.

It is, generally speaking, very destitute of water, and the excess of lime in long continued droughts often destroys vegetation. There are, however, oases of surpassing beauty, such as that described in Lieutenant Michler's journal. There is another on the road which I opened

Site of Fort Davis—Limpia Mountains.

from the Presidio del Norte to the Leon springs, called the Puerto del Paisano. This is a valley on the northern slope of the principal range of the Limpia mountains, watered by a limpid stream from crystalline rocks, clothed with luxuriant grass, sufficient to graze a million of

TORO-MUCHO.
CHIEF OF A BAND OF KIOWAYS

cattle. On the hill-tops overlooking the valley, live oak and pine grow in abundance, but are much distorted and wind-shaken, and generally unfit for building purposes.

This road, which will be found traced on the map, was opened for the double purpose of communicating with my parties on the lower Rio Grande, and of shortening the distance from San Antonio to Chihuahua. The route followed by the merchant trains is by the way of El Paso, a distance greater by 300 miles. It is possible a shorter route may be found, but our explorations led us to believe this was the shortest one where a permanent supply of water could be obtained.

Fort Davis has been established since our survey. There is now a constantly travelled road connecting Fort Davis and Chihuahua, via Presidio del Norte.

Several other roads have been opened through this region—one other by myself, one by Colonel Johnston, and one by Lieutenant Michler; all having for their object a more direct communication with the lower Rio Bravo. A good wagon road is said to exist along the Comanche trail, figured on the map, but this I doubt.

The area included in the southern bend forms of itself a distinct drainage, and is one of those basins peculiar to the interior of the continent. It is called by the Mexicans the Bolson de Mapimi, and its waters run into the Lake Jaqui, the rendezvous and stronghold of the Comanches and Kioways, who annually plunder Durango and the neighboring States of Mexico. It is here they collect and divide the plunder, consisting of women, children, and animals. Here, also, they leave their rifles, depending alone upon the lance in their depredations upon the Mexicans.

The immediate neighborhood of the Presidio del Norte, situated in the southern bend above described, is very dry, owing, I think, in some measure, to the manner in which the mountains recede from the valley at that point. The summer we passed there, clouds, discharging water and electricity copiously, were almost daily seen following the ranges of mountains, about ten miles to the south, while not a drop fell upon the Presidio for some weeks. Indeed, so great were the rains to the south, that the Conchos was swollen, and about the 10th of August the whole valley of the Rio Bravo, below its junction, was inundated. This is said to occur annually.

There is sometimes an overflow in June, from the melting of the snows at the head of the Rio Bravo, and it is to these two overflows that the country is indebted for the little capacity it possesses for agricultural pursuits. A narrow belt of alluvial soil is moistened, upon which corn and vegetables are raised.

For a description of the valley of the river from the Presidio del Norte to the cañon, where the San Antonio and El Paso road first strikes it, I give an extract from the official report of assistant von Hippel:

"From Presidio del Norte to Vado de Piedras, a distance of twenty-four miles, the valley of the Rio Bravo has a course from southeast to northwest, and is from three to four miles in width. It is a good grazing country, and the soil is of easy cultivation. This valley is enclosed by hills on the American side, and on the Mexican side by a large mountain range.

"Vado de Piedras is a Mexican military colony, containing some three hundred persons. Here are large cultivated fields, which are watered by acequias, and yield abundant crops of wheat and corn. The place takes its name from the rocky ford of the river opposite the town, which is quite shallow at the ordinary stage of the water.

"Here the river takes a course nearly north, through a valley, varying in width from one-half to one and a half miles, till it comes to Pilaris, forty-five miles from Vado de Piedras. Pilaris was once a military colony, and, from abundant signs still visible, the smelting of silver ore was carried on extensively. It has long been deserted, and I could not learn from what mountains in the vicinity the ore was procured. The river continues the same general course through a valley, bounded by high ridges of mountains, for some eighteen miles, when it enters a large cañon of six miles in length. On emerging from this it changes its course to northwest, through an open valley of eight miles in length, the bearing of which is north and south.

"It now passes between low hills for some eight miles, when it breaks through an immense mountain range, where its banks are of perpendicular rock, of from four to five hundred feet in height. In this cañon are many rapids, and one fall of some six feet, making navigation impossible, except at a very high stage of water.

"One mile above the cañon, on the American side, is a level plateau of rock, about one-half mile square, near the centre of which are two warm springs, their cavities having a funnel-shape, and of great depth. The temperature of the water in them is about 180° Fahrenheit. From these springs the river continues a northwest course, through a narrow valley, for twenty-four miles, to the cañon where the San Antonio road leaves it."

From the cañon up to El Paso, a distance of eighty or ninety miles, the valley of the river will average from six to ten miles in width, and is, almost everywhere within the water-level of the river, capable of cultivation. On the American side, however, there is no settlement

Socorro, Texas.

until within a few miles of San Elceario, a distance of sixty miles from the cañon. On the Mexican side there are two small military colonies—Guadalupe and San Ignacio—of about five hundred inhabitants each. From San Elceario up to El Paso, a distance by the sinuosities of the river of thirty miles, but by air-line of only twenty miles, is almost one continuous settlement of Mexicans and Pueblo Indians, with here and there an American farmer or trader. I estimate the whole population of the valley as follows:

| | |
|---|---|
| El Paso | 4,000 |
| Franklin | 200 |
| Socorro | 300 |
| San Elceario | 1,200 |
| Guadalupe | 800 |
| San Ignacio | 500 |
| Total | 7,000 |

I have included under the head of El Paso the Indian town of Sinecu, which is in the eastern part of the settlement, and is stated to have been built by the aborigines, before the occupation of the country by the Spaniards.

There are some families of pure Spanish descent in this valley, but the population is generally of a mixed character—a cross of the Indian and Spaniard. They are mostly engaged in agriculture and commerce. Before the ports on the lower Rio Bravo were opened, there was sometimes as much as two million dollars' worth of goods passed into the northern States of Mexico by the way of El Paso; at present, I suppose there is not more than $500,000 or $1,000,000, and of import about $70,000. The grapes, peaches, figs, melons, and the fruits generally of this valley, are of very superior quality. There are two descriptions of grapes—one white, the other large and blue; both are very luscious, having no trace of the musky taste of American grapes, and in skilful hands make delicious wine and good brandy. When I first visited New Mexico, in 1846, that whole country was supplied with wine and brandy from El Paso. It is now mostly consumed in the country, or sent to Chihuahua. The wine as at present made will not bear transportation, and as a general rule is but an imperfect test of what the grape can produce. The town of El Paso is itself but one extended vineyard in the hands of many proprietors. The culture of the grape, and its product of wine, would be much increased but for the difficulty of procuring vessels in which to place it for transportation. There is no wood in that whole region from which casks can be manufactured, and there is not yet sufficient demand to authorize the erection of founderies for making glass bottles.

The meteorological table which I have given in the general sketch is not a fair exhibit of the hygrometric character of this region; that record was kept in the last year of the great drought, which extended through 1849-'50-'51. In the succeeding years much more rain fell, but I had no party stationary at any one point, and therefore the record of 1851 was given as that which extended over the greatest space.

In the summer of 1852 the rains were frequent and copious. While occupied at the cañon, in the astronomical determination of that station, a deluge occurred which will long be remembered by those present.

In the middle of the night of June 25, the sky was overcast and our labors at the observatory obstructed. We had all retired to bed, when I was awakened by a roaring noise, which I supposed to be wind. I called to Mr. Burns, who was in charge of my zenith telescope, to take the usual precautions against high wind. He answered that it was not wind, but water; adding, if we did not leave camp pretty soon we should all be drowned. I had made the selection of my camp on a spot which I supposed secure from any possible inundation, but on stepping out of my blankets, found myself knee-deep in water, which was rapidly rising. My first impulse was to seize the chronometer and note-books of the survey, and make for the small eminence upon which the observatory was placed. Only two persons were near enough to assist me, Mr. Gardner and my cook, and neither of them could swim. As we advanced, the water came up to the chin, and the soft ground under foot gave way. It was with the greatest difficulty we reached the hill with our precious load. The night was inky dark, but I caused fires to be built, when all hands immediately went to work, and by the time day broke we had secured nearly everything of value. The only public property lost was some belonging to the escort, composed of raw recruits, many of whom could not speak a word of English, and who, in the absence of their commanding officer, took to the hills, and could not be brought down till day-light. A tremendous rain on the adjacent mountain had fallen during the early part of the night, and the accumulated waters finding insufficient drainage, made for themselves a new channel, which unfortunately passed through our camp.

Throughout that whole region traces of the same kind of deluges can be found, where for months and years not a particle of running water is ever seen. These traces receive the name of arroyos, and I think may be taken generally as evidences of a country subject to long droughts, only interrupted at long intervals by heavy falls of rain.

On a more recent visit to El Paso, in the summer of 1855, the rains were very frequent and heavy. On one occasion several adobe houses were washed down, and, with few exceptions, every house in the place was damaged and rendered leaky. This town, although built in the sixteenth century, and possessing a very considerable trade, does not contain a single stone, brick, or wooden building. The houses, of one story, are built of adobe, (mud and straw,) and the tops covered with tile, grass, or mud, supported by undressed cottonwood logs. They resemble very much the ruins of the houses described in the oases of Syria, and particularly in the dimensions of the rooms, which are accommodated to the rude carpentry of semi-civilized nations. However long a room may be, it is never more than twenty or thirty feet wide, the span of a stick of timber, without the aid of king-posts.

Drawn by A. de Vaudricourt.

Lith. of SARONY & Co. New York.

THE PLAZA AND CHURCH OF EL PASO.

# CHAPTER VI.

## SKETCH OF TERRITORY ACQUIRED BY TREATY OF DECEMBER 30, 1853.

AREA.—HOW WATERED.—FACE OF THE COUNTRY.—PLAYAS.—VALLEYS AND THEIR CAPACITY FOR AGRICULTURE.—ABANDONED SETTLEMENTS.—MINERAL WEALTH.—PIMOS INDIANS.—DESCRIPTION OF SKETCHES.—VIEWS.

The territory acquired under the treaty of December 30, 1853, lies between the parallels of 31° 20′ and 33° 30′, and between the meridians of 106° 30′ and 104° of longitude measured from Greenwich, and contains 26,185 square miles.

Its eastern part is bounded by the Rio Bravo; its northern by the Rio Gila. The interior of the area is traversed by two rivers, which run northwest and empty into the Gila. These are the San Pedro and the Santa Cruz.

A smaller rivulet, lying to the east of both of these, called the San Domingo, takes its rise near the middle of the territory and runs in a northwest direction, emptying into the Gila. This last named river, like the Santa Cruz, is of uncertain flow, and in dry seasons only stands in pools, or is found running under ground, making it necessary for the traveller or grazier to dig for water. There are numerous springs scattered about in the mountains which dot this area, but as they do not usually occur in the levels or mesas, it is somewhat difficult to reach them.

The mountains which traverse this territory run mostly in the same general direction as the river—that is so say, northwest and southeast. The most remarkable feature in the mountain system of this region, is that the elevations are mostly isolated, and have received the local designation of "Lone Mountains," so that a traveller passing from the Rio Bravo to the Pimo villages may, by deflecting slightly from a straight line, pass most of the way over a mesa, the different planes of which vary but slightly in elevation, and are usually from 3,000 to 4,000 feet above the sea.

It is that peculiarity which gives this territory a leading interest as affording a practicable passage for a national railway to the Pacific, and the facility of making a military road over easy gradients to unite the posts in the valley of the Rio Bravo with those on the Gila and in California.

These levels, although usually covered with a luxuriant growth of nutritious grasses, are mostly destitute of water; hence, the traveller is now obliged to seek his road over a more rugged surface in the mountains, where water is to be found. These levels, however, are the recipients of the drainage of the surrounding mountains, and water can be had by sinking wells at no great depth below the surface.

South of the Picacho de los Mimbres the Rio Mimbres, which is a large lively stream in the mountains, disappears entirely in its course to the south, in a large open plain, which presents to the eye of the distant observer the appearance of a meadow.

West as far as 112° meridian of longitude, the soil of the levels and hills is everywhere good, and, except in the playas, covered with a luxuriant growth of nutritious grass, mostly the grama.

The playas are large flats where water accumulates, and salts deleterious to vegetation are disengaged from the soil. They are not, however, very extensive, nor do they occur very often.

West of the 112th meridian, the soil becomes very sandy; the mountains of igneous rocks are bare of vegetation, and as we approach the Gulf of California, except in the immediate beds of the Gila and Colorado, the country becomes a hopeless desert—destitute alike of both water and vegetation—and from the best information I can collect, this is the character of the eastern coast of the Gulf of California as far down as the island of Tiburon, (almost to Mazatlan.) Of this particular section the memoir of Lieutenant Michler, which follows this, will give a more detailed description.

It is very possible the whole of the new territory, except the region of desert country referred to above, may be brought under the influence of artesian wells and made productive ; but until that is the case, agriculture must be confined to the beds of the river, where the land is below the water-level. There are many tracts of this kind of surpassing richness, but of limited extent, on the Rio Bravo, on the Rio Gila, on the San Pedro, and on the Santa Cruz. Those which are most conspicuous, and which are at present in a very advanced state of cultivation, are the Mesilla Valley on the Rio Bravo, the Valleys of Tucson and Tomacacori on the Santa Cruz, and the settlement of the Pimos on the Gila river.

Throughout the whole course of the San Pedro there are beautiful valleys susceptible of irrigation, and capable of producing large crops of wheat, corn, cotton, and grapes; and there are on this river the remains of large settlements which have been destroyed by the hostile Indians, the most conspicuous of which are the mining town of San Pedro and the town of San Cruz Viejo. There are also to be found here, in the remains of spacious corrals, and in the numerous wild cattle and horses which still are seen in this country, the evidences of its immense capacity as a grazing country.

Removed from the river-beds, at the base of the mountains, where perpetual springs are found, are also to be seen the remains of large grazing establishments; the most famous of which is the ranch of San Bernardino, which falls half in the United States and half in Mexico. I have been informed that this establishment was owned in Mexico, and when in its most flourishing condition boasted as many as one hundred thousand head of cattle and horses. They have been killed or run off by the Indians, and the spacious buildings of adobe which accommodated the employés of this vast grazing farm are now washed nearly level with the earth.

Wherever water is sufficient, this whole region presents marvellous advantages for the raising of stock, owing to the character and quantity of the grass, the mildness of the winters, and its almost perfect exemption from flies and mosquitoes.

### MINERAL WEALTH.

Retaining a vivid recollection of the constantly threatened desertion of our work in California, and the inconveniences which sometimes actually occurred, growing out of the gold mania which raged there in 1849, just as we were commencing to run the line, I kept the search for gold and other precious metals as much out of view as possible, scarcely allowing it to be the subject of conversation, much less of actual search ; for I well knew if this mania was once to seize my party, it would be attended with the worst consequences; consequently, our investigations into the mineral wealth of the region have not been as thorough as they otherwise would have been.

Enough was ascertained, however, to convince us that the whole region was teeming with the precious metals. We everywhere saw the remains of mining operations, conducted by the

Spaniards, and more recently by the Mexicans. At this moment several companies from California are prospecting with success, and one company is working a mine in the Sierra del Ajo, west of Tucson. There are the remains of mines in the Mimbres mountains, rich in copper and gold; in the San Pedro mountains, between the San Pedro and Santa Cruz rivers, and on the Santa Cruz river a few miles north of the boundary, there are the remains of a mill for crushing gold quartz. These came under my own observation; and we had many reports of mines to the north, and invitations to visit them, which it was inconvenient to accept. We had what I consider authentic accounts of silver being found in *placers* in the Ajo mountains a little north of the line; although I have never before heard or read of silver being found in placers. I was informed upon authority which I could not permit myself to doubt, that a solid lump of virgin silver had been picked up in that region weighing eighteen ounces. Gold had been found in placers in the new territory in small quantities, in the Mimbres mountains, in the Chirricahui, and in the hills bordering the Santa Cruz river, between the boundary and the Calabasas ranch; and quite a rich placer is found in the mountains to the south of the line near Cocospera. Argentiferous galena, iron ore and meteoric iron are found in several localities. The analysis of Dr. Easter which is appended to this report will give the values of such of the metals as are collected.

I hope nothing I may say will induce persons to run off in unprofitable searches in these distant and unprotected regions. To guard against this it may be well to state, the country is now full of *prospecters* from California, who will undoubtedly discover anything worth knowing.

There are causes which must operate against the speedy development of the mineral wealth of this country, no matter how rich it may prove. One is the hostility of the Indians, which makes it unsafe for parties of less than fifteen or twenty to traverse the country; another is its remoteness from navigation and the scarcity of water.

There are within this territory four settlements; one the Mesilla Valley settlement, containing about fifteen hundred inhabitants of the mixed Spanish and Indian races, all engaged in the pursuit of agriculture.

At Tucson there is a settlement consisting of about seventy families, engaged in the same way. South of Tucson there is a small settlement at San Xavier of semi-civilized Indians, called Papagos; and further on, at Tomacacori, a small settlement of Germans.

San Xavier was once a Jesuit mission, and there remains in a very good state of preservation a large and handsome church.

The most considerable and interesting settlement in the new territory is composed of a confederacy of semi-civilized Indians, the Pimos and Coco Maricopas. Their population is variously estimated at from five to ten thousand. The military commandant at Santa Cruz estimated the number of warriors which they could muster at two thousand. They are located on the Gila river, and form the most efficient barrier for the people of Sonora against the incursions of the savages who inhabit the mountains to the north of the Gila, and who sometimes extend their incursions as far south as Hermosilla, in the State of Sonora.

I became acquainted with these people in 1846, and in another work eulogized their advanced state of civilization, their proficiency in agriculture and the art of war, and their morality. While at Los Nogales, our last astronomical station near the 111th meridian of longitude, a delegation, consisting of the chiefs and head-men, visited my camp, nearly two hundred miles distant from their homes, to consult as to the effect upon them and their interests of the treaty with Mexico, by which they were transferred to the jurisdiction of the United States. I give below a copy of the statement made at the meeting, where it will be seen I said all in my power to silence their apprehensions. They have undoubtedly a just claim to their lands, and if dispossessed will make a war on the frontier of a very serious character.

I hope the subject will soon attract the attention of Congress, as it has done that of the Executive, and that some legislation will be effected securing these people in their rights. They have always been kind and hospitable to emigrants passing from the old United States to California, supplying them freely, and at moderate prices, with wheat, corn, melons, and cotton blankets of their own manufacture.

CAMP AT LOS NOGALES, *June* 29, 1855.

Capt. Antonio Azul, head chief of the Pimos; Capt. Francisco Luke, Coco Maricopa chief; Capt. Malai, Coco Maricopa chief; Capt. Shalan, a chief of Gila Pimos; Capt. Ojo de Burro, war-chief of Pimos; Capt. Tabaquero, a chief of Gila Pimos; Capt. La Boca de Queja, a chief of Gila Pimos; Capt. José Victoriano Lucas, head chief of San Xavier Pimos; Capt. José Antonio, chief of San Xavier Pimos, have this day visited my camp for the purpose of ascertaining in what manner the cession of the territory, under the treaty with Mexico, will affect their rights and interests. I have informed them that, by the terms of the treaty, all the rights that they possessed under Mexico are guarantied to them by the United States; a title to lands that was good under the Mexican government is good under the United States government. I informed them that, in the course of five or ten months, perhaps sooner, the authorities of the United States would come into the ceded territory and relieve the Mexican authorities; until that time, they must obey the Mexican authorities, and co-operate with them, as they have done heretofore, in defending the territory against the savage Apaches.

I have examined the testimonials given by numerous American emigrants to Azul and his captains, bearing testimony to the kindness and hospitality of himself, and the Pimo and Coco Maricopa Indians generally. I can myself bear testimony to the truth of these statements. I therefore call upon all good American citizens to respect the authority of Azul and his chiefs.

W. H. EMORY,
*U. S. Commissioner, Major U. S. A.*

ANTONIO AZUL, *alias* CHE-T-A-CA-MOOSE.
FRANCISCO LUKE, " SEE-COOL-MAT-HAIS.
MALAI.
SHALAN, " KI-MAH.
OJO DE BURRO, " WAH-LA-WHOOP-KA.
TABAQUERO, " VIR-AH-KA-TA.
LA BOCA DE QUEJA, " KI-HO-CHIN-KO.
JOSÉ VICTORIANO LUCAS.
JOSÉ ANTONIO.

I furnished the head-chief a copy of this paper and gave him for distribution among his subalterns, some silver dollars, and all the blankets and cloths which could be spared from our camp.

I conclude this chapter by giving a series of views along the line, sketched by Mr. John E. Weyss. These views commence at the point where the boundary line leaves the Rio Bravo, and terminate at the 111th meridian of longitude. They were taken to perpetuate the evidences of the location of the boundary, in the event of the Indians removing the monuments erected on the ground. They give also a very good idea of the topography of the country.

VIEW OF MONUMENT MOUNTAIN

NOTES TO ACCOMPANY SKETCHES, (VIEWS ALONG THE BOUNDARY LINE ON PARALLEL 31° 47′ AND 31° 20′ NORTH LATITUDE), BY JOHN E. WEYSS, FROM STARTING POINT ON THE RIO BRAVO TO 111TH MERIDIAN OF LONGITUDE.

*Sketch No.* 1 presents a view of the initial point on the Rio Grande, the observer looking west along the line, parallel 31° 47′ N. The flag indicates the point where the line crosses the mountain known as the "Muleras." Directly west of this mountain, the line crosses a very sandy valley, supposed to be a former bed of the Rio Grande, and strikes the table land (some 200 feet above the river) about three miles from the initial point. Here sketches Nos. 2 and 3 were taken, looking respectively east and west.

*Sketch No.* 2 is a back view, looking towards the initial point, again showing where the line crosses the Muleras mountain, and also, in the back-ground, the mountains near Franklin, east of the river.

*Sketch No.* 3 is a view taken at the same point as No. 2 ; that is, where the line first strikes the table-land, but in the direction of the line westward. The line here leads over an apparently endless level table-land, which is very sandy and generally without grass, but thickly covered with clumps of bushes and small sand-hills four or five feet high. On the horizon, exactly in the line, is visible the top of an isolated mountain, serving beautifully as a natural monument. The mountains seen on the right hand are the "Sierra del Potrillo."

*Sketch No.* 4 is taken from the top of the isolated mountain that the line strikes, as represented in sketch No. 3. By this view, the observer looks east along the line towards the initial point. The volcanic mountain range on the left of the flag is called "Sierra Seca." The two mountains behind this Sierra are the topmost peaks of the Sierra del Potrillo, represented in sketch No. 3. The Sierra, quite on the back-ground, shows the mountains near Franklin, and those on the right of the flag are the mountains near El Paso.

*Sketch No.* 5 is a near view of the Monument mountain before mentioned, on which is shown, by the flag, the exact point struck by the boundary line. This view was taken from a point west of this mountain, and about a mile from it.

*Sketch No.* 6 is a view also taken near, and from the west side of Monument mountain, but looking westward along the line. At this mountain the table-land ceases, and the line passes over a series of hills for about 2.5 miles, the highest of which is not more than 300 feet, with so gentle an ascent as to be easily crossed with loaded wagons. Passing these hills, the line leads into a broad valley, bounded on the west by the Sierra del Carrizalillo. About a mile from the foot of these hills the sand begins to disappear, and fertile soil takes its place. The pasturage of this valley was everywhere luxuriant; and in its lowest part, nearly midway between Monument mountain and the Sierra del Carrizalillo, about one mile south of the boundary line, are the "ojos adjuntos," the first permanent water near the line west of the Rio Grande, and about sixty-four miles from the initial point. The "ojos adjuntos" are a series of lagoons formed by many springs, of which fifteen were counted, all affording clear water. They are connected, and all together present a sheet of water from one and a half to two miles long, by from one-third to one-half mile broad, and four to five feet deep; their direction is north and south. The most northern springs, as also the lagoons which they form, are some four or five feet higher than the surrounding prairie. It is possible that these springs are but the re-appearance of the Rio Mimbres. Fine grama grass surround these lagoons and springs, but no bushes. From the "ojos adjuntos" to the foot of the Carrizalillo hills, there is a gentle ascent of the prairie. In the prolongation of the line towards this last named Sierra, it passes six miles south of the "Sierra del Tabaco," and north of, but very near, two small isolated hills, where the magnetic needle underwent a variation of 2° 30′; the needle was affected by this magnetic influence at the distance of three miles, on each side of these hills. The mountains on the left of the flag in this view, are the Sierra de la Boca Grande; those directly on the back-ground, the Sierra del Carrizalillo, where the line crosses; and those on the right hand belong to the Sierra del Tabaco.

*Sketch No.* 7 gives a view of the Carrizalillo hills where they are crossed by the line. It leads up a steep valley across these hills, through an open valley, into another series of hills, where the parallel 31° 47′ terminates. This termination is marked by a monument, a view of which is given in sketch No. 8.

*Sketch No.* 8.—From this point southward the meridians connecting the parallels 31° 47′ and 31° 20′ constitute the boundary line. This sketch gives a view westward, from the terminal point of line on parallel 31° 47′, and not along the line.

*Sketch No.* 9 represents a view of the line, on the meridian, from the monument marking the terminal point on parallel 31° 47′. The flag marks the direction across the hills.

*Sketch No.* 10 is taken from the point where the flag stands in sketch No. 9. This view is south along the meridian. The high mountains on the left are the Sierra de la Boca Grande. The distant hill ranges beyond the plain, and covered by the flag are the hills on which is erected the monument marking the beginning of the boundary on parallel 31° 20′. The hills on the right hand belong to those adjoining "Ojo del Perro." The boundary line here runs through a large valley or plain; the Sierra de la Boca Grande lying on the east, and the Sierra de la Hacha, and that of Ojo del Perro, on the west. Nearly in the middle of this valley, and about 172 miles east of the boundary line, are situated the Ojos de los Mosquitos, five in number, which, though furnishing an abundant supply of clear water, soon sink below the surface. The pasturage of this valley is good in some places; but the soil is generally sandy, and many spots are destitute of vegetation. As the mountains are approached, the soil becomes gravelly and bushes abound.

*Sketch No.* 11 presents a view of the hills on which is located the monument marking the initial point of the line on parallel 31° 20′. The view looks south along the meridian, and the flag marks the spot where the monument is erected.

*Sketch No.* 12 is a back view from the monument, looking north along the meridian. The rocky bluffs on the left are a part of the mountains near Ojo del Perro. Further on, and in the middle ground, are seen the Sierra de la Hacha, and entirely in the back-ground appear the hill ranges on which terminates the line on parallel 31° 47′.

*Sketch No.* 13 is taken from the same point as No. 12, but looks west along the parallel 31° 20′. All the hills here represented belong to the Sierra del Ojo del Perro. The spring giving name to the sierra is situated at the foot of the second mountain on the right of the flag, and is about seven miles west of the monument, and north of the flag one and a half.

*Sketch No.* 14 is a view taken from the place marked by the flag in sketch No. 13, looking eastward. The range behind the flag embraces the hill on which is located the monument, as shown in sketch No. 13. The mountain range in the back-ground on the left is Sierra de la Boca Grande. From this flag westward the boundary line runs for a few miles over a series of round hills, and, after crossing a wide valley, strikes the high Sierra de San Luis. The soil of this valley is light and sandy, except in the middle it is covered with grass and other vegetation.

It contains a large prairie-dog town, and, constituting the receptacle of an extensive drainage, would be passed with much difficulty during the rainy season. A series of springs were discovered near the middle of the valley, and about one mile south of the line. They form a little creek, but are lost in the sand in a run of less than two miles.

*Sketch No.* 15.—A near view of the San Luis mountains where they are crossed by the line; sketched from the intersection of the line and the road leading from Janos to Santa Cruz.

*Sketch No.* 16.—This view is sketched from the monument near San Luis springs, looking eastward. The flag shows where the line crosses the mountain.

*Sketch No.* 17 is taken from the same point as No. 16, but in the opposite direction. The top of the mountain on the back-ground, directly over the monument, is the first over which the line runs near the Guadalupe Pass.

*Sketch No.* 18 is a near view of the mountain whose top rests on the horizon in sketch No. 17. The flag indicates where it is struck by the line.

*Sketch No.* 19 looks west along the line, and is taken from the point marked by the flag in No. 18.

*Sketch No.* 20 is drawn from the point indicated by flag in No. 19. It looks westward, and the single peak in the back-ground belongs to the mountain ridge west of San Bernardino; and the sierras still further off are the San José and Éspinola, on the left and right, respectively.

*Sketch No.* 21 is a view looking eastward from the point where the line crosses the road through the Guadalupe Pass.

*Sketch No.* 22 is a view from the monument near the springs of San Bernardino, looking west along the boundary, and giving a nearer view of the peak seen from the Guadalupe cañon, and represented in sketch No. 20.

*Sketch No.* 23.—A back view taken from the same point as No. 22, but looking eastward towards the Guadalupe cañon.

*Sketch No.* 24.—In this the observer again looks west, and is shown where the line crosses the first mountain-ridge west of San Bernardino. The mountain on the left of the flag is the peak referred to in sketches Nos. 20 and 22.

*Sketch No.* 25.—This view is sketched from the point indicated by the flag in Sketch No. 24. The high mountain on the left fore-ground represents the before-mentioned peak. The high sierra in the back-ground on the flag is the San José; that on the right the Sierra de Éspinola. Rain-water was found at the foot of the hill where the flag stands, and was the only water near the line between San Bernardino and Rio San Pedro, a distance of fifty-five miles. The Rio San Pedro flows along the eastern base of the Sierra de Éspinola.

*Sketch No.* 26 is a view taken at the foot of the hill on which the flag stands in sketch No. 25; it looks west along the parallel. From this hill, as far as the banks of the Rio San Pedro, the line runs over a rolling prairie of a light, sandy soil, sometimes covered with bushes, sometimes bare, and fine patches of pasturage occurring here and there.

*Sketch No.* 27.—View looking west along the line from from flag-staff in sketch No. 26.

*Sketch No.* 28.—Sketched from flag in view No. 27, also looking westward. The mountains on the left edge of which the flag rests, and marks the line, are the Sierra de Éspinola.

*Sketch No.* 29.—This view looks westward, and is taken on the east bank of the Rio San Pedro, where it is crossed by the line. At this point, approaching from the east, the traveller comes within a mile of the river before any indications of a stream are apparent. Its bed is marked by trees and bushes, but it is some sixty or one hundred feet below the prairie, and the descent is made by a succession of terraces. Though affording no very great quantity of water, this river is backed up into a series of large pools by beaver-dams, and is full of fishes. West of the river there are no steep banks or terraces, the prairie presenting a gentle ascent. Here again the flag represents where the line touches the Sierra de Éspinola. The mountains in the back-ground on the left of the flag are directly east of Santa Cruz.

*Sketch No.* 30 is taken from the monument situated north of Santa Cruz, and is a back view, showing the flag on Sierra de Éspinola.

*Sketch No.* 31.—A view from the same monument, but looking westward. The mountains in the right-hand corner of the back-ground are the Santa Rita.

*Sketch No.* 32.—This is a view near Los Nogales, and shows where the line crosses the road leading from Tucson to Imuris. It looks south from the monument. The mountains in the back-ground are called the Sierra del Pajarito.

1

VIEW OF THE INITIAL POINT OF THE BOUNDARY LINE ON THE RIO BRAVO DEL NORTE - LOOKING WEST.

2

VIEW ALONG THE BOUNDARY LINE - LOOKING EAST FROM MONUMENT No. 3 ON PARALLEL 31°47'.

3

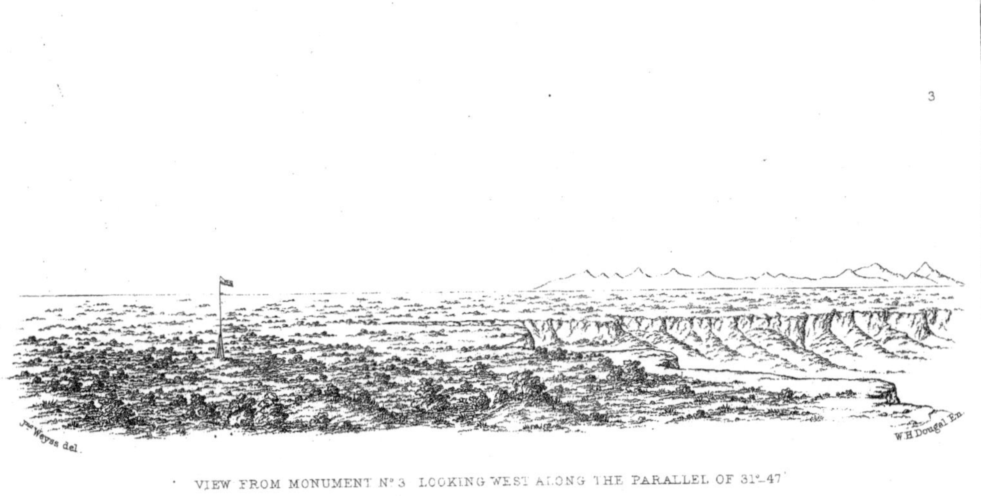


VIEW FROM MONUMENT N° 3 LOOKING WEST ALONG THE PARALLEL OF 31°-47'

4

VIEW FROM MONUMENT N° 4--LOOKING EAST ALONG THE PARALLEL OF 31°-47'

5

VIEW FROM MONUMENT Nº 5—LOOKING EAST ALONG THE PARALLEL OF 31°-47'.

6

VIEW FROM MONUMENT Nº 5—LOOKING WEST ALONG THE PARALLEL OF 31°-47'.

7

VIEW OF THE CARRIZALILLO HILLS WHERE CROSSED BY THE BOUNDY LINE ON PARALLEL 31° 47' – LOOKING WEST.

8

VIEW FROM THE MONUMENT MARKING THE TERMINAL POINT OF BOUNDARY ON PARALLEL 31° 47' – LOOKING WEST
(not along the Boundary)

9

VIEW FROM THE MONUMENT MARKING THE TERMINAL POINT OF BOUNDARY ON PARALLEL 31° 47′ – LOOKING SOUTH.
ALONG THE MERIDIAN.

10

[ from flag on above sketch ]
DISTANT VIEW OF THE HILLS ON WHICH IS LOCATED THE MONUMENT MARKING THE INITIAL POINT
OF THE BOUNDARY LINE ON PARALLEL 31° 20′ - LOOKING SOUTH
ALONG THE MERIDIAN.

11

NEAR VIEW OF THE INITIAL POINT OF THE BOUNDARY LINE ON PARALLEL 31°20' LOOKING SOUTH ALONG THE MERIDIAN.

12

VIEW FROM INITIAL POINT OF BOUNDARY LINE ON PARALLEL 31°20' LOOKING NORTH ALONG THE MERIDIAN.

14

VIEW FROM HILL RANGE REFERRED TO IN Nº 13 BACK TO INTERSECTION

13

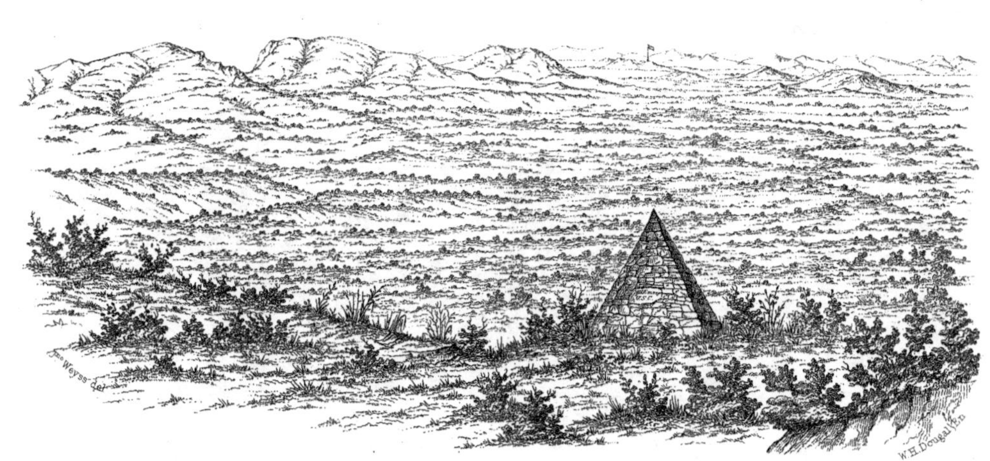


VIEW FROM INTERSECTION OF MERIDIAN AND PARALLEL OF 30°20'-LOOKING WEST ALONG THE PARALLEL TO THE FIRST RANGE OF HILLS.

15

VIEW ALONG PARALLEL 31° 20′ FROM MONUMENT ON THE JANOS ROAD TO THE POINT WHERE THE LINE CROSSES ST LOUIS MTS

16

VIEW FROM EMORY'S MONUMENT SOUTH OF ST LUIS SPRINGS BACK TO THE SAME POINT ON THE MOUNTAINS

17

VIEW FROM EMORY'S MONUMENT SOUTH OF THE SAN LUIS SPRINGS LOOKING WEST ALONG THE PARALLEL OF 31°20'

18

VIEW LOOKING WEST OF THE POINT WHERE THE PARALLEL OF 31°20' FIRST STRIKES THE GUADELUPE CANON

19

FIRST VIEW OF THE GUADALUPE CAÑON ALONG THE BOUNDARY LINE ON PARALLEL 31° 20'–LOOKING WEST.

20

SECOND VIEW OF THE GUADALUPE CAÑON ALONG THE BOUNDARY LINE ON PARALLEL 31° 20'–LOOKING WEST

21

VIEW OF THE POINT WHERE THE LINE CROSSES THE ROAD IN THE GUADALUPE CANON - LOOKING EAST ALONG THE PARALLEL 31°20'

22

VIEW FROM EMORY'S MONUMENT AT THE SAN BERNARDINO SPRINGS - LOOKING WEST ALONG THE PARALLEL OF 31°20'

23

VIEW FROM EMORY'S MONUMENT AT THE SAN BERNARDINO SPRINGS-LOOKING EAST ALONG THE PARALLEL OF 31°20′

24

VIEW ALONG THE LINE 31°20′ LOOKING WEST WHERE IT CROSSES THE FIRST RANGE OF HILLS WEST OF SAN BERNARDINO

25

VIEW FROM THE MONUMENT NEAR SAN BERNARDINO LOOKING WEST ALONG THE PARALLEL 31° 20'

26

VIEW ON THE PRAIRIE BETWEEN SAN BERNARDINO AND THE SAN PEDRO, LOOKING WEST ALONG THE PARALLEL 31° 20' (No 1)

27

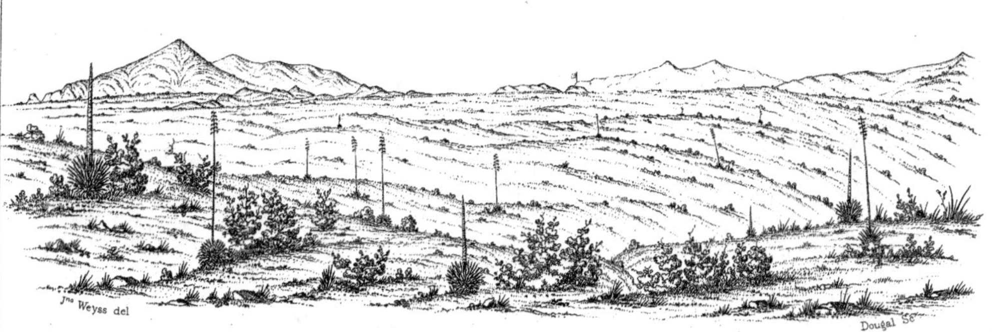


VIEW ON THE PRAIRIE BETWEEN SAN BERNARDINO AND THE SAN PEDRO, LOOKING WEST ALONG THE PARALLEL 31° 20' (No 2)

28

VIEW ON THE PRAIRIE BETWEEN SAN BERNARDINO AND THE SAN PEDRO, LOOKING WEST ALONG THE PARALLEL 31° 20' (No 3)

29

VIEW FROM THE MONUMENT ON THE RIO SAN PEDRO, LOOKING WEST ALONG THE PARALLEL 31° 20'

30

VIEW FROM EMORYS MONUMENT NORTH OF SANTA CRUZ, LOOKING EAST ALONG THE PARALLEL 31° 20'

31

VIEW FROM EMORYS MONUMENT NORTH OF SANTA CRUZ, LOOKING WEST ALONG THE PARALLEL 31° 20'

32

VIEW FROM THE MONUMENT NEAR LOS NOGALES LOOKING SOUTH
( not along the line )

# CHAPTER VII.

## FROM THE 111TH MERIDIAN OF LONGITUDE TO THE PACIFIC OCEAN.

### REPORT OF LIEUT. MICHLER.

FORT YUMA.—COLORADO AND GILA.—SLOUGHS OR ARROYOS.—SITE OF AN OLD PRESIDIO.—BOUNDARY LINE.—SAND BELT.—DESERT.—PANORAMA OF MOUNTAIN RANGES.—MIRAGE.—BOTTOM LAND AND VEGETATION.—EARTHQUAKES AND MUD VOLCANOES.—CLIMATE.—DUST STORMS.—INDIANS.—INITIAL POINT ON THE COLORADO.—TINAJAS ALTAS.—TULE.—SALADO.—AGUA DULCE.—QUITOBAQUITA.—CABEZA PRIETA.—SONOYTA.—ROAD ALONG THE GILA.—MARICOPAS.—PIMOS.—TUCSON.—SAN JAVIER.—TUBAC.—TOMOCACORI.—SOPORI.—ARIBACA.—SIERRAS ALONG THE AZIMUTH LINE.—PAPAGOS.—"TIERRA CALIENTE" OF SONORA.—SANTA MONICA.—SANTA ISABEL.—HEIGHT AND ABRUPTNESS OF MOUNTAIN RIDGES.—EASTERN SLOPE.—COLORADO DESERT.—NEW RIVER.—DISTANCES.

OFFICE UNITED STATES AND MEXICAN BOUNDARY SURVEY,
*Washington, July* 29, 1856.

SIR: The following extract is taken from your orders to me, dated Washington, D. C., August 29, 1854: "You are charged with the important service of running that part of the boundary line between the United States and Mexico which commences on the Colorado river, twenty English miles below or south of the junction of that river and the Gila, until you meet the party running the line under my immediate direction, from El Paso westward."

Having complied with your instructions, I now have the honor to submit to you a report of the manner in which the work has been executed, and describe that portion of the country to which our duty particularly confined us, and the Indian tribes frequenting the immediate neighborhood of the line.

Sailing from New York on September 20, 1854, myself and assistants proceeded, via Aspinwall, Panama and San Francisco, to San Diego. All necessary instruments having been provided before leaving the eastern cities, preparations for the transportation, subsistence, and organization of a party occupied my attention in the last named places. These completed, we left San Diego on the 16th of November, for Fort Yuma, which place was reached, after journeying over mountains and deserts, on the 9th of December. This road, the most difficult I have ever travelled for heavily-loaded wagons, has been already spoken of in your military reconnoissances in New Mexico and California, and a further description would be unnecessary. Its distance, measured with a viameter, is 217 miles.

On the right bank of the Colorado, and in a bend opposite the mouth of the Gila, rises up a low irregular hill, from seventy to eighty feet in height; on the water-side there is a perpendicular cliff; the other sides are less steep, but equally rugged. This hill is of Plutonic origin, and presents a bleak, dreary appearance. The surface is covered with sharp, volcanic rocks, cutting like glass under the tread, and is destitute of every form of vegetation, except the euphorbia, a rank poison, and used by the Indians as an antidote against the bite of the rattlesnake. Such is the site of the military post of Fort Yuma. This hill, cleft by the Colorado at its junction with the Gila, and extending a short distance, unites with a larger mass of the same formation. A mile further south is another isolated hill, about 250 feet high, called Sierra Prieta, with its base imbedded in the white sands of the desert. These hills were once one and the same; one river runnning around its north, and the other its south base, (their old beds being still traceable,) and both uniting on the west. By some freak in the laws of nature, an eruption in the bowels of the earth caused an upheaving of this whole section of country, and changed the beds of these rivers: the one now runs due south, and the other due north, before uniting. Their currents act on the same line and are diametrically opposed, and as the waters meet, neither willing to yield, they open a passage through the highest part of the hill, turning at right angles to their original courses and flowing towards the west. The cleft thus made is about 240 feet in width. The Colorado furnishes more than two-thirds of the water. At an average stage at the junction, the quantity discharged per second was found, from a mean of several experiments, to be 6,249 cubic feet, and the velocity three feet per second. At the same point the depth of the channel is about eighteen feet. It then widens, and becomes more shallow. By daily observations with the barometer, the level of the rivers at their confluence was found to be 275 feet above that of the sea at San Diego. The Colorado, as its name signifies, is of a reddish color, and carries down immense quantities of sand and mud. The water is sweet, and excellent for drinking, but does not bear keeping long, as it soon putrifies. The Gila is clearer, and its temperature warmer, but somewhat brackish in its taste, owing to the large quantity of earthy salts held in solution.

For twenty miles above the post the Colorado spreads out into a wide and low sheet of water; but above that point, to the entrance of the Great Cañon, it becomes more narrow and deep. An expedition under Major Heintzelman ascended this river in boats in September, 1852. Another is contemplated, when it is the purpose to carry a steamboat up as far as possible, provided the government will render some assistance by an appropriation sufficiently large to insure the safety of the boat. The belief is entertained and strongly advocated, that the Colorado will be the means of supplying the Mormon territory, instead of the great extent of land transportation now used for that purpose. Its head-waters approach the large settlements in Utah, and may one day become the means of bearing away the produce and stock of these pioneers of the far West. With this idea prominent in the minds of speculators, a city on paper, bearing the name of "Colorado City," has already been surveyed, the streets and blocks marked out, and many of them sold. It is situated on the left bank, opposite Fort Yuma.

From the description given me of the Great Cañon, it must resemble in appearance and character those along the Rio Bravo del Norte, upon which I have already reported.

The Colorado is said to have but few tributaries; the Gila has several, emptying in above and below the Pimos villages. The annual rise in both rivers usually takes place in the months of May and June, sometimes as late as July, and is caused by the melting of the snows in the mountains near their head-waters; the freshets are not of long duration. Frequently the one stream will be up and the other down. The Gila becomes so low that a sand-bar forms at its mouth during the summer, and at no time does it supply much water. The Colorado, on the contrary, is navigable for small steamers, drawing two and two and a half feet water, as high up as Fort Yuma. Sailing-vessels take stores from the Pacific through the Gulf of California, and up the river, sixty miles above its mouth, to Point Invincible, or near Hardy's Colorado, and there discharge their cargoes upon the river steamers; the latter then transport them ninety miles to the junction—the present contract price per ton being seventy-five dollars, and the boat carrying from fifty to sixty tons. This is a great saving, as the cost of transportation of stores by trains across the desert is enormous. The navigation is pretty good, but, like all streams of the same nature, the channel frequently changes, owing to the shifting sands and the instability of its banks. The nature of the latter varies; thirty miles above the junction, the river is walled in by mountains throughout nearly its whole extent; and fifteen miles lower down, it passes for a short distance through the Santa Isabel range. From there to the salt marshes near the mouth, except at the junction with the Gila, the banks are alluvial, caving in and shifting with every rise and fall; they become very low and flat, and are overflowed for miles during spring tides; a heavy *bore* then rushes in, swell upon swell, and renders it very dangerous for small boats. The tides ascend for thirty-seven miles. The lowest depth of the channel is three feet, its mean or average stage of water six, and its highest about twenty feet. During very high freshets the water flows back for many miles through the arroyos or sloughs which intersect the country: large lagunas or lakes are thus formed, such as the "Big Laguna," and "New River" or "Providence creek," found on the road from San Diego, and also Hardy's false Colorado; these remain filled for a long time—some nearly the entire year. Whenever they occur a broad slough, north and west of the post, is filled, and completely isolates it from the main land, communication being had only by means of boats.

There are only three kinds of fish, that are at all palatable, caught in the Colorado—the hump-back, trout, and buffalo—all very soft and of a muddy flavor, full of small bones and of most inferior quality.

Fort Yuma is well located for defence against the Indians; the only point (Sierra Prieta) commanding it is beyond the reach of arrows. It affords a distant and fine view of the surrounding country. In the very interesting report of Major Heintzelman, made to the commanding general of the Pacific department, in July, 1853, he says: "The post is on the site of a Presidio established about seventy-seven years ago by the Spaniards. Padre Pedro Garces came out here with a San Gabriel Indian, and reported this a favorable position for a mission. The next year he and Padre Kino came out with troops and established a mission at the junction, and José Maria Ortegas, son of Don Francisco Ortegas, captain and commandante of the expedition of the discoverers of Alta California, founded the Presidio. The position is described between the sierras of San Pedro and San Pablo. A little east of north from here, forty-five miles, on the top of a ridge of barren mountains, is a detached rock, several hundred feet high, resembling a dome, which may have given it the name of St. Peter; and in a direction west of north, about eighteen miles distant, on another range of mountains, rises a solitary rock, five hundred feet high, which we have called Chimney Peak, and which must have borne the other name."

Our camp lay opposite the military post, on the left bank of the Colorado, between the Plutonic ridge on the east, and a low range of sand and gravel hills, called the Yuma hills, on the west; these latter end abruptly at the water's edge, no trace of them being seen on the opposite side, and extend south to the base of the Sierra Prieta. They were interesting from the beautiful specimens of quartz found upon them, among which were fortification and moss agates, chalcedony, jasper, and opals, and various fine pieces of petrifactions of mezquite, cottonwood, and indigenous plants, and one of palm-wood. Seven miles and a half by the river, below the post, is another high, prominent, and isolated hill, called Pilot Knob, similar in general appearance and formation to those spoken of. The boundary line from the initial point on the Pacific ocean runs tangent to the southern base of this butte, until it intersects the middle of the Colorado, a short distance below the south ferry. An iron monument formerly marked the line near this place, on a high knoll, but has been broken into a thousand pieces by the Indians; its locality, however, is well defined. From this point of intersection the boundary follows down the middle of the stream to a point 20 English miles, in a straight line, below the junction of the Gila and Colorado.

Near Pilot Knob, a large belt of white, glistening sand encroaches upon the river to within a short distance of its right bank; it is fifteen miles long by five wide, and about forty feet high; from its gradual approachment, it threatens to dislodge the river and efface its present bed. Twelve miles above the junction, a spur of the "Sierra de la Gila," a mass of sharp, angular, igneous rocks, thrown together in the most incongruous shapes, sets into the Rio Gila; its bearing is northwest and southeast, and it extends as far as the eye can see. From the base of this mountain, along its whole length, extends out towards the Gila and Colorado a level plain of gravel and sand, in breadth from twenty to fifty miles, and stretching far south until it mingles with the hillocks of white sand which define the eastern shore, along the Gulf of California. It limits the bottom-lands, sometimes touching the river, as at Ogden's landing, and again recedes, leaving a fertile tract of several miles in width. The latter is from two to ten feet above the surface of the water, and the former rises in bluff banks from twenty to forty feet in height. The plain is a perfect desert, marked by an entire absence of water, and destitute of vegetation, save some few sickly plants: the Larrea Mexicana and the Fouquiera, the natural growth of such barren localities, only add to the gloomy sensation produced by the scorched sterility spread out to view, with jagged ridges of hills lying in the back-ground. The bottom-land on the right bank of the Colorado is bounded by a similar plain, which extends south to the base of the mountains of Lower California. This whole country is truly a desolate region; rich, however, in geological and mineralogical material.

Standing on the top of the Sierra Prieta, you have a magnificent panorama of the high peaks, rugged sides, and angular outlines of the mountain ranges which encircle you. From this point, looking westward and following the points of the compass round towards the north, your eye first rests upon Avie Quah-la-Altwa, (Avie signifying mountain, in the Indian tongue,) or Pilot Knob, as known to emigrants; a little further on, Avie A-re-ña Hampan, connecting with the low ranges of white sand-hills already spoken of; then Avie Qui-a-sa viño; to the northwest a light and a dark range, Avie Qui-a-sa and Avie Haz-e-nas; afterwards Avie Sut-ma-mou-ra—all isolated ridges. Ranging across the north is Avie Mil-li-ket, its highest peak called by the Americans "Chimney Peak," and by the old Jesuits "San Pablo." The Indian name is in honor of a learned and wise chief, who became a deity after his death. He occupies a large cavern in the mountains, the entrance to which is guarded by a raccoon, a pet during his stay upon earth; the path which leads from the cave to the river bank is said to be distinctly marked by his foot-prints. He seems to enjoy long intervals of sleep, and when aroused from his slumbers by the wickedness of his worshippers, he is believed to change his position, and the act of rolling over causes the rumbling earthquakes which are frequently felt throughout this section of country. During the last shock experienced there, it is reported that a large piece of the peak of Mil-li-ket, solid rock as it is, was broken off, and rolled into the plain beneath. The Indians, considering it a part of their religious duty, make regular visits to the spot, like Mahomedans to the shrine of Mahomet. To the east of Mil-li-ket is another remarkable-looking peak, called Pin-chie, the allegorical allusion scarcely bearing mention; the two are almost in juxtaposition. Avie Mil-li-ket is quite an extended range, and is about twenty-four or five miles north of Fort Yuma. To the northeast, and about forty-five miles distant, is Avie Tok-a-va or Dome mountain, or

Sierra de San Pedro, a solid rock many feet in height, and resembling the dome of a cathedral. Some god is supposed to inhabit this range. Near it is a second peak, called the "broken dome." To the east, and extending south, are Cone mountain, of the Santa Isabel range, and the Sierra de la Gila; Antelope peak is the principal one of the latter. To the southeast, mountain after mountain rises up; to the south, those of Lower California are plainly visible, so high that snow envelopes their tops; and when the southwest winds blow, they are more chilly than those from the north, bearing along with them the cold air of the snow-clad peaks. From a distance these mountain ranges look rugged in the extreme, although here and there, as you watch the play of the sun, you see reflected back perpendicular walls of smooth, white rock.

The atmosphere is so clear that you are able to see at long distances. In the morning a beautiful sight is afforded by the mirage. It has the effect, apparently, of raising the mountains and bringing them more plainly to view, and many are the fantastic and peculiar shapes that are represented.

We turn from this barren view and look with pleasure upon the bright green foliage which marks the course of the Colorado. The river-bottom, varying in width, is generally broad and fertile—an alluvial deposite, covered with a thick growth of timber. Large cotton-wood trees, different varieties of willow thickly matted together, and impenetrable thickets of arrow and grease-wood, grow near the river; further back the mezquite of two kinds—the flat-pod and the screw-bean—thrive and flourish. The bottom is intersected by innumerable lagoons and sloughs, which during the annual rises fill to overflowing, and irrigate the soil. The earth is consequently impregnated with the salts of potash, magnesia, and soda, which are held in solution by the water. No vegetation will grow beyond the influence of these overflows, and when a white efflorescence appears upon the surface of the ground it is useless to plant, as nothing edible for man or beast will grow there.

The delta of the Colorado and Gila is below high-water mark, and is subjected to overflows. The soil is a mixture of clay and sand. There are some few varieties of grass very scatteringly distributed. The distance from Fort Yuma to the mouth of the Colorado is about one hundred and sixty miles. The whole of the country strongly resembles the Rio Bravo del Norte in the general appearance of its vegetable forms; varieties of cacti, the maguey plant, Larrea Mexicana, and the fouquiera, are all found here. Although both regions are probably of the same geological structure, they are not equal in richness, that upon the Rio Grande being the most fertile. To add to the interest of this section of our land, we find it is subject to earthquakes, by which it is sometimes depressed and sometimes elevated. To quote from a very interesting account given by Major Heintzelman of a visit made to the scene in November, 1852, he says: "The low ground was full of cracks, from many of which there gushed forth sulphurous water, mud, and sand. At the time, great changes were made in the river-bed. The earthquake appears to have been occasioned by an accumulation of gases and steam in the caverns of the earth. The elasticity of these forced an escape through a pond forty-five miles below, on the desert between the river and coast mountains, the repeated escapes causing rumbling and shocks. It is an old orifice, that has been closed several years, so that the first effort occasioned the most violent explosion. The steam rose in a beautiful snowy jet more than a hundred feet in the air, and spread, appearing above the tops of the mountains like a white cloud, and gradually disappeared. This was repeated several times, but on a much smaller scale."

When the Major visited the place three months later, "these jets took place at irregular intervals of fifteen or twenty minutes, and had a beautiful effect as they rose, mingled with the black water and mud of the ponds. The temperature in the principal pond was 118°, and in a smaller one 135°. One of the mud-holes from which gas escaped was 170°. The air was filled with sulphuretted hydrogen, and in the crevices were beautiful yellow crystals of sulphur. The ground was covered with a white efflorescence, tinged with red and yellow."

The climate of this region is in accordance with everything else relating to it. Encamped there during the three winter months, we found the weather generally mild, although the changes in temperature were very great; the thermometer during part of this time as high as 90° Fahrenheit, and then as low as 30°. The days were sometimes uncomfortably warm, and the nights intensely cold. Living and sleeping in tents all the time, we seldom had occasion to have a camp-fire except at early dawn. Owing to the clearness of the skies, the radiation is extremely rapid, and ice forms quickly.

Having returned the following August to Fort Yuma, the thermometer in the shade at the post was found to be 116° Fahrenheit, and over 120° in the shade along the river. The heat, commencing to be excessive in May, becomes almost unendurable in the months of June, July, and August. Even in winter the sun is so hot, and the direct as well as reflected light upon the sand-plains so dazzling, that, excepting a couple of hours after daybreak and an hour before sunset, it is only possible to see objects through the best instrumental telescopes in the most distorted shapes—a thin white pole appearing as a tall column of the whitest fleece.

In this belt of country rain seldom falls; in the distance dark clouds may be seen hanging over the California and Sonoranian mountains, but they seldom visit the intermediate localities. During the whole of one year they had but two inches of rain. After our arrival a few drops from some passing cloud fell in the two winter months, December and January, and in the following February .07 of an inch. The coast rains take place during the winter; and the rainy season in Sonora, the Mexican state south of the boundary line, in the months of July, August, and September. Spring, in the intermediate section, puts forth its thick green foliage in February, without any rains to refresh and cool the parched ground.

Instead of storms of rain during the winter and spring, they have those of dust and sand. These are caused by high and strong winds sweeping over the desert plains, coming principally from the northwest, raising and carrying before them, like mist, clouds of pulverized sand and dust. You can watch them in their progress as they approach for hours beforehand, and when they reach you the dust penetrates into every crevice, the finest silk not being impervious to it. They last generally a day; sometimes three. The winds blow up quickly and violently, and it is useless to attempt to work with nice instruments. These dust-storms were our great drawbacks, as it was impossible to see many feet distant, and then only at the risk of being blinded. The gusts of wind which produce this unpleasant effect in winter are in summer like the simoons of the Sahara—they sweep over and scorch the land, burning like the hot blasts of a furnace.

Think of those officers and soldiers who are so unfortunate as to be stationed at Fort Yuma. Two companies of artillery now garrison the post; their quarters have heretofore been Mexican *jacals*—upright mezquite poles, plastered with mud and covered with a thatching of arrow-wood; like so much powder, a single spark ignites them, and they burn like a flash in the pan. Dust and rain, as well as the eyes of the curious, penetrate through the crevices, the sun only being denied admission. When I left they were engaged in building new quarters of adobes, (sun-dried brick.) As every other comfort is denied them, their dwellings at least should be substantial and cool.

Arthur Schott del.

Lith. of SARONY, MAJOR & KNAPP, New York

DIEGEÑOS.

Among the curiosities of the country are its aborigines. On the road from San Diego to Fort Yuma we passed through several Indian settlements of the Diegeño tribe, at San Pasqual, Santa Isabella, San Felipe, &c. These Indians were converted by the Jesuits, who many years ago organized missions throughout this country; they became partly civilized, and were industrious and happy, and collected many comforts about them. Naturally lazy, and incapable of self-government, and deeply imbued with all the traits of the wild Indian, they easily degenerated after the missions had fallen from under the rule of the church, and have become absolutely worse than in their original condition. Then they were simply children of nature, following the bent of their inclinations, with few comforts, and fewer wants; now they have learned sufficient to be exceedingly avaricious and unscrupulous—a herd of drones and beggars, their dispositions thievish, and forever on the watch to commit some petty larceny. They call themselves "Christianos." The degradation of the Indian woman is only surpassed by that of those off-scourings of creation, the male white population who wander over the country.

The women are beautifully developed, and superbly formed, their bodies as straight as an arrow; their features, however, are coarse and uninviting, their persons filthy, and their actions still more disgusting. They imitate the whites in dress, and in a single Indian group you see the odds and ends of clothing from all parts of the globe most fancifully and grotesquely worn. Don Tomas, the chief of the Santa Isabella Pueblos, is quite a fine-looking person, and has considerable reputation as a man and warrior. He goes about dressed in a full-dress soldier's coat and shirt, but no breeches; carries an old sabre as a sword of justice and rod of correction, judging from the way I saw him use the flat of it on the back of a drunken Indian.

The opposite picture is a lithograph of a Diegeño, wife and child—the one leading and the other riding a mule—as we met them travelling to the "Agua Caliente," near Warner's rancho.

There are many Indian tribes scattered throughout this part of California; but I will confine my remarks particularly to those dwelling on the Colorado and Gila. From about sixty miles above Fort Yuma to within a few miles of the most southern point of that part of the Colorado forming the boundary, live the Cuchanos, or Yumas. A belt of land of some few miles in width, forms neutral ground between them and the Cocopas; the latter living below, and near the mouth of the Colorado, within the limits of Mexico, and the former almost entirely in the United States. These, together with the Maricopas, who now live up the Gila among the Pimos, originally formed one tribe. Disagreeing upon the choice of chiefs, they separated; until recently, they have been deadly enemies, carrying on a war of extermination to the knife. The continued warfare with each other has compelled them to manifest a seeming friendship for the whites, has occasioned great loss of life and property, and been detrimental to their increase. In consequence of their great suffering, the Cuchanos have found it necessary and expedient to live near the post; every day, numbers are seen loitering about the parade-ground, and through the quarters of officers and men. These tribes speak the same dialect, follow the same habits and customs, and dress in the same manner and of the same materials. The Maricopas, however, are fast becoming embodied with the Pimos, and seldom visit their kinsmen. The Yumas and Cocopas are said to be very treacherous races; they conquer not by fair and honorable contest, but by craft and cunning, and midnight attack; they steal upon their enemies under the cover of night, and beat out the brains of their unsuspecting foes with clubs; or, under the garb of friendship and peace, invite each other to feasts, and suddenly fall upon and kill their guests; or, taking advantage of the absence of the warriors from their villages, massacre the remaining men, old women, and small children, and carry off as prisoners the more youthful women and larger children. They look upon this kind of warfare as right and honorable. They follow their war expeditions on foot, possessing only a few horses.

Their hunting as well as war weapons are bows and arrows, clubs and knives. I have not seen a rifle or gun of any kind among them. The bow is made of willow; the arrows are of reed, part of the shaft of arrow-wood—the point tipped with a head of hard stone, either jasper or agate, small, but neatly and sharply edged; they are winged with the gay feathers of the various birds of this country. Their clubs are of mezquite wood, three or four feet long. On one occasion, as Major Fitzgerald was escorting a train up the river, he discovered them moving their families; pressing them too hard, they turned upon his command, and, in defiance of powder and ball, attacked it with clubs at the very bayonet's point and forced the soldiers to retire.

An instance of the stratagem and bad faith practised by these different tribes upon each other, was told me by the officers at the post. The Cocopas planned the massacre of all the captains of the Cuchanos in 1851, to accomplish which they intended inviting them to a feast and slaying them. The plan was overheard and told the Cuchanos; the latter fell upon the former the same night, killing several men, and carrying off women and children. To repay them, the Cocopas made a visit to the Cuchanos to recover their prisoners, and again invited the latter to a feast, who unsuspectingly accepted; during their absence, the Cocopas fell upon their villages and reciprocated the treatment they had previously received. Macedon, the principal chief of the Cuchanos, was killed on this occasion; he was much beloved by his tribe, and is spoken of as an intelligent and high-minded Indian; his death is said to have occasioned much grief. This was the time of the outbreak of Antonio Garras, who had leagued all the tribes of Indians of South California against the whites, intending by a simultaneous and well-concerted attack, to annihilate the Americans and drive them from the country. He was afterwards taken and shot by the military at San Diego, where his grave is pointed out to the passer-by.

On several occasions, the officers commanding at Fort Yuma have been instrumental in securing peace; but the Indians being naturally suspicious of each other, it does not continue long. A treaty was made between them whilst we were encamped on the Colorado. The Cuchanos were anxious for, and had often sent down their women to propose one. Owing to the number of intermarriages among the tribes, this is the usual mode of proceeding. At last, through the influence of Major Thomas, a day was appointed for both parties to meet at the post. Francisco, an intelligent, splendid-looking young Indian, and brother to the murdered Macedon, was sent down the river to bring up the Cocopas chiefs. Four of them and their women arrived on board the steamboat. José, Jepita, Coyote, and Colorado, representing the Cocopas, and Pasqual, an immense man, near six feet four inches in height, Caballo-en-pelo, and Vincente, figured on the part of the Cuchanos. All made speeches; and when assenting to any particular view advanced, on either side, they commenced with the principal chief, and passing round the whole circle from one to another, in the order of rank, each one expressed his approval by the monosyllable, "good." After the words of the treaty had been agreed upon, the Major asked each one to make a sign or mark opposite his name. Before having time to explain its purport Jepita jumped up, and, with very energetic language and appropriate gesture, stated that their word was as good as their mark; but that they would make any of their signs, such as "kneeling upon one knee," "raising the hand to heaven," or "embracing." Immediately putting his words into effect, he walked up to Pasqual, and taking his large frame in his arms, gave him a long and tight embrace. After the ceremony was over, rations were issued to them, which they devoured with right good will. They then went about begging for old clothes, and in the evening celebrated one of their games.

The association of the Indian with the white tends to cause a rapid decrease by the introduction of diseases among them heretofore unknown; war, too, among themselves is a great exterminator, but has the advantage of making them more dependent upon the whites. Thinking the military will protect all, they draw near to the posts, and from presents learn the use of various articles of clothing and food; these, now regarded as luxuries, will, in time, become to them necessities. They, too, learn and see the advantages which the whites possess over them in every respect, and are not slow either to admit or account for it. They say that whites and Indians at one time were all one tribe, equally well informed, and acquainted with the use of implements of husbandry and of all useful articles. Differing upon the choice of a chief, they quarrelled, and during the night the whites stole a march upon them, carrying away everything, and leaving the poor Indian in the dark. These Indians are of a dark brown color; during the cold weather, of dull and dirty appearance, but in summer bright and glossy from bathing in the river. They are most expert swimmers. They are of the medium height, well formed, and slender; not muscular, the deltoid muscles alone being largely developed, arising from the peculiar mode of throwing the arms while swimming; active and clean-limbed; their features not disagreeable, although they have large noses, thick lips, and high cheek-bones; their chests are well developed and figures manly, indicating activity but not strength. The women are under the medium height: their figures are fine and plump; the bust is well developed, the mamma firm; the arms finely moulded; the hands small and pretty; the legs beautifully formed and well rounded, and nicely-turned ankles; the feet are natually small, but become much enlarged by not being protected. Altogether they present a very voluptuous appearance. Their deportment is modest, and their carriage and bearing erect and graceful. They all travel on foot, and when going long distances, at a slow trot.

An essential article of dress worn by the men is a piece of coarse cotton cloth, three or four feet long, passed between the legs, the ends drawn over a cord tied around the waist, and then allowed to fall loosely down. The women wear a very becoming and a very pretty dress. They take the inner bark of willow, cut into strips about an inch wide and sufficiently long to extend from the waist to the knee. A number of these pieces are woven together at one end and selvedged, the edge long enough to go half-way round the body; two of these pieces—the one called the a-be-hike, and the other the al-ter-dick—are secured in front and behind by means of a girdle of strips composed of the same material, and covering the body from the hips to the knees. The front portion is woven plain, but the back into an angular shape, with a lump at each side, answering the same purpose and appearing like a bustle. On this protuberance the women carry their children of two or three years of age, a rope passing around the groins of the child and the ends tied together in front of the mother; as she approaches you, nothing is seen but a little foot dangling down on each side. The belles of the tribe, however, when they can obtain the material, make the front of white woolen cord; they take a white blanket, pick the wool loose, and twist it into cords of some thickness, and use this in place of the willow-bark; they tip the ends of the cords with bits of red flannel; the girdle is then made of cords of the same kind, only variegated with different colors, red, white, and blue. When they lie down to sleep, they strip and cover themselves with their clothes, having nothing beneath them; in winter they keep warm by lying near a fire. The hair of both males and females is cut square across the forehead above the eyes, the sides and back left long; the men wear it very long, as it is considered a great ornament, and braid it in rolls; the latter are used for the purpose of securing their bows, arrows, and clothes above water when swimming a river. The women do not wear it as long as the men. They speak of one of their celebrities, now dead, with great respect, as the warrior with the very long hair. Both sexes paint; the usual colors are vermilion, black, and blue. A very few are tattooed; this operation is performed by pricking the skin with the sharp point of a flint, and sprinkling in the wound the dust of charcoal. Very few ornaments are used. The chiefs of the various bands seem to have a distinct official badge, consisting of pearl-shells suspended by rings from the nose. Both men and women are passionately fond of glass beads.

Although their language is not sweet, the sounds being guttural and harsh, still their names are very pretty. Three of the belles of the tribe were named Ma-vah, He-pa, and Le-och. There appears to be no marriage ceremony. If a man and woman like each other, they live together; if they afterwards disagree they can separate, provided there be no children, and even then they can marry again should both parties consent. Unmarried women are taken care of by the tribes; children can go from one hut or family to another, and will be fed and cared for as belonging to the tribe. Nor do they have any funeral ceremonies. When a death occurs they move their villages, although sometimes only a short distance, but never occupying exactly the same locality. The dead is burned; the body, dressed and surrounded with all the personal effects, is placed upon a funeral pile and consumed. No disposition is ever made of the ashes. A feast is celebrated, and if the deceased is possessed of any horses they are killed and eaten; his possessions are said to be bad, and are burnt or destroyed. The female relations of the departed mourn for many days, manifesting their grief by tearing out their hair, cutting their bodies, and destroying everything they possess, not even saving a vestige of their garments. If any member of the tribe should kill another, whether in the heat of battle or in cold blood, he returns to his home and atones for the necessity of having been compelled to commit the deed by keeping a fast for one moon; on such occasions he eats no meat—only vegetables—drinks only water, knows no woman, and bathes frequently during the day to purify the flesh.

Among these tribes they have a ceremony for celebrating the arrival of a virgin to the age of puberty. When the old women ascertain the fact, the whole tribe collect together and celebrate the occasion with a feast. The applicant for womanhood is placed in an oven or closely covered hut; this is made by digging a hole, in which they lay heated stones, covering them with twigs and bushes, upon which the novice is placed; hot water is then thrown upon the stones, and when completely steamed and saturated with profuse perspiration, she plunges into the river and takes a bath. This process is kept up for three days, maintaining a fast all the time. The feast celebrated, the girl is considered a woman, and is ready for marriage; maidens, however, do not generally marry early. They become fully developed at about twelve or fourteen, and grow so rapidly that in a few years they look coarse and fat. Previous to a birth, the mother leaves her village for some short distance and lives by herself until a month after the child is born; the band to which she belongs then assembles and selects a name for

Arthur Schott del.

Lith of Sarony & C^o New York

YUMAS.

FIGURE TO THE LEFT, "PORTRAIT OF LEOCH."

Arthur Schott del.

Lith of SARONY, MAJOR & KNAPP. New York

CO-CO-PAS.

the little one, which is given with some trivial ceremony, and the mother then returns with it to her home.

Nothing is known of their religion. At one time they profess to worship the sun and moon; at another they say the Indian and white man have the same God; then you find them making pilgrimages to the sepulchre of some departed chieftain, celebrated for deeds of valor or civic honors.

As to their government, they are divided into bands, each having its own head. There is one principal hereditary chief presiding over the whole. Each of the former, with the advice of its members, decides upon all affairs relating directly to the band to which he belongs. Any important business affecting the whole, is acted upon by a council of chiefs—the principal chieftain governing their deliberations. Each chief punishes delinquents by beating them across the back with a stick. Criminals brought before the general council for examination, if convicted, are placed in the hands of a regularly appointed executioner of the tribe, who inflicts such punishment as the council may direct.

An execution took place among the Cuchanos whilst we were in their neighborhood, which created great sorrow among us all. An Indian boy named "Bill" was in the habit of going up and down the river on board the steamboat, and frequently visited the post and our camp. Being very smart and good-natured, he became a great favorite; and speaking some little English and Spanish, could act as interpreter. He was secretly accused and tried before the council for "being under the influence of evil spirits"—the evidence going to show, that for the sake of frightening a little child he had forewarned it of its death on the following day, which, in reality, accidentally took place. He was convicted and sentenced to be executed. Whilst seated on the ground with three others of his tribe, laughing, talking, and playing cards, the executioner walked up behind him and struck him three blows upon the forehead and each temple killing him instantly.

Their games are few. The principal one is called mo-upp, or in Spanish, redondo, played with two poles fifteen feet long, and a ring some few inches in diameter. They play another with sticks, like jack-straws; also monte and other games of cards, but know no ball plays. Old and young join in the games. Different from most Indians, they seem to be good-natured, laughing and talking all the time. They are very affectionate towards each other, and it is not unusual to see them walking with their arms around each other's waists.

Music is not much cultivated among them. They sing some few monotonous songs, and the beaux captivate the hearts of their lady-loves by playing on a flute made of cane. They manufacture but few articles. The women make baskets of willow, and also of tule, which are impervious to water; also earthen ollas or pots, which are used for cooking and for cooling water; they answer the latter purpose very well—being porous, the water oozes out and evaporates on the surface. The men make headstalls and reatas for horses.

Although constantly in the water, these Indians never use canoes, but swim from shore to shore; and in the event of moving their families some distance down stream, they place them on rafts of wood or balsas of rushes, push them out in the channel, and trust to the current, directing their movements with a pole.

Owing to the mild climate and the absence of rains, they require but little shelter, and their houses are of the meanest construction. Sometimes they make them of upright poles a few feet in height, crossed horizontally by others on the top, upon which rest brush and dirt. The side to the prevailing wind is sloped towards the ground. They usually select a sandy spot, as it is warmer in winter and cooler in summer.

Major Heintzelman, in speaking of their agriculture, says "it is simple; with an old axe, (if they are so fortunate as to possess one,) knives, and fire, a spot likely to overflow is cleared; after the waters subside, (those of the annual rise,) small holes are dug at proper intervals, a few inches deep, with a sharpened stick, having first removed the surface for an inch or two, as it is apt to cake; the ground is tasted; if salt, rejected, and if not, the seeds are planted. No further care is required but to remove the weeds, which grow most luxuriantly wherever the water has been. They cultivate watermelons, muskmelons, pumpkins, corn, and beans. The watermelons are small and indifferent, muskmelons large, and pumpkins good; these latter they cut and dry for winter use. Wheat is planted in the same manner, near the lagoons, in December or January, and ripens in May or June. It has a fine plump grain and well-filled heads. They also grow grass-seed for food; it is prepared by pounding the seed in wooden mortars made of mezquite, or in the ground. With water the meal is kneaded into a mass, and then dried in the sun. The mezquite bean is prepared in the same manner, and will keep to the next season. The pod-mezquite begins to ripen the latter part of June; the screw-bean a little later. Both contain a great deal of saccharine matter; the latter is so full, it furnishes, by boiling, a palatable molasses; and from the former, by boiling and fermentation, a tolerably good drink may be made. The great dependence of the Indian for food, besides the product of his fields, is the mezquite-bean. Mules form a favorite article of food; but horses are so highly prized, they seldom kill them, unless pressed by hunger or required by their customs." A lithographic sketch accompanies this report, depicting the appearance and dress of the Yumas, or Cuchanos.

Apart from my own observations of the Indians of the Colorado, I am very much indebted for my acquaintance with their habits and customs to the very interesting report of Major Heintzelman, from which I have taken the liberty to make some extracts, and also to frequent conversations with Major George H. Thomas, Dr. Robert J. Abbott, and other officers of the army stationed at Fort Yuma during our sojourn in its neighborhood. It may be pardonable in me to render here, by a passing word, an acknowledgment of the great kindness and consideration shown myself and assistants by all those officers whom we had the good fortune to meet after reaching the shores of the Pacific. Our wants were always kindly supplied, and all they could do was done, to expedite the work.

On examination, after arriving at Fort Yuma, it was found that the instruments were disarranged, and in some instances broken, in consequence of the numerous changes in the mode of transportation, and the rough road travelled over; they were, however, soon repaired, as well as circumstances would permit, and the work commenced very shortly after reaching the field of our operations.

Surveys of the meanderings of the rivers Gila and Colorado for short distances above their junction, and of the latter river from the junction down to the head of ship navigation, together with the roads in the neighborhood, were made by assistant surveyor A. C. V. Schott, assisted by Messrs. E. A. Phillips, C. Michler, and T. Cozzens. Owing to the thick underbrush along the banks, the work proved tedious.

Astronomical and meteorological observations were daily made by myself, assisted by Mr. G. Power, and the computations made by Mr. J. O'Donoghue. At the same time I carried on the triangulation "to a point on the Colorado river twenty English miles below its junction with the

Gila." In consequence of the thick growth of timber along the river, this was effected on the sand plain until near the terminal point. The timber on the bottom-land there is nearly two miles in width, and lines of sight for the theodolite had to be cut through it to approach the river. This obstruction delayed the work some time, and numerous dust-storms also impeded its progress, preventing the possibility of using any instrument for several days at a time.

On the 14th February, 1855, we moved the main camp from opposite Fort Yuma, in order to be more in the vicinity of our work; a beautiful mezquite grove near a laguna of fresh water was selected. This spot was close to the edge of the sand plain, and the nearest desirable one to the terminal point of the triangulation, about two miles distant in a direct line. It is the site of Fitzgerald's battle-ground, twenty-two miles, by the road, below Fort Yuma. We were here joined by our escort, company I, 1st artillery, officered by First Lieutenant (now captain) Francis E. Patterson, and Second Lieutenant Henry W. Closson.

By the 4th of March the triangulation and survey were all completed, an observatory erected near the initial point of the new azimuth line, (running eastward to the intersection of the 111th meridian west of Greenwich, with the parallel 31° 20′ north latitude,) and astronomical observations with the transit and zenith instrument commenced. Our lucky stars did not, however, prove to be in the ascendency; first, clouds obscured them, and then the rising waters of the Colorado did not leave us long undisturbed. There came a freshet from the Gila, far up in the mountains, causing the Colorado to rise very slowly—so slowly that we anticipated no danger. The sloughs began to fill up between the observatory and the camp; the men bridged them, and still we hoped to see the water recede before forcing us to move. Day after day it continued to advance upon us until the night of the 19th, when the instruments were packed and moved to a higher point, five hundred yards distant. By this time the water had entered the observatory, and to reach it we were compelled to wade waist-deep for nearly the whole of that distance. An extract from my notes of the 20th says: "Compelled again to move the instruments and carry them up to camp; every slough is filled, all rapidly rising, and several swimming deep; rafts built to transport the men over them; all the men in water up to their breasts, and instruments only kept dry by being carried on their heads. About noon all safely in camp; water within fifty feet of it, and everybody getting ready to leave. At sunset the river still continues rising, and gradually approaches camp, but so slowly that we are still in doubt. At 2 o'clock a. m., decided to take to the sand-hills; the long roll was beaten, the camp struck, the train loaded, and all moved on the high plain. Behind us lay a desert of sand forty miles across, and in front was spread a sheet of water several miles in breadth. From fifteen hundred feet the Colorado had widened to at least five miles."

After being forced from our position, the river commenced falling back into its old channel. The bottom-land had become so boggy, it was many days before we were able to reach our observatory. In the mean time, that portion of the Mexican commission appointed to co-operate with me arrived. The party was composed of Don Francisco Jimenez, 1st engineer, in charge, assisted by Señores Manual Alemán and Augustine Diaz, 2d engineers. Captain Hilarion Garcia and Lieutenant Romero were the officers of the escort.

Having already made much progress in the work, Mr. Jimenez consented to adopt the initial point fixed by me. He also accepted its longitude as determined by my triangulation. Having succeeded at length in reaching the river, we were both enabled to commence observing for latitude on the night of the 1st of April. After ten nights of successive observations a mean of the results of each party was taken as the final determination. The latitude of this initial point on the Colorado is 32° 29′ 44″.45 north, and the longitude of same 114° 48′ 44″.53 west of Greenwich. The computed azimuth of the line connecting this point with the intersection of the 111th meridian and parallel 31° 20′ north, forming part of the boundary between the United States and Mexico, is at the initial point 71° 20′ 43″.8 southeast, and at the intersection 69° 19′ 45″.94 northwest, and its length 237.63565 English miles. The mean of eighty barometrical observations at this point is 29.871 inches, — .020 for non-periodic error = 29.851; the non-periodic error was obtained by comparison with observations made at San Diego. The height of this point above the level of the sea at San Diego is 156.3 feet; its distance below the junction by the meanderings of the river is 27.9 miles, making the mean fall of the river between these two points 4.26 feet per mile.

The magnetic variation of the initial point in March, 1855, was 12° 37′ 30″ east of north.

As it was impossible to mark the exact initial point in the middle of the stream, Mr. Jimenez and myself established the first monument 3,164.84 feet distant from it, in the direction of the line, at its intersection with the meridian of the observatory. The azimuth of this monument is 71° 20′ 25″ southwest. Monument II, of cast iron, and pyramidal in form, is placed on the edge of the sand plain, as this position is more permanent and free from the action of freshets in the Colorado. I give its astronomical position: Latitude 32° 29′ 01″.48 north, and longitude 114° 46′ 14″.43 west of Greenwich. The azimuth of the line is 71° 19′ 23″.18 southeast; its distance from the initial point is 4,522.9 yards. This monument erected, everything was in readiness to prolong the line. An agreement was drawn up between both parties to facilitate the tracing and marking of the line by working conjointly.

From the junction to Sonoyta, a Mexican and Indian rancheria, or village, situated near the middle of the line, two roads run. The first one, which we will now describe, crosses the desert west of the Sierra de la Gila, in a southeast direction, to a pass through one of its ridges leading to water-holes, called by the Mexicans, "Tinajas Altas." These are natural wells formed in the gullies, or arroyos, on the sides of the mountains, by dams composed of fragments of rocks and sand washed down by heavy rains; they are filled up during the rainy seasons, and frequently furnish travellers with water for many months of the year, being, in fact, their only dependence. There are eight of these tinajas, one above the other, the highest two extremely difficult to reach; as the water is used from the lower ones you ascend to the next higher, passing it down by means of buckets. It is dangerous to attempt the highest, as it requires a skilful climber to ascend the mountain, which is of granitic origin, the rocks smooth and slippery. Although no vegetation marks the place, still it is readily found. A variety of birds frequent the spot, principally the small, delicate humming-bird. The "palo de fierro" and the "palo verde" grow near the base of the mountain.

The distance to the "Tinajas" is forty-five miles, over the desert plain already described; the first twelve through the heaviest kind of white sand, and it is next to an impossibility for a train to pass over it, even by doubling teams—twelve mules to each wagon. Sixteen miles and a half further on you reach the "Tinajas del Tule," situated in the mountains of the same name, called so from the few scattered blades of coarse grass growing in their vicinity. The water here is found in an arroyo, walled in by huge high masses of granitic rocks, which present a peculiar appearance, as they lie in smooth whitish lumps huddled together in every possible way. The road winds through the ridges of this sierra for many miles, and then passes over a plain in an easterly course until it turns the southern base of the "Cerro Salado." From this point it follows up the valley of a subterraneous creek, (at two points of which sweet, or slightly brackish, water can be had by digging) to an Indian village called Quitobaquita, fifty-four miles from "Tule." Midway between these two places is a low mezquite flat called "Las Playas," containing charcos, or holes, which are filled during the rainy season with water.

The second road from the junction, known by the name of the "Cabeza Prieta" route, from passing near "Tinajas," in the mountain of that name, after continuing up the Gila for forty miles, leaves it and joins the first at "Las Playas." At Quitobaquita there are fine springs running for the greater part of the year.

The road continues along the course of the subterraneous stream until you reach the Rancho de Sonoyta, thirteen miles and a half further on. From the junction to within a short distance of this place, a heavy road of one hundred and thirty miles, you look on a desert country. Near Sonoyta it is well covered with mezquite timber; in the valley, to the east of the town, there is some salt grass; but to the west, as far as the Colorado, scarce a blade is to be seen. A dull, wide waste lies before you, interspersed with low sierras and mounds, covered with black igneous rocks. The soil is a mixture of sand and gravel; the reflection from its white surface adds still greater torment to the intense and scorching heat of the sun. Well do I recollect the ride from Sonoyta to Fort Yuma and back, in the middle of August, 1855. It was the most dreary and tiresome I have ever experienced. Imagination cannot picture a more dreary, sterile country, and we named it the "Mal Pais." The burnt lime-like appearance of the soil is ever before you; the very stones look like the scoriæ of a furnace; there is no grass, and but a sickly vegetation, more unpleasant to the sight than the barren earth itself; scarce an animal to be seen—not even the wolf or the hare to attract the attention, and, save the lizard and the horned frog, naught to give life and animation to this region. The eye may watch in vain for the flight of a bird; to add to all is the knowledge that there is not one drop of water to be depended upon from Sonoyta to the Colorado or Gila. All traces of the road are sometimes erased by the high winds sweeping the unstable soil before them, but death has strewn a continuous line of bleached bones and withered carcases of horses and cattle, as monuments to mark the way.

Although I travelled over it with only four men in the most favorable time, during the rainy season of Sonora, our animals well rested and in good condition, still it was a difficult undertaking. On our way to the post from Sonoyta we met many emigrants returning from California, men and animals suffering from scarcity of water. Some men had died from thirst, and others were nearly exhausted. Among those we passed between the Colorado and the "Tinajas Altas," was a party composed of one woman and three men, on foot, a pack-horse in wretched condition carrying their all. The men had given up from pure exhaustion and laid down to die; but the woman, animated by love and sympathy, had plodded on over the long road until she reached water, then clambering up the side of the mountain to the highest tinaja, she filled her bota, (a sort of leather flask,) and scarcely stopping to take rest, started back to resuscitate her dying companions. When we met them, she was striding along in advance of the men, animating them by her example.

On our return we had to ride to the "Tinajas Altas," forty-five miles, the first night to reach water; and the second one over sixty-three to "Agua Dulce," where we managed to obtain some by digging. During this time our poor mules plodded through the heavy sand without rest or food.

It was over this country one portion of the new boundary line was to be traced; the road of which I have just spoken runs immediately along the line, and is the only practicable one connecting California and Sonora.

Before completing the work immediately on the river, a party had been sent out to make a reconnoissance in the direction of the line, and principally to examine the country for water. Anxious to have no delay, as the hot weather was fast coming on, and the river-bottom having become so infested with mosquitoes as to make life unendurable and labor of any kind impracticable, we commenced prolonging the line without awaiting the return of the reconnoitring party. Mr. Phillips, in the performance of this duty, reached the Tinajas, but there found very little water, and what there was, difficult of access; and, although directed to some new water-holes by a Papago Indian, still he only found sufficient to last a short time for a small number of men and animals. Mr. Alemán, of the Mexican commission, also endeavored to travel the road; but meeting the party first sent out, and hearing their report of the entire absence of water from the river to Sonoyta, was compelled to turn back.

The escort and provision train likewise made an attempt, but it was found almost impossible to advance more than a few miles with the heavily-loaded wagons. My own success was little better; starting from our camp with a light spring-wagon and six good mules, I managed to make twenty-five miles in twenty-eight hours' constant travel; an express then reached me from Mr. Alemán, informing me of the unfavorable account of the search for water.

Not finding it feasible to carry out our plan of operations, the parties of both commissions retraced their steps to the Gila. Every effort had been made to prosecute the work, under the most trying circumstances, but we found it useless to contend against impossibilities. It was then agreed by Mr. Jimenez and myself "to cease operations at the west end, and to proceed along the Gila to the east end of the azimuth line, there to fix the point of intersection of the parallel 31° 20′ north latitude with the 111th meridian west of Greenwich, and afterwards to trace the line from that point westward as far as practicable."

On May 5th both parties, American and Mexican, took the road leading up the Gila; this journey was a long and tedious one, our mules having been thoroughly used up in their service on the desert. During the whole winter they had had but scanty grazing, and to find any at all had to be driven ten miles up the Gila. As there are but three or four families of whites living on the Colorado, and those only in charge of ferries, they did not pretend to cultivate the soil and raise grain; and at the post they had only sufficient for their own use. For some little barley, shipped at San Francisco and brought round by water, I paid twelve cents a pound, and for hay one hundred dollars per ton.

The condition of our animals compelled us to make but short marches each day, to enable them to recruit.

As the road we followed has been travelled and reported upon by others, I shall not dwell long upon the subject. It continues the greater part of the distance in the valley of the Gila, occasionally leaving it for a few miles to go upon the sand plains bordering the bottom-land, or where hills jut into the water's edge, such as "Los Metates," "Lomas Negras," or "Lomas del Muerto," either following round their bases or crossing them. The last named is really the only difficult place in the road, but a trying one for mules and wagons. It is 110 miles above Fort Yuma, and consists of steep, rugged buttes, which, in a low stage of the river, can be avoided by crossing to the other side, but in high water must be passed over. Here are several severe ascents and descents, one at an angle of forty-five degrees, where it is necessary to let wagons down by ropes; they are also covered with vesicular rocks, making them exceed-

Arthur Schott del.

Lith of SARONY MAJOR & KNAPP New York.

PIMO WOMEN.

ingly rough. The valley of this part of the Gila is the same in appearance as that of the Colorado; the soil seems to be more sandy, and contains more alkaline matter; a white efflorescence covers nearly the whole surface. Little grass grows excepting in spots subject to overflow. The same freshet which molested us so much at the initial point here proved a benefit, as we were only able to find grazing where the river had risen over its banks.

I have been told by those who frequently travel along this part of the river, that you may not be fortunate enough once in twenty years to find more than a little bunch-grass, and that only by driving your animals to the plains, four or five miles back from the river. By constant search, we discovered sufficient for our purposes. The growth does not vary much. For the first time, we see the "cereus giganteus," as it rises fifteen or twenty feet above the head.

One hundred and forty miles above the junction we pass a place called "Tezotal." Several miles before reaching it you find limestone rock intermingled with seams of trap. Here the river makes a large bend to the north, and the road pursues a direct course over a *jornada* of forty miles without water, until you reach the Maricopa wells. After leaving these wells you again travel for twenty-nine miles along and occasionally touching the river; you also pass through several Indian villages of the Pimos and Maricopas. The former are further advanced in the art of agriculture, and are surrounded with more comforts, than any uncivilized Indian tribe I have ever seen. Besides being great warriors, they are good husbandmen and farmers, and work laboriously in the field. The women are very industrious, not only attending to their household duties, but they also work superior baskets, cotton blankets, belts, balls, &c. Their huts are very comfortable, being of an oval shape, not very high, built of reeds and mud, and thatched with tule or wheat-straw. They are the owners of fine horses and mules, fat oxen and milch cows, pigs and poultry, and are a wealthy class of Indians.

The Pimos consider themselves the regular descendants of the Aztecs, and claim "Montezuma" to have been of their tribe. One of their legends speaks of his leaving them on horseback on his prilgrimage to found a new country. As the Aztecs in all human probability never saw any horses until their introduction into Mexico by the Spaniards, this seems to be a fabrication. The Aztecs, too, had a form of religious service, but the Pimos to this day have none.

As we journeyed along this portion of the valley of the Gila we found lands fenced in, and irrigated by many miles of acequias, and our eyes were gladdened with the sight of rich fields of wheat ripening for the harvest—a view differing from anything we had seen since leaving the Atlantic States. They grow cotton, sugar, peas, wheat, and corn; from the last two, parched and ground, they make a meal, which, mixed with water, forms a cooling and palatable drink. From the large emigration passing through they have learned the value of American coin, and you can use it in the purchase of anything. Encamping one day at the village of their principal chief, "Cola Azul," a swarm of them soon infested the camp, bringing different articles for sale or barter. In a short time we had laid in a large supply of corn, much needed for our poor worn-out mules.

A little hillock stands near the village, used as a look-out, from which you have a beautiful view of rich cultivated fields. As I sat upon a rock, admiring the scene before me, an old grey-headed Pimo took great pleasure in pointing out the extent of their domains.

They were anxious to know if their rights and titles to lands would be respected by our government, upon learning that their country had become part of the United States.

From the Gila to Tucson—a military colony of the Mexicans on the extreme frontier—is a second jornada, seventy miles in extent. Near the middle of it you pass a detached sierrra called

"Picacho," or peak, an upheaval of volcanic rocks. Tinajas are here found which remain filled with water for short periods after the rainy season.

Several miles before reaching Tucson you strike the bed of the Santa Cruz river, but the stream is subterraneous until you reach the town. The latter is inhabited by a few Mexican troops and their families, together with some tame Apache Indians. It is very prettily situated in a fine fertile valley at the base of the Sierra de Santa Catarina. Some fine fields of wheat and corn were ready for the sickle. Many varieties of fruit and all kinds of vegetables were also to be had, upon which we indulged our long-famished appetites. The Apaches, under the direction of the Mexicans, do most of the labor in the fields.

Circumstances were such that my party and escort were compelled to remain encamped near this town for nearly the entire month of June. During this time we became the recipients of every attention and civility from Captain Garcia, who commanded the place, and from his family. We cannnot find words to express our thanks for their uniform kindness and constant efforts to make the time pass pleasantly.

The month was judiciously occupied in repairing the train and recruiting the mules. Having learned previously on the Gila of the presence of the commissioner and the parties immediately under his charge at his camp near Los Nogales, sixty-nine miles distant from Tucson, my party was directed to stop, while I continued on to have an interview with him.

The road lay in the valley of the Santa Cruz as far as the "Rancho de las Calabasas," between high mountains. On the east are the Santa Catarina, with its top covered with lofty pines, and the Santa Rita rich in minerals; and on the west are the Sierra Rica and the Sierra Atascosa.

A fine specimen of meteoric iron brought from the Santa Rica is to be seen at Tucson, and is used as a blacksmith's anvil. It is massive, and quite malleable.

You pass through the towns of San Javier and Tubac, and the mission of Tomocacari. The first place has been ceded by the Mexicans to the Papago Indians. A beautiful church, with its exterior walls richly ornamented, carved, and stuccoed, and the interior handsomely decorated and painted in bright colors, with many paintings in fresco, still stands as a monument to the zealous labor and religious enthusiasm of the Jesuits of the past century.

Tubac is a deserted village. The wild Apache lords it over this region, and the timid husbandman dare not return to his home.

The mission of Tomocacari, another fine structure of the mother church, stands, too, in the midst of rich fields; but fear prevents its habitation, save by two or three Germans, who have wandered from their distant fatherland to this out of the way country.

Leaving the Santa Cruz river at the rancho, and following up the pretty little valley of Los Nogales for several miles, brought me to the camp of the United States commissioner. It was a gratifying sight, and refreshing to the senses, as I traversed these valleys, to see them clothed with rich green verdure, and contrast them with the bleached barrenness of the Colorado and Gila.

On my arrival, I found the observations for determining the latitude and longitude of the intersection of the parallel and meridian nearly completed, under the order of the United States commissioner, and, a short time after, a pyramidal monument of dressed stone was erectcd to mark its position. At this point Mr. Jimenez and myself again commenced operations, on the 26th of June, to trace and mark the azimuth line running westward. By this time there were some indications of the commencement of the rainy reason, for which we had been anxiously waiting. At any other period of the year it would have been impossible to attempt this section of the work, as there is little or no permanent water in the neighborhood of or along the whole length of this line of two hundred and thirty-seven miles.

Whilst the work was progressing, Lieut. Patterson moved with the escort and train from Tucson, via Tubac and Sopori, to Aribaca. Ojo del Agua de Sopori is a spring, twelve miles from Tubac, in a westerly direction; it once irrigated the valley of the same name, which was cultivated by Mexicans. We found a solitary peach tree, loaded with fruit, and signs of acequias, relics of other days. The stream is a small and pretty one. A league from it, in the Sierra Atascosa, rich mines of copper, silver, and gold, are said to exist. Its mineral resources have not yet been thoroughly examined, on account of the Apache Indians. Only the night before reaching "Sopori," a large party of them passed within a short distance of our camp, driving before them a drove of horses and mules. Within a day's ride of Tubac, through the "Sonora Pass," they have large herds of these, together with cattle and milch cows.

Eighteen miles and a half from "Sopori" (an Indian name) you reach a deserted Mexican rancho, in the valley of Aribaca; the latter is narrow, lying east and west, and bounded by high granite hills, limited on the east by the Sierra del Pais. These are all said to be rich in mineral wealth. Within four miles, and south of the deserted rancho, are to be found large excavations made by men previously engaged in mining; piles of metallic ore lay near the springs where they had been engaged in smelting.

The valley was mantled with rich green pasturage; immediately bordering it are hills covered with fine grama grass and a low growth of mezquite. Numerous springs lie concealed among the tule, with here and there a willow or a cotton-wood to mark their localities. A mule trail runs south from this place to Tubutama, a small town in Sonora, crossing the line about thirteen miles from Aribaca, and within four miles of the "Ojos Escondidos," lying at the base of the sierra of that name. To the northwest is a range of mountains crowned with a high peak of solid rock, called by the Papago Indians "Baboquivari," or "Water on the Mountain;" in winter it is covered with snow and ice, although at its base lies the "Tierra Caliente." It is a most prominent and unmistakeable land-mark, and during the triangulation of the line was of the greatest service, as it could be seen from different points more than one hundred miles apart.

The main escort and train remained in camp at Aribaca until near the middle of August. A few men, under Mr. C. Michler, were sent west to Sonoyta with supplies to re-provision the party on the line, and to make a reconnoissance of the road made by the wagons from Tubac to that place. Lieutenant Closson, with twelve men, formed their escort. Mr. Jiminez and Mr. Alemán accompanied them, for the purpose of going to Quitobaquita to establish its astronomical position, according to agreement entered into with the United States commissioner.

The sierras to the west were reported to be detached, and not continuous, so that, by winding around their bases, a good, although circuitous wagon road might be found; between them are generally broad and level valleys. The heavy rains in that direction offered great hopes of an abundance of water on the road.

Having shown the movements of the different parties, I return to the party on the line. This was necessarily very small on account of the anticipated scarcity of water. To reduce as much as possible the size of the pack-train, there were no more men employed than were absolutely necessary to do the work, without any regard to protection or defence against the Indians.

Leaving the "Potrero" in the valley of Los Nogales, where my party had been encamped for a few days, we started for the monument at the intersection of the parallel 31° 20′, and the

111th meridian. Our trail led up a pretty little valley towards the west for eight miles, when we reached the base of the "Sierra de los Pajaritos" (the Mountain of Little Birds;) following up one of the arroyos or gullies of this chain, we were soon locked in on all sides by high hills; the ravine through which we continued to wind for four miles became rocky, narrow, and difficult to pass, until we reached some small springs, "Los Ojos de Alizos." At this point we left the arroyo, and by clambering up a steep ascent gained the crest of the hills; riding or walking along it as best we could, and passing from hill to hill, each higher as we advanced, we finally reached the point where the monument stands. The hill on the side of which it is erected is low compared to the high peaks in its immediate vicinity; its locality is not easily discovered. Our instrument being placed in position, the azimuth of the new line (69° 19′ 45.9″ northwest) was measured from a meridian established by assistant Clark; a large live-oak growing on the adjoining ridge was found to be in the direction of the line, and answered the purpose of a monument, (No. XIX from the Rio Colorado.) Señor A. Diaz, with a party, operated conjointly with us in the prolongation of this line.

As if in response to our earnest wishes for rain, to be able to continue the work, we had scarcely commenced our labors before the heavens poured down refreshing showers, which we saw with pleasure extended along the line. The commencement of the rainy season is in reality the beginning of spring. The vegetation during the actual months of spring and summer is so parched by the excessively hot suns, that the country present the same appearance as is produced by the effects of frost in our more northern climates. The seeds seem to rest in the earlier part of the season, in order to germinate and beautify the autumn and winter.

"The Sierra de los Pajaritos" is said to form part of the Arizone mountains, reported to be the richest in Mexico. Many specimens of copper, gold and silver are found on the surface, and they are no doubt rich in ore. The hills are covered with live-oak trees, and are overspread with a rich growth of grama grass; they are capped by masses of conglomerate rocks. Monument XVIII, distant from XIX, a little over three miles, is situated on the same sierra.

The country here presents a new aspect. Powerful volcanic irruptions have at some earlier period of the world's history produced great disturbances in this part of the earth. Strata of limestone once horizontal, are now curved and bent by the force of this action, and masses of igneous rocks have been upheaved through the fissures opened on the surface. Here you find granite rocks, and near them beds of trap; and not far from both, limestone; then again all fused in one conglomeration. It was impossible to approach the station nearer than three miles with the riding and pack mules; the instruments had to be transported by hand for that distance up a rugged hill covered with vesicular and scoriaceous rocks.

Monument XVII is placed on the "Sierra de Sonora," seventeen miles from XVIII. Three days were occupied in travelling this short distance. The trail for the first two was over almost impassable mountains; massive rocks and steep precipices constantly impeded the progress of and turned the party out of its course, making the route circuitous as well as hazardous; rough ascents were surmounted, steep ravines followed down, and deep gullies passed; the mules had actually to be dragged along.

At the end of the second day the party found some small springs—"Los Ojos Escondidos"—on the trail to Tubutama, and encamped on them. On the third, the trail was still over high hills, but not so difficult; and some springs—"Los Ojos de Granizo"—a short distance from the monument, were reached. The animals had become so injured and lame by the sharp angular rocks, that they had to be taken into Aribaca to be reshod, and many of them to be replaced by others.

VIEW FROM MONUMENT Nº XIX, ON THE SIERRA DEL PAJARITO, LOOKING EAST TOWARDS THE MONUMENT AT THE INTERSECTION OF 111TH MERIDIAN AND PARALLEL 31°. 20' NORTH.

VIEW FROM MONUMENT Nº XIX, LOOKING WEST TOWARDS MONUMENT Nº XVIII, IN THE PUERTO DE LA SIERRA DEL PAJARITO.

A. Schott, del. J.D. Smillie.

VIEW FROM MONUMENT XVIII, IN THE PUERTO DE LA SIERRA DEL PAJARITO, LOOKING WEST TOWARDS MONUMENT XVII, ON THE CERRO DE SONORA.

A. Schott, del. J.D. Smillie

VIEW FROM MONUMENT XVIII, IN THE PUERTO DE LA SIERRA DEL PAJARITO, LOOKING EAST TOWARDS MONUMENT XIX.

VIEW FROM MONUMENT Nº XVII, ON THE CERRO DE SONORA, LOOKING WEST TOWARDS MONUMENT Nº XV. ON THE SIERRA DEL POZO VERDE.

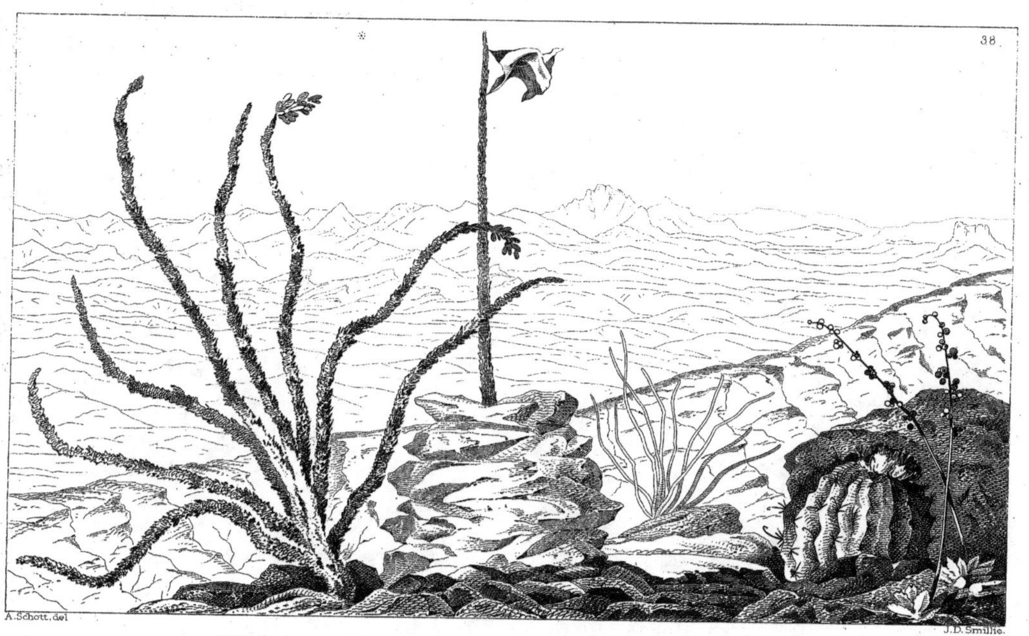


VIEW FROM MONUMENT Nº XVII, LOOKING EAST TOWARDS MONUMENT Nº XVIII.

VIEW FROM LINE (½ MILE WEST OF MONUMENT Nº XVI,) LOOKING N.W. TOWARDS 'BABUQUIBARI'.

VIEW FROM MONUMENT Nº XVI, LOOKING S. E. TOWARDS THE 'CERROS DE LOS OJOS ESCONDIDOS'.

A. Schott Del   Dougal En

VIEW FROM MONUMENT Nº XV ON THE 'SIERRA VERDE', LOOKING EAST TOWARDS MONUMENTS XVI, XVII & XVIII.

A. Schott Del.   Dougal En

VIEW FROM MONUMENT Nº XV. LOOKING WEST TOWARDS MONUMENT Nº XIV.

VIEW FROM MONUMENT Nº XIV, ON THE SIERRA DE LA UNION LOOKING EAST TOWARDS MONUMENT Nº XV.

VIEW FROM MONUMENT Nº XIV, LOOKING WEST TOWARDS MONUMENT Nº XII.

A. Schott Del — Dougal. En

VIEW FROM MONUMENT Nº XIII NEAR SIERRA DE COBOTA, LOOKING EAST TOWARDS MONUMENT Nº XIV

A. Schott Del — Dougal En

VIEW FROM MONUMENT Nº XIII LOOKING WEST TOWARDS MONUMENT Nº XII

A. Schott Del — Dougal En

VIEW FROM MONUMENT № XIII NEAR SIERRA DE COBOTA, LOOKING EAST TOWARDS MONUMENT № XIV

A. Schott Del — Dougal En

VIEW FROM MONUMENT № XIII LOOKING WEST TOWARDS MONUMENT № XII

A. Schott Del — Dougal En

VIEW FROM MONUMENT Nº XII ON THE EAST RIDGE OF SIERRA DE LA NARIZ, LOOKING EAST TOWARDS MONUMENT Nº XIV

A. Schott Del — Dougal En

VIEW FROM MONUMENT Nº XII LOOKING WEST TOWARDS MONUMENT Nº X

A. Schou Del. Dougal En.

VIEW FROM MONUMENT Nº X, ON THE WEST RIDGE OF SIERRA DE LA NARIZ, LOOKING EAST TOWARDS MONUMENT Nº XII.

A. Schou Del. Dougal En.

VIEW FROM MONUMENT Nº X, LOOKING WEST TOWARDS MONUMENT Nº IX.

VIEW FROM MONUMENT No. IX, ON THE SIERRA DE SONOYTA, LOOKING EAST TOWARDS MONUMENT No. X.

VIEW FROM MONUMENT No. IX, LOOKING WEST TOWARDS MONUMENTS VIII, VII, VI & V.

53

A. Schott Del.

Dougal En.

VIEW FROM MONUMENT Nº VIII, NEAR LOS OJOS DE QUITOBAQUITA, LOOKING EAST TOWARDS MONUMENT Nº IX.

54

A. Schott Del.

Dougal En.

VIEW FROM MONUMENT Nº VIII, LOOKING WEST TOWARDS MONUMENTS Nºs VII & VI.

VIEW FROM MONUMENT Nº VI, ON THE 'CUCHILLA DE LAS CHOYAS', LOOKING EAST TOWARDS MONUMENT Nº IX

VIEW FROM MONUMENT Nº VI, LOOKING WEST TOWARDS MONUMENT Nº V

VIEW FROM MONUMENT Nº V, ON THE SIERRA DEL TULE, LOOKING WEST TOWARDS MONUMENT Nº IV.

VIEW FROM MONUMENT Nº V. LOOKING EAST TOWARDS MONUMENT Nº VI.

A. Shott del. J.D. Smillie

VIEW FROM MONUMENT Nº IV. ON THE SIERRA DE LAS TINAJAS ALTAS, LOOKING EAST TOWARDS MONUMENT Nº V.

A. Shott del. J.D. Smillie.

VIEW FROM MONUMENT Nº IV. LOOKING WEST TOWARDS MONUMENT Nº III.

VIEW FROM IRON MONUMENT, Nº II, NEAR THE EDGE OF THE COLORADO DESERT LOOKING EAST TOWARDS MONUMENT Nº IV.

VIEW FROM IRON MONUMENT Nº II, LOOKING SOUTH WEST TOWARDS THE CORDILLERAS OF LOWER CALIFORNIA.

A. Schott del. J. D. Smillie.

VIEW FROM THE INITIAL POINT OF AZIMUTH LINE ON THE RIO COLORADO DEL OESTE, LOOKING NORTH TOWARDS "AVIE-MIL-LI-KET" OR "SIERRA DE SAN PABLO."

A. Schott. del. J. D. Smillie.

VIEW FROM YUMA HILLS, BELOW THE JUNCTION OF THE COLORADO AND GILA LOOKING EAST TOWARDS "SIERRA DE SAN PEDRO" OR "DOME MOUNTAIN."

A few feet south of the line is a prominent peak of the "Sierra de Sonora," which serves as a good natural object to mark it. A league from it are "Los Ojos de Granizo," (Springs of Hail;) their position is indicated by Monument XVI, erected on a hill two hundred metres to the north of them, as well as by some few willow and other trees. The soil is very rich in their neighborhood; the vegetation is profuse, and there is an abundance of fine grama grass; live-oak, and occasionally cedar, are seen on the hills. Whilst encamped here, heavy storms of wind, hail, and rain, were experienced; the valley where the party lay was so quickly flooded as to endanger all the camp equipage, as well as instruments; tents were blown down, and many articles carried away by the hurricane. Notwithstanding the inconvenience attending them, the rains were welcome, as they refreshed and cooled the atmosphere, which was oftentimes heated to 110° Fahrenheit. Some strange specimens of natural history were found at this place; among them, what is called by the Mexicans "El Scorpion," a large, slothful lizard, in shape a miniature alligator, marked with red, black, and white belts—a hideous-looking animal. The *alicante* and *coralilla* snakes were also caught, and added to the collection of natural history.

Leaving Los Ojos de Granizo, our trail lay over a wide and rich valley, running north and south, and extending along the east base of the "Sierra Babuquivari." Crossing it, brings you to the base of "Sierra del Pozo Verde," on which is erected Monument XV, a little more than nine miles from XVI. A trail leads round its southern extremity to Agua del Pozo Verde, (Green Well,) lying at the foot of the western slope, a little east of south, and about two miles distant from the monument. Permanent water is found here; and, although a large number of animals soon exhaust it, still it fills up in a very few hours. This is the site of an old rancheria of the Papago Indians. Numerous "metates" for grinding corn are lying about. The grave of one of their chiefs, who had been killed by the Apaches, was found near camp. A thousand arrows were buried with him, placed there as a token that his death would be avenged by his tribe. The Indians respect these graves, and the deadly threats which they contain, and will not remove a single arrow from the number, although it is a warning of hate and hostility.

The "Sierra del Pozo Verde" is very high, and overlooks wide valleys east and west of it. It is of granitic formation, and covered with a rich growth of grass, and plants of various kinds. The *suwarrow* grows on it in abundance; also the Fonquiera and many varieties of cacti, bearing beautiful flowers. The fruit of the suwarrow is delightful; it is shaped like the pomegranate, and when opened, presents the same beautiful carnation red; the seeds are very small and numerous, and of a black color; only the pulp and seeds are eaten. The Pimos and Papagos use it for food; also a small white cactus, which just peeps above the ground. Many antelope were seen about this place. The glare of our fires attracted a large number of rattlesnakes; the whole place seemed infested with them. We judged them to be a new species from their tiger-colored skins; they were exceedingly fierce and venomous. On the deserts of the Colorado we had often seen others with horns, or small protuberances above the eyes; and Dr. Abbott had taken from the body of still another species quite a number of small ones, among which was a monstrosity with two perfectly formed heads attached to one neck. When you lie down on your blankets, stretched on the ground, you know not what strange bedfellow you may have when you awake in the morning. My servant insisted upon encircling my bed with a reata of horse-hair to protect me from their intrusions. Snakes are said to have a perfect repugnance to being pricked by the extremities of the hair. The paisano, or chapparal cock, surrounds his antagonist, while asleep, with a chain of cactus thorns; when the preparations are all made the bird flutters over the head of the snake to arouse it to action; the latter, in its vain efforts to escape, is irritated to such a degree, by running against the barrier encompassing it, that it ends its existence by burying its fangs in its own body.

From Sierra del Pozo Verde we moved on to Monument XIV, on the "Sierra de la Union," sixteen miles and a half from the last. The country between the two sierras was, as usual, a broad plain; but there is a great contrast between the east and west portions; the first seven miles were exceedingly rich, and covered with a fine growth of mezquite grass and underbrush, but the remainder of the distance was entirely bare of any kind of vegetation until we reached the base of the mountains, where we found the usual growth of palo verde, palo de fierrò, cacti, &c. The bleached appearance of the soil, together with the excessive heat of the sun, reminded us of the Colorado desert.

The sierra is of igneous origin, with a considerable mixture of lime. Its western slope, instead of having the arid and desolate appearance of the eastern one, was fresh and green. Crossing it, we encamped at its base, near "Los Ojos de Yestas."

The next monument, XIII, is placed at the point of intersection of the line and the road made by the few wagons previously sent to Sonoyta, and not far distant from the "Papago Rancheria de Cobota." It is 11.8 miles from Monument XIV, and stands in a valley, limited by the Sierra de la Union and the "Cerritos de los Linderos." The boundary runs a few feet south of a high peak of the former, and between two prominent horns of the latter, both positions making good natural points of reference. This valley resembles the last in every respect. A deep gap in the mountain, near the Cerritos, affords a good pass, and the trail then goes out upon a broad plain, bounded on the west by the "Sierra de la Nariz," (Mountain of the Nose.) This plain is nearly level, and covered with low mezquite, and a few withered plants; its white surface, perfectly destitute of grass or of any verdure, gives it a dismal appearance. There is no water except in charcos, or ponds, filled by drainage after heavy rains. The same description answers for the country west of the Sierra de la Nariz, in the prolongation of the line, until you strike the valley of Sonoyta. Monuments were erected along this portion of the boundary, as follows:

No. XII, on the east ridge of Sierra de la Nariz; No. X, on the west ridge; and No. XI, on the wagon road made by our supply train, passing along the narrow valley between the two; from XIII to XII is 27.70 miles; XII to X, 4.3 miles.

These mountains are masses of black igneous rock, and difficult to clamber up. The eastern slopes are gradual, but the western are perpendicular ledges.

Monument No. IX stands on the Sierra de Sonoyta, 14.5 miles from X, and about one mile and a half north from the town of Sonoyta.

We found encamped near Sonoyta, the small party sent forward with provisions. Their road had been a circuitous and a hard one. The sierras had proved disconnected, and running in parallel ridges from northwest to southeast, with small valleys between them. Not being able to pass with wagons through the rough gaps frequently occurring in the mountains, they managed to wind round the bases, which are short and abrupt. A westerly course was preserved as much as the nature of the country would permit. Only a few small springs were discovered, and but one large well, regularly walled in by the Indians at Cobota. Had it not been for the heavy showers which fell almost every day, it would have been impossible for the

Arthur Schott del.

Lith. of SARONY, MAJOR & KNAPP, New York

PAPAGOS.

Arthur Schott, del.

ARENEÑOS.
(SUBTRIBE OF THE PAPAGOS.)

party to have found sufficient water to supply their wants. At the time we reached there, Mr. Jimenez was engaged in observing for latitude and longitude at Quitobaquita.

The valley of Sonoyta is not very wide, but affords pasturage for large numbers of cattle. Numerous springs course through it for short distances, and then sink into subterraneous channels. These, together with the "Ojos Escondidos," "Pozo Verde," the well at Cobota, and the springs at Quitobaquita, furnish the only water on the line that can be relied upon; nor are these always sure, as experience taught us. There is no timber within several miles of the settlement; firewood has to be brought on the back of the patient *burro*.

The town of Sonoyta is the door of the State of Sonora, from the California side. It is a resort for smugglers, and a den for a number of low, abandoned Americans, who have been compelled to fly from justice. Some few Mexican rancheros had their cattle in the valley near by. It is a miserable poverty-stricken place, and contrasts strangely with the comparative comfort of an Indian village of Papagos within sight.

The Papagos wander over the country from San Javier as far west as the Tinajas Altas. They were at one time a formidable tribe, and waged unceasing war against the Mexicans. Having sustained repeated losses, they at length sought their God, who is said to dwell upon the high peak of Babuquivari, to ask his aid and countenance in their last grand fight with their enemies. They assembled their families and herds of horses and cattle within an amphitheatre enclosed by the mountain ridges, and battled it manfully for many days at its entrance; but their God could not turn the fate of war, and they suffered an overpowering defeat; since that time they have been quiet and peaceable.

We passed many deserted Papago rancherias; they are generally situated some distance from water, as there seems to be a superstition about living near it; the women, who do all the labor, have to bring it in ollas, or earthen vessels, a long way, bearing it on their heads; they are compelled to keep very large ones filled, which are sunk in the ground, and capable of holding a great many gallons. This tribe is comparatively well off in worldly goods; they plant and grow corn and wheat, and possess cattle, and many fine horses. Nature supplies them with numerous useful plants which grow spontaneously; from the suwarrow (Cereus Giganteus) and pitaya they make an excellent preserve by simply boiling the fruit down without sugar, and also a candy of the same material. They collect from a low bush growing wild, seeds called "Chie," which are coated with a gummy substance; placed in water these become partly dissolved, and make a cool and refreshing drink, a refreshment much needed in that warm country. The women are better dressed than most Indian women; they all wear skirts of manta or calico, covering the body from the hips down. They appear to be a good, quiet, and inoffensive tribe. A sub-tribe of the Papagos, called Areneños, live on the salt lakes near the Gulf of California, and principally subsist upon fish.

North of Sonoyta, and about forty miles distant, is a rugged serrated range of mountains called "Sierra del Ajo," represented to be rich in copper, gold and silver. A company was engaged in attempts at mining, but, from the scarcity of water, with little hopes of success. The great distance necessary to transport the ore on pack-mules before reaching navigation, will render their efforts futile and unprofitable.

The section west from Sonoyta to the Colorado has already been described. In August we were enabled to complete that portion of the work, and although engaged upon it during the wet season, barely sufficient water was to be had for our wants. The heat had become so great as to compel us to operate entirely with signal-fires by night. Monuments are placed near Quitobaquita, Agua

Dulce, Tule, and Tinajas Altas, to mark the boundary. The line runs a few feet south of the springs at Quitobaquita, north of Agua Dulce and Agua Salada, and south of the Tinajas del Tule and Tinajas Altas. The sierras on which these two last are located were troublesome to work on ; their summits are so peaked as to make it difficult to find a place sufficiently large upon which to stand or place an instrument. Those who visited these stations to determine them, had to console themselves by sitting up all night after their work was done, as there was not sufficient space to stretch themselves out.

The big horn mountain goats frequent this region, and the noise of their horns as they butt them together in fight is often heard among the rocks.

Mr. Schott has made a large and interesting collection of botanical plants and of natural history, besides making careful examinations of the geology of the country ; he has also taken the views of the scenery along the line, which accompany this report.

It was a happy day that witnessed the termination of the field-work. On the 25th of August both parties left Sonoyta for Altar, and thence via Santa Anna to Magdalena, in the State of Sonora. The tracing and marking and triangulation of the line having been completed, Mr. Jimenez and myself compared at this last place the data for fixing the respective distances between stations, and the positions of the prominent topographical features of the country.

The section marked "B," (see Astronomical and Geodetical work,) shows the results of calculations of the latitudes and longitudes of points in the triangulation made to determine the "azimuth line of twenty English miles," together with tables showing the lengths of iron rods, A and B, used for measuring the base line; tables for laying off the circumference of the circle having its centre at the junction of the Gila and Colorado, and radius of twenty miles ; tabulation of results for the latitude of the initial point on the Colorado ; astronomical determinations of positions on the azimuth line between the Colorado and 111th meridian ; and distances between monuments. Tabulated distances along the routes in the neighborhood of the boundary line from the Pacific ocean to the Gulf of Mexico also accompany this report.

At Imuris, a few miles from Magdalena, we found Lieutenant Patterson, encamped with the escort and train, having left Aribaca in August, and reached there via Tubac and Los Nogales. When at this last place, the Apaches, splendidly mounted upon fine horses, made a descent upon his animals and endeavored to stampede them. Although the Indians, in war-dress and uttering unearthly yells, dashed up within fifteen feet of the mules, then in excellent condition and well-rested, still their efforts were unsuccessful.

At Imuris the parties of both commissions separated—the one to return to the city of Mexico, the other to cross the continent to the Gulf of Mexico, and thence to Washington city.

I take great pleasure in reporting to the commissioner the very agreeable relations, both official and social, which constantly existed during a difficult work, with those gentlemen of the Mexican commission with whom we were so long and intimately associated.

From Imuris we travelled the road up the San Ignacio river by Cocospera, a deserted mission, to the rancho de San Lazaro, where we struck the main southern emigrant road. If space permitted, I should like to dwell upon the rich valleys of the "Tierra Caliente" of Sonora, the towns of Altar, Santa Anna, Magdalena, Imuris, San Ignacio, and Cocospera, through which we journeyed on our way home ; upon their highly cultivated fields of grain and sugar-cane, irrigated by miles of acequias, and their gardens loaded with richly flavored fruit of the tropics as well as of the more temperate zones. At Magdalena we saw in the same garden, apples, peaches, apricots, pomegranates, figs, grapes, lemons and oranges. Leaving San Lazaro, we followed the road, via Santa Cruz, Janos, and Corralitos, to El Paso, and thence took the southern route through Texas to San Antonio de Bexar. From San Diego, on the Pacific ocean, via Fort Yuma, Tucson, Santa Cruz, Janos, El Paso, and San Antonio, to Indianola, on the Gulf of Mexico, measured by viameter, the distance is 1,727.32 miles. From San Diego, via Fort Yuma, Sonoyta, Altar, Imuris, Santa Cruz, Janos, El Paso, and San Antonio, to Indianola, the distance is 1,695.22 miles.*

My party arrived at this place November 30, 1855; a few days after, it was discharged, and the property belonging to the commission disposed of by sales. I reached Washington January 10, 1856.

To the officers of my escort, and to my assistants, I feel deeply indebted for their urbanity in all my companionship with them, and for their untiring efforts in the performance of their duties.

I am, sir, very respectfully, your obedient servant,

N. MICHLER,
*Lieut. Corps Top. Engineers, U. S. Army.*

Major W. H. EMORY, U. S. A.,
*U. S. Commissioner.*

---

RECONNOISSANCE TO THE MOUTH OF THE GILA RIVER, FROM SAN DIEGO, CALIFORNIA, SEPTEMBER 11 TO DECEMBER 10, 1849.—BY C. C. PARRY, M. D.

On the 11th September, 1849, the astronomical party of the United States boundary commission, detailed by Major W. H. Emory for the determination of the point of junction of the Gila and Colorado rivers, left the Mission San Diego, en route across the mountains.

A more direct course than that usually taken was concluded on, leading northeast by the Rancho Santa Monica, to intersect the road usually travelled at Santa Maria.

Soon after leaving the mission grounds, we commence the ascent of the first rocky range, leading by steep slopes to a height of several hundred feet above the river valley; thence, passing over upland terraced plains, to descend a broken slope on the opposite (eastern) side.

The rock exposures show a form of porphyritic greenstone, of close, compact texture, and uniform bluish color. As exposed in the line of the river course, which lies to our left, it exhibits abrupt broken walls, through which the river makes its way, forming, near its exit from the range, a distinct fall of ten or twelve feet in a distance of two hundred yards. At this point commences the line of irrigating ditch, which formerly supplied the cultivated grounds adjoining the Mission of San Diego, distant two miles or more. The only traces of this aqueduct now remaining consist of broken patches of masonry, seen at several points along the right bank of the stream.

This greenstone range, having an average width of two to five miles, terminates on the east in an open basin valley, bounded on its western aspect by granite rocks, whose grey, mottled appearance shows a marked contrast to the uniform bluish aspect of the porphyry range.

Our route thence, observing a general northeast course, passes diagonally over the wide basin-valley below, reaching, at a distance of twelve miles from the mission, the Rancho Santa Monica. This rancho occupies the left bank of the upper San Diego river, attached to which is a very considerable section of rich bottom-land, capable of irrigation. The higher lands, and mountain slopes adjoining, furnish the requisite pasture ground to extensive herds of cattle and

* The distance can be shortened and the road improved by following the line of Lieutenant Parke's exploration through the new territory. W. H. E.

horses. From this point, continuing a northeast course, the main stream of the San Diego river is crossed; thence you pass up a more northerly branch. On this route we soon approach an immense mountain wall, lying on our right, and blocking up our way eastward. The ascent of this was accomplished at a depressed point in the general range, leading by a rude, unbroken track along the edges of a ravine. The general height of the ridge, some eight hundred feet above the valley, was at last attained by doubling teams, and frequent manual assistance.

Our route thence led along, and beyond, the line of broken valleys and irregular ridges, showing frequently depressed basins, over upland plains, to the Rancho Santa Maria. The rock exposure was quite uniform, being composed of crystalline feldspathic granite, coarsely grained, or showing occasionally a close sienitic texture. The computed height of the Rancho Santa Maria, above the sea, is 1,353 feet. It occupies the western edge of an extensive upland plain, from which is distinctly visible towards the east, at a distance of fifteen to twenty miles, the broken line of the dividing ridge of this mountain range.

On the northern border of this plain lies the lower course of the Rio Santa Isabel, flowing hence in an irregular western course, and finally forming the San Diegito river, which empties into the ocean some twenty miles above San Diego. The open plain is destitute of timber, being covered mainly with pasture growth. The California live-oak (Quercus agrifolia) grows on all the adjoining mountain slopes. Continuing along the line of the main road to Santa Isabel, being the same followed by General Kearny in 1846, the day before the battle of San Pasqual, a gradually increasing elevation brings us in the midst of the attractive mountain scenery of this portion of California. We here pass amid groves of live-oak, verdant shrubbery, and rich pasturage, set off in the back-ground by high rocky cliffs, or disclosing, in the distance, pine-fringed heights, distinctly marked against the clear sky. At Santa Isabel we encounter a clear running stream, coursing through an open valley, surrounded by lofty mountains; those directly to the east form the dividing crest of the range.

From this point there is a "cut-off" leading by a direct east course, over the mountain ridge, which rejoins the wagon road at San Felipe. To this route, being least known, we shall confine our remarks. Passing then directly up the main course of the Rio Santa Isabel, we follow a plain bridle-path, which, passing by frequent ascents, at first steep and broken, amid rocky exposures of granite, soon expands into quite an open valley. This valley is bounded on either side by steep mountains, along the sides of which, as we proceed upwards, pines make their appearance. Our trail, crossing from one side to another of the lively brook dignified with the title of the Rio Santa Isabel, brings us into the main road, about six miles above the settlements, and near the dividing crest of the main ridge. Just below this is situated the rancho of a Mr. Williams. The country here has a fresh mountain look; the air is cool and bracing. The rock exposures at this point show a form of quartz granite, frequently imbedding crystals of tourmaline.

The view from the higher peaks in this vicinity, reaching probably a height of 5,000 feet or more above the sea, is strikingly grand. We here overlook, to the westward, the broken mountain ranges stretching in a dim line seaward; to the east the descent is more abrupt, and the view shows the bare outline of the desert mountains, projecting in irregular spurs into the desert plain, or standing as isolated ridges in the dull brown expanse below.

The descent from the ridge to the east is by abrupt pitches along the sides of a steep ravine, opening out below into a dry waterless valley; this valley, thence expanding, forms the open plain of San Felipe, surrounded by dull ashy-colored mountains.

The distance, by this pass, from Santa Isabel to San Felipe, is twelve miles, while the wagon road between these two points is twenty-five miles, or more, in length.

The geological formation exhibited along the eastern slope of the mountain range at this point shows a very sensible change, and in place of the usual forms of feldspathic or quartz granite we meet with a more prevalent character of micaceous granite, in which the scales of mica are frequently of large size, and very confusedly intermixed. With this also occur mica and talcose slates, traversed by quartz veins. At this point, then, we have an approach to the gold formation, and in the section of country thus limited, exist the fairest prospects of mineral discoveries.

The country thus characterized is, however, barren and desolate in the extreme; water is scarce, and pasturage of the poorest description. Thorny cacti and arid shrubbery usurp the soil, not only of the mountain clefts, but also of the open valleys. At this point, indeed, we may say, the desert proper commences; for it is here we have the first appearance of the desert plants *Larrea Mexicana* and *Fouquiera Splendens.*

On leaving the last rocky exposures to enter on the open desert plain, we pass some distance down the bed of Cariso creek; along the course of which are exposed the high bluffs of sand, marl, and clay, exhibiting a fine sectional view of the tertiary formation on which the desert plateau is based. At the point where the road leaves the bed of the creek, to mount to the desert table-land, some 150 feet above, fossil marine shells of *Ostrea* are found, and gypsum makes its appearance in extensive beds. The upper layer of the table-land shows a variable thickness, composed of water-worn pebbles, derived from the adjoining mountains. Near the mountain base, this plateau has a height of about 500 feet above the level of the Colorado river. The surface extends in a gentle slope towards the Colorado, or eastward, about the distance of twenty-five miles, where it reaches its lowest depression at the Lagoon or "New river" basin, which is in fact a part of the extended alluvial tracts belonging to the Colorado river.

The proof of this latter fact is seen in the barometric observations, showing a depression at this point, below the level of the Colorado river in high water, and also by tracing a direct connexion between the overflow of this latter stream and the appearance of water at New river. The numerous depressions found along the course of this alluvial tract have, moreover, all the character of the sedimentary soil of the Colorado bottoms, supporting, though more sparsely, the same character of vegetation, and showing, frequently, fluviatic shells, identical with those now found at lagoons and sloughs adjoining the river.

This "New river" tract also receives the drainage of a large scope of desert country, which is sometimes visited by heavy showers of rain. It retains this rain-water, and river overflows, for several months; when both these sources fail, it becomes a perfectly dry bed, or contracts into quaggy saline marshes.

When we stopped here, in the latter part of September, copious local rains had filled these lake reservoirs, which, with previous extensive river overflows, had enriched the soil and caused a rank growth of annual grama grass. This afforded a fine grazing camp for our animals for two months.

Directly south from our camp at this place, and about eight miles distant, lies a high mountain range, having a direction nearly east and west. To the western and most prominent point of this range the name of "Signal Mountain" was given. This range is made up of a form of sienitic rock, associated with recent lava. Its surface is bare, and presents a forbidding outline of dark weathered rock, variously marked by furrows, and shows an irregular crest, gradually sloping towards the east.

Our route hence to the Colorado river leaves this depressed alluvial tract to the south, and passes again over the hard, gravelly surface of the desert table-land till we come upon the regular wooded bottoms of the main river. These bottom-grounds are everywhere bounded by a distinct line of the desert table-land, which forms bluffs of greater or less height. The character of these bluffs is often obscured by drifting sand, which is constantly encroaching on the lower tracts.

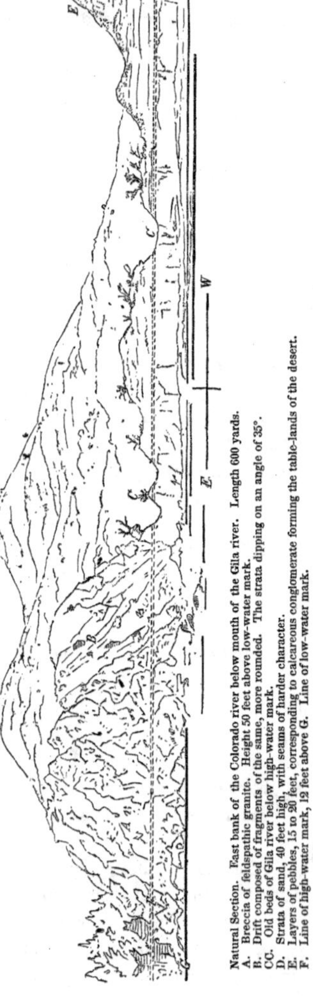

Natural Section. East bank of the Colorado river below mouth of the Gila river. Length 600 yards.
A. Breccia of feldspathic granite. Height 50 feet above low-water mark.
B. Drift composed of fragments of the same, more rounded. The strata dipping on an angle of 35°.
CC. Old beds of Gila river below high-water mark.
D. Strata of sand, 40 feet high, with seams of harder character.
E. Layers of pebbles, 15 to 20 feet, corresponding to calcareous conglomerate forming the table-lands of the desert.
F. Line of high-water mark, 12 feet above G. Line of low-water mark.

This upper bottom-land is densely wooded with mezquite, which here finds its most congenial soil, and spreads its thorny branches on all sides, forming impenetrable thickets. To this higher level succeeds a lower surface of moist soil, supporting cotton-wood and willow, both of which extend to the immediate edges of the stream.

In passing up the river on its right bank to the junction of the Gila, we encounter a rocky ridge abutting directly on the river bank; thence rising inland into high rugged peaks, it forms the "Pilot Knob" range. The character of the rock, as exposed on the river bank, is *gneiss*, having a distinct laminated structure. This character gradually passes into a form of *sienite*, composing the principal mass of the adjoining mountain ridge.

The immediate junction of the Gila and Colorado rivers is marked by a formation different from any elsewhere noticed. It consists of rounded knolls, which rise from fifty to one hundred and fifty feet above the river level, and are strewn over with the erratic deposites belonging to the desert formation. Its internal structure is thus in a great measure concealed. In the cleft made by the passage of the Colorado, just below the junction, the central nucleus is brought to view, and exhibits a form of epidote rock, occurring as an irregular breccia, and showing evidence of internal disturbance below.

The Colorado river, below the junction, is barely five hundred feet across. The Gila, near its mouth, is one hundred and fifty feet wide. The depth of channel in each is very variable.

The alluvial delta lying north of the junction of these two rivers is considerably below high-water mark. It thus furnishes soil suitable for cultivation, and is occupied as such by the Yumas Indians. Some two miles above the junction, on the right bank of the Colorado, are marks of an old river bed, which, in the time of floods, is filled with an obstructed body of water, forming frequent sloughs and lagoons along its course. The ground thus irrigated is occupied by another branch of the Yumas tribe for cultivation; the chief productions being maize, beans, pumpkins, and melons.

At the time of our arrival, in the month of October, it was the harvest season. The river overflows usually occur in the month of July. During the early part of the month of October the weather was oppressively sultry; the thermometer at mid-day frequently rising to 100° in the shade. The sky was remarkably clear, and the atmosphere extremely dry. During the month of November the air became sensibly cooler, especially at night; the thermometer sinking below 50° Fahrenheit. Heavy dews and fog at times, with cloudy weather and occasional showers, rendered the atmosphere more moist. Strong winds were frequent from the north, raising immense clouds of dust along the course of the river.

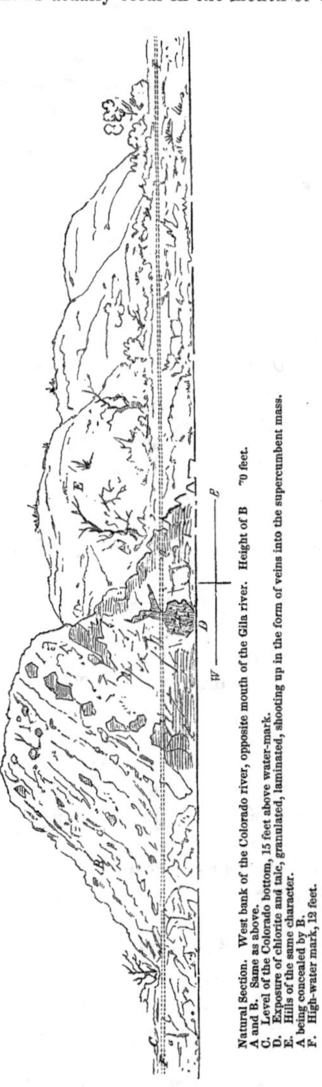


Natural Section. West bank of the Colorado river, opposite mouth of the Gila river. Height of B 70 feet.
A and B. Same as above.
C. Level of the Colorado bottom, 15 feet above water-mark.
D. Exposure of chlorite and talc, granulated, laminated, shooting up in the form of veins into the supercumbent mass.
E. Hills of the same character.
A being concealed by B.
F. High-water mark, 12 feet.

The water in the river channel varied but little during our stay, occasionally rising several inches, in consequence of heavy rains, and again sinking to the ordinary low-water level. Along the sides of the cañon, through which the river passes, below the junction of the Gila, there is plainly seen a line of high-water mark, showing an elevation of twelve feet or more above the usual level.

The character of the soil adjoining the river banks, derived from the sediment of river overflows and the light material borne by winds from the adjoining desert plateaux, causes along the bed of the stream the frequent formation of shifting sand-bars. These are perpetually changing with the variable river current. The process of deposition and removal is thus continually going on, rendering the river bed exceedingly variable and unequal in its depth and permanence.

The view of the adjoining country from any high elevation discloses a scene of unqualified barrenness and bleak sterility. The horizon is everywhere bounded by the bare outline of distant mountains, forming jagged and serrated ridges, or rising into various-shaped domes and chimney peaks. Intermediate, stretches the broad and desolate table-land, with its dead-brown aspect; while the more attractive river bottoms are seen clothed with a straggling growth of mezquite, or reflecting from turbid waters the overhanging willow and the lofty cotton-wood.

On the 1st of December, having completed our observations, we struck camp for our return to San Diego. The frequent rains of the previous month caused an abundance of water at convenient points along our road. In the bottoms of New river our teams were compelled to drag over muddy tracks. The opportune supply of desert grama grass, which made this locality the recruiting station for our animals during our stay on the Colorado, was now entirely exhausted.

Leaving the wagon trains to follow out the ordinary road across the mountains, our advance party, under Lieutenant Coutts, left the wagon route at Cariso creek, to mount the height of the range, by a direct ascent, to the west. Following out at first a gradual slope by which we advanced towards a re-entering angle in the steep rocky range, we accomplished with ease nearly half the height of the mountain ridge. The rest of the ascent was literally climbing up steep rocky slopes, or winding along rude ravines ; the height was finally gained, and was some 2,500 feet above the desert plain below. Thence our route led by a gentle slope towards the west, passing along beautifully shaded valleys, watered by clear flowing streams, and brought us to the coast near the initial point of boundary on the Pacific.

---

*Major Emory's Report Resumed.*

In 1846, I made a report of a rapid reconnoissance of the country here described by Dr. Parry. I preferred giving this description, taken from a different point of view, to reproducing my own sketch.

Dr. Parry accompanied me under the first organization as physician to the boundary commission, and also undertook the duties of zoologist and botanist. In the summer of 1854, when the second commission was organized under the new treaty with Mexico, the same position was offered him, but was declined. The appointment was then conferred on Dr. C. B. R. Kennerly.

In the list of officers of the expedition, (given on page 24,) the name of Dr. Kennerly is inadvertently omitted.

I cannot conclude the account of this part of the country, relating to the boundary, without some reference to a sad affair which occurred at the crossing of the Colorado, while the parties under my orders were engaged at that point, and which, at the time, excited much interest in the army and elsewhere. I refer to the death of the brave and accomplished Captain Thorn, of the army.

In the fall of 1849, Captain Thorn was detailed to escort, with his command, from the frontier of Missouri to California, the collector of the port of San Francisco. As may be supposed, the march was full of difficulties. When between Santa Fé and the Gila, the party was attacked by a force of Indians, which was gallantly repulsed by Captain Thorn and his command.

Arrived at the Colorado, most of the party fagged out and dispirited, Captain Thorn was obliged to use extraordinary exertion in crossing it. There was but one boat; and with that zeal and hardihood which characterized this officer in the discharge of all his duties, he stripped off his uniform, and took the personal direction of the boat. After having crossed and recrossed repeatedly, in ferrying over his command, and the party he escorted, the boat sank. The captain, although a good swimmer, became entangled with a Mexican who was in the boat, probably in the chivalrous attempt to save him, went down, and was swept away by the current.

I was at the time in my camp, distant one hundred and fifty miles, where a soldier came in and reported the circumstance, stating that the body had not been found when he left. I immediately despatched an Indian runner to Lieutenant Coutts, who commanded a company of dragoons engaged in escorting a surveying party of the boundary commission, to turn out his whole force, and search the river to its mouth for the recovery of the captain's body. He succeeded in obtaining it some miles below the crossing, where it was found by the Indians, and had it carefully placed in a coffiin, with the intention of bringing it to my camp; but in passing through San Diego, the officers of the 2d infantry, to which regiment Captain Thorn then belonged, who were stationed there, claimed the body, and took possession of it.

Previous to setting out on the expedition to California, I applied to have Captain Thorn assigned to duty with my command. This and other considerations made me desirous of recovering his body and sending it to his friends; but I could interpose no claim over that of the officers of his own regiment. I close this brief account of the circumstances attending the loss of a valued friend and brave brother officer by giving the letter of Lieutenant Coutts, which accompanied his remains:

CAMP CALHOUN, CALIFORNIA, *November* 11, 1849.

MAJOR: I have succeeded in making a box that will probably carry the remains of the lamented Captain Thorn to San Diego. In the absence of all material and conveniences for effecting this desired object properly, my carpenters have done better than I expected of them. I send the whole under the charge of Mr. Wiatt, a citizen, with one of my teamsters and a dragoon. They will procure a fresh team at Salvation camp, and should reach San Diego by the 23d instant. It will not, of course, be necessary for the teamster and dragoon to return.

* * * * * * * * * * *

I have the honor to be, your obedient servant,

CAVE J. COUTTS,

*Lieutenant 1st Dragoons, commanding Escort.*

Maj. W. H. EMORY,

*Commanding Escort to Boundary Commission, Camp Riley, California.*

---

*Tabulated distances of routes along and in the neighborhood of the boundary line between the United States and Mexico, from the Pacific ocean to the Gulf of Mexico, measured by viameters, by Lieut. N. Michler, Lieut. Parke, and Assistant Chandler.*

| From— | To— | Distance. | Distance from starting point. | Total distance. |
|---|---|---|---|---|
| | | *Miles.* | *Miles.* | *Miles.* |
| Newtown or New San Diego | Old San Diego | 2 | 2 | |
| Old San Diego | Fisher's Rancho | 8.95 | 10.95 | |
| Fisher's Rancho | Panasquitas | 8.02 | 18.97 | |
| Panasquitas | San Pasqual | 18.87 | 37.84 | |
| San Pasqual | Laguna | 12 | 49.84 | |
| Laguna | Santa Isabel | 11.40 | 61.24 | |
| Santa Isabel | Warner's Rancho | 10.33 | 71.57 | |
| Warner's Rancho | San Felipe | 15.88 | 87.45 | |
| San Felipe | Vallecito | 17.85 | 105.30 | |
| Vallecito | Carrizo creek | 16.60 | 121.90 | |
| Carrizo creek | Big Laguna | 26.41 | 148.31 | |
| Big Laguna | New River | 5.83 | 154.14 | |
| New river | Little Laguna | 4.50 | 158.64 | |
| Little Laguna | Alamo Mocho | 16.44 | 175.08 | |
| Alamo Mocho | Cook's Well | 21.94 | 197.02 | |
| Cook's Well | Fort Yuma | 20 | 217.02 | |
| Newtown | Fort Yuma | | | 217.02 |

TABLE—Continued.

| From— | To— | Distance. | Distance from starting point. | Total distance. |
|---|---|---|---|---|
| | | *Miles.* | *Miles.* | *Miles.* |
| Fort Yuma | 1st Laguna | 7.7 | | |
| 1st Laguna | 2d Laguna | 1.3 | 9 | |
| 2d Laguna | 3d Laguna | 10.8 | 19.8 | |
| 3d Laguna | 4th Laguna, camp near New Initial Point. | 1.5 | 21.3 | |
| Fort Yuma | Rowlett's Rancho | 2.63 | 2.63 | |
| Rowlett's Rancho | Camp No. 4 | 4.86 | 7.49 | |
| Camp No. 4 | Camp No. 5 | 20.88 | 28.37 | |
| Camp No. 5 | Camp No. 6 | 14.79 | 43.16 | |
| Camp No. 6 | Los Metates | 2 | 45.16 | |
| Los Metates | Camp No. 7 | 14.84 | 60 | |
| Camp No. 7 | Camp No. 8 | 11.50 | 71.50 | |
| Camp No. 8 | Lomas Negras, Camp No. 9 | 16.72 | 88.22 | |
| Lomas Negras | Camp No. 10 | 13 | 101.22 | |
| Camp No. 10 | Camp No. 11 | 9.50 | 110.72 | |
| Camp No. 11 | Camp No. 12 | 10.50 | 121.22 | |
| Camp No. 12 | Camp No. 13 | 10 | 131.22 | |
| Camp No. 13 | Camp No. 14, at Tezotal | 10.50 | 141.72 | |
| Camp No. 14, at Tezotal | Camp No. 15, Maricopa Wells | 40 | 181.72 | |
| Camp No. 15, Maricopa Wells | Camp No. 16, Pimo village of Cola Azul. | 15 | 196.72 | |
| Camp No. 16, Pimo village of Cola Azul. | Camp No. 17, last point of the Gila. | 14 | 210.72 | |
| Camp No. 17, last point of Gila | Picacho on the Jornada | 35 | 245.72 | |
| Pichaco on the Jornada | Tucson | 35 | 280.72 | |
| Fort Yuma | Tucson | | | 280.72 |
| Tucson | San Xavier | 9 | | |
| San Xavier | Agua de la Canoa | 25 | 34 | |
| Agua de la Canoa | Ford of Santa Cruz river | 12 | 46 | |
| Ford of Santa Cruz river | Tubac | 2.50 | 48.50 | |
| Tucson | Tubac | | | 48.50 |
| San Xavier | Cienega de los Pimos | 24 | | |
| Cienega de los Pimos | San Pedro river | 23.52 | 47.52 | |
| San Pedro river | Quercus Cañon | 6 | 53.52 | |
| Quercus Cañon | Plaza de los Pimos, Croton Spring | 30.76 | 84.28 | |
| Plaza de los Pimos | Puerto de Dado | 30 | 114.28 | |
| Puerto del Dado | Cienega del Sauz | 25.30 | 139.58 | |
| Cienega del Sauz | Ojo de la Vaca | 54.05 | 193.63 | |
| Ojo de la Vaca | Rio Mimbres | 17 | 210.63 | |
| Rio Mimbres | Cook's Spring | 17.60 | 228.23 | |
| Cook's Spring | Mesilla | 53.11 | 281.34 | |
| Mesilla | Fort Fillmore | 2.50 | 283.84 | |
| Fort Fillmore | Franklin | 40 | 323.84 | |
| *San Xavier | Franklin | | | 323.84 |
| Tubac | Ojo del Agua de Sopori | 10.25 | 10.25 | |
| Ojo del Agua de Sopori | Aribaca | 18.25 | 28.50 | |
| Aribaca | Ojos de las Boquillas | 9.10 | 37.60 | |
| Ojos de las Boquillas | Laguna | 25.08 | 62.68 | |
| Laguna | Coyotes | 9.70 | 72.38 | |
| Ojos de los Coyotes | Charcos de Alvarez | 16.49 | 88.87 | |
| Charcos de Alvarez | Rancho de Cobota | 25.73 | 114.60 | |
| Rancho de Cobota | Puerto de la Nariz | 44.85 | 159.45 | |
| Puerto de la Nariz | Sonoyta | 24.55 | 184 | |

*The distances from San Xavier to Franklin were furnished by Lieut. J. G. Parke, Top. Engineers, U. S. A.

TABLE—Continued.

| From— | To— | Distance. | Distance from starting point. | Total distance. |
|---|---|---|---|---|
| | | *Miles.* | *Miles.* | *Miles.* |
| Tubac | Mission of Tomocacari | 2. 61 | 2. 61 | |
| Mission of Tomocacari | Rancho de las Calabasas | 10. 37 | 12. 98 | |
| Tubac | Calabasas | | | 12. 98 |
| Rancho de las Calabasas | Observatory at Los Nogales | 8 | 8 | |
| Observatory at Los Nogales | Monument on Line | 3. 97 | 11. 97 | |
| Monument on Line | Agua Zarca | 11. 39 | 23. 36 | |
| Agua Zarca | Casita | 14. 79 | 38. 15 | |
| Casita | Los Alisos | 3. 73 | 41. 88 | |
| Los Alisos | Imuris | 11. 37 | 53. 25 | |
| Rancho de las Calabasas | Rancho de San Lazaro | 35 | 35 | |
| Rancho de San Lazaro | Santa Cruz | 7. 18 | 42. 18 | |
| Rancho de las Calabasas | Santa Cruz | | | 42. 18 |
| Newtown | Fort Yuma | 217. 02 | | |
| Fort Yuma | Tucson | 280. 72 | 497. 74 | |
| Tucson | Tubac | 48. 50 | 546 24 | |
| Tubac | Rancho de las Calabasas | 12. 98 | 559. 22 | |
| Rancho de las Calabasas | Santa Cruz | 42. 18 | 601. 40 | |
| Newtown | Santa Cruz, via Ft. Yuma & Tucson | | | 601. 40 |
| Fort Yuma | Camp near New Initial Point on Rio Colorado. | | 21. 30 | |
| Tubac | Sonoyta | | 184 | |
| Rancho de las Calabasas | Imuris | | 53. 25 | |
| Fort Yuma | Point of departure from Gila | 2. 63 | 2. 63 | |
| Point of departure from Gila | Las Cuevitas | 26. 45 | 29. 08 | |
| Las Cuevitas | Las Tinajas Altas | 16. 49 | 45. 57 | |
| Las Tinajas Altas | El Corral | 15. 33 | 60. 90 | |
| El Corral | El Tule | 1. 15 | 62. 05 | |
| El Tule | La Salada | 44. 89 | 106. 94 | |
| La Salada | Agua Dulce | 2. 89 | 109. 83 | |
| Agua Dulce | Quitobaquita | 6. 54 | 116. 37 | |
| Quitobaquita | Santo Domingo | 5. 70 | 122. 07 | |
| Santo Domingo | Rancho de Sonoyta | 7. 73 | 129. 80 | |
| Rancho de Sonoyta[a] | Pozo del Macias | 47. 15 | 176. 95 | |
| Pozo del Macias | Rancho del Soñi | 8. 70 | 185. 65 | |
| Rancho del Soñi | Las Caborqueñas | 22. 69 | 208. 34 | |
| Las Caborqueñas | Rancho del Bamori | 15. 83 | 224. 17 | |
| Rancho del Bamori | Las Tinajitas | 6. 73 | 230. 90 | |
| Las Tinajitas | Altar | 4. 65 | 235. 55 | |
| Fort Yuma | Altar | | | 235. 55 |
| Altar | Charco de San Raphael | 8 | 8 | |
| Charco de San Raphael | Rancho del Ocuca | 18. 4 | 26. 4 | |
| Rancho del Ocuca | Pueblo de Santa Anna | 21. 38 | 47. 78 | |
| Pueblo de Santa Anna | Pueblo de Santa Marta | 2. 84 | 50. 62 | |
| Pueblo de Santa Marta | Pueblo de San Lorenzo | 4. 68 | 55. 30 | |
| Pueblo de San Lorenzo | Pueblo de la Magdalena | 4. 76 | 60. 06 | |
| Pueblo de la Magdalena | San Ignacio | 4. 78 | 64. 84 | |
| San Ignacio | Imuris | 6. 62 | 71. 46 | |
| Altar | Imuris | | | 71. 46 |

[a] The distances from Fort Yuma to Sonoyta were furnished by Don Francisco Jimenez, Mexican commission.

TABLE—Continued.

| From— | To— | Distance. | Distance from starting point. | Total distance. |
|---|---|---|---|---|
| | | *Miles.* | *Miles.* | *Miles.* |
| Altar | Charco San Raphael | 8 | 8 | |
| Charco San Raphael | Rancho de las Boquillas | 16 | 24 | |
| Rancho de las Boquillas | Laguna near Lomita | 3. 10 | 27. 10 | |
| Laguna near Lomita | Rancho de los Alamitos | 3. 16 | 30. 26 | |
| Rancho de las Alamitos | Ford of San Ignacio | 2. 67 | 32. 93 | |
| Ford of San Ignacio | Rancho de Arequabo | 2. 38 | 35. 31 | |
| Rancho de Arequabo | Rancho Espinosa | 12. 80 | 48. 11 | |
| Rancho Espinosa | Pueblo Santa Anna | 13. 28 | 61. 39 | |
| Imuris | Rancho de Babasaqui | 5 | 5 | |
| Rancho de Babasaqui | Cocospera | 15. 81 | 20. 81 | |
| Cocospera | San Lazaro | 17. 28 | 38. 09 | |
| San Lazaro | Santa Cruz | 7. 18 | 45. 27 | |
| Imuris | Santa Cruz | | | 45. 27 |
| Newtown | Fort Yuma | 217. 02 | | |
| Fort Yuma | Altar | 235. 55 | 452. 57 | |
| Altar | Imuris | 71. 46 | 524. 03 | |
| Imuris | Santa Cruz | 45. 27 | 569. 30 | |
| Newtown | Santa Cruz, via Ft. Yuma and Altar | | | 569. 30 |
| Santa Cruz | 1st tributary of San Pedro | 13. 50 | | |
| 1st tributary San Pedro | 2d...do......do..(des'ted rancho) | 16 | 29. 50 | |
| 2d...do......do...(deserted rancho) | 3d...do......do | 1. 97 | 31. 47 | |
| 3d...do......do | 4th...do......do | 0. 50 | 31. 97 | |
| 4th...do......do | 5th...do......do..(Sauz) | 3 | 34. 97 | |
| 5th...do......do...(Sauz) | 6th...do......do | 9. 81 | 44. 78 | |
| 6th...do......do | Ash creek | 22. 32 | 67. 10 | |
| Ash creek | San Bernardino | 30. 16 | 97. 26 | |
| San Bernardino | Entrance of Guadalupe cañon | 9. 27 | 106. 53 | |
| Entrance of Guadalupe cañon | Camp in the cañon | 12. 73 | 119. 26 | |
| Camp in the cañon | San Luis Springs | 11. 70 | 130. 96 | |
| San Luis Springs | San Francisco | 16. 10 | 147. 06 | |
| San Francisco | Pelatado | 27. 13 | 174. 19 | |
| Pelatado | Janos | 10. 50 | 184. 69 | |
| Janos | Corralitas | 20. 26 | 204. 95 | |
| Corralitas | Mines of San Pedro | 19 | 223. 95 | |
| Mines of San Pedro | Santa Maria | 27. 18 | 251. 13 | |
| Santa Maria | Salado | 27 | 278. 13 | |
| Salado | Samalurca | 36. 31 | 314. 44 | |
| Samalurca | El Paso | 25. 02 | 339. 46 | |
| Santa Cruz | El Paso | | | 339. 46 |
| Janos | Las Lagunitas | 8. 7 | | |
| Las Lagunitas | Palos Blancos | 13. 8 | 22. 5 | |
| Palos Blancos | Espia | 14. 1 | 36. 6 | |
| Espia | Desechado | 18. 8 | 55. 4 | |
| Desechado | Carrizalillo | 19. 3 | 74. 7 | |
| Carrizalillo | Mountain Camp | 22. 6 | 97. 3 | |
| Mountain Camp | Ojo de Vaca | 20 | 117. 3 | |
| Ojo de Vaca | Rio Mimbres | 18. 7 | 136 | |
| Rio Mimbres | Cook's Spring | 19. 7 | 155. 7 | |
| Cook's Spring | Cañon Camp | 28. 1 | 183. 8 | |
| Cañon Camp | Mesilla Ford | 30. 5 | 214. 3 | |
| Mesilla Ford | Alamos | 21 | 235. 3 | |
| Alamos | Franklin | 21. 5 | 256. 8 | |
| Janos[a] | Franklin, (opposite El Paso) | | | 256. 8 |

[a] The distances from Janos to Franklin were furnished by Mr. Chandler, assistant United States boundary commission.

TABLE—Continued.

| From— | To— | Distance. | Distance from starting point. | Total distance. |
|---|---|---|---|---|
| | | *Miles.* | *Miles.* | *Miles.* |
| Franklin, (opposite El Paso) | Fort Bliss | 2 | | |
| Fort Bliss | Isleta | 12.14 | 14.14 | |
| Isleta | Socorro | 3.10 | 17.24 | |
| Socorro | San Elceario | 5.45 | 22.69 | |
| San Elceario | Last camp on Rio Grande | 59.80 | 82.49 | |
| Last camp on Rio Grande | Eagle Springs | 31.42 | 113.91 | |
| Eagle Springs | Van Horn's Wells | 19.74 | 133.65 | |
| Van Horn's Wells | Dead Man's Hole | 32.83 | 166.48 | |
| Dead Man's Hole | Barrel Spring | 13.58 | 180.06 | |
| Barrel Spring | Fort Davis | 18.42 | 198.48 | |
| Fort Davis | Varela Springs | 28 | 226.48 | |
| Varela Springs | Leon Springs | 33.86 | 260.34 | |
| Leon Springs | Comanche Springs | 8.88 | 269.22 | |
| Comanche Springs | Ojos Escondidos | 19.40 | 288.62 | |
| Ojos Escondidos | Arroyo Escondido | 8.58 | 297.20 | |
| Arroyo Escondido | First camp on Pecos | 16.26 | 313.46 | |
| First camp on Pecos | Ferry of Pecos | 38.26 | 351.72 | |
| Ferry of Pecos | Live Oak creek | 7.29 | 359.01 | |
| Live Oak creek | Howard's Springs | 30.44 | 389.45 | |
| Howard's Springs | First camp on San Pedro | 44 | 433.45 | |
| First camp on San Pedro | 2d crossing of San Pedro | 19.50 | 452.95 | |
| 2d crossing of San Pedro | Palos Blancos | 18.39 | 471.34 | |
| Palos Blancos | Painted Caves | 15.73 | 487.07 | |
| Painted Caves | 1st crossing San Pedro | 2.54 | 489.61 | |
| 1st Crossing of San Pedro | San Felipe | 10.22 | 499.83 | |
| San Felipe | Arroyo Pedro | 8.80 | 508.63 | |
| Arroyo Pedro | Zoquete creek | 3.81 | 512.44 | |
| Zoquete creek | Piedra Pinta | 8.86 | 521.30 | |
| Piedra Pinta | Las Moras, (Fort Clark) | 7 | 528.30 | |
| Las Moras (Fort Clark) | Elm creek | 7.13 | 535.43 | |
| Elm creek | Turkey creek | 15.23 | 550.66 | |
| Turkey creek | Nueces | 10.27 | 560.93 | |
| Nueces | Head of Leona | 9.04 | 569.97 | |
| Head of Leona | Rio Frio | 6.08 | 576.05 | |
| Rio Frio | Comanche creek | 8.46 | 584.51 | |
| Comanche creek | Sabinal | 5 | 589.51 | |
| Sabinal | Rancheros creek | 3.94 | 593.45 | |
| Rancheros creek | Rio Seco, (Dhanis) | 8.38 | 601.83 | |
| Rio Seco, (Dhanis) | Quihi | 15.28 | 617.11 | |
| Quihi | Castroville | 10 | 627.11 | |
| Castroville | Leon | 18 | 645.11 | |
| Leon | San Antonio | 6.53 | 651.64 | |
| El Paso | San Antonio | | | 651.64 |
| San Antonio | Port Lavaca | | | 128.50 |
| San Antonio | Indianola | | | 138 |

TABLE—Continued.

SUMMARY.

| From— | To— | Distance. | Distance from starting point. | Total distance. |
|---|---|---|---|---|
| | | *Miles.* | *Miles.* | *Miles.* |
| New San Diego, via Fort Yuma and Altar. | Santa Cruz | 569. 30 | | |
| Santa Cruz | El Paso | 339. 46 | 908. 76 | |
| El Paso | San Antonio | 651. 64 | 1, 560. 40 | |
| San Antonio | Indianola | 138. 00 | 1, 698. 40 | |
| New San Diego | Indianola | | | 1, 698. 40 |
| New San Diego, via Fort Yuma and Tucson. | Santa Cruz | 601. 40 | | |
| Santa Cruz | El Paso | 339. 46 | 940. 86 | |
| El Paso | San Antonio | 651. 64 | 1, 592. 50 | |
| San Antonio | Indianola | 138 | 1, 730. 50 | |
| New San Diego | Indianola | | | 1, 730. 50 |
| New San Diego | Fort Yuma | 217. 02 | | |
| Fort Yuma | San Xavier | 289. 72 | 506. 74 | |
| San Xavier | Franklin | 323. 84 | 830. 58 | |
| Franklin | San Antonio | 651. 64 | 1, 482. 22 | |
| San Antonio | Indianola | 138. 00 | 1. 620. 22 | |
| New San Diego | Indianola | | | 1, 620 22 |

# CHAPTER VIII.

## ASTRONOMICAL AND GEODETIC WORK.

---

### PREFACE.

1. Classes of observations.
2. Longitude.
3. Latitude.
4. Geodetic measurement of azimuth lines.
5. Tracing of parallels.
6. Computations.

### A.—Determination of Boundary Line from the Initial Point on the Pacific Ocean to junction of the Gila and Colorado.

1. Longitude of Camp Riley, near Initial Point, on the Pacific.
2. Longitude of junction of Gila and Colorado.
3. Latitude of Camp Riley,
4. Latitude of junction of Gila and Colorado.
5. Triangulation, transferring the determination at Camp Riley to Initial Point, on the Pacific.
6. Azimuth of straight line from Initial Point, on Pacific, to junction of Gila and Colorado.

### B.—Determination of Boundary Line from Rio Colorado to intersection of 111th meridian of longitude west of Greenwich and parallel 31° 20′ N.

1. Azimuth line—astronomical positions.
2. Triangulation for determining longitude of Initial Point on the Colorado.
3. Tabulated results of latitude.
4. Distances between monuments.

### C.—Determinations of the Boundary Line along parallels 31° 47′ and 31° 20′ N.

1. Latitude and longitude of Los Nogales, near intersection of 111th meridian and 31° 20′.
2. Latitude near the head of Santa Cruz river.
3. Latitude of San Bernardino.
4. Latitude of San Luis springs.
5. Latitude of Agua del Perro.
6. Latitude of Espia.
7. Latitude and longitude of Carrizalillo.
8. Latitude of Initial Point on Rio Grande.
9. Azimuths for laying off the Prime Vertical at above stations.
10. Elements for marking parallels of latitude 31° 20′ and 31° 47′.

### D.—Boundary Line formed by the Rio Grande.

1. Of Longitudes:
   - *a.* Frontera.
   - *a′.* San Elceario.
   - *b.* El Paso del Norte.
   - *c.* Mouth of cañon where road from San Antonio to El Paso strikes the Rio Grande.
   - *d.* Presidio del Norte.
   - *e.* Fort Duncan.
   - *f.* Ringgold barracks.
   - *g.* Mouth of the Rio Bravo del Norte.
2. Of Latitudes:
   - *a.* Frontera.
   - *b.* San Elceario.
   - *c.* Mouth of cañon where road from San Antonio to El Paso strikes the Rio Grande.
   - *d.* Presidio del Norte.
   - *e.* Fort Duncan.
   - *f.* Ringgold barracks.
   - *g.* Mouth of Rio Grande.

### E.—Table of Latitudes and Longitudes of points on and near the Boundary Line between the United States and Mexico.

# PREFACE.

## I. Classes of Observations.

The observations for the determination of the latitude and longitude were of two classes—the first being those which were made at primary stations with the largest instruments that could be conveniently transported by land; the second, those made at places of less importance, determined by reflecting instruments, and by the transmission of chronometers from the nearest primary stations, or by flashes of gunpowder, observed simultaneously. Eighteen stations of the first class were established across the continent at the following places, named in their order, from west to east:

1. Camp Riley, near initial point, on the Pacific coast; 2. Junction of the Gila and Colorado; 3. On the Colorado, where the line leaves that river; 4. Quitobaquita; 5. Los Nogales, near 111th meridian of longitude; 6. San Bernardino, near parallel 31° 20′; 7. San Luis springs, near parallel 31° 20′; 8. Agua del Perro; 9. Espia; 10. Carrizalillo, near parallel 31° 47′; 11. Frontera; 12. San Elceario; 13. Initial point of boundary on parallel 31° 47′; 14. Cañon where the San Antonio road leaves the Rio Bravo; 15. Presidio del Norte; 16. Eagle Pass, (Fort Duncan;) 17. Ringgold Barracks; 18. Mouth of Rio Bravo.

I do not enumerate the very many points of lesser importance determined by the sextant and chronometer, as no special notice is required of the means used in their determination. It may be as well to state, however, that in all cases where observations were made for latitude with reflecting instruments, stars were taken, both north and south, and at altitudes as nearly equal as could be obtained; and when local time was obtained by these instruments, stars were taken both east and west, of nearly equal altitudes, and as near the prime vertical as they could be found. In this way we attempted to avoid the errors arising from refraction and from the eccentricity of the instrument.

In some cases, where I had direct comparisons with results obtained by the large instrument, I ascertained that the latitude of a place determined by the Gambey sextant in the proper hands, in a single night, might be relied upon to within 3″ or 5″; and if the observation was repeated for two nights, the result might be relied upon to be within 2″ of the true position.

## II. Longitude.

The longitudes of 1, 2, 4, 5, 10, 11, 12, 15, 16, 17, 18, were obtained by observations on the transit of the moon and moon culminating stars, with a telescope of forty-six inches' focal length, by Troughton & Simms, of London, and with a smaller one of thirty-six inches' focal length. Occultations were observed, whenever practicable; but, owing to the impossibility of obtaining corresponding observations, they proved of little value; indeed, but few were observable. Occultations are no doubt of the greatest value where corresponding observations at some established point are observed; but for the general purposes of a survey, conducted in distant regions, they are not a sure reliance. They occur too seldom; and to see the instant of immersion and emersion of a star requires great steadiness in the telescope, which in the field can be rarely obtained, owing to the difficulty of protecting the telescope from the wind, and of getting a firm support.

After giving what I considered a fair trial in the field to all the methods now known, it was concluded to place the chief reliance on the transit of the moon. If, however, it happens to me to be again in charge of extensive operations of the kind, I shall make some effort to improve the instruments for the observation of lunar distances. I am satisfied it is in that direction itinerant observers must look for improved methods and facilities in obtaining longitude.

When the reflecting instruments are made so as to be placed more firmly and quickly in any given plane, and the methods of computing lunar distances are improved and simplified, it will be in the power of the observer any clear night, when the moon is above the horizon, to multiply his observations so as to obtain close results. The instruments in present use have not sufficient power to observe near contacts of the moon and stars; and in the attempts which have been made to increase the power of the telescope, the instrument becomes insupportable by the hand for repeated or nice observations.

In all cases where it was not necessary to declare the result on the spot, as at those stations at the extremities of azimuth lines, and at stations such as the 111th meridian of longitude, which formed turning-points in the boundary, the longitude was deduced from corresponding observations made at Greenwich. In some few cases we obtained corresponding observations at the American observatories; but the observations were not sufficiently continuous at any of these last-named observatories to enable us to rely upon them. And I have here to repeat (what I have heretofore expressed to the American Association for the Advancement of Science) my obligations to Astronomer Royal Airy for the trouble he has taken to furnish the corresponding observations in MSS. before they were published at Greenwich.

In the personal account, mention is made of the agreement made with the Mexican commissioner to declare the 111th meridian, from computations based on the data afforded by the Greenwich Ephemeris,* before receiving the corresponding observations. This arrangement was a necessity arising from our isolated position near the centre of the continent, cut off from all intercourse except by expresses protected by armed escorts. To have awaited the reception of the corresponding observations would have detained us fully eighteen months, at great expense—a result not contemplated by either the United States or Mexican governments, and not contemplated by the treaty, which provided against any possible errors in the location of the line by declaring, "that line shall alone be established upon which the commissioners may fix; their consent in this particular being considered decisive and an integral part of this treaty, without necessity of ulterior ratification or approval, and without room for interpretation of any kind by either of the parties contracting."

The observations at 1, 11, 13, 14, 15, 17, were made by myself in person; those at 2, by Lieutenant Whipple; at 4, by Señor Jimenez, first engineer Mexican boundary commission; at 5, 10, and 16, by Assistant John H. Clark; at 18, by Assistants Gardner and Clark; and at 12, by Lieutenant W. F. Smith. At most of the stations the observations were carried through at least three lunations; but, it will be seen, the result was not changed materially after the first lunation.

The longitude of the point where the boundary leaves the Rio Bravo was transferred from Frontera by triangulation; and the longitude of El Paso and of No. 14 (the cañon) were respectively transferred from Frontera and San Elceario by flashes of gunpowder simultaneously

* When this agreement was made, no copy of the American Ephemeris had been received, nor was I aware it had been published.

observed. It was my desire to extend this beautiful and accurate mode of obtaining differences of longitude to many other stations; but in a country without settlements, and traversed by bands of savages who kill at sight, it was impossible to do so, as every party that went out had to be escorted by ten or fifteen armed men.

Where neither of the above means could be resorted to, longitude was obtained by transmission of chronometers from some established point. This method, so successful at sea, where the motion is uniform and smooth, has objections on land, principally the impossibility of moving chronometers without deranging the rate. Every method of transporting them was tried—on carriages, on foot, and on horseback; and an ordinary spring-carriage was found to be the best. No test can be applied to check an error in determining longitude by the transmission of chronometers; for even with three chronometers it is possible for all to be affected in the same way, though of course not in the same degree—that is to say, all may run, while travelling, too fast or too slow; and when you halt, may resume their former rates.

The observations at the two stations 11 and 12—Frontera and San Elceario—being about the centre of the continent, and in a geographical point of view more important than any others, were combined to arrive at the results given.

| | | |
|---|---|---|
| The longitude of Frontera from moon culminations, extending through four lunations, computed from the predicted place of the moon and moon culminating stars, given in the Greenwich Ephemeris for 1851–'52............ | | $=7^h\ 05^m\ 55^s.3$ |
| The same, after applying the correction due for corresponding observations made at Greenwich and furnished in MSS. from the Observatory at that place, is— | | |
| For the 1st lunation, December and January, 1851–'52...... | 7 06 11.38 | |
| 2d " January and February, 1852............ | 13.34 | |
| 3d " February and March, " ......... | 14.73 | |
| 4th " March and April, " ......... | 12.48 | |
| Mean........................................................................... | | 7 06 12.98 |
| Difference due to correction........................................................ | | + 17.68 |
| The longitude of San Elceario deduced from observations on forty moon culminations, extending through three lunations, computed from the predicted place of the moon and moon culminating stars, given in the Greenwich Ephemeris for 1852 .................................................................. | | $7^h\ 04^m\ 46^s.55$ |
| The same, after applying the correction due for corresponding observations made at Greenwich, is— | | |
| For the 1st lunation, January and February, 1852............ | 7 05 02.52 | |
| 2d " February and March, " ............ | 04.31 | |
| 3d " April, " ............ | 03.44 | |
| Mean ........................................................ | 7 05 03.42 | |
| By combining these observations with corresponding ones at Cambridge, Mass., we get......................................................................... | | 7 05 04.3 |
| Difference due to correction........................................................ | | + 17.75 |

The coincidence between these differences is satisfactory. The computations were made by independent computers: the first, by Assistant J. H. Clark; the second, by Assistant J. O'Donoghue. The observations for the first were made by myself; those at San Elceario by Lieutenant W. F. Smith.

To give greater effect to the results, and to establish beyond the probability of future change the longitude of Frontera—which is about the longitude of the middle of the continent, and is a primary station on the survey of the boundary—an attempt was made to connect the observatory of San Elceario with that of Frontera by flashes of gunpowder, and the following is the result. It should be observed that the Frontera here mentioned is not the Frontera of the old maps of North America. Frontera signifies a frontier town, but in this instance is the name given by its proprietor to a newly-constructed hut, built immediately on the ratification of the treaty of Guadalupe Hidalgo, at a point some eight miles above El Paso, where it was supposed the boundary under that treaty would leave the Rio Bravo. The difference of longitude between Frontera and San Elceario, observed by flashes on the nights of the 14th, 18th, 19th February, and 14th March, 1852, was found to be as follows:

| Date. | No. of observat'ns each night. | Diff. of long., El Paso, east of Frontera. | No. of observat'ns each night. | Diff. of long., San Elceario, east of Frontera. |
|---|---|---|---|---|
| 1852. | | *s.* | | *m. s.* |
| February 14 | 14 | 16.03 | 13 | 1 7.16 |
| 18 | 15 | 16.06 | 15 | 1 7.54 |
| 19 | 12 | 15.84 | 15 | 1 7.36 |
| March 14 | 12 | 15.84 | 14 | 1 7.15 |
| | Mean of 53 observations = 15.94 | | Mean of 57 observations = 1 7.30 | |

The difference of longitude by observations on the moon and moon culminating stars is $1^m$ $08^s.58$, which agrees with that determined by flashes within $1^s.3$. Now, assuming the difference determined by flashes as correct, and giving equal weight to the observations at each station, the longitude of Frontera will be diminished by $0^s.65$, and that of San Elceario will be increased by the same quantity; so that the final result will be:

| | |
|---|---|
| Frontera, west of Greenwich | $7^h$ $06^m$ $12^s.33$ |
| San Elceario " " | 7 05 $04^s.95$ |

The longitude of the observatory at El Paso erected by the Mexican commission, two hundred feet south and five hundred feet west of the Cathedral tower, was determined by flashes observed simultaneously by Señor Salazar and myself on the nights stated in the preceding part of this article, to be $15^s.94$ east of Frontera; hence the longitude of El Paso, $7^h$ $05^m$ $56^s.39$.

A discussion of the longitudes of the Presidio del Norte and of Eagle Pass, on the Rio Grande, shows a difference between the longitude obtained by using the Greenwich Ephemeris and that obtained by using the corresponding observations at Greenwich, to be in the first case $+ 19^s$, and in the second $+ 17^s.1$. Comparing these with the same quantities obtained at Frontera and San Elceario, made in the same year, it will be seen that there is a coincidence, showing that in this case the error in the predicted place of the moon is nearly uniform for the same year.

The difference between the longitudes obtained in 1849, those computed from data in the

Greenwich Ephemeris, and those obtained by corresponding observations at Greenwich, was pretty generally + 12$^s$. This confirms the importance of a thorough revision of the lunar tables. The uniformity observable in these results shows, I hope, the probability of detecting the error, and eliminating or reducing it.

I have deposited in the Department of the Interior two volumes containing, in tabulated form, all the individual observations and computations upon which the results obtained on the boundary for longitude are founded. I give a leaf from these volumes, to show the manner in which the observations were made and computed. It has been suggested to me to present them for publication; but as each would make a volume nearly the size of the Greenwich Observations, I have contented myself, in this publication, with presenting in tabulated form the separate results, and in two cases—at the initial point on the Pacific, and at the mouth of the Rio Bravo—I have extended the table so as to show in detail the manner in which all the observations and computations have been tabulated. It has been found convenient, also, to incorporate with these tables the computations by which the azimuth lines forming portions of the boundary were determined.

## III. Latitudes.

The latitudes of all the primary astronomical stations, except four, were determined either by myself or by Assistant J. H. Clark, with the zenith telescope. Two of the four excepted were determined by Lieutenant Whipple, the other two by Lieutenant Michler. I have placed in the Department of the Interior four volumes containing the individual observations and the computations for the latitude of the primary stations. In regard to the publication of these volumes, the same remarks that were made above in reference to the longitudes apply here. I give a leaf from them also, to show the mode of tabulating and computing the observations.

The tables attached hereto present a recapitulation of all the results for the latitudes of the primary stations, including the station determined by Lieutenant Michler, by circum-meridian altitudes of northern and southern stars observed with a sextant, and those determined by Lieutenant Whipple, by observing the transit of stars over the prime vertical.

The method habitually used on the boundary for obtaining latitude—that by the measurement of the difference of zenith distance of stars near the zenith, and nearly equidistant, north and south—is now so generally used and approved as to make no particular notice of it necessary. It was first adopted by Captain Talcott, in 1835, on the survey of the Ohio boundary. It was resumed by myself on the northeastern boundary; and some of my results coming under the eye of Professor Bache, he concluded to try it on the Coast Survey, and called on me for any suggestion I might have to make in reference to the form. I made the suggestions which resulted in the form in which the instrument is now made by Troughton & Simms, of London, and is that which I used on the present boundary survey.

Attached to the table combining the results of the observations at each station is a table showing the correction applied to the places of stars, derived either from actual observations of stars at the Washington Observatory, and politely furnished for the use of the boundary survey, or from the Twelve-year Catalogue of the Greenwich Observatory.

A comparison of the results obtained by the zenith telescope, with the errors developed in the declination of stars of the British Association catalogue, will show the rapid march field operations have made, in point of accuracy, upon the observations at the fixed observatories.

While the results confirm the excellence of the zenith telescope for field operations, they indicate the necessity of a more extended and accurate catalogue of stars.

## IV. Geodetic Measurement.

The azimuth lines were ascertained by observations on the elongation of Polaris, and the measurement on the face of the earth was made with several different instruments. Those in California with a transit by Ertel & Son, Munich; with a horizontal limb of fifteen inches diameter, graduated to read to 10″. The instruments used in tracing the parallel of latitude were a ten-inch azimuth circle, by Gambey, of Paris; two by Bruner; and one by Draper, of Philadelphia. Some of the barometers used were by Bunten, of Paris; but they were chiefly made by James Green, of New York. They, together with the thermometers, were compared with the standard at the Smithsonian Institution, both before and after being used.

In tracing the parallels of latitude 31° 47′ and 31° 20′, and also in prolonging the azimuth line across California, and from the Rio Colorado to the 111th meridian of longitude, it frequently happened that it was convenient to take the meridians determined by the transit instrument, but most usually they were taken from the measurements of the elongation of Polaris.

## V. Tracing the Parallels.

The parallels were determined by tracing a tangent to the prime vertical at any given point, and measuring the ordinates to the parallel. The use of the tangent instead of the chord was preferred, because the measurement of the ordinates, confided to a variety of assistants, presented always an increasing series, and was less liable to lead to confusion; a precaution very necessary in a country where water is scarce, and where parties operating have constantly to be on the alert against attacks of Indians. A general sketch of the stations established in latitude to trace these parallels is stated in the agreement with the Mexican commissioner, which will be found under the head of Personal Account, in Chapter II, and it is therefore unnecessary to repeat it here.

Great as were the embarrassments in other respects, the absence of trees gave us great facility in tracing these lines, and enabled us easily to correct errors resulting from producing long lines.

In the determinations of latitude along the same parallel, it will be seen we used the same instrument, and, as far as practicable, the same sets of stars; so we were quite certain of getting correct differences of latitude between two stations. In no case was it attempted to produce the same tangent in one direction more than thirty miles, and it was then always compared with the tangent from the new latitude station. The parallel of latitude thus deduced by separate and independent operations seldom differed more than a few feet; and in no case was the discrepancy sufficiently great to make it necessary to retrace our steps. The tangents, being few in number, were generally laid off by myself, and prolonged by the principal assistant surveyors, who were furnished with tables of ordinates and angles, which will be found in the appendix, that enabled us at once, and by simple measurements, to establish points in the parallels forming the boundary.

## VI. Computations.

The computations were all made in the field originally, and subsequently revised in the office.

The observations made in California were computed in the field by myself, Lieutenant Whipple, and James Nooney. They were all subsequently revised by Professor Hubbard, and the new element of corresponding observations introduced into the computations for longitude. The observations on the Rio Bravo were computed in the field by myself and Assistants J. H. Clark and J. O'Donoghue, and revised in the office by Captain George Thom, corps of topographical engineers, and Assistant C. N. Thom.

The observations on the parallels 31° 47′ and 31° 20′ were all computed in the field by Principal Assistant J. H. Clark, Lieutenant Turnbull, corps of topographical engineers, and Assistant Hugh Campbell, and revised in the office by the same.

The observations at the point where the line strikes the Rio Colorado were made and computed by Lieutenant Michler and Assistant J. O'Donoghue.

## A.

*Determination of the line forming the boundary between the United States and the republic of Mexico, from the Initial Point on the Pacific ocean to the point where the "Gila river empties into the Colorado." By Brevet Major William H. Emory, Chief Astronomer.*

This portion of the boundary consists of a straight line from a point on the Pacific ocean, one marine league south of the port of San Diego, to the junction of the Gila and Colorado. The most obvious way of determining the direction of this line was to connect the two points by triangulation, and in this way ascertain their relative positions on the face of the earth, and compute the azimuth of the line joining them. But the character of the intervening country made it impossible to pursue this mode of operating when the time and means at the disposal of the joint commission were considered. Triangulation is the surest, but it is the slowest and most expensive method of surveying, even in old-settled countries, where the stations to be selected are easily accessible in wagons. In the country under consideration obstacles presented themselves almost insurmountable. The whole distance, about 148 miles, may be divided into two nearly equal parts, differing in character, but both equally unfavorable to geodetic operations. The first, rising in steppes from the sea, and covered with spinose vegetation, attains, in abrupt ascents, the height of five or six thousand feet in the short space of thirty miles. From this point, for about thirty miles, the country is occupied by a succession of parallel ridges, striking the boundary nearly at right angles, and separated by deep, and sometimes impassable chasms. It then falls abruptly to near the level of the sea. The remainder of the line stretches across the desert of shifting sand at the head of the Gulf of California, destitute, for the most part, of both water and vegetation.

The following is the order in which are arranged the subjects embraced in the determination of the line:

1. The longitude of Camp Riley, near the Initial Point.
2. The longitude of Camp near the junction of the Gila and Colorado.
3. The latitude of Camp Riley, near the Initial Point.
4. The latitude of Camp near the junction of the Gila and Colorado.
5. Transfer of the latitude and longitude of Camp Riley, by triangulation, to the Initial Point.
6. Azimuth of straight line from Initial Point, on Pacific, to junction of Gila and Colorado.

Numbers 1, 3, 5, and 6 are by myself. Numbers 2 and 4 are by Lieutenant Whipple.

The tracing of the line on the ground was partly by myself and Lieutenant Whipple, but chiefly by Captain E. L. F. Hardcastle, corps topographical engineers.

The computation of the azimuth of the line was made in the field. In this computation the earth was supposed to be a spheroid of revolution of the following dimensions, which are those determined by Bessel from all the measurements up to that time, (1849,) and the elements given by him were converted into English measure by adopting the following value of the metre, viz:

| | |
|---|---|
| 39.6850 inches; logarithm | 1.5951741293. |
| Equatorial radius | = 6974129.339 yards. |
| Polar radius | = 6950815.059 " |

I am indebted to Professor Airy for the observations at Greenwich for 1849; and for the recomputation of the longitude and the application of the correction due to the corresponding observations on moon and moon culminating stars, I am indebted to the assistance of Professor J. S. Hubbard, of the National Observatory.

## I. LONGITUDE OF CAMP RILEY, NEAR THE INITIAL POINT.

The observations with the transit instrument have been reduced in the following manner:

The equatorial intervals of the transit wires having been determined as accurately as possible, the imperfect transits were corrected, by applying to the mean of the observed wires the mean of their equatorial intervals, multiplied by the secant of the stars' declination.

For circum-polar stars, each wire was reduced separately, and the mean of the results taken. In the case of the moon, allowance was made for its motion by the method and tables of Bessel. (Tabulæ Regiomontanæ, pp. LII and 537.)

Denoting by $a$ the constant of correction for azimuth of the instrument, by $b$ the constant for level, and by $c$ that for collimation, and by $d$ the star's right ascension, $\delta$ its declination and $z$ its zenith distance, and by $t$ the chronometer time of its transit, and by $\Delta t$ the correction of the chronometer at the time $t$, we have the known formula—

$$\alpha = t + \Delta t + a \sin. z. \sec. \delta + b. \cos. z. \sec. \delta + c. \sec. \delta.$$

If $\varphi$ denote the latitude of the observer, and if

$$m = b. \cos. \varphi + a. \sin. \varphi,$$
$$n = b. \sin. \varphi - a. \cos. \varphi,$$

the expression above becomes—

$$\alpha = t + \Delta t + m + n. \tan. \delta + c. \sec. \delta,$$

or

$$\alpha = t + \Delta t + m + (n + c.) \tan. \delta + c. (\sec. \delta - \tan. \delta)$$

which last form has been employed in the reductions.

In the observations at Camp Riley, $c = o$ for nearly the whole series, and is small enough at all times to have no effect in the last term of the formula; in the other series, one or two cases occur where it has been necessary to take this last term into account.

Where, as in the present case, only the right ascension of the body is wanted, the quantities $\Delta t$ and $m$ being constant for the evening, may be combined together, and then the last term of one equation, always small, and vanishing at no great distance from the equator, being introduced when necessary, and the requisite correction for the chronometer rate being applied, it is evident that but two equations are necessary for the determination of the unknown quantities. One is generally furnished by a circum-polar star; the other by the mean of the equations, corresponding to all the stars near the moon's path, in order the more completely to remove all chance of constant error from the desired result. The equations being solved, furnish the quantities given below, and which have been applied to the observations.

The first column contains the date; the second the name of the object observed; the third shows the position of the instrument, (lamp east or west.) Next follow columns 4, 5, 6, 7, 8, 9, 10, the seconds of observed transit, and column 11, the mean of the transit over as many wires as have been observed. Column 12 contains the correction to be applied to this mean for an imperfect transit; column 13 the correction for instrumental error, or the quantity $(n + c)$ tan. $\delta + c$. (sec. $\delta$ — tan. $\delta$,) the last term of which is generally equal to $o$; and column 14 gives the correction of chronometer, and the constant term of instrumental correction, or the quantity $\Delta\ t + m$.

In cases where a mean-time chronometer has been used, this column includes also the reduction of mean to sidereal time, the quantities in all the preceding columns being in mean time. In column 15 is given the sum of the quantities; in columns 11, 12, 13, and 14 are the observed right ascension of the object; and the last column shows the tabular right ascension, taken in the order of preference from the Nautical Almanac, the Greenwich Twelve-year Catalogue, or the Catalogue of the British Association.

The next step was to deduce the required corrections of the assumed longitude of the place, by comparing the observed AR. of the moon with that corresponding to the assumed longitude already determined very approximately by computations in the field. For this purpose, the tabular AR. was interpolated from the moon culminating list of the Nautical Almanac, using fourth differences, and it was found that the assumed longitude corresponded perfectly to the results from the uncorrected tabular place of the moon. But the extracts from the observations at Greenwich, given below, show a correction of the latter to be necessary; and this being applied, the corresponding correction of the assumed longitude was determined and also applied.

*Constant values employed in the reductions.*

OBSERVATORY AT CAMP RILEY.

*Equatorial intervals of transit wires.*

| I. | II. | III. | IV. | V. | VI. | VII. |
|---|---|---|---|---|---|---|
| s. | s. | s. | s. | s. | s. | s. |
| + 51.163 | + 33.971 | + 17.165 | + 0.22 | — 17.092 | — 34.089 | — 51.141. |

| | $n + c$. | $\Delta t + m$. | | $n + c$ | $\Delta t + m$. |
|---|---|---|---|---|---|
| | s. | s. | | s. | h. m. s. |
| July 27.... | 0.000 | + 11.99 | *Sept. 5... | +2.716 | —2 25 29.02 |
| 28.... | 0.000 | + 12.50 | 24... | +1.388 | —2 24 54.55 |
| 29.... | 0.000 | + 12.48 | 27... | +1.041 | —2 24 47.68 |
| 30.... | 0.000 | + 12.45 | 28... | +0.792 | —2 24 45.66 |
| 31.... | — 0.770 | + 12.20 | 29... | +1.125 | —2 24 43.83 |
| Aug. 2.... | — 0.726 | + 12.63 | 30... | +1.204 | —2 24 42.23 |
| 3.... | — 0.726 | + 10.85 | Oct. 23... | +0.934 | —2 23 54.74 |
| 26.... | — 1.852 | + 6.32 | 25... | +1.471 | —2 23 48.95 |
| 27.... | — 2.694 | + 6.30 | 28... | +1.128 | —2 23 40.42 |
| 28.... | — 2.231 | + 6.28 | 29... | +1.764 | —2 23 38.85 |
| 29.... | — 1.778 | + 5.87 | Nov. 1... | +1.764 | —2 23 31.26 |
| Sept. 3.... | — 2.613 | + 1.84 | 2... | +1.764 | —2 23 28.09 |
| 4.... | — 2.427 | + 0.49 | 5... | 0.000 | —2 23 22.54 |

OBSERVATORY NEAR JUNCTION OF THE GILA AND COLORADO RIVERS.

*Equatorial intervals of transit wires.*

| I. | II. | III. | IV. | V. | VI. | VII. |
|---|---|---|---|---|---|---|
| s. | s. | s. | s. | s. | s. | s. |
| + 52.790 | + 35.078 | + 17.467 | + 0.44 | — 17.489 | — 35.180 | — 52.710. |

| | $n + c$. | $\Delta t + m$. | | $n + c$. | $\Delta t + m$. |
|---|---|---|---|---|---|
| | s. | m. s. | | s. | m. s. |
| Oct. 3.... | — 1.339 | + 41.79 | Nov. 1.... | — 0.802 | — 45.76 |
| 4.... | — 1.026 | + 39.05 | 2.... | — 0.199 | — 49.99 |
| 5.... | — 0.450 | + 12 2.06 | 3.... | 0.000 | — 52.07 |
| 6.... | — 0.000 | + 31.52 | 4.... | 0.000 | — 54.11 |
| 7.... | — 0.878 | + 29.66 | 5.... | — 0.411 | — 55.17 |
| 23.... | — 29.100 | + 8.79 | 6.... | 0.000 | — 57.31 |
| 24.... | — 1.410 | — 12.15 | 20.... | 0.773 | + 12 22.04 |
| 25.... | — 0.450 | — 27.80 | 22.... | 0.000 | — 1 29.88 |
| 26.... | — 0.437 | — 29.86 | 23.... | 0.000 | — 1 32.22 |
| 27.... | — 0.147 | — 34.19 | 24.... | + 0.672 | — 1 35.09 |
| 28.... | — 0.297 | — 36.50 | 25.... | 0.000 | — 1 37.36 |
| 29.... | — 0.607 | — 39.04 | 27.... | — 4.370 | + 12 25.83 |
| 30.... | — 1.435 | — 41.56 | 29.... | — 4.270 | — 1 42.73 |
| 31.... | — 1.238 | — 45.01 | | | |

* The value of $\Delta t$ adopted for the mean-time chronometer being the complement of the time value, it becomes necessary to change the sign of $(n + c.)$

*Longitude of Camp Riley: By William Hemsly Emory.*

| DATE. | OBJECT. | LAMP. | CHRONOMETER TIMES OF TRANSIT. I. | II. | III. | IV. | V. | VI. | VII. | MEAN OF OBS'D WIRES | CORRECTION FOR— Imperfect transits. | Instrument. | Chronometer. | OBSERVED A.R. | TABULAR A.R. |
|---|---|---|---|---|---|---|---|---|---|---|---|---|---|---|---|
| 1849. | | | s. | s. | s. | s. | s. | s. | s. | h. m. s. | m. s. | s. | s. | h. m. s. | s. |
| July 26 | ε Bootis ........ | | 16.0 | 35.0 | 54.0 | 13.2 | 32.5 | 52.0 | 11.2 | 14 38 13.41 | .......... | 0.00 | + 11.14 | 14 38 24.55 | 24.61 |
| | $\alpha^{2}$ Libræ .......... | | 29.2 | 47.0 | 5.0 | 22.5 | 40.5 | 58.5 | 16.0 | 14 42 23.67 | .......... | 0.00 | 11.14 | 14 42 33.81 | 33.74 |
| 27 | Moon, 1st L.... | | ...... | ...... | ...... | ...... | 39.5 | 57.5 | 15.0 | 15 2 57.33 | — 38.66 | 0.00 | + 11.96 | 15 2 33.63 | ...... |
| | β Libræ.......... | | ...... | 9.2 | 26.2 | 43.4 | 1.0 | 18.0 | 35 0 | 15 8 52.13 | — 8.63 | 0.00 | 11.97 | 15 8 55.47 | 55.00 |
| | α Serpentis....... | | 48.8 | 6.0 | 23.2 | 38.8 | 56.8 | 14.0 | 28.0 | 15 36 39.37 | .......... | 0.00 | 11.99 | 15 36 51.36 | 51.69 |
| | θ Libræ.......... | | 11.6 | 29.2 | 46.4 | 4.0 | 22.4 | 39.6 | 54.8 | 15 45 4.00 | .......... | 0.00 | 11.99 | 15 45 15.99 | 16.14 |
| 28 | α Serpentis ....... | W. | 47.2 | 5.0 | 22.0 | 39.0 | 56.5 | 13.5 | 30.5 | 15 36 39.10 | ......... | 0.00 | + 12.49 | 15 36 51.59 | 51.67 |
| | θ Libræ .......... | | ...... | 28.2 | 46.0 | 4 0 | 22.0 | 39.2 | 56.8 | 15 45 12.70 | — 8.88 | 0.00 | 12.49 | 15 45 16.31 | 16.13 |
| | Moon, 1st L.... | | 43.0 | 1.5 | 19.5 | 37.6 | 56.0 | 13.5 | 32.0 | 15 51 37.59 | .......... | 0 00 | 12.49 | 15 51 50.08 | ...... |
| | $\beta^{1}$ Scorpii ........ | | 35.8 | 54.0 | 12.0 | 29.6 | 47.8 | 6.5 | 24.0 | 15 56 29.96 | .......... | 0.00 | 12.49 | 15 56 42.45 | 42.04 |
| | δ Ophiuchi ....... | | 24.5 | 42.2 | 58.6 | 16 0 | 33 0 | 50.0 | 7.5 | 16 6 15.97 | .......... | 0.00 | 12.50 | 16 6 28.47 | 28.16 |
| | α Scorpii.......... | | 2.0 | 20.6 | 40.8 | 59.2 | 18.4 | 36.4 | 53.8 | 16 19 58.74 | .......... | 0.00 | 12.50 | 16 19 11.24 | 11.87 |
| | (5579).......... | | 46.8 | 4.2 | 22.8 | 40.0 | 58.8 | 16 8 | 34.2 | 16 32 40.52 | ......... | 0 00 | 12.50 | 16 32 53.02 | 53.11 |
| | η Ophiuchi....... | | ...... | ...... | 15.5 | 33.2 | 50.8 | 8.6 | 26.0 | 17 1 50.82 | — 17.67 | 0.00 | 12.51 | 17 1 45.66 | 45.80 |
| 29 | Moon, 1st L.... | W. | 46.0 | 5.0 | ...... | 41.5 | 58.5 | 17.5 | 35.4 | 16 41 43.98 | — 3.06 | 0.00 | + 12.47 | 16 41 53.39 | ...... |
| | *Anonymous.... | | ...... | ...... | 51.5 | 9.5 | 27.0 | 44.5 | 2.5 | 17 2 27.00 | — 17.67 | 0.00 | 12.47 | 17 2 21.80 | ...... |
| 30 | (5579) .......... | W. | 47.0 | 5.0 | 23.0 | 41.0 | 59.0 | ...... | 34.0 | 16 32 34.83 | + 5.95 | 0.00 | + 12.45 | 16 32 53 23 | 53.08 |
| | η Ophiuchi....... | | 39.8 | 58.0 | 15.2 | 33.0 | 51.0 | 8.6 | 26 0 | 17 1 33.09 | .......... | 0.00 | 12.45 | 17 1 45.54 | 45.78 |
| | Moon, 1st L.... | | 45.2 | 4.0 | 22.2 | 40.5 | 58.4 | 17.2 | 36.2 | 17 32 40.53 | .......... | 0.00 | 12.45 | 17 32 52.98 | ...... |
| 31 | (5579) .......... | | 47.5 | 5.0 | 23.0 | 40.5 | 58.5 | 15.5 | 33.5 | 16 32 40.50 | .......... | + 0.25 | + 12.21 | 16 32 52.96 | 53.07 |
| | α Herculis ... .... | | 42.8 | 0.8 | 18.2 | 36.2 | 53.2 | 11.2 | 29.0 | 17 7 35.92 | .......... | — 0.20 | 12.20 | 17 7 47.92 | 47.85 |
| | Moon, 1st L.... | | 38.0 | 51.0 | 9.6 | 28.0 | 46.0 | 4.5 | 23.0 | 18 24 27.87 | .......... | + 0.28 | 12.19 | 18 24 40.34 | ...... |
| | α Lyræ.......... | | ...... | ...... | ...... | ...... | ...... | 24.0 | 46.0 | 18 32 35.00 | — 54.57 | — 0.63 | 12.19 | 18 31 51.99 | 51.95 |
| Aug. 1 | α Serpentis....... | W. | 49.2 | 6.0 | 23.2 | 40.4 | 57.2 | 14.8 | 31.6 | 15 36 40.34 | .......... | — 0.09 | + 11.76 | 15 36 52.01 | 51.62 |
| | $\beta^{1}$ Scorpii......... | | 36.0 | 54.0 | 10.4 | 30.0 | 48.8 | 6.4 | 24.4 | 15 56 30.00 | .......... | + 0.28 | 11.76 | 15 56 42.04 | 41.99 |
| | δ Ophiuchi ....... | | 25.2 | 42.0 | 58.4 | ...... | 31.6 | 50.0 | 8.0 | 16 6 15.87 | .......... | + 0.05 | 11.76 | 16 6 27.68 | 28.12 |
| 2 | γ Draconis ....... | W. | 33.5 | 2.0 | 29.0 | 56.5 | 23.6 | 51.0 | 18.5 | 17 52 56.30 | .......... | — 0.78 | + 12.63 | 17 53 8.15 | 8.26 |
| | $\mu^{1}$ Sagittarii....... | | ...... | 57.0 | 15.2 | 33.5 | 52.0 | 10.0 | 29.0 | 18 4 42.78 | — 9.14 | + 0.24 | 12.63 | 18 4 46.51 | 46.69 |
| | δ Ursæ Minoris... | | ...... | 36.0 | 24.0 | 12.0 | 59.0 | 47.5 | 37.0 | 18 23 35.92 | —2 23.97 | — 10.48 | 12.63 | 18 21 14.10 | 13.50 |
| | 51 (Hev.) Cep., S.P. | | 37.0 | 32.5 | 32.0 | 23.0 | 16.0 | 15.5 | ...... | 18 24 26.00 | +2 57.32 | + 12.96 | 12.63 | 18 27 48.91 | 52.21 |
| | β Lyræ ...... .... | | ..... | 39.5 | 59.5 | 20.0 | 40.5 | ...... | 20.0 | 18 44 29.92 | — 10.19 | — 0.41 | 12.63 | 18 44 31.95 | 32 72 |
| | ζ Aquilæ ......... | | 25.5 | 42.5 | ...... | 18.2 | 35.5 | 53.0 | 10.8 | 18 58 17.93 | .......... | — 0.15 | 12.63 | 18 58 30.41 | 30.65 |
| | $\rho^{1}$ Sagittarii....... | | 51.4 | 9.0 | 27.0 | 45.0 | 2.8 | 20.5 | 38.3 | 19 12 44.86 | .......... | + 0.20 | 12.63 | 19 12 57.69 | 57.54 |
| | $e^{1}$ Sagittarii....... | | 1.0 | 18.5 | 36.5 | 54.0 | 12.0 | 30.0 | 47.5 | 19 31 54.21 | .......... | + 0.19 | 12.63 | 19 31 7.03 | 6.73 |
| | ζ Sagittarii........ | | ...... | 37.5 | 55.5 | 13.0 | 31.0 | 48.0 | 6.5 | 19 49 21.92 | — 8.87 | + 0.18 | 12.63 | 19 49 25.86 | 25.81 |
| † | Moon, 1st L ... | E. | 16.4 | 34.4 | 52.8 | 11.2 | 29.2 | 47.5 | 6.0 | 20 9 11.07 | .......... | + 0.19 | 12.63 | 20 9 23.89 | ...... |
| | ρ Capricorni ...... | | 10.8 | 28.5 | 46.5 | 4.5 | 22.5 | 40.0 | 58.0 | 20 20 4.40 | .......... | + 0.21 | 12.63 | 20 20 17.24 | 17.31 |
| | μ Aquarii......... | | 28.5 | 46.0 | 3.0 | 20.2 | 37.5 | 55.0 | 12.0 | 20 44 20.31 | .......... | + 0.11 | 12.63 | 20 44 33.05 | 33.08 |
| 3 | $\alpha^{1}$ Capricorni...... | E. | ...... | 33.2 | 50.0 | 8.0 | 26.5 | ...... | 1.0 | 20 9 11.74 | — 3.52 | + 0.18 | + 10.87 | 20 9 19.27 | 19.19 |
| | $\alpha^{2}$ Capricorni...... | | ..... | 56.7 | 13.5 | 31.5 | 50.0 | .... | 24.5 | 20 9 35.24 | — 3.52 | + 0.18 | 10.87 | 20 9 42.77 | 43.06 |
| | ρ Capricorni...... | | 12.5 | 30.0 | 48.4 | 6.0 | 24.0 | 42.0 | 0.2 | 20 20 6.14 | .......... | + 0.26 | 10.85 | 20 20 17.25 | 17.29 |
| | η Capricorni...... | | 45.8 | 3.8 | 21.8 | 40.0 | ...... | ...... | ...... | 20 55 12.85 | + 27.30 | + 0.29 | 10.83 | 20 55 51.27 | 50.99 |
| | Moon, 1st L.... | | ...... | 49.0 | ...... | ...... | ...... | 1.6 | ...... | 21 1 25.30 | + 0.07 | + 0.22 | 10.82 | 21 1 36.41 | ...... |
| 4 | ε Ursæ Minoris... | E. | 13.5 | 21.8 | 28.0 | 35.0 | 42.0 | 49.5 | 56.0 | 17 1 35.11 | .......... | — 5.78 | + 9.99 | 17 1 39.32 | 39.09 |
| | β Draconis........ | | 30.5 | 58.0 | 26.5 | 54.5 | 22.8 | 50.2 | 18.5 | 17 26 54.43 | .......... | — 1.02 | 9.98 | 17 27 3.39 | 3.27 |
| | 58 Ophiuchi ....... | | ...... | 39.0 | 57.0 | 15.6 | 34.0 | 52.0 | 10.4 | 17 34 24.67 | — 9.17 | + 0.31 | 9.98 | 17 34 25.79 | 25.70 |
| | 4 Sagittarii ....... | | 31.0 | 49.5 | 8.5 | 27.0 | 45 4 | 4.4 | ...... | 17 50 17.63 | + 9.32 | + 0.35 | 9.97 | 17 50 37.27 | 37.25 |
| | γ Draconis........ | | ...... | ..... | ...... | 58.8 | 26.4 | 53.6 | 21.5 | 17 53 40.08 | — 41.10 | — 0.98 | 9.97 | 17 53 7.97 | 8.22 |
| | $\mu^{1}$ Sagittarii....... | | ...... | ...... | ...... | 36.5 | 54.5 | 12.8 | ...... | 18 4 54.60 | — 18.28 | + 0.30 | 9.97 | 18 4 46.59 | 46.68 |
| | δ Ursæ Minoris... | | ..... | ...... | ...... | 16.0 | ...... | ...... | ...... | 18 21 16.00 | — 0.37 | — 13.18 | 9.96 | 18 21 12.41 | 12.95 |
| | 51 (Hev.) Cephei.. | | 38.0 | ...... | ...... | 27.0 | ...... | ...... | ...... | 18 18 32.50 | +8 51.47 | + 16.30 | 9.96 | 18 27 50.23 | 52.92 |
| | α Lyræ ...... .... | | 37.0 | 59.0 | 21.0 | 42.6 | 4.5 | 26.8 | 48.0 | 18 31 42.70 | .......... | — 0.63 | 9.96 | 18 31 52.03 | 51.91 |
| | β Lyræ . . . | | 22.2 | 43.0 | 2.8 | ...... | ...... | 4.4 | 24.5 | 18 44 19.38 | + 4.11 | — 0.51 | + 9.95 | 18 44 32.93 | 32.71 |

* Observed by mistake for η Ophiuchi.

† Instrument reversed.

## *Longitude of Camp Riley*—Continued.

| DATE. | OBJECT. | LAMP. | CHRONOMETER TIMES OF TRANSIT. I. | II. | III. | IV. | V. | VI. | VII. | MEAN OF OBS'D WIRES | CORRECTION FOR— Imperfect transits. | Instrument. | Chronometer. | OBSERVED A.R. | TABULAR A.R. |
|---|---|---|---|---|---|---|---|---|---|---|---|---|---|---|---|
| 1849. | | | s. | s. | s. | s. | s. | s. | s. | h. m. s. | m. s. | s. | s. | h. m. s. | s. |
| Aug. 19* | ε Ursæ Minoris... | W. | ...... | 20.4 | 27.6 | 34.8 | 42.4 | 49.0 | 56 0 | 17 2 38.37 | —1 3.51 | — 6.99 | + 7.47 | 17 1 35.34 | 36.61 |
| | β Draconis ....... | | 32.6 | 0.4 | 28.0 | 56.4 | 24.4 | 52.4 | 20.4 | 17 26 56.37 | ......... | — 1.23 | 7.47 | 17 27 2.61 | 2.86 |
| | 58 Ophiuchi........ | | 22.4 | 40.4 | 58.8 | 17.4 | 35.6 | 54.0 | 12.4 | 17 34 17.30 | ......... | + 0.37 | 7.47 | 17 34 25.14 | 25.53 |
| | 4 Sagittarii........ | | 33.6 | 51.6 | 10.0 | 28.6 | 47.2 | 6.0 | 25.0 | 17 50 28.86 | ......... | + 0.42 | 7.47 | 17 50 36.75 | 37.09 |
| | $\mu^{1}$ Sagittarii....... | | 44.0 | 2.0 | 20.4 | 38.8 | 57.2 | 15.4 | 33.2 | 18 4 38.71 | ......... | + 0.37 | 7.47 | 18 4 46.55 | 46.53 |
| | δ Ursæ Minoris... | | ..... | 41.6 | 30.4 | 16.6 | 3.8 | 49.2 | 38 4 | 18 23 40.00 | —2 23.92 | — 15.96 | 7.47 | 18 21 7.59 | 8.20 |
| | ζ Aquilæ.......... | | ...... | ...... | ...... | ...... | 40.4 | 58.0 | 16.0 | 18 59 58.13 | — 35.10 | — 0.23 | 7.47 | 18 59 30.27 | 30.53 |
| | δ Aquilæ.......... | | 57.0 | 14.0 | 30.8 | 48.0 | 5.6 | 22 4 | 38.8 | 19 17 48.09 | ......... | — 0.05 | 7.47 | 19 17 55.51 | 55.54 |
| | γ Aquilæ......... | | 8.4 | 26.0 | 43.2 | 0.4 | 18.0 | 34.6 | 51.6 | 19 39 0.31 | ......... | — 0.17 | 7.47 | 19 39 7.61 | 7.36 |
| | α Aquilæ.......... | | 28.6 | 45.5 | 3.2 | 20.4 | 37.6 | 54 8 | 12.0 | 19 43 20.30 | ......... | — 0.14 | 7.47 | 19 43 27.63 | 27.48 |
| | $\alpha^{1}$ Capricorni..... | | 19.0 | 36.0 | 53.8 | 11.2 | 28.5 | 46.0 | 3.5 | 20 9 11.20 | ......... | + 0.22 | 7.47 | 20 9 18.89 | 19.20 |
| | $\alpha^{2}$ Capricorni..... | | 43.0 | 1 0 | 18.0 | 35.2 | 52.5 | 9.0 | 27.8 | 20 9 35.21 | ......... | + 0.22 | 7.47 | 20 9 42.90 | 43.07 |
| | α Cygni......... | | 2.0 | 26.0 | 50.0 | 14.0 | 38.0 | 2.4 | 26.5 | 20 36 14 13 | ......... | — 0.94 | 7.47 | 20 36 20.66 | 20.11 |
| | $61^{1}$ Cygni.......... | | 59.6 | 22.0 | 42.8 | 4.8 | 26.2 | 48.0 | 9.6 | 21 0 4.72 | ......... | — 0.74 | 7.47 | 21 0 11.45 | 11.07 |
| | ζ Cygni.......... | | 27.5 | 48.0 | 8.0 | 26.8 | 48.0 | 6.0 | 26.0 | 21 6 26.90 | ......... | — 0.54 | 7.4[illegible] | 21 6 33.83 | 33.59 |
| | ι Capricorni..... | | 51.4 | 9.5 | 26.4 | 44.8 | 3.0 | 20.6 | 38.0 | 21 13 44.81 | ......... | + 0.30 | 7.47 | 21 13 52.58 | 52.67 |
| 26 | η Ophiuchi....... | W. | 45.5 | 3.0 | 20.5 | 38.4 | 56.0 | 13.5 | 31.5 | 17 1 38.34 | ......... | + 0.51 | + 6.32 | 17 1 45.17 | 45.42 |
| | α Herculis....... | | 49.0 | 6.8 | 23.8 | 41.8 | 59.5 | 16.8 | 34.5 | 17 7 41.74 | ......... | — 0.48 | 6.32 | 17 7 47.58 | 47.47 |
| | Moon, 1st L.... | | 7.0 | 25.4 | 43.5 | 2.0 | 20.2 | 38.4 | 57.0 | 17 13 1.93 | ......... | + 0.60 | 6.32 | 17 13 8.85 | ...... |
| | 58 Ophiuchi........ | | 22.8 | 41.4 | 59.8 | ...... | 36.0 | ...... | ...... | 17 33 55.00 | + 22.91 | + 0.73 | 6.32 | 17 34 24.96 | 25.42 |
| | $\mu^{1}$ Sagittarii...... | | ...... | ...... | 21.5 | 39.8 | 57.8 | ...... | 34.2 | 18 4 53.32 | — 13.68 | + 0.71 | 6.32 | 18 4 46.67 | 46.43 |
| | λ Sagittarii....... | | 37.8 | 57.0 | 16.0 | 35.0 | 53.8 | 12.5 | 31.4 | 18 18 34.80 | ......... | + 0.88 | 6.32 | 18 18 42.00 | 41.65 |
| | α Lyræ.......... | | 41.5 | 3 5 | 24.5 | 46.5 | 8.4 | 30.0 | 52.0 | 18 31 46.63 | ......... | — 1.48 | 6.32 | 18 31 51.47 | 51.55 |
| | $\nu^{1}$ Sagittarii....... | | 3 6 | 22.0 | 40.0 | 58.6 | 17.5 | 35.5 | 54.0 | 18 44 58.74 | ......... | + 0.78 | 6.32 | 18 45 5.84 | 5.73 |
| | ζ Aquilæ......... | | 32.4 | 49.5 | 7.0 | 24.5 | 42.0 | 59.5 | 17.0 | 18 58 24.56 | ......... | — 0.45 | 6.32 | 18 58 30.43 | 30.45 |
| 27 | η Ophiuchi...... | W. | 45.8 | 3.0 | 20.8 | 38.0 | 56.0 | 13.6 | 31.5 | 17 1 38.38 | ......... | + 0.75 | + 6.30 | 17 1 45.43 | 45.40 |
| | α Herculis....... | | 49.0 | 6.5 | 23.8 | 41.5 | 59.5 | 17.0 | 34.4 | 17 7 41.67 | ......... | — 0.70 | 6.30 | 17 7 47.27 | 47.45 |
| | θ Ophiuchi....... | | 42.4 | 1.5 | 20.4 | 39.0 | 58.0 | 16.8 | 35.4 | 17 12 39.07 | ......... | + 1.25 | 6.30 | 17 12 46.62 | 46.74 |
| | α Ophiuchi....... | | 59.6 | 17.0 | 34 0 | 51.5 | 9.5 | 26.5 | 43.5 | 17 27 51.66 | ......... | — 0.61 | 6.30 | 17 27 57.35 | 57.36 |
| | 58 Ophiuchi........ | | 23.0 | 41.0 | 59.4 | 18.0 | 36.5 | 54.8 | 13.0 | 17 35 17.96 | ......... | + 1.06 | 6.30 | 17 35 25.32 | 25.40 |
| | 4 Sagittarii........ | | 33.5 | 52.5 | 11.0 | 29.4 | 48.0 | 7.0 | 25.4 | 17 50 29.54 | ......... | + 1.19 | 6.30 | 17 50 37.03 | 36.97 |
| | Moon, 1st L.... | | 33.0 | 51.4 | 10.0 | 28.2 | 47.0 | 5.4 | 23.6 | 18 4 28.37 | ......... | + 0.92 | 6.30 | 18 4 35.59 | ...... |
| | λ Sagittarii....... | | 37.5 | 56.8 | 15.0 | 34.0 | 53.4 | 12.0 | 30.5 | 18 18 34.17 | ......... | + 1.28 | 6.30 | 18 18 41.75 | 41.64 |
| | ζ Aquilæ.......... | | 32.0 | 49.4 | 7.2 | 25.0 | 42.5 | 59.8 | 17.8 | 18 58 24.96 | ......... | — 0.65 | 6.30 | 18 58 30.61 | 30.43 |
| 28 | $\mu^{1}$ Sagittarii....... | W. | 44.0 | 2.6 | 21.8 | 39.2 | 57.0 | 16.0 | 34.0 | 18 4 39.23 | ......... | + 0.86 | + 6.28 | 18 4 46.37 | 46.40 |
| | λ Sagittarii....... | | ...... | 56.6 | 15.2 | 34.0 | 53.2 | 12.5 | 30.5 | 18 18 43.67 | — 9.45 | + 1.06 | 6.28 | 18 18 41.56 | 41.62 |
| | α Lyræ.......... | | 41.2 | 3.4 | 25.2 | 46.8 | 9.0 | 30.6 | 52.5 | 18 31 46.96 | ......... | — 1.78 | 6.28 | 18 31 51.46 | 51.51 |
| | Moon, 1st L..... | | 34.0 | 52.2 | 11.0 | 29.4 | 48.0 | 6.0 | ...... | 18 56 20.10 | + 9.23 | + 0.76 | 6.28 | 18 56 36.37 | ...... |
| | π Sagittarii........ | | ...... | 6.5 | 24.0 | 42.4 | 0.5 | ...... | ...... | 19 0 33.35 | + 9.14 | + 0.87 | 6.28 | 19 0 49 64 | 49.46 |
| | γ Aquilæ......... | | 9.4 | 26.8 | ...... | ...... | ...... | ...... | ...... | 19 38 18.10 | + 43.26 | — 0.40 | 6.28 | 19 39 7.24 | 7.28 |
| *29 | 4 Sagittarii....... | E. | 33.4 | 52 4 | 11.0 | 29.4 | 48.2 | 6.8 | 25.2 | 17 50 29.51 | ......... | + 0.78 | + 5.87 | 17 50 36.16 | 36.94 |
| | $\mu^{1}$ Sagittarii...... | | 45.0 | 3.0 | 21.4 | 39.4 | 58.0 | 16.5 | 33.8 | 18 4 39.51 | ......... | + 0.69 | 5.87 | 18 4 46.07 | 46.39 |
| | λ Sagittarii....... | | 38.6 | 57.0 | 16.0 | 34.6 | 53.6 | 12.5 | 31.5 | 18 18 34.83 | ......... | + 0.85 | 5.87 | 18 18 41.55 | 41.61 |
| | α Lyræ.......... | | 42.0 | 4.0 | 25.0 | 47.2 | 9.4 | 31.0 | 53.0 | 18 31 47.37 | ......... | — 1.42 | 5.87 | 18 31 51.82 | 51.59 |
| | ο Sagittarii....... | | ...... | 57.5 | 16.0 | ...... | ...... | ...... | 29.0 | 18 55 34.17 | 0.00 | + 0.72 | 5.87 | 18 55 40.76 | 40.62 |
| | ζ Aquilæ......... | | ...... | ...... | ...... | 25.2 | 42.6 | 0.0 | 17.5 | 18 58 51.32 | — 26.32 | — 0.43 | 5.87 | 18 58 30.44 | 30.41 |
| | ρ Sagittarii........ | | 57 2 | 16.0 | 33.8 | 51.2 | ...... | ...... | ...... | 19 12 24.55 | + 26.92 | + 0.58 | 5.87 | 19 12 57.92 | 57.37 |
| | δ Aquilæ.......... | | 57.8 | 15.2 | 31.8 | ...... | 6.5 | 23.2 | 40.0 | 19 17 49.08 | 0.00 | — 0.09 | 5.87 | 19 17 54.86 | 55.44 |
| | γ Aquilæ......... | | 9.5 | 27.0 | 44.0 | 1.8 | 19.2 | 36.0 | 53.2 | 19 39 1.53 | ......... | — 0.32 | 5.87 | 19 39 7.08 | 7.28 |
| | Moon, 1st L..... | | 56.8 | 15.4 | 34.0 | 52.6 | 11.5 | 30.0 | 48.0 | 19 48 52.61 | ......... | + 0.57 | 5.87 | 19 48 59.05 | ...... |
| | $\alpha^{1}$ Capricorni...... | | 21.0 | 38.0 | 56.0 | 13.5 | 31.0 | ...... | 6.0 | 20 9 7.58 | + 5.83 | + 0.41 | 5.87 | 20 9 19.69 | 19.15 |
| | $\alpha^{2}$ Capricorni...... | | 44.5 | 3.2 | 20.2 | 37.6 | ...... | ...... | 29.5 | 20 9 27.00 | + 10.51 | + 0.41 | 5.87 | 20 9 43.79 | 43.02 |
| | β Capricorni...... | | 34.8 | 52.4 | 10.0 | 27.6 | 45.0 | 3.0 | 20.6 | 20 12 27.63 | ......... | + 0.48 | 5.87 | 20 12 33.98 | 34.12 |
| | α Cygni.......... | | 3.3 | 27.0 | 50.0 | 15.0 | 39.2 | 3.5 | 27.5 | 20 36 15.07 | ......... | — 1.76 | 5.87 | 20 36 19.18 | 20.02 |
| 30 | $\mu^{1}$ Sagittarii....... | W. | 45.2 | 3.5 | 21.5 | 39.8 | 58.2 | 16.5 | 34.5 | 18 4 39.89 | ......... | + 0.80 | + 5.48 | 18 4 46.17 | 46.37 |
| | δ Ursæ Minoris.. | | ...... | 57.5 | 46.5 | ...... | ...... | ...... | ...... | 18 14 22.00 | +7 11.69 | — 35.14 | 5.48 | 18 21 5.03 | 4.22 |
| | α Lyræ.......... | | 42.6 | 4.8 | 26.0 | 47.8 | 9 8 | 31.0 | 53.0 | 18 31 47.86 | ......... | — 1.67 | + 5.48 | 18 31 51.67 | 51.47 |

* Instrument reversed.

## *Longitude of Camp Riley*—Continued.

| DATE. | OBJECT. | LAMP. | CHRONOMETER TIMES OF TRANSIT. I. | II. | III. | IV. | V. | VI. | VII. | MEAN OF OBS'D WIRES | CORRECTION FOR— Imperfect transits. | Instrument. | Chronometer. | OBSERVED A.R. | TABULAR A.R. |
|---|---|---|---|---|---|---|---|---|---|---|---|---|---|---|---|
| 1849. | | | s. | s. | s. | s. | s. | s. | s. | h. m. s. | m. s. | m. s. | m. s. | h. m. s. | s. |
| Sept. 1 | $c^1$ Sagittarii ....... | W. | ...... | ...... | ...... | 2.0 | 20.0 | 37.5 | 55.0 | 19 32 28.62 | — 26.69 | + 0.66 | + 3.97 | 19 32 6.56 | 6.57 |
| | γ Aquilæ ......... | | 12.0 | 29.0 | 46.8 | 4.0 | 21.4 | 37.8 | 55.8 | 19 39 3.83 | ......... | — 0.40 | 3.97 | 19 39 7.40 | 7.27 |
| | α Aquilæ ......... | | 31.8 | 49.4 | 6.5 | 23.5 | 40.5 | 57.8 | 15.4 | 19 43 23.50 | ......... | — 0.33 | 3.97 | 19 43 27.14 | 27.39 |
| | $g^1$ Sagittarii....... | | 27.8 | 45.5 | 3.2 | 21.2 | 39.0 | 57.0 | 14.5 | 19 49 21.17 | ......... | + 0.63 | 3.97 | 19 49 25.77 | 25.69 |
| | α Cygni .......... | | 6.0 | 30.8 | 54.4 | 18.0 | 42.2 | 6.0 | 30.4 | 20 36 18.26 | ......... | — 2.19 | 3.97 | 20 36 20.04 | 20.01 |
| 3 | π Sagittarii....... | W. | 51.6 | 10.0 | 28.0 | 46.4 | 4.8 | 23.4 | 41.2 | 19 0 46.48 | ......... | + 1.02 | + 1.98 | 19 0 49.48 | 49.38 |
| | $\rho^1$ Sagittarii....... | | 0.2 | 18.4 | 36.5 | 54.5 | 12.4 | 30.0 | 48.4 | 19 12 54.34 | ......... | + 0.86 | 1.96 | 19 12 57.16 | 57.30 |
| | δ Aquilæ ......... | | 2.5 | 19.4 | 36 0 | 53.4 | 10.5 | 27.2 | 44.4 | 19 17 53.34 | ......... | — 0.13 | 1.95 | 19 17 55.16 | 55.38 |
| | γ Aquilæ ......... | | 13.6 | 31.0 | 48.4 | 6.0 | 23.2 | 40.0 | 57.8 | 19 39 5.72 | ......... | — 0.47 | 1.94 | 19 39 7.19 | 7.22 |
| | α Aquilæ ......... | | ...... | 51.2 | 8.8 | 26.0 | 42.6 | 0.4 | 17.4 | 19 43 34.40 | — 8.62 | — 0.39 | 1.93 | 19 43 27.32 | 27.35 |
| | g Sagittarii ....... | | 30.0 | 47.0 | 5.0 | 23.0 | 40.5 | 58.0 | 16.4 | 19 49 22.84 | ......... | + 0.74 | 1.93 | 19 49 25.51 | 25.67 |
| | $\alpha^1$ Capricorni...... | | 24.0 | 41.5 | 59.0 | 17.0 | 34.0 | 51.6 | 9 2 | 20 9 16.61 | ..... .... | + 0.60 | 1.92 | 20 9 19.13 | 19.11 |
| | $\alpha^2$ Capricorni...... | | 48.0 | 5.2 | 23.0 | 40.0 | 57.5 | 16.0 | 33.0 | 20 9 40.39 | ......... | + 0.60 | 1.92 | 20 9 42.91 | 42.98 |
| | 75 Draconis........ | | ...... | 13.5 | 2.0 | 50.0 | ...... | 25.0 | 13.5 | 20 38 32.80 | — 43.08 | — 16.31 | 1.90 | 20 37 35.31 | 35.50 |
| | 76 Draconis........ | | 31.5 | 32.4 | 35.2 | 36.6 | 39.2 | 40.4 | 43.0 | 20 53 36.90 | ......... | — 18.51 | 1.89 | 20 53 20.28 | 19.78 |
| | β Cephei ......... | | 23.5 | 12.5 | 1.8 | 52.0 | 42.0 | 31.0 | 21.0 | 21 26 51.97 | ......... | — 7.14 | 1.87 | 21 26 46.70 | 46.49 |
| | 7663 . . . . | | 42.2 | 10.4 | 37.5 | 6.0 | 33.0 | 2.4 | 28.8 | 21 54 5.73 | ......... | — 13.24 | 1.85 | 21 53 54.34 | 50.33 |
| | 3495, S. P....... | | ...... | ...... | 46.5 | 0.4 | 17.5 | 31.8 | 45.4 | 22 9 16.32 | —3 16.23 | + 29.96 | 1.84 | 22 6 31.89 | 35.63 |
| | λ Aquarii ...... .. | | 53.0 | 10.4 | 27.4 | 44.6 | 2.0 | 19.2 | 36.2 | 22 44 44.69 | ......... | + 0.38 | 1.81 | 22 44 46.88 | 46.84 |
| | α Piscis Australis | | 18.0 | 37.5 | 57.8 | 17.2 | 36.5 | 56.2 | 16.6 | 22 49 17.12 | ......... | + 1.53 | 1.81 | 22 49 20.46 | 20.56 |
| | α Pegasi .......... | | 23.4 | 41.4 | 58.8 | 16.5 | 34.0 | 51.5 | 9.0 | 22 57 16.37 | ......... | — 0.67 | 1.80 | 22 57 17.50 | 17.47 |
| | φ Aquarii .... .... | | 39.0 | 56.4 | 13.4 | 30.4 | 47.6 | 4.8 | 22.4 | 23 6 30.57 | ......... | + 0.31 | 1.79 | 23 6 32 67 | 32.82 |
| | 96 Aquarii .... .... | | ...... | ...... | 18.0 | 35.0 | 52.0 | 9.0 | 26.4 | 23 11 52.08 | — 17.12 | + 0 27 | 1.78 | 23 11 37.01 | 36.83 |
| | ι Piscium ....... | | 21.6 | 37.8 | 55.2 | 12.5 | 29.8 | 47.0 | 4.2 | 23 32 12.58 | ......... | — 0.22 | 1.76 | 23 32 14.12 | 13.97 |
| | 20 Piscium ........ | | 20.8 | 37.6 | 55.0 | 11.5 | 28.5 | 45.8 | 3.0 | 23 40 11.74 | ......... | + 0.16 | 1.76 | 23 40 13.66 | 13.48 |
| | 27 Piscium ........ | | 6.4 | 23.0 | 40.0 | 57.2 | 14.5 | 31.5 | 48.7 | 23 50 57.33 | ......... | + 0.20 | 1.75 | 23 50 59.28 | 59.34 |
| | 33 Piscium ........ | | 45.5 | 2.6 | 20.0 | 37.0 | 54.0 | 11.2 | 28.2 | 23 57 36.93 | ......... | + 0.30 | 1.75 | 23 57 38.98 | 39.17 |
| | α Andromedæ .... | | ...... | ...... | 18.8 | 38.0 | 57.5 | 17.0 | ..... | 47.82 | — 9.65 | — 1.40 | 1.75 | 38.52 | 38.69 |
| | γ Pegasi.......... | | 36.6 | 54.8 | 12.2 | 29.4 | 47.4 | 4.8 | 22.5 | 5 29.67 | ......... | — 0.67 | 1.75 | 5 30.75 | 30.84 |
| | Moon, 2d L..... | | 11.5 | 28.5 | 46.4 | 4.0 | 21.5 | 38.5 | 56.4 | 12 3.83 | ......... | + 0.06 | 1.74 | 12 5.63 | ...... |
| | 10 Ceti ............ | | ...... | ...... | 37.0 | 54.0 | 11.0 | 28.0 | 45.0 | 19 11.00 | — 17.03 | + 0.04 | 1.74 | 19 55.75 | 55.53 |
| | 13 Ceti ............ | | 38.0 | 55.2 | 12.4 | 29.6 | 46.5 | 3.6 | 21.0 | 27 29.90 | ......... | + 0.20 | 1.73 | 27 31.83 | 31.17 |
| | β Ceti ............ | | 6.5 | 24.5 | 42.0 | ...... | 18.5 | 35.8 | ...... | 35 51.22 | + 9.00 | + 0 89 | 1.73 | 36 2.84 | 2.91 |
| | δ Piscium ........ | | 1.0 | 18.4 | 35.5 | 52.5 | 10.0 | 27.0 | 44.0 | 40 52 64 | ......... | — 0.31 | 1.72 | 40 54.05 | 53.87 |
| | 20 Ceti ............ | | 27.0 | 44.0 | 1.0 | 18.5 | 35.4 | 52.4 | 10.0 | 45 18.33 | ......... | + 0.09 | 1.71 | 45 20.13 | 20.19 |
| | Polaris.......... | | ...... | ...... | 24.0 | 26.4 | 17.0 | 13.0 | 12.6 | 1 18 18.60 | —10 53.80 | —1 40.00 | 1.70 | 1 5 46.50 | 50.78 |
| 4 | 27 Piscium ........ | W. | 7.4 | 24.4 | 41.4 | 59.6 | 16.0 | 32 5 | 49.8 | 23 50 58.59 | ......... | + 0.19 | + 0 55 | 23 50 59.33 | 59.35 |
| | 33 Piscium ........ | | 47.0 | 4.0 | 21.4 | 38.0 | 55.5 | 12.6 | 29.6 | 23 57 38.30 | ......... | + 0.28 | 0.54 | 23 57 39.12 | 39.10 |
| | γ Pegasi.......... | | 38.0 | 55.6 | 13.4 | 31.0 | 48.5 | 6.2 | 23 6 | 5 30.90 | ......... | — 0.62 | 0.54 | 5 30.82 | 30.83 |
| | 10 Ceti ............ | | 4.0 | 21.8 | 38.4 | 55.2 | 12 4 | 29.0 | 46.0 | 18 55.26 | ......... | + 0.04 | 0.52 | 18 55.82 | 55.54 |
| | 13 Ceti ............ | | 39.4 | 56.4 | 13.5 | 30.6 | 47.6 | 5.0 | ...... | 27 22.08 | + 8.55 | + 0.19 | 0.51 | 27 31.33 | 31.18 |
| | β Ceti ............ | | 8.0 | 25.6 | 43.4 | 2.0 | 20.0 | 37.4 | 55.4 | 36 1.70 | ..... .... | + 0.83 | 0.51 | 36 3.04 | 2.93 |
| | δ Piscium ........ | | 2.4 | 19.4 | 36.4 | 53.8 | 11.0 | 28.0 | 45.0 | 40 53.71 | ......... | — 0.29 | 0.50 | 40 53.92 | 53.88 |
| | ε Piscium ........ | | 18.0 | 35.0 | 52.0 | 9.4 | 26.4 | 43.4 | 0.6 | 55 9.26 | ......... | — 0.30 | 0.49 | 55 9.45 | 9.34 |
| | e Piscium ........ | | 46.8 | 4.0 | 20.4 | 38.0 | 55.0 | 12.4 | 29.6 | 1 0 38.17 | ......... | — 0.21 | 0.49 | 1 0 38.45 | 39.05 |
| | Moon, 2d L. ... | | ...... | 24.0 | 41.5 | 59.0 | 16.5 | 34.0 | 51.4 | 1 5 7.73 | — 8.73 | — 0.13 | 0.48 | 1 4 59.35 | ...... |
| | μ Piscium ........ | | 27.8 | 44.8 | 2.0 | 19.0 | 36.0 | 53.4 | 10.6 | 1 22 19.09 | ......... | — 0.23 | 0.46 | 1 22 19.32 | 19.16 |
| | ν Piscium ........ | | 45.8 | 2.8 | 20.0 | 36.8 | 54.0 | 11.2 | 28.0 | 1 33 36.94 | ......... | — 0.21 | 0.45 | 1 33 37.18 | 37.19 |
| | ο Piscium ........ | | ...... | ...... | 11.0 | 28.0 | 45.4 | 2.8 | 20.0 | 1 37 45.44 | — 17.21 | — 0.36 | 0.45 | 1 37 28.32 | 27.94 |
| | φ Phœnicis....... | | ...... | ...... | 41.5 | 5.0 | 28.5 | 52.0 | 15.0 | 1 48 28.40 | — 23.37 | + 2.28 | 0 44 | 1 48 7.75 | 8.00 |
| | α Arietis ......... | | 48.0 | 6.8 | 25.0 | 43.5 | 2.0 | 20.0 | 38.5 | 1 58 43.40 | ......... | — 1.02 | 0.43 | 1 58 42.81 | 43.07 |
| | μ Fornacis....... | | 15.4 | 35.5 | 55.0 | 15.4 | 34.4 | 55.0 | 15.5 | 2 6 15.31 | ......... | + 1.48 | 0.42 | 2 6 17.21 | 17.34 |
| *5 | 10 Ceti ............ | W. | 12.4 | 28.6 | 46.0 | 2.8 | 19.6 | 37.0 | 54.0 | 15 43 2.91 | ......... | + 0.04 | +8 35 52.89 | 18 55.84 | 55.55 |
| | 13 Ceti ........... | | 46.0 | 2.4 | 20.0 | 37.0 | 54.0 | 11.2 | 28.0 | 15 51 36.94 | ......... | + 0.21 | 35 54.30 | 27 31.45 | 31.19 |
| | Polaris.......... | | ...... | 47.6 | 30.8 | 24.0 | ...... | ..... | ...... | 16 20 30.80 | +10 51.96 | —1 44.00 | 36 0.58 | 1 5 39.34 | 51.68 |
| | $\theta^1$ Ceti ............ | | 36.4 | 54.0 | 11.0 | 28.4 | 45.2 | 2.6 | 20.0 | 16 40 28.22 | ......... | + 0.43 | 36 2.32 | 1 16 30.97 | 31.07 |
| | μ Piscium ........ | | 25.0 | 42 0 | 59.0 | 16.0 | 33.4 | 50.4 | 7.6 | 16 46 16.20 | ......... | — 0.26 | 36 3.27 | 1 22 19.21 | 19.17 |
| | ν Piscium ........ | | 41.0 | 58.2 | 15.2 | 32.4 | 49.4 | 6.6 | 23.6 | 16 57 32.34 | ......... | — 0.22 | + 36 ´5.13 | 1 33 37.25 | 37.20 |

* Observed with mean-time chronometer No. 76.

*Longitude of Camp Riley*—Continued.

| DATE. | OBJECT. | LAMP. | CHRONOMETER TIMES OF TRANSIT. I. | II. | III. | IV. | V. | VI. | VII. | MEAN OF OBS'D WIRES | CORRECTION FOR— Imperfect transits. | Instrument. | Chronometer. | OBSERVED A.R. | TABULAR A.R. |
|---|---|---|---|---|---|---|---|---|---|---|---|---|---|---|---|
| 1849. | | | s. | s. | s. | s. | s. | s. | s. | h. m. s. | s. | s. | h. m. s. | h. m. s. | s. |
| Sept. 5 | ο Piscium ........ | W. | 31.2 | 48.2 | 5.8 | 23.0 | 40.0 | 57.2 | 14.0 | 17 1 22.77 | ......... | − 0.40 | + 36 5.75 | 1 37 28.12 | 27.95 |
| | Moon, 2d L..... | | 5.0 | 22.0 | 39.5 | 57.4 | 15.0 | 32.0 | 50.0 | 17 22 57.27 | ......... | − 0.36 | 36 9.35 | 1 59 6.16 | ...... |
| | $\xi^{1}$ Ceti....... .... | | 1.2 | 18.2 | 35.2 | 52.6 | 9.8 | 27.0 | 44.0 | 17 28 52.57 | ......... | − 0.39 | + 8 36 10.27 | 2 5 2.45 | 2.74 |
| | 713 B. A. C..... | | ...... | 2.0 | 23.4 | 44.4 | 5.4 | 27.0 | 48.0 | 17 34 55.03 | − 10.60 | + 2.02 | 36 11.24 | 2 10 57.69 | 58.46 |
| | $\zeta^{2}$ Ceti.......... | | 7.0 | 23.4 | 40.6 | 57.8 | 15.2 | 32 4 | 49.4 | 17 43 57.97 | ......... | − 0.37 | 36 12.75 | 2 20 10.35 | 10.73 |
| | 783 B. A. C..... | | 43.2 | 4.6 | 26.0 | 47.3 | 8 5 | 30.0 | 51.2 | 17 49 47.24 | ......... | + 2.05 | 36 13.72 | 2 26 3.01 | 4.09 |
| | ι Eridani .... .... | | 19.0 | 41.5 | 4.0 | 26.5 | 48.6 | 11.4 | 33.4 | 17 58 26.34 | ......... | + 2.32 | 36 15.14 | 2 34 43.80 | 44.55 |
| *7 | δ Ursæ Minoris.... | W. | 21.0 | 9.0 | 57.8 | ...... | 31.5 | 19.0 | 8.6 | 18 21 44.48 | ......... | ......... | ......... | ......... | ...... |
| | 51 (Hev.) Cephei .. | | 33.5 | ...... | 24.0 | 20.0 | ...... | 12.0 | 6.4 | 18 28 31.18 | ......... | ......... | ......... | ......... | ...... |
| | 6625 B. A. C.... | | 19.0 | 30.5 | 42.4 | 55.0 | 7.0 | 18.8 | 31.0 | 19 14 54.81 | ......... | ......... | ......... | ......... | ...... |
| | λ Ursæ Minoris.... | | 17.6 | 42.5 | 7.0 | 30.4 | 49.2 | 11.2 | 45.2 | 20 16 29.01 | ......... | ......... | ......... | ......... | ...... |
| †17 | $\gamma^{1}$ Sagittarii....... | W. | 10.8 | 30 0 | 49.2 | 7.6 | 26.4 | 44.0 | 3.2 | 18 45 7.33 | ......... | ......... | ......... | ......... | ...... |
| | $\xi^{2}$ Sagittarii....... | | 53.5 | 11.5 | 29.3 | 48.0 | 6.0 | 24.2 | 42.0 | 18 48 47.80 | ......... | ......... | ......... | ......... | ...... |
| | ο Sagittarii ....... | | 47.0 | 5.8 | 24.0 | 42.0 | 0.4 | 18.6 | 37.0 | 18 55 42.11 | ......... | ......... | ......... | ......... | ...... |
| | ζ Aquilæ ......... | | ...... | ...... | ...... | ...... | ...... | 6.0 | 23.5 | 18 57 14.75 | ......... | ......... | ......... | ......... | ...... |
| | δ Aquilæ ......... | | 5.2 | 22.4 | 39.4 | 56.5 | 13.8 | 30.6 | 47.8 | 19 17 56.53 | ......... | ......... | ......... | ......... | ...... |
| | β Cygni .......... | | 41.8 | 1.5 | 21.0 | 40.2 | 59.6 | 18.8 | 38.0 | 19 24 40.13 | ......... | ......... | ......... | ......... | ...... |
| | $n^{2}$ Sagittarii ....... | | 38.4 | 58.0 | 16.8 | 35.4 | 54.0 | 13.4 | 31.8 | 19 27 35.40 | ......... | ......... | ......... | ......... | ...... |
| | α Aquilæ ......... | | ...... | ...... | ...... | 27.5 | 45.0 | 2.0 | 19.8 | 19 43 53.58 | ......... | ......... | ......... | ......... | ...... |
| | c Sagittarii........ | | 29.0 | 48.4 | 8.0 | 27.0 | 46.5 | 6.0 | 24.8 | 19 53 27.10 | ......... | ......... | ......... | ......... | ...... |
| 18 | ζ Aquilæ ......... | W. | 39.6 | 57.2 | 15.0 | 32.4 | 50.0 | 7.8 | 25.0 | 18 58 32.43 | ......... | ......... | ......... | ......... | ...... |
| | $\beta^{1}$ Sagittarii ...... | | 40.0 | 4.0 | 27.6 | 52.4 | ...... | 40.2 | 4.0 | 19 10 8.03 | ......... | ......... | ......... | ......... | ...... |
| | β Cygni .......... | | 44.0 | 3.6 | 23.0 | 41.8 | 1.6 | 20.6 | 39.8 | 19 24 42 06 | ......... | ......... | ......... | ......... | ...... |
| | γ Aquilæ ......... | | 17.8 | 35.0 | 52.4 | 9.6 | 27.0 | 44.0 | 1.4 | 19 39 9.60 | ......... | ......... | ......... | ......... | ...... |
| | 57 Sagittarii ....... | | ...... | 54.0 | 12.2 | 30.4 | 48.4 | 6.5 | 24.5 | 19 43 39.33 | ......... | ......... | ......... | ......... | ...... |
| | $\alpha^{2}$ Capricorni . .... | | 53.2 | 10.0 | 27.4 | 45.0 | 2.6 | 20.0 | 37.2 | 20 9 45.06 | ......... | ......... | ......... | ......... | ...... |
| | π Capricorni...... | | ...... | 8.8 | 27.0 | 45.2 | 3.0 | 21.0 | 38.6 | 20 18 53.93 | ......... | ......... | ......... | ......... | ...... |
| | γ Capricorni...... | | 37.5 | 55.5 | 13.8 | 31.5 | 49.5 | 8.0 | 25.8 | 20 31 31.61 | ......... | ......... | ......... | ......... | ...... |
| | α Cygni .......... | | 9.2 | 33.5 | 57 5 | 22.0 | 45.8 | 9.8 | 33.5 | 20 36 21.62 | ......... | ......... | ......... | ......... | ...... |
| | μ Aquarii.... .... | | 43.5 | 1.0 | 18.0 | 35.0 | 52.4 | 10.0 | 27.0 | 20 44 35.27 | ......... | ......... | ......... | ......... | ...... |
| | η Capricorni...... | | 58.7 | 17.0 | 34.8 | 53.2 | 11.5 | 29.5 | 47.8 | 20 55 53.21 | ......... | ......... | ......... | ......... | ...... |
| | ζ Cygni .......... | | 36.0 | 56.0 | 15.5 | 35.3 | 55.0 | 14.7 | 34.0 | 21 6 35.20 | ......... | ......... | ......... | ......... | ...... |
| ‡20 | δ Ursæ Minoris... | E. | 35.2 | 25.2 | 10.4 | 57.2 | ...... | ...... | ...... | 18 13 47.00 | ......... | ......... | ......... | ......... | ...... |
| | δ Ursæ Minoris... | W. | ...... | ...... | ...... | ...... | 47.2 | 31.2 | 22.4 | 18 30 33.60 | ......... | ......... | ......... | ......... | ...... |
| | $\gamma^{1}$ Sagittarii....... | | 16.5 | 34.5 | 53.0 | 12.0 | 30.0 | 48.8 | 7.4 | 18 45 11.74 | ......... | ......... | ......... | ......... | ...... |
| | ζ Aquilæ .... .... | | 44.0 | 1.6 | 19.0 | 36.4 | 54.4 | 12.0 | 29.0 | 18 58 36.63 | ......... | ......... | ......... | ......... | ...... |
| | $\beta^{1}$ Sagittarii....... | | 43.4 | 7.8 | 31.4 | 56.0 | 20.0 | 44.0 | 7.6 | 19 11 55.74 | ......... | ......... | ......... | ......... | ...... |
| | δ Aquilæ .... .... | | 10.6 | 27.6 | 44.8 | 2.0 | 19.0 | 35.5 | 53.0 | 19 18 1.79 | ......... | ......... | ......... | ......... | ...... |
| | β Cygni .......... | | 48.5 | 8.0 | 27.0 | 46.4 | 5.8 | 24.8 | 44.0 | 19 24 46.36 | ......... | ......... | ......... | ......... | ...... |
| §22 | Moon, 1st L.... | W. | 16.6 | 34.4 | 53.2 | 11.4 | 29.6 | 48.0 | 6.4 | 7 10 11.37 | ......... | ......... | ......... | ......... | ...... |
| 23 | Moon, 1st L.... | W. | 26.0 | 44.4 | 3.4 | 21.4 | 39.8 | 58.4 | 16.8 | 7 57 21.46 | ......... | ......... | ......... | ......... | ...... |
| 24 | λ Sagittarii........ | W. | 34.8 | 53.6 | 12.4 | 31.2 | 50.0 | 8.8 | 29.6 | 8 28 31.20 | ......... | − 0.66 | + 9 50 10.66 | 18 18 41.20 | 41.13 |
| | Moon, 1st L.... | | 59.4 | 18.6 | 36.4 | 54.8 | 13.4 | 32.0 | 50.0 | 8 44 54.94 | ......... | − 0.48 | 9 50 13.35 | 18 35 7.81 | ...... |
| | $\nu^{1}$ Sagittarii........ | | 55.6 | 13.6 | 32.0 | 50.8 | 9.2 | 28.6 | 46.0 | 8 54 50.83 | ......... | − 0.59 | 9 50 14.99 | 18 45 5.23 | 5.25 |
| | ο Sagittarii........ | | 29.2 | 46.6 | ...... | ...... | ...... | ...... | ...... | 9 4 37.90 | + 45.77 | − 0.56 | 9 50 16.72 | 18 55 39.83 | 40.09 |
| | α Aquilæ ......... | | 10.8 | 28.0 | 45.2 | 2.4 | 19.6 | 36.8 | 53.4 | 9 53 2.32 | ......... | + 0.21 | 9 50 24.55 | 19 43 27.08 | 27.05 |
| 27 | ζ Aquilæ ......... | W. | ...... | ...... | 0.4 | 18.0 | 35.2 | 52.4 | 10.2 | 8 56 35.24 | − 17.47 | + 0.35 | 10 2 11.72 | 18 58 29.81 | 29.92 |
| | $\beta^{1}$ Sagittarii....... | | 24.2 | 48.0 | 12.0 | 35.6 | 59.6 | 23.6 | 48.6 | 9 9 35.94 | ......... | − 0.97 | 10 2 13.90 | 19 11 48.78 | 48.88 |
| | δ Aquilæ ......... | | 49.0 | 6.4 | 23.0 | 40.0 | 57.2 | 14.0 | 30.8 | 9 15 40.06 | ......... | + 0.11 | 10 2 14.90 | 19 17 55.08 | 55.01 |
| | β Cygni .......... | | 25.2 | 44.8 | 3.6 | 22.8 | 42.0 | 1.2 | 20.0 | 9 22 22.80 | ......... | + 0.61 | 10 2 6.09 | 19 24 39.42 | 39.78 |
| | $h^{2}$ Sagittarii........ | | 20.8 | 39.6 | 58.4 | 16.8 | 35.8 | 54.4 | 13.2 | 9 25 17.00 | ......... | − 0.42 | 10 2 16.47 | 19 27 33.05 | 33.09 |
| | γ Aquilæ.......... | | 56.4 | 13.8 | 30.8 | 48.0 | 5.0 | 22.0 | 39.6 | 9 36 47.94 | ......... | + 0.25 | 10 2 18.37 | 19 39 6.57 | 6.86 |
| ‡ | β Capricorni...... | E. | 16.8 | 35.2 | 58.2 | 10.4 | 28.0 | 45.6 | 3.2 | 10 10 10.34 | ......... | − 0.34 | 10 2 23.85 | 20 12 33.85 | 33.68 |
| | π Capricorni...... | | ...... | ...... | ...... | 18.4 | 36.0 | 54.2 | 12.0 | 10 16 45.15 | − 27.01 | − 0.41 | 10 2 24.86 | 20 18 42.59 | 42.82 |
| | ν Capricorni...... | | 9.0 | 27.4 | 44.4 | 2.4 | 20.8 | 38.0 | 56.4 | 10 29 2.63 | ......... | − 0.41 | +10 2 26.95 | 20 31 29.17 | 29.46 |

* Resumed sidereal chronometer No. 420. † Instrument adjusted in azimuth. ‡ Instrument reversed. § Mean-time chronometer No. 76.

## *Longitude of Camp Riley*—Continued.

| DATE. | OBJECT. | LAMP. | CHRONOMETER TIMES OF TRANSIT. I. | II. | III. | IV. | V. | VI. | VII. | MEAN OF OBS'D WIRES | CORRECTION FOR— Imperfect transit. | Instrument. | Chronometer. | OBSERVED A.R. | TABULAR A.R. |
|---|---|---|---|---|---|---|---|---|---|---|---|---|---|---|---|
| 1849. | | | s. | s. | s. | s. | s. | s. | s. | h. m. s. | s. | s. | h. m. s. | h. m. s. | s. |
| Sept. 27 | ε Aquarii | E. | 12.4 | 30.0 | 47.2 | 4.4 | 21.6 | 38.8 | 56.0 | 10 37 4.34 | ......... | − 0.24 | +10 2 28.27 | 20 39 32 37 | 32.20 |
| | μ Aquarii | | 12.0 | 29.6 | 46.8 | 4.0 | 21.6 | ...... | 55.4 | 10 41 58.23 | + 6.38 | − 0.60 | 10 2 29.09 | 20 44 33.10 | 32 85 |
| | η Capricorni | | 25.6 | 44.0 | 2.0 | 20.4 | 38.4 | 56.4 | 14.8 | 10 53 20.23 | ......... | − 0.40 | 10 2 30.94 | 20 55 50.72 | 50.81 |
| | ν Aquarii | | 0.8 | 18.0 | 35.6 | 52.8 | 10.4 | 27.6 | 44.8 | 10 58 52.86 | ......... | − 0.28 | 10 2 31.85 | 21 1 24.43 | 24.33 |
| | ζ Cygni | | 1.4 | 20.8 | 40.4 | 0.0 | 19.8 | 39.2 | 58.4 | 11 4 0.00 | ......... | + 0.53 | 10 2 32.69 | 21 6 33.22 | 33.25 |
| * | Moon, 1st L | | 40.4 | 58.4 | 16.4 | 34.4 | 52.4 | 10.2 | 28.0 | 11 8 34.31 | ......... | − 0.21 | 10 2 33.44 | 21 11 7.54 | ...... |
| 28 | ζ Cygni | W. | 3.2 | 22.4 | 42.4 | 2.4 | 21.6 | 40.8 | 0.8 | 11 0 1.94 | ......... | + 0.45 | +10 6 30.85 | 21 6 33.24 | 33.23 |
| | ι Capricorni | | 27.4 | 45.0 | 2.8 | 20.5 | 38.4 | 56.0 | 14.0 | 11 7 20.59 | ......... | − 0.25 | 10 6 32.05 | 21 13 52.39 | 52.38 |
| | β Aquarii | | 14.0 | 31.6 | 48.0 | 5.4 | 22.4 | 39.6 | ...... | 11 16 56.83 | + 8.55 | − 0.09 | 10 6 33.66 | 21 23 38.95 | 38.96 |
| | Moon, 1st L | | 34.0 | 52.8 | 10.8 | 28.0 | 46.8 | 3.6 | 22.4 | 11 56 28.34 | ......... | − 0.16 | 10 6 39.89 | 22 3 8.07 | ...... |
| 29 | ζ Cygni | W. | ...... | 24.8 | 45.0 | 3.8 | 23.6 | 43.2 | 2.4 | 10 56 13.80 | − 9.76 | + 0.64 | +10 10 28.54 | 21 6 33.32 | 33.21 |
| | β Aquarii | | 16.0 | 33.0 | 50.0 | ...... | 24.4 | 41.2 | 58.0 | 11 13 7.10 | 0.00 | − 0.12 | 10 10 31.35 | 21 23 38.33 | 38.95 |
| | γ Capricorni | | 20.0 | 37.8 | 55.4 | 13.6 | 31.2 | 49.2 | 6.8 | 11 21 13.43 | ......... | − 0.35 | 10 10 32.68 | 21 31 45.76 | 45.71 |
| | δ Capricorni | | 18.0 | 36 0 | 53.6 | 11.6 | 29.2 | 46.8 | 4.8 | 11 28 11.43 | ......... | − 0.34 | 10 10 33.83 | 21 38 44.92 | 44.65 |
| | ι Aquarii | | 49.8 | 7.6 | 24.8 | 42.4 | 0.0 | 17.8 | 35.2 | 11 47 42.51 | ......... | − 0.29 | 10 10 37.05 | 21 58 19.27 | 19.27 |
| | θ Aquarii | | 24.2 | 41.6 | 58.8 | 16.0 | 33.2 | 50.0 | 7.6 | 11 58 15.91 | ......... | − 0.17 | 10 10 38.78 | 22 8 54.52 | 54.42 |
| | γ Aquarii | | 23.4 | 40.4 | 57.6 | 14.8 | 31.6 | 48.4 | 5.6 | 12 3 14.54 | ......... | − 0.04 | 10 10 39.60 | 22 13 54.10 | 54.07 |
| | σ Aquarii | | 8.8 | 26.0 | 43.6 | 1.0 | 18.0 | 35.6 | 53.2 | 12 12 0.90 | ......... | − 0 23 | 10 10 41.05 | 22 22 41.72 | 41.78 |
| | ζ Pegasi | | 24.0 | 41.6 | 58.8 | 16.0 | 33.2 | 50.4 | 7.6 | 12 23 15.80 | ......... | + 0.20 | 10 10 42.90 | 22 33 58.90 | 58.77 |
| | λ Aquarii | | 10.8 | 28.0 | 45.2 | 2.4 | 19.6 | 36.8 | 54.0 | 12 34 2.40 | ......... | − 0.17 | 10 10 44.68 | 22 44 46.91 | 46.84 |
| | α Piscis Australis | | 36.8 | 56.4 | 16.0 | 35.6 | 55.6 | 15.2 | 35.0 | 12 38 35.80 | ......... | − 0.66 | 10 10 45.43 | 22 49 20.57 | 20.56 |
| | Moon, 1st L | | 38.0 | 55.8 | 13.6 | 31.0 | 48.8 | 6.4 | 23.8 | 12 44 31.06 | ......... | − 0.15 | 10 10 46.13 | 22 55 17.04 | ...... |
| | $\psi^2$ Aquarii | | 28.4 | 45.6 | 3.0 | 20.4 | 37.6 | 54.8 | 12.0 | 13 0 20.26 | ......... | − 0.21 | 10 10 49.01 | 23 11 9.06 | 9.04 |
| †30 | λ Aquarii | E. | 13.2 | 30.8 | 47.8 | 5.0 | 22.4 | 39.6 | 56.8 | 12 30 5.09 | ......... | − 0.18 | +10 14 42.18 | 22 44 47.09 | 46.85 |
| | α Piscis Australis | | 38.8 | 58.4 | 18.4 | 38.0 | 58.0 | 17.6 | 37.4 | 12 34 38.09 | ......... | − 0.71 | 10 14 42.93 | 22 49 20.31 | 20.56 |
| | α Pegasi | | 40.0 | 58.0 | 15.6 | 33.0 | 50.4 | 8.0 | 25.6 | 12 42 32.94 | ......... | + 0.31 | 10 14 44.24 | 22 57 17.49 | 17.49 |
| | Moon, 1st L | | 7.2 | 24.8 | 42.0 | 59.4 | 17.0 | 34.0 | 51.6 | 13 32 59.43 | ......... | − 0.07 | 10 14 52.24 | 23 47 51.60 | ...... |
| Oct. 4 | α Arietis | E. | 42.4 | 0.8 | 18.8 | 37.2 | 55.6 | 14.0 | 32.4 | 15 27 37.31 | ......... | ......... | ......... | ......... | ...... |
| | $\xi^1$ Ceti | | 4.8 | 22.0 | 38.8 | 56.0 | 13.2 | 30.2 | 47.4 | 15 33 56.06 | ......... | ......... | ......... | ......... | ...... |
| | $\xi^2$ Ceti | | 10.8 | 27.6 | 44.4 | 1.6 | 18.4 | 36.0 | 52.8 | 15 49 1.66 | ......... | ......... | ......... | ......... | ...... |
| | 783 | | 50.0 | ...... | 32.4 | ...... | ...... | ...... | ...... | 15 54 11.20 | ......... | ......... | ......... | ......... | ...... |
| | γ Ceti | | ...... | ...... | ...... | 48.8 | 6.0 | 23.6 | 40.4 | 15 57 14.70 | ......... | ......... | ......... | ......... | ...... |
| | 832 | | 25.2 | 48.0 | 10.4 | 32.4 | 54.8 | 17.6 | 39.6 | 16 3 32.57 | ......... | ......... | ......... | ......... | ...... |
| | π Arietis | | 49.6 | 6.8 | 24.0 | 41.8 | 59.6 | 17.8 | 35.2 | 16 9 42.11 | ......... | ......... | ......... | ......... | ...... |
| ‡ | α Ceti | | ...... | 38.0 | ...... | ...... | ...... | ...... | ...... | 38.00 | ......... | ......... | ......... | ......... | ...... |
| 5 | γ Aquilæ | E. | ...... | 30.8 | 48.0 | 5.2 | 22.4 | 39.6 | 56.4 | 9 5 13.73 | ......... | ......... | ......... | ......... | ...... |
| | α Aquilæ | | 32.8 | 50.0 | 7.6 | 24.8 | 42.0 | ...... | 16.0 | 9 9 18.87 | ......... | ......... | ......... | ......... | ...... |
| | $\zeta^1$ Sagittarii | | 29.2 | 46.8 | 4.4 | 21.6 | 39.6 | 57.2 | 14.8 | 9 15 21.94 | ......... | ......... | ......... | ......... | ...... |
| §8 | α Cygni | | 2.8 | 26.8 | 50.4 | 14.4 | 39.2 | 2.4 | 26.0 | 9 50 14.57 | ......... | ......... | ......... | ......... | ...... |
| 23 | γ Aquilæ | E. | 50.0 | 7.6 | 24.4 | 41.6 | 59.2 | 16.4 | 33.6 | 7 53 41.83 | ......... | − 0.17 | +11 45 24.82 | 19 39 6.48 | 6.38 |
| | α Aquilæ | | 9.6 | 26.4 | 44.0 | 0.8 | 18.0 | 35.6 | 52.6 | 7 58 1.00 | ......... | − 0.14 | 11 45 25.53 | 19 43 26.39 | 26.53 |
| | $\zeta^1$ Sagittarii | | ...... | 22.8 | 40.4 | 58.0 | 16.0 | 33.4 | 50.8 | 8 4 6.90 | − 8.84 | + 0.27 | 11 45 26.51 | 19 49 24.86 | 24.88 |
| | Moon, 1st L | | 54.0 | 12.4 | 30.8 | 49.0 | 7.6 | 25.6 | 44.6 | 8 11 49.14 | ......... | + 0.30 | 11 45 27.80 | 19 57 17.24 | ...... |
| | $\alpha^2$ Capricorni | | 20.0 | 37.6 | 54.4 | 12.0 | 29.6 | 47.0 | 4.4 | 8 24 12.14 | ......... | + 0 22 | 11 45 29.67 | 20 9 42.03 | 42.23 |
| | β Capricorni | | 9.8 | 27.4 | 45.2 | 2.6 | 20.4 | 38.0 | 55.6 | 8 27 2 71 | ......... | + 0.25 | 11 45 30.31 | 20 12 33.27 | 33.34 |
| | π Capricorni | | 16.8 | 34.8 | 52.8 | 10.8 | 28.8 | 46.8 | 4.4 | 8 33 10.74 | ......... | + 0.32 | 11 45 31.31 | 20 18 42.37 | 42.38 |
| | ν Capricorni | | 1.6 | 19.6 | 37.2 | 55.0 | 13.2 | 31.2 | 49.2 | 8 45 55.28 | ......... | + 0.32 | 11 45 33.40 | 20 31 29.00 | 29.03 |
| †25 | μ Aquarii | W. | 7.2 | 24.8 | 42.4 | 59 2 | 16.6 | 33.6 | 50.8 | 8 50 59.23 | ......... | + 0.24 | +11 53 33.20 | 20 44 32.67 | 32.42 |
| | η Capricorni | | 20.4 | 38.8 | 57.0 | 14.8 | 33.2 | 51.2 | 9.2 | 9 2 14.94 | ......... | + 0.53 | 11 53 35.04 | 20 55 50.51 | 50.36 |
| | ν Aquarii | | 56.0 | 13.2 | 30.0 | 48.0 | 5.4 | 22.4 | 39.6 | 9 7 47.80 | ......... | + 0.30 | 11 53 35.95 | 21 1 23.05 | 23.91 |
| | 29 Capricorni | | 55.0 | 12.8 | 30.4 | 48.0 | 5.8 | 23.2 | 40.8 | 9 13 48.00 | ......... | + 0.31 | 11 53 36.92 | 21 7 25.23 | 25.23 |
| | ι Capricorni | | 20.0 | 38.0 | 55.8 | 13.8 | 31.6 | 49.4 | 7.2 | 9 20 13.69 | ......... | + 0.45 | 11 53 37.96 | 21 13 52.10 | 52.06 |
| | β Aquarii | | 7.3 | 24.4 | 41.2 | 58.8 | 16.0 | 32.8 | ..... | 9 29 50.08 | + 8.55 | + 0 16 | 11 53 39.54 | 21 23 38.33 | 38.58 |
| | γ Capricorni | | 10.4 | 28 0 | 46.0 | 4.0 | 22.0 | 39.6 | 57 2 | 9 38 3.90 | ......... | + 0.45 | 11 53 40.85 | 21 31 45.20 | 45.35 |
| | Moon, 1st L | | 11.0 | 29.2 | 47.2 | 5.2 | 22.8 | 40.4 | 58.8 | 9 46 4.95 | ......... | + 0.33 | 11 53 42.23 | 21 39 47.51 | ...... |
| | ι Aquarii | | 40.0 | 58.0 | 15.6 | 33.2 | 50.8 | 8.4 | 26.0 | 10 4 33.14 | ......... | + 0.37 | +11 53 45.19 | 21 58 18.70 | 18.95 |

* Interrupted by dense clouds. † Instrument reversed. ‡ Interrupted by clouds. § Sky obscured by dense clouds.

*Longitude of Camp Riley*—Continued.

| DATE. | OBJECT. | LAMP. | CHRONOMETER TIMES OF TRANSIT. I. | II. | III. | IV. | V. | VI. | VII. | MEAN OF OBS'D WIRES | CORRECTION FOR— Imperfect transits. | Instrument. | Chronometer. | OBSERVED A.R. | TABULAR A.R. |
|---|---|---|---|---|---|---|---|---|---|---|---|---|---|---|---|
| 1849. | | | *s.* | *s.* | *s.* | *s.* | *s.* | *s.* | *s.* | *h. m. s.* | *s.* | *s.* | *h. m. s.* | *h. m. s.* | *s.* |
| Oct. 28 | μ Aquarii ........ | W. | 11.2 | 28.4 | 46.0 | 2.8 | 20.4 | 37.2 | 54.4 | 8 39 2.91 | .......... | + 0.24 | +12 5 29.70 | 20 44 32.85 | 32.37 |
| | η Capricorni...... | | 24.4 | 42.8 | 0.8 | 18.8 | 37.2 | 54.8 | 13.2 | 8 50 18.86 | .......... | + 0.53 | 12 5 31.55 | 20 55 50.94 | 50.31 |
| | ξ Cygni .......... | | 1.6 | 21.2 | 40.8 | 0.4 | 20.0 | 39.6 | 59.2 | 9 1 0.40 | .......... | — 0.81 | 12 5 33.28 | 21 6 32.87 | 32.67 |
| | 20 Piscium ........ | | 24.4 | 41.6 | 58.4 | 15.6 | 32.4 | 49.2 | 6.4 | 11 34 15.43 | .......... | + 0.09 | 12 5 58.24 | 23 40 13.76 | 13.51 |
| | 27 Piscium ........ | | 8.4 | 25.2 | 42.2 | 59.2 | 16.4 | 33.6 | 50.4 | 11 44 59.34 | .......... | + 0.11 | 12 5 59.98 | 23 50 59.43 | 59.43 |
| | α Andromedæ .... | | ...... | ...... | 18.8 | 38.4 | 57.6 | 16.8 | 36.0 | 11 54 57.52 | — 19.28 | — 0 77 | 12 6 1.54 | 39.01 | 38.80 |
| | γ Pegasi.......... | | 36.4 | 53.6 | 11.6 | 29.2 | 46.4 | 4.0 | 21.6 | 11 59 28.97 | .......... | — 0.37 | 12 6 2.33 | 5 30.93 | 30.98 |
| | Moon, 1st L.... | | 26.8 | 44.0 | 2.0 | 19.2 | 36.8 | 54.4 | 11.6 | 12 9 19.26 | .......... | + 0.03 | 12 6 3.95 | 15 23.24 | ...... |
| | 10 Ceti ............ | | ...... | 17.2 | 34.4 | 51.2 | 8.0 | 25.2 | 42.0 | 12 12 51.14 | .......... | + 0.02 | 12 6 4.52 | 18 55.68 | 55.76 |
| | 13 Ceti ............ | | 34.0 | 51.2 | 8.0 | 25.2 | 42.8 | 59.6 | 16.4 | 12 21 25.31 | .......... | + 0.11 | 12 6 5.91 | 27 31.33 | 31.45 |
| | δ Piscium ........ | | 54.4 | 11.6 | 28.8 | 46.0 | 3.2 | 20.4 | 37.6 | 12 34 46.00 | .......... | — 0.17 | 12 6 8.09 | 40 53.92 | 54.22 |
| | 20 Ceti ............ | | 20 2 | 37.2 | 54.4 | 11.6 | 28.4 | 45.2 | 2.4 | 12 39 11.34 | .......... | + 0.05 | 12 6 8.79 | 45 20.18 | 20.56 |
| 29 | δ Piscium ........ | W. | 57.2 | 14.2 | 31.6 | 48.8 | 5.6 | 23.2 | 39.8 | 12 30 48.63 | .......... | — 0.17 | +12 10 5.60 | 40 54.06 | 54.21 |
| * | 20 Ceti ............ | E. | 22.8 | 39 6 | 57.0 | 14 4 | 31.2 | 48.0 | 4.8 | 12 35 14.00 | .......... | + .05 | 12 10 6.33 | 45 20.38 | 20.56 |
| | ε Piscium ........ | | 10.6 | 27.6 | 45.0 | 2.0 | 19.2 | 36.0 | 53 2 | 12 45 2.00 | .......... | + 0.18 | 12 10 7.94 | 55 10.12 | 9.76 |
| | Moon, 1st L.... | | 35.0 | 52.4 | 9 2 | 26.8 | 44.4 | 2.4 | 19.2 | 12 59 27.06 | .......... | — 0 09 | 12 10 10.31 | 1 9 37.28 | ...... |
| | θ¹ Ceti ..... ...... | | 28.0 | 45.4 | 2.4 | 19.6 | 36.8 | 54.4 | 11.6 | 13 6 19.74 | .......... | + 0.23 | 12 10 11.44 | 1 16 31.41 | 31.57 |
| | μ Piscium ........ | | 16.4 | 33.6 | 50.4 | 7.6 | 24.8 | 41.8 | 58.8 | 13 12 7.63 | .. ....... | — 0.13 | 12 10 12.39 | 1 22 19.89 | 19.71 |
| | ν Piscium ....... | | 32.4 | 49.8 | 6.4 | 23.6 | 40.8 | 58.0 | 14.8 | 13 23 23.69 | .......... | — 0.12 | 12 10 14.24 | 1 33 37.81 | 37.80 |
| | ο Piscium ........ | | 22.4 | 40.0 | 57.2 | 14.4 | 31.6 | 48.8 | 6.0 | 13 27 14.34 | .......... | — 0.21 | 12 10 14.87 | 1 37 29.00 | 28.77 |
| Nov. 1 | ξ Tauri........... | W. | 45.2 | 1.6 | 19.0 | 36.0 | 53.6 | 11.2 | 28.4 | 14 56 36.43 | .......... | — 0.23 | +12 22 26.82 | 3 19 3.02 | 2.80 |
| | e Tauri........... | | 41.2 | 58.8 | 15.6 | 33.2 | 50.4 | 8.0 | 25.2 | 15 17 33.20 | .......... | — 0.27 | 12 22 30.26 | 3 40 3.19 | 3.12 |
| | λ Tauri...... .... | | 58.0 | 16.0 | 33.2 | 50.4 | 8.0 | 25.2 | 42.4 | 15 29 50.46 | .......... | — 0.31 | 12 22 32.28 | 3 52 22.43 | 22.59 |
| | Moon, 2d L..... | | 28.8 | 47.2 | 5.2 | 23.6 | 41.6 | 59.6 | 17.8 | 15 46 23.40 | .......... | — 0.41 | 12 22 35.00 | 4 8 57.99 | ...... |
| | ε Tauri........... | | 21.2 | 39.4 | 57.6 | 15.6 | 33.4 | 51.2 | 9.6 | 15 57 15.43 | .......... | — 0.49 | 12 22 36.78 | 4 19 51.72 | 51.82 |
| | α Tauri........... | | 48.4 | 6.0 | 23.8 | 41.6 | 59.2 | 17.0 | 34.4 | 16 4 41.49 | .......... | — 0.42 | 12 22 38.01 | 4 27 19.08 | 19.09 |
| 2 | ε Tauri........... | W. | 22.8 | 40.8 | 59.2 | 17.2 | 34.8 | 52.8 | 10.8 | 15 53 16.92 | .......... | — 0.49 | +12 26 35.87 | 4 19 52.30 | 51.83 |
| | α Tauri........... | | 50.0 | 7.8 | 24.8 | 42.8 | 0.2 | 18.0 | 35.8 | 16 0 42.77 | .......... | — 0.42 | 12 26 37.09 | 4 27 19.44 | 19.11 |
| | ο¹ Orionis......... | | 30.8 | 48.4 | 6.0 | 23.6 | 41.2 | 58.4 | 16.0 | 16 17 23.50 | .......... | — 0.36 | 12 26 39.83 | 4 44 2.97 | 3.02 |
| | ι Tauri........... | | 32.0 | 50.6 | 8.8 | 26.8 | 45.2 | 3.2 | 21.6 | 16 27 26.89 | .......... | — 0.56 | 12 26 41.48 | 4 54 7.81 | 7.92 |
| | 11 Orionis ......... | | ...... | ...... | 0.4 | 18.4 | 36.2 | 53.4 | 11.0 | 16 29 35.88 | — 17.59 | — 0.39 | 42 26 41.79 | 4 55 59.69 | 60.03 |
| | β Orionis......... | | 44.0 | 1.4 | 18.4 | 35.6 | 52.8 | 10.0 | 27.2 | 16 40 35.63 | .......... | + 0.21 | 12 26 43.65 | 5 7 19.49 | 19.81 |
| † | Moon, 2d L..... | | 58.4 | 16.8 | 35.2 | 53.6 | 12.0 | 30.4 | 48.8 | 16 45 53.60 | .......... | — 0.47 | 12 26 44.54 | 5 12 37.67 | ...... |
| *5 | 68 Geminorum..... | E. | 9.2 | 27.2 | 44.8 | 2.2 | 20.0 | 38.0 | 55.2 | 18 46 2.37 | .......... | 0.00 | +12 39 5.05 | 7 25 1.94 | 1.99 |
| | α Canis Minoris.. | | 34.0 | 51.6 | 8.4 | 25.6 | 42.8 | 58.8 | 16.8 | 18 52 25.43 | .......... | 0.00 | 12 39 0.06 | 7 31 26.06 | 26.09 |
| | β Geminorum .... | | ...... | 26.8 | 46.0 | 5.2 | 24.6 | 44.0 | 3.4 | 18 57 15.00 | — 9.67 | 0.00 | 12 39 1.39 | 7 36 6.72 | 6.90 |
| | 15 Argus .......... | | 7.8 | 26.4 | 45.2 | 3.8 | 22.4 | 40.4 | 59.4 | 19 22 3.63 | .......... | 0.00 | 12 39 5.49 | 8 1 9.12 | 8.99 |
| | d¹ Cancri .......... | | 43.4 | 1.6 | 19.6 | 37.4 | 55.6 | 13.4 | 31.2 | 19 35 37.46 | .......... | 0.00 | 12 39 7.72 | 8 14 45.18 | 45.09 |
| | Moon, 2d L..... | | 50.8 | 9.2 | 27.2 | 45.2 | 3.6 | 22.0 | 40.2 | 19 43 45.46 | .......... | 0.00 | 12 39 9.06 | 8 22 54.52 | ...... |
| | δ Cancri .......... | | 2.8 | 21.2 | 39.2 | 56.8 | 14.8 | 33.2 | 50.8 | 19 56 56.97 | .......... | 0.00 | 12 39 11.22 | 8 36 8.19 | 8.13 |
| | ε Hydræ.......... | | 45.8 | 2.8 | 19.8 | 37.2 | 54.4 | 11.6 | 28.4 | 19 59 37.14 | .......... | 0.00 | 12 39 11.66 | 8 38 48.80 | 48.73 |
| | α Cancri.......... | | 9.6 | 27.2 | 44.4 | 2.0 | 19.2 | 36.8 | 54.0 | 20 11 1.90 | .......... | 0.00 | +12 39 13.54 | 8 50 15.44 | 15.52 |
| 6 | δ Cancri.......... | E. | 2.4 | 20.4 | 38.4 | 56.4 | 14.0 | 32.4 | 50.4 | .......... | .......... | .......... | .......... | .......... | ...... |
| | α Cancri.......... | | 9.2 | 27.4 | 44.0 | 1.2 | 18.8 | 36.4 | 53.2 | .......... | .......... | .......... | .......... | .......... | ...... |
| | α Hydræ.......... | | 1.2 | 18.8 | 35.6 | 52.8 | 10.0 | 27.2 | 44.4 | .......... | .......... | .......... | .......... | .......... | ...... |
| 29 | 20 Piscium ....... | E. | 3.2 | 20.0 | 36.8 | 54.0 | 10.8 | 28.0 | 45.2 | .......... | .......... | .......... | .......... | .......... | ...... |
| | α Andromedæ .... | | 18.0 | 37.6 | 56.8 | 16.0 | 35.2 | 55.2 | 13.6 | .......... | .......... | .......... | .......... | .......... | ...... |
| | γ Pegasi.......... | | 14.8 | 32.8 | 50.0 | 7.2 | 25.2 | 42.8 | 0.4 | .......... | .......... | .......... | .......... | .......... | ...... |
| | 10 Ceti ............ | | 38.8 | 56.0 | 13.2 | 30.0 | 47.2 | 4.0 | 20.8 | .......... | .......... | .......... | .......... | .......... | ...... |
| | 13 Ceti ............ | | 12.8 | 30.0 | 47.2 | 4.0 | 21.2 | 38.4 | 55.2 | .......... | .......... | .......... | .......... | .......... | ...... |
| | β Ceti ............ | | 40.0 | 57.6 | 16.0 | 33.6 | 51.6 | 9.6 | 27.6 | .......... | .......... | .......... | .......... | .......... | ...... |

* Instrument reversed.

† Wire VI indistinct.

From the "Greenwich Observations" for 1849 we obtain the following observed corrections of the AR. of the moon's bright limb:

| | | | s. | | | | s. |
|---|---|---|---|---|---|---|---|
| July | 27 | 1st L. | —0.51 | Sept. | 22 | 1st L. | —0.68 |
| | 28 | | .55 | | 25 | | .15 |
| | 29 | | .48 | | 26 | | .22 |
| | 30 | | .48 | | 30 | | .56 |
| | 31 | | .26 | Oct. | 2 | 2d L. | .67 |
| Aug. | 1 | | .44 | | 4 | | .65 |
| | 3 | | .18 | | 5 | | .47 |
| | 3 | 2d L. | .73 | | 8 | | .32 |
| | 4 | | .38 | | 9 | | .67 |
| | 6 | | .38 | Oct. | 28 | 1st L. | .60 |
| | 8 | | .54 | | 29 | | .67 |
| | 11 | | .62 | | 31 | | .73 |
| Aug. | 23 | 1st L. | —1.22 | Nov. | 1 | 2d L. | .50 |
| | 24 | | .68 | | 4 | | .60 |
| | 29 | | .46 | | 5 | | .74 |
| | 31 | | .47 | | | | |
| Sept. | 5 | 2d L. | .22 | | | | |
| | 8 | | .41 | | | | |
| | 9 | | .51 | | | | |

*Longitude of Camp Riley by corresponding observations.*

| | h. m. s. | | h. m. s. | | h. m. s. |
|---|---|---|---|---|---|
| July 27 | 7 48 37.98 | Aug. 3 | 7 48 51.51 | Oct. 28 | 7 48 24.48 |
| 28 | 23.51 | 29 | 39.97 | 29 | 15.13 |
| 29 | 7.45 | Sept. 5 | 6.99 | Nov. 1 | 13.41 |
| 30 | 37.60 | 30 | 18.27 | 5 | 25.37 |
| 31 | 39.29 | | | | |

| | | h. m. s. |
|---|---|---|
| Mean | | 7 48 24.70 |
| Probable error of result | = | ± 2.32 |
| Probable error of single observation | = | ± 8.05 |

The following have been adopted as corrections for the respective lunations:

| | s. | | s. |
|---|---|---|---|
| July 27 to August | — 0.47 | September 22 to October | — 0.48 |
| August 23 to September | — 0.54 | October 28 to November | — 0.63 |

Applying these corrections to the computed AR. of the moon's limb for each date of observation, and comparing with the observed AR., we obtain:

| | h. m. s. | | h. m. s. | | h. m. s. |
|---|---|---|---|---|---|
| July 27 | 7 48 36.81 | Aug. 28 | 7 48 21.77 | Sept. 30 | 7 48 17.73 |
| 28 | 20.90 | 29 | 41.89 | Oct. 23 | 34.80 |
| 29 | 6.88 | Sept. 3 | 9.77 | 25 | 22.50 |
| 30 | 37.32 | 4 | 18.54 | 28 | 25.02 |
| 31 | 45.08 | 5 | 15.12 | 29 | 14.09 |
| Aug. 2 | 29.28 | 24 | 41.90 | Nov. 1 | 16.17 |
| 3 | 39.60 | 27 | 34.61 | 2 | 18.00 |
| 26 | 23.07 | 28 | 22.98 | 5 | 22.75 |
| 27 | 36.91 | 29 | 21.85 | | |

| | h. m. s. |
|---|---|
| Mean | 7 48 25.98 |
| Longitude of Camp Riley, computed in the field from the predicted place of the moon in the Greenwich ephemeris for 1849 | 7 48 13.1 |
| Difference | 12.88 |

| | s. |
|---|---|
| Probable error of a single observation | ± 7.21 |
| Probable error of result | ± 1.44 |

## II.—*Longitude of junction of the Gila and Colorado: By Lieut. A. W. Whipple.*

| DATE. | OBJECT. | LAMP. | CHRONOMETER TIMES OF TRANSIT. I. | II. | III. | IV. | V. | VI. | VII. | MEAN OF OBS'D WIRES | CORRECTIONS FOR— Imperfect transits. | Instrument. | Chronometer. | OBSERVED A.R. | TABULAR A.R. |
|---|---|---|---|---|---|---|---|---|---|---|---|---|---|---|---|
| 1849. | | | s. | s. | s. | s. | s. | s. | s. | h. m. s. | s. | s. | m. s. | h. m. s. | s. |
| Oct. 3 | α Arietis ......... | E. | 5.5 | 24.5 | 44.5 | 3.0 | 22.0 | 40.0 | 59.5 | 1 58 2.71 | .......... | − 0.56 | + 0 41.83 | 1 58 43.98 | 43.62 |
| | 64 Ceti............ | | 52.0 | 9.5 | 27.0 | 45.0 | 3.0 | 20.5 | 38.0 | 2 2 45.00 | .......... | 0.15 | 41.83 | 2 3 26.68 | 26.82 |
| | Moon, 2d L.... | | 52.0 | 10.5 | ...... | ...... | 5.0 | 23.5 | 42.0 | 2 33 50.60 | − 3.64 | 0.23 | 41.81 | 2 34 28.54 | ...... |
| | α Ceti............ | | 52.0 | 10.0 | 27.5 | 44.5 | 2.0 | 20.0 | 37.5 | 2 53 44.79 | .......... | 0.08 | 41.80 | 2 54 26.51 | 26.33 |
| | δ Arietis ......... | | 25.5 | 44.5 | 3.5 | 21.5 | 40.5 | 59.5 | 17.5 | 3 2 21.79 | .......... | 0.46 | 41.79 | 3 3 3.12 | 3.33 |
| | α Persei.......... | | 37.0 | 4.0 | 31.0 | 57.5 | 24.5 | 52.0 | 19.0 | 3 12 57.86 | .......... | 1.56 | 41.78 | 3 13 38.09 | 38.40 |
| | ξ Tauri ..... .... | | 27.5 | 45.0 | 3.5 | 21.0 | 38.5 | 56.5 | 14.5 | 3 18 20.93 | .......... | 0.22 | 41.76 | 3 19 2.47 | 2.32 |
| 4 | μ Ceti............ | | 18.0 | 35.5 | 53.5 | 11.5 | 29.5 | 46.5 | 5.0 | 2 36 11.36 | .......... | − 0.17 | + 0 39.61 | 2 36 50.30 | 50.11 |
| | α Ceti............ | | 54.5 | 13.5 | 29.5 | 46.5 | 5.0 | 22.5 | 40.0 | 2 53 47.36 | .......... | 0.06 | 39.09 | 2 54 26 39 | 26.35 |
| | δ Arietis ......... | | 29.0 | 47 5 | 6.0 | 25.0 | 43.5 | 2.0 | 20.5 | 3 2 24.79 | .......... | 0.36 | 39.08 | 3 3 3.51 | 3.34 |
| | α Persei.......... | | ...... | 7.0 | 34.0 | 0.0 | 27.0 | 54.5 | 22 0 | 3 13 14.08 | − 13.50 | 1.19 | 39.07 | 3 13 38.46 | 38.43 |
| | ξ Tauri .......... | | 30.0 | 48.0 | 5.5 | 23.0 | 41.0 | 59.0 | 17.0 | 3 18 23 34 | .......... | 0.17 | 39.06 | 3 19 2.23 | 2.34 |
| | s Tauri........... | | 40.0 | 58.0 | 16.5 | 34.0 | 51.5 | 9.5 | 28.0 | 3 21 33.93 | .......... | 0.20 | 39.05 | 3 22 12.78 | 12.66 |
| | Moon, 2d L.... | | 30.0 | 49.0 | 7.5 | 26.0 | 44.5 | 3.0 | 21.0 | 3 32 25.86 | .......... | 0.25 | 39.04 | 3 33 4.65 | ...... |
| | e Tauri .......... | | ...... | ...... | ...... | ..... | 41.0 | 59.5 | 17.5 | 3 39 59.33 | − 35.74 | 0.19 | 39.03 | 3 40 2.43 | 2.60 |
| | λ Tauri .......... | | 49.5 | 7.0 | 25.0 | 43.0 | 1.0 | 19.0 | 37.0 | 3 51 43.07 | .......... | 0.22 | 39.01 | 3 52 21.86 | 22.04 |
| 5 | α Arietis ......... | E. | 45.0 | 4.5 | 23.5 | 42.0 | 1 5 | 20.5 | 39.5 | 1 46 42.36 | .......... | − 0.67 | + 12 2.06 | 1 58 43.75 | 43.65 |
| | ξ¹ Ceti............ | | 8.5 | 26.5 | 44.0 | 1.5 | 19.5 | 37.5 | 55.0 | 1 53 1.79 | .......... | 0.51 | 2.06 | 2 5 3.34 | 3.12 |
| | α Ceti............ | | 31.5 | 49.5 | 7.0 | 24.5 | 42.5 | 59.5 | 17.5 | 2 42 24.57 | .......... | 0.48 | 2.06 | 2 54 26.15 | 26.37 |
| | α Persei.......... | W. | 15.5 | 42.0 | 9.5 | 36.5 | 2.5 | 29.5 | 56.5 | 3 1 36.00 | .......... | + 0.18 | 2.06 | 3 13 38.24 | 38.46 |
| | ξ Tauri .......... | | 6.0 | 24.0 | 42.0 | 59.5 | 18.0 | 35.5 | 53.5 | 3 6 59.79 | .......... | 0.38 | 2.06 | 3 19 2.23 | 2.36 |
| | e Tauri .......... | | ...... | 24.5 | 42.5 | 0.5 | 18.0 | 35.5 | 53.5 | 3 28 9.08 | − 8.94 | 0.37 | 2.06 | 3 40 2.57 | 2.63 |
| | λ Tauri .......... | | 26.0 | 43.5 | 1.5 | 20.0 | 37.5 | 55.5 | 13.5 | 3 40 19.64 | .......... | 0.37 | 2.06 | 3 52 22.07 | 22.07 |
| | α Tauri .......... | | 21.5 | 39.5 | 57.5 | 16.5′ | 34.5 | 52.5 | 11.5 | 4 15 16.21 | .......... | 0.35 | 2.06 | 4 27 18.62 | 18.47 |
| | Moon, 2d L.... | | 40.0 | 59.0 | 17.5 | 36.5 | 55.5 | 14.5 | 33.5 | 4 21 36.64 | .......... | 0.35 | 2.06 | 4 33 39.05 | ...... |
| | o¹ Orionis......... | | ...... | 23.5 | 42.0 | 0.0 | 18.0 | 36.0 | 54.5 | 4 32 9.00 | − 9.05 | 0.36 | 2.06 | 4 44 2.37 | 2.36 |
| | ι Tauri........... | | 8.5 | 27.5 | 46.5 | 5.0 | 23.5 | 42.5 | 1.5 | 4 42 5.00 | .......... | 0.32 | 2.06 | 4 54 7.38 | 7.20 |
| 6 | γ Tauri .......... | W. | 48.8 | 7.2 | 25.6 | 43.6 | 1.6 | 19.6 | 28.0 | 4 10 43.49 | ......... | 0.00 | + 31.67 | 4 11 15.16 | 15.15 |
| | α Tauri .......... | | 52.0 | 10.8 | 28.8 | 46.8 | 5.2 | 23.6 | 41.6 | 4 26 46.97 | .......... | 0.00 | 31.64 | 4 27 18.61 | 18.50 |
| | o¹ Orionis......... | | 36.4 | 54.8 | 13.6 | 31.2 | 48.8 | 7 2 | 25.2 | 4 43 31.03 | .......... | 0.00 | 31.61 | 4 44 2.64 | 2.39 |
| | ι Tauri .......... | | 38.8 | 58.0 | 16.8 | 35.6 | 54.4 | 13.6 | 32.0 | 4 53 35.60 | .......... | 0.00 | 31.58 | 4 54 7.18 | 7.22 |
| | α Aurigæ......... | | 49.6 | 14.8 | 39.6 | 5.2 | 30.0 | 54.8 | 20.4 | 5 5 4.91 | .......... | 0.00 | 31.55 | 5 5 36.46 | 36.04 |
| | o Tauri .......... | | 8.8 | 25.4 | 46.4 | 5.2 | 24.0 | 43.2 | 2.4 | 5 18 5.06 | .......... | 0.00 | 31.52 | 5 18 36.58 | 36.68 |
| | δ Orionis......... | | 55.6 | 11.2 | 30.4 | 48.0 | 5.6 | 23.2 | 40.8 | 5 23 48.83 | .......... | 0.00 | 31.50 | 5 24 20.33 | 19.95 |
| | ζ Tauri .......... | | 10.8 | 30.8 | 49.6 | 8.4 | 26.8 | 46.0 | 4.8 | 5 28 8.17 | .......... | 0.00 | 31.48 | 5 28 39.65 | 37.97 |
| | Moon, 2d L.... | | 12.0 | 30.8 | 49.6 | 8.8 | 27.0 | 46.4 | 5.0 | 5 35 8.66 | .......... | 0.00 | 31.45 | 5 35 40.05 | ...... |
| | α Orionis......... | | ...... | ...... | ...... | ...... | 48.0 | 6.0 | 23.6 | 5 47 5.87 | − 35.40 | 0.00 | 31.43 | 5 47 1.90 | 2.14 |
| | η Geminorum..... | | 20.0 | 38.4 | 57.6 | 16.4 | 35.6 | 54.4 | 14.0 | 6 5 16.63 | .......... | 0.00 | 31.49 | 6 5 48.02 | 48.31 |
| | μ Geminorum .... | | 23.2 | 42.4 | 1.2 | 20.4 | 39.2 | 58 4 | 17.6 | 6 13 20.34 | .......... | 0.00 | 31.37 | 6 13 51.71 | 51.83 |
| 7 | α Aurigæ......... | W. | ...... | ...... | ...... | ...... | 32.0 | 58.0 | 23 2 | 5 5 37.73 | − 50.39 | − 0.90 | + 29.74 | 5 5 36.18 | 36.08 |
| | δ Orionis......... | | ...... | ...... | ...... | 50.0 | 8.0 | 25.6 | 43.2 | 5 24 16.70 | − 26.34 | + 0.01 | 29.71 | 5 24 20.08 | 19.97 |
| | ζ Tauri .......... | | 12.8 | 33.2 | 52.0 | 10.8 | 30.4 | ...... | 7.6 | 5 28 4.47 | + 6.26 | − 0.34 | 29.70 | 5 28 40.09 | 40.00 |
| | α Orionis ......... | | 39.6 | ...... | 14.2 | 32.8 | 50.4 | 8.0 | 26.0 | 5 46 38.50 | − 5.91 | 0.11 | 29.68 | 5 47 2.16 | 2.17 |
| | η Geminorum..... | | 21.6 | 40.4 | 0.4 | 19.6 | 38 0 | 56.8 | 16.4 | 6 5 19.03 | .......... | 0.36 | 29.66 | 6 5 48.33 | 48.34 |
| | μ Geminorum .... | | 26.0 | 44.0 | 4.0 | 23.2 | 41.6 | 0.8 | 20.0 | 6 13 22.80 | .......... | 0.37 | 29.65 | 6 13 52.08 | 51.86 |
| | Moon, 2d L.... | | 44.4 | 4.0 | 23.2 | ...... | ...... | ...... | 39.2 | 6 37 27.70 | + 14.26 | 0.30 | 29.63 | 6 38 11.29 | ..... |
| | ζ Geminorum .... | | ...... | ...... | 23.2 | 42.0 | 0.8 | 19.6 | ...... | 6 54 51.40 | − 9.39 | 0.33 | 29.61 | 6 35 11.29 | 11.67 |
| 23 | α Aquilæ......... | W. | 28.8 | 46.8 | 4.8 | 22.4 | 39.6 | 57.6 | 15.6 | 19 43 22.23 | .......... | − 4.34 | + 8.79 | 19 43 26.68 | 26.54 |
| | β Aquilæ......... | | 56.8 | ...... | 32.0 | 49.6 | 7.2 | 25.2 | 42.0 | 19 47 55.47 | − 5.90 | − 3.08 | 8.79 | 19 47 55.28 | 55.38 |
| | Moon, 1st L.... | | ...... | ...... | ...... | 36.0 | 55.2 | 14.0 | 33.2 | 19 57 4.60 | − 28.39 | + 9.76 | 8.79 | 19 56 54.76 | ...... |
| | α² Capricorni ..... | | ...... | 50.4 | 9.2 | 26.0 | 43.6 | 2.8 | 20.8 | 20 9 35.60 | − 9.02 | + 6.72 | 8.79 | 20 9 42.09 | 42.24 |
| | α Cygni........... | | 24.8 | 49.2 | 14.8 | 38.8 | 3.2 | 28.0 | 53.2 | 20 36 38.86 | .......... | − 28.85 | 8.79 | 20 36 18.80 | 18.80 |
| | η Capricorni ..... | | 34.4 | 53.2 | 12.0 | 31.2 | 49.6 | 8.0 | 27.2 | 20 55 30.80 | .......... | + 10.85 | 8.79 | 20 55 50.44 | 50.39 |
| | 61¹ Cygni .......... | | 17.6 | 40.0 | 1.6 | 23.6 | 46.0 | 9.2 | 32.0 | 21 0 24.29 | .......... | − 2.75 | 8.79 | 21 0 10.33 | 10.13 |
| | ζ Cygni .......... | | 40.0 | 0.0 | 20.4 | 40.4 | 0.8 | 20.4 | 40.8 | 21 6 40.40 | .......... | − 16.55 | + 8.79 | 21 6 32.64 | 32.77 |

## *Longitude of junction of the Gila and Colorado*—Continued.

| DATE. | OBJECT. | LAMP. | CHRONOMETER TIMES OF TRANSIT. I. | II. | III. | IV. | V. | VI. | VII. | MEAN OF OBS'D WIRES | CORRECTIONS FOR— Imperfect transits. | Instrument. | Chronometer. | OBSERVED A.R. | TABULAR A.R. |
|---|---|---|---|---|---|---|---|---|---|---|---|---|---|---|---|
| 1849. | | | s. | s. | s. | s. | s. | s. | s. | h. m. s. | m. s. | m. s. | s. | h. m. s. | s. |
| Oct. 23 | α Cephei ......... | W. | 54.4 | 31.6 | 8.8 | 46.0 | 23.2 | 8.0 | 38.0 | 21 15 47.14 | .......... | − 54.62 | + 8.79 | 21 15 1.31 | 0.63 |
| | β Aquarii ........ | | 33.2 | 51.2 | 9.2 | 26.8 | 44.0 | 1.6 | 20.0 | 21 23 26.57 | .......... | + 3.18 | 8.79 | 21 23 38.54 | 38.62 |
| | β Cephei ......... | | 21.2 | 12.0 | 3.2 | 54.4 | 45.2 | 36.0 | 28.0 | 21 27 54.[illegible]9 | .......... | −1 19.57 | 8.79 | 21 26 43.51 | 44.30 |
| | ε Pegasi ......... | | 51.6 | 8.8 | 26 8 | 44.4 | 2.0 | 19.6 | ...... | 21 36 35.53 | + 8.91 | − 4.70 | 8.79 | 21 36 48.53 | 48.51 |
| | α Aquarii......... | | 2.0 | 19.6 | 37.2 | 54.8 | 12.0 | 29.6 | 47.2 | 21 57 54.63 | .......... | + 0.54 | 8.79 | 21 58 3.96 | 3.96 |
| | ζ Pegasi ......... | | ...... | 20.0 | 38.0 | 55.2 | 12.8 | 31.2 | 48.8 | 22 34 4.33 | − 8.92 | − 5.16 | 8.79 | 22 33 59.04 | 58.56 |
| 24 | π Capricorni...... | W. | ...... | 17.2 | 35.6 | 54.0 | 12.0 | 30.8 | 49.6 | 20 19 3.20 | − 9.27 | + 0.48 | − 12.15 | 20 18 42.26 | 42.36 |
| * | Moon, 1st L.... | | ...... | 50.0 | 8.8 | 27.6 | 46.0 | 5.2 | 24.0 | 20 48 36.93 | − 9.34 | 0.42 | 12.15 | 20 48 15.86 | ...... |
| | η Capricorni...... | | 6.0 | 24.4 | 43.2 | 2.4 | 20.6 | 39.2 | 58.4 | 20 56 2.03 | .......... | 0.53 | 12.15 | 20 55 50.41 | 50.41 |
| | 29 Capricorni...... | | 42.8 | 0.8 | 19.2 | 37.2 | 55.2 | 14.0 | 32.0 | 21 7 37.31 | .......... | 0.40 | 12.15 | 21 7 25.56 | 25.24 |
| | ι Capricorni...... | | 9.0 | 27.2 | 45.6 | 4.2 | 20.6 | 41.2 | 59.2 | 21 14 3.86 | .......... | 0.44 | [illegible].15 | 21 13 52.15 | 52.08 |
| | β Aquarii......... | | ...... | ...... | ...... | ...... | 8.0 | 25.6 | 43.6 | 21 24 25.73 | − 35.32 | 0.15 | 12.15 | 21 23 38.41 | 38.60 |
| | ε Pegasi ........ | | 7.2 | 25.2 | 43.2 | 0.8 | 18.4 | 36.4 | 54.0 | 21 37 0.74 | .......... | − 0.23 | 12.15 | 21 36 48.36 | 48.49 |
| | ζ Pegasi.......... | | 17.6 | 35.2 | 53.2 | 10.8 | 28 8 | 46.4 | 4.8 | 22 34 10.97 | .......... | − 0.25 | 12.15 | 22 33 58.57 | 58.54 |
| 25 | η Capricorni...... | E. | 22.0 | 40.8 | 59.6 | 18.4 | 36.8 | 56.0 | 14.4 | 20 56 18.29 | .......... | ..... .... | − 27.80 | 20 55 50.49 | 50.36 |
| | 61 Cygni .......... | | 32 0 | 54.4 | 16.8 | ...... | 0.8 | 23.2 | 40.8 | 21 0 38.00 | − 0.01 | 0.00 | 27.80 | 21 0 10.19 | 10.09 |
| | 29 Capricorni...... | | 58.4 | 17.2 | 35.2 | 53.2 | 12.0 | 29.6 | 48.0 | 21 7 53.37 | .......... | 0.00 | 27.80 | 21 7 25.57 | 25.23 |
| † | ι Capricorni...... | | 24.8 | 45.2 | 1.6 | 20.0 | 38.4 | 57.2 | 15.6 | 21 14 20.11 | .......... | 0.00 | 27.80 | 21 13 52.31 | 52.06 |
| | β Aquarii......... | | 13.6 | 31.2 | 49.2 | 6.4 | 24.0 | 42.0 | 59.6 | 21 24 6.57 | .......... | 0.00 | 27.80 | 21 24 38.77 | 38.58 |
| | Moon, 1st L.... | | ...... | 16.8 | 35.2 | 53.6 | 12.2 | 31.2 | 49.2 | 21 40 3.03 | − 9.93 | 0.00 | 27.80 | 21 39 25.30 | ...... |
| | ι Aquarii .... .... | | 52.0 | 10.4 | 28.8 | 46.8 | 4.4 | 23.2 | 41.2 | 21 58 46.69 | .......... | 0.00 | 27.80 | 21 58 18.89 | 18.95 |
| ‡ | σ Aquarii......... | | 15.2 | 32.8 | 50.0 | 8.8 | 26.8 | 44.6 | 2.4 | 22 23 8 66 | .......... | 0.00 | 27.80 | 22 22 40.86 | 41.52 |
| | ζ Pegasi.......... | | 32.8 | 50.8 | 8.4 | 26.4 | 44.0 | 2.2 | 20.0 | 22 34 26.37 | .......... | 0.00 | 27.80 | 22 33 58.57 | 58.53 |
| | λ Aquarii.. ...... | | 20.8 | 38.8 | 56.4 | 14.4 | 32 0 | 49.6 | 7.6 | 22 45 14.23 | .......... | 0.00 | 27.80 | 22 44 46.43 | 46.62 |
| | α Piscis Australis. | | 46.8 | 7.2 | 28.0 | 48.0 | 8.8 | 28.4 | 48.8 | 22 49 48.00 | .......... | 0.00 | 27.80 | 22 49 20.20 | 20.31 |
| 26 | λ Ursæ Minoris... | W. | ...... | ...... | ...... | 52.8 | 33.4 | 21.4 | 29.6 | 20 36 4.30 | −22 17.45 | + 22.08 | − 29.86 | 20 13 39.07 | 34.04 |
| | 29 Capricorni...... | | 0.4 | 18.4 | 36.8 | 55.2 | 13.2 | 31.2 | 50.0 | 21 7 56.03 | .......... | − 0.12 | 29.86 | 21 17 25.05 | 25.21 |
| | ι Capricorni...... | | 26.8 | ...... | 3.6 | 22.0 | 39.6 | 58.6 | 17.4 | 21 14 28.00 | − 6.15 | − 0.14 | 29.86 | 21 13 51.85 | 52.05 |
| | β Cephei ......... | | ...... | ...... | 22.4 | 13.6 | 4.0 | 55.6 | 46.8 | 21 28 4.48 | 51.15 | + 1.19 | 29.86 | 21 26 44.66 | 44.13 |
| | γ Capricorni...... | | 20.0 | 38.2 | 57.2 | 15.4 | 33.2 | 52.0 | 10.8 | 21 32 15.26 | .......... | − 0.14 | 29.86 | 21 31 45.26 | 45.33 |
| | δ Capricorni...... | | 19.2 | 37.6 | 55.6 | 14.8 | 32.8 | 50.8 | 9.6 | 21 39 14.34 | .......... | − 0.13 | 29 86 | 21 38 44.35 | 44.27 |
| | ι Aquarii .... .... | | 54.4 | 12.8 | 30.8 | 48.8 | 6.8 | 25.2 | 43.6 | 22 58 48.91 | .......... | − 0.13 | 29.86 | 21 58 18.92 | 18.94 |
| | σ Aquarii......... | | 18.0 | 35.6 | 53.6 | 12.0 | 29.6 | 47.2 | 5.6 | 22 23 11.66 | .......... | − 0.09 | 29.86 | 22 22 41.71 | 41.45 |
| | Moon, 1st L.... | | 16.2 | 34.0 | 52.8 | 18.8 | 28.8 | 47.2 | 5.6 | 22 31 10.77 | .......... | − 0.08 | 29.86 | 22 30 40.83 | ...... |
| | λ Aquarii......... | | ...... | 41.2 | 58.8 | 16.8 | 34.4 | 52.0 | 10.0 | 22 45 25.53 | − 8.88 | − 0.06 | 29.86 | 22 44 46.73 | 46.61 |
| | α Ursæ Maj., S. P. | | 58.4 | 36.8 | 15.4 | 52.8 | 30.8 | 9.2 | 47.2 | 22 54 52.94 | .......... | − 0.84 | 29.86 | 22 54 22.24 | 21.60 |
| 27 | λ Ursæ Minoris... | E. | ...... | ...... | ...... | 12.4 | 52.0 | 59.2 | 58.4 | 20 36 30.50 | −22 18.00 | − 7.41 | − 33.82 | 20 13 31.27 | 32.80 |
| | 29 Capricorni...... | | 4.0 | 22.6 | 40.8 | 58.8 | 17.2 | 35.2 | 53.6 | 21 7 58.89 | .......... | + 0.04 | 33.90 | 21 7 24.98 | 25.20 |
| | ι Capricorni...... | | 30.4 | 49.2 | 7.6 | 26.0 | 44.4 | 2.8 | 21.2 | 21 14 25.94 | .......... | + 0.04 | 33.97 | 21 14 52.01 | 52.03 |
| | β Cephei.......... | | ...... | ...... | 27.2 | 18.4 | 9.2 | 0.8 | 52.0 | 21 28 9.52 | − 51.14 | − 0.40 | 34.01 | 21 26 43.97 | 44.07 |
| | ι Aquarii......... | | 58.8 | 16.8 | 34.8 | 52 8 | 10.8 | 28.8 | 46.8 | 21 58 52.80 | .......... | + 0.04 | 34.09 | 21 58 18.75 | 18.92 |
| | σ Aquarii......... | | 21.6 | 40.0 | 57.6 | 15.6 | 33.6 | 51.6 | 9.2 | 22 23 15.60 | .......... | + 0.03 | 34.14 | 22 22 41.49 | 41.43 |
| | λ Aquarii......... | | 27.2 | 42.2 | 3.2 | 20.8 | 38.4 | 56.0 | 14.0 | 22 45 20.69 | .......... | + 0.02 | 34.19 | 22 44 46.52 | 46.60 |
| | α Piscis Australis. | | 53.6 | 14.0 | 34.4 | 54.8 | 15.2 | 35.6 | 55.6 | 22 49 54.74 | .......... | + 0.08 | 34.20 | 22 49 20.62 | 20.28 |
| | Moon, 1st L.... | | 2.0 | 20.0 | 38.0 | 56.0 | 14.0 | 32.0 | 50.0 | 23 22 56.00 | .......... | + 0.01 | 34.29 | 23 22 21.72 | ...... |
| | 20 Piscium ........ | | 55.6 | 12.8 | 30.4 | 47.6 | 5.6 | 23.2 | 40.8 | 23 40 48.00 | .......... | + 0.01 | 34.34 | 23 40 13.67 | 13.52 |
| | 27 Piscium ........ | | 40.8 | 58.0 | 16.4 | 33.6 | 51.2 | 8.8 | 26.4 | 23 51 33.60 | .......... | + 0.01 | 34.37 | 23 50 59.24 | 59.44 |
| | β Ceti............ | | 42.0 | 0.8 | 19.2 | 37.6 | 56.2 | 15.2 | 33.6 | 0 36 37.80 | .......... | + 0.05 | 34.48 | 0 36 3.37 | 3.24 |
| | Polaris ......... | | 44.4 | 9.2 | 31.2 | 40.8 | ..... | ...... | ...... | 0 49 46.40 | +16 55.02 | − 5.83 | 34.53 | 0 5 61.04 | 59.55 |
| 28 | 29 Capricorni..... | E. | 6.8 | 24.8 | 42.8 | 0.8 | 18.8 | 37.6 | 56.0 | 21 8 1.09 | .......... | − 0.08 | − 36.08 | 21 7 24.93 | 25.19 |
| | β Aquarii.... .... | | 22.0 | 39.6 | 57.2 | 14.8 | 32.4 | 50.0 | 8.0 | 21 24 14.86 | .......... | − 0.03 | 36.14 | 21 23 38.69 | 38.54 |
| | β Cephei.......... | | ...... | 36.4 | 29.6 | 20.4 | 10.8 | 2.0 | 53.6 | 21 27 45.47 | − 25.56 | + 0.81 | 36.15 | 21 26 44.57 | 44.01 |
| | δ Capricorni...... | | 15.6 | 44.0 | 2.2 | 20.4 | 38.8 | 57.2 | 15.6 | 21 39 20.54 | .......... | − 0.09 | 36.19 | 21 38 44.26 | 44.24 |
| | σ Aquarii......... | | 24.4 | 42.4 | 0.0 | 18.0 | 36.0 | 54.0 | 12.0 | 22 23 18.11 | .......... | − 0.06 | 36.37 | 22 22 41.68 | 41.42 |
| | λ Aquarii .... .... | | ...... | 47.6 | 7.4 | 23.2 | 40.4 | 58.4 | 16.4 | 22 45 32.23 | − 8.88 | − 0.04 | 36.44 | 22 44 46.87 | 46.59 |
| | α Ursæ Minoris... | | 4.4 | 42.8 | 21.2 | 58.8 | 36.0 | 15.2 | 52.4 | 22 54 58.69 | .......... | − 0.57 | 36.48 | 22 54 21.64 | 21.66 |
| | γ Cephei ..... ... | | 4.8 | 21.2 | 38.0 | ...... | ...... | 28.4 | ...... | 23 32 38.10 | +1 16.95 | + 1.26 | − 36.61 | 23 33 19.70 | 19 30 |

* Wire IV recorded 23.6s. † Wire IV recorded 51.2s. ‡ Wire VI recorded 40.6s.

## *Longitude of junction of the Gila and Colorado*—Continued.

| DATE. | OBJECT. | LAMP. | CHRONOMETER TIMES OF TRANSIT. I. | II. | III. | IV. | V. | VI. | VII. | MEAN OF OBS'D WIRES | CORRECTIONS FOR— Imperfect transits. | Instrument. | Chronometer. | OBSERVED A.R. | TABULAR A.R. |
|---|---|---|---|---|---|---|---|---|---|---|---|---|---|---|---|
| 1849. | | | s. | s. | s. | s. | s. | s. | s. | h. m. s. | m. s. | s. | s. | h. m. s. | s. |
| Oct. 28 | 20 Piscium........ | E. | 57.2 | 14.8 | 32.8 | 50.0 | 7.2 | 25.0 | 43.2 | 23 40 50.03 | ......... | − 0.02 | − 36.64 | 23 40 13.37 | 13.51 |
| | 27 Piscium........ | | 43.2 | 0.8 | 18.4 | 36.0 | 53.6 | 11.6 | 29.2 | 23 51 36 11 | ......... | − 0.02 | 36.68 | 23 50 59.41 | 59.42 |
| | Moon, 1st L.... | | 42.8 | 1.2 | 20.0 | 38.0 | 56.0 | 14.0 | 30.2 | 0 15 37.71 | ......... | − 0.01 | 36.76 | 0 15 0.94 | .... . |
| | β Ceti............ | | 44.4 | 2.8 | 21.6 | 40.4 | 58.8 | 17.2 | 36.0 | 0 36 40.17 | ......... | − 0.10 | 36.84 | 0 36 3.23 | 3.24 |
| | 20 Ceti........... | | 4.8 | 22.0 | 40.8 | 57.2 | 14 8 | 32.0 | 50.0 | 0 45 57.37 | ......... | − 0.01 | 36.87 | 0 45 20.49 | 20.56 |
| | Polaris......... | | 31.6 | 51.2 | 11.2 | ...... | ...... | ...... | ...... | 0 43 51.33 | +22 33.44 | + 11.41 | 36.94 | 1 5 59.24 | 59.38 |
| | $\theta^1$ Ceti............ | | 15.2 | 32.8 | 50.8 | 8.4 | 26.4 | 44.0 | 2.0 | 1 17 8.51 | ......... | − 0.05 | 36.98 | 1 16 31.48 | 31.57 |
| 29 | α Capricorni...... | W. | 3.2 | 20.3 | 39.2 | 56.8 | 15.9 | 29.6 | ...... | 20 9 47.50 | + 9.02 | + 0.14 | − 38.74 | 20 9 17.92 | 18.26 |
| | $\alpha^2$ Capricorni...... | | 27.2 | 45.8 | 3.4 | 21.2 | 39 3 | ...... | ...... | 20 18 3.38 | + 18.04 | + 0.14 | 38.75 | 20 9 42.81 | 42.13 |
| | π Capricorni...... | | 26.0 | 44 4 | 2.8 | 21.2 | 40.0 | 58.0 | 17.2 | 20 19 21.37 | ......... | + 0.21 | 38.77 | 20 18 42.81 | 42.28 |
| | α Cephei......... | | 48.8 | 26.0 | 3.2 | 40.8 | 17.6 | 55.6 | 33.2 | 21 15 40.74 | ......... | − 1.14 | 38.87 | 21 15 0.73 | 0.38 |
| | β Aquarii......... | | 24.8 | 42.8 | ...... | 18.0 | 35.6 | 53.2 | 10.8 | 21 24 20.87 | − 2.93 | + 0.07 | 38.88 | 21 23 39.13 | 38.52 |
| | β Cephei......... | | ..... | ...... | 33.6 | 25.0 | 15.2 | 6.4 | 58.0 | 21 28 15.68 | − 51.14 | − 1.66 | 38.89 | 21 26 43.99 | 43.95 |
| | ε Pegasi.......... | | 34.4 | 52.4 | 10.0 | 27.6 | 45.6 | 3.4 | 21.6 | 21 37 27.89 | ......... | − 0.09 | 38.90 | 21 36 48.90 | 48.41 |
| | ι Aquarii........ | | 4.0 | 22.8 | 40.4 | 58.4 | 16.4 | 34.8 | 52.8 | 21 58 58.51 | ......... | + 0.16 | 38.94 | 21 58 19.73 | 18.88 |
| | σ Aquarii......... | | 24.0 | 43.6 | 2.4 | 20.0 | 37.6 | 55.6 | 13.6 | 22 23 19.54 | ......... | + 0.12 | 38.98 | 22 22 40.68 | 41.46 |
| | ξ Pegasi.......... | | 43.2 | 1.6 | 19.6 | 37.2 | 54.8 | 13.2 | 30.8 | 22 34 37.20 | ......... | − 0.10 | 39.00 | 22 33 58.10 | 58.48 |
| | λ Aquarii......... | | 31.6 | 49.2 | 7.6 | 25.2 | 42.8 | 0.4 | ...... | 22 45 16.13 | + 8.88 | + 0.08 | 39.02 | 22 44 46.07 | 46.57 |
| | α Ursæ Minoris... | | 3.2 | 41.2 | 19.2 | 58.0 | 35.6 | 13.6 | 52.0 | 22 54 57.54 | ......... | + 1.12 | 39.03 | 22 54 19.63 | 21.71 |
| | β Ceti............ | | 46.0 | 4.8 | 23.2 | 41.6 | 0.4 | 18.8 | 37.6 | 0 36 41.77 | ......... | + 0.20 | 39.20 | 0 36 2.77 | 3.24 |
| | δ Piscium......... | | 40.0 | 57.6 | 16.0 | 33.2 | 50.8 | 8.8 | 26.4 | 0 41 33.26 | ......... | − 0.08 | 39.21 | 0 40 53.97 | 54.21 |
| | Moon, 1st L.... | | 59.8 | 17.6 | 35.6 | 53.6 | 11.6 | 29.6 | 47.6 | 1 9 53.63 | ......... | − 0.04 | 39.25 | 1 9 14.34 | ...... |
| | $\theta^1$ Ceti............ | | 17.2 | 34.8 | 52.8 | 10.8 | 28.0 | 46.0 | 4.0 | 1 17 10.51 | ......... | + 0.09 | 39.27 | 1 16 31.33 | 31.57 |
| | μ Piscium........ | | 5.6 | 23.6 | 41.6 | 58.8 | 16.8 | 34.0 | 52.0 | 1 22 58.91 | ......... | − 0.06 | 39.28 | 1 22 19.57 | 19.71 |
| | ν Piscium......... | | 24.0 | 42.0 | 59 6 | 17.2 | 34.2 | 52.0 | 10.0 | 1 34 17.00 | ......... | − 0.06 | 39.30 | 1 33 37.64 | 37.80 |
| | ο Piscium........ | | 14.8 | 32.8 | 50.4 | 8.4 | 26.4 | 43.6 | 1.6 | 1 38 8.29 | ......... | − 0.08 | 39.39 | 1 37 28.91 | 28.77 |
| 30 | ι Piscium........ | W. | ...... | ...... | ...... | ...... | 11.2 | 30.8 | 48.4 | 23 33 30.13 | − 35.24 | − 0.12 | − 41.56 | 23 32 13.21 | 13.94 |
| | 20 Piscium........ | | 2.0 | 20.0 | 37.2 | 54.8 | 12.8 | 30.4 | 48.0 | 23 40 55.03 | ......... | + 0.09 | 41.58 | 23 40 13.54 | 13.49 |
| | 27 Piscium........ | | 48.0 | 5.6 | 23.2 | 40.8 | 58.4 | 16.0 | 34.0 | 23 51 40.86 | ......... | + 0.11 | 41.67 | 23 50 59 36 | 59.41 |
| | α Andromedæ .... | | 21.6 | 41.2 | 1.6 | 21.2 | 40.8 | 0.8 | 20.8 | 0 1 21.14 | ......... | − 0.77 | 41.63 | 0 0 38.74 | 38.78 |
| | γ Pegasi.......... | | 18.8 | 36.8 | 54.8 | 12.8 | 30.8 | 48.8 | 7.6 | 0 6 12.91 | ......... | − 0.37 | 41.63 | 0 5 30.91 | 30.97 |
| | α Cassiopeæ..... | | 13.6 | 44.0 | 15.6 | 46.8 | 17.2 | 48.8 | 20.8 | 0 32 46.69 | ......... | − 2.10 | 41.69 | 0 32 2.90 | 3.00 |
| | β Ceti............ | | 49.2 | 7.2 | 26.0 | 44.4 | 2.8 | 21.2 | 40 4 | 0 36 44.46 | ......... | + 0.39 | 41.70 | 0 36 3.15 | 3.23 |
| | δ Piscium........ | | 42 8 | 0.8 | 18.4 | 36.0 | 53.6 | 11.6 | 29.2 | 0 41 36.06 | ......... | − 0.17 | 41.71 | 0 40 54.18 | 54.20 |
| | 20 Ceti........... | | 9.6 | 27.2 | 44.4 | 2.0 | 19.6 | 37.6 | 54.8 | 0 46 2.17 | ......... | + 0.05 | 41.72 | 0 45 20.50 | 20.55 |
| | α Arietis......... | | 29.2 | 48.4 | 7.2 | 26.4 | 45.2 | 4.4 | 23.6 | 1 59 26.34 | ......... | − 0.60 | 41.88 | 1 58 43.86 | 43.88 |
| | Moon, 1st L... | | 25 2 | 43.6 | 1.6 | 19.6 | 38.0 | 56.0 | 14.4 | 2 6 19.77 | ......... | − 0 21 | 41.89 | 2 5 37.67 | ...... |
| | ξ Ceti........... | | 0.4 | 18.4 | 36.4 | 53.6 | 11.2 | 29.2 | 47.2 | 2 20 53.77 | ......... | − 0.20 | 41.92 | 2 20 11.65 | 11.47 |
| | α Ceti............ | | 15.6 | 33.2 | 51.2 | 8.8 | 26.0 | 44.0 | 1.6 | 2 55 8.63 | ......... | − 0.09 | 41.99 | 2 54 26.55 | 26.72 |
| | δ Arietis........ | | 50.4 | 9.2 | 28.0 | 46.8 | 6.8 | 23.6 | 42.0 | 3 3 46.69 | ......... | − 0.50 | 42.01 | 3 3 4.18 | 3.76 |
| | α Persei.......... | | 2.0 | 29.2 | 55.6 | 22.8 | 49.6 | 16.8 | 44.0 | 3 14 22.86 | ......... | − 1.67 | 42.04 | 3 13 39.15 | 39.05 |
| | ξ Tauri........... | | 51.6 | 9.6 | 27.2 | 44.8 | 2.4 | 20.4 | 38.4 | 3 19 44.91 | ......... | − 0.23 | 42.05 | 3 19 2.63 | 2.78 |
| 31 | δ Capricorni...... | E. | 34.0 | 52.0 | 10.0 | ...... | ...... | ...... | ...... | 21 38 52.00 | + 36.68 | + 0.37 | − 45.01 | 21 38 44.04 | 41.07 |
| | λ Aquarii......... | | 38.0 | 56.0 | 14.0 | 31.2 | 49.2 | 6.8 | 24.8 | 22 45 31.43 | ......... | + 0.18 | 45.03 | 22 44 46.49 | 46.47 |
| | α Piscis Australis. | | 3.6 | 24.0 | 44.0 | 4.4 | 24.8 | 45.6 | 6.0 | 22 50 4.63 | ......... | + 0.73 | 45.04 | 22 49 20.22 | 20.23 |
| | α Pegasi.......... | | 8.0 | 26.0 | 44.0 | 2.0 | 20.0 | 38.0 | 56.0 | 22 58 2.00 | ......... | − 0.32 | 45.17 | 22 57 16.51 | 17.22 |
| | ι Piscium........ | | 6.4 | 23.6 | 41.2 | 59.2 | 17.2 | 34.8 | 52.0 | 23 32 59.20 | ......... | − 0.10 | 45.24 | 23 32 13.86 | 13.93 |
| | 20 Piscium........ | | 5.6 | 23.6 | 40.8 | 58.0 | 16.0 | 33.6 | 51.2 | 23 40 58.40 | ......... | + 0.08 | 45.26 | 23 40 13.22 | 13.36 |
| | 27 Piscium........ | | 51.6 | 9.6 | 27.6 | 44.0 | 2.4 | 20.0 | 37.6 | 23 51 44.74 | ......... | + 0.09 | 45.29 | 23 50 59 54 | 59.30 |
| | α Andromedæ .... | | 24.4 | 44.8 | 4.8 | ...... | 44.8 | 4.8 | 24.8 | 0 1 24.73 | − 0.01 | − 0.67 | 45.31 | 0 0 38.74 | 38.78 |
| | γ Pegasi.......... | | 22.8 | 40.8 | 58.8 | 16.8 | 34.8 | 52.8 | 10.8 | 0 6 16.80 | ......... | − 0.32 | 45.33 | 0 5 31.15 | 30.96 |
| | Polaris......... | | 36.0 | 0.0 | 19.6 | 29.6 | 40.6 | 4.4 | 29.6 | 1 7 31.40 | ......... | − 47.62 | 45.43 | 1 5 58.35 | 58.74 |
| | ν Piscium........ | | 30 0 | 48.0 | 6.0 | ..... | ...... | ...... | ...... | 1 33 48.00 | + 35.24 | − 0.10 | 45.49 | 1 33 37.65 | 37.78 |
| | α Arietis......... | | 32.4 | 51.2 | 10.8 | 29.6 | 48.8 | ...... | 26.8 | 1 59 23.27 | + 6.36 | − 0 52 | 45.53 | 1 58 43.58 | 43.88 |
| | $\xi^1$ Ceti........... | | 56.0 | 14.0 | 31.2 | 48.8 | 6.8 | 24.8 | 42.0 | 2 5 49.09 | ......... | − 0.18 | 45.55 | 2 5 3.36 | 3.36 |
| | $\xi^2$ Ceti........... | | 3.6 | 22.0 | 39.2 | 56.8 | 14.4 | 32.8 | 50.0 | 2 20 56.97 | ......... | − 0.17 | 45.59 | 2 20 11.21 | 11.48 |
| | α Ceti........... | | 20.0 | ..... | ...... | ...... | 29.6 | 47.6 | ..... | 2 55 12.40 | + 0.13 | − 0.07 | 45.63 | 2 54 26.83 | 26.73 |
| | Moon, 2d L... | | 45.6 | 4.0 | 22.0 | 40.4 | ...... | ...... | ...... | 3 7 13.00 | + 27.64 | − 0.27 | − 45.67 | 3 6 54.70 | ...... |

## *Longitude of junction of the Gila and Colorado*—Continued.

| DATE. | OBJECT. | LAMP. | CHRONOMETER TIME OF TRANSIT. I. | II. | III. | IV. | V. | VI. | VII. | MEAN OF OBS'D WIRES | CORRECTIONS FOR— Imperfect transits. | Instrument. | Chronometer. | OBSERVED A.R. | TABULAR A.R. |
|---|---|---|---|---|---|---|---|---|---|---|---|---|---|---|---|
| 1849. | | | *s.* | *s.* | *s.* | *s.* | *s.* | *s.* | *s.* | *h. m. s.* | *m. s.* | *s.* | *s.* | *h. m. s.* | *s.* |
| Nov. 1 | Polaris ......... | W. | ...... | 41.6 | 0.8 | 17.0 | 29.2 | 48.4 | 13.2 | 1 12 55.03 | — 38.97 | — 30.80 | — 46.76 | 1 5 58.50 | 58.51 |
| | μ Piscium ........ | | 13.6 | 31.2 | 49.2 | 6.8 | 24.0 | 41.6 | 59.6 | 1 23 6.57 | .......... | 0.07 | 46.78 | 1 22 19.72 | 19.67 |
| | ν Piscium ........ | | 32.0 | 49.6 | 7.2 | 24.4. | 42.0 | 59.6 | 17.6 | 1 34 24.63 | .......... | 0.07 | 46.79 | 1 33 37.77 | 37.77 |
| | α Arietis ......... | | 34.0 | 53.6 | 12.0 | 31.6 | 50.0 | 9.2 | 28.0 | 1 59 31.20 | .......... | 0.34 | 46.82 | 1 58 44.04 | 43.89 |
| | $\xi^1$ Ceti........... | | 57.2 | 15.2 | 32.4 | 50.4 | 8.0 | 25.6 | 43.6 | 2 5 50.34 | .......... | 0.11 | 46.84 | 2 5 3.39 | 3.37 |
| | $\xi^2$ Ceti........... | | 5.6 | 22.8 | 40.8 | 58.4 | 16.0 | 33.6 | 51.6 | 2 20 58.40 | .......... | 0.11 | 46.86 | 2 20 11.43 | 11.49 |
| | χ Ceti........... | | 26.4 | 43.6 | 1.6 | 18.8 | 36.8 | 54.0 | 12.0 | 2 36 19.03 | .......... | 0.04 | 46.88 | 2 35 32.11 | 32 07 |
| | α Ceti........... | | 20.8 | 38.4 | 56.0 | 14.0 | 30.8 | 48.8 | 6.4 | 2 55 13.60 | .......... | 0.05 | 46.90 | 2 54 26.65 | 26.74 |
| | δ Arietis.......... | | 55.6 | 13.6 | 32.6 | 51.2 | 9.6 | 28.0 | 47.2 | 3 3 51.03 | ....... .. | 0.28 | 46.91 | 3 3 3.84 | 3.80 |
| | α Polaris ......... | | 6.4 | 32.8 | 0.4 | 27.2 | 54.0 | 20.8 | 47.6 | 3 14 27.03 | .......... | 0.93 | 46.92 | 3 13 39.18 | 39.09 |
| | ξ Tauri... ....... | | 56.0 | 14.0 | 32.0 | 50.0 | 7.2 | 25.2 | 43.2 | 3 19 49.66 | .......... | 0.13 | 46.93 | 3 19 2.60 | 2.80 |
| | e Tauri........... | | 56.4 | 14.4 | 32.4 | 50.4 | 8.0 | 26.0 | 44.0 | 3 40 50.23 | .......... | 0.15 | 46.96 | 3 40 3.12 | 3.11 |
| | λ Tauri........... | | 16.0 | 34.0 | 52.0 | 10.0 | 28.0 | 46.0 | 4.0 | 3 53 10.00 | .......... | 0.17 | 46 98 | 3 52 22.85 | 22.55 |
| | Moon, 2d L..... | | 23.2 | 42.4 | 1.2 | 19.6 | 38.0 | 57.2 | 16 0 | 4 9 19.66 | .......... | 0.23 | 46.99 | 4 8 32.44 | ...... |
| | γ Tauri........... | | 8.8 | 26.8 | 44.8 | 2.8 | 20.8 | 38.8 | 56.8 | 4 12 2.80 | .......... | 0 22 | 47.00 | 4 11 15.58 | 15.75 |
| | α Tauri .......... | | 11.6 | 29.6 | 48.0 | 6.8 | 24.4 | 42.8 | 0.8 | 4 28 6.29 | .......... | 0.23 | 47.02 | 4 27 19.04 | 19.09 |
| | $o^1$ Orionis......... | | 55.6 | 14.0 | 32.0 | 50.0 | 8.0 | 26.0 | 44.0 | 4 44 49.96 | ..... . . | 0.20 | 47.04 | 4 44 2.70 | 2.97 |
| | ι Tauri........... | | 59.2 | 17.6 | 36.4 | 55.6 | 14.0 | 32.8 | 52.0 | 4 54 55.37 | .......... | 0.31 | 47.05 | 4 54 8.01 | 7.80 |
| 2 | α Tauri........... | E. | ...... | ...... | ...... | 8 8 | 27.6 | 45.6 | 4.0 | 4 28 36.50 | — 27.42 | + 0.06 | — 49.99 | 4 27 19.15 | 19.10 |
| | $o^1$ Orionis......... | | 58.4 | 16.4 | 34.8 | 52.4 | 10.8 | 28.8 | 46.8 | 4 44 52.63 | .......... | 0 05 | 50.01 | 4 44 2.67 | 3.02 |
| | ι Tauri........... | | 0.8 | 19.6 | 38.8 | 57.6 | 16.8 | 35.6 | 54.4 | 4 54 57.66 | .......... | 0.08 | 50.02 | 4 54 7.72 | 7.92 |
| | Moon, 2d L..... | | 4.4 | 23.6 | 42.4 | 1.6 | 20.8 | 39.2 | 58.4 | 5 13 1.49 | .......... | 0.06 | 50.05 | 5 12 11.50 | ...... |
| | β Tauri........... | | 38.8 | 58.8 | 18.8 | 38.8 | 58.8 | 18.8 | 38.8 | 5 17 38.80 | .......... | 0.01 | 50.06 | 5 16 48.85 | 48.61 |
| | δ Orionis... ..... | | 18.0 | 36.0 | 52.8 | 10.8 | 28.4 | 45.6 | 3.6 | 5 25 10.74 | .......... | 0.00 | 50.07 | 5 24 20.67 | 20.62 |
| * | ζ Tauri ......... | | 34.0 | 53.0 | 12.0 | 30.4 | 49.6 | 8.8 | 27.2 | 5 29 30.71 | .......... | 0.08 | 50.08 | 5 28 40.71 | 40.70 |
| † | α Orionis......... | | 59.6 | 17.6 | 35.6 | 53.8 | 10.8 | 28.4 | 46.0 | 5 47 53.11 | ......... | 0.02 | 50.10 | 5 47 3.03 | 2.86 |
| | η Geminorum.... | | 41.6 | 0.8 | 20.0 | 39.2 | 58.0 | 17.2 | 36.0 | 6 6 38.97 | .......... | 0.08 | 50.12 | 6 5 48.93 | 48.90 |
| | δ Ursæ Minoris... | | ...... | ...... | 35.6 | 32.0 | 25.6 | 24.0 | 23.2 | 6 26 28.08 | —4 56.60 | — 3.36 | 50.15 | 6 20 37.97 | 38.03 |
| | 51 (Hev.) Cephei . | | 58.0 | 11.6 | 20.4 | 22.4 | 29.2 | 36.4 | 42.4 | 6 29 22.91 | .......... | + 4.15 | 50.15 | 6 28 36.91 | 36.92 |
| 3 | e Tauri........... | W. | 1.2 | 19.2 | 37.2 | 55.2 | 12.8 | 30.8 | 48.8 | 3 40 55.03 | .......... | 0.00 | — 52.07 | 3 40 2.96 | 3.13 |
| | $\gamma^1$ Eridani......... | | 0.0 | 18.0 | 36.0 | 54.0 | 12.0 | 30.4 | 48.4 | 3 51 54.11 | .......... | 0.00 | 52.09 | 3 51 2.02 | 2.10 |
| | γ Tauri. ......... | | 13.2 | 31.6 | 49.6 | 7.6 | 26.0 | 44.4 | 2.4 | 4 12 7.83 | . ....... | 0.00 | 52.11 | 4 11 15.72 | 15.77 |
| | α Tauri........... | | 16.8 | 34.8 | 52.8 | 11.2 | 29.6 | 47.6 | 6.8 | 4 28 11.37 | .......... | 0.00 | 52.13 | 4 27 19.24 | 19.12 |
| | $o^1$ Orionis......... | | 1.2 | 19.2 | 37.2 | 55.2 | 13.2 | 31.2 | 49.2 | 4 44 55.20 | .......... | 0 00 | 52.15 | 4 44 3.05 | 3.03 |
| | α Aurigæ......... | | 13.6 | 38.8 | 4.0 | 29.2 | 53.6 | 19.2 | 44.8 | 5 6 29.03 | .... ..... | 0.00 | 52.17 | 5 5 36.86 | 37.01 |
| | o Tauri...... .... | | 32.8 | 51.6 | 10.8 | 29.6 | 48.4 | 7.6 | 26.8 | 5 19 29.66 | .......... | 0.00 | 52.19 | 5 18 37.47 | 37.44 |
| | δ Orionis......... | | 20.4 | 37.6 | 55.2 | 13.2 | 30.0 | 48.0 | 5 6 | 5 25 12.86 | .......... | 0.00 | 52.20 | 5 24 20.66 | 20.64 |
| | ζ Tauri........... | | 36.8 | 55.6 | 14.4 | 32.8 | 51.6 | 10.4 | 29.2 | 5 29 32.97 | .......... | 0.00 | 52.21 | 5 28 40.76 | 40.72 |
| | α Orionis......... | | 2.0 | 20.0 | 37.6 | 55.2 | 12 8 | 34.4 | 48.4 | 5 47 55.20 | .......... | 0.00 | 52.23 | 5 47 2.97 | 2.88 |
| | η Geminorum..... | | 44.0 | 3.2 | 22.0 | 41.2 | 0.0 | 19.2 | 38.4 | 6 6 41.14 | .......... | 0.00 | 52.25 | 6 5 48.89 | 48.92 |
| | μ Geminorum..... | | 47.6 | 6.8 | 26.4 | 44.8 | ...... | ...... | ...... | 6 14 16.40 | + 28.52 | 0.00 | 52.27 | 6 13 52.65 | 52.67 |
| | Moon, 2d L..... | | 37.2 | 56.4 | 15.6 | 34.8 | 53.2 | 12.8 | 32.0 | 6 17 34.57 | .......... | 0.00 | 52.28 | 6 16 42.29 | ...... |
| | γ Geminorum..... | | 59.6 | 18.0 | 36.0 | 54.8 | 12.8 | 30.8 | 49.6 | 6 29 54.51 | .......... | 0.00 | 52.29 | 6 29 2.22 | 2.25 |
| | α Canis Majoris .. | | 29.6 | 48.0 | 6.0 | 24.8 | 42.8 | 1.2 | 20.0 | 6 39 24.63 | .......... | 0.00 | 52.31 | 6 38 32.32 | 32.15 |
| 4 | γ Tauri........... | E. | 15 2 | 33.2 | 51.6 | 9.6 | 27.6 | 46.0 | 4.4 | 4 12 9.66 | .... ..... | 0 00 | — 54.11 | 4 11 15.55 | 15.79 |
| | α Tauri........... | | 18.0 | 36.4 | 54.8 | 13.2 | 31.6 | 50.0 | 8.0 | 4 28 13.14 | .......... | 0.00 | 54.13 | 4 27 19.01 | 19.14 |
| ‡ | $o^1$ Orionis......... | | 2.8 | 20.8 | 38.8 | 56.8 | 15.6 | 33.2 | 51.6 | 4 44 57.09 | ........ . | 0.00 | 54.15 | 4 44 2.94 | 3.05 |
| | ι Tauri.... .... . | | 5.6 | 24.0 | 43.2 | 2.0 | 20.8 | 40.0 | 58.4 | 4 55 2.00 | .......... | 0.00 | 54.18 | 4 54 7.82 | 7.96 |
| | α Aurigæ. ........ | | 15.4 | 40.8 | 6.4 | 31.2 | 56.4 | 21.2 | 46.8 | 5 6 31.17 | .......... | 0.00 | 54.20 | 5 5 36.97 | 37.04 |
| | β Tauri........... | | 42.8 | 2.8 | 22.8 | 42.8 | 2.8 | 22.8 | 42.8 | 5 17 42.80 | .......... | 0.00 | 54.22 | 5 16 48.58 | 48 66 |
| | δ Orionis......... | | 22.4 | 40.0 | 57.6 | 14.8 | 32.0 | 50.0 | 7.6 | 5 25 14.91 | .......... | 0.00 | 54.22 | 5 24 20.69 | 20.66 |
| | α Leporis .... .... | | ...... | ...... | 43.2 | 1.2 | 20.2 | 38.0 | 56.8 | 5 27 19.88 | — 18.47 | 0.00 | 54.25 | 5 26 7.16 | 7.05 |
| | α Orionis. ........ | | 3.6 | 21.6 | 39.6 | 57.6 | 14.8 | 32.8 | 50.4 | 5 47 57.20 | ......... | 0.00 | 54 27 | 5 47 2.93 | 2.90 |
| | η Geminorum .... | | 46.4 | 5.4 | 24.4 | 43.6 | 2.4 | 21.2 | 40.0 | 6 6 43.34 | .......... | 0.00 | 54.28 | 6 5 49.06 | 48.95 |
| | μ Geminorum .... | | 49.6 | 8.8 | 28.0 | 47.2 | 6.0 | 25.2 | 44 0 | 6 14 46.97 | .......... | 0.00 | 54.30 | 6 13 52.67 | 52.70 |
| | δ Ursæ Min., S. P. | | ...... | ...... | ...... | 33.6 | 28.8 | ...... | 22.8 | 6 28 5.07 | —6 35.73 | 0.00 | 54.31 | 6 20 35.03 | 37.30 |
| | 51 (Hev.) Cephei... | | ...... | ...... | 24 8 | ...... | 38.0 | 43.6 | ...... | 6 33 35.47 | 4 4.67 | 0.00 | 54.31 | 6 28 36.49 | 37.86 |
| | γ Geminorum .... | | ...... | 20.0 | 38.8 | 56.4 | 14.8 | 33.2 | 52.0 | 6 30 5.87 | 9 18 | 0.00 | — 54.32 | 6 29 2.37 | 2.28 |

* Wire II recorded 52.0*s*. † Wire IV recorded 54.8*s*. ‡ Wire II recorded 18.8*s*.

*Longitude of junction of the Gila and Colorado*—Continued.

| DATE. | OBJECT. | LAMP. | CHRONOMETER TIMES OF TRANSIT. I. | II. | III. | IV. | V. | VI. | VII. | MEAN OF OBS'D WIRES | CORRECTIONS FOR— Imperfect ransits. | Instrument. | Chronometer. | OBSERVED A.R. | TABULAR A.R. |
|---|---|---|---|---|---|---|---|---|---|---|---|---|---|---|---|
| 1849. | | | s. | s. | s. | s. | s. | s. | s. | h. m. s. | m. s. | s. | m. s. | h. m. s. | s. |
| Nov. 4 | α Canis Majoris... | E. | 32.0 | 50.0 | 8.4 | 26.8 | 46.8 | 3.6 | 21.6 | 6 39 26.74 | .......... | 0.00 | — 54.33 | 6 38 32.41 | 32.18 |
| | ε Canis Majoris... | | 38.4 | 58.4 | 18.4 | 38.4 | 58.4 | ...... | ...... | 6 53 18.40 | + 20.05 | 0.00 | 54.34 | 6 52 44.11 | 43.85 |
| | ζ Geminorum ... | | 10 0 | 28.8 | 47.6 | 6.0 | 24.8 | 44.0 | 2.8 | 6 56 6.29 | .......... | 0.00 | 54.34 | 6 55 11.95 | 11.99 |
| | λ Geminorum .... | | 26.8 | 45.2 | 4.0 | 22.0 | 40.0 | 58.8 | 16.5 | 7 10 21.90 | .......... | 0.00 | 54.35 | 7 9 27.55 | 27.53 |
| | δ Geminorum .... | | ...... | ...... | ...... | 3.2 | 22.4 | 41.2 | 0.0 | 7 12 31.70 | — 28.45 | 0.00 | 54.35 | 7 11 8.90 | 8.93 |
| | Moon, 2d L..... | | 32.4 | 51.6 | 10.4 | 29.6 | 48.8 | 7.6 | 26.8 | 7 21 29.60 | .......... | 0 00 | 54.36 | 7 20 35.24 | ...... |
| | 68 Geminorum .... | | 1.2 | 19.2 | 38.0 | 56.0 | 14.4 | 32.8 | 50.8 | 7 25 56.06 | .......... | 0.00 | 54.37 | 7 25 1.69 | 1.98 |
| | α Canis Majoris... | | 26.8 | 45.2 | 2.8 | 20.4 | 38.4 | 56.0 | 14.0 | 7 32 20.51 | .......... | 0.00 | 54 38 | 7 21 26 13 | 26.06 |
| | β Geminorum .... | | 1.2 | 21.2 | 41.6 | 1.2 | 21.2 | 41.2 | 1.2 | 7 37 1.26 | .......... | 0.00 | 54.39 | 7 36 6.87 | 6.87 |
| 5 | μ Geminorum .... | W. | 50.4 | 9.6 | 28.8 | 48.0 | 7.2 | 26.0 | 45.2 | 6 14 47.86 | .......... | + 0.17 | — 55.17 | 6 13 52.86 | 52.73 |
| | δ Ursæ Min., S. P. | | ...... | ...... | ...... | 37.6 | 35.2 | ...... | 26.4 | 6 28 13.07 | —6 34.77 | — 6.92 | 55.18 | 6 20 36.10 | 36.95 |
| | 51 (Hev.) Cephei .. | | ..... | ...... | ...... | ...... | 30.8 | 35.2 | 43.2 | 6 41 36.40 | 12 12.23 | + 8.55 | 55.18 | 6 28 37.54 | 38.28 |
| | γ Geminorum .... | | 2.0 | 20.4 | 38.8 | 57.2 | 15.6 | 34.0 | 42.4 | 6 29 57.20 | .......... | 0.12 | 55.18 | 6 29 2.14 | 2.30 |
| | α Canis Majoris... | | ...... | ...... | 9.2 | 27.6 | 45.6 | 3.6 | 22.4 | 6 39 45.68 | — 18.33 | — 0.12 | 55.20 | 6 38 32.03 | 32.21 |
| | ε Canis Majoris... | | ...... | ...... | 19.6 | 39.2 | 59.2 | 19.2 | 39.6 | 6 53 59.36 | 20.05 | 0.23 | 55.22 | 6 52 43.86 | 43.88 |
| | λ Geminorum .... | | 27.6 | 46.0 | 4.0 | 22.8 | 40.8 | 59.2 | 17.6 | 7 10 22.55 | .......... | + 0.12 | 55.25 | 7 9 27.42 | 27.55 |
| | 68 Geminorum .... | | 2.0 | 20.0 | 38.4 | 56.8 | 14.8 | 33.6 | 52.0 | 7 25 56.80 | .......... | 0.12 | 55.27 | 7 25 1.65 | 2.00 |
| | α Canis Minoris... | | 28.8 | 44.8 | 3.6 | 21.6 | 39.2 | 56.8 | 15.2 | 7 32 21.43 | .......... | 0.04 | 55.28 | 7 31 26.19 | 26.09 |
| | β Geminorum .... | | 2.4 | 22.0 | 42.4 | 2.0 | 22.0 | 42.0 | 2.0 | 7 37 2.14 | .......... | 0.22 | 55.28 | 7 36 7.05 | 6.90 |
| | 15 Argus .......... | | 6 8 | 26.0 | 45.6 | 4.4 | 23.2 | 42.8 | 2.4 | 8 2 4.46 | .......... | — 0.18 | 55.31 | 8 1 8.97 | 8.99 |
| | ζ Cancri .... .... | | 35.2 | 53.6 | 12.0 | 30.4 | 49.2 | 7.6 | 26.0 | 8 4 30.57 | .......... | + 0.13 | 55.31 | 8 3 35.39 | 35.13 |
| | Moon, 2d L..... | | 28.0 | 47.2 | 6.0 | 25.2 | 43.6 | 2.4 | 21.2 | 8 23 24.80 | .......... | 0.12 | 55.33 | 8 22 29.59 | ...... |
| | δ Cancri ......... | | 7.6 | 26.0 | 44.0 | 3.6 | 21.6 | 40.4 | 59.2 | 8 37 3.20 | .......... | 0.13 | 55.36 | 8 36 7.97 | 8.03 |
| | ε Hydræ ......... | | 50.8 | 8.8 | 26.4 | 44.0 | 1.6 | 19 2 | 37.2 | 8 39 44.00 | .......... | 0.05 | 55.36 | 8 38 48.69 | 48.73 |
| | α Cancri ......... | | 16.8 | 34.8 | 52.8 | 10.8 | 28.8 | 46.8 | 4.8 | 8 51 10.80 | .......... | 0.09 | 55.38 | 8 50 15.15 | 15.43 |
| 6 | α Canis Majoris... | E. | 34.0 | 53.6 | 11.6 | 29.6 | 48.0 | 6.4 | 24.8 | 6 39 29.71 | .......... | 0.00 | — 57.31 | 6 38 32.40 | 32.23 |
| | ε Canis Majoris... | | 41.2 | 1.2 | 21.2 | 41.2 | 1.2 | 21.2 | 41.2 | 6 53 41.20 | .......... | 0.00 | 57.33 | 6 52 43.87 | 43.91 |
| | ζ Geminorum .... | | ...... | ...... | 50.4 | 9.2 | 28.0 | 47.2 | 5.6 | 6 56 28.08 | — 18.80 | 0.00 | 57.33 | 6 55 11.95 | 12.05 |
| | λ Geminorum .... | | 30.0 | 48.0 | 6.0 | 24.4 | 43.6 | 1.6 | 20.0 | 7 10 24.80 | .......... | 0.00 | 57.37 | 7 9 27.43 | 27.57 |
| | β Canis Minoris... | | 4.0 | 22.0 | 40.0 | 57.6 | 16.0 | 33.6 | 51.2 | 7 19 57.77 | .......... | 0.00 | 57.38 | 7 19 0.39 | 0.33 |
| | 68 Geminorum .... | | 4.0 | 22.8 | 41.2 | 59.2 | 17.6 | 36.0 | 54.0 | 7 25 59.26 | .......... | 0.00 | 57.39 | 7 25 1.87 | 2.02 |
| | α Canis Minoris... | | 30.8 | 48.4 | 6.0 | 23.6 | 41.6 | 59.2 | 16.8 | 7 32 23.77 | .......... | 0.00 | 57.39 | 7 31 26.38 | 26.12 |
| | β Geminorum .... | | 4.4 | 24.4 | 44.4 | 4.4 | 24.4 | 44.4 | 4.4 | 7 37 4.40 | .......... | 0.00 | 57.39 | 7 36 7.01 | 6.94 |
| | 15 Argus .......... | | ...... | ...... | 47.2 | 6.4 | 26.0 | 45.2 | 4.8 | 8 2 25.92 | — 19.22 | 0.00 | 57.42 | 8 1 9.28 | 9.02 |
| | β Cancri ......... | | 26.0 | 44.0 | 1.6 | 18.8 | ...... | 54.8 | 12.8 | 8 9 16.33 | + 2.94 | 0.00 | 57.43 | 8 8 21,84 | 21.84 |
| | θ Cancri ......... | | ...... | 21.2 | 40.0 | 58.4 | 16.8 | 35.6 | 54.0 | 8 24 7.66 | — 9.28 | 0.00 | 57.45 | 8 23 0.93 | 1.19 |
| | δ Cancri ......... | | 10.0 | 28.0 | 47.2 | 5.6 | 24.0 | 42.4 | 1.2 | 8 37 5.49 | .......... | 0.00 | 57.47 | 8 36 8.02 | 8.16 |
| | ε Hydræ.......... | | ...... | 10.8 | 28.8 | 46.0 | 3.6 | 22.0 | 39.6 | 8 39 55 13 | — 8.86 | 0.00 | 57.47 | 8 38 48.80 | 48.76 |
| | α Cancri ......... | | 19.2 | 37.2 | 55.2 | 12.8 | 31.2 | 49.2 | 7.2 | 8 51 13.14 | .......... | 0.00 | 57.49 | 8 50 15.65 | 15.55 |
| | ξ Cancri ......... | | 42.4 | 1.6 | 20.8 | ...... | 58.4 | 18.0 | 37.2 | 9 1 39.73 | — 0.01 | 0.00 | 57.50 | 9 0 42.22 | 42.29 |
| | Moon, 2d L..... | | 38.4 | 57.2 | 15.6 | 34.0 | 52.8 | 11.2 | 29.6 | 9 22 34.11 | .......... | 0.00 | 57.53 | 9 21 36.58 | ...... |
| *20 | Moon, 1st L .... | E. | 5.5 | 24.5 | 43.0 | 1.8 | 20.5 | 39.5 | 58.5 | 20 16 1.90 | .......... | + 0.24 | + 12 22.04 | 20 28 24.18 | ...... |
| | ζ Cygni........... | | 9.5 | 30.0 | 50.0 | 10.0 | 30.5 | 50.5 | 11.0 | 20 54 10.21 | .......... | — 0.44 | 12 22.04 | 21 6 31.81 | 32.24 |
| | ι Capricorni...... | | 34.5 | 52.5 | 11.0 | 29.5 | 47.5 | 6.3 | 24.5 | 21 1 29.40 | .......... | + 0.24 | 12 22.04 | 21 13 51.68 | 51.65 |
| | α Cephei ......... | | ...... | ...... | ...... | ...... | 15.5 | 54.0 | 30.8 | 21 3 53.43 | —1 14.70 | — 1.45 | 12 22.04 | 21 14 59.32 | 59.43 |
| | β Aquarii .... .... | | 23.0 | 40.5 | 58.5 | 16.2 | 33.5 | 51.5 | 9.8 | 21 11 16.14 | .......... | + 0.08 | 12 22.04 | 21 23 38.26 | 38.20 |
| | β Cephei ......... | | ...... | ...... | 32.0 | 32.8 | 13.8 | 5.0 | 56.0 | 21 15 13.92 | — 51.14 | — 2.11 | 12 22.04 | 21 27 42.71 | 42.60 |
| | ε Pegasi.......... | | 32.5 | 50.5 | 8.5 | 26.0 | 44.0 | 1.5 | 19.5 | 21 24 26.07 | .......... | 0.12 | 12 22.04 | 21 36 47.99 | 48.09 |
| †22 | Moon, 1st L .... | E. | 34.4 | 52.8 | 11.2 | 29.2 | 47.6 | 6.4 | 24.4 | 22 10 29.43 | .......... | 0.00 | — 1 29.88 | 22 8 59.55 | ...... |
| | σ Aquarii......... | | 17.2 | 35.4 | 52.8 | 10.8 | 28.8 | 46.8 | 4.8 | 22 24 10.91 | .......... | 0.00 | 1 29.88 | 22 23 41.03 | 40.98 |
| | ζ Pegasi.......... | | 34.4 | 52.4 | 10.4 | ...... | 45.6 | 3.6 | 21.6 | 22 35 28.00 | — 0.01 | 0.00 | 1 29.88 | 22 38 58.11 | 58.15 |
| ‡23 | α Aquarii......... | E. | 42.8 | 0.8 | 18.4 | 35.6 | 52.8 | 10.8 | 28.8 | 21 59 35.71 | .......... | 0.00 | — 1 32.22 | 21 58 3.49 | 3.53 |
| | θ Aquarii......... | | 32.4 | 50.4 | 8.4 | 26.4 | 44.4 | 2.4 | 20.8 | 23 10 26.46 | .......... | 0.00 | 1 32.24 | 22 8 54.22 | 53.58 |
| | σ Aquarii......... | | 19.6 | 37.6 | 55.6 | 13.6 | 30.8 | 48.8 | 7.2 | 23 24 13.31 | .......... | 0.00 | 1 32.26 | 22 32 41.05 | 40.97 |
| | ζ Pegasi ......... | | 37.2 | 54.8 | 12.4 | 30.4 | 48.4 | 6.0 | 24.0 | 23 35 30.46 | .......... | 0.00 | 1 32.28 | 22 33 58.18 | 58.14 |
| | λ Aquarii .... .... | | 25.2 | 43.2 | 1.2 | 18.8 | 36.0 | 54 0 | 12.0 | 23 46 18.63 | .......... | 0.00 | 1 32.29 | 22 44 46.34 | 46.25 |
| | α Piscis Australis.. | | 50.8 | 11.2 | 32.0 | 52.4 | 12.4 | 32.4 | 53.2 | 23 50 52.06 | .......... | 0.00 | — 1 32.30 | 22 49 19.76 | 19.87 |

* Chronometer 2475. † Chronometer 719. ‡ Wire IV recorded 34.6s. All these wires increased 10s.

*Longitude of junction of the Gila and Colorado*—Continued.

| DATE. | OBJECT. | LAMP. | CHRONOMETER TIMES OF TRANSIT. I. | II. | III. | IV. | V. | VI. | VII. | MEAN OF OBS'D WIRES | CORRECTIONS FOR— Imperfect transits. | Instrument. | Chronometer. | OBSERVED A.R. | TABULAR A.R. |
|---|---|---|---|---|---|---|---|---|---|---|---|---|---|---|---|
| 1849. | | | *s.* | *s.* | *s.* | *s.* | *s.* | *s.* | *s.* | *h. m. s.* | *s.* | *s.* | *m. s.* | *h. m. s.* | *s.* |
| Nov. 23 | Moon 1st L..... | E. | 46.0 | 4.0 | 22.0 | 40.0 | 58.4 | 16.4 | 34.4 | 23 0 40.17 | .......... | 0.00 | — 1 32.30 | 22 59 7.87 | ...... |
| | φ Aquarii......... | | 11.2 | 29.2 | 46.2 | 4.4 | 22.0 | 40.0 | 58.0 | 23 8 4.43 | .......... | 0.00 | 1 32.31 | 23 6 32.12 | 32.27 |
| | χ Aquarii......... | | 47.2 | 4.8 | 22.8 | 40.8 | 58.8 | 16.4 | 34.4 | 23 12 40.74 | .......... | 0.00 | 1 32.32 | 23 11 8.42 | 3.34 |
| 24 | σ Aquarii......... | E. | 22.0 | 40.0 | 58.0 | 16.0 | 34.0 | 52.0 | 10.0 | 22 24 16.00 | .......... | + 0.14 | — 1 35.09 | 22 22 41.05 | 40.95 |
| | ξ Pegasi.......... | | 39.2 | 57.6 | 15.6 | 3).2 | 52.8 | 8.8 | 26.8 | 22 35 33.43 | .......... | — 0.12 | 1 35.11 | 22 33 58.20 | 58.13 |
| | λ Aquarii......... | | 27.6 | 46.0 | 3.6 | 21.2 | 38.4 | 56.8 | 14.4 | 22 46 21.14 | .......... | + 0.10 | 1 35.12 | 22 44 46.12 | 46.24 |
| | α Piscis Australis. | | 53.6 | 14.0 | 34.0 | 54.4 | 14.8 | 35.6 | 55.6 | 22 50 54.57 | .......... | 0.39 | 1 35.12 | 22 49 19.84 | 19.86 |
| | φ Aquarii........ | | 14.0 | 32.0 | 49.6 | 7.2 | 24.8 | 42.4 | 0.4 | 23 8 7.20 | .......... | 0.08 | 1 35.15 | 23 6 32.13 | 32.25 |
| | χ Aquarii......... | | 50.0 | 8.0 | 26.0 | 43.6 | 1.2 | 19.6 | 37.2 | 23 12 43.66 | .......... | 0.12 | 1 35.15 | 23 12 8.63 | 8.33 |
| | 20 Piscium......... | | 55.2 | 13 2 | 30.8 | 48.4 | 6.0 | 23.6 | 40.8 | 23 41 28.29 | .......... | 0.04 | 1 35.18 | 23 40 13.15 | 13.24 |
| | Moon, 1st L ... | | 34.0 | 52.0 | 10.0 | 28.0 | 46.0 | 4.0 | 22.0 | 23 51 28.00 | .......... | 0.09 | 1 35.21 | 23 49 52 88 | ...... |
| | 33 Piscium......... | | 20.8 | 38 8 | 56.4 | 14.0 | 31.6 | 49.2 | 6.8 | 23 59 13.94 | .......... | 0.08 | 1 35.22 | 23 57 38.80 | 38.75 |
| | γ Pegasi.......... | | 11.6 | 30.0 | 48.0 | 6.0 | 24.0 | 42.0 | 0.8 | 0 7 6.06 | .......... | — 0.17 | 1 35.23 | 0 5 30.66 | 30.76 |
| 25 | 20 Piscium......... | W. | 57.6 | 15.6 | 32.2 | 50.8 | 8.0 | ...... | 43.2 | 23 41 44.73 | + 5.86 | 0.00 | — 1 37.36 | 23 40 13.23 | 13.22 |
| | 27 Piscium......... | | 42.8 | 0.4 | 18.4 | 35.6 | 53.6 | 12.4 | 28.8 | 23 52 36.00 | .......... | 0.00 | 1 37.38 | 23 50 58.62 | 59.06 |
| | 33 Piscium......... | | 22.8 | 40.8 | 58.4 | 16.4 | 34.0 | 51.6 | 9.6 | 23 59 16.23 | .......... | 0.00 | 1 37.38 | 23 57 38.85 | 38.74 |
| | α Andromedæ .... | | ...... | 36.0 | 56.0 | 16.4 | 36.0 | 56.0 | 16.0 | 0 2 26.13 | — 9.97 | 0.00 | 1 37.39 | 0 0 38.77 | 38.52 |
| | γ Pegasi.......... | | 14.0 | 32.0 | 50.0 | 8.0 | 26.0 | 44.0 | 2.0 | 0 7 8.00 | ......... | 0.00 | 1 37.39 | 0 5 30 61 | 30.75 |
| | δ Piscium......... | | 38.4 | 56.0 | 14.0 | 31.6 | ...... | ...... | ...... | 0 42 5.00 | + 26.52 | 0.00 | 1 37.44 | 0 40 54.08 | 53.96 |
| | Moon, 1st L .... | | ...... | 58.8 | 16.8 | 34.8 | 52.8 | 10.4 | 28.4 | 0 43 43.67 | — 8.96 | 0.00 | 1 37.44 | 0 41 57.27 | ..... |
| | 20 Ceti............ | | ...... | 22.4 | 40.0 | 58.0 | 15.6 | 52.8 | 50.8 | 0 47 6.60 | 8.79 | 0.00 | 1 37.44 | 0 45 20.37 | 20.26 |
| 27 | Moon, 1st L.... | E. | 57.0 | 15.5 | 33.5 | 52.0 | 10.0 | 28.5 | 47.0 | 2 20 51.93 | .......... | — 0.68 | + 12 25.83 | 2 33 17.08 | ...... |
| | μ Ceti............ | | 32.0 | 50.0 | 8.0 | 25.5 | 43.5 | 1.5 | 19.0 | 2 24 25.64 | .......... | 0.69 | 12 25.83 | 2 36 50.78 | 50.58 |
| | α Ceti............ | | 8.0 | 26.0 | 43.5 | 1.0 | 18.5 | 36.5 | 54.0 | 2 42 1.07 | .......... | 0.25 | 12 25.83 | 2 54 26.65 | 26.90 |
| | δ Arietis ......... | | 43.5 | 2.5 | 21.0 | 39.5 | 58.0 | 17.0 | 35.5 | 2 50 39.57 | .......... | 1.44 | 12 25.83 | 3 3 3.96 | 3.92 |
| | α Persei........... | | 57.5 | 24.5 | 51.5 | 18.0 | 45.0 | 12.5 | 39.5 | 3 1 18.36 | ......... | 4.81 | 12 25.83 | 3 13 39.98 | 39.38 |
| 29 | e Tauri........... | E. | 43.2 | 11.2 | 29.2 | 46.2 | ...... | ...... | ...... | 3 41 19.95 | + 26.81 | — 0.80 | — 1 42.73 | 3 40 3.23 | 3.41 |
| | λ Tauri........... | | ...... | ...... | 49.2 | 6.4 | 24.8 | 42.4 | ...... | 3 54 15.70 | — 8.91 | 0.91 | 1 42.75 | 3 52 23.06 | 22.92 |
| | γ Tauri........... | | 5.2 | 23.6 | 42.0 | 0.0 | 18.0 | 36.4 | 54.4 | 4 13 59.94 | .......... | 1.17 | 1 42.77 | 4 12 16.00 | 16.10 |
| | α Tauri........... | | 8.8 | 26.8 | 45.2 | 3.2 | 22.0 | 40 4 | 58.4 | 4 29 3.54 | .......... | 1.24 | 1 42.79 | 4 27 19.51 | 19.53 |
| | Moon, 1st L.... | | 20.4 | 38.8 | 58.0 | 16.4 | 35.2 | 54.4 | 13.2 | 4 39 16.63 | .......... | 1.31 | 1 42.81 | 4 37 32.51 | ...... |
| | ι Tauri .......... | | 56.4 | 15.2 | 34.0 | 52.8 | 12.0 | 30.8 | 49.6 | 4 55 52.97 | .......... | 1.67 | 1 42.82 | 4 54 8.48 | 8.33 |
| | α Aurigæ......... | | 9.2 | 34.4 | 59.6 | 24.8 | 50.4 | 15.2 | 40.8 | 5 7 24.91 | .......... | 4.40 | 1 42.84 | 5 5 37.67 | 37.67 |

The following are the results from the observations at the observatory near the junction of the Gila and Colorado:

| | | *h. m. s.* | | | *h. m. s.* |
|---|---|---|---|---|---|
| Oct. | 3 | 7 38 47.04 | Nov. | 1 | 7 38 30.58 |
| | 4 | 37.61 | | 2 | 32.39 |
| | 5 | 33.82 | | 3 | 29.66 |
| | 6 | 27.69 | | 4 | 28.44 |
| | 7 | 33.70 | | 5 | 30.30 |
| | 23 | 5.84 | | 6 | 22.42 |
| | 24 | 31.95 | | 20 | 32.43 |
| | 25 | 37 40.18 | | 22 | 27.53 |
| | 26 | 38 31.64 | | 23 | 23.44 |
| | 27 | 26.66 | | 24 | 45.40 |
| | 28 | 23.62 | | 25 | 14.99 |
| | 29 | 16.17 | | 27 | 25.72 |
| | 30 | 21.74 | | 29 | 25.25 |
| | 31 | 9.14 | | | |

| | *h. m. s.* |
|---|---|
| Mean | 7 38 25.75 |
| Longitude of the same, computed in the field from the Greenwich ephemeris for 1849 | 7 38 12.53 |
| Difference | 13.22 |

| | *s.* |
|---|---|
| Probable error of single observation | ± 8.71 |
| Probable error of mean result | ± 1.71 |

III.—*Latitude of Camp Riley, near Initial Point on Pacific, determined*

| Date. | 5461<br>5507 | 5596<br>5620 | 5658<br>5708 | 5765<br>5937 | 6094<br>6129 | 6091<br>6482 | 6091<br>6528 | 6246<br>6482 | 6246<br>6528 | 6428<br>6642 | 6428<br>6647 | 6476<br>6642 | 6476<br>6647 | 6724<br>6741 | 6761<br>6814 | 6867<br>6893 |
|---|---|---|---|---|---|---|---|---|---|---|---|---|---|---|---|---|
| | " | " | " | " | " | " | " | " | " | " | " | " | " | " | " | " |
| July 25 | ........ | 45.09 | ........ | 45.41 | 45.50 | ........ | ........ | ........ | ........ | 40.36 | 42.56 | 44.30 | ........ | 37.52 | ........ | ........ |
| 26 | ........ | 47.04 | ........ | 43.80 | ........ | ........ | ........ | ........ | ........ | ........ | ........ | ........ | ........ | ........ | ........ | ........ |
| 27 | 44.97 | 49.50 | ........ | 40.50 | ........ | ........ | ........ | ........ | ........ | ........ | ........ | ........ | ........ | ........ | ........ | ........ |
| 28 | ........ | 45.66 | ........ | 42.85 | ........ | ........ | ........ | ........ | ........ | ........ | ........ | ........ | ........ | ........ | ........ | ........ |
| Aug. 2 | ........ | 44.82 | ........ | 42.10 | 43.82 | ........ | 44.20 | ........ | ........ | 39.31 | 42.67 | 43.18 | 46.55 | ........ | ........ | ........ |
| 3 | 45.14 | ........ | ........ | ........ | ........ | 44.49 | 44.46 | ........ | ........ | ........ | ........ | ........ | ........ | ........ | ........ | ........ |
| 4 | 44.54 | ........ | ........ | 43.20 | ........ | ........ | ........ | ........ | ........ | ........ | ........ | ........ | ........ | ........ | ........ | ........ |
| 6 | 43.49 | 45.52 | ........ | ........ | ........ | ........ | ........ | ........ | ........ | ........ | ........ | ........ | ........ | ........ | ........ | ........ |
| 7 | 46.69 | ........ | ........ | 41.96 | ........ | ........ | ........ | ........ | ........ | ........ | ........ | ........ | ........ | ........ | ........ | ........ |
| 11 | ........ | ........ | 41.18 | 46.06 | ........ | ........ | ........ | 44.80 | 46.33 | ........ | ........ | ........ | ........ | 39.64 | ........ | 46.61 |
| 13 | ........ | ........ | ........ | ........ | ........ | ........ | ........ | 43.01 | 43.17 | ........ | ........ | ........ | ........ | 44.12 | ........ | 41.72 |
| 14 | ........ | ........ | ........ | 42.41 | ........ | 45.58 | 45.14 | ........ | ........ | ........ | ........ | ........ | ........ | 41.38 | ........ | 42.62 |
| 17 | ........ | ........ | ........ | 42.47 | ........ | 43.91 | 41.82 | ........ | ........ | ........ | ........ | ........ | ........ | ........ | ........ | 47.36 |
| 18 | ........ | ........ | ........ | 45.08 | ........ | 42.35 | 42.94 | ........ | ........ | ........ | ........ | ........ | ........ | 38.68 | ........ | 44.27 |
| | 44.97 | 46.27 | 41.18 | 43.26 | 44.66 | 44.08 | 43.71 | 43.91 | 44.75 | 39.84 | 42.62 | 43.74 | 46.55 | 40.27 | 41.32 | 44.52 |

| Date. | 5918<br>5985 | 6091<br>6482 | 6091<br>6528 | 6246<br>6482 | 6246<br>6528 | 6652<br>6754 | 6661<br>6754 | 6678<br>6754 | 6865<br>6952 | 7035<br>7082 | 7035<br>7125 | 7055<br>7088 | 7055<br>7125 | 7176<br>7324 | 7193<br>7324 | 7421<br>7476 |
|---|---|---|---|---|---|---|---|---|---|---|---|---|---|---|---|---|
| | " | " | " | " | " | " | " | " | " | " | " | " | " | " | " | " |
| Aug. 21 | 46.67 | ........ | 45.39 | ........ | ........ | ........ | ........ | ........ | ........ | ........ | ........ | ........ | ........ | ........ | ........ | ........ |
| 22 | ........ | 43.05 | 43.42 | 44.79 | 45.25 | ........ | ........ | 39.55 | 40.92 | 44.66 | ........ | 45.83 | ........ | 35.75 | ........ | ........ |
| 23 | 44.63 | 39.27 | ........ | ........ | ........ | 40.34 | 41.56 | 39.45 | 37.60 | 44.07 | ........ | 45.05 | ........ | ........ | ........ | ........ |
| 24 | 46.96 | 44.43 | 45.00 | 42.24 | 46.21 | ........ | ........ | ........ | 41.17 | 49.69 | 47.72 | 48.59 | 46.62 | 36.17 | 38.60 | 46.34 |
| 25 | 46.22 | 45.05 | 48.66 | ........ | ........ | 43.13 | 44.34 | 42.65 | 41.71 | 44.72 | 43.51 | 44.55 | 43.26 | ........ | ........ | ........ |
| Sept. 4 | ........ | 44.63 | 44.00 | ........ | ........ | 43.08 | 42.59 | 41.12 | 42.83 | ........ | ........ | 44.93 | 41.46 | 38.87 | 40.94 | 42.06 |
| 5 | ........ | 47.68 | 41.45 | ........ | ........ | ........ | ........ | 39.00 | 37.72 | ........ | ........ | ........ | ........ | ........ | ........ | ........ |

There are 190 results obtained from observations on eighty-two different stars.

| | ° ′ ″ |
|---|---|
| By giving the same weight to each observation (mean of all the observations) we have for the latitude ... | 32 35 43.53 |
| Latitude by giving to each pair a weight depending on the number of observations, (most probable)...... | 32 35 43.54 |
| General mean of each night........................................................................ | 32 35 43.73 |
| General mean of each pair......................................................................... | 32 35 43.56 |
| General mean of all the observations.............................................................. | 32 35 43.53 |

*with a Zenith Telescope of 46-inch focal length: By W. H. Emory.*

| 6959<br>7107 | 6959<br>7121 | 6959<br>7160 | 7193<br>7318 | 7418<br>7455 | 7547<br>7595 | 7651<br>7689 | 7759<br>7788 | 7827<br>7875 | 7908<br>7961 | 7997<br>8058 | 8056<br>8147 | 8058<br>8147 | 8268<br>8315 | Mean of each night's observations. |
|---|---|---|---|---|---|---|---|---|---|---|---|---|---|---|
| ″ | ″ | ″ | ″ | ″ | ″ | ″ | ″ | ″ | ″ | ″ | ″ | ″ | ″ | ° ′ ″ |
| 44.36 | 43.55 | 44.14 | 47.69 | 44.25 | 39.57 | 42.68 | 40.91 | ........ | ........ | ........ | ...... | ...... | ...... | 32 35 43.19 |
| ........ | ........ | ........ | ........ | ........ | ........ | ........ | ........ | ........ | ........ | ........ | ...... | ...... | ...... | 45.42 |
| ........ | ........ | ........ | ........ | ........ | ........ | ........ | ........ | ........ | ........ | ........ | ...... | ...... | ...... | 44.99 |
| ........ | ........ | ........ | ........ | ........ | ........ | ........ | ........ | ........ | ........ | ........ | ...... | ...... | ...... | 44.26 |
| ........ | ........ | ........ | ........ | 43.04 | 40.81 | ........ | 39.55 | ........ | 44.37 | ........ | 46 39 | ...... | ...... | 43.14 |
| ........ | ........ | ........ | ........ | ........ | ........ | ........ | ........ | ........ | ........ | ........ | ...... | ...... | ...... | 44.70 |
| ........ | ........ | ........ | ........ | ........ | ........ | ........ | ........ | ........ | ........ | ........ | ...... | ...... | ...... | 43.87 |
| ........ | ........ | ........ | ........ | ........ | ........ | ........ | ........ | ........ | ........ | ........ | ...... | ...... | ...... | 44.51 |
| ........ | ........ | ........ | ........ | ........ | ........ | ........ | ........ | ........ | ........ | ........ | ...... | ...... | ...... | 44.33 |
| 47.20 | 46.85 | 47.21 | 46.48 | 41.98 | 40.85 | 43.07 | 40.50 | ........ | 40.52 | ........ | ...... | ...... | ...... | 43.95 |
| 44.56 | 45.36 | ........ | ........ | ........ | 38.89 | 45.02 | 39.00 | 42 58 | 40.81 | ........ | ...... | 41.94 | 43.84 | 42.62 |
| 45.01 | 46.00 | 46.24 | ........ | ........ | ........ | ........ | ........ | ........ | ........ | ........ | ...... | ...... | ...... | 44.30 |
| 42.78 | 41.83 | 43.63 | ........ | 43.76 | ........ | 44.17 | 39.07 | 42.16 | 38.52 | ........ | ...... | ...... | ...... | 42.52 |
| 44.87 | 45.91 | 46.37 | ........ | 41.70 | ........ | 46.83 | 40.66 | 46.70 | ........ | 41.85 | ...... | 44.12 | 43.84 | 43.74 |
| | | | | | | | | | | | | | | 32 35 43.97 Mean of each night. |
| 44.80 | 44.92 | 45.52 | 47.08 | 42.95 | 40.03 | 44.35 | *39.95 | 43.81 | 41.05 | 41.85 | 46.39 | 43.03 | 43.84 | 32 35 43.63 Mean of each pair. |
| | | | | | | | | | | | | | | 32 35 43.80 Mean of observa'ns. |

* Rejected. 7759 not well determined.

| 7567<br>7598 | 7605<br>7522 | 7605<br>7547 | 7629<br>7696 | 7629<br>7698 | 7659<br>7696 | 7659<br>7698 | 7815<br>7912 | 7971<br>8024 | 7971<br>8083 | 8125<br>8227 | 8268<br>8315 | Mean of each night's observations. |
|---|---|---|---|---|---|---|---|---|---|---|---|---|
| ″ | ″ | ″ | ″ | ″ | ″ | ″ | ″ | ″ | ″ | ″ | ″ | ° ′ ″ |
| ........ | ........ | ........ | ........ | ........ | ........ | ........ | ........ | ........ | ........ | ........ | ........ | 32 35 46.03 |
| ........ | 41.10 | 44.87 | ........ | 36.42 | ........ | 43.23 | 46.33 | 39.92 | 42.00 | 42.15 | ........ | 42.30 |
| ........ | ........ | ........ | ........ | 39.40 | ........ | 46.76 | 44.43 | 40.41 | 37.90 | 43.39 | ........ | 41.60 |
| 49.14 | ........ | ........ | 40.76 | 40.40 | 47.93 | 47.57 | 49.93 | 43.21 | 42.68 | 44.73 | 44.18 | 44.79 |
| ........ | ........ | ........ | ........ | ........ | ........ | ........ | ........ | ........ | ........ | ........ | ........ | 44.34 |
| 42.83 | ........ | ........ | ........ | 37.13 | ........ | 45.00 | 45.80 | 40.43 | 39.24 | 43.08 | 43.77 | 42.31 |
| ........ | ........ | ........ | ........ | ........ | ........ | ........ | ........ | ........ | ........ | ........ | ........ | 41.46 |
| | | | | | | | | | | | | 32 35 43.26 Mean of each night. |
| | | | | | | | | | | | | 32 35 46.48 Mean of each pair. |
| | | | | | | | | | | | | 32 35 43.32 Mean of observ'ns. |

| | ″ |
|---|---|
| Probable error in determinations of the latitude from a single pair.................................. | 1.48 |
| Limit of probable error in determinations of the latitude from the results of all the pairs............ | 0.198 |

## IV.—*Observations for latitude at Observatory near the junction of the Gila and Colorado rivers: By Lieut. A. W. Whipple.*

| Date. | 7480 7528 | 7547 7595 | 7950 7997 | 8058 8146 | 8280 8312 | 7 66 | 6867 6893 | 7107 7120 | 7176 7206 | 7302 7310 | |
|---|---|---|---|---|---|---|---|---|---|---|---|
| 1849. | ° ′ ″ | ° ′ ″ | ° ′ ″ | ″ | ° ′ ″ | ° ′ ″ | ″ | ″ | ″ | ″ | ° ′ ″ |
| | | | | | | | | | | | *32 43 27.36 |
| Oct. 6 | | 32 43 37.81 | 32 43 38.61 | | 32 43 48.97 | 32 43 51.92 | | | | | 32 43 37.16 |
| 7 | 28.44 | | | | | | | | | | 32 43 41.60 |
| 8 | 25.74 | | 42.49 | 41.31 | 44.24 | 47.93 | | | | | 32 43 43.17 |
| 9 | 29.04 | | 40.56 | 43.40 | 47.48 | 51.31 | | | | 40.43 | 32 43 44.94 |
| 10 | | 35.37 | | 43.21 | 42.82 | 50.93 | 44.31 | 41.96 | 36.82 | | 32 43 51.31 |
| 11 | | | 41.72 | 44.66 | 43.23 | 50.31 | | 41.39 | 38.10 | | 32 43 44.31 |
| 12 | 27.40 | 39.34 | 46.27 | 46.04 | | 54.44 | | 42.59 | 39.11 | | 32 43 42.63 |
| 13 | 26.05 | 36.54 | | | | | | 44.59 | 37.78 | 39.96 | 32 43 37.95 |
| 15 | | 37.76 | 39.97 | 40.39 | 42.88 | | | | | 39.47 | 32 43 39.92 |
| Mean for each pair. | 32 43 27.36 | 37.16 | 41.60 | 43.17 | 44.94 | 51.31 | 44.31 | 42.63 | 37.95 | 39.92 | |
| Mean of nine pairs | | | | | | | | | | | 32 43 42.54 |

* Rejected.

## V.—*Triangulation by which the observed latitude and longitude of Camp Riley was transferred to the Initial Point of the boundary on the Pacific: By Major Emory.*

### MEASUREMENT OF THE BASE LINE.

(*Unit of measure, a metre graduated by Gambey, of Paris.*)

| | |
|---|---|
| 1st measurement, with rods made of seasoned red wood | 4536.7895 metres. |
| 2d measurement, with steel wires belonging to Señor Salazar, surveyor of the Mexican commission | 4536.60 " |
| | 2) 3895 |
| Result adopted | 4536.6947 |

### SOLUTION OF THE TRIANGLE.

| Stations. | No. of observations. | Observed angles. | Distribution and error. | Spherical excess. | Plane angles and distances. | Logarithms. |
|---|---|---|---|---|---|---|
| | | ° ″ ″ | ″ | | ° ′ ″ | |
| East base | 24 | 37 25 57.5 | + 0.033 | 00 | 37 25 57.53 | 9.7837811 |
| West base | 16 | 107 34 1.2 | + 0.033 | 00 | 107 34 1.23 | |
| Initial point | 24 | 35 0 1.2 | + 0.033 | 00 | 35 0 1.23 | 9.7585949 |
| | | | + 0.1 | | | |
| East base to west base | | | | | 4536.39 | 3.6567391 |
| East base to initial point | | | | | 7540.59 | 3.8774051 |
| West base to initial point | | | | | 4807.56 | 3.6819252 |

### *Calculation of the Geographical Position of the Initial Point.*

Azimuth of the line from east base to initial point determined by measurement of angle made with meridian of the observatory, and also by various measurements of the elongations of Polaris: Counting from the south towards the west, 24° 31′ 31″.

Latitude of east base situated precisely in the meridian of observatory at Camp Riley, and determined, by direct measurement, to be south of it 1″.2; north latitude, 32° 35′ 42″.33.

East base to initial point = K = 7540.59 metres, H = 32° 35′ 42″.33.

P = 117° 03′ 16″.5; Z = 24° 31′ 31″.

| | | | |
|---|---|---|---|
| Log. K............ | = 3.8774051 | 1st term H = | 32° 35′ 42″.33 |
| Log. $\frac{1}{\text{N sin. } 1''}$ | = 8.5093882 | 2d term H = | 3′ 42″.76 |
| Log. $u''$............ | = 12.3868933 | 3d term H = | |
| | | Lat. Initial Point = | 32° 31′ 59″.57 |

| | |
|---|---|
| (2d term H) log. (1 + E² cos.² H) | = 0.0020139 |
| Log. $u''$ | = 2.3868933 |
| Log. cos. Z | = 9.9589355 |
| Log. 2d term | = 2.3478427 |
| 2d term | = 222″.76 |

| | |
|---|---|
| Log. $u''$ | = 2.3868933 |
| Log. sin. Z | = 9.6181471 |
| | 12.0050504 |
| Log. cos. H | = 9.9258689 |
| | 2.0791815 = log. 120″ |

| | |
|---|---|
| P............. | = 117° 03′ 16″.5 |
| $\frac{u'' \text{ sin. Z}}{\text{Cos. H.}}$ | = 2′ 00″ |
| Long. Int. Pt. | = 117° 05′ 16″.5 |

| | |
|---|---|
| 3d term H log. $u''$ | = 2.3868933 |
| Log. sin. Z | = 9.6181471 |
| | 2.0050404 |
| | 2 |
| Log. $(u'' \text{ sin. Z})^2$ | = 4.0100808 |
| Log. $(1 + e^2 \text{ cos.}^2 \text{ H})$ | = 0.0020139 |
| Log. $\frac{\text{Sin. } 1''}{2}$ | = 4.3845449 |
| Log. tang. H......... | = 9.8057664 |
| | 8.2024060 |

*Calculation of the Geographical Position of Station "West Base."*

Measured azimuth of base line = Z = 61° 57′ 28″.5. Base line = K = 4536.69 metres.

| | |
|---|---|
| 1st term H......... | = 32° 35′ 42″.33 |
| 2d term H......... | = 1′ 09″.23 |
| 3d term H......... | = 0′ 00″.00 |
| H. or W. base | = 32° 34′ 33″.10 |

| | |
|---|---|
| Log. K.................. | = 3.6567391 |
| Log. $\frac{1}{\text{N. sin. } 1''}$ | = 8.5093882 |
| Log. $u''$.................. | = 2.1661273 |
| Log. $(1 + e^2 \text{ cos.}^2 \text{ H})$ | = 0.0020139 |
| Log. cos. Z......... | = 9.6722077 |
| | 1.8403489 |
| 2d term | = 69″.23 |

Log. $u''$............... $= 2.1661273$
Log. sin. Z........ $= 9.9457651$

$2.1118924$

Log. cos. H $= 9.9256623$

$2.1862301$

2d term P $= 153''.54 = 2'\ 33''.54$

P................. $= 117°\ 03'\ 16''.5$
2d term.......... $= \quad 2'\ 33''.54$

P. or long. of West Base $= 117°\ 05'\ 50''.04$

3d term—
Log. $u''$............... $= 2.1661273$
Log. sin. Z......... $= 9.9457651$

$2.1118924$

$2$

Log. $(u'' \text{ sin. Z})^2$ $= 4.2237848$
Log. $(1 + e^2 \cos.^2 \text{H})$ $= 0.0020139$
Log. $\frac{\text{Sin. } 1''}{2}$ $= 4.3845449$
Log. tang. H......... $= 9.8057664$

$8.4141100$

*Calculation of the Azimuth of the line from Initial Point of the Boundary to East Base.*

Log K $= 3.8774050 = 7540.59.$ $Z' = 180 + Z - \frac{u'' \text{ sin. Z}}{\text{Cos. L}'} \text{ sin. } \frac{1}{2}\,(\text{L} + \text{L}')$

$\frac{1}{\text{N. sin. } 1''}$ $= 8.5093881$
Sin. Z $= 9.6181471$

$2.0049402$

Cos. L′ $= 9.9258689$

$2.0790713$

$\frac{\text{Sin. L} + \text{L}'}{2}$ $= 9.7309790$

$64''.57 = 1.8100503$

Measured Z $=$ $24°\ 31'\ 16''$
$+\ 15$ err. in meridian.

$24°\ 31'\ 31''$
$180°$

$204°\ 31'\ 31''$
$1'\ 04''.5$

$Z' = 204°\ 30'\ 26''.5$

VI.—*Azimuth of straight line from Initial Point on the Pacific to junction of Gila and Colorado.*

In the computation for the direction of the line, the longitude of the initial point and the longitude of the junction of the Gila and Colorado are taken as determined in the field by the observations compared with the moon's place, as given in the Nautical Almanac (Greenwich.) On arriving at Washington, I obtained from Professor Airy his corresponding observations, made at Greenwich, and it will be seen that a change has been made in the absolute longitude of both places, but fortunately no material change is discoverable in the relative longitude of the two places. Now, an inspection of the formula used will show that the *difference* in longitude is the element used in determining the azimuth of the line connecting the two points. Hence the change deduced from comparison with the corresponding Greenwich observations does not affect this result.

The preceding pages show the process by which the latitude and longitude of Camp Riley was transferred to the initial point of the boundary on the Pacific.

A word on the subject of the transfer to the "junction" of the latitude and longitude of the observatory near that point; the distance between them was so small that the transfer may be considered as having been accomplished by direct measurement.

Lieutenant Whipple's report to me, November 30, 1849, gives—

| | ° ′ ″ |
|---|---|
| The longitude of observatory, $7^h\ 38^m\ 12^s.53$; in arc | 114 33 07.95 |
| The longitude of junction | 114 32 51.61 |
| Difference | 16.34 |

| | ° ′ ″ |
|---|---|
| Latitude of observatory, (see report of November 24) | 32 43 43.96 |
| Latitude of junction | 32 43 32.3 |
| Difference | 11.66 |

These, corresponding with my computations founded on the same data, were adopted; but it must be observed, to prevent future misunderstanding, that it was impracticable to measure the azimuth from the junction of the two rivers, (then under water,) and a point, B, (see sketch,) was selected in the azimuth produced, ascertained by direct measurement to be 73.5 feet south and 1,070 feet west of the junction, and here the monument was placed and the azimuth measured from it. The geographical position of this monument is, consequently,

| | ° ′ ″ |
|---|---|
| In north latitude | 32 43 31.6 |
| Uncorrected longitude | 114 33 04.3 |

The computation of the azimuth and length of the line of boundary extending from the initial point on the Pacific coast, near San Diego, to the junction of the Gila and Colorado, was based on the following assumption:

| | ° ′ ″ |
|---|---|
| Latitude of initial point on the Pacific | 32 31 59.63 |
| Latitude of junction of Gila and Colorado | 32 43 32.2 |
| Difference of longitude | 2 32 24.9 |

We compute the azimuth and distance by the formulæ given by *Puissant, Traitê de Geodesie,* Ed. III, Vol. 2, p. 316, using the following notation:

$a =$ equatorial radius $\qquad e =$ ellipticity $= \dfrac{a^2 - b^2}{b^2}$

$b =$ polar radius $\qquad$ Log. $e = 7.8273187$

$Z' =$ azimuth at the Gila, reckoned from the S. round by W.

$Z'' =$ azimuth at the initial point $\qquad \sigma =$ distance in arc.

$$\tan.\ l' = \frac{b}{a}\tan.\ L' \qquad \tan.\ l'' = \frac{b}{a}\tan.\ L''$$

In the spherical triangle formed by $l'$, $l''$, and P, we now compute the angles $180° - Z'$ and $Z'' - 180°$, the arc $\sigma$, and also $l$, = the latitude of the foot of the perpendicular from the pole, and obtain for a first approximation:

$$Z' = 85°\ 33'\ 25''.05 \qquad \sigma = 7739''.75$$

$$Z'' - 180° = 84°\ 11'\ 25''.21 \qquad l = 32°\ 54'\ 22''.69$$

Next we compute the correction $d\,P$, to be applied to the spheroidal difference of longitude P, by the formula

$$d\,P = -\,\sigma\,(\tfrac{1}{2}\,e - \tfrac{3}{8}\,e^2)\cos.\,l = +\,21''.72$$

And we get................ $P + d\,P = 2°\ 32'\ 46''.62$

Substituting this into the former computation, we obtain

$Z' = 85°\ 34'\ 14''.41$ $\qquad \sigma = 7758''.10$

$Z'' - 180° = 84°\ 12'\ 02''.89$ $\qquad l = 32°\ 54'\ 16''.71$

And by a second substitution of the latter values we obtain, finally,

$Z' = 85°\ 34'\ 14''.49$ $\qquad d\,P = +\,21''.77$

$Z'' - 180° = 84°\ 12'\ 02''.95$ $\qquad \sigma = 7758''.15$

We also compute $\sigma'$ and $\sigma''$, the arcs from $l'$ and $l''$ to the foot of the perpendicular $l$, viz: $\sigma' = 6°\ 52'\ 31''.5$ ; $\sigma'' = 9°\ 01'\ 49''.7$ ; and obtain the distance $s$ in metres by the expression

$$\frac{s}{b} = \sigma\,(1 + \tfrac{1}{4}\,e\sin.^2 l - \tfrac{3}{64}\,e^2\sin.^4 l) + (\sin.\,2\,\sigma'' - \sin.\,2\,\sigma')\,(\tfrac{1}{8}\,e\sin.^2 l - \tfrac{1}{32}\,e^2\sin.^4 l) - \cdots$$

| | | |
|---|---|---|
| 1st term .............. | $= +$ | 239187.0 |
| 2d term............... | $= +$ | 113.8 |
| 3d term............... | $= -$ | 0.0 |
| Distance $s$............ | $=$ | 239300.8 metres = 261692.0 yards = 148.689 miles. |

Azimuth at initial point on Pacific coast ............................................ $= 84°\ 12'\ 02''.95$

Azimuth at junction of Gila and Colorado............................................ $= 85°\ 34'\ 14''.49$

Length of line of boundary connecting above points.............................. = 148.689 miles

## B.

*Determinations of boundary line from the Rio Colorado of the west, to the intersection of the* 111*th meridian of longitude, west of Greenwich, and parallel* 31° 20′ *north latitude: By Lieutenant N. Michler, Topographical Engineers U. S. A.*

### I.—Azimuth line—astronomical positions.

The longitude of the initial point on the Rio Colorado, twenty English miles below its junction with the Gila, as agreed upon by Lieutenant N. Michler, Topographical Engineers United States Army, on the part of the United States, and Francisco Jimenez, first engineer of the Mexican commission, on the part of Mexico, was determined to be 114° 48′ 44.53″ west of Greenwich.

This result was obtained by transferring the longitude of the monument near the junction to the initial point, by Lieutenant Michler's triangulation of the "twenty English miles," the longitude of said monument having been previously obtained from observations by Lieutenant A. W. Whipple, Topographical Engineers, Assistant United States Boundary Survey, deduced from corresponding observations at Greenwich.

| | ° ′ ″ | |
|---|---|---|
| Longitude of the monument ......................................... | 114 36 22.20 | W. of Greenwich. |
| Difference of longitude between monument and initial point | + 12 22.33 | |
| Longitude of initial point ............................................ | 114 48 44.53 | |

| | ° ′ ″ | |
|---|---|---|
| The latitude of the initial point on the Rio Colorado was found to be.......................................................... | 32 29 44.45 | North. |

This latitude was obtained by a mean of results from observations with zenith telescopes by Lieutenant Michler and Señor Jimenez, at their respective observatories near the initial point, (reduced to Lieutenant Michler's observatory,) as follows:

| | ° ′ ″ | |
|---|---|---|
| Determination by Señor Jimenez | 32 29 41.53 | |
| Determination by Lieutenant Michler | 32 29 41.77 | |
| Mean latitude | 32 29 41.65 | North. |

This latitude of the observatory was then transferred to the initial point, by triangulation, by Lieutenant Michler. By transferring the latitude of the monument near the junction to the same observatory, by two different triangulations, one by Lieutenant Michler and the other by Señor A. Diaz, second engineer Mexican commission, the following were the results:

| | ° ′ ″ | |
|---|---|---|
| Known latitude of the monument near the junction | 32 43 31.58 | North. |
| Difference of latitude between monument and observatory, by Lieutenant Michler's triangulation | — 13 48.95 | |
| Latitude of observatory | 32 29 42.63 | North. |
| Known latitude of the monument near the junction | 32 43 31.58 | North. |
| Difference of latitude between monument and observatory, by Señor Diaz's triangulation | — 13 48.39 | |
| Latitude of observatory | 32 29 43.19 | North. |
| | 32 29 42.63 | " |
| Difference | 00.56 | |

The azimuth of the line from the junction of the Colorado and Gila, to Lieutenant Michler's observatory, is, at the latter point, 36° 14′ 10″ northeast, and its length 104024.34 feet.

The azimuth of the boundary line from the initial point on the Colorado to the intersection of the 111th meridian, west of Greenwich, and the parallel of 31° 20′ north latitude, is at the initial point 71° 20′ 43″.8 southeast, and at the point of intersection of parallel and meridian 69° 19′ 45″.94 northwest; the length of this line = 382844.87 metres, = 418684.3 yards, = 237.63565 English miles.

Monument No. II, made of cast-iron plates, and pyramidal in form, was placed on the edge of the desert, at a distance from the initial point of 4522.9 yards; its latitude was computed to be 32° 29′ 01″.48 north; its longitude 114° 46′ 14″.43 west of Greenwich. The azimuth of the boundary line at this point was computed to be 71° 19′ 23″.18 southeast.

The longitude of the observatory of the Mexican commission at Quitobaquita, near monuments VII and VIII, as determined by Señor Jimenez, first engineer, from ten lunar culminations, commencing July 23, 1856, and ending August 2, 1856, inclusive, was found to be 112° 52′ 25″.73 (7*h.* 31*m.* 29.775*s.*) west of Greenwich.

The latitude of observatory at Quitobaquita, as determined by Señor Jimenez, first engineer, from forty observations upon eight pairs of stars with zenith telescope, was found to be 31° 56′ 26″.57 north.

II.—*Results of calculations of geodetic latitudes and longitudes of points of triangulation of a line "twenty English miles in length," extending from the Monument, near the junction of the Gila and Colorado, to the Initial Point of the new azimuth line. Triangulation by Lieut. N. Michler, Topographical Engineers U. S. A. Computer, John O'Donoghue. Instrument, Bruner Theodolite.*

| Name of station. | Letter of station. | Name of side. | Name of angle. | Azimuth. | Angle of station. | Length of sides in feet. | Difference of latitude + north. | Difference of latitude — south. | Difference of longitude + west. | Difference of longitude — east. | Latitude of station. | Longitude of station. |
|---|---|---|---|---|---|---|---|---|---|---|---|---|
| | | | | ° ′ ″ | ° ′ ″ | | ′ ″ | ′ ″ | ′ ″ | ′ ″ | ° ′ ″ | ° ′ ″ |
| Monument | M | M C | ........... | 10 13 15.7 S.W. | ............... | 4,921.16 | ............ | — 0 47.9230 | + 0 10.2223 | ............ | 32 43 31.6 | 114 36 22.20 |
| Sierra Prieta | C | C H | F C H | 21 40 37 S.E. | 156 53 9 | 22,988.95 | ............ | — 3 31.4058 | ............ | — 1 39.3261 | 32 42 43.677 | 114 36 32.4223 |
| | H | H K | C H K | 48 3 25 S.W. | 110 16 51.5 | 19,247.3 | ............ | — 2 7.3320 | + 2 47.3941 | ............ | 32 39 12.2712 | 114 34 53.0962 |
| | K | K Q | H K Q | 20 29 39 S.W. | 207 32 15.6 | 6,606.97 | ............ | — 1 1.2414 | + 0 27.0420 | ............ | 32 37 4.9392 | 114 37 40.4903 |
| | Q | Q R | K Q R | 67 16 26 S.W. | 133 12 58.8 | 4,030.91 | ............ | — 0 15.4117 | + 0 43.4621 | ............ | 32 36 3.6978 | 114 38 7.5323 |
| | R | R W | Q R W | 2 3 12 S.E. | 249 19 14.7 | 7,161.32 | ............ | — 1 10.8210 | ............ | — 0 2.9990 | 32 35 48.2861 | 114 38 50.9944 |
| East stations | W | W V | R W V | 32 28 8 S.W. | 145 28 41.4 | 6,825.12 | ............ | — 0 56.9812 | + 0 42.8146 | ............ | 32 34 37.4651 | 114 38 47.9954 |
| | V | V X′ | W V X′ | 32 2 22 S.W. | 180 25 23 | 5,460.98 | ............ | — 0 32.7200 | + 0 33.8478 | ............ | 32 33 40.4839 | 114 39 30.8100 |
| | X′ | X′ Y′ | V X′ Y′ | 56 56 52 S.W. | 155 5 11.5 | 2,459.80 | ............ | — 0 13.2763 | + 0 24.0835 | ............ | 32 33 7.7639 | 114 40 4.6578 |
| | Y′ | Y′ Z′ | X′ Y′ Z′ | 37 44 30 S.W. | 199 12 8.8 | 9,677.29 | ............ | — 1 15.7318 | + 1 9.1879 | ............ | 32 32 54.4876 | 114 40 28.7413 |
| | Z′ | Z′ B′ | Y′ Z′ B′ | 25 35 37 S.W. | 192 8 16.3 | 14,028.38 | ............ | — 2 5.2035 | + 1 10.7553 | ............ | 32 31 38.7558 | 114 41 37.9292 |
| | B′ | B′ D′ | Z′ B′ D′ | 78 29 51 S.W. | 127 5 7.9 | 16,530.94 | ............ | — 0 45.7492 | + 3 9.1158 | ............ | 32 29 33.5523 | 114 42 48.6845 |
| | D′ | D′ F′ | B′ D′ F′ | 63 50 36 S.W. | 142 17 35 | 12,568.51 | + 0 54.8439 | ............ | + 2 11.7016 | ............ | 32 28 47.8031 | 114 45 57.8003 |
| Observatory near initial point, on Colorado | F′ | ........... | ........... | ............... | ............... | ............ | ............ | ............ | ............ | ............ | 32 29 42.6470 | 114 48 9.5019 |
| Monument | M | M F | ........... | 15 59 42.8 N.W. | ............... | 2,513.09 | + 0 23.9047 | ............ | + 0 8.1074 | ............ | 32 43 31.6 | 114 36 22.20 |
| Flag Staff (Fort Yuma) | F | F P | P F G | 83 55 37 S.W. | 99 55 25.4 | 33,944.60 | ............ | — 0 35.7091 | + 6 35.1297 | ............ | 32 43 55.5047 | 114 36 30.3074 |
| Pilot Knob | P | G P | F P G | 51 11 20 S.E. | 44 56 36.7 | 33,808.90 | ............ | — 3 29.7844 | ............ | — 5 8.1915 | 32 43 19.7956 | 114 43 5.4371 |
| | G | G L | P G L | 18 22 1 S.W. | 249 30 34.7 | 19,223.25 | ............ | — 3 0.5360 | + 1 10.8218 | ............ | 32 39 50.0112 | 114 37 57.2456 |
| | L | L S | G L S | 43 30 0 S.W. | 205 8 37.2 | 4,216 71 | ............ | — 0 30.2684 | + 0 33.9338 | ............ | 32 36 49.4752 | 114 39 8.0674 |
| West stations | S | Q T | L S T | 8 55 17 S.W. | 145 25 35.6 | 9,492.13 | ............ | — 1 32.7926 | + 0 17.2045 | ............ | 32 36 19.2068 | 114 39 42.0012 |
| | T | T W | S T W | 20 11 14 S.W. | 191 16 6.2 | 10,055.98 | ............ | — 1 33.3977 | + 0 40.5466 | ............ | 32 34 46.4142 | 114 39 59.2057 |
| | W | W Z | T W Z | 57 49 27 S.W. | 217 38 34.5 | 9,572.11 | ............ | — 0 50 4506 | + 1 34.6498 | ............ | 32 33 13.0165 | 114 40 39.7523 |
| | Z | Z A′ | W Z A′ | 37 13 59 S.W. | 159 24 23.3 | 10,754.1 | ............ | — 1 31.7140 | + 1 22.2532 | ............ | 32 32 22.5259 | 114 42 14.4021 |
| | A′ | A′ C′ | Z A′ C′ | 69 25 20 S.W. | 212 12 5 | 15,339.12 | ............ | — 0 53.3885 | + 2 47.6849 | ............ | 32 30 50.8519 | 114 43 36.6553 |
| | C′ | C′ F′ | A′ C′ F′ | 80 33 0 S.W. | 191 9 10 | 9,131.91 | ............ | — 0 14.8490 | + 1 45.1842 | ............ | 32 29 57.4634 | 114 46 24.3402 |
| Observatory near initial point, on Colorado | F′ | ........... | ........... | ............... | ............... | ............ | ............ | ............ | ............ | ............ | 32 29 42.6144 | 114 48 9.5224 |
| First determination by east stations of triangles | | | | | | | | | | | 32 29 42.6470 | 114 48 09.5019 |
| Second determination by west stations of triangles | | | | | | | | | | | 32 29 42.6144 | 114 48 09.5224 |
| | | | | | | | | | | | 85.2614 | 19.0243 |
| Mean latitude and longitude of observatory near initial point | | | | | | | | | | | 32 29 42.6307 | 114 48 09.512 |

"The base line of the triangulation of the twenty English miles to a point on the Colorado from its junction with the Gila," was measured by Lieut. N. Michler, corps topographical engineers, with two iron rods, "A" and "B," corresponding with rod "B," in the possession of Mr. R. D. Cutts, U. S. Coast Survey, the length of which is 4.0002457 metres at 32° Fahrenheit. The length of one metre, at 32° Fahrenheit, is equal to 39.3685034 inches at 62° Fahrenheit of the standard made by Troughton.

Rate of expansion of rods for 1° Fahrenheit, .000006963535.

The total length of the base, as computed by John O'Donoghue, computer, is 5,867 feet 5.9 inches.

*Table showing the length of rods, at different temperatures, of the American and English Imperial Standard.*

| Temperature of iron rods. | Length of rods at this temperature, of American standard. | Length of rods at this temperat'e, of the English imperial standard. | Temperature of iron rods. | Length of rods at this temperature, of American standard. | Length of rods at this temperat'e, of the English imperial standard. |
|---|---|---|---|---|---|
| ° | *Inches.* | *Inches.* | ° | *Inches.* | *Inches.* |
| 52 | 157.5056195 | 157.512060 | 62 | 157.5165855 | 157.523070 |
| 53 | .5067161 | .513161 | 63 | .5176821 | .524171 |
| 54 | .5078127 | .514262 | 64 | .5187787 | .525272 |
| 55 | .5089093 | .515363 | 65 | .5198753 | .526373 |
| 56 | .5100059 | .516464 | 66 | .5209719 | .527474 |
| 57 | .5111025 | .517565 | 67 | .5220685 | .528575 |
| 58 | .5121991 | .518666 | 68 | .5231651 | .529676 |
| 59 | .5132957 | .519767 | 69 | .5242617 | .530777 |
| 60 | .5143923 | .520868 | 70 | .5253583 | .531878 |
| 61 | .5154889 | .521969 | | | |

*Table showing the quantity to be taken from the length of the measuring-rod at the different elevations.*

| Angle of elevation. | Sum to be subtracted from the length of the rod. | Angle of elevations. | Sum to be subtracted from the length of the rod. |
|---|---|---|---|
| ° ′ | *Inches.* | ° ′ | *Inches.* |
| 0 00 | 0.0000000 | 0 35 | 0.0081595 |
| 0 05 | 0.0001733 | 0 40 | 0.0106641 |
| 0 10 | 0.0006615 | 0 45 | 0.0134995 |
| 0 15 | 0.0014964 | 0 50 | 0.0166656 |
| 0 20 | 0.0026612 | 0 55 | 0.0201626 |
| 0 25 | 0.0041585 | 1 00 | 0.0239903 |
| 0 30 | 0.0061275 | | |

The point "F′" was Lieut. Michler's observatory, and distant from the junction of the Colorado and Gila, in a straight line, 104024.34 feet; the azimuth of this line, at the point "F′," is 36° 14′ 10″ N. E., and its length is 1575.66 feet short of twenty miles. (See results of calculations of geodetic latitudes and longitudes of points of triangulation, &c.)

The latitude of point "F′," as obtained from triangulation, is 32° 29′ 42″.64 N., and longitude 114° 48′ 09″.51 west of Greenwich. The latitude used, however, is that obtained from observations with zenith telescope, and is 32° 29′ 41″.65 N.; but the longitude taken is that obtained by triangulation.

The initial point, in the middle of the Colorado, was determined by prolonging the line from the junction, passing through "F′" 1575.66 feet, measured with the two iron rods, "A" and

"B," thus laying off a radius of twenty miles. At the extremity of this line, a perpendicular was erected, or, in other words, a tangent was drawn to the circumference of a circle with that radius and the junction as a centre, and, by means of the following table, the circle was described.

*Co-ordinates of points of the circle.*

| Abscissas in feet, measured along the tangent. | | Corresponding ordinates, in feet, measured on perpendiculars to the tangent. | Abscissas in feet, measured along the tangent. | | Corresponding ordinates, in feet, measured on perpendiculars to the tangent. |
|---|---|---|---|---|---|
| *Feet.* | | | *Feet.* | | |
| 0 | = | 0. 00 | 1, 300 | = | 8. 29 |
| 100 | = | 0. 04745 | 1, 400 | = | 9. 30 |
| 200 | = | 0. 19 | 1, 500 | = | 10. 67 |
| 300 | = | 0. 427 | 1, 600 | = | 12. 148 |
| 400 | = | 0. 759 | 1, 800 | = | 15. 37 |
| 500 | = | 1. 186 | 2, 000 | = | 18. 90 |
| 600 | = | 1. 708 | 2. 200 | = | 22. 96 |
| 700 | = | 2. 325 | 2, 400 | = | 27. 33 |
| 800 | = | 3. 037 | 2, 600 | = | 33. 00 |
| 900 | = | 3. 843 | 3, 000 | = | 42. 66 |
| 1, 000 | = | 4. 74 | 5, 000 | = | 118. 10 |
| 1, 100 | = | 5. 74 | 10, 000 | = | 472. 2 |
| 1, 200 | = | 6. 83 | | | |

*A table to lay out on the ground a portion of the circumference of a circle whose radius is twenty miles.*

First take a point twenty miles from the mouth of the Gila, and having the direction of the line joining this point and the mouth of the Gila, protract a straight line, making an angle of 88° 34′ 02″.8522 with this line; or prolong a line that will make an angle of 1° 25′ 57″.1478 with the tangent to the circle at the point; then run 5,280 feet on this line, and this will give you a second point on the circle; then place your instrument alternately at the second and first points, and lay off the following angles with this chord of a mile long, and their intersections will be so many points in the circumference of the circle.

| | First point. | Second point. | Intermediate points of circumference. |
|---|---|---|---|
| | ° ′ ″ | ° ′ ″ | |
| 1 | 0 06 36. 70 | 1 19 20. 44 | 1st. |
| 2 | 0 13 13. 41 | 1 12 43. 74 | 2d. |
| 3 | 0 19 50. 11 | 1 6 7. 03 | 3d. |
| 4 | 0 26 26. 81 | 0 59 30. 33 | 4th. |
| 5 | 0 33 3. 52 | 0 52 53. 63 | 5th. |
| 6 | 0 39 40. 22 | 0 46 16. 92 | 6th. |

Having come to a point more than half way, reverse the readings, and they will give you other points commencing near the second point. The greatest distance of the periphery from this chord is about thirty-three feet.

III.—*Tabulation of results for the latitude of astronomical station at the Initial Point on the Rio Colorado, twenty English miles below its junction with the Gila, derived from observations made with zenith telescope of Wurdemann, on sixteen pairs of stars. Observer, Lieut. N. Michler, Corps Topographical Engineers, U. S. Army. Computer, John O'Donoghue.*

| Date. | 1st pair. | 2d pair. | 3d pair. | 4th pair. | 5th pair. | 6th pair. | 7th pair. | 8th pair. | 9th pair. |
|---|---|---|---|---|---|---|---|---|---|
| | N. 582 G. C.<br>S. 560 G. C. | N. 705<br>S. 713 | N. 791<br>S. 793 | N. 796<br>S. 804 | N. 796<br>S. 805 | N. 812<br>S. 833 | N. 850<br>S. 845 | N. 859<br>S. 864 | N. 924<br>S. 934 |
| 1855. | ° ′ ″ | ° ′ ″ | ° ′ ″ | ° ′ ″ | ° ′ ″ | ° ′ ″ | ° ′ ″ | ° ′ ″ | ° ′ ″ |
| March 17...... | ............. | 32 29 37.16 | ............. | 32 29 38.63 | 32 29 36.77 | 32 29 41.21 | ............. | ............. | ............. |
| 18...... | 32 29 40.96 | 42.06 | ............. | 41.11 | 38.60 | ............. | 32 29 38.71 | ............. | ............. |
| April 2...... | ............. | ............. | 32 29 45.94 | ............. | ............. | 42.14 | ............. | 32 29 38.24 | ............. |
| 3...... | ............. | 48 57 | ............. | 40.45 | 37.97 | ............. | 45.68 | ............. | ............. |
| 4...... | ............. | ............. | ............. | ............. | 48.87 | ............. | 44.05 | ............. | ............. |
| 5...... | ............. | 47.68 | ............. | 38.34 | ............. | 41.23 | 39.80 | ............. | 32 29 36.37 |
| 6...... | ............. | ............. | ............. | 42.64 | 40.13 | ............. | 44.12 | 40.00 | 44.96 |
| Lat. by a mean of each pair.. | 32 29 40.96 | 32 29 43.87 | 32 29 45.94 | 32 29 40.23 | 32 29 40.47 | 32 29 41.53 | 32 29 42.47 | 32 29 39.12 | 32 29 40.67 |

*Tabulation of results*—Continued.

| Date. | 10th pair. | 11th pair. | 12th pair. | 13th pair. | 14th pair. | 15th pair. | 16th pair. | 1st result. | Final result. |
|---|---|---|---|---|---|---|---|---|---|
| | N. 1010<br>S. 1012 | N. 1044<br>S. 1026 | N. 1044<br>S. 1046 | N. 1062<br>S. 1089 | N. 1063<br>S. 1089 | N. 1064<br>S. 1089 | N. 1157<br>S. 1175 | Latitude by a mean of all the pairs. | |
| 1855. | ° ′ ″ | ° ′ ″ | ° ′ ″ | ° ′ ″ | ° ′ ″ | ° ′ ″ | ° ′ ″ | ° ′ ″ | ° ′ ″ |
| March 17...... | ............. | ............. | ............. | ............. | ............. | ............. | ............. | ............. | ............. |
| 18...... | ............. | ............. | ............. | ............. | ............. | ............. | ............. | ............. | ............. |
| April 2...... | ............. | 32 29 38.25 | ............. | ............. | ............. | ............. | 32 29 46.74 | ............. | ............. |
| 3...... | ............. | 40.80 | 32 29 38.90 | ............. | ............. | ............. | ............. | ............. | ............. |
| 4...... | 32 29 47.32 | 39.80 | ............. | ............. | ............. | ............. | ............. | ............. | ............. |
| 5...... | ............. | ............. | ............. | ............. | ............. | ............. | ............. | ............. | ............. |
| 6...... | ............. | ............. | 38.55 | 32 29 40.04 | 32 29 41.19 | 32 29 39.45 | ............. | ............. | ............. |
| Lat. by a mean of each pair.. | 32 29 47.32 | 32 29 39.62 | 32 29 38.73 | 32 29 40.04 | 32 29 41.19 | 32 29 39.45 | 32 29 46.74 | 32 29 41.77 | 32 29 41.77 |

REMARKS.—The zenith telescope suffered very material injury in its transportation, in consequence of the counterpoise having been separated from the instrument by the breaking of a screw, and knocked about among the other parts. The tangent screws were mostly bent, the micrometer slightly injured, and the spider lines and levels all broken. Being in a country where the levels could not be replaced, the not very sensitive ones of a large bronze theodolite had to be substituted for those broken, and the other injuries repaired by such means as were at hand.

*Computations from observations on Polaris, western elongation, for the determination of the value of one division of the micrometer attached to zenith telescope, by Wurdemann, for the U. S. Boundary Commission. March* 23, 1855.

| No. | Micrometer readings. | Times of observat'n by chron'r. | Time from elongation. | Correct'n for H. | Reduced time. | Nos. | Difference of time. | Difference of time in arc. | Reduction to the equator. | Diff. of micrometer readings. | Resulting values of one division. |
|---|---|---|---|---|---|---|---|---|---|---|---|
| | | *h. m. s.* | *m.* | *s.* | *h. m. s.* | | *m. s.* | ° ′ ″ | ′ ″ | | ″ |
| 1 | 300 | 6 15 48.0 | 20.91 | 1.8 | 6 15 49.8 | 1 to 6 | 8 29.7 | 2 7 25.5 | 3 15.0 | 300 | 0.65000 |
| 2 | 250 | 17 12.0 | 19.52 | 1.4 | 17 13.4 | 5 | 7 6.2 | 1 46 33.0 | 2 43.1 | 250 | 0.65200 |
| 3 | 150 | 20 5.8 | 16.62 | 0.9 | 20 6.7 | 4 | 5 42.4 | 1 25 36.0 | 2 11.0 | 150 | 0.65500 |
| 4 | 100 | 21 31.5 | 15.19 | 0.7 | 21 32.2 | 3 | 4 16.9 | 1 4 13.5 | 1 38.3 | 100 | 0.65500 |
| 5 | 50 | 22 55.5 | 13.79 | 0.5 | 22 56.0 | 2 | 1 23.6 | 20 54.0 | 32.0 | 50 | 0.64000 |
| 6 | 00 | 24 19.2 | 12.40 | 0.3 | 24 19.5 | 2 to 6 | 7 6.1 | 1 46 31.5 | 2 43.0 | 250 | 0.65280 |
| 7 | 100 | 27 9.2 | 9.56 | 0.1 | 27 9.3 | 6 to 14 | 16 44.7 | 4 11 10.5 | 6 25.1 | 600 | 0.64183 |
| 8 | 150 | 28 34.0 | 8.10 | 0.1 | 28 34.1 | 13 | 15 20.5 | 3 50 7.5 | 5 51.9 | 550 | 0.63982 |
| 9 | 250 | 31 20.0 | 5.38 | 0.0 | 31 20.0 | 12 | 13 59.5 | 3 29 52.5 | 5 21.0 | 500 | 0.64200 |
| 10 | 350 | 34 11.0 | 2.53 | 0.0 | 34 11.0 | 11 | 12 35.5 | 3 8 52.5 | 4 49.0 | 450 | 0.64222 |
| 11 | 450 | 36 55.0 | 0.18 | 0.0 | 36 55.0 | 10 | 9 51.5 | 2 27 52.5 | 3 46.2 | 350 | 0.64639 |
| 12 | 500 | 38 19.0 | 1.59 | 0.0 | 38 19.0 | 9 | 7 0.5 | 1 45 7.5 | 2 41.1 | 250 | 0.64440 |
| 13 | 550 | 39 40.0 | 2.94 | 0.0 | 39 40.0 | 8 | 4 14.6 | 1 3 39.0 | 1 37.4 | 150 | 0.64933 |
| 14 | 600 | 41 4.2 | 4.34 | 0.0 | 41 4.2 | 7 to 14 | 13 54.9 | 3 28 43.5 | 5 19.3 | 500 | 0.63860 |

Mean $= \frac{9\ 04939}{14} = 0''.64638$ by 1st series. Sum = 9.04939

*Remarks.*

Chronometer slow.................................................... = 28*m*. 41*s*.490

Time, by chronometer, of western elongation of Polaris.......................... = 6*h*. 36*m*. 43*s*.350

Declination of star.................................................... = 88° 32′ 17″.4

Observer, Lieut. N. Michler, Top. Engineers, U. S. A. Computer, Hugh Campbell.

## *Computations for the value of one division of the micrometer, &c.*—Continued.

| No. | Micrometer readings. | Time of observat'n by mic'ter. | Time from elongation. | Correct'n for H. | Reduced time. | Nos. | Difference of time. | Difference of time in arc. | Reduction to the equator. | Diff. of micrometer readings. | Value of one divis'n of the micrometer. |
|---|---|---|---|---|---|---|---|---|---|---|---|
| | | *h. m. s.* | *m.* | *s.* | *h. m. s.* | | *m. s.* | ° ′ ″ | ′ ″ | | ″ |
| 1 | 300 | 6 15 48.0 | 20.91 | 1.8 | 6 15 49.8 | 7 to 13 | 13 54.9 | 3 7 40.5 | 4 47.1 | 450 | 0.63800 |
| 2 | 250 | 17 12.0 | 19.52 | 1.4 | 17 13.4 | 12 | 12 30.7 | 2 47 25.5 | 4 16.1 | 400 | 0.64025 |
| 3 | 150 | 20 5.8 | 16.62 | 0.9 | 20 6.7 | 11 | 11 9.7 | 2 26 25.5 | 3 44.0 | 350 | 0.64000 |
| 4 | 100 | 21 31.5 | 15.19 | 0.7 | 21 32.2 | 10 | 9 45.7 | 1 45 25.5 | 2 41.4 | 250 | 0.64560 |
| 5 | 50 | 22 55 5 | 13.79 | 0.5 | 22 56.0 | 8 to 14 | 12 30.1 | 3 7 31.5 | 4 46.9 | 450 | 0.63533 |
| 6 | 0 | 24 19.2 | 12.40 | 0.3 | 24 19.5 | 13 | 11 5.9 | 2 46 28.5 | 4 14.7 | 400 | 0.63675 |
| 7 | 100 | 27 9.2 | 9.56 | 0.1 | 27 9.3 | 12 | 9 44.9 | 2 26 13.5 | 3 43.7 | 350 | 0.63914 |
| 8 | 150 | 28 34.0 | 8.10 | 0.1 | 28 34.1 | 11 | 8 20.9 | 2 5 13.5 | 3 11.6 | 300 | 0.63866 |
| 9 | 250 | 31 20.0 | 5.38 | 0.0 | 31 20.0 | 14 to 1 | 25 14.4 | 6 18 36.0 | 9 38.3 | 900 | 0.64255 |
| 10 | 350 | 34 11.0 | 2.53 | 0.0 | 34 11.0 | 13 to 2 | 22 26.6 | 5 36 39.0 | 8 34.4 | 800 | 0.64300 |
| 11 | 450 | 36 55.0 | 0.18 | 0.0 | 36 55.0 | 12 to 3 | 18 12.3 | 4 33 4.5 | 6 57.5 | 650 | 0.64230 |
| 12 | 500 | 38 19.0 | 1.59 | 0.0 | 38 19.0 | 11 to 4 | 15 22.8 | 3 50 42.0 | 5 52.8 | 550 | 0.63600 |
| 13 | 550 | 39 40.0 | 2.94 | 0.0 | 39 40.0 | 14 to 2 | 23 50.8 | 5 57 42.0 | 9 6.5 | 850 | 0.64294 |
| 14 | 600 | 41 4.2 | 4.34 | 0.0 | 41 4.2 | 13 to 3 | 19 33.3 | 4 53 19.5 | 7 28.4 | 700 | 0.64066 |

Mean $= \frac{8.96018}{14} = 0''.64001$ by 2d series. Sum = 8.96018

| | ″ | | |
|---|---|---|---|
| 1st series................ | = 0.64638 | 1st sum............... | = 9.04939 |
| 2d series................ | = 0.64001 | 2d sum................ | = 8.96018 |
| Mean.................... | = 0.643195 | | $\frac{18.00957}{28} = 0''.643198$ = mean of 28 combinations. |

| | ″ |
|---|---|
| 1st mean.......................................... | = 0.643195 |
| 2d mean.......................................... | = 0.643198 |
| Result by Polaris.................................. | = 0.643196 |

Observer, Lieut. N. Michler, Top. Engineers, U. S. A. Computer, Hugh Campbell.

*Computations from observations on δ Ursæ Minoris, eastern elongation, for the value of one division of the micrometer. March 23, 1855.*

| No. | Micrometer readings. | Time of observat'n by chron'r. | Time from elongation. | Correct'n for H. | Reduced time. | No. | Micrometer readings. | Time of observat'n by chronometer. | Time from elongation | Correct'n for H. | Reduced time. |
|---|---|---|---|---|---|---|---|---|---|---|---|
| | | h. m. s. | m. | s. | h. m. s. | | | h. m. s. | m. | s. | h. m. s. |
| 1 | 400 | 11 46 25.0 | 3.9 | 0.0 | 11 46 25.0 | 19 | 1000 | 12 03 06.0 | 12.7 | 0.4 | 12 03 05.4 |
| 2 | 350 | 46 59.5 | 3.4 | 0.0 | 46 59.9 | 20 | 1050 | 03 40.5 | 13.1 | 0.4 | 03 40.1 |
| 3 | 300 | 47 36.5 | 2.8 | 0.0 | 47 36.5 | 21 | 1100 | 04 15.8 | 13.9 | 0.5 | 04 15.3 |
| 4 | 250 | 48 13.5 | 2.1 | 0.0 | 48 13.5 | 22 | 1150 | 04 52.5 | 14.4 | 0.6 | 04 51.9 |
| 5 | 200 | 48 50.0 | 1.5 | 0.0 | 48 50.0 | 23 | 1250 | 06 04.0 | 15.6 | 0.7 | 06 03.3 |
| 6 | 150 | 49 23.0 | 1.0 | 0.0 | 49 23.0 | 24 | 1300 | 06 40.8 | 16.3 | 0.8 | 06 40.0 |
| 7 | 100 | 49 58.8 | 0.4 | 0.0 | 49 58.8 | 25 | 1350 | 07 16.0 | 16.8 | 0.9 | 07 15.1 |
| 8 | 50 | 50 35.0 | 0.2 | 0.0 | 50 35.0 | 26 | 1400 | 07 51.6 | 17.4 | 1.0 | 07 50.6 |
| 9 | 0 | 51 08.5 | 0.7 | 0.0 | 51 08.5 | 27 | 1500 | 08 58.0 | 18.5 | 1.2 | 08 56.8 |
| 10 | 50 | 51 43.0 | 1.3 | 0.0 | 51 43.0 | 28 | 1550 | 09 33.0 | 19.1 | 1.3 | 09 31.7 |
| 11 | 100 | 52 19.0 | 1.9 | 0.0 | 52 19.0 | 29 | 1600 | 10 08.0 | 19.7 | 1.4 | 10 06.6 |
| 12 | 300 | 54 46.0 | 4.3 | 0.0 | 54 46.0 | 30 | 1700 | 11 21.8 | 20.9 | 1.8 | 11 20.0 |
| 13 | 350 | 55 19.0 | 4.9 | 0.0 | 55 19.0 | 31 | 1800 | 12 31.5 | 22.1 | 2.0 | 12 29.5 |
| 14 | 450 | 56 32.0 | 6.0 | 0.0 | 56 32.0 | 32 | 1850 | 13 07.0 | 22.7 | 2.3 | 13 04.7 |
| 15 | 550 | 57 45.0 | 7.3 | 0.0 | 57 45.0 | 32 | 1900 | 13 44.5 | 23.3 | 2.3 | 13 42.2 |
| 16 | 750 | 12 00 04.5 | 9.6 | 0.1 | 12 00 04.4 | 34 | 1950 | 14 19.6 | 23.9 | 2.6 | 14 17.0 |
| 17 | 850 | 01 17.0 | 10.9 | 0.2 | 01 16.8 | 35 | 2000 | 14 57.0 | 24.5 | 2.8 | 14 54.0 |
| 18 | 900 | 01 51.6 | 11.4 | 0.2 | 01 51.4 | | | | | | |

*Remarks.*

Time by chronometer of eastern elongation of δ Ursæ Minoris........................ 11h. 50m. 24s.760
Chronometer slow.................................................................. = 28m. 41s.49
Declination of star .................................................................. = 86° 35′ 32″.5.

*Combination of results for the determination of one division of the micrometer, derived from observations on δ Ursæ Minoris near eastern elongation.*

| Nos. | Microm'er divisions. | Differences of times. | Differences of times in arc. | Reduction to the equator. | Values of one division. | Nos. | Microm'er divisions. | Differences of times. | Differences of times in arc. | Reduction to the equator. | Values of one div'n. |
|---|---|---|---|---|---|---|---|---|---|---|---|
| | | m. s. | ° ′ ″ | ′ ″ | ″ | | | m. s. | ° ′ ″ | ′ ″ | ″ |
| 1 to 18 | 1300 | 15 26.4 | 3 51 36.0 | 13 45.3 | .63484 | 1 to 35 | 2400 | 28 29.2 | 7 07 18.0 | 25 20.0 | .63333 |
| 2 to 19 | 1350 | 16 05.9 | 4 01 28.5 | 14 20.5 | .63888 | 2 to 34 | 2300 | 27 17.5 | 6 49 22.5 | 24 16.5 | .63317 |
| 3 to 20 | 1350 | 16 03.6 | 4 00 54.0 | 14 18.4 | .63585 | 3 to 33 | 2200 | 26 08.0 | 6 32 00.0 | 23 15.0 | .63409 |
| 4 to 21 | 1350 | 16 01.8 | 4 00 27.0 | 14 17.8 | .63547 | 4 to 32 | 2100 | 24 53.5 | 6 13 22.5 | 22 09.0 | .63285 |
| 5 to 22 | 1350 | 16 01.9 | 4 00 28.5 | 14 16.9 | .63474 | 5 to 31 | 2000 | 23 39.5 | 5 54 52.5 | 21 03.3 | .63165 |
| 6 to 23 | 1400 | 16 40.3 | 4 10 04.5 | 14 51.0 | .63642 | 6 to 30 | 1850 | 21 57.0 | 5 29 15.0 | 19 32.4 | .63373 |
| 7 to 24 | 1400 | 16 41.2 | 4 10 18.0 | 14 51.9 | .63771 | 7 to 29 | 1700 | 20 07.8 | 5 01 57.0 | 17 55.4 | .63288 |
| 8 to 25 | 1400 | 16 40.1 | 4 10 01.5 | 14 50.9 | .63635 | 8 to 28 | 1600 | 18 56.7 | 4 44 10.5 | 16 52.3 | .63269 |
| 9 to 26 | 1400 | 16 42.1 | 4 10 31.5 | 14 52.7 | .63764 | 9 to 27 | 1500 | 17 48.3 | 4 27 04.5 | 15 51.5 | .63433 |
| 10 to 27 | 1450 | 17 13.8 | 4 18 27.0 | 15 20.8 | .63503 | 10 to 26 | 1350 | 16 08.6 | 4 02 09.0 | 14 22.8 | .63911 |
| 11 to 28 | 1450 | 17 12.7 | 4 18 10.5 | 15 19.8 | .63433 | 11 to 25 | 1250 | 14 57.0 | 3 44 15.0 | 13 19.2 | .63935 |
| 12 to 29 | 1300 | 15 20.6 | 3 50 09.0 | 13 40.1 | .63077 | 12 to 24 | 1000 | 11 54.8 | 2 58 42.0 | 10 37.0 | .63700 |
| 13 to 30 | 1350 | 16 01.0 | 4 00 15.0 | 14 16.1 | .63474 | 13 to 23 | 900 | 10 45.0 | 2 41 15.0 | 9 35.9 | .63988 |
| 14 to 31 | 1350 | 15 57.5 | 3 59 22.5 | 14 13.0 | .63185 | | | | | | |
| 15 to 32 | 1300 | 15 19.7 | 3 49 55.5 | 13 39.3 | .63023 | 1st series—mean | | | | | 0.63492 |
| 16 to 33 | 1100 | 13 00.3 | 3 15 04.5 | 11 36.3 | .63300 | 2d series—mean | | | | | 0.63466 |
| 17 to 34 | 1100 | 13 00.2 | 3 15 03.6 | 11 35.2 | .63200 | Result by δ Ursæ Minoris | | | | | 0.63479 |
| 18 to 35 | 1100 | 13 02.8 | 3 15 42.0 | 11 37.5 | .63409 | Result by Polaris | | | | | 0.64319 |
| | | | | | Mean = 0.63466 | Final result | | | | | 0.63899 |

Value of one division of the micrometer from observations on Polaris (western elongation) and δ Ursæ Minoris (eastern elongation) is 0″.63899.

Observer, Lieut. N. Michler, U. S. Topographical Engineers. Computer, Hugh Campbell.

IV.—*Table showing the triangulated distances, in metres and yards, between the different monuments of the survey of that portion of the boundary line running from the Initial Point, on the Colorado river, to the intersection of the parallel* 31° 20′ 00″ *north latitude, and the meridian* 111° 00′ 00″ *west of Greenwich.*

Triangulation by Lieut. N. MICHLER, Mr. A. C. V. SCHOTT, and Señor A. DIAZ.

| | Metres. | Yards. | Remarks. |
|---|---|---|---|
| From Initial Point, on the Colorado river, to Monument I... | 964.62 | 1054.9214 | Monument I, in River bottom, near the bank. |
| Monument I to Monument II .............. | 3171.12 | 3467.9793 | Monument II, Iron monument, on desert. |
| Monument II to Monument III .............. | 829.81 | 907.4913 | Monument III, erected on desert. |
| Monument III to Monument IV .............. | 72170.00 | 78926.0790 | Monument IV, Sierra de las Tinajas Altas. |
| Monument IV to Monument V .............. | 44393.34 | 48549.1515 | Monument V, Sierra del Tule. |
| Monument V to Monument VI ... .......... | 57633.12 | 63028.3523 | Monument VI, Sierra del Agua Dulce. |
| Monument VI to Monument VII .............. | 13203.04 | 14439.0215 | Monument VII, near Rancho de Quitobaquita. |
| Monument VII to Monument VIII .............. | 877.61 | 959.7660 | Monument VIII, near Rancho de Quitobaquita. |
| Monument VIII to Monument IX .............. | 17298.65 | 18918.0354 | Monument IX, Sierra de Sonoyta. |
| Monument IX to Monument X .............. | 23405.35 | 25596.4044 | Monument X, west ridge of Sierra de la Nariz. |
| Monument X to Monument XI ........... .. | 4180.00 | 4571.3040 | Monument XI, on the wagon road from Cobota to Sonoyta. |
| Monument XI to Monument XII .............. | 2793.97 | 3055.5230 | Monument XII, east ridge of Sierra de la Nariz. |
| Monument XII to Monument XIII .............. | 44698.76 | 48883.1629 | Monument XIII, on the road from Tubac to Cobota. |
| Monument XIII to Monument XIV .............. | 18986.27 | 20763.6403 | Monument XIV, Sierra de la Union. |
| Monument XIV to Monument XV .............. | 26493.60 | 28973.7560 | Monument XV, Sierra del Pozo Verde. |
| Monument XV to Monument XVI ............. | 14592.57 | 15958.6301 | Monument XVI, near Ojos de los Granizos. |
| Monument XVI to Monument XVII .............. | 3519.11 | 3848.5458 | Monument XVII, Sierra de Sonora. |
| Monument XVII to Monument XVIII .............. | 27962.77 | 30580.4599 | Monument XVIII, Sierra de los Pajaritos. |
| Monument XVIII to Monument XIX .............. | 5261.97 | 5754 5609 | Monument XIX, Sierra de los Pajaritos. |
| Monument XIX to intersection of parallel 31° 20′ N. latitude, and meridian 111° west of Greenwich.. | 409.19 | 447.4957 | Monument (intersection of meridian and parallel) Sierra de los Pajaritos. |
| Total length of line ............ .......... | 382844.87 | 418684.2807 | |

## C.

*Astronomical observations for establishing the 111th meridian of longitude west of Greenwich, and for determining the parallels 31° 47′ and 31° 20′ north latitude: By John H. Clark.*

The four manuscript volumes which have been submitted to the U. S. Commissioner, embrace a complete tabulation of all the observations, both for latitude and longitude, made along the parallels of 31° 47′ and 31° 20′. It will be seen, by a reference to these volumes, that each of the stations has been determined in latitude with a zenith telescope, (T. & S.,) by about one hundred observations, and two in longitude, with a transit of thirty-six inches focal length, by observations on the moon and moon culminating stars.

In accordance with the direction of the Commissioner, the stars for latitude were at first selected exclusively from the Greenwich Twelve-year catalogue. At Espia, however, it was found that this catalogue no longer afforded, in that portion of the heavens then observable, a sufficient number of pairs that would fulfil the conditions required for satisfactory results. It was therefore deemed expedient, in the exigencies of the survey, to rely subsequently almost wholly upon the British Association catalogue.

It was found, by combining the results of observations on about thirty pairs of stars taken from this catalogue, that any error in the final result arising from errors of polar distances was materially reduced; and although, by comparing the means of the observations on each pair, there seemed to be in some cases errors of polar distances developed, all the results were nevertheless incorporated to obtain the one adopted; nor was a single observation rejected because of its apparent inconsistency or want of parallelism with any previous or subsequent result obtained by it or by any other pair, except at one station, (Agua del Perro,) where the instrument was mounted on a rock, (no timber being attainable,) and the observations otherwise rendered objectionable by the violence of the wind. Thus the result of every pair, whether high or low, and without reference to the "general run," has been included in the "means" used to obtain the latitude adopted.

A subsequent and careful revision in the office of the computations made in the field has disclosed no considerable error.

A brief summary of the observations and results of all the stations, and a reference to the tables which are appended, are here given:

1. The observations at Los Nogales for determining the 111th degree of longitude west of Greenwich, extending through two lunations, and computed from data furnished by the Nautical Almanac, gave the result as shown by Table I, 110° 51′ 01″.95, ($7^h$ $23^m$ $24^s$.13). The latitude deduced from 120 observations on 29 pairs of stars, taken from the British Association catalogue, is (see Table II) 31° 21′ 00″.48.

2. Seventy-three observations on 23 pairs of stars, selected from British Association catalogue, give for the latitude of the station near the head of Rio Santa Cruz, (Table III) 31° 17′ 56″.33.

3. At San Bernardino there were 57 observations on 21 pairs from British Association catalogue, and the latitude deduced therefrom, (Table IV,) 31° 19′ 40″.38.

4. The result deduced from 97 observations on 28 pairs of stars gives for the latitude of San Luis spring (Table V) 31° 20′ 31″.51.

5. At Agua del Perro there were 81 observations on 25 pairs of stars selected from both cata-

logues, (British Association catalogue and Greenwich catalogue,) and the latitude deduced, (Table VI,) 31° 20′ 57″.56.

6. The observations at Espia, made on 23 pairs of stars, partly from the Greenwich Twelve-year catalogue and partly from the British Association catalogue, amount to 81, and give for the latitude (Table VII) 31° 20′ 56″.45.

7. The latitude of Carrizalillo, resulting from 72 observations on 14 pairs of stars, selected entirely from the Greenwich Twelve-year catalogue, is (Table VIII) 31° 50′ 55″.23; longitude, (Table IX) $7^h\ 11^m\ 44^s.26 = 107°\ 56'\ 03''.9$.

8. The result for the initial point on the Rio Grande, obtained from 108 observations on 22 pairs of stars, selected also exclusively from the Greenwich Twelve-year catalogue, is (Table X) 31° 46′ 51″.29.

TABLE I.

*Results for longitude of astronomical station at Las Nogales, east of the intersection of the* 111*th degree of longitude and the parallel of* 31° 20′ *north latitude.*

| Date. | Authority for elements used. | Results for moon's 1st limb. | Date. | Authority for elements used. | Results for moon's 2d limb. | Date. | Authority for elements used. | Results for moon's 1st limb. | Date. | Authority for elements used. | Results for moon's 2d limb. |
|---|---|---|---|---|---|---|---|---|---|---|---|
| 1855. | | *h. m. s.* | 1855. | | *h. m. s.* | 1855. | | *h. m. s.* | 1855. | | *h. m. s.* |
| May 24 | N. A. A. Rs. | 7 23 19.20 | May 30 | N. A. A. Rs. | 7 23 23.24 | June 22 | N. A. A. Rs. | 7 23 42.93 | June 28 | N. A. A. Rs. | 7 23 16.76 |
| 25 | ......do...... | 20.41 | 31 | ......do...... | 26.71 | 28 | ......do...... | 15.88 | 30 | ......do...... | 17.14 |
| 26 | ......do...... | 27.92 | | | | | | | July 1 | ......do...... | 20.78 |
| 28 | ......do...... | 32.87 | | | | | | | | | |
| 29 | ......do...... | 25.78 | | | | | | | | | |
| Mean longitude from moon's 1st limb............*7h. 23m. 25.24s.* | | | Mean longitude from moon's 2d limb............*7h. 23m. 24.97s.* Mean longitude from moon's 1st limb............*7h. 23m. 25.24s.* | | | Mean longitude from moon's 1st limb............*7h. 23m. 29.40s.* | | | Mean longitude from moon's 2d limb............*7h. 23m. 18.23s.* Mean longitude from moon's 1st limb............*7h. 23m. 29.40s.* | | |

| | *h. m. s.* | | *h. m. s.* |
|---|---|---|---|
| Mean longitude from 1st lunation.......................... | 7 23 25.10 | Mean longitude from 2d lunation.......................... | 7 23 23.81 |
| Mean longitude from 2d lunation.......................... | 23.81 | | |
| Longitude of Station.......................... | 7 23 24.45 | | |

| Date. | Results for longitude during two lunations. | Date. | Results for longitude during two lunations. |
|---|---|---|---|
| 1855. | *h. m. s.* | 1855. | *h. m. s.* |
| May 24 | 7 23 19.200 | May 31 | 7 23 26.710 |
| 25 | 7 23 20.410 | June 22 | 7 23 42.930 |
| 26 | 7 23 27.920 | 28 | 7 23 15.884 |
| 28 | 7 23 32.870 | 28 | 7 23 16.764 |
| 29 | 7 23 25.780 | 30 | 7 23 17.140 |
| 30 | 7 23 23.240 | July 1 | 7 23 20.780 |

Longitude of Los Nogales by a mean of the above results, (the one adopted,) *7h. 23m. 24.136s.*

TABLE II.

*Tabulation of results for the latitude of astronomical station at Los Nogales derived from observations made with a zenith telescope (T. & S.) on twenty-nine pairs of stars: By J. H. Clark, Principal Assistant.*

| Date. | 1st pair. | 2d pair. | 3d pair. | 4th pair. | 5th pair. | 6th pair. | 7th pair. | 8th pair. | 9th pair. | 10th pair. | 11th pair. | 12th pair. |
|---|---|---|---|---|---|---|---|---|---|---|---|---|
| | B. A. C. * S. 3995 † N. 4026 | B. A. C. S. 3995 N. 4028 | B. A. C. S. 4110 N. 4026 | B. A. C. N. 4128 S. 4142 | B. A. C. S. 4248 N. 4282 | B. A. C. N. 4282 S. 4318 | B. A. C. N. 4282 S. 4319 | B. A. C. S. 4388 N. 4408 | B. A. C. S. 4388 N. 4415 | B. A. C. S. 4388 N. 4595 | B. A. C. S. 4388 N. 4600 | B. A. C. N. 4408 S. 4575 |
| 1855. | ″ | ″ | ″ | ″ | ″ | ″ | ″ | ″ | ″ | ″ | ″ | ″ |
| May 23 | ......... | ......... | ......... | ......... | 60.45 | 60.42 | ......... | 63.78 | 63.33 | ......... | ......... | ......... |
| 25 | ......... | ......... | ......... | ......... | ......... | ......... | ......... | ......... | ......... | ......... | ......... | ......... |
| 26 | ......... | ......... | ......... | ......... | ......... | ......... | ......... | ......... | ......... | ......... | ......... | ......... |
| 29 | 58.62 | 60.30 | 64.96 | 58.75 | 60.28 | 60.76 | 60.85 | 63.33 | 64.87 | 63.39 | 65.18 | 59.92 |
| 30 | 58.59 | 59.34 | 64.61 | ......... | 58.12 | 58.96 | 59.36 | 59.83 | 61.64 | 59.05 | 60.37 | 59.05 |
| June 5 | ......... | ......... | ......... | ......... | 59.35 | 60.68 | 60.14 | 62.74 | 64.01 | 62.13 | 63.38 | 60.43 |
| 7 | ......... | ......... | ......... | ......... | 59.45 | 61.59 | 61.00 | 62.73 | 63.38 | 61.89 | 62.92 | 60.35 |
| Mean of each pair | 58.60 | 59.82 | 64.78 | 58.75 | 59.53 | 60.48 | 60.33 | 62.28 | 63.44 | 61.61 | 62.96 | 59.93 |

TABLE II—Continued.

| Date. | 13th pair. | 14th pair. | 15th pair. | 16th pair. | 17th pair. | 18th pair. | 19th pair. | 20th pair. | 21st pair. | 22d pair. | 23d pair. | 24th pair. |
|---|---|---|---|---|---|---|---|---|---|---|---|---|
| | B. A. C. N. 4415 S. 4575 | B. A. C. S. 4575 N. 4595 | B. A. C. S. 4575 N. 4600 | B. A. C. N. 4714 S. 4723 | B. A. C. S. 4737 N. 4741 | B. A. C. S. 4810 N. 4943 | B. A. C. N. 4803 S. 4823 | B. A. C. N. 4961 S. 4991 | B. A. C. S. 5075 N. 5131 | B. A. C. N. 5157 S. 5189 | B. A. C. N. 5175 S. 5234 | B. A. C. S. 5244 N. 5259 |
| 1855. | ″ | ″ | ″ | ″ | ″ | ″ | ″ | ″ | ″ | ″ | ″ | ″ |
| May 23 | ......... | 60.93 | 62.66 | 58.32 | 59.38 | ......... | 59.95 | 61.21 | 61.04 | 56.67 | ......... | 61.73 |
| 25 | ......... | 56.44 | 57.70 | 59.07 | 57.85 | ......... | 60.31 | 62.19 | 60.14 | 56.88 | ......... | 62.63 |
| 26 | ......... | 59.55 | 60.29 | 58.42 | 59.21 | ......... | 60.58 | 62.05 | 59.01 | 55.63 | ......... | 62.22 |
| 29 | 61.38 | 59.89 | 61.69 | ......... | ......... | ......... | ......... | ......... | ......... | ......... | ......... | ......... |
| 30 | 60.86 | 58.78 | 59.61 | 60.67 | 56.66 | 60.34 | ......... | 60.52 | ......... | ......... | ......... | ......... |
| June 5 | 61.75 | 59.86 | 61.12 | 60.28 | ......... | ......... | 61.33 | 62.80 | 61.43 | ......... | 59.49 | 61.83 |
| 7 | 61.00 | 59.51 | 60.54 | 59.91 | 59.38 | ......... | 62.23 | 63.50 | 62.52 | ......... | 59.89 | 62.14 |
| Mean of each pair | 61.24 | 59.28 | 60.51 | 59.44 | 58.49 | 60.34 | 60.88 | 62.04 | 60.82 | 56.39 | 59.69 | 62.11 |

TABLE II—Continued.

| Date. | 25th pair. | 26th pair. | 27th pair. | 28th pair. | 29th pair. | Latitude by a mean of each night. | 1st result. | 2d result. | 3d result. | Final result. |
|---|---|---|---|---|---|---|---|---|---|---|
| | B. A. C. S. 5284 N. 5338 | B. A. C. S. 5367 N. 5388 | B. A. C. S. 5368 N. 5388 | B. A. C. S 5504 N. 5568 | B. A. C. S. 5507 N. 5568 | | Latitude by a mean of each pair. | Lat. by a mean of all the observations. | Lat. by a mean of the results for each night. | Mean of 1st, 2d, and 3d results. |
| 1855. | ″ | ″ | ″ | ″ | ″ | ° ′ ″ | ° ′ ″ | ° ′ ″ | ° ′ ″ | ° ′ ″ |
| May 23 | 60.64 | 59.54 | 58.97 | 58.27 | 59.74 | 31 20 60.33 | | | | |
| 25 | 58.89 | 59.68 | 58.86 | 58.62 | 60.10 | 31 20 59.22 | | | | |
| 26 | 60.75 | 59.86 | 59.63 | ......... | ......... | 31 20 59.76 | | | | |
| 29 | ......... | ......... | ......... | ......... | ......... | 31 20 61.61 | | | | |
| 30 | ......... | ......... | ......... | ......... | ......... | 31 20 59.79 | | | | |
| June 5 | 61.80 | 60.97 | 60.19 | 59.05 | 60.19 | 31 20 61.13 | | | | |
| 7 | 62.38 | 61.22 | 60.45 | ......... | ......... | 31 20 61.33 | | | | |
| Mean of each pair. | 60.83 | 60.25 | 59.62 | 58.64 | 60.01 | | 31 20 60.45 | 31 20 60.55 | 31 20 60.45 | 31 20 60.48 |

* S., star south of the zenith. † N., star north of the zenith.

TABLE III.

*Tabulation of results for the latitude of astronomical station at head of Santa Cruz river, derived from observations made with a zenith telescope (T. & S.) on twenty-three pairs of stars: By J. H. Clark, Principal Assistant, assisted by C. N. Turnbull, Lieut. Corps Top. Eng'rs, U. S. A.*

| Date. | 1st pair. | 2d pair. | 3d pair. | 4th pair. | 5th pair. | 6th pair. | 7th pair. | 8th pair. | 9th pair. | 10th pair. |
|---|---|---|---|---|---|---|---|---|---|---|
| | B. A. C. 3523 S. 3533 N. | B. A. C. 3548 N. 3650 S. | B. A. C. 3742 S. 3811 N. | B. A. C. 3869 S. 3952 N. | B. A. C. 3995 S. 4026 N. | B. A. C. 3995 S. 4028 N. | B. A. C. 4057 N. 4156 S. | B. A. C. 4059 N. 4156 S. | B. A. C. 4177 N. 4242 S. | B. A. C. 4248 S. 4282 N. |
| 1855. | ″ | ″ | ″ | ″ | ″ | ″ | ″ | ″ | ″ | ″ |
| May 10………… | 58.28 | ………… | 57.59 | ………… | ………… | ………… | ………… | 53.19 | 53.41 | ………… |
| 11………… | ………… | 53.59 | 57.23 | ………… | 55.72 | 56.57 | 52.99 | 53.16 | 54.84 | 56.55 |
| 12………… | ………… | ………… | ………… | 56.52 | 56.76 | 57.23 | ………… | ………… | ………… | ………… |
| 13………… | ………… | ………… | ………… | 56.09 | 55.75 | 57.07 | 51.81 | 51.18 | 55.64 | ………… |
| 14………… | ………… | ………… | ………… | ………… | 55.39 | 56.60 | 52.74 | 52.00 | 52.82 | 54.77 |
| Mean of each pair. | 58.28 | 53.59 | 57.41 | 56.50 | 55.90 | 56.86 | 52.51 | 52.38 | 54.19 | 55.66 |

TABLE III—Continued.

| Date. | 11th pair. | 12th pair. | 13th pair. | 14th pair. | 15th pair. | 16th pair. | 17th pair. | 18th pair. | 19th pair. | 20th pair. |
|---|---|---|---|---|---|---|---|---|---|---|
| | B. A. C. 4282 N. 4318 S. | B. A. C. 4345 N. 4388 S. | B. A. C. 4345 N. 4575 S. | B. A. C. 4346 N. 4388 S. | B. A. C. 4346 N. 4575 S. | B. A. C. 4388 S. 4408 N. | B. A. C. 4388 S. 4415 N. | B. A. C. 4388 S. 4595 N. | B. A. C. 4388 S. 4600 N. | B. A. C. 4408 N. 4575 S. |
| 1855. | ″ | ″ | ″ | ″ | ″ | ″ | ″ | ″ | ″ | ″ |
| May 10………… | 57.38 | ………… | ………… | ………… | ………… | 58.93 | 59.49 | ………… | ………… | ………… |
| 11………… | 56.47 | 58.02 | 56.37 | 59.38 | 57.73 | 57.26 | 57.00 | 56.42 | 56.77 | 55.58 |
| 12………… | ………… | 56.03 | ………… | 56 56 | ………… | ………… | ………… | ………… | ………… | ………… |
| 13………… | 55.50 | 57.59 | 55.35 | 58.53 | 56.32 | 61.20 | 60.72 | 56.90 | 58.54 | 57.86 |
| 14………… | 57.31 | 55.96 | 54.92 | 56.81 | 55.73 | 58.08 | 58.47 | 57.95 | 59.37 | 57.06 |
| Mean of each pair. | 56.66 | 56.90 | 55.54 | 57.82 | 56.59 | 58.86 | 58.92 | 57.08 | 58.22 | 56.83 |

TABLE III—Continued.

| Date. | 21st pair. | 22d pair. | 23d pair. | Latitude by a mean of each night. | 1st result. | 2d result. | 3d result. | Final result. |
|---|---|---|---|---|---|---|---|---|
| | B. A. C. 4415 N. 4575 S. | B. A. C. 4575 S. 4595 N. | B. A. C. 4575 S. 4600 N. | | Latitude by a mean of each pair. | Latitude by a mean of all the observations. | Latitude by a mean of the results for each night. | Mean of 1st, 2d, and 3d results. |
| 1855. | ″ | ″ | ″ | ° ′ ″ | ° ′ ″ | ° ′ ″ | ° ′ ′ | ° ′ ″ |
| May 10………… | ………… | 53.60 | 54.74 | 31 17 56.36 | | | | |
| 11………… | 55.26 | 54.77 | 55.09 | 31 17 56.03 | | | | |
| 12………… | ………… | ………… | ………… | 31 17 56.62 | | | | |
| 13………… | 58.51 | 54.65 | 57.55 | 31 17 56.67 | | | | |
| 14………… | 57.46 | 56.94 | 58.20 | 31 17 56.24 | | | | |
| Mean of each pair. | 57.07 | 54.99 | 56.39 | | 31 17 56.30 | 31 17 56.32 | 31 17 56.38 | 31 17 56.33 |

TABLE IV.

*Tabulation of results for the latitude of astronomical station at San Bernardino, derived from observations made with a zenith telescope (T. & S.) on twenty-one pairs of stars: By J. H. Clark, Principal Assistant, assisted by H. Campbell.*

| Date. | 1st pair. | 2d pair. | 3d pair. | 4th pair. | 5th pair. | 6th pair. | 7th pair. | 8th pair. | 9th pair. |
|---|---|---|---|---|---|---|---|---|---|
| | B. A. C. 3327 S. 3364 N. | B. A. C. 3416 N. 3500 S. | B. A. C. 3523 S. 3533 N. | B. A. C. 3548 N. 3650 S. | B. A. C. 3560 N. 3650 S. | B. A. C. 3742 S. 3811 N. | B. A. C. 3842 S. 3856 N. | B. A. C. 3919 S. 3953 N. | B. A. C. 3953 N. 3992 S. |
| 1855. | " | " | " | " | " | " | " | " | " |
| April 27......... | 40.71 | 37.16 | 41.89 | 40.35 | 40.52 | ............. | ............. | 40.74 | 41.51 |
| 28......... | 40 07 | 38.01 | 42.35 | ............. | ............. | ............. | ............. | ............. | ............. |
| 29......... | 42.09 | 35.24 | ............. | 42.03 | 40.27 | 43.05 | 41.85 | 41.18 | 36.99 |
| 30......... | 38.31 | 35.52 | 40.79 | ............. | 42.80 | 40.66 | 41.04 | 40.35 | ............. |
| May 2......... | ............. | ............. | ............. | ............. | ............. | 40.44 | 41.37 | ............. | ............. |
| Mean of each pair | 40.29 | 36.48 | 41.67 | 41.29 | 41.19 | 41.38 | 41.75 | 40.75 | 39.25 |

TABLE IV—Continued.

| Date. | 10th pair. | 11th pair. | 12th pair. | 13th pair. | 14th pair. | 15th pair. | 16th pair. | 17th pair. | 18th pair. |
|---|---|---|---|---|---|---|---|---|---|
| | B. A. C. 3995 S. 4026 N. | B. A. C. 3995 S. 4028 N. | B. A. C. 4059 N. 4156 S. | B. A. C. 4177 N. 4242 S. | B. A. C. 4248 S. 4282 N. | B. A. C. 4282 N. 4318 S. | B. A. C. 4282 N. 4319 S. | B. A. C. 4388 S. 4408 N. | B. A. C. 4388 S. 4415 N. |
| 1855. | " | " | " | " | " | " | " | " | " |
| April 27......... | ............. | ............. | ............. | ............. | ............. | ............. | ............. | ............. | ............. |
| 28......... | ............. | ............. | ............. | ............. | ............. | ............. | ............. | ............. | ............. |
| 29......... | ............. | ............. | 38.00 | 38.35 | 38.77 | 39.64 | 39.65 | 44.03 | 45.51 |
| 30......... | 38.25 | 41.38 | 35.98 | 38.18 | 39.39 | 39.66 | 40.27 | 41.68 | 43.21 |
| May 2......... | 40.87 | 41.12 | 41.98 | ............. | 40.23 | 38.18 | 38.73 | 41.07 | 43.45 |
| Mean of each pair | 39.56 | 41.25 | 38.65 | 38.26 | 39.46 | 39.16 | 39.55 | 42.26 | 44.05 |

TABLE IV—Continued.

| Date. | 19th pair. | 20th pair. | 21st pair. | Latitude by a mean of each night. | 1st result. | 2d result. | 3d result. | Final result. |
|---|---|---|---|---|---|---|---|---|
| | B. A. C. 4479 N. 4513 S. | B. A. C. 4575 S. 4595 N. | B. A. C. 4575 S. 4600 N. | | Latitude by a mean of each pair. | Latitude by a mean of all the observations. | Latitude by a mean of the results for each night. | Latitude by a mean of 1st, 2d, and 3d results. |
| 1855. | " | " | ' | ° ' " | ° ' " | ° ' " | ° ' " | ° ' " |
| April 27............. | ............. | ............. | ............. | 31 19 40.45 | | | | |
| 28............. | ............. | ............. | ............. | 31 19 40.14 | | | | |
| 29............. | 40.69 | 40.07 | 42.45 | 31 19 40.55 | | | | |
| 30............. | 40.84 | 39.77 | 41.50 | 31 19 39.97 | | | | |
| May 2............. | ............. | ............. | ............. | 31 19 40.74 | | | | |
| Mean of each pair.... | 40.76 | 39.92 | 41.97 | | 31 19 40.42 | 31 19 40.35 | 31 19 40.37 | 31 19 40.38 |

TABLE V.

*Tabulation of results for the latitude of astronomical station at San Luis Springs, derived from observations made with a zenith telescope (T. & S.) on twenty-eight pairs of stars: By J. H. Clark, Principal Assistant, assisted by Lieut. Turnbull.*

| Date. | 1st pair. | 2d pair. | 3d pair. | 4th pair. | 5th pair. | 6th pair. | 7th pair. | 8th pair. | 9th pair. | 10th pair. | 11th pair. | 12th pair. |
|---|---|---|---|---|---|---|---|---|---|---|---|---|
| | B. A. C.<br>3170 S.<br>3290 N. | B. A. C.<br>3170 S.<br>3297 N. | B. A. C.<br>3204 S.<br>3290 N. | B. A. C.<br>3204 S.<br>3297 N. | B. A. C.<br>3327 S.<br>3364 N. | B. A. C.<br>3416 N.<br>3500 S. | B. A. C.<br>3523 S.<br>3533 N. | B. A. C.<br>3548 N.<br>3650 S. | B. A. C.<br>3560 N.<br>3650 S. | B. A. C.<br>3742 S.<br>3811 N. | B. A. C.<br>3842 S.<br>3856 N. | B. A. C.<br>3919 S.<br>3953 N. |
| 1855. | " | " | " | " | " | " | " | " | " | " | " | " |
| April 17.......... | 32.20 | 33.05 | 32.45 | 33.21 | 31.53 | 28.12 | 31.40 | 29.95 | 32.72 | 32.64 | 32.62 | 30.12 |
| 18.......... | 33.16 | 34.18 | 32.58 | 33.61 | 30.95 | 27.82 | 32.54 | 29.34 | 31.88 | 31.91 | 34.00 | 30.73 |
| 19.......... | 31.59 | 33.99 | 32.19 | 34.29 | 31.43 | 28.02 | 31.93 | 28.74 | 31.15 | 33.57 | 32.12 | 32.34 |
| 20.......... | ........ | ........ | ........ | ........ | 32.11 | 29.05 | 33.90 | 32 39 | 33.57 | 33.14 | 32.84 | 31.15 |
| 21.......... | 33.12 | ........ | 32.63 | ........ | 30.59 | 29.09 | 32.98 | 28.37 | 30.63 | 32.09 | 34.17 | 30.97 |
| Mean of each pair.. | 32.51 | 33.71 | 32.46 | 33.70 | 31.32 | 28.42 | 32.55 | 29.75 | 31.99 | 32.67 | 33.15 | 31.06 |

TABLE V—Continued.

| Date. | 13th pair. | 14th pair. | 15th pair. | 16th pair. | 17th pair. | 18th pair. | 19th pair. | 20th pair. | 21st pair. | 22d pair. | 23d pair. | 24th pair. |
|---|---|---|---|---|---|---|---|---|---|---|---|---|
| | B. A. C.<br>3953 N.<br>3992 S. | B. A. C.<br>3995 S.<br>4026 N. | B. A. C.<br>3995 S.<br>4028 N. | B. A. C.<br>2894 S.<br>2984 N. | B. A. C.<br>2984 N.<br>3000 S. | B. A. C.<br>2984 N.<br>3002 S. | B. A. C.<br>4059 N.<br>4156 S. | B. A. C.<br>4248 S.<br>4282 N. | B. A. C.<br>4282 N.<br>4318 S. | B. A. C.<br>4282 N.<br>4319 S. | B. A. C.<br>4345 N.<br>4388 S. | B. A. C.<br>4346 N.<br>4388 S. |
| 1855. | " | " | " | " | " | " | " | " | " | " | " | " |
| April 17.......... | 26.95 | 32.33 | 33.10 | ........ | ........ | ........ | ........ | ........ | ........ | ........ | ........ | ........ |
| 18.......... | 27.18 | ........ | ........ | 31.47 | 30.65 | 32.45 | 27.26 | 31 55 | 31.65 | 31.47 | 31.35 | 32.54 |
| 19.......... | 28.51 | ........ | ........ | ........ | 26.80 | 30.56 | 27.08 | 32.31 | 33.38 | 33.23 | ........ | ........ |
| 20.......... | 27.14 | ........ | ........ | ........ | 28.41 | 31.06 | ........ | 31.45 | 32.96 | 33.75 | ........ | ........ |
| 21.......... | 27.63 | ........ | ........ | ........ | ........ | ........ | 28.08 | 34.36 | 34.20 | 34.10 | ........ | ........ |
| Mean of each pair.. | 27.48 | 32.33 | 33.10 | 31.47 | 29.28 | 31.35 | 27.47 | 32.41 | 33.04 | 33.13 | 31.35 | 32.54 |

TABLE V—Continued.

| Date. | 25th pair. | 26th pair. | 27th pair. | 28th pair. | Latitude by a mean of each night. | 1st result. | 2d result. | 3d result. | Final result. |
|---|---|---|---|---|---|---|---|---|---|
| | B. A. C.<br>4408 N.<br>4388 S. | B. A. C.<br>4415 N.<br>4388 S. | B. A. C.<br>3062 S.<br>3085 N. | B. A. C.<br>4177 N.<br>4242 S. | | Latitude by a mean of each pair. | Latitude by a mean of all the observations. | Lat. by a mean of the results for each night. | Mean of 1st, 2d, and 3d results. |
| 1855. | " | " | " | " | ° ′ ″ | ° ′ ″ | ° ′ ″ | ° ′ ″ | ° ′ ″ |
| April 17.......... | ........ | ........ | ........ | ........ | 31 20 31.49 | | | | |
| 18.......... | 33.12 | 34.61 | ........ | ........ | 31 20 32.00 | | | | |
| 19.......... | 33.36 | 33.39 | 27.62 | 29.71 | 31 20 31.27 | | | | |
| 20.......... | 32.90 | 34.18 | 29.28 | 27.54 | 31 20 31.43 | | | | |
| 21.......... | 32.55 | 33.99 | ........ | 29.03 | 31 20 31.58 | | | | |
| Mean of each pair... | 32.98 | 34.04 | 28.45 | 28.76 | | 31 20 31.51 | 31 20 31.48 | 31 20 31.55 | 31 20 31.51 |

TABLE VI.

*Tabulation of results for the latitude of astronomical station at Agua del Perro, derived from observations made with a zenith telescope (T. & S.) on twenty-five pairs of stars: By J. H. Clark, Principal Assistant, assisted by H. Campbell.*

| Date. | 1st pair. | 2d pair. | 3d pair. | 4th pair. | 5th pair. | 6th pair. | 7th pair. | 8th pair. | 9th pair. | 10th pair. | 11th pair. |
|---|---|---|---|---|---|---|---|---|---|---|---|
| | G. C. 638 S. 675 N. | G. C. 638 S. 677 N. | G. C. 638 S. 678 N. | B. A. C. 2493 S. 2504 N. | B. A. C. 2540 S. 2592 N. | B. A. C. 2984 N. 3000 S. | B. A. C. 2605 S. 2715 N. | B. A. C. 2894 S. 2984 N. | B. A. C. 2984 N. 3002 S. | B. A. C. 3062 S. 3085 N. | B. A. C. 3170 S. 3290 N. |
| 1855. | " | " | " | " | " | " | " | " | " | " | " |
| April 4 | ..... | ..... | ..... | ..... | ..... | ..... | ..... | 56.03 | 58.70 | 58.35 | 57.34 |
| 5 | 57.24 | 57.12 | 59.89 | ..... | 60.82 | 56.73 | ..... | 57.08 | 58.86 | 57.71 | 59.42 |
| 6 | ..... | ..... | ..... | 57.22 | 56.62 | 54.38 | ..... | 56.98 | 55.94 | 56.27 | 57.39 |
| 7 | ..... | ..... | ..... | 55.44 | 60.14 | 55.57 | 57.67 | 57.50 | 57.26 | 55.94 | 60.61 |
| 8 | ..... | ..... | ..... | ..... | ..... | ..... | 57.78 | 57.69 | ..... | 55.94 | 57.08 |
| Mean of each pair | 57.24 | 57.12 | 59.89 | 56.33 | 59.19 | 55.56 | 57.72 | 57.05 | 57.69 | 56.84 | 58.36 |

TABLE VI—Continued.

| Date. | 12th pair. | 13th pair. | 14th pair. | 15th pair. | 16th pair. | 17th pair. | 18th pair. | 19th pair. | 20th pair. | 21st pair. | 22d pair. |
|---|---|---|---|---|---|---|---|---|---|---|---|
| | B. A. C. 3170 S. 3297 N. | B. A. C. 3204 S. 3290 N. | B. A. C. 3204 S. 3297 N. | B. A. C. 3327 S. 3364 N. | B. A. C. 3416 N. 3500 S. | B. A. C. 3523 S. 3533 N. | B. A. C. 3548 N. 3650 S. | B. A. C. 3560 N. 3650 S. | B. A. C. 3742 S. 3811 N. | B. A. C. 3842 S. 3856 N. | B. A. C. 3919 S. 3953 N. |
| 1855. | " | " | " | " | " | " | " | " | " | " | " |
| April 4 | 58.36 | 56.73 | ..... | 56.28 | 54.84 | 60.49 | 55.94 | 58.48 | ..... | ..... | ..... |
| 5 | 60.22 | ..... | 60.35 | 56.17 | 55.98 | 58.73 | 55.63 | 58.12 | 57.43 | 60.24 | 55.80 |
| 6 | 58.58 | 57.54 | 58.74 | 57.44 | ..... | ..... | 56.35 | 58.29 | ..... | 59.82 | 56.14 |
| 7 | ..... | 58.42 | 59.50 | 56.80 | 56.42 | 57.28 | 55.95 | ..... | 58.55 | 60.65 | ..... |
| 8 | ..... | 59.39 | ..... | 57.06 | 53.62 | 58.61 | 54.57 | 57.38 | 56.90 | 58.64 | 55.76 |
| Mean of each pair | 58.91 | 58.02 | 59.53 | 56.75 | 55.21 | 58.77 | 55.68 | 58.06 | 57.62 | 59.83 | 55.90 |

TABLE VI—Continued.

| Date. | 23d pair. | 24th pair. | 25th pair. | Latitude by a mean of each night. | 1st result. | 2d result. | 3d result. | Final result. |
|---|---|---|---|---|---|---|---|---|
| | B. A. C. 3953 N. 3992 S. | B. A. C. 3995 S. 4026 N. | B. A. C. 3995 S. 4028 N. | | Latitude by a mean of each pair. | Latitude by a mean of all the observations. | Lat. by a mean of the results for each night. | Mean of 1st, 2d, and 3d results. |
| 1855. | " | " | " | ° ′ " | ° ′ " | ° ′ " | ° ′ " | ° ′ " |
| April 4 | ..... | ..... | ..... | 31 20 57.41 | | | | |
| 5 | 55.27 | ..... | ..... | 31 20 57.44 | | | | |
| 6 | ..... | 58.77 | 59.85 | 31 20 57.43 | | | | |
| 7 | 58.76 | 57.44 | 58.97 | 31 20 57.83 | | | | |
| 8 | ..... | ..... | ..... | 31 20 57.08 | | | | |
| Mean of each pair | 57.01 | 58.10 | 59.41 | | 31 20 57.67 | 31 20 57.58 | 31 20 57.43 | 31 20 57.56 |

TABLE VII.

*Tabulation of results for the latitude of astronomical station at Espia, derived from observations made with a zenith telescope (T. & S.) on twenty-three pairs of stars: By J. H. Clark, Principal Assistant, assisted by Lieut. Turnbull.*

| Date. | 1st pair. | 2d pair. | 3d pair. | 4th pair. | 5th pair. | 6th pair. | 7th pair. | 8th pair. | 9th pair. | 10th pair. |
|---|---|---|---|---|---|---|---|---|---|---|
| | G. C. 638 S. 675 N. | G. C. 638 S. 677 N. | G. C. 638 S. 678 N. | B. A. C. 2540 S. 2592 N. | B. A. C. 2605 S. 2715 N. | B. A. C. 2894 S. 2984 N. | B. A. C. 2984 N. 3000 S. | B. A. C. 3002 S. 2984 N. | B. A. C. 3062 S. 3085 N. | B. A. C. 3170 S. 3290 N. |
| 1855. | " | " | " | " | " | " | " | " | " | " |
| March 24 | ........ | ........ | ........ | ........ | ........ | ........ | ........ | ........ | ........ | ........ |
| 25 | 53.39 | ........ | 53.36 | ........ | 56.77 | 57.15 | ........ | 57.25 | 53.70 | ........ |
| 26 | 54.74 | 55.01 | 56.47 | ........ | 54.84 | 56.53 | 55.05 | 55.09 | 54.33 | ........ |
| 27 | 54.11 | 53.68 | 55.39 | ........ | 54.77 | 57.94 | 55.80 | 57.53 | 56.84 | ........ |
| 29 | 55.97 | 56.16 | 57.67 | 57.36 | ........ | 58.15 | 55.75 | 57.01 | 55.64 | 57.17 |
| 31 | ........ | ........ | ........ | ........ | ........ | 56.92 | 55.38 | 56.68 | 55.17 | ........ |
| Mean of each pair... | 54.55 | 54.95 | 55.72 | 57.36 | 55.46 | 57.33 | 55.49 | 56.71 | 55.13 | 57.17 |

TABLE VII—Continued.

| Date. | 11th pair. | 12th pair. | 13th pair. | 14th pair. | 15th pair. | 16th pair. | 17th pair. | 18th pair. | 19th pair. | 20th pair. |
|---|---|---|---|---|---|---|---|---|---|---|
| | B. A. C. 3170 S. 3297 N. | B. A. C. 3204 S. 3290 N. | B. A. C. 3204 S. 3297 N. | B. A. C. 3327 S. 3364 N. | B. A. C. 3416 N. 3500 S. | B. A. C. 3523 S. 3533 N. | B. A. C. 3610 N. 3666 S. | B. A. C. 3742 S. 3811 N. | B. A. C. 3842 S. 3856 N. | B. A. C. 3919 S. 3953 N. |
| 1855. | " | " | " | " | " | " | " | " | " | " |
| March 24 | ........ | ........ | ........ | ........ | ........ | ........ | 58.35 | 56.10 | ........ | 57.59 |
| 25 | ........ | 56.32 | 57.84 | 57.08 | 54.91 | 56.32 | 58.92 | 57.68 | 57.94 | 56.33 |
| 26 | ........ | 56.21 | 57.02 | 56.19 | 54.51 | 58.89 | 57.42 | 57.15 | ........ | 57.28 |
| 27 | ........ | 57.49 | ........ | 55.81 | 54.87 | 58.21 | 58.21 | 57.78 | ........ | ........ |
| 29 | 58.67 | 56.85 | 58.35 | 57.08 | 56.19 | 55.86 | 59.09 | 57.58 | 59.03 | 56.31 |
| 31 | ........ | ........ | ........ | ........ | ........ | ........ | ........ | ........ | ........ | ........ |
| Mean of each pair... | 58.67 | 56.71 | 57.53 | 56.64 | 55.12 | 57.32 | 58.39 | 57.25 | 58.48 | 56.87 |

TABLE VII—Continued.

| Date. | 21st pair. | 22d pair. | 23d pair. | Latitude by a mean of each night. | 1st result. | 2d result. | 3d result. | Final result. |
|---|---|---|---|---|---|---|---|---|
| | B. A. C. 3992 S. 3953 N. | B. A. C. 3995 S. 4026 N. | B. A. C. 3995 S. 4028 N. | | Latitude by a mean of each pair. | Latitude by a mean of all the observations. | Latitude by a mean of the results for each night. | Latitude by a mean of 1st, 2d, and 3d results. |
| 1855. | " | " | " | ° ′ ″ | ° ′ ″ | ° ′ ″ | ° ′ ″ | ′ ″ |
| March 24 | 54.28 | ........ | ........ | 31 20 56.58 | | | | |
| 25 | 53.26 | 56.70 | 58.03 | 31 20 56.14 | | | | |
| 26 | 53.27 | 57.14 | 58.94 | 31 20 56.23 | | | | |
| 27 | ........ | ........ | ........ | 31 20 56.31 | | | | |
| 29 | 53.78 | 56.33 | 57.69 | 31 20 56.95 | | | | |
| 31 | ........ | ........ | ........ | 31 20 56.13 | | | | |
| Mean of each pair... | 53.67 | 56.89 | 58.22 | | 31 20 56.56 | 31 20 56.43 | 31 20 56.37 | 31 20 56.45 |

## TABLE VIII.

*Tabulation of results for the latitude of astronomical station at Carrizalillo, derived from observations made with a zenith telescope (T. & S.) on fourteen pairs of stars: By J. H. Clark, Principal Assistant, assisted by H. Campbell.*

| Date. | 1st pair. | 2d pair. | 3d pair. | 4th pair. | 5th pair. | 6th pair. | 7th pair. | 8th pair. | 9th pair. | 10th pair. | 11th pair. |
|---|---|---|---|---|---|---|---|---|---|---|---|
| | G. C. 389 N. 400 S. | G. C. 414 N. 400 S. | G. C. 419 N. 400 S. | G. C. 461 N. 505 S. | G. C. 570 N. 556 S. | G. C. 586 N. 589 S. | G. C. 653 N. 689 S. | G. C. 747 N. 714 S. | G. C. 747 N. 715 S. | G. C. 797 N. 792 S. | G. C. 822 N. 863 S. |
| 1855. | ″ | ″ | ″ | ″ | ″ | ″ | ″ | ″ | ″ | ″ | ″ |
| Feb'y 24 | | | | | 55.09 | | | | 56.72 | 52.15 | 54.78 |
| 25 | | 55.11 | 55.95 | | | | | | | 54.10 | 52.26 |
| 26 | 55.64 | 52.00 | 54.29 | | | | | | | 54.84 | 54.10 |
| 27 | 54.41 | 53.77 | 55.87 | | 57.73 | 53.50 | | | | 54.59 | 53.41 |
| March 2 | | | | | 54.71 | 55.06 | 57.89 | | 55.41 | 56.59 | |
| 3 | | | | 56.99 | 54.64 | 55.29 | 56.75 | | 57.71 | 55.39 | |
| 5 | | | | 56.09 | 53.07 | 54.00 | 54.83 | | 54.83 | 52.50 | 52.52 |
| 6 | | | | | 54.41 | | 57.26 | 56.82 | 57.16 | 54.64 | 53.86 |
| 7 | | | | 56.70 | 53.62 | 55.95 | 56.80 | | 58.27 | 54.47 | 54.74 |
| 8 | | | | 57.87 | 54.86 | 54.43 | | | | 53.87 | 54.12 |
| 12 | | | | | 54.84 | 55.23 | 56.03 | 55.83 | 55.48 | 56.39 | |
| Mean of each pair | 55.02 | 53.62 | 55.37 | 56.91 | 54.77 | 54.78 | 56.59 | 56.32 | 56.51 | 54.50 | 53.72 |

## TABLE VIII—Continued.

| Date. | 12th pair. | 13th pair. | 14th pair. | Latitude by a mean of each night. | 1st result. | 2d result. | 3d result. | Final result. |
|---|---|---|---|---|---|---|---|---|
| | G. C. 869 N. 871 S. | G. C. 880 N. 939 S. | 797 N., G. C. 2995 S., B. A. C. | | Latitude by a mean of each pair. | Latitude by a mean of all the observations. | Lat. by a mean of the results for each night. | Latitude by a mean of 1st, 2d, and 3d results. |
| 1855. | ″ | ″ | ″ | ° ′ ″ | ° ′ ″ | ° ′ ″ | ° ′ ″ | ° ′ ″ |
| Feb'y 24 | 55.91 | | | 31 50 54.93 | | | | |
| 25 | 54.71 | | | 31 50 54.42 | | | | |
| 26 | 54.78 | | | 31 50 54.61 | | | | |
| 27 | 56.62 | | | 31 50 54.98 | | | | |
| March 2 | | | | 31 50 55.93 | | | | |
| 3 | | | | 31 50 56.13 | | | | |
| 5 | 54.57 | 54.26 | | 31 50 54.07 | | | | |
| 6 | 56.55 | | | 31 50 55.81 | | | | |
| 7 | 55.41 | | | 31 50 55.74 | | | | |
| 8 | 55.38 | | | 31 50 55.09 | | | | |
| 12 | | | 55.94 | 31 50 55.67 | | | | |
| Mean of each pair | 55.74 | 54.26 | 55.94 | | 31 50 55.29 | 31 50 55.19 | 31 50 55.21 | 31 50 55.23 |

TABLE IX.

*Results for longitude of Carrizalillo, east of terminal point of parallel* 31° 47′ *north latitude. Observer, J. H. Clark: Computer, H. Campbell.*

| Date. | Authority for elements used. | Results for longitude from moon's 1st limb. | Date. | Authority for elements used. | Results for longitude from moon's 2d limb. |
|---|---|---|---|---|---|
| 1855. | | *h. m. s.* | 1855. | | *h. m. s.* |
| Feb. 23 | N. A. | 7 11 36.138 | March 3 | N. A. | 7 11 56.145 |
| 24 | ---------- | 46.304 | 4 | ---------- | 51.290 |
| 25 | ---------- | 47.792 | 7 | ---------- | 41.910 |
| 26 | ---------- | 35.111 | | | |
| 27 | ---------- | 43.990 | | | |
| March 1 | ---------- | 41.259 | | | |
| 2 | ---------- | 42.667 | | | |
| | | *h. m. s.* | | | *h. m. s.* |
| Mean longitude from moon's 1st limb | | 7 11 41.894 | Mean longitude from moon's 2d limb | | 7 11 49.781 |
| | | | Mean longitude from moon's 1st limb | | 41.894 |
| Mean longitude | | | | | 7*h.* 11*m.* 45.84*s.* |

| Date. | Results for longitude from moon's 1st and 2d limbs. | Remarks. |
|---|---|---|
| | *h. m. s.* | |
| Feb. 23 | 7 11 36.138 | |
| 24 | 46.304 | |
| 25 | 47.792 | |
| 26 | 35.111 | |
| 27 | 43.990 | |
| March 1 | 41.259 | |
| 2 | 42.667 | |
| 3 | 56.145 | |
| 4 | 51.290 | |
| 7 | 41.910 | |

Mean longitude adopted ---------- 7*h.* 11*m.* 44.26*s.*

TABLE X.

*Tabulation of results for the latitude of astronomical station at the Initial Point on the Rio Grande, derived from observations made with zenith telescope, (T. & S.,) on twenty-two pairs of stars: By J. H. Clark, principal assistant, assisted by H. Campbell.*

| Date. | 1st pair. | 2d pair. | 3d pair. | 4th pair. | 5th pair. | 6th pair. | 7th pair. | 8th pair. | 9th pair. | 10th pair. |
|---|---|---|---|---|---|---|---|---|---|---|
| | G. C. 18 N. 170 S. | G. C. 18 N. 251 S. | G. C. 135 N. 186 S. | G. C. 170 S. 277 N. | G. C. 194 N. 244 S. | G. C. 203 N. 244 S. | G. C. 204 S. 267 N. | G. C. 230 S. 267 N. | G. C. 244. S. 252 N. | G. C. 251 S. 277 N. |
| 1854. | " | " | " | " | " | " | " | " | " | " |
| Dec'r 27 | ........... | ........... | 51.20 | ........... | ........... | 49.17 | ........... | ........... | 48.04 | ........... |
| 28 | ........... | ........... | 52.07 | ........... | ........... | 50.21 | ........... | ........... | 49.85 | ........... |
| 29 | ........... | ........... | 49.75 | ........... | ........... | 51.60 | ........... | ........... | 50.30 | ........... |
| 1855. | | | | | | | | | | |
| Jan'y 1 | ........... | ........... | 51.78 | ........... | ........... | 52.07 | ........... | ........... | 50.87 | ........... |
| 2 | 50.06 | 49.46 | ........... | 50.43 | ........... | ........... | ........... | ........... | ........... | 50.10 |
| 3 | ........... | ........... | 50.70 | ........... | ........... | 51.89 | ........... | ........... | 51.44 | ........... |
| 6 | ........... | ........... | 51.42 | ........... | ........... | 51.58 | ........... | ........... | 50.31 | ........... |
| 9 | ........... | ........... | 50.73 | ........... | ........... | 53.00 | ........... | ........... | ........... | ........... |
| 11 | ........... | ........... | ........... | ........... | ........... | ........... | 50.67 | 52.02 | ........... | ........... |
| 13 | ........... | ........... | ........... | ........... | 50.99 | 50.77 | ........... | ........... | 50.63 | ........... |
| 14 | ........... | ........... | ........... | ........... | 52.28 | 50.74 | ........... | ........... | 50.88 | ........... |
| 15 | ........... | ........... | ........... | ........... | 53.79 | 53.09 | ........... | ........... | 52.42 | ........... |
| Mean of each pair... | 50.06 | 49.46 | 51.09 | 50.43 | 52.35 | 51.41 | 50.67 | 52.02 | 50.52 | 50.10 |

TABLE X—Continued.

| Date. | 11th pair. | 12th pair. | 13th pair. | 14th pair. | 15th pair. | 16th pair. | 17th pair. | 18th pair. | 19th pair. | 20th pair. |
|---|---|---|---|---|---|---|---|---|---|---|
| | G. C. 267 N. 271 S. | G. C. 311 N. 345 S. | G. C. 370 S. 389 N. | G. C. 389 N. 400 S. | G. C. 400 S. 414 N. | G. C. 400 S. 419 N. | G. C. 430 N. 448 S. | G. C. 461 N. 505 S. | G. C. 556 S. 570 N. | G. C. 586 N. 589 S. |
| 1854. | " | " | " | " | " | " | " | " | " | " |
| Dec'r 27 | 50.73 | 51.56 | 52.28 | ........... | 51.25 | 53.40 | 51.10 | 52.54 | 52.04 | 51.89 |
| 28 | 51.69 | 51.97 | 50.21 | ........... | 51.92 | ........... | 53.65 | ........... | 50.55 | 51.77 |
| 29 | ........... | 50.84 | 49.10 | ........... | 50.04 | 53.05 | 52.21 | ........... | ........... | ........... |
| 1855. | | | | | | | | | | |
| Jan'y 1 | 50.91 | ........... | 52.35 | ........... | 52.39 | ........... | 53.16 | ........... | ........... | ........... |
| 2 | ........... | 51.82 | 51.17 | ........... | 51.25 | ........... | 51.76 | ........... | 51.88 | 50.68 |
| 3 | ........... | ........... | 50.30 | ........... | 51.33 | ........... | 50.77 | ........... | 52.11 | 50.87 |
| 6 | 51.58 | 52.23 | 51.84 | ........... | 48.86 | ........... | 50.80 | ........... | 51.44 | 50.19 |
| 9 | 50.61 | 52.30 | 51.40 | ........... | 50.29 | ........... | ........... | ........... | ........... | ........... |
| 11 | 50.67 | 52.51 | ........... | 53.13 | 52.16 | 53.92 | 53.29 | ........... | ........... | ........... |
| 13 | 50.42 | ........... | 51.07 | ........... | 51.23 | 52.86 | 50.56 | ........... | ........... | ........... |
| 14 | 51.32 | 49.88 | ........... | ........... | 50.64 | 51.85 | 50.67 | ........... | ........... | ........... |
| 15 | 52.11 | 53.88 | 50.19 | ........... | 51.25 | 53.16 | 49.95 | ........... | ........... | ........... |
| Mean of each pair... | 51.11 | 51.85 | 50.99 | 53.13 | 51.05 | 53.04 | 51.62 | 52.54 | 51.60 | 51.08 |

TABLE X—Continued.

| Date. | 21st pair. G. C. 653 N. 661 S. | 22d pair. G. C. 652 N. 661 S. | Latitude by a mean of each night. | 1st result. Latitude by a mean of each pair. | 2d result. Latitude by a mean of all the observations. | 3d result. Latitude by a mean of the results for each night. | Final result. Mean of 1st, 2d, and 3d results. |
|---|---|---|---|---|---|---|---|
| 1854. | ″ | ″ | ° ′ ″ | ° ′ ″ | ° ′ ″ | ° ′ ″ | ° ′ ″ |
| Dec'r 27.......... | 50.71 | .............. | 31 46 51.22 | | | | |
| 28.......... | .............. | .............. | 31 46 51.39 | | | | |
| 29.......... | .............. | .............. | 31 46 50.86 | | | | |
| 1855. | | | | | | | |
| Jan'y 1.......... | .............. | .............. | 31 46 51.93 | | | | |
| 2.......... | .............. | 50.01 | 31 46 50.78 | | | | |
| 3.......... | 49.50 | .............. | 31 46 50.99 | | | | |
| 6.......... | .............. | 51.85 | 31 46 51.12 | | | | |
| 9.......... | .............. | .............. | 31 46 51.39 | | | | |
| 11.......... | .............. | .............. | 31 46 52.29 | | | | |
| 13.......... | .............. | .............. | 31 46 51.06 | | | | |
| 14.......... | .............. | .............. | 31 46 51.13 | | | | |
| 15.......... | .............. | .............. | 31 46 52.17 | | | | |
| Mean of each pair... | 50.10 | 50.93 | | 31 46 51.23 | 31 46 51.30 | 31 46 51.35 | 31 46 50.29 |

## 9.—*Azimuths for laying off the prime vertical of stations from* 1 *to* 8, *inclusive.*

*Measurements for establishing the prime vertical at the initial point of parallel* 31° 47′.

JANUARY 7, 1855.

| Reading of azimuth circle instrument in true meridian, previously determined by transit observations. | | | | Reading of azimuth circle instrument in prime vertical. | | | |
|---|---|---|---|---|---|---|---|
| Ver. A. | B. | C. | D. | A. | B. | C. | D. |
| ° ′ ″ | ° ′ ″ | ° ′ ″ | ° ′ ″ | ° ′ ″ | ° ′ ″ | ° ′ ″ | ° ′ ″ |
| 90 00 00 | 180 00 05 | 270 00 07 | .............. | 180 00 00 | 270 00 15 | 359 59 55 | 89 59 40 |
| 89 59 55 | 180 00 00 | 269 59 55 | 359 59 45 | 180 00 05 | 270 00 15 | 360 00 10 | 90 00 00 |
| 89 59 55 | 180 00 00 | 270 00 05 | 360 00 05 | .............. | .............. | .............. | .............. |
| 89 59 56.6 | 180 00 01.6 | 270 00 02.3 | 359 59 55 | 180 00 02.5 | 270 00 15 | 360 00 02.5 | 89 59 50 |

*Observations for the determination of the true meridian at San Luis Springs.*

APRIL 20, 1855.

| Time of observation by chronometer 2419, sidereal. | Reading of azimuth circle, telescope directed on star. Ver. 1. | 2. | 3. | 4. | Reading of azimuth circle when plane of instrument stands in true meridian. Ver. 1. | 2. | 3. | 4. | Computed azimuth of Polaris west of north at each observation. | Remarks. |
|---|---|---|---|---|---|---|---|---|---|---|
| h. m. s. | ° ′ ″ | ° ′ ″ | ° ′ ″ | ° ′ ″ | ° ′ ″ | ° ′ ″ | ° ′ ″ | ° ′ ″ | ° ′ ″ | |
| 11 42 18 | 181 29 15 | 271 29 10 | 1 29 15 | 91 29 15 | 179 58 23.9 | 269 58 19.4 | 359 58 19.4 | 89 58 20.9 | 1 30 54.1 | Chronometer 2419 is fast 2*h*. 42*m*. 0.57*s*. |
| 11 54 14.7 | 181 26 30 | 271 26 25 | 1 26 15 | 91 26 25 | 179 58 14.7 | 269 58 09.7 | 359 58 00 | 89 58 09.9 | 1 28 15.3 | The reading of azimuth circle when telescope |
| 12 05 00.9 | 181 24 10 | 271 24 10 | 1 24 00 | 91 24 05 | 179 58 28.9 | 269 58 28.9 | 359 58 19 | 89 58 24 | 1 25 41.10 | was directed on signal = zero. |
| | | | | | 179 58 22.5 | 269 58 19.3 | 359 58 12.8 | 89 58 18.2 | | Error of signal from true meridian west of north = 1′ 41″.8. |

| | ′ ″ |
|---|---|
| Ver. No. 1.................................................................. | 1 37.5 |
| 2.................................................................. | 1 40.7 |
| 3.................................................................. | 1 47.2 |
| 4.................................................................. | 1 41.8 |
| Mean.................................................................. | 1 41.8 |

## 9.—*Azimuths for laying off the prime vertical, &c.*—Continued.

*Observations for the determination of the true meridian at San Luis Springs.*

APRIL 22, 1855.

| Time by chronometer 2419, sidereal. | Reading of azimuth circle, telescope directed on star. | | | | Reading of azimuth circle, telescope directed on signal. | | | | Reading of azimuth circle when plane of inst. stands in true meridian. | | | | Computed azim'h of Polaris west of N. at each observation. | Results |
|---|---|---|---|---|---|---|---|---|---|---|---|---|---|---|
| | Ver. 1. | 2. | 3. | 4. | Ver. 1. | 2. | 3. | 4. | Ver. 1. | 2. | 3. | 4. | | |
| h. m. s. | ° ′ ″ | ° ′ ″ | ° ′ ″ | ° ′ ″ | ° ′ ″ | ° ′ ″ | ° ′ ″ | ° ′ ″ | ° ′ ″ | ° ′ ″ | ° ′ ″ | ° ′ ″ | ° ′ ″ | ′ ″ |
| 11 51 26.6 | 91 27 20 | 181 27 10 | 271 27 20 | 1 27 30 | 90 00 15 | 180 00 00 | 270 00 10 | 0 00 25 | 89 58 24.8 | 179 58 14.8 | 269 58 24.8 | 0 58 34.8 | 1 28 55.20 | 1 47.70 |
| 12 11 55.7 | 91 22 30 | 181 22 10 | 271 22 25 | 1 22 35 | 90 00 30 | 180 00 05 | 270 00 35 | 0 00 55 | 89 58 36.1 | 179 58 16.1 | 269 58 31.1 | 0 58 41.1 | 1 23 53.9 | 1 58.67 |
| 12 31 05.7 | 91 17 40 | 181 17 25 | 271 17 35 | 1 17 50 | ........ | .......... | .......... | ........ | 89 59 05.1 | 179 58 50.1 | 269 59 00.1 | 0 59 15 | 1 18 34.9 | 57.42 |
| 12 41 20.6 | 91 14 40 | 181 14 25 | 271 14 40 | 1 14 50 | 90 01 00 | 180 00 45 | 270 01 05 | 0 01 20 | 89 59 10 | 179 58 55 | 269 59 10 | 0 59 20 | 1 15 30 | 1 57.50 |
| | | | | | 90 00 35 | 180 00 16.6 | 270 00 36.6 | 0 00 53.3 | 89 58 49.0 | 179 58 34.0 | 269 58 46.5 | 0 58 57.72 | .......... | 1 40.32 |

| | ′ ″ |
|---|---|
| Error of signal from true meridian West of North.................................... | 1 40.32 |
| Result April 20.................................................................... | 1 41.80 |
| Error of signal by a mean of two nights' observations......................... | 1 41.06 |

*Observations for the determination of the true meridian at San Bernardino.*

APRIL 28, 1855.

| Time of observation by chronometer 2419, sidereal. | Reading of azimuth circle, telescope directed on star. | | | | Reading of azimuth circle, telescope directed on signal. | | | | Mean difference of readings at each observation. | Azimuth of Polaris at each observation deduced from east elongation. | Error of signal from true meridian by each observation. |
|---|---|---|---|---|---|---|---|---|---|---|---|
| | Ver. 1 | 2 | 3 | 4 | Ver. 1 | 2 | 3 | 4 | | | |
| h. m. s. | ° ′ ″ | ° ′ ″ | ° ′ ″ | ° ′ ″ | ° ′ ″ | ° ′ ″ | ° ′ ″ | ° ′ ″ | ° ′ ″ | ° ′ ″ | ′ ″ |
| 21 51 01.4 | 89 59 50 | 179 59 35 | 269 59 40 | 0 00 45 | 91 11 40 | 181 11 35 | 271 11 45 | 1 12 05 | 1 11 48.75 | 1 42 52.46 | 30 63.71 |
| 22 01 07.9 | 89 59 35 | 179 59 40 | 269 59 45 | 0 00 15 | 91 11 30 | 181 11 27.5 | 271 11 40 | 1 12 00 | 1 11 50.6 | 1 42 40.76 | 30 50.16 |
| 22 08 06.9 | 89 59 50 | 179 59 45 | 270 00 02 | 0 00 20 | 91 11 30 | 181 11 27.5 | 271 11 40 | 1 12 00 | 1 11 40 | 1 42 25.68 | 30 45.68 |
| 22 13 51.6 | 90 00 05 | 179 59 40 | 270 00 07.5 | 0 00 25 | 91 11 30 | 181 11 27.5 | 271 11 40 | 1 12 00 | 1 11 35 | 1 42 08.96 | 30 33.96 |

Error of signal from true meridian E. of N. = 30′ 48″.37.

APRIL 29, 1855.

| Time of observation by chronometer 2419, sidereal. | Reading of azimuth circle, telescope directed on star. | | | | Reading of azimuth circle, telescope directed on signal. | | | | Mean difference of readings at each observation. | Azimuth of Polaris at each observation deduced from east elongation. | Error of signal from true meridian by each observation. |
|---|---|---|---|---|---|---|---|---|---|---|---|
| | Ver. 1 | 2 | 3 | 4 | Ver. 1 | 2 | 3 | 4 | | | |
| h. m. s. | ° ′ ″ | ° ′ ″ | ° ′ ″ | ° ′ ″ | ° ′ ″ | ° ′ ″ | ° ′ ″ | ° ′ ″ | ° ′ ″ | ° ′ ″ | ′ ″ |
| 21 54 47.1 | 359 59 15 | 89 59 10 | 179 59 20 | 269 59 35 | 1 11 45 | 91 11 32.5 | 181 11 42 | 271 11 50 | 1 12 22.37 | 1 42 49.57 | 30 27.20 |
| 22 01 37 | 359 59 20 | 89 59 10 | 179 59 15 | 269 59 35 | 1 11 45 | 91 11 32.5 | 181 11 42 | 271 11 50 | 1 12 22.34 | 1 42 40.00 | 30 17.66 |
| 22 20 02.9 | 0 00 22 | 90 00 02.5 | 180 00 22.5 | 270 00 32.5 | 1 11 35 | 91 11 15 | 181 11 40 | 271 11 45 | 1 11 13.87 | 1 41 46.83 | 30 32.96 |

Error of signal from true meridian E. of N. = 30′ 25″.94.

## 9.—*Azimuths for laying off the prime vertical, &c.*—Continued.

*Observations for the determination of the true meridian at San Bernardino*—Continued.

APRIL 30, 1855.

| Time of observation by chronometer 2419, sidereal. | Reading of azimuth circle, telescope directed on star. | | | | Reading of azimuth circle, telescope directed on signal. | | | | Mean difference of readings at each observation. | Azimuth of Polaris at each observation deduced from east elongation. | Error of signal from true meridian by each observation. |
|---|---|---|---|---|---|---|---|---|---|---|---|
| | Ver. 1 | 2 | 3 | 4 | Ver. 1 | 2 | 3 | 4 | | | |
| h. m. s. | ° ′ ″ | ° ′ ″ | ° ′ ″ | ° ′ ″ | ° ′ ″ | ° ′ ″ | ° ′ ″ | ° ′ ″ | ° ′ ″ | ° ′ ″ | ′ ″ |
| 21 35 38.5 | 358 47 55 | 88 48 00 | 178 47 45 | 268 47 40 | 359 59 45 | 89 59 50 | 179 59 40 | 269 59 20 | 1 11 48.75 | 1 42 47.33 | 30 58.58 |
| 21 49 08.6 | 358 47 45 | 88 47 40 | 178 47 45 | 268 47 30 | 359 59 45 | 89 59 50 | 179 59 35 | 269 59 25 | 1 11 58.75 | 1 42 53.35 | 30 54.60 |
| 22 09 35.8 | 358 47 45 | 88 47 55 | 178 47 40 | 268 47 35 | 359 59 42 | 89 59 40 | 179 59 25 | 269 59 20 | 1 11 48.12 | 1 42 22.04 | 30 33.92 |

| | ′ ″ |
|---|---|
| Error of signal from true meridian . . . . . . . . | 30 49.03 |
| April 29, signal from true meridian . . . . . . . | 30 25.94 |
| April 28, signal from true meridian . . . . . . . | 30 48.37 |
| Mean error of signal from true meridian E. of N. | 30 41.11 |

*Observations for the determination of the true meridian at camp near the head of the Santa Cruz river.*

MAY 10, 1855.

| Time of observation by chronometer 2419, sidereal. | Reading of azimuth circle, telescope directed on star. | | | | Reading of azimuth circle, telescope directed on signal. | | | | Mean difference of readings at each observation. | Azimuth of Polaris at each observation deduced from east elongation. | Error of signal from true meridian by each observation. |
|---|---|---|---|---|---|---|---|---|---|---|---|
| | Ver. 1 | 2 | 3 | 4 | Ver. 1 | 2 | 3 | 4 | | | |
| h. m. s. | ° ′ ″ | ° ′ ″ | ° ′ ″ | ° ′ ″ | ° ′ ″ | ° ′ ″ | ° ′ ″ | ° ′ ″ | ° ′ ″ | ° ′ ″ | ° ′ ″ |
| 21 44 51.8 | 170 03 15 | 260 03 20 | 350 03 22.5 | 80 03 30 | 179 59 45 | 269 59 45 | 359 59 50 | 89 59 55 | 9 56 26.87 | 1 42 52.09 | 8 13 34.78 |
| 21 55 32.9 | 170 03 15 | 260 03 10 | 350 03 15 | 80 03 20 | 179 59 45 | 269 59 30 | 359 59 50 | 89 59 50 | 9 56 28.70 | 1 42 54.67 | 8 13 34.03 |
| 22 10 37.8 | 170 03 15 | 260 03 10 | 350 03 17 | 80 03 25 | 179 59 45 | 269 59 35 | 359 59 50 | 89 59 55 | 9 56 29.50 | 1 42 35.48 | 8 13 54.50 |

Error of signal on true meridian West of North, 8° 13′ 41″.10.

*Observations at the intersection of the parallel* 31° 20′ *and the* 111*th*° *of longitude west from Greenwich for the determination of the true meridian.*

JUNE 14, 1855.

| Time of observation by chronometer 2419, sidereal. | Reading of azimuth circle, telescope directed on star. | | | Reading of azimuth circle, telescope directed on signal. | | | Mean difference of readings at each observation. | Azimuth of Polaris at each observation deduced from east elongation. | Error of signal from true meridian by each observation. | Remarks. |
|---|---|---|---|---|---|---|---|---|---|---|
| | Ver. 1 | 2 | 3 | Ver. 1 | 2 | 3 | | | | |
| h. m. s. | ° ′ ″ | ° ′ ″ | ° ′ ″ | ° ′ ″ | ° ′ ″ | ° ′ ″ | ° ′ ″ | ° ′ ″ | ° ′ ″ | |
| 21 43 12.5 | 120 18 45 | 0 18 45 | 240 19 10 | 117 59 00 | 257 59 15 | 237 58 45 | 2 19 50 | 1 42 52.4 | 36 57 46 | Chronometer 2419 fast 2*h.* 54*m.* 20*s.* |
| 21 51 34.5 | 120 19 30 | 0 19 30 | 240 19 15 | 117 59 15 | 257 59 15 | 237 59 30 | 2 20 05 | 1 43 01.7 | 37 03 26 | |

Azimuth of signal by a mean of two observations on Polaris East of North, 37′ 00″.36.

## 9.—*Azimuths for laying off the prime vertical, &c.*—Continued.

*Observations at the intersection of the parallel* 31° 20′ *and the* 111*th*° *of longitude west from Greenwich, &c.*—Continued.

JUNE 15, 1855.

| Time of observation by chronometer 2419, sidereal. | Reading of azimuth circle, telescope directed on star. | | Reading of azimuth circle, telescope directed on signal. | | Mean difference of readings at each observation. | Azimuth of Polaris at each observation deduced from east elongation. | Error of signal from true meridian by each observation. | Remarks. |
|---|---|---|---|---|---|---|---|---|
| | Ver. 1 | 2 | Ver. 1 | 2 | | | | |
| h. m. s. | ° ′ ″ | ° ′ ″ | ° ′ ″ | ° ′ ″ | ° ′ ″ | ° ′ ″ | ′ ″ | |
| 21 22 10.5 | 312 10 50 | 132 10 55 | 309 52 15 | 129 52 20 | 2 18 35 | 1 41 52.7 | 36 42.30 | Chronometer 2419 fast 2*h*. 54*m*. 25*s*. |
| 21 27 23.5 | 312 11 15 | 132 11 05 | 309 52 15 | 120 52 20 | 2 18 52 | 1 42 12.35 | 36 39.65 | Azimuth of signal by a mean of ten observation |
| 21 44 22.5 | 312 11 45 | 132 12 10 | 309 52 10 | 129 52 30 | 2 19 37.5 | 1 42 54.27 | 36 43.24 | on Polaris East of North, 36′ 55″.59. |
| 21 50 58 | 312 12 10 | 132 12 25 | 309 52 10 | 129 52 30 | 2 19 57.5 | 1 43 01.29 | 36 55.21 | |
| 21 55 48 | 312 12 15 | 132 12 20 | 309 52 10 | 129 52 30 | 2 19 57.5 | 1 43 03.24 | 36 54.26 | |
| 21 58 47 | 312 12 40 | 132 12 20 | 309 52 10 | 129 52 25 | 2 20 15 | 1 43 03.07 | 37 11.93 | |
| 22 06 46 | 312 12 00 | 132 12 20 | 309 52 10 | 129 52 25 | 2 19 52.5 | 1 42 57.41 | 36 54.04 | |
| 22 10 38 | 312 11 55 | 132 12 10 | 309 52 10 | 129 52 25 | 2 19 45 | 1 42 52.05 | 36 52.95 | |
| 22 19 06.5 | 312 12 00 | 132 12 15 | 309 52 10 | 129 52 25 | 2 19 50 | 1 42 34.03 | 37 15.97 | |
| 22 25 07 | 312 11 30 | 132 11 45 | 309 52 00 | 129 52.30 | 2 19 22.5 | 1 42 16.13 | 37 06.37 | |

| | ′ ″ |
|---|---|
| Result June 14th.......................................................... | 37 06.36 |
| Result June 15th.......................................................... | 36 55.59 |
| Azimuth of signal by a mean of two nights' observations on Polaris............ | 36 57.97 |

## 10.—*Elements for marking parallels of latitude* 31° 20′ *and* 31° 47′.

PARALLEL 31° 20′.

| Distances from point of beginning (on tangent.) | | Length of offset from tangent (= difference of latitude.) | | Latitude of points on tangent. | Azimuth of tangent at several points bearing North East. | Longitude of points *five miles* apart on the parallel of 31° 20′. |
|---|---|---|---|---|---|---|
| Miles. | Feet. | In arc. | In feet. | | | |
| | | ″ | | ° ′ ″ | ° ′ ″ | ° ′ ″ |
| 0 | 0 | 0.000 | 0.000 | 31 20 00.00 | 90 00 00.0 | 0 00 00.00 |
| 1 | 0 | 0.004 | 0.4 | 00.00 | 89 59 43.3 | 1 00.88 |
| 5 | 0 | 0.100 | 10.1 | 19 59.90 | 57 21.7 | 5 04.413 |
| 10 | 0 | 0.401 | 40.5 | 59.60 | 54 43.4 | 10 08.826 |
| 15 | 0 | 0.902 | 91.1 | 59.10 | 52 05.0 | 15 13.24 |
| 20 | 0.8 | 1.604 | 162.0. | 58.40 | 49 26.8 | 20 16.75 |
| 25 | 1.2 | 2.506 | 253.2 | 57.50 | 46 48.5 | 25 22.06 |
| 30 | 1.7 | 3.609 | 364.6 | 56.39 | 44 10.2 | 30 26.48 |
| 35 | 2.6 | 4.913 | 496.4 | 55.09 | 41 32.0 | 35 30.89 |
| 40 | 4.3 | 6.417 | 648.4 | 53.58 | 38 53.7 | 40 35.33 |
| 45 | 6.0 | 8.121 | 820.5 | 51.88 | 36 15.9 | 45 39.70 |
| 50 | 7.7 | 10.026 | 1013.0 | 49.97 | 33 37.2 | 50 44.13 |
| 55 | 10.3 | 12.131 | 1225.7 | 47.87 | 30 58.9 | 55 48.54 |
| 60 | 13.8 | 14.437 | 1458.7 | 45.56 | 28 21.6 | 1 00 52.96 |
| 64 +972 ft. | 16.6 | 16.522 | 1669.3 | 43.48 | 26 08.2 | 1 05 07.69 |
| 100 | 62.4 | 40.115 | 4056.2 | 19.89 | 07 15.0 | 1 41 28.26 |

## 10.—*Elements for marking parallels, &c.*—Continued.

### PARALLEL 31° 47′.

| Distance, in miles, from the point of beginning. | Length of offset (= difference of latitude.) | | Latitude at the end of any distance on the tangent. | Azimuth of the tangent at any distance bearing North East. | Longitude of the point of the parallel determined by each offset. |
|---|---|---|---|---|---|
| | In arc. | In feet. | | | |
| | ″ | | ° ′ ″ | ° ′ ″ | ′ ″ |
| 1 | 0.004 | 0.4 | 31 47 00.00 | 89 59 43.0 | 1 01.17 |
| 5 | 0.102 | 10.3 | 46 59.90 | 57 18.9 | 5 05.88 |
| 10 | 0.408 | 41.2 | 59.59 | 54 37.8 | 10 11.75 |
| 15 | 0.918 | 92.7 | 59.08 | 51 56.7 | 15 17.63 |
| 20 | 1.632 | 164.9 | 58.37 | 49 15.5 | 20 23.50 |
| 25 | 2.550 | 257.6 | 57.45 | 46 34.5 | 25 29.37 |
| 30 | 3.673 | 371.1 | 56.33 | 43 53.0 | 30 25.24 |
| 35 | 5.000 | 505.2 | 55.00 | 41 12.2 | 35 41.11 |
| 40 | 6.530 | 659.8 | 53.47 | 38 31.2 | 40 46.97 |
| 45 | 8.265 | 835.0 | 51.74 | 35 50.0 | 45 52.83 |
| 50 | 10.203 | 1030.9 | 49.80 | 33 09.0 | 50 58.68 |
| 55 | 12.346 | 1247.4 | 47.65 | 30 08.0 | 56 04.53 |
| 60 | 14.692 | 1484.4 | 45.31 | 27 47.0 | 61 10.37 |

Log. N in feet................ = 7.3210287
Log. $(1 + e^2 \cos.{}^2 L)$ ........ = 0.0021098
Log. 2 sin 1″................ = 4.9866049
Log. sin 1″.................. = 4.6855749

1° of parallel................ = 104,069.2 yds.
10′ of parallel................ = 17,344.87 "
1′ of parallel................ = 1,734.487 "
1″ of parallel................ = 28.908 "
1″ of parallel................ = 86.724 feet.

$$L - l = D^2 \frac{\text{tang. } L\ (1 + e^2 \cos L)}{N^2\ 2 \sin 1''}$$

$$Z = 90° - D \text{ tang. } l \frac{1}{N \sin 1''}$$

$$\text{Diff. long.} = D \frac{1}{N \sin 1''}\ \frac{1}{\cos l}$$

D = distance in feet, measured on tangent.
L = lat. of points of beginning of ditto.
$l$ = lat. of any point of tangent.
Z = azimuth of tangent line at any point.

Log. $(L - l)$ = log. $(D^2)$ + 0.1579269
Log. 2 sin 1″ = 4.9866049
Log. sin 1″ = 4.6855749

### MEMORANDA.

| | | |
|---|---|---|
| | | ° ′ ″ |
| One hundred miles of parallel of 31° 47′ .................................... | = | 1 41 57.55 |
| Longitude of initial point of parallel on Rio Bravo, (by survey from Frontera.) .. | | 106 31 26.50 |
| Longitude of terminal point of parallel 31° 47′................................ | | 108 13 24.05 |
| Longitude of terminal point of parallel 31° 20′, (by treaty).................... | = | 111 00 00.00 |
| | | ° ′ ″ |
| Length of parallel 31° 20′—in arc............................................ | = | 2 46 35.95 |
| Do..........do......in yards.................................................. | | 288964.03 |
| Do..........do......in feet................................................... | | 866892.10 |
| Do..........do......in miles and feet......................................... | = | 164 miles + 972 feet. |
| One degree of parallel of latitue 31° 47′..................................... | = | 103,570.85 yards. |
| One minute of........do........do............................................. | | 1,726.18 " |
| One second of........do........do............................................. | | 28.77 " |
| Or in feet.................................................................... | = | 86.310 |
| One degree of parallel of latitude 31° 20′.................................... | = | 104,069.2 yards. |
| One minute of........do..........do............................................ | | 1,734.487 " |
| One second of........do..........do............................................ | | 28.908 " |
| Or in feet.................................................................... | = | 86.724 |
| From parallel 31° 20′ to 31° 47′ = 27′........................................ | = | 31 miles + 5.37 feet. |
| One degree of meridian (middle latitude being 31° 33½)........................ | = | 121,248.43 yards. |
| One minute of ....do..........do..........do.................................. | | 2,020.807 " |
| One second of ....do..........do..........do.................................. | | 33.680 " |
| Or in feet.................................................................... | = | 101.04 |

# ASTRONOMICAL POSITIONS

ALONG

# THE RIO BRAVO DEL NORTE.

---

D.—BOUNDARY LINE FORMED BY THE RIO BRAVO DEL NORTE.

Office of Survey of the United States and Mexican Boundary,
*Washington, D. C., May* 22, 1856.

Sir: In my communication of February 9, 1856, I presented to you the final results for the longitudes of the astronomical station, established under your direction in the year 1853, near the mouth of Rio Bravo del Norte, the same having been computed with corresponding observations made at Greenwich, Philadelphia High School, and Radcliffe observatories.

I have now to present, in a tabular form, the individual results of all the observations made by you and under your orders for the longitudes and latitudes of the primary astronomical positions on and near the Rio Bravo del Norte, established in connexion with the survey of the United States and Mexican boundary.

I.—Longitudes.

The positions thus determined are eight in number, being enumerated as follows in the order of place from the west:

*a*. Frontera.

$a^1$. San Elceario.

*b*. El Paso del Norte.

*c*. Mouth of Cañon.

*d*. Presidio del Norte.

*e*. Fort Duncan, Texas.

*f*. Ringgold Barracks.

*g*. Mouth of Rio Bravo del Norte.

All the observations made at these places, together with the computations, as well as the elements and data used therein, are *herewith* presented in a tabular form, comprising the corresponding observations made at Greenwich, Cambridge, Philadelphia High School, and Radcliffe observatories.*

Attached to this is also a recapitulation of the results, from which are deduced the final longitude adopted for each station, the papers being marked *a*, $a^1$, *b*, *c*, *d*, *e*, *f*, *g*, to each of which I will briefly call your attention.

*a*. *Frontera*.—The observations at this place extend through four lunations, commencing December 29, 1851, and ending April 6, 1852; making, as combined in table (I,) the longitude=$7^h\ 6^m\ 13^s.02$ west of Greenwich.

* These computations are to be deposited in the Department of the Interior, in manuscript form.

$a^1$. *San Elceario.*—Moon culminations were observed at this place simultaneous with those observed at Frontera. These observations extend through a period of five lunations, commencing January 29, and ending June 3, 1852; making, as combined in table (II,) the longitude of San Elceario=$7^h$ $5^m$ $4^s.43$ west of the meridian of Greenwich.

This result, however, as well as that above given for Frontera, has been corrected by combining with them the difference of longitude of these places, as determined by flashes of gunpowder simultaneously observed at Frontera, El Paso del Norte, and San Elceario, on the nights of February 14, 18, 19, and March 14, 1852, (see table III,) by which it appears that San Elceario is east of Frontera=$1^m$ $7^s.30$, whilst that deduced from moon culminations, $1^m$ $8^s.59$; difference,=$1^s.29$.

The longitudes of Frontera and San Elceario, as determined from moon culminations, being corrected by half the difference $\frac{1^s.29}{2}$, gives for the final adopted longitude of Frontera $7^h$ $6^m$ $12^s.37$; San Elceario, $7^h$ $5^m$ $5^s.07$.

*b. El Paso del Norte* being, as determined by flashes, $15^s.94$ east of Frontera, it is therefore in longitude=$7^h$ $5^m$ $56^s.43$ west of the meridian of Greenwich.

*c.* The astronomical station "near the *mouth of the Cañon,*" on the left bank of Rio Bravo del Norte, is in longitude=$7^h$ $2^m$ $29^s.06$; having been determined, in the absence of moon culminations, by thirteen flashes of gunpowder, simultaneously observed at that station and San Elceario, on the night of June 21, 1852, to be $2^m$ $36^s.0$ east of San Elceario.—(See table IV.)

*d.* The astronomical station near *Presidio del Norte,* on the left bank of Rio Bravo del Norte, was determined by a series of moon culminations, observed during a period of two lunations, commencing July 26, 1852, and ending August 29, 1852, determining its position to be $6^h$ $57^m$ $39^s.02$ west of the meridian of Greenwich.—(See table V.)

*e.* The astronomical station near *Fort Duncan,* Texas, was determined to be in longitude $6^h$ $42^m$ $1^s.78$ west of the meridian of Greenwich, from observed moon culminations, commencing October 19, and ending October 27, 1852, combined as per table herewith marked VI.

*f. Ringgold Barracks* is in longitude $6^h$ $35^m$ $6^s.19$, as determined by moon culminations observed on ten nights during the months of June and July, 1853, the several results being combined as per table herewith, marked VII.

*g.* The longitude of the astronomical station near the *mouth of the Rio Bravo del Norte* has already been discussed by me, as presented to you in report of February 19, 1856, (herewith appended, marked *g,*) to which I refer you for the conclusion of the subject of the longitudes of the primary points on the Rio Bravo; it explains in detail the manner in which all the observations and computations have been tabulated, for which reason I have not herein before made reference thereto.

## II. Latitudes.

The two volumes herewith* (marked *Latitudes,*) contain, in a tabulated form, all the individual observations made by yourself with the zenith instrument, for determining the latitudes of all the primary astronomical stations on and near the Rio Bravo del Norte, from Frontera down to its mouth, with the exception of San Elceario and Fort Duncan; of these two, the former was determined in 1851, by Lieutenant Whipple, topographical engineers, by transits of stars over the prime vertical, and the latter in 1852, by Lieutenant Michler, topographical engineers, by circum-meridian altitudes of N. and S. stars observed with a sextant.

* To be deposited in the Department of the Interior.

The tables appended present a recapitulation of all the results for the latitudes of the primary stations, giving results which have been adopted, as follows, viz:

*a. Frontera*, by a mean of 106 observations made by W. H. Emory, on twenty-four pairs of stars observed near the zenith, is determined by combining the results, as in table herewith, marked VIII, to be in latitude = 31° 48′ 44″.53.

The table marked IX, indicates the corrections derived from actual observations of the stars at the Washington Observatory, which corrections have been applied as indicated in table IX*a*.

*b. San Elceario** was determined by Lieutenant Whipple in 1851, by twenty prime vertical observations on eight stars, to be in latitude 31° 35′ 12″.62, the individual results being combined as shown in table X.

*c.* Astronomical station near the *mouth of Cañon* is in latitude 31° 2′ 26″.15, as determined by Major Emory in 1852, from fifty observations on twenty-one pairs of stars near the zenith; the individual results being combined as shown in table marked XI. Table XI*a*, shows the corrections which have been applied as indicated in table XI, in order to introduce the stars' elements as given in the "Twelve-Year Catalogue."

*d.* Astronomical station near *Presidio del Norte* is in latitude 29° 34′ 7″.13, as determined by Major W. H. Emory in 1852, from 121 observations on twenty-six pairs of stars near the zenith, combined as shown in table marked XII. Table XII*a*, shows the corrections which have been applied as indicated in table XII, in order to introduce the stars' positions as given in the "Twelve-Year Catalogue."

*e. Fort Duncan* (Eagle Pass) is in latitude 28° 42′ 43″.67, as determined by Lieutenant N. Michler, topographical engineers, in 1852, from eighty-seven altitudes of north and south stars, observed with a sextant, combined as in table marked XIII.

*f. Ringgold Barracks* (observatory) is in latitude 26° 22′ 27″.79, as determined by Major Emory in 1853, from 107 observations on thirty-two pairs of stars near the zenith, combined as shown in table marked XIV. Table XIV*a*, shows the corrections which have been applied as indicated in table XIV, in order to give to the stars their positions furnished in the "Twelve-Year Catalogue."

*g.* The astronomical station near the *mouth of Rio Bravo del Norte* is in latitude 25° 57′ 21″.83, as determined by Major W. H. Emory in 1853, from 129 observations on twenty pairs of stars near the zenith, combined as shown in table marked XV.

The papers herewith have been arranged in this manner with a view to facilitate you in preparing them for such further use as you may deem best.

Very respectfully, your obedient servant,

GEO. THOM,

*Captain Topographical Engineers.*

Major Wm. H. Emory, *United States Commissioner.*

* This place was subsequently determined by myself, not knowing that Lieutenant Whipple had observed there; but finding he had done so, I gave his observations priority.—W. H. E.

TABLE I.

*Tabulation of results* for longitude of astronomical station at Frontera observatory, derived from observations made with the bronzed transit and sidereal chronometer No. 2440, (by Parkinson & Frodsham:) By Major Wm. H. Emory, Chief Astronomer and Surveyor United States and Mexican boundary survey.*

| Date. | Moon's first limb. | Date. | Moon's sec'd limb. |
|---|---|---|---|
| 1851. | h. m. s. | 1852. | h. m. s. |
| Dec. 29 | 7 06 05.1 | Jan. 7 | 7 06 08.7 |
| 30 | 08.2 | 8 | 22.0 |
| 31 | 13.1 | 9 | 15.4 |
| 1582. | | 10 | 06.4 |
| Jan. 1 | 09.0 | | 21.2 |
| 3 | 13.2 | | |
| Mean.......... | h. m. s. =7 06 08.66 | Mean—2d limb ... | h. m. s. =7 06 14.74 |
| | | Mean—1st limb... | = 08.66 |
| Mean longitude from first lunation .................. | | | h. m. s. =7 06 11.70 |

| Date. | Moon's first limb. | Date. | Moon's sec'd limb. |
|---|---|---|---|
| 1852. | h. m. s. | 1852. | h. m. s. |
| Feb. 28 | 7 06 06.0 | Mar. 4 | 7 06 20.0 |
| 29 | 08.1 | 5 | 13.8 |
| Mar. 1 | 17.8 | 6 | 09.6 |
| 2 | 14.1 | 8 | 14.8 |
| 3 | 13.3 | | |
| 4 | 19.7 | | |
| 5 | 17.4 | | |
| Mean............ | h. m. s. =7 06 13.77 | Mean—2d limb ... | h. m. s. =7 06 14.55 |
| | | Mean—1st limb... | = 13.77 |
| Mean longitude from third lunation.................... | | | h. m. s. =7 06 14.16 |

| Date. | Moon's first limb. | Date. | Moon's sec'd limb. |
|---|---|---|---|
| 1852. | h. m. s. | 1852. | h. m. s. |
| Jan. 29 | 7 06 16.6 | Feb. 4 | 7 06 10.2 |
| 30 | 11.2 | 5 | 06.3 |
| Feb. 1 | 17.7 | 7 | 14.2 |
| 2 | 19.6 | 9 | 13.6 |
| 4 | 09.1 | 10 | 07.7 |
| | | 11 | 17.1 |
| Mean.......... | h. m. s. =7 06 14.96 | Mean—2d limb ... | h. m. s. =7 06 11.52 |
| | | Mean—1st limb... | = 14.96 |
| Mean longitude from second lunation................ | | | h. m. s. =7 06 13.24 |

| Date. | Moon's first limb. | Date. | Moon's sec'd limb. |
|---|---|---|---|
| 1852. | h. m. s. | 1852. | h. m. s. |
| Mar. 31 | 7 06 08.6 | April 4 | 7 06 13.9 |
| April 1 | 05.6 | 5 | 13.9 |
| 2 | 16.1 | 6 | 19.8 |
| Mean............ | h. m. s. =7 06 10.1 | Mean—2d limb ... | h. m. s. =7 06 15.87 |
| | | Mean—1st limb... | = 10.10 |
| Mean longitude from fourth lunation.................. | | | h. m. s. =7 06 12.98 |

| Lunation. | Longitude deduced. |
|---|---|
| | h. m. s. |
| First............................................ | 7 06 11.70 |
| Second .......................................... | 7 06 13.24 |
| Third ........................................... | 7 06 14.16 |
| Fourth........................................... | 7 06 12.98 |
| * Longitude of Frontera.......................... | h. m. s. =7 06 13.02 |

* Reduced from Greenwich observations for 1851–'52.

TABLE II.

*Tabulation of results for longitude of astronomical station at San Elceario, Texas, derived from observations made with transit (by Troughton & Simms) and mean solar chronometer No. 76, (by Charles Young:) By Lieut. William F. Smith, topographical engineers, and by J. Lawson, under the direction of Major W. H. Emory, chief astronomer and surveyor of the United States and Mexican boundary survey.*

| Date. | Authority for elements used. | Moon's 1st limb. | Resulting longitude from observations on moon's 1st l'b. |
|---|---|---|---|
| 1852. | | *h. m. s.* | *h. m. s.* |
| Jan. 29 | Greenwich Right Ascensions | 7 05 06.07 | |
| | Cambridge observations..... | 7 05 05.77 | 7 05 05.96 |
| | Cambridge Right Ascensions. | 7 05 06.04 | |
| 30 | Greenwich Right Ascensions | 7 04 59.80 | |
| | Greenwich observations..... | 7 04 59.09 | 7 04 59.45 |
| 31 | Greenwich Right Ascensions. | ................ | 7 05 01.30 |
| Feb. 1 | Greenwich Right Ascensions. | 7 04 58.70 | |
| | Greenwich observations..... | 7 04 59.70 | 7 04 59.20 |
| 2 | Greenwich Right Ascensions. | ................ | 7 05 03.50 |
| 4 | Greenwich Right Ascensions. | ................ | 7 05 01.80 |

Mean longitude from moon's 1st limb = 7*h.* 05*m.* 01*s.*87

| Date. | Authority for elements used. | Moon's 2d limb. | Resulting longitude from observations on moon's 2d l'b. |
|---|---|---|---|
| | | *h. m. s.* | *h. m. s.* |
| Feb. 8 | Greenwich Right Ascensions. | ................ | 7 05 04.4 |
| 9 | Greenwich Right Ascensions. | ................ | 7 05 02.1 |
| 11 | Greenwich Right Ascensions. | ................ | 7 05 01.9 |
| 12 | Greenwich Right Ascensions. | ................ | 7 05 06.9 |

Mean longitude from moon's 2d limb = 7*h.* 05*m.* 03*s.*83
Mean longitude from moon's 1st limb = 7*h.* 05*m.* 01*s.*87

Mean longitude from 1st lunation = 7*h.* 05*m.* 02*s.*85.

| Date. | Authority for elements used. | Moon's 1st limb. | Resulting longitude from observations on moon's 1st l'b. |
|---|---|---|---|
| 1852. | | *h. m. s.* | *h. m. s.* |
| Feb. 28 | Greenwich Right Ascensions. | ................ | 7 05 02.7 |
| 29 | Greenwich Right Ascensions. | 7 05 03.6 | |
| | Greenwich observations. ... | 7 05 02.4 | 7 05 03.0 |
| March 1 | Greenwich Right Ascensions. | 7 05 06.6 | |
| | Washingt'n Right Ascensions | 7 05 04.2 | 7 05 05.4 |
| 2 | Greenwich Right Ascensions. | 7 05 08.4 | |
| | Greenwich observations..... | 7 05 08.9 | |
| | Washingt'n Right Ascensions | 7 05 07.1 | 7 05 07.22 |
| | Cambridge Right Ascensions. | 7 05 03.3 | |
| | Cambridge observations..... | 7 05 08.4 | |
| 4 | Greenwich Right Ascensions. | ................ | 7 05 04.3 |
| 5 | Greenwich Right Ascensions. | 7 05 05.6 | |
| | Greenwich observations..... | 7 05 05.2 | 7 05 05.4 |

Mean longitude from moon's 1st limb = 7*h.* 05*m.* 04*s.*67

| Date. | Authority for elements used. | Moon's 2d limb. | Resulting longitude from observations on moon's 2d l'b. |
|---|---|---|---|
| 1852. | | *h. m. s.* | *h. m. s.* |
| March 5 | Greenwich Right Ascensions. | 7 05 06.8 | |
| | Greenwich observations..... | 7 05 08.5 | 7 05 07.65 |
| 7 | Greenwich Right Ascensions. | ................ | 7 05 09.8 |

Mean longitude from moon's 2d limb = 7*h.* 05*m.* 08*s.*73
Mean longitude from moon's 1st limb = 7*h.* 05*m.* 04*s.*67

Mean longitude from 2d lunation = 7*h.* 05*m.* 06*s.*70.

TABLE II—Continued.

| Date. | Authority for elements used. | Moon's 1st limb. | Resulting longitude from observations on moon's 1st l'b. | Date. | Authority for elements used. | Moon's 2d limb. | Resulting longitude from observations on moon's 2d l'b. |
|---|---|---|---|---|---|---|---|
| 1852. | | *h. m. s.* | *h. m. s.* | 1852. | | *h. m. s.* | *h. m. s.* |
| March 29 | Greenwich Right Ascensions. | ............... | 7 05 02.1 | April 4 | Greenwich Right Ascensions. | ............... | 7 05 07.9 |
| 30 | Greenwich Right Ascensions. | ............... | 7 05 11.5 | 5 | Greenwich Right Ascensions. | ............... | 7 05 01.5 |
| April 1 | Greenwich Right Ascensions. | 7 05 05.8 | | 6 | Greenwich Right Ascensions. | ............... | 7 05 01.5 |
| | Greenwich observations..... | 7 05 07.6 | 7 05 07.63 | | | | |
| | Cambridge Right Ascensions. | 7 05 10.4 | | | | | |
| | Cambridge observations..... | 7 05 06.7 | | | | | |
| 2 | Greenwich Right Ascensions. | 7 05 05.6 | 7 05 07.75 | | | | |
| | Greenwich observations..... | 7 05 09.9 | | | | | |

Mean longitude from moon's 1st limb = 7*h.* 05*m.* 07*s*.24.

Mean longitude from moon's 2d limb = 7*h.* 05*m.* 03*s*.80.
Mean longitude from moon's 1st limb = 7*h.* 05*m.* 07*s*.24.

Mean longitude from third lunation = 7*h.* 05*m.* 05*s*.27.

| Date. | Authority for elements used. | Moon's 1st limb. | Resulting longitude from observations on moon's 1st l'b. | Date. | Authority for elements used. | Moon's 1st limb. | Resulting longitude from observations on moon's 1st l'b. |
|---|---|---|---|---|---|---|---|
| 1852. | | *h. m. s.* | *h. m. s.* | 1852. | | *h. m. s.* | *h. m. s.* |
| April 29 | Greenwich Right Ascensions. | 7 05 00.5 | | April 30 | Cambridge Right Ascensions. | 7 05 02.8 | 7 05 03.05 |
| | Cambridge Right Ascensions. | 7 05 05.7 | 7 05 02.73 | | Cambridge observations. ... | 7 05 03.3 | |
| | Cambridge observations..... | 7 05 02.0 | | | | | |

Mean longitude from moon's 1st limb = 7*h.* 05*m.* 02*s*.89.

| Date. | Authority for elements used. | Moon's 1st limb. | Resulting longitude from observations on moon's 1st l'b. | Date. | Authority for elements used. | Moons 2d limb. | Resulting longitude from observations on moon's 2d l'b. |
|---|---|---|---|---|---|---|---|
| 1852. | | *h. m. s.* | *h. m. s.* | 1852. | | *h. m. s.* | *h. m. s.* |
| May 28 | Greenwich Right Ascensions. | 7 05 03.3 | | June 3 | Greenwich Right Ascensions. | ..... .......... | 7 05 01.4 |
| | Cambridge Right Ascensions. | 7 05 02.9 | 7 05 02.63 | | | | |
| | Cambridge observations..... | 7 05 01.7 | | | | | |
| 29 | Greenwich Right Ascensions. | ............... | 7 05 10.20 | | | | |
| 31 | Greenwich Right Ascensions. | 7 05 00.6 | 7 05 01.10 | | | | |
| | Greenwich observations..... | 7 05 01.6 | | | | | |
| June 1 | Greenwich Right Ascensions. | ............... | 7 05 02.30 | | | | |

Mean long. from moon's 1st limb.................. = 7*h.* 05*m.* 04*s*.06
Mean long. from moon's 1st limb, by preceding lunation = 7*h.* 05*m.* 02*s*.89

Mean long. from moon's 2d limb.................. = 7*h.* 05*m.* 01*s*.40
Mean of last two lunations from moon's first limb.... = 7*h.* 05*m.* 03*s*.48

Mean longitude from fourth and fifth lunations = 7*h.* 05*m.* 02*s*.44.

| | | *h. m. s.* |
|---|---|---|
| Longitude of San Elceario from first lunation.................................... | = | 7 05 02.85 |
| Do.........do.......from second lunation.................................... | = | 7 05 06.70 |
| Do.........do.......from third lunation.................................... | = | 7 05 05.27 |
| Do.... .....do.......from fourth and fifth lunations.................................... | = | 7 05 02.44 |

Longitude of San Elceario = 7*h.* 05*m.* 04*s*.43.

TABLE III.

*Difference of longitude between Frontera and San Elceario, by flashes of gunpowder, made on the 14th February, 1852.*

| No. of flash. | Name of station. | Name of chronometer. | Time of flash by chronometer. | Chronometer, fast or slow, of mean solar or sidereal time. | Mean solar time of flash at each station. | Difference of longitude. |
|---|---|---|---|---|---|---|
| | | | h. m. s. | m. s. | h. m. s. | m. s. |
| 1 | Frontera | P. & F. 2440 sidereal | 5 07 32.8 | 27 52.08 Sidereal chronometer 2440 fast of sidereal time at Frontera, derived from its error on the 10th and 18th | 7 02 40.36 | 1 07.24 |
| | San Elceario | C. Y. 76 solar | 7 01 12.0 | 2 35.60 Mean solar chronometer 76 slow of mean time at San Elceario | 7 03 47.60 | |
| 2 | Frontera | 2440 sidereal | 5 09 31.0 | | 7 04 38.24 | *1 06.26 |
| | San Elceario | 76 solar | 7 03 09.9 | | 7 05 44.50 | |
| 3 | Frontera | 2440 sidereal | 5 11 46.5 | | 7 06 53.37 | 1 07.63 |
| | San Elceario | 76 solar | 7 05 25.4 | | 7 08 01.00 | |
| 4 | Frontera | 2440 sidereal | 5 13 30.5 | | 7 08 37.09 | 1 06.91 |
| | San Elceario | 76 solar | 7 07 08.4 | | 7 09 44.00 | |
| 5 | Frontera | 2440 sidereal | 5 15 31.3 | | 7 10 37.56 | 1 07.24 |
| | San Elceario | 76 solar | 7 09 09.2 | | 7 11 44.80 | |
| 6 | Frontera | 2440 sidereal | 5 20 31.3 | | 7 15 36.74 | 1 07.06 |
| | San Elceario | 76 solar | 7 14 08.2 | | 7 16 43.80 | |
| 7 | Frontera | 2440 sidereal | 5 22 32.0 | | 7 17 36.87 | 1 07.43 |
| | San Elceario | 76 solar | 7 16 08.7 | | 7 18 44.30 | |
| 8 | Frontera | 2440 sidereal | 5 24 34.3 | | 7 19 39.07 | 1 07.13 |
| | San Elceario | 76 solar | 7 18 10.6 | | 7 20 46.20 | |
| 9 | Frontera | 2440 sidereal | 5 26 32.8 | | 7 21 37.25 | 1 07.05 |
| | San Elceario | 76 solar | 7 20 08.7 | | 7 22 44.30 | |
| 10 | Frontera | 2440 sidereal | 5 28 32.3 | | 7 23 36.42 | 1 06.92 |
| | San Elceario | 76 solar | 7 22 07.8 | | 7 24 43.40 | |
| 11 | Frontera | 2440 sidereal | 5 33 34.8 | | 7 28 38.10 | 1 07.30 |
| | San Elceario | 76 solar | 7 27 09.8 | | 7 29 45.40 | |
| 12 | Frontera | 2440 sidereal | 5 35 32.8 | | 7 30 35.77 | 1 06.99 |
| | San Elceario | 76 solar | 7 29 07.16 | | 7 31 42.76 | |
| 13 | Frontera | 2440 sidereal | 5 37 33.8 | | 7 32 36.45 | 1 07.07 |
| | San Elceario | 76 solar | 7 31 07.92 | | 7 33 43.52 | |
| 14 | Frontera | 2440 sidereal | 5 39 34.6 | | 7 34 36.92 | 1 07.08 |
| | San Elceario | 76 solar | 7 33 08.4 | | 7 35 44.00 | |
| 15 | Frontera | 2440 sidereal | 5 41 47.3 | | 7 36 49.25 | *1 06.75 |
| | San Elceario | 76 solar | 7 35 20.4 | | 7 37 56.00 | |

* Reject.

Difference of longitude deduced from 13 flashes of gunpowder, February 14 ........ 1 m. 07.15 s.

TABLE III—Continued.

*Difference of longitude between Frontera and San Elceario, by flashes of gunpowder, made on the 18th February,* 1852.

| No. of flash. | Name of station. | Name of chronometer. | Time of flash by chronometer. | Chronomete, fast or slow, of mean solar or sidereal time. | Mean solar time of flash at each station. | Difference of longitude. |
|---|---|---|---|---|---|---|
| | | | *h. m. s.* | *m. s.* | *h. m. s.* | *m. s.* |
| 1 | Frontera ........................ | P. & F. 2440 sidereal ....... | 5 25 02.6 | Sidereal chronometer 2440 is fast sidereal time at Frontera........................ 28 09.46 | 7 04 06.33 | 1 07.17 |
| | San Elceario . .................. | C. Y. 76 solar .............. | 7 02 40.80 | Mean solar chronometer 76 slow of mean time at San Elceario...................... 2 33.00 | 7 05 13.50 | |
| | | | 7 02 40.2 *d* | | | |
| 2 | Frontera ........................ | 2440 sidereal ........... | 5 27 02.5 | | 7 06 05.90 | 1 07.77 |
| | San Elceario .................... | 76 solar ............... | 7 04 40.4 | | 7 07 13.67 | |
| | | | L. 40.8 | | | |
| | | | C. 40.8 | | | |
| 3 | Frontera ........................ | 2440 sidereal............ | 5 29 27.0 | | 7 08 30.17 | 1 07.53 |
| | San Elceario .................... | 76 solar ............... | 7 07 04.6 | | 7 09 37.70 | |
| | | | 7 07 00.8 *d* | | | |
| 4 | Frontera ........................ | 2440 sidereal........... | 5 31 03.5 | | 7 10 06.41 | 1 07.7 |
| | San Elceario .................... | 76 solar ............... | 7 08 41.2 | | 7 11 14.20 | |
| | | | 7 08 41.2 | | | |
| 5 | Frontera ........................ | 2440 sidereal............ | 5 33 04.8 | | 7 12 07.38 | 1 07.45 |
| | San Elceario .................... | 76 solar ............... | 7 10 41.9 | | 7 13 14.83 | |
| | | | 7 10 41.9 | | | |
| | | | 7 10 41.7 | | | |
| 6 | Frontera ........................ | 2440 sidereal............ | 5 38 04.9 | | 7 17 06.66 | 1 07.54 |
| | San Elceario .................... | 76 solar ............... | 7 15 41.2 | | 7 18 41.20 | |
| | | | 7 15 41.2 | | | |
| | | | 7 15 41.2 | | | |
| 7 | Frontera ........................ | 2440 sidereal............ | 5 40 05.5 | | 7 19 06.93 | 1 07.27 |
| | San Elceario .................... | 76 solar ............... | 7 17 41.2 | | 7 20 14.20 | |
| | | | 7 17 41.2 | | | |
| | | | 7 17 41.2 | | | |
| 8 | Frontera ........................ | 2440 sidereal............ | 5 42 05.6 | | 7 21 06.55 | 1 07.60 |
| | San Elceario .................... | 76 solar ............... | 7 19 41.16 | | 7 22 14.15 | |
| | | | 7 19 41.2 | | | |
| | | | 7 19 41.1 | | | |
| 9 | Frontera ........................ | 2440 sidereal............ | 5 44 05.8 | | 7 23 06.42 | 1 07.78 |
| | San Elceario .................... | 76 solar ............... | 7 21 41.2 | | 7 24 14.20 | |
| | | | 7 21 41.2 | | | |
| | | | 7 21 41.2 | | | |
| 10 | Frontera ........................ | 2440 sidereal............ | 5 46 06.8 | | 7 25 07.09 | 1 07.38 |
| | San Elceario .................... | 76 solar ............... | 7 23 41.5 | | 7 26 14.47 | |
| | | | 7 23 41.5 | | | |
| | | | 7 23 41.4 | | | |
| 11 | Frontera ........................ | 2440 sidereal............ | 5 51 07.3 | | 7 30 06.76 | 1 07.44 |
| | San Elceario .................... | 76 solar ............... | 7 28 41.2 | | 7 31 14.20 | |
| | | | 7 28 41.2 | | | |
| | | | 7 28 41.2 | | | |
| 12 | Frontera ........................ | 2440 sidereal............ | 5 53 07.5 | | 7 32 06.63 | 1 07.57 |
| | San Elceario .................... | 76 solar ............... | 7 30 41.2 | | 7 33 14.20 | |
| | | | 7 30 41.2 | | | |
| | | | 7 30 41.2 | | | |
| 13 | Frontera ........................ | 2440 sidereal............ | 5 55 07.8 | | 7 34 06.60 | 1 07.50 |
| | San Elceario .................... | 76 solar ............... | 7 32 41.1 | | 7 35 14.10 | |
| | | | 7 32 41.1 | | | |
| | | | 7 32 41.1 | | | |
| 14 | Frontera ........................ | 2440 sidereal............ | 5 57 08.3 | | 7 36 06.77 | 1 07.63 |
| | San Elceario .................... | 76 solar ............... | 7 34 41.4 | | 7 37 14.40 | |
| | | | 7 34 41.4 | | | |
| | | | 7 34 41.4 | | | |
| 5 | Frontera ........................ | 2440 sidereal............ | 5 59 08.4 | | 7 38 06.55 | 1 07.65 |
| | an Elceario .................... | solar ............... | 7 36 41.2 | | 7 39 14.20 | |
| | | | 7 36 41.2 | | | |
| | | | 7 36 41.2 | | | |

Mean difference of longitude by 15 flashes of gunpowder, February 18............. 1*m.* 07.54*s.*

TABLE III—Continued.

*Difference of longitude between Frontera and San Elceario, by flashes of gunpowder, made on the 19th of February, 1852.*

| No. of flash. | Name of station. | Name of chronometer. | Time of flash by chronometer. | Chronometer, fast or slow, of mean solar or sidereal time. | Mean solar time of flash at each station. | Difference of longitude. |
|---|---|---|---|---|---|---|
| | | | h. m. s. | | h. m. s. | m. s. |
| 1 | Frontera | P. & F. 2440 sidereal | 5 28 06.3 | Sidereal chronometer 2440 is fast of sidereal time at Frontera, m. s. 28 14.43 | 7 03 08.67 | 1 04.99 |
| | San Elceario | C. Y. 76 solar | 7 01 41.3d | Solar chronometer 76 is slow of mean time at San Elceario, 2 32.6 | 7 04 13.66 | |
| 2 | Frontera | 2440 sidereal | 5 30 08.3 | | 7 05 10.33 | 1 07.63 |
| | San Elceario | 76 solar | 7 03 45.6 | | 7 06 17.96 | |
| | | | 7 03 43.6d | | | |
| 3 | Frontera | 2440 sidereal | 5 32 09.4 | | 7 07 11.10 | 1 07.29 |
| | San Elceario | 76 solar | 7 05 46.0 | | 7 08 18.39 | |
| | | | 7 05 46.0 | | | |
| | | | 7 05 46.1 | | | |
| 4 | Frontera | 2440 sidereal | 5 34 09.2 | | 7 09 10.68 | 1 07.27 |
| | San Elceario | 76 solar | 7 07 45.5 | | 7 10 17.95 | |
| | | | 7 07 45.6 | | | |
| | | | 7 07 45.6 | | | |
| 5 | Frontera | 2440 sidereal | 5 36 09.8 | | 7 11 10.95 | 1 07.41 |
| | San Elceario | 76 solar | 7 09 46.0 | | 7 12 18.36 | |
| | | | 7 09 46.0 | | | |
| | | | 7 09 46.0 | | | |
| 6 | Frontera | 2440 sidereal | 5 41 10.8 | | 7 16 11.12 | 1 07.54 |
| | San Elceario | 76 solar | 7 14 46.3 | | 7 17 18.66 | |
| | | | 7 14 46.3 | | | |
| | | | 7 14 46.3 | | | |
| 7 | Frontera | 2440 sidereal | 5 43 10.6 | | 7 18 10.70 | 1 07.36 |
| | San Elceario | 76 solar | 7 16 45.6 | | 7 19 18.06 | |
| | | | 7 16 45.6 | | | |
| | | | 7 16 45.8 | | | |
| 8 | Frontera | 2440 sidereal | 5 45 10.8 | | 7 20 10.57 | 1 07.42 |
| | San Elceario | 76 solar | 7 18 45.6 | | 7 21 17.99 | |
| | | | 7 18 45.6 | | | |
| | | | 7 18 45.7 | | | |
| 9 | Frontera | 2440 sidereal | 5 47 12.5 | | 7 22 11.94 | 1 07.22 |
| | San Elceario | 76 solar | 7 20 46.72 | | 7 23 19.16 | |
| | | | 7 20 46.8 | | | |
| | | | 7 20 46.8 | | | |
| 10 | Frontera | 2440 sidereal | 5 49 11.8 | | 7 24 10.91 | 1 07.45 |
| | San Elceario | 76 solar | 7 22 46.0 | | 7 25 18.36 | |
| | | | 7 22 46.0 | | | |
| | | | 7 22 46.0 | | | |
| 11 | Frontera | 2440 sidereal | 5 54 51.3 | | 7 29 49.29 | 1 07.07 |
| | San Elceario | 76 solar | 7 28 24.0 | | 7 30 56.36 | |
| 12 | Frontera | 2440 sidereal | 5 56 12.8 | | 7 31 10.56 | 1 07.40 |
| | San Elceario | 76 solar | 7 29 45.6 | | 7 32 17.96 | |
| | | | 7 29 45.6 | | | |
| | | | 7 29 45.6 | | | |
| 13 | Frontera | 2440 sidereal | 5 58 14.6 | | 7 33 12.03 | 1 07.54 |
| | San Elceario | 76 solar | 7 31 47.2 | | 7 34 19.57 | |
| | | | 7 31 47.2 | | | |
| | | | 7 31 47.2 | | | |
| 14 | Frontera | 2440 sidereal | 6 00 13.3 | | 7 35 10.41 | 1 07.38 |
| | San Elceario | 76 solar | 7 33 45.4 | | 7 36 17.79 | |
| | | | 7 33 45.5 | | | |
| | | | 7 33 45.4 | | | |
| 15 | Frontera | 2440 sidereal | 6 02 14.3 | | 7 37 11.08 | 1 07.13 |
| | San Elceario | 76 solar | 6 35 47.7* | | 7 38 18.21 | |
| | | | 6 35 45.9 | | | |
| | | | 6 35 45.8 | | | |

* Rejected.

Mean difference of longitude by 15 flashes of gunpowder, February 19, 1m. 07s.36.

TABLE III—Continued.

*Difference of longitude between Frontera and San Elceario, by flashes of gunpowder, made on the 14th March, 1852.*

| No. of flash. | Name of station. | Name of chronometer. | Time of flash by chronometer. | Chronometer, fast or slow, of mean solar or sidereal time. | Mean solar time of flash at each station. | Difference of longitude. |
|---|---|---|---|---|---|---|
| | | | h. m. s. | m. s. | h. m. s. | m. s. |
| 1 | Frontera | P. & F. 2440 sidereal | 7 01 06.8 | 30 05.32 (Sidereal chronometer 2440 fast of sidereal time at Frontera) | 6 59 41.57 | 1 07.44 |
| | San Elceario | C. Y. 76 solar | L. 6 58 36.0 | 2 13.11 (Mean solar chronometer 76 slow of mean time at San Elceario) | 7 00 49.01 | |
| | | | C. 6 58 35.8 | | | |
| 2 | Frontera | 2440 sidereal | 7 03 07.4 | | 7 01 41.84 | 1 07.27 |
| | San Elceario | 76 solar | L. 7 00 36.0 | | 7 02 49.11 | |
| | | | C. 7 00 36.0 | | | |
| 3 | Frontera | 2440 sidereal | 7 05 07.5 | | 7 03 41.62 | 1 07.09 |
| | San Elceario | 76 solar | L. 7 02 35.6 | | 7 04 48.71 | |
| | | | C. 7 02 35.6 | | | |
| 4 | Frontera | 2440 sidereal | 7 07 08.2 | | 7 05 41.99 | 1 07.12 |
| | San Elceario | 76 solar | L. 7 04 36.0 | | 7 06 49.11 | |
| | | | C. 7 04 36.0 | | | |
| 5 | Frontera | 2440 sidereal | 7 09 08.5 | | 7 07 41.96 | 1 06.65 |
| | San Elceario | 76 solar | L. 7 06 35.5 | | 7 08 48.61 | |
| | | | C. 7 06 35.5 | | | |
| 6 | Frontera | 2440 sidereal | 7 14 08.8 | | 7 12 41.56 | 1 07.20 |
| | San Elceario | 76 solar | L. 7 11 35.6 | | 7 13 48.76 | |
| | | | C. 7 11 35.7 | | | |
| 7 | Frontera | 2440 sidereal | 7 16 09.5 | | 7 14 41.94 | 1 07.12 |
| | San Elceario | 76 solar | L. 7 13 36.0 | | 7 15 49.06 | |
| | | | C. 7 13 35.9 | | | |
| 8 | era | 2440 sidereal | 7 18 09.5 | | 7 16 41.61 | 1 07.10 |
| | San Elcearia | 76 solar | L. (Lost.) | | 7 17 48.71 | |
| | | | C. 7 15 35.6 | | | |
| 9 | Frontera | 2440 sidereal | 7 20 09.6 | | 7 18 41.37 | 1 07.29 |
| | San Elceario | 76 solar | 7 17 35.6 | | 7 19 48.66 | |
| | | | 7 17 35.5 | | | |
| 10 | Frontera | 2440 sidereal | 7 22 10.3 | | 7 20 41.74 | 1 07.37 |
| | San Elceario | 76 solar | L. 7 19 36.0 | | 7 21 49.11 | |
| | | | C. 7 19 36.0 | | | |
| 11 | Frontera | 2440 sidereal | (Lost.) | | (Lost.) | |
| | San Elceario | 76 solar | L. 7 24 36.0 | | 7 26 49.11 | |
| | | | C. 7 24 36.0 | | | |
| 12 | Frontera | 2440 sidereal | 7 29 11.2 | | 7 27 41.38 | 1 06.93 |
| | San Elceario | 76 solar | L. 7 26 35.2 | | 7 28 48.31 | |
| | | | 7 26 35.2 | | | |
| 13 | Frontera | 2440 sidereal | 7 31 11.6 | | 7 29 41.45 | 1 07.26 |
| | San Elceario | 76 solar | L. 7 28 35.6 | | 7 30 48.71 | |
| | | | C. 7 28 35.8 | | | |
| 14 | Frontera | 2440 sidereal | 7 33 12.3 | | 7 31 41.82 | 1 07.09 |
| | San Elceario | 76 solar | L. 7 30 35.8 | | 7 32 48.91 | |
| | | | C. 7 30 35.8 | | | |
| 15 | Frontera | 2440 sidereal | 7 35 13.4 | | 7 33 42.59 | 1 07.27 |
| | San Elceario | 76 solar | L. 7 32 36.7 | | 7 34 49.86 | |
| | | | C. 7 32 36.8 | | | |

Mean of 14 observations, March 14, 1852 ................................ = 1m. 07.15s.

The record of the flashes, to establish the difference of longitude between Frontera and San Elceario, is given as a means of determining the weight to be attached to this mode of observing. Assuming the result to be correct, it gives a very satisfactory coincidence between the results obtained for longitude at Frontera and San Elceario, by moon culminations, by two independent positions, with different instruments and different observers.

The record is omitted for other stations, but the results are given in the following table:

TABLE IV.

*Recapitulation of differences of longitude of several astronomical stations on the Rio Bravo, found by flashes of gunpowder.*

| Date. | No. of flashes. | Difference of long. between Frontera & El Paso. | No. of flashes. | Difference of long. between Frontera & San Elceario. | Difference of long. betweeen El Paso & San Elceario. | No. of flashes. | Difference of long. between San Elceario and mouth of Cañon. |
|---|---|---|---|---|---|---|---|
| 1852. | | s. | | m. s. | s. | | m. s. |
| Feb. 14 | 14 | 16.03 | 13 | 1 07.16 | 51.13 | | |
| 18 | 15 | 16.06 | 15 | 1 07.54 | 51.48 | | |
| 19 | 12 | 15.84 | 15 | 1 07.36 | 51.52 | | |
| Mar. 14 | 12 | 15.84 | 14 | 1 07.15 | 51.31 | | |
| June 21 | .. | ..... | .. | ........ | ..... | 13 | 2 36.01 |

TABLE V.

*Long. of station near Presidio del Norte, computed from observations with transit, by W. H. Emory.*

| With tabular R. A. in Nautical Almanac. | | | With Greenwich observed R. A. | | |
|---|---|---|---|---|---|
| 1852. | | h. m. s. | 1852. | | h. m. s. |
| July 26 | Observations on moon's 1st limb.......... | =6 57 18.17 | July 26 | Observations on moon's 1st limb.......... | =6 57 37.53 |
| 27 | .........do............do............... | = 27.32 | 27 | .........do............do............... | = 47.67 |
| 28 | .........do............do............... | = 37.41 | 28 | .........do............do............... | = 55.76 |
| 29 | .........do............do............... | = 17.00 | 29 | .........do............do............... | = 34.50 |
| Aug. 24 | .........do............do............... | = 24.76 | Aug. 24 | .........do............do............... | = 44.76 |
| 25 | .........do............do............... | = 17.56 | 25 | .........do............do............... | = 39.02 |
| 27 | .........do............do............... | = 06.04 | 27 | .........do............do............... | = 41.35 |
| 28 | .........do............do............... | = 03.41 | 28 | .........do............do............... | = 20.30 |
| | Sum.............................. | = 8)151.67 | | Sum.............................. | = 8)320.89 |
| | Mean.............................. | =6 57 18.96 | | Mean.............................. | =6 57 40.11 |
| July 30 | Observations on moon's 2d limb.......... | =6 57 22.82 | July 30 | Observations on moon's 2d limb.......... | =6 57 39.66 |
| 31 | .........do............do............... | = 11.67 | 31 | .........do............do............... | = 28.78 |
| Aug. 1 | .........do............do............... | = 35.48 | Aug. 1 | .........do............do............... | = 43.27 |
| 2 | .........do............do............... | = 06.73 | 2 | .........do............do............... | = 32.89 |
| 3 | .........do............do............... | = 25.13 | 3 | .........do............do............... | = 40.42 |
| 4 | .........do............d ............... | = 36.06 | 4 | .........do............do............... | = 47.38 |
| 29 | .........do............do............... | = 08.70 | 29 | .........do............do............... | = 33.10 |
| | Sum.............................. | = 7)146.59 | | Sum.............................. | = 7)265.50 |
| | Moon's 2d limb—mean.............. | =6 57 20.94 | | Moon's 2d limb—mean.............. | =6 57 37.93 |
| | Moon's 1st limb—m an.............. | =6 57 18.96 | | Moon's 1st limb—mean.............. | =6 57 40.11 |
| | Sum.............................. | = 39.90 | | Sum.............................. | = 78.04 |
| | Mean.............................. | =6 57 19 95 | | Mean.............................. | =6 57 39.02 |
| | Correction to be applied for tabular error. | = +11.26 | | | |
| | Long. of station near Presidio del Norte, computed with elements from N. A... | =6 57 31.21 | | Long. of station near Presidio del Norte | =6 57 39.02 |

TABLE V—Continued.

*Comparison of results for longitude of station near Presidio del Norte, for each date of observation, as computed with Tab. R. A. in Nautical Almanac and Greenwich observations.*

| Date of observation. | Long. computed with N. Almanac R. A. | Long. computed with Greenwich observations. | Greenwich observations + N. Almanac, or difference. |
|---|---|---|---|
| 1852. | *h. m. s.* | *h. m. s.* | *s.* |
| July 26...... | 6 57 18.17 | 6 57 37 53 | + 19.36 |
| 27...... | 27.32 | 47.67 | 20.35 |
| 28...... | 37.41 | 55.76 | 18.35 |
| 29...... | 17.00 | 34.50 | 17.50 |
| 30...... | 22.82 | 39.66 | 16.84 |
| 31...... | 11.67 | 28.78 | 17.11 |
| Aug. 1...... | 35.48 | 43.27 | 7.79 |
| 2...... | 06.73 | 32.89 | 26.16 |
| 3...... | 25.13 | 40.42 | 15.29 |
| 4...... | 36.06 | 47.38 | 11.32 |
| 24...... | 24.76 | 44.76 | 20.00 |
| 25...... | 17.56 | 39.02 | 21.46 |
| 27...... | 06.04 | 41.35 | 35.31 |
| 28...... | 03.41 | 20.30 | 16.89 |
| 29...... | 6 57 08.70 | 6 57 33.10 | + 24.40 |
| | Sum.................................... | | = 15)288.13 |
| | Mean.................................... | | = + 19s.21 |

*Comparison of mean results for longitude, obtained from observations on moon's limbs, as computed with Tab. R. A. in Nautical Almanac and Greenwich observations.*

| | |
|---|---|
| FIRST. | *h. m. s.* |
| Mean of results of observations on moon's first limb, computed from Tabular Right Ascensions in Nautical Almanac.............. | 6 57 18.96 |
| Mean of results of observations on moon's first limb, computed from Greenwich observations.................................. | 6 57 40.11 |
| Difference, or Greenwich observations + Nautical Almanac.................................... | = + 21.15 |
| SECOND. | |
| Mean of results of observations on moon's second limb, computed from Tabular Right Ascensions in Nautical Almanac........... | 6 57 20.94 |
| Mean of results of observations on moon's second limb, computed from Greenwich observations.................................. | 6 57 37.93 |
| Difference, or Greenwich observations + Nautical Almanac.................................... | = + 16.99 |

*Corrections to be applied to results obtained from computations (with tabular R. A. in Nautical Almanac) of observations made near Presidio del Norte.*

| | |
|---|---|
| | *h. m. s.* |
| Observed difference of longitude between Greenwich and Cambridge, July 28.................................. | = 4 44 19.06 |
| Established longitude of Cambridge, west of Greenwich.................................. | = 4 44 29.60 |
| Observed longitude east of established longitude.................................. | 10.54 |
| Observed difference of longitude between Greenwich and Cambridge, August 24.................................. | = 4 44 17.62 |
| Established longitude of Cambridge, west of Greenwich.................................. | = 4 44 29.60 |
| Observed longitude east of established longitude.................................. | 11.98 |
| Difference, July 28.................................. | = 10.54 |
| Do....Aug. 24.................................. | = 11.98 |
| Sum.................................. | = 22.52 |
| Mean correction to be applied.................................. | + 11.26 |

TABLE V—Continued.

RECAPITULATION.

*Difference of results for longitude of station near Presidio del Norte, as obtained from computations of observed moon culminations, with tabular R. A. in Nautical Almanac and Greenwich observations*, 1852.

| | h. m. s. |
|---|---|
| Longitude computed from tabular R. A. in Nautical Almanac | = 6 57 19.95 |
| Longitude computed from Greenwich observations | = 6 57 39.02 |
| Difference between Nautical Almanac and Greenwich observations | = 19.07 |
| Observed longitude of Cambridge *east* of established longitude | = 11.26 |
| Difference | = 7.81 |
| Longitude computed from tabular R. A. in Nautical Almanac, with corrections applied | = 6 57 31.21 |
| Longitude computed from Greenwich observations | = 6 57 39.02 |
| Difference | = 7.81 |
| Longitude of station near Presidio del Norte | = 6 57 39.02 |

TABLE VI.

*Tabulation of results for longitude of astronomical station near Fort Duncan, derived from observations made with* 30-*inch transit (by Troughton & Simms) and sidereal chronometer No.* 2440, *(by Parkinson & Frodsham:) By J. H. Clark, under the direction of Major W. H. Emory, Chief Astronomer and Surveyor of United States and Mexican boundary survey.*

| Date. | Authority for elements used. | Moon's 1st limb. | Resulting longitude from observations on moon's 1st limb. | Date. | Authority for elements used. | Moon's 2d limb. | Resulting longitude from observations on moon's 2d limb. |
|---|---|---|---|---|---|---|---|
| 1852. | | h. m. s. | h. m. s. | 1852. | | h. m. s. | h. m. s. |
| Oct. 19 | G. observations.. | .................. | 6 42 06.7 | Oct. 27 | G. observations.. | .................. | 6 41 46.2 |
| 20 | .......do......... | .................. | 12.4 | 28 | .......do......... | .................. | 6 42 01.3 |
| 21 | .......do........ | 6 42 00.5 | 6 41 57.25 | 29 | .......do......... | .................. | 6 41 53.3 |
| 21 | C. observations.. | 6 41 54.0 | | 30 | .......do......... | .................. | 6 42 04.4 |
| 22 | G. observations.. | 6 42 09.5 | 6 42 06.90 | 31 | .......do......... | .................. | 6 42 02.6 |
| 22 | C. observations.. | 04.3 | | Nov. 1 | .......do......... | .................. | 6 42 04.9 |
| 23 | G. observations . | 6 41 58.2 | 6 41 57.70 | 2 | .......do......... | .................. | 6 41 46.5 |
| 23 | C. observations.. | 57.2 | | | | | |
| 25 | G. observations.. | 6 42 09.5 | 6 42 07.60 | | | | |
| 25 | C. observations. | 05.7 | | | | | |
| 26 | G. observations.. | 18.0 | 6 42 15.65 | | | | |
| 26 | C. observations.. | 13.3 | | | | | |
| 27 | G. observations.. | .................. | 6 41 49.1 | | | | |
| Mean longitude from moon's 1st limb = 6*h*. 42*m*. 04*s*.16. | | | | Mean longitude from moon's 2d limb = 6*h*. 41*m*. 57*s*.03 | | | |

By giving double weight to the results of observations on moon's 1st limb, we have longitude = 6*h*. 42*m*. 01*s*.78

Longitude of astronomical station near Fort Duncan = 6*h*. 42*m*. 01*s*.78

TABLE VII.

*Tabulation of results for longitude of astronomical station at Ringgold barracks, derived from observations made with 30-inch transit (maker unknown) and sidereal chronometer No. 2440, (by Parkinson & Frodsham:) By Major W. H. Emory, Chief Astronomer and Surveyor of United States and Mexican boundary survey, assisted by G. C. Gardner and J. H. Clark.*

| Date. | Authority for elements used. | Moon's limb observed. | Resulting longitude. |
|---|---|---|---|
| 1853. | | | *h. m. s.* |
| June 17 | Greenwich observations............ | First ............... | 6 35 05.90 |
| 18 | Philadelphia High School ........... | ...do.................. | 03.42 |
| 20 | ......do...........do................ | Second.............. | 03.36 |
| 25 | Greenwich observations........... | ...do.................. | 08.39 |
| July 14 | ......do...........do................ | First ................ | 02.61 |
| 15 | ......do...........do................ | . .do.................. | 10.49 |
| 16 | ......do...........do................ | ...do.................. | 07.41 |
| 18 | Philadelphia High School.......... | ...do.................. | 07.98 |

Longitude of Ringgold barracks = 6*h.* 35*m.* 06*s*.19.

*Discussion of the longitude of astronomical station (g) near the mouth of the Rio Bravo del Norte.*

Office of Survey of United States and Mexican Boundary,
*Washington, D. C., February* 9, 1856.

Sir: In presenting to you the final results of the computations for the longitude of the astronomical station established under your direction in 1853, near the mouth of Rio Bravo del Norte, I have been delayed for want of all the corresponding moon culminations observed at Greenwich throughout the four lunations.

The observations which were commenced by yourself and continued by Messrs. G. C. Gardner and J. H. Clark, extend through four lunations, commencing August 12, and ending November 22, 1853. The longitude resulting from the first three lunations was computed by Mr. C. N. Thom from corresponding observations at Greenwich observatory, furnished in manuscript, in 1853, by Professor Airy, astronomer royal, as well as from the corresponding observations made at Philadelphia High School observatory during the same period—giving for the position of the astronomical station, in longitude, 6*h.* 28*m.* 30*s*.5 west from Greenwich observatory.

Having recently received the printed observations of 1853, made at Greenwich and Radcliffe observatories, the observations of the fourth lunation have also been computed by Mr. Thom, and the results combined with those previously deduced from the first three lunations, without producing any change in the result hitherto adopted, as above given.

The instruments used at this station were a 46-inch transit, made by Troughton & Simms, of London, and an excellent sidereal box-chronometer, made by Parkinson & Frodsham. The transit was mounted on a massive brass stand, which rested on a pine log, imbedded about eight feet in the sand, the whole sheltered by a temporary wooden structure.

The accompanying tables, marked A, exhibit all the observations in detail, with the corrections for instrumental errors as applied, together with the several results deduced from the observations of each night. The tables marked B, C, D, exhibit the computations of those instrumental errors, with their adopted results, as follows:

1. The computed values of the equatorial intervals of each wire from the middle wire—the illumination being east—are (see table B):

| I. | II. | III. | IV. | V. | VI. | VII. |
|---|---|---|---|---|---|---|
| $51^s.13$ | $34^s.03$ | $17^s.09$ | $00^s.00$ | $17^s.19$ | $34^s.14$ | $51^s.32$ |

with a probable error for each value of $\pm 0^s.005$. The equatorial reduction of the mean of the seven wires to the middle wire $= - 0^s.06 \pm 0.00$.

2. The computed value of the error of collimation of the middle wire, as deduced from a mean of twenty-five observations, made on the nights of October 27, 28, and 29, (see table C,) is $= + 0^s.16 \pm 0^s.01$; hence the collimation of the mean of wires, $= + 0^s.10 \pm 0^s.01 =$ (in arc) $+1''.5 \pm 0''.1$.

This value for the collimation of mean of wires has been applied to all the observations of the four lunations, in consideration of the improbability of any perceptible change in that element of the instrumental errors, due to the superior mechanism of the instrument.

3. The azimuthal deviation, however, has been applied to the observations of each night, a then observed, on account of the unavoidable instability of the foundation of the instrument stand, and shown by the changes of deviation exhibited in column 13 of table A.

4. The equatorial value of the divisions marked on the level used with this instrument has been determined from observations made August 19, 1853, the result being $= 1''.065$ (in arc) for one division (see table D.)

The chronometer rate adopted was obtained by reducing to $0^h$ sidereal time the error for each night by interpolation; and although the rate therefrom deduced is very satisfactory and regular for the period of any one lunation, it perceptibly continues to increase throughout the series, being for the

| | |
|---|---|
| First lunation, in August.................................. | $= + 1^s.18$ |
| Second lunation, in September............................ | $= + 1^s.70$ |
| Third lunation, in October................................. | $= + 2^s.89$ |
| Fourth lunation, in November............................ | $= + 4^s.60$ |

In reducing the observations, therefore, the actual rate for the day of observation has been used, as shown in column 18 (table A) of the tabulated computations.

In applying the corrections due to errors of collimation, level, and azimuth, the tables marked E have greatly facilitated the reduction—all which are combined in column 15 (table A) of the tabulated computations, showing the "corrected transits" of stars.

The value for "sidereal time of moon's semi-diameter passing meridian of station," shown in column 19, (table A,) has been computed by interpolation, and applied to corrected transit of the limb observed, giving the corrected transit of its centre; which element has been used in computing, by interpolation, the change of the moon's position.

The positions of the moon, as observed with the transit circle at Greenwich observatory, have served to give, by interpolation, its position for all the nights on which it was observed at the mouth of the Rio Bravo, furnishing reliable and satisfactory results; and these positions were adopted in preference to those deduced from the altazimuth observations, which differ in most cases from those actually observed by the transit circle. The positions adopted, as well as those observed at Philadelphia High School and Radcliffe observatories, during the period stated, are given in table F, being the data used in computing the longitude.

The several results for longitude, computed from the observations of each night, are exhibited in table G; the mean of which is $6^h\ 28^m\ 30^s.48 \pm 0^s.56$, being deduced from forty observations combined with the Greenwich observations, ten with Philadelphia High School, and four with

Radcliffe observations, in which equal weight is given to the results deduced from the Greenwich and Radcliffe observations; whilst double weight has been given to those deduced from Philadelphia High School observations, in consideration of its relative distance from the mouth of Rio Bravo, rendering the moon's position, as observed at Philadelphia High School observatory, so much more reliable than that deduced from Greenwich observations, wherein the law of its motion has not been strictly applied.

The probable error, whilst it may furnish an approximate estimate of the value of the result of any one series, cannot certainly be a very reliable guide, unless applied to a continued series of observations, made under various changes of condition, such as may eliminate all possible or probable errors to which observations are subjected.

In the results tabulated I have therefore introduced all such as appear reliable, giving to each its estimated value in the final result, without any regard to its "probable error," as it does not appear what personal or other constant errors may have crept into any or all the observations which have been combined in the computations. In adopting this plan, I am glad to find myself sustained by a paper in the "Astronomical Journal," of January 9, 1856, over the signature of Professor Airy, astronomer royal.

I have therefore to recommend that, until corrected by the application of more accurate laws of the moon's motion, or additional observations, that $6^h\ 28^m\ 30^s.5$ should continue to be adopted for the longitude of the astronomical station, west from the meridian of Greenwich observatory.

Very respectfully, your obedient servant,

GEORGE THOM,
*Captain Topographical Engineers.*

Major W. H. Emory, *United States Commissioner.*

Note.—By way of experiment, the accompanying tables, marked H, I, and K, are presented, exhibiting the results combined in different ways, without, as it appears, materially changing the result given above.

1. In table H, showing the results of the moon's limbs separately combined—giving to those results their relative values adopted for each night, (as in table G,) the mean of I and II limbs being... = 6*h*.28*m*.30*s*.52
2. In table I, showing those results deduced from actual corresponding observations only, and giving to those results their relative values adopted for each night, the mean of the whole being...... = 6*h*.28*m*.30*s*.38
3. In table K, showing the results deduced from actual corresponding observations only, of each limb separately combined—giving to those results their relative values adopted for each night—a mean of the two limbs being............ = 6*h*.28*m*.30*s*.45

GEORGE THOM,
*Captain Topographical Engineers.*

## TABLE A.

*Meridian transit observations made at mouth of the Rio Grande with 46-inch transit, (by Troughton & Simms,) and sidereal chronometer No. 2440, (by Parkinson & Frodsham,) and computations of apparent right ascension and longitude deduced therefrom. By G. C. Gardner and J. H. Clark, obs'rs; C. N. Thom, comp.*

| Date. | No. for reference. | Name of object. | Illuminated end of axis. | Seconds of transit over the seven wires. I. | II. | III. | IV. | V. | VI. | VII. | Concluded transit over the mean of the seven wires. | Error of— Collima'n, (azimuth.) | Level. | Corrected transit. | Tabular right ascension of known stars and moon's centre. | Chronometer apparently fast of sider'l time. | Adopted chronometer fast at 0h. sider'l time and (gaining rate.) | Sidereal time of semi-diam. passing meridian of station. | Apparent right ascension of centre deduced from observations made at Royal Observ., Greenwich. | Long. west of Greenwich deduced from observations of each night. |
|---|---|---|---|---|---|---|---|---|---|---|---|---|---|---|---|---|---|---|---|---|
| | | | | s. | s. | s. | s. | s. | s. | s. | h. m. s. | " | " | h. m. s. | h. m. s. | h. m. s. | m. s. | m. s. | h. m. s. | h. m. s. |
| 1853. Aug. 12 | 1 | Moon's 1st limb. | E. | ...... | ...... | 16.2 | 34.8 | 53.3 | 12.0 | 30.6 | 17 44 34.72 | + 2.44 (− 5.59) | + 1.65 | 17 44 34.72 | 15.44 24.73 | ........... | 45 28.00 | 1 11.56 | 15 44 14.26 | 6 28 35.04 |
| | 2 | ψ Ophiuchi....... | | 04.6 | 22.8 | 41.2 | 59.3 | 17.4 | 35.3 | 53.6 | 18 00 59.17 | + 1.50 | 1.65 | 18 00 59.08 | 16 15 31.72 | 1 45 27.36 | (+ 1.00) | ......... | ............ | ........... |
| | 3 | α Scorpii......... | | 55.8 | 14.8 | 34.2 | 53.0 | 11.8 | 30.7 | 50.2 | 18 05 52.93 | − 1.59 | 1.65 | 18 05 52 80 | 16 20 25.54 | 1 45 27.26 | | ......... | ............ | ........... |
| | 4 | G. C. 1402...... | | 06.6 | 27.2 | 47.5 | 08.4 | 28.8 | 49.4 | 10.3 | 18 26 08.31 | | 1.65 | 18 26 08.11 | 16 40 40.81 | 1 45 27.30 | | ......... | ............ | ........... |
| | 5 | G. C. 1418...... | | 19.3 | 36.8 | 54.2 | 11.4 | 28.6 | 45.8 | 03.3 | 18 36 11.34 | | + 1.65 | 18 36 11.24 | 16 50 44.17 | 1 45 27.07 | | ......... | ............ | ........... |
| 13 | 6 | Moon's 1st limb. | E. | 28.6 | 47.7 | 06.8 | 26.0 | 45.2 | 04.2 | 23.3 | 18 46 25.97 | + 1.50 | + 4.81 | 18 46 25.85 | 16 45 08.76 | ........... | ......... | 1 13.62 | 16 45 08.12 | 6 28 40.00 |
| | 7 | θ Ophiuchi.... ... | | 34.3 | 53.2 | 11.8 | 30.8 | 49.5 | 08.3 | 27.2 | 18 58 30.73 | (− 8.93) | 4.81 | 18 58 30.55 | 17 13 00.89 | 1 45 29.66 | 45 30.06 | ......... | 17 13 00.91 | ........... |
| | 8 | b Ophiuchi....... | | 59.6 | 18.3 | 36.8 | 55.5 | 14.2 | 32.7 | 51.6 | 19 02 55.53 | | 4.74 | 19 02 55.36 | 17 17 25.50 | 1 45 29.86 | (+ 2.25) | ......... | 17 17 25.48 | ........... |
| | 9 | G. C. 1532...... | | 11.4 | 28.6 | 45.5 | 02.6 | 20.2 | 36.8 | 54.3 | 19 26 02.77 | | 4.40 | 19 26 02.81 | 17 40 32.93 | 1 45 29.88 | | ......... | ............ | ........... |
| | 10 | γ Draconis ....... | | 19.5 | 46.8 | 14.4 | 42.2 | 09.4 | 36.6 | 04.3 | 19 38 41.89 | | 4.40 | 19 38 42.88 | 17 53 13.37 | 1 45 29.51 | | ......... | ............ | ........... |
| | 11 | G. C. 1575..... | | 02.3 | 19.7 | 37.2 | 54.3 | 11.6 | 28.8 | 46.4 | 19 45 54.33 | | + 4.40 | 19 45 54.54 | 18 00 25.26 | 1 45 29.28 | | ......... | ............ | ........... |
| 15 | 12 | $\nu^1$ Sagittarii. ...... | W. | 58.2 | 16.5 | 34.6 | 53.3 | 12.2 | 30.3 | 48.6 | 20 30 53.39 | − 1.50 | + 0.82 | 20 30 52.85 | 18 45 19.73 | 1 45 33.12 | 45 33.40 | ......... | ............ | ........... |
| | 13 | $\xi^2$ Sagittarii....... | | ...... | 56.8 | 14.4 | 33.3 | 51.6 | 09.8 | 28.3 | 20 34 33.2 | (− 8.59) | 0.82 | 20 34 32.78 | 18 48 59.55 | 1 45 33.23 | (+ 2.26) | ......... | ............ | ........... |
| | 14 | Moon's 1st limb. | | 12.3 | 31.9 | 51.2 | 10.7 | 30.3 | 49.8 | 09.3 | 20 57 10.79 | | 0.82 | 20 57 10.23 | 18 55 05.69 | ........... | | 1 14.85 | 18 55 04.71 | 6 28 35.91 |
| | 15 | $\kappa^2$ Sagittarii ....... | | 24.8 | 43.8 | 02.5 | 21.6 | 40.3 | 59.2 | 18.0 | 21 13 21.46 | | 0.82 | 21 13 20.90 | 19 27 47.78 | 1 45 33.12 | | ......... | ............ | ........... |
| | 16 | γ Aquilæ.......... | | 59.4 | 16.6 | 34.0 | 51.6 | 09.2 | 26.3 | 43.3 | 21 24 51.49 | | 1.11 | 21 24 51.29 | 19 39 18.25 | 1 45 33.04 | | ......... | ............ | ........... |
| | 17 | β Sagittarii ....... | | 33.7 | 53.3 | 11.8 | 31.2 | 50.4 | 09.8 | 29.3 | 21 33 31.36 | | 1.29 | 21 33 30.79 | 19 47 57.71 | 1 45 33.08 | | ......... | ............ | ........... |
| | 18 | $\alpha^2$ Capricorni ...... | | 37.3 | 54.6 | 11.8 | 29.4 | 47.3 | 04.6 | 22.3 | 21 55 29.61 | | 1.84 | 21 55 29.24 | 20 09 55.92 | 1 45 33.32 | | ......... | ............ | ........... |
| | 19 | α Pavonis ........ | | 03.4 | 35.0 | 05.8 | 37.6 | 09.6 | 40.9 | 12.8 | 21 59 37.87 | | + 1.92 | 21 59 36.68 | 20 14 03.48 | 1 45 33.20 | | ......... | ............ | ........... |
| 16 | 20 | $h^2$ Sagittarii........ | E. | 26.6 | 45.4 | 04.3 | 22.9 | 41.8 | 00.7 | 19.6 | 21 13 23.04 | + 1.50 | + 2.20 | 21 13 22.16 | 19 27 47.78 | 1 45 34.38 | 45 34 58 | ......... | ............ | ........... |
| | 21 | γ Aquilæ ......... | | 00.8 | 18.2 | 35.3 | 52.6 | 10.0 | 27.3 | 44.5 | 21 24 52.67 | (− 19.21) | 2.20 | 21 24 52.56 | 19 39 18.25 | 1 45 34.31 | (+ 0.88) | ......... | ............ | ........... |
| | 22 | α Aquilæ ......... | | 21.5 | 38.6 | 55.8 | 13.2 | 30.8 | 47.7 | 05.3 | 21 29 13.27 | | 2.20 | 21 29 13.11 | 19 43 38.66 | 1 45 34.45 | | ......... | ............ | ........... |
| | 23 | b Sagittarii........ | | 35.4 | 54.8 | 13.6 | 33.0 | 52.6 | 12.1 | 31.2 | 21 33 33.24 | | 2.20 | 21 33 32.98 | 19 47 57.70 | 1 45 34.58 | | ......... | ............ | ........... |
| | 24 | Moon's 1st limb. | | 05.3 | 24.1 | 43.3 | 02.6 | 21.8 | 41.5 | 00.3 | 22 02 02.70 | | 1.65 | 22 02 01.81 | 20 00 26.51 | ........... | | 1 13 45 | 20 00 25.36 | 6 28 39.85 |
| | 25 | ρ Capricorni ...... | | 12.2 | 30.0 | 47.6 | 05.7 | 23.8 | 42.0 | 59.8 | 22 06 05.87 | | 1.10 | 22 06 05.08 | 20 20 30.56 | 1 45 34.52 | | ......... | ............ | ........... |
| | 26 | α Cygni ......... | | 49.2 | 13.3 | 37.2 | 01.3 | 25.5 | 49.3 | 13.4 | 22 22 01.31 | | + 1.10 | 22 22 02.15 | 20 36 27.51 | 1 45 34.64 | | ......... | ............ | ........... |

REMARKS.—Equatorial intervals of each wire from the middle wire, (illumination east.)

| I. | II. | III. | V. | VI. | VII. |
|---|---|---|---|---|---|
| 51s.13 | 34s.03 | 17s.09 | 17s.19 | 34s.14 | 51s.32 |

Equatorial reduction of mean of wires to middle wire.... ............................ = − 0s.06 ± 0s.00

Collimation of middle wire...................................................................... = + 0s.16 ± 0s.01

Collimation of mean of wires.................................................................... = + 0s.10 ± 0s.01 (in arc = + 1".5 ± 0".1

### *Meridian transit observations made at mouth of Rio Grande, &c.*—Continued.

| Date. | Number for reference. | Name of object. | Illuminated end of axis. | Seconds of transit over the seven wires. | | | | | | | Concluded transit over the mean of the seven wires. | Error of— | | Corrected transit. | Tabular right ascension of known stars and moon's centre. | Chronometer apparently fast of sider'l time. | Adopted chronometer fast at 0h. sider'l time and (gaining rate.) | Sidereal time of semi-diam. passing meridian of station. | App. R. A. of centre deduced from observations made at | | Long. west of Greenwich deduced from observations of each night. |
|---|---|---|---|---|---|---|---|---|---|---|---|---|---|---|---|---|---|---|---|---|---|
| | | | | I. | II. | III. | IV. | V. | VI. | VII. | | Collima'n, (azimuth.) | Level. | | | | | | High School Observatory, Phila. | Royal Observatory, Gr'nwich. | |
| | | | | s. | s. | s. | s. | s. | s. | s. | h. m. s. | " | " | h. m. s. | h. m. s. | h. m. s. | m. s. | m. s. | h. m. s. | h. m. s. | h. m. s. |
| 1853. Aug. 17a | 27 | β Capricorni | W. | 30.2 | 47.6 | 05.3 | 22.8 | 40.8 | 58.4 | 16.0 | 21 58 23.01 | — 1.50 | + 0.96 | 21 58 22.42 | 20 12 47.15 | 1 45 35.32 | 45 35.16 | ... | ... | 20 12 47.10 | ... |
| | 28 | ρ Capricorni | | 12.4 | 30.6 | 48.2 | 06.3 | 24.3 | 42.4 | 00.3 | 22 06 06.36 | (— 12.10) | 0.96 | 22 06 05.72 | 20 20 30.57 | 1 45 35.15 | (+ 0.37) | ... | ... | ... | ... |
| | 29 | α Cygni | | 49.9 | 13.8 | 37.6 | 02.3 | 26.5 | 50.0 | 14.2 | 22 22 02.01 | | 0.96 | 22 22 02.31 | 20 36 27.50 | 1 45 34.81 | | ... | ... | ... | ... |
| | 30 | 61¹ Cygni | | 50.8 | 12.7 | 34.3 | 56.0 | 17.8 | 39.3 | 01.2 | 22 45 56.01 | | 1.26 | 22 45 56.20 | 21 00 20.96 | 1 45 35.24 | | ... | ... | ... | ... |
| | 31 | ξ Cygni | | 19.0 | 38.8 | 58.4 | 18.5 | 37.8 | 57.6 | 17.0 | 22 52 18.16 | | 1.34 | 22 52 18.21 | 21 06 43.06 | 1 45 35.15 | | ... | ... | ... | ... |
| | 32 | G. C. 1900 | | 47.8 | 05.8 | 23.3 | 41.6 | 59.4 | 17.2 | 35.3 | 22 59 41.49 | | 1.46 | 22 59 40.88 | 21 14 06.32 | 1 45 34.56 | | ... | ... | ... | ... |
| | 33 | Moon's 1st limb. | | 52.0 | 11.4 | 29.9 | 48.8 | 07.6 | 26.2 | 45.1 | 23 03 48.71 | | 1.48 | 23 03 48.05 | 21 03 08.82 | ... | | 1 11.12 | ... | 21 03 07.50 | 6 28 29.28 |
| | 34 | Moon's 2d limb. | | 14.7 | 38.3 | 52.3 | 10.9 | 30.0 | 48.6 | 07.2 | 23 06 11.07 | | 1.51 | 23 06 10.41 | 21 03 08.82 | ... | | 1 11.12 | ... | 21 03 07.50 | ... |
| | 35 | ε Pegasi | | 43.7 | 01.2 | 17.8 | .... | 52.8 | 10.3 | 27.8 | 23 22 35.67 | — 2.44 | 1.51 | 23 22 35.37 | 21 37 00.18 | 1 45 35.19 | | ... | ... | ... | ... |
| | 36 | δ Capricorni | | ...... | 57.8 | 15.3 | 33.8 | 51.3 | 08.8 | 26.7 | 23 24 33.34 | | 1.65 | 23 24 32.68 | 21 38 57.68 | 1 45 34.92 | | ... | ... | ... | ... |
| | 37 | μ Capricorni | | 02.3 | 19.6 | 37.3 | 54.8 | 12.2 | 29.7 | 47.5 | 23 30 54.77 | — 1.50 | + 2.06 | 23 30 54.25 | 21 45 18.95 | 1 45 35.30 | | ... | ... | ... | ... |
| 18 | 38 | δ Capricorni | E. | 40.2 | 58.3 | 16.0 | 33.5 | 51.6 | 09.3 | 27.4 | 23 24 33.76 | + 1.50 | + 2.06 | 23 24 33.09 | 21 38 57.69 | 1 45 35.32 | 45 35.32 | ... | ... | 21 38 57.77 | ... |
| | 39 | α Gruis | | 20.6 | 46.2 | 11.6 | 36.7 | 02.4 | 27.5 | 52.7 | 23 44 36.81 | (— 18.67) | 2.06 | 23 44 35.24 | 21 59 00.10 | 1 45 35.14 | (+ 0.05) | ... | ... | ... | ... |
| | 40 | Moon's 2d limb. | | 54.3 | 12.6 | 30.5 | 48.7 | 07.3 | 25.4 | 43.8 | 24 03 48.94 | | 2.06 | 24 03 48.28 | 22 01 57.03 | ... | | 1 08.51 | ... | 22 01 55.78 | 6 28 20.69 |
| | 41 | σ Aquarii | | 37.8 | 55.2 | 12.4 | 29.9 | 47.5 | 04.8 | 22.3 | 24 08 29.99 | | 1.89 | 24 08 29.43 | 22 22 54.10 | 1 45 35.33 | | ... | ... | ... | ... |
| | 42 | ζ Pegasi | | 53.4 | 10.8 | 28.2 | 45.6 | 03.3 | 20.2 | 37.7 | 24 19 45.60 | | 1.35 | 24 19 45.44 | 22 34 10.03 | 1 45 35.41 | | ... | ... | ... | ... |
| | 43 | G. C. 2047 | | 36.2 | 54.6 | 13.5 | 32.3 | 50.8 | 09.3 | 28.3 | 24 28 32.14 | | 1.00 | 24 28 32.28 | 22 42 57.19 | 1 45 35.09 | | ... | ... | ... | ... |
| | 44 | δ Aquarii | | 35.4 | 53.6 | 11.3 | 28.9 | 47.0 | 04.5 | 22.4 | 24 32 29.01 | | 0.82 | 24 32 28.29 | 22 46 52.88 | 1 45 35.41 | | ... | ... | ... | ... |
| | 45 | α Piscis Australis. | | 10.5 | 30.3 | 50.2 | 09.6 | 29.8 | 49.5 | 09.3 | 24 35 09.89 | | + 0.68 | 24 35 08.84 | 22 49 33.56 | 1 45 35.28 | | ... | ... | ... | ... |
| 19 | 46 | σ Aquarii | W. | 37.7 | 55.4 | 12.6 | 30.3 | 47.7 | 05.2 | 26.6 | 24 08 30.21 | — 1.50 | — 0.27 | 24 08 29.22 | 22 22 54.11 | 1 45 35.11 | 45 35.26 | ... | 22 22 54.10 | ... | ... |
| | 47 | ζ Pegasi | | 53.6 | 11.3 | 28.4 | 45.8 | 03.3 | 20.5 | 38.0 | 24 19 45.84 | (— 21.45) | 0.27 | 24 19 45.31 | 22 34 10.04 | 1 45 35.27 | (+ 0.75) | ... | ... | ... | ... |
| | 48 | δ Aquarii | | 35.7 | 53.6 | 11.2 | 29.1 | 47 3 | 04.8 | 22.7 | 24 32 29.26 | | 0.27 | 24 32 28.08 | 22 46 52.89 | 1 45 35.19 | | ... | 22 46 52.87 | ... | ... |
| | 49 | α Piscis Australis. | | 10.8 | 30.7 | 50.3 | 10.4 | 30.5 | 49.8 | 09.9 | 24 35 10.34 | | 0.27 | 24 35 08.86 | 22 49 33.58 | 1 45 35 28 | | ... | ... | ... | ... |
| | 50 | α Pegasi | | 11.3 | 29.2 | 46.4 | 04.3 | 22.0 | 39.3 | 57.2 | 24 43 04.24 | | 0.27 | 24 43 03.86 | 22 57 28.59 | 1 45 35.27 | | ... | ... | ... | ... |
| | 51 | ψ Aquarii | | 29.0 | 46.3 | 03.4 | 20.6 | 38 2 | 55.0 | 11.9 | 24 52 20.63 | | 0.27 | 24 52 19.75 | 23 06 44.72 | 1 45 35.03 | | ... | 23 06 44.49 | ... | b6 28 22.33 |
| | 52 | Moon's 2d limb. | | 34.2 | 51.7 | 09.5 | 27.6 | 45.3 | 03.3 | 20.6 | 24 57 27.46 | | — 0.27 | 24 57 26.47 | 22 56 39.41 | ... | | 1 06.08 | c23 07 34.76 | 22 56 38.29 | d6 28 33.62 |
| 20 | 53 | α Piscis Australis. | E. | 12.1 | 31.8 | 51.6 | 11.5 | 31.3 | 51.3 | 11.3 | 0 35 11.56 | + 1.50 | + 0.82 | 0 35 10.48 | 22 49 33.59 | 1 45 36.89 | 45 36.81 | ... | ... | ... | ... |
| | 54 | α Pegasi | | 12.7 | 30.6 | 48.2 | 05.6 | 23.3 | 40.8 | 57.7 | 0 43 05.70 | (—18.19) | — 0.82 | 9 43 05.50 | 22 57 28.60 | 1 45 36.90 | (+ 1.42) | ... | ... | ... | ... |
| | 55 | φ Aquarii | | 30.3 | 47.6 | 04.8 | 21.8 | 39.5 | 56.6 | 13.6 | 0 52 22.03 | | 0.82 | 0 52 21.44 | 23 06 44.74 | 1 45 36.70 | | ... | ... | ... | ... |
| | 56 | ψ² Aquarii | | 06.4 | 23.6 | 41.2 | 58.3 | 15.9 | 33.2 | 50.4 | 0 56 58.43 | | 0.82 | 0 56 57.76 | 23 11 20.86 | 1 45 36.90 | | ... | ... | ... | ... |
| | 57 | 33 Piscium | | 36.7 | 53.8 | 11.1 | 27.8 | 45.3 | 02.4 | 19.8 | 1 43 28.13 | | 1.81 | 43 27.48 | 23 57 50.66 | 1 45 36.82 | | ... | ... | ... | ... |
| | 58 | Moon's 2d limb. | | 57.3 | 14.6 | 32.6 | 49.6 | 07.3 | 24.7 | 42.9 | 1 47 49.67 | | 2.06 | 1 47 49.03 | 23 47 50.04 | ... | | 1 04.30 | ... | 23 47 49.06 | 6 28 14.71 |
| | 59 | 12 Ceti | | 20.3 | 37.6 | 54.3 | 11.6 | 28.8 | 46.0 | 02.7 | 2 08 11.90 | | — 2.06 | 2 08 11.26 | 0 22 34.28 | 1 45 36.98 | | ... | ... | ... | ... |

| | | | | | | | | | | | | | | | | | | | | | |
|---|---|---|---|---|---|---|---|---|---|---|---|---|---|---|---|---|---|---|---|---|---|
| 21 | 60 | 33 Piscium | W. | 37.8 | 55.3 | 12.2 | 29.4 | 47.0 | 03.7 | 20.9 | 1 43 28.90 | — 1.50 | + 0.13 | 1 43 28.50 | 23 57 50.68 | 1 45 37.82 | 45 38.11 | | | | |
| | 61 | α Andromedæ | | 29.8 | 49.3 | 08.6 | 28.2 | 47.6 | 06.7 | 26.1 | 1 46 28.04 | (— 8.52) | 0.13 | 1 46 27.91 | 0 00 49.92 | 1 45 37.99 | (+ 1.61) | | | | |
| | 62 | 12 Ceti | | 21.6 | 38.8 | 55.5 | 12.7 | 30.2 | 47.6 | 04.3 | 2 08 12.96 | | 0.13 | 2 08 12.58 | 0 22 34.30 | 1 45 38.28 | | | | | |
| | 63 | 20 Ceti | | 19.1 | 36.3 | 52.9 | 10.3 | 27.6 | 44.4 | 01.8 | 2 31 10.34 | | 0.22 | 2 31 09.99 | 0 45 31.66 | 1 45 38.33 | | | 0 45 31.75 | | b6 28 27.27 |
| | 64 | Moon's 2d limb. | | 02.6 | 20.2 | 37.1 | 54.9 | 12.5 | 29.7 | 47.3 | 2 35 54.90 | | 0.24 | 2 35 54.57 | 0 36 25.73 | | | 1 03.20 | e0 46 19.72 | 0 36 24.88 | d6 28 35.90 |
| | 65 | ε Piscium | | 07.8 | 25.2 | 42.3 | 59.4 | 16.8 | 34.0 | 50.9 | 2 40 59 49 | | + 0.27 | 2 40 59.22 | 0 55 21.00 | 1 45 38.22 | | | 0 55 20.96 | | |
| 22 | 66 | α Andromedæ | E. | 31.8 | 50.9 | 10.5 | 30.0 | 49.6 | 08.4 | 28.2 | 1 46 29.91 | + 1.50 | + 1.65 | 1 46 30.18 | 0 00 49.93 | 1 45 40.25 | 45 40.03 | | | | |
| | 67 | γ Pegasi | | 29.6 | 47.3 | 04.7 | 22.3 | 40.3 | 57.5 | 15.4 | 1 51 22.44 | (—16.63) | 1.65 | 1 51 22.42 | 0 05 42.26 | 1 45 40.16 | (+ 1.43) | | | | |
| | 68 | θ Ceti | | 31.2 | 48.3 | 05.4 | 22.7 | 40.0 | 57.6 | 14.8 | 3 02 22.86 | | 1.59 | 3 02 22.40 | 1 16 42.37 | 1 45 40.03 | | | | | |
| | 69 | G. C. 135. | | 44.7 | 07.6 | 30.2 | 52.4 | 15.5 | 37.6 | 00.5 | 3 13 52.64 | | 1.37 | 3 13 53.25 | 1 28 13.35 | 1 45 39 90 | | | | | |
| | 70 | ν Piscium | | 37.6 | 54.8 | ...... | ...... | ...... | 03.3 | 20.8 | 3 19 29.05 | + 2.44 | 1.26 | 3 19 28.89 | 1 33 48.76 | 1 45 40.13 | | | | | |
| | 71 | Moon's 2d limb. | | 54.3 | 12.1 | 29.2 | 46.8 | 04.3 | 22.0 | 39.3 | 3 22 46.86 | + 1.50 | + 1.23 | 3 22 46.66 | 1 23 30.03 | | | 1 02.72 | | 1 23 29.32 | 6 28 27.22 |
| 23 | 72 | ο Piscium | W. | 39.6 | 46.8 | 03.8 | 21.2 | 38.7 | 55.6 | 12.9 | 3 23 21.23 | — 1.50 | + 2.33 | 3 23 20.88 | 1 37 39.91 | 1 45 40.97 | 45 40.98 | | | | |
| | 73 | G. C. 195 | | 04.3 | 21.6 | 38.4 | 55.6 | 13.3 | 30.3 | 47.4 | 3 50 55.84 | (—18.97) | 2.33 | 3 50 55.49 | 2 05 14.42 | 1 45 41.07 | (+ 1.07) | | | | |
| | 74 | Moon's 2d limb. | | 32.3 | 50.3 | 07.7 | 25.7 | 43.4 | 01.0 | 18.3 | 4 09 25.53 | | 1.92 | 4 09 25.24 | 2 10 05.09 | | | 1 02.96 | | 2 10 04.52 | 6 28 33.54 |
| | f75 | B. A. C. 845 | | 51.0 | 08.6 | 25.4 | 42.8 | 00.3 | 17.5 | 34.8 | 4 22 42.91 | | 1.59 | 4 22 42.53 | 2 37 01.52 | 1 45 41.08 | | | | 2 37 01.45 | |
| | f76 | π Arietis | | 54.9 | 12.9 | 30.6 | 48.5 | 06.4 | 24.2 | 42.2 | 4 26 48.53 | | 1.51 | 4 26 48.32 | 2 41 07.21 | 1 45 41.11 | | | | 2 41 07.21 | |
| 24 | 77 | B. A. C. 845 | E. | 52.2 | 09.4 | 26.6 | 43.8 | 01.3 | 18.5 | 36.3 | 4 22 44.01 | + 1.50 | + 0.55 | 4 22 43.83 | 2 37 01.48 | 1 45 42.35 | 45 42.17 | | | | |
| | 78 | π Arietis | | 56.1 | 13.7 | 31.8 | 49.3 | 07.4 | 25.2 | 43.2 | 4 26 49.53 | (— 15.72) | 0.59 | 4 26 49.50 | 2 41 07.24 | 1 45 42.27 | (+ 1.47) | | | 2 41 07.23 | |
| | 79 | G. C. 254 | | 37.8 | 56.2 | 14.3 | 32.6 | 50.8 | 09.0 | 27.6 | 4 36 32.61 | | 0.55 | 4 36 32.66 | 2 50 50.48 | 1 45 42.18 | | | | | |
| | 80 | α Ceti | | 28.8 | 46.0 | 02.8 | 19.9 | 36.8 | 54.3 | 11.5 | 4 40 20.01 | | + 0.24 | 4 40 19.71 | 2 54 37.36 | 1 45 42.35 | | | | | |
| | 81 | ζ Arietis | | 16.6 | 34.8 | 52.8 | 11.2 | 29.9 | 47.6 | 06.0 | 4 52 11.27 | | — 0.37 | 4 52 11.25 | 3 06 28.88 | 1 45 42.40 | | | | 3 06 28.85 | |
| | 82 | Moon's 2d limb. | | 52.2 | 10.4 | 27.7 | 46.3 | 04.3 | 22.3 | 40.2 | 4 56 46.20 | | 0.99 | 4 56 46.03 | 2 57 07.66 | | | 1 03.75 | | 2 57 07.07 | 6 28 32.10 |
| | 83 | α Persei | | ...... | 41.8 | 08.4 | 34.3 | 00.9 | 26.6 | 53.3 | 4 59 34.38 | | — 1.23 | 4 59 35.06 | 3 13 52.67 | 1 45 42.39 | | | | | |
| Sept. 12g | 84 | β Lyræ | W. | 54.8 | 15.3 | 35.8 | 56.2 | 16.6 | 36.8 | 57.3 | 20 30 56.11 | — 1.50 | + 0.68 | 20 30 56.01 | 18 44 40.47 | 1 46 15.54 | 46 15.70 | | | | |
| | 85 | ο Sagittarii | | 14.7 | 33.3 | 51.5 | 10.0 | 28.4 | 46.9 | 05.2 | 20 42 10.00 | (— 2.42) | 0.68 | 20 42 09.79 | 18 55 54.03 | 1 46 15.76 | (+ 1.20) | | | | |
| | 86 | π Sagittarii | | 23.8 | 42.3 | 00.3 | 18.7 | 37.2 | 55.2 | 14.3 | 20 47 18.83 | | 0.68 | 20 47 18.62 | 19 01 02.98 | 1 46 15.64 | | | | | |
| | 87 | δ Aquilæ | | 31.4 | 48.6 | 05.3 | 22.8 | 39.6 | 56.8 | 14.0 | 21 04 22.64 | | 0.68 | 21 04 22.52 | 19 18 06.85 | 1 46 15.68 | | | | | |
| | 88 | γ Aquilæ | | 41.6 | 59.2 | 16.0 | 33.5 | 50.8 | 08.3 | 25.7 | 21 25 33.59 | | 0.92 | 21 25 33.50 | 19 39 18.00 | 1 46 15.50 | | | | | |
| | 89 | Moon's 1st limb. | | 54.3 | 13.7 | 32.9 | 52.6 | 11.8 | 31.0 | 50.2 | 21 39 52.36 | | 1.10 | 21 39 52.16 | 19 37 45.84 | | | 1 13.30 | | 19 37 45.20 | 6 28 30.23 |
| | 90 | σ Capricorni | | 18.2 | 36.4 | 54.2 | 12.6 | 30.5 | 48.5 | 06.7 | 21 57 12.44 | | 1.10 | 21 57 12.27 | 20 10 56.68 | 1 46 15.59 | | | | | |
| | 91 | π Capricorni | | 18.3 | 36.4 | 54.0 | 12.3 | 30.2 | 48.4 | 06.3 | 22 05 12.27 | | + 1.10 | 22 05 12.11 | 20 18 56.44 | 1 46 15.67 | | | | | |
| 13 | 92 | σ Capricorni | E. | 18.8 | 37.1 | 55.3 | 12.8 | 31.4 | 49.2 | 07.7 | 21 57 13.19 | + 1.50 | + 0.27 | 21 57 13.03 | 20 10 56.64 | 1 46 16.36 | 46 16.34 | | 20 10 56.41 | 20 10 56.67 | |
| | 93 | π Capricorni | | 18.8 | 36.8 | 54.8 | 12.9 | 30.8 | 47.8 | 06.9 | 22 05 12.81 | (— 5.27) | 0.27 | 22 05 12.66 | 20 18 56.34 | 1 46 16.23 | (+ 0.67) | | 20 18 56.29 | 20 18 56.43 | b6 28 30.48 |
| | 94 | Moon's 1st limb. | | 27.6 | 46.7 | 05.8 | 21.8 | 43.8 | 02.3 | 21.6 | 22 41 24.66 | | 0.27 | 22 41 24.51 | 20 40 04.07 | | | 1 11.31 | h20 52 39.82 | 20 40 03.21 | d6 28 30.60 |
| | 95 | ζ Cygni | | 00.2 | 19.8 | 39.3 | 58.7 | 18.8 | 38.3 | 57.9 | 22 52 59.00 | | 0.27 | 22 52 59.10 | 21 06 42.92 | 1 46 16.18 | | | | | |
| | 96 | ξ Capricorni | | 39.6 | 58.2 | 16.6 | 35.3 | 53.8 | 12.3 | 30.8 | 23 04 35.23 | | 0.16 | 23 04 35.06 | 21 18 18.49 | 1 49 16.57 | | | 21 18 18.22 | | |
| | 97 | β Aquarii | | 16.4 | 33.4 | 50.3 | 07.6 | 25.0 | 42.2 | 59.5 | 23 10 07.77 | | 0.11 | 23 10 07.70 | 21 23 51.30 | 1 46 16.40 | | | | | |
| | 98 | ε Capricorni | | 15.1 | 33.3 | 51.4 | 09.3 | 27.8 | 45.8 | 04.2 | 23 15 09.56 | | 0.05 | 23 15 09.40 | 21 28 53.04 | 1 46 16.15 | | | | 21 28 53.25 | |
| | 99 | G. C. 1931 | | 15.3 | 09.3 | 27.3 | 45.6 | 03.8 | 21.6 | 40.0 | 23 20 45.56 | | + 0.00 | 23 20 45.40 | 21 34 29.10 | 1 46 16 30 | | | | | |

a Moon's second limb imperfect. b Deduced from corresponding observations made at Greenwich Observatory. c + 66.21 = computed time of moon's semi-diam. passing meridian.
d Deduced from corresponding observations made at Phila. High School Observatory. e 63.15 s. = computed time of moon's semi-diam. passing meridian. f Cloudy during the observations on Nos. 75 and 76.
g Sept. 12, very hazy. No culmination could be taken previous to this because of the bad weather. h 71s.46 computed time of moon's semi-diameter passing meridian.

*Meridian transit observations made at mouth of Rio Grande, &c.*—Continued.

| Date. | No. for reference. | Name of object. | Illuminated end of axis. | Seconds of transit over the seven wires. | | | | | | | Concluded transit over the mean of the seven wires. | Error of— | | Corrected transit. | Tabular right ascension of known stars and moon's centre. | Chronometer apparently fast of sider'l time. | Adopted chronometer fast at 0h. sider'l time and (gaining rate.) | Sidereal time of semi-diam. passing meridian of station. | App. R. A. of centre deduced from observations made at— | | Long. west of Greenwich deduced from observations of each night. |
|---|---|---|---|---|---|---|---|---|---|---|---|---|---|---|---|---|---|---|---|---|---|
| | | | | I. | II. | III. | IV. | V. | VI. | VII. | | Collima'n, (azimuth.) | Level. | | | | | | High School Observatory, Phila. | Royal Observatory, Gr'nwich. | |
| 1853. | | | | s. | s. | s. | s. | s. | s. | s. | h. m. s. | " | " | h. m. s. | h. m. s. | h. m. s. | m. s. | m. s. | h. m. s. | h. m. s. | h. m. s. |
| Sept. 14a | 100 | ζ Cygni ........ | W. | 01.0 | 20.8 | 40.3 | 00.2 | 19.4 | 39.3 | 59.1 | 22 53 00.10 | − 1.50 | − 0.68 | 22 52 59.82 | 21 06 42.91 | 1 46 16.91 | 46 17.04 | ........ | ........ | ........ | ........ |
| | 101 | ζ Capricorni ...... | | ...... | 59.2 | 17.3 | 35.6 | 54.5 | 12.8 | 31.3 | 23 04 35.94 | (− 5.48) | 0.68 | 23 04 35.44 | 21 18 18.48 | 1 46 16.96 | (+ 1.28) | ........ | ........ | ........ | ........ |
| | 102 | β Aquarii ........ | | 17.2 | 34.4 | 51.3 | 08.7 | 25.8 | 43.0 | 00.3 | 23 10 08.67 | | 0.68 | 23 10 08.34 | 21 23 51.30 | 1 46 17.00 | | ........ | ........ | ........ | ........ |
| | 103 | ε Capricorni ...... | | 15.9 | 34.3 | 52.3 | 10.8 | 28.8 | 47.1 | 04.7 | 23 15 10.56 | | 0.68 | 23 15 10.14 | 21 28 53.24 | 1 46 16.90 | | ........ | ........ | ........ | ........ |
| | 104 | ε Pegasi ........ | | 25.6 | 42.8 | 00.0 | 17.5 | 34.8 | 52.3 | 09.3 | 23 23 17.47 | | 0.68 | 23 23 17.22 | 21 37 00.19 | 1 46 17.03 | | ........ | ........ | ........ | ........ |
| | 105 | μ Capricorni ...... | | 43.5 | 01.4 | 18.7 | 36.7 | 54.3 | ...... | ...... | 23 31 36.54 | | 0.73 | 23 31 36.16 | 21 45 19.05 | 1 46 17.11 | | ........ | ........ | ........ | ........ |
| | 106 | Moon's 1st limb. | | 31.6 | 50.3 | 08.4 | 27.0 | 45.5 | 03.8 | 22.2 | 23 39 26.97 | | 0.78 | 23 39 26.57 | 21 39 03.06 | ........... | | 1 08.88 | ........... | 21 39 01.98 | 6 28 37.08 |
| | 107 | ι Aquarii ........ | | 56.4 | 14.2 | ...... | ...... | ...... | ...... | ...... | 23 44 49.45 | | − 0.82 | 23 44 48.99 | 21 58 31.99 | 1 46 17.00 | | ........ | ........ | ........ | ........ |
| 15 | 108 | μ Capricorni ...... | E. | ...... | ...... | ...... | 37.8 | 55.7 | 13.4 | 31.2 | 23 31 38.17 | + 1.50 | − 0.27 | 23 31 38.03 | 21 45 19.05 | 1 46 18.98 | 46 18.91 | ........ | ........ | ........ | ........ |
| | 109 | ι Aquarii ........ | | 58.3 | 15.8 | 33.3 | ...... | 08.8 | 26.4 | 44.2 | 23 44 51.05 | (− 6.87) | 0.27 | 23 44 50.90 | 21 58 31.99 | 1 46 18.99 | (+ 1.93) | ........ | ........ | ........ | ........ |
| | 110 | G. C. 1993 ...... | | 34.2 | 51.4 | 08.6 | 26.0 | 43.3 | 00.5 | 17.7 | 23 55 25.96 | | 0.27 | 23 55 25.78 | 22 09 06.85 | 1 46 18.93 | | ........ | ........ | ........ | ........ |
| | 111 | G. C. 2019 ...... | | ...... | 49.2 | 09.8 | 30.2 | 50.6 | 10.7 | 31.5 | 0 09 30.08 | | 0.27 | 0 09 29.79 | 22 23 11.09 | 1 46 18.70 | | ........ | ........ | ........ | ........ |
| | 112 | ζ Pegasi ........ | | 37.3 | 54.6 | 12.0 | 29.2 | 46.6 | 03.8 | 21.3 | 0 20 29.26 | | 0.22 | 0 20 29.22 | 22 34 10.18 | 1 46 18.94 | | ........ | ........ | ........ | ........ |
| | 113 | Moon's 1st limb. | | 54.6 | 12.3 | 30.2 | 48.4 | 06.3 | 24.2 | 42.0 | 0 33 48.29 | | 0.14 | 0 33 48.09 | 22 34 18.61 | ........... | | 1 06.56 | ........... | 22 34 17.31 | 6 28 37.19 |
| | b114 | Moon's 2d limb. | | 06.5 | 24.4 | 41.8 | 00.3 | 18.3 | 36.3 | 53.8 | 0 36 00.20 | | 0.13 | 0 36 00.00 | 22 34 18.61 | ........... | | 1 06.56 | ........... | 22 34 17.31 | ........... |
| | 115 | φ Aquarii ........ | | ...... | 29.5 | 46.8 | 04.3 | 21.4 | 38.5 | 55.6 | 0 53 03.98 | | 0.13 | 0 53 03.88 | 23 06 44.97 | 1 46 18.91 | | ........ | ........ | ........ | ........ |
| | 116 | ψ³ Aquarii ........ | | 48.3 | 06.0 | 22.8 | 40.3 | 57.7 | 14.8 | 32.6 | 0 57 40.34 | | − 0.13 | 0 57 40.16 | 23 11 21.11 | 1 46 19.05 | | ........ | ........ | ........ | ........ |
| 16 | 117 | φ Aquarii ........ | W. | ...... | 32.3 | ...... | 06.5 | 23.3 | 40.2 | 57.6 | 0 53 06.20 | − 1.50 | + 0.82 | 0 53 05.79 | 23 06 44.97 | 1 46 20.82 | 46 20.98 | ........ | ........ | ........ | ........ |
| | 118 | ψ³ Aquarii ........ | | 50.8 | 07.8 | 25.3 | 42.6 | 59.8 | 17.3 | 34.6 | 0 57 42.60 | (− 8.27) | 0.82 | 0 57 42.21 | 23 11 21.11 | 1 46 21.10 | (2.20) | ........ | 23 11 21.32 | ........... | c6 28 30.72 |
| | 119 | Moon's 1st limb. | | 04.5 | 22.3 | 39.8 | 57.4 | 14.8 | 32.6 | 50.3 | 1 24 57.39 | | 0.82 | 1 24 57.02 | 23 26 11.40 | ........... | | 1 04.68 | d23 36 38.50 | 23 26 09.87 | e6 28 23.86 |
| | 120 | Moon's 2d limb. | | 14.2 | 31.8 | 49.4 | 07.1 | 24.8 | 42.3 | 59.6 | 1 27 07.03 | | 0.82 | 1 27 06.66 | 23 26 11.40 | ........... | | 1 04.68 | d23 36 38.50 | 23 26 09.87 | ........... |
| | 121 | 33 Piscium ........ | | ...... | 38.3 | 55.3 | ...... | ...... | ...... | 04.2 | 1 44 12.67 | | 0.95 | 1 44 12.26 | 23 57 51.03 | 1 46 21.05 | | ........ | 23 57 51.10 | 23 57 51.21 | ........... |
| | 122 | α Andromedæ ..... | | 13.3 | 32.6 | ...... | 12.0 | ...... | 50.2 | 09.8 | 1 47 11.58 | | 1.05 | 1 47 11.46 | 0 00 50.27 | 1 46 21.19 | | ........ | ........ | ........ | ........ |
| | 123 | γ Pegasi ........ | | 11.2 | 28.6 | 46.3 | 04.0 | 21.7 | 39.3 | 57.0 | 1 52 04.01 | | 1.23 | 1 52 03.87 | 0 05 42.60 | 1 46 21.27 | | ........ | ........ | ........ | ........ |
| | 124 | β Ceti ........... | | 42.5 | 00.4 | 18.3 | 36.8 | 54.6 | 12.8 | 39.8 | 2 22 36.60 | | + 1.23 | 2 22 36.19 | 0 36 14.90 | 1 46 21.29 | | ........ | ........ | ........ | ........ |
| 17f | 125 | γ Pegasi ........ | E. | 13.2 | 30.6 | 48.3 | 06.0 | 23.8 | 41.3 | 59.3 | 1 52 06.07 | + 1.50 | − 0.41 | 1 52 06.09 | 0 05 42.61 | 1 46 23.48 | 46 23.31 | ........ | ........ | ........ | ........ |
| | 126 | Moon's 2d limb. | | 59.6 | 16.8 | 34.4 | 51.6 | 09.2 | 26.5 | 44.2 | 2 15 51.76 | (− 3.47) | 0.41 | 2 15 51.34 | 0 15 27.89 | ........... | (+ 2.45) | 1 03.41 | ........... | 0 15 26.56 | 6 28 24.66 |
| | 127 | β Ceti ........... | | 44.7 | 02.8 | 20.9 | 38.5 | 56.8 | 14.7 | 33.1 | 2 22 38.79 | | 0.34 | 2 22 38.70 | 0 36 14.92 | 1 46 23.78 | | ........ | ........ | ........ | ........ |
| | 128 | 20 Ceti ........... | | 04.3 | 21.5 | 38.3 | 55.7 | 12.8 | 29.8 | 47.2 | 2 31 55.66 | | 1.24 | 2 31 55.65 | 0 45 32.13 | 1 46 23.44 | | ........ | 0 45 32.14 | 0 45 32.21 | ........... |
| | 129 | G. C. 62 ........ | | 58.3 | 18.2 | 37.5 | 57.3 | ...... | 37.2 | ...... | 2 37 57.55 | | 0.17 | 2 37 57.51 | 0 51 33.81 | 1 46 23.70 | | ........ | ........ | ........ | ........ |
| | 130 | G. C. 66 ........ | | 53.3 | 10.5 | 27.6 | 44.6 | 02.3 | 19.3 | 36.6 | 2 41 44.89 | | − 0.13 | 2 41 44.78 | 0 55 21.42 | 1 46 23.36 | | ........ | ........ | ........ | ........ |
| | 131 | G. C. 121 ....... | | 03.5 | 20.8 | 37.7 | 55.0 | 12.3 | ...... | 46.8 | 3 08 55.02 | | + 0.01 | 3 08 55.10 | 1 22 31.48 | 1 46 23.62 | | ........ | ........ | ........ | ........ |

| | | | | | | | | | | | | | | | | | | | | | |
|---|---|---|---|---|---|---|---|---|---|---|---|---|---|---|---|---|---|---|---|---|---|
| 18g | 132 | δ Piscium | W. | 40.7 | ...... | 15.3 | 32.4 | 49.8 | 06.3 | 24.3 | 2 27 32.48 | − 1.50 | − 0.96 | 2 27 32.01 | 0 41 05.90 | 1 46 25.96 | 46 25.89 | ...... | 0 41 05.93 | 0 41 06.05 | ...... |
| | 133 | G. C. 66 | | 56.3 | 13.8 | 30.8 | 48.3 | 05.3 | 22.4 | 39.8 | 2 41 48.10 | (− 7.09) | 0.96 | 2 41 47.78 | 0 55 21.43 | 1 46 26.35 | (+ 2.81) | ...... | ...... | ...... | c 6 28 29.69 |
| | 134 | Moon's 2d limb | | 21.6 | 39.3 | 56.6 | 13.8 | 31.3 | 48.8 | 06.3 | 3 03 13.96 | | 1.07 | 3 03 13.62 | 1 03 04.57 | ...... | | 1 02.83 | h 1 12 52.18 | 1 03 03.29 | e 6 28 36.03 |
| | 135 | G. C. 121 | | 06.7 | 24 0 | 40.5 | 58.3 | 15.5 | 32.6 | 49.8 | 3 08 58.20 | | 1.10 | 3 08 57.86 | 1 22 31.46 | 1 46 26.40 | | ...... | ...... | ...... | ...... |
| | 136 | ν Piscium | | 24.8 | 42.0 | 58.8 | 16.2 | 33.3 | 50.3 | 07.7 | 3 20 16.16 | | 1.10 | 3 20 15.82 | 1 33 49.33 | 1 46 26.49 | | ...... | 1 33 49.36 | ...... | ...... |
| | 137 | ο Piscium | | 15.3 | 32.6 | 49.8 | 07.2 | 24.3 | 41.5 | 58.8 | 3 24 07.07 | | 1.10 | 3 24 06.75 | 1 37 40.46 | 1 46 26.18 | | ...... | 1 37 40.43 | 1 37 40.57 | ...... |
| | 138 | G. C. 181 | | 14.3 | 36.8 | 00.2 | 22.8 | 45.5 | 08.4 | 31.2 | 3 41 22.74 | | − 1.10 | 3 41 22.35 | 1 54 56.37 | 1 46 25.98 | | ...... | ...... | ...... | ...... |
| Oct. 8 | 139 | ξ Cygni | E. | 10.2 | 29.7 | 49.4 | 09.3 | 28.8 | 48.5 | 08.3 | 22 54 09.17 | + 1.50 | − 0.52 | 22 54 09.19 | 21 06 42.57 | 1 47 26.62 | 47 26.98 | ...... | ...... | ...... | ...... |
| | 140 | ε Pegasi | | 34.8 | 52.1 | 09.3 | 26.6 | 44.3 | 01.5 | 18.5 | 23 24 26.73 | (− 10.81) | 1.10 | 23 24 26.54 | 21 36 59.98 | 1 47 26.56 | (+ 2.73) | ...... | ...... | ...... | ...... |
| | 141 | G. C. 1993 | | 42.2 | 59.3 | 16.6 | 33.7 | 50.8 | 08.4 | 25.7 | 23 56 33.81 | | 0.48 | 23 56 33.47 | 22 09 06.69 | 1 47 26.78 | | ...... | ...... | ...... | ...... |
| | 142 | G. C. 1999 | | 41.8 | 58.8 | 15.6 | 33.0 | 50.2 | 07.3 | 24.3 | 0 01 33.00 | | − 0.12 | 0 01 32.76 | 22 14 06.01 | 1 47 26.75 | | ...... | ...... | ...... | ...... |
| | 143 | G. C. 2019 | | 37.3 | 57.8 | 17.9 | 38.4 | 58.8 | 18.9 | 39.8 | 0 10 38.41 | | + 0.44 | 0 10 37.81 | 22 23 10.95 | 1 47 26.86 | | ...... | ...... | ...... | ...... |
| | 144 | ξ Pegasi | | 44.6 | 02.4 | 19.3 | 36.9 | 54.3 | 11.7 | 29.2 | 0 21 36.91 | | 1.10 | 0 21 36.87 | 22 34 10.08 | 1 47 26.79 | | ...... | ...... | ...... | ...... |
| | 145 | α Piscis Australis | | 01.8 | 21.8 | 41.3 | 01.5 | 21.3 | 40.8 | 00.6 | 0 37 01.30 | | 1.10 | 0 37 00.77 | 22 49 23.74 | 1 47 27.03 | | ...... | ...... | ...... | ...... |
| | 146 | α Pegasi | | 02.6 | 20.3 | 37.8 | 55.3 | 13.3 | 30.8 | 48.5 | 0 44 55.51 | | + 1.10 | 0 44 55.46 | 22 57 28.74 | 1 47 26.72 | | ...... | ...... | ...... | ...... |
| 9 | 147 | ο Sagittarii | W | 28.3 | 46.5 | 05.0 | 23.4 | 41.8 | 00.1 | 18.6 | 20 43 23.39 | + 1.59 | + 0.13 | 20 43 22.83 | 18 55 53.55 | 1 47 29.28 | 47 29.39 | ...... | ...... | ...... | ...... |
| | 148 | π Sagittarii | | 37.4 | 55.6 | 13.6 | 32.3 | 50.4 | 07.8 | 27.3 | 20 48 32.19 | (− 13.74) | 0.13 | 20 48 31.65 | 19 01 02.51 | 1 47 29.14 | (2.08) | ...... | ...... | ...... | ...... |
| | 149 | Moon's 1st limb | | 21.5 | 41.0 | 00.3 | 19.6 | 39.4 | 58.6 | 17.8 | 21 22 19.74 | | 0.13 | 21 22 19.75 | 19 18 52.07 | ...... | | 1 13.85 | ...... | 19 18 51.49 | 6 28 38.86 |
| | 150 | α Aquilæ | | 15.6 | 32.4 | 49.3 | 07.3 | 24.6 | 41.8 | 59.2 | 21 31 07.17 | + 1.50 | 0.07 | 21 31 06.98 | 19 43 38.00 | 1 47 28.98 | 47 29.39 | ...... | ...... | ...... | ...... |
| | 151 | b Sagittarii | | 29.3 | 48.3 | 07.5 | 26.8 | 46.3 | 05.4 | 24.7 | 21 35 26.90 | (− 13.74) | + 0.04 | 21 35 26.17 | 19 47 57.04 | 1 47 29.13 | (+ 2.08) | ...... | ...... | 19 47 57.06 | ...... |
| | 152 | c Sagittarii | | 10.3 | 29.8 | 49.2 | 08.4 | 27.6 | 47.3 | 06.6 | 21 41 08.46 | | | 21 41 07.73 | 19 53 38.59 | 1 47 29.14 | | ...... | ...... | ...... | ...... |
| | 153 | a² Capricorni | | 32.5 | 49.8 | 07.4 | 24.8 | 42.6 | 59.7 | 17.7 | 21 57 24.93 | | | 21 57 24.44 | 20 09 55.39 | 1 47 29.05 | | ...... | ...... | ...... | ...... |
| 10i | 154 | b Sagittarii | W. | 30.6 | ...... | ...... | 28.4 | 47.8 | 07.3 | 26.3 | 21 35 26.65 | − 1.50 | − 0.27 | 21 35 27.65 | 19 47 57.02 | 1 47 30.63 | 47 31.14 | ...... | ...... | ...... | ...... |
| | 155 | c Sagittarii | | 11.5 | 31.3 | 50.6 | 09.8 | 29.3 | 48.7 | 08.2 | 21 41 09.91 | (− 13.28) | + 0.20 | 21 41 09.00 | 19 53 38.57 | 1 47 30.43 | (+ 2.53) | ...... | ...... | ...... | ...... |
| | 156 | a² Capricorni | | 34.3 | 51.8 | 09.0 | 26.9 | 44.4 | 01.8 | 19.3 | 21 57 26.79 | | 1.50 | 21 57 26.20 | 20 09 55.38 | 1 47 30.82 | | ...... | ...... | ...... | ...... |
| | 157j | Moon's 1st limb | | 20.8 | 40.8 | 59.3 | 18.6 | 38.0 | 56.9 | 15.3 | 22 24 18.53 | | 1.92 | 22 24 17.85 | 20 21 37.14 | ...... | | 1 11.80 | ...... | 20 21 36.54 | 6 28 40.56 |
| 12k | 158 | δ Capricorni | E. | 41.6 | 59.4 | 17.3 | 34.8 | 52.7 | 10.6 | 28.6 | 23 26 35.00 | + 1.50 | + 1.65 | 23 26 34.58 | 21 38 57.47 | 1 47 37.11 | 47 37.76 | ...... | ...... | ...... | ...... |
| | 159 | μ Capricorni | | 03.5 | 21.2 | 38.7 | 56.3 | 14.0 | 31.6 | 49.4 | 23 32 56.39 | (− 12.82) | 1.43 | 23 32 56.01 | 21 45 18.82 | 1 47 37.19 | (+ 3.07) | ...... | ...... | ...... | ...... |
| | 160 | α Gruis | | 21.8 | 46.9 | 12.5 | 37.7 | 03.6 | 28.8 | 54.8 | 23 46 38.01 | + 1.01 | | 23 46 36.97 | 21 58 59.87 | 1 47 37.10 | | ...... | ...... | ...... | ...... |
| | 161 | G. C. 1993 | | 52.3 | 09.8 | 26.8 | 44.0 | 01.3 | 18.5 | 36.2 | 23 56 44.13 | | 0.68 | 23 56 43.77 | 22 09 06.65 | 1 47 37.12 | | ...... | ...... | ...... | c 6 28 24.11 |
| | 162 | Moon's 1st limb | | 16.8 | 34.5 | 52.3 | 10.6 | 28.7 | 46.8 | 05.1 | 0 17 10.69 | | 0.68 | 0 17 10.24 | 22 16 21.30 | ...... | | 1 06.84 | l 22 27.27.06 | 22 16 20.66 | e 6 28 24.96 |
| | 163 | ξ Pegasi | | 55.6 | 12.8 | 30.0 | 47.5 | 04.8 | 22.3 | 39.4 | 0 21 47.49 | | 0.68 | 0 21 47.39 | 22 34 10.05 | 1 47 37.34 | | ...... | ...... | ...... | ...... |
| | 164 | τ² Aquarii | | 35.6 | 53.4 | 10.7 | 28.3 | 46.2 | 03.8 | 21.3 | 0 29 28.47 | | 0.68 | 0 29 28.05 | 22 41 50.49 | 1 47 37.56 | | ...... | 22 41 50.70 | ...... | ...... |
| | 165 | δ Aquarii | | 37.3 | 55.5 | 13.1 | 30.9 | 48.8 | 06.3 | 24.4 | 0 34 30.90 | | 0.68 | 0 34 30.44 | 22 46 53.00 | 1 47 37.44 | | ...... | 22 46 53.03 | ...... | ...... |
| | 166 | α Piscis Australis | | 12.2 | 32.3 | 52.0 | 11.8 | 31.5 | 51.3 | 11.4 | 0 37 11.79 | | 0.68 | 0 37 11.12 | 22 49 33.70 | 1 47 37.42 | | ...... | ...... | ...... | ...... |
| | 167 | α Pegasi | | 13.3 | 30.8 | 48.4 | 06.0 | 23.6 | 41.3 | 59.3 | 0 45 06.10 | | + 0.68 | 0 45 06.07 | 22 57 28.71 | 1 47 37.26 | | ...... | ...... | ...... | ...... |
| 13 | 168 | τ² Aquarii | W. | 38.8 | 56.3 | 13.6 | 31.5 | 49.3 | 07.0 | 24.4 | 0 29 31.56 | − 1.50 | + 0.27 | 0 29 31.06 | 22 41 50.48 | 1 47 40.58 | 47 40.59 | ...... | ...... | ...... | ...... |
| | 169 | δ Aquarii | | 40.5 | 58.3 | 16.2 | 34.3 | 51.9 | 09.6 | 27.3 | 0 34 34.01 | (− 9.28) | 0.27 | 0 34 33.48 | 22 46 52.99 | 1 47 40.49 | (+ 2.70) | ...... | 22 46 53.12 | ...... | ...... |
| | 170 | α Piscis Australis | | 15.4 | 35.6 | 54.8 | 15.1 | 34.7 | 54.4 | 14.3 | 0 37 14.90 | | 0.27 | 0 37 14.21 | 22 49 33.70 | 1 47 40.51 | | ...... | ...... | ...... | ...... |
| | 171 | α Pegasi | | 16.3 | 34.4 | 51.6 | 09.6 | 27.0 | 44.8 | 02.3 | 0 45 09.43 | | + 0.27 | 0 45 09.22 | 22 57 28.71 | 1 47 40.51 | | ...... | ...... | ...... | ...... |

*a* Fleecy clouds were flying over during the observations. *b* The perfect limb. *c* Deduced from corresponding observations made at Greenwich Observatory.
*d* 64.77*s.* = computed time of moon's semi-diam. passed meridian. *e* Deduced from observations made at Philadelphia High School Academy. *f* Clouds have prevented a full set of observations to-night.
*g* No low star could be taken in consequence of the clouds. *h* 63*s*.84 = computed time of moon's semi-diam. passing meridian. *i* Clouds prevent further observations. *j* Very cloudy.
*k* Clouds and rain prevent observations being made bright. *l* 66.98*s.* = computed time of moon's semi-diam. passing meridian.

## *Meridian transit observations made at mouth of Rio Grande, &c.*—Continued.

| Date. | Number for reference. | Name of object. | Illuminated end of axis. | Seconds of transit over the seven wires. I. | II. | III. | IV. | V. | VI. | VII. | Concluded transit over the mean of the seven wires. | Error of— Collima'n, (azimuth.) | Level. | Corrected transit. | Tabular right ascension of known stars and moon's centre. | Chronometer apparently fast of sider'l time. | Adopted chronometer fast at 0h. sider'l time and (gaining rate.) | Sidereal time of semi-diam. passing meridian of station. | App. R. A. of centre deduced from observations made at— High School Observatory, Phila. | Royal Observatory, Gr'nwich. | Long. west of Greenwich deduced from observations of each night. |
|---|---|---|---|---|---|---|---|---|---|---|---|---|---|---|---|---|---|---|---|---|---|
| 1853. | | | | s. | s. | s. | s. | s. | s. | s. | h. m. s. | " | " | h. m. s. | h. m. s. | h. m. s. | m s. | m. s. | h. m. s. | h. m. s. | h. m. s. |
| Oct. 13 | 172 | G. C. 2086 ...... | W. | 34.2 | 51.4 | 08.3 | 25.7 | 43.2 | 00.3 | 17.3 | 0 54 25.77 | − 1.50 | + 0.27 | 0 54 25.35 | 23 06 44.90 | 1 47 40.45 | 47 40.59 | ........ | ........ | ........ | ........ |
| | 173 | G. C. 2092 ...... | | 09.8 | 27.3 | 44.6 | 02.3 | 19.3 | 36.5 | 54.2 | 0 59 02.00 | (− 9.28) | 0.47 | 0 59 01.55 | 23 11 21.17 | 1 47 40.38 | (+ 2.70) | ........ | ........ | ........ | a6 28 20.87 |
| | 174 | Moon's 1st limb. | | 28.6 | 46.3 | 04.4 | 21.8 | 39.3 | 56.7 | 14.9 | 1 08 21.71 | | 0.82 | 1 08 21.28 | 23 08 16.56 | ........ | | 1 04.80 | b22 18 43.58 | 23 08 15.90 | c6 28 28.00 |
| | 175 | 20 Piscium ........ | | 15.2 | 32.4 | 49.1 | 06.3 | 23.6 | 40.8 | 57.7 | 1 28 06.44 | | 0.82 | 1 28 06.08 | 23 40 25.49 | 1 47 40.59 | | ........ | 23 40 25.43 | ........ | ........ |
| | 176 | 27 Piscium ...... | | 00.8 | 18.2 | 35.0 | 52.3 | 09.6 | 26.3 | 43.5 | 1 38 52.24 | | 0.82 | 1 38 51.88 | 23 51 11.25 | 1 47 40.63 | | ........ | 23 51 11.21 | ........ | ........ |
| | 177 | G. C. 2153 ...... | | 40.3 | 57.8 | 14.8 | 32.2 | 49.3 | 06.4 | 23.5 | 1 45 32.04 | | + 0.82 | 1 45 31.60 | 23 57 51 21 | 1 47 40.39 | | ........ | ........ | ........ | ........ |
| 17 | 178 | α Eridani........ | E. | 32.5 | 04.8 | 36.4 | 09.3 | ...... | ...... | ...... | 3 20 08.83 | + 1.50 | − 0.55 | 3 20 08.63 | 1 32 17.71 | 1 47 50.92 | 47 50.86 | ........ | ........ | ........ | ........ |
| | 179 | α Piscium........ | | 29.2 | 46.3 | 03.4 | 20.3 | 37.3 | 54.3 | 11.6 | 3 42 20.34 | (− 3.90) | + 1.38 | 3 42 20.41 | 1 54 29.46 | 1 47 50.95 | (+ 2.56) | ........ | 1 54 29.38 | ........ | ........ |
| | 180 | ξ[1] Ceti............ | | 14.7 | 31.9 | 49.0 | 06.6 | 23.8 | 41.1 | 58.3 | 3 53 06.49 | | 2.33 | 3 53 06.66 | 2 05 15.56 | 1 47 51.10 | | ........ | 2 05 15.47 | ........ | a6 28 25.89 |
| | 181 | Moon's 2d limb. | | 01.6 | 19.3 | 36.8 | 54.8 | 12.7 | 30.2 | 47.9 | 4 19 54.76 | | 2.33 | 4 19 54.95 | 2 18 17.81 | ........ | | 1 03.10 | e2 28 07.46 | 2 18 17.07 | c6 28 34.37 |
| | 182 | B. A. C. 845 .... | | 01.8 | 19.3 | 36.6 | 53.6 | 11.0 | 28.3 | 45.0 | 4 24 53.77 | | 1.88 | 4 24 53.91 | 2 37 02.71 | 1 47 51.20 | | ........ | 2 37 02.75 | 2 37 02.71 | ........ |
| | 183 | π Arietis.......... | | 06.0 | 23.5 | 41.8 | 59.7 | 17.3 | 34.8 | 53.3 | 4 28 59.49 | | 1.50 | 4 28 59.65 | 2 41 08.44 | 1 47 51.21 | | ........ | ........ | ........ | ........ |
| | 184 | α Ceti............ | | 38.5 | 55.4 | 12.3 | 29.5 | 46.8 | 03.9 | 20.8 | 4 42 29.60 | | 1.50 | 4 42 29.69 | 2 54 38.56 | 1 47 51.13 | | ........ | ........ | ........ | ........ |
| | 185 | G. C. 274........ | | 44.6 | 04.3 | 23.8 | 43.8 | 03.3 | 22.8 | 42.6 | 4 53 43.60 | | + 0.28 | 4 53 43.47 | 3 05 52.32 | 1 47 51.15 | | ........ | ........ | ........ | ........ |
| 18 | 186 | B. A. C. 845 .... | W. | 04.6 | 22.2 | 39.3 | 56.7 | 13.9 | 31.3 | 48.5 | 4 24 56.79 | − 1.50 | + 0.27 | 4 24 56.52 | 2 37 02.72 | 1 47 53.80 | 47 53.42 | ........ | ........ | 2 37 02.72 | ........ |
| | 187 | π Arietis.......... | | 08.6 | 26.8 | 44.3 | 02.3 | 20.3 | 38.1 | 55.8 | 4 29 02.31 | (− 9.08) | 0.44 | 4 29 02.14 | 2 41 08.46 | 1 47 53.68 | (+ 2.88) | ........ | 2 41 08.44 | ........ | a6 28 20.6 |
| | 188 | Moon's 2d limb.. | | 01.3 | 19.2 | 36.8 | 55.3 | 13.4 | 31.5 | 49.3 | 5 07 55.26 | | 2.06 | 5 07 55.20 | 3 05 54.03 | ........ | | 1 04.06 | g3 15 59.50 | 3 05 53.28 | c6 28 24.09 |
| | 189 | η Tauri........... | | 46.0 | 04.4 | 22.6 | 41.8 | 00.5 | 18.8 | 37.7 | 5 26 41.69 | | 2.06 | 5 26 41.70 | 3 38 47.99 | 1 47 53.71 | | ........ | ........ | 3 38 48.03 | ........ |
| | 190 | 32 Tauri........... | | 12.3 | 31.3 | 49.5 | 07.8 | 26.3 | 44.8 | 03.2 | 5 36 07.89 | | 1.55 | 5 36 07.94 | 3 48 14.10 | 1 47 53.84 | | ........ | 3 48 13.97 | ........ | ........ |
| | 191 | γ[1] Eridani......... | | 14.2 | 31.8 | 49.3 | 06.8 | 24.0 | 42.3 | 59.6 | 5 39 06.94 | | 1.38 | 5 39 06.51 | 3 51 12.71 | 1 47 53.80 | | ........ | ........ | ........ | ........ |
| | 192 | G. C. 344....... | | 02.3 | 20.4 | 38.6 | 57.2 | 15.8 | 33.8 | 52.1 | 5 43 57.17 | | 1.10 | 5 43 57.09 | 3 56 03.35 | 1 47 53.74 | | ........ | ........ | ........ | ........ |
| | 193 | G. C. 362...... | | 29.4 | 47.4 | 04.5 | 22.3 | 40.3 | 57.8 | 15.7 | 5 59 22.49 | | + 1.10 | 5 59 22.34 | 4 11 28.51 | 1 47 53.83 | | ........ | ........ | ........ | ........ |
| 19 | 194 | η Tauri .......... | E. | 49.3 | 07.8 | 26.4 | 45.3 | 03.7 | 22.5 | 41.3 | 5 26 45.19 | + 1.50 | − 0.41 | 5 26 45.24 | 3 38 48.01 | 1 47 57.23 | 47 56.62 | ........ | 3 38 48.16 | 3 38 48.05 | ........ |
| | 195 | 32 Tauri .......... | | 16.0 | 34.3 | 52.6 | 11.4 | 29.6 | 48.2 | 06.5 | 5 36 11.23 | (− 13.24) | + 0.09 | 5 36 11.28 | 3 48 14.13 | 1 47 57.15 | (+ 3.30) | ........ | 3 48 14.05 | ........ | ........ |
| | 196 | γ[1] Eridani......... | | 17.6 | 35.1 | 52.5 | 10.3 | 27.7 | 45.4 | 03.3 | 5 39 10.27 | | 0.26 | 5 39 09.80 | 3 51 12.73 | 1 47 57.07 | | ........ | ........ | ........ | ........ |
| | 197 | G. C. 344....... | | 05.3 | 23.8 | 42.2 | 00.4 | 19.0 | 37.4 | 55.8 | 5 44 00.56 | | 0.55 | 5 44 00.64 | 3 56 03.38 | 1 47 57.26 | | ........ | ........ | ........ | a6 28 24.86 |
| | 198 | Moon's 2d limb. | | 34.6 | 53.2 | 11.6 | 30.5 | 49.3 | 07.5 | 26.3 | 5 57 30.43 | | 0.55 | 5 57 30.49 | 3 54 56.86 | ........ | | 1 05.32 | h4 05 23.77 | 3 54 56.38 | c6 28 27 56 |
| | 199 | G. C. 363....... | | 18.2 | 38.5 | 59.3 | 20.2 | 40.4 | 01.3 | 22.3 | 6 00 20.03 | | 0.68 | 6 00 19.25 | 4 12 22.01 | 1 47 57.24 | | ........ | ........ | ........ | ........ |
| | 200 | G. C. 370 ....... | | 35.5 | 53.6 | 12.3 | 30.8 | 49.3 | 07.7 | 26.4 | 6 05 30.80 | | 0.91 | 6 05 30.92 | 4 17 33.75 | 1 47 57.17 | | ........ | ........ | ........ | ........ |
| | 201 | α Tauri . ........ | | 35.6 | 53.5 | 11.3 | 29.0 | 46.8 | 04.4 | 22.3 | 6 15 28.99 | | 1.37 | 6 15 29.02 | 4 27 31.95 | 1 47 57.07 | | ........ | 4 27 31.95 | ........ | ........ |
| | 202 | G. C. 400 ....... | | 29.8 | 48.3 | 06.8 | 25.2 | 43.7 | 02.3 | 20.9 | 6 21 25.29 | | + 1.65 | 6 21 25.47 | 4 33 28.25 | 1 47 57.22 | | ........ | ........ | ........ | ........ |
| 20 | 203 | θ[2] Tauri .......... | W. | 26.7 | 44.5 | 02.3 | 20.2 | 37.6 | 55.3 | 13.0 | 6 08 19.94 | − 1.50 | + 0.55 | 6 08 19.80 | 4 20 19.05 | 1 48 00.75 | 48 00.03 | ........ | ........ | ........ | ........ |

| | | | | | | | | | | | | | | | | | | | | | | |
|---|---|---|---|---|---|---|---|---|---|---|---|---|---|---|---|---|---|---|---|---|---|---|
| | 204 | α | Tauri ...... .... | | 39.3 | 57.6 | 14.9 | 33.2 | 50.6 | 08.3 | 26.5 | 6 15 32.91 | (— 6.43) | 1.30 | 6 15 32.82 | 4 27 31.97 | 1 48 00.85 | (+ 3.46) | ........ | ............ | ............ | ............ |
| | 205 | | G. C. 400 ....... | | 33.3 | 52.3 | 10.4 | 29.3 | 47.8 | 06.3 | 24.8 | 6 21 29.17 | | 0.13 | 6 21 29.16 | 4 33 28.28 | 1 48 00.88 | | ........ | ............ | ............ | ............ |
| | 206 | | G. C. 405........ | | 56.0 | 14.3 | 31.8 | 50.1 | 08.0 | 26.0 | 44.3 | 6 40 50.07 | | 2.75 | 6 30 50.11 | 4 42 49.32 | 1 48 00.71 | | ........ | ............ | ............ | ............ |
| | 207 | | Moon's 2d limb. | | ..... | 16.8 | 34.8 | 54.3 | 13.3 | 32.2 | 51.3 | 6 48 54.41 | | 1.65 | 6 48 54.34 | 4 45 45.58 | ............ | | 1 06.59 | ............ | 4 45 45.37 | 6 28 42.03 |
| | 208 | ο | Tauri .......... | | 56.7 | 15.2 | 33.4 | 52.0 | 10.3 | 28.6 | 47.3 | 7 06 51.93 | | 1.65 | 7 06 51.81 | 5 18 51.05 | 1 48 00.76 | | ........ | ............ | ............ | ............ |
| | 209 | α | Leporis ........ | | 24.4 | 42.6 | 00.3 | 18.3 | 36.3 | 54.2 | 12.2 | 7 14 18.33 | | 1.92 | 7 14 18.01 | 5 26 16.93 | 1 48 01.08 | | ........ | ............ | ............ | ............ |
| | 210 | ξ | Tauri .... ...... | | 00.3 | 18.5 | 36.4 | 55.3 | 13.6 | 31.8 | 49.9 | 7 16 55.11 | | 2.04 | 7 16 55.10 | 5 28 54.19 | 1 48 00.91 | | ........ | ............ | ............ | ............ |
| | 211 | | G. C. 493 ....... | | 07.2 | 25.6 | 44.4 | 03.3 | 22.1 | 40.5 | 59.4 | 7 28 03.21 | | + 2.47 | 7 28 03.27 | 5 40 02.34 | 1 48 00.93 | | ........ | ............ | ............ | ............ |
| i21 | 212 | ο | Tauri .......... | E. | ...... | 18.3 | 36.8 | 55.3 | 13.8 | 32.4 | 50.6 | 7 06 55.26 | + 1.50 | — 0.55 | 7 06 55.15 | 5 18 51.08 | ............ | 48 03.55 | ... .... | ............ | ............ | ............ |
| | 213 | α | Leporis......... | | 27.8 | 46.2 | 03.6 | 21.6 | 39.7 | 57.8 | 15.8 | 7 14 21.79 | (— 12.68) | + 0.18 | 7 14 21.28 | 5 26 16.96 | 1 48 04.32 | (+ 3.68) | ........ | ............ | ............ | ............ |
| | 214 | ξ | Tauri .......... | | ...... | 22.0 | 40.1 | 58.3 | 16.8 | 35.2 | 53.5 | 7 16 58.48 | | 0.50 | 7 16 58.60 | 5 28 54.22 | 1 48 04.38 | | ........ | ............ | ............ | ............ |
| | 215 | | Moon's 2d limb. | | 00.6 | 19.7 | 38.5 | 57.8 | ...... | 36.6 | ...... | 7 41 57.94 | | + 0.68 | 7 41 58.10 | 5 38 19.40 | ............ | | 1 07.66 | ............ | 5 38 19.19 | 6 28 41.25 |
| 22 | 216 | α | Columbæ....... | W. | 28.5 | 49.3 | 09.6 | 30.3 | 50.8 | 11.7 | 31.8 | 7 22 30.29 | — 1.50 | + 1.23 | 7 22 29.99 | 5 34 21.67 | 1 48 08.32 | 48 07.40 | ........ | ............ | ............ | ............ |
| | 217 | α | Orionis......... | | 31.6 | 49.3 | 06.2 | 23.3 | 41.0 | 57.8 | 15.3 | 7 35 23.50 | (— 3.31) | 1.23 | 7 35 23.41 | 5 47 15.08 | 1 48 08.33 | (+ 3.75) | ........ | ............ | ............ | ............ |
| | 218 | η | Geminorum ... | | 15.6 | 34.3 | 52.3 | 11.3 | 29.4 | 47.8 | 06.4 | 7 54 11.01 | | 1.23 | 7 54 10.98 | 6 06 02.48 | 1 48 08.50 | | ........ | ............ | ............ | ............ |
| | 219 | μ | Geminorum .... | | 19.3 | 37.5 | 56.3 | 14.7 | 33.3 | 52.0 | 10.2 | 8 02 14.76 | | 2.10 | 8 02 14.79 | 6 14 06.34 | 1 48 08.45 | | ........ | ............ | ............ | ............ |
| | 220 | | G. C. 587....... | | 07.2 | 26.3 | 44.6 | 03.8 | 22.8 | 41.8 | 00.4 | 8 23 03.84 | | 2.10 | 8 23 03.88 | 6 34 55.49 | 1 48 08.39 | | ........ | ............ | ............ | ............ |
| | 221 | | Moon's 2d limb. | | 17.2 | 36.7 | 55.5 | 14.8 | 34.3 | 53.9 | 13.0 | 8 36 15.06 | | 2.71 | 8 36 15.15 | 6 32 15.86 | ............ | | 1 08.28 | ............ | 6 32 15.65 | 6 28 11.11 |
| | 222 | ξ | Geminorum .... | | 38.6 | 57.2 | 15.6 | 33.7 | 52.3 | 10.3 | 28.5 | 8 43 33.74 | | + 3.02 | 8 43 33.82 | 6 55 25.38 | 1 48 08.44 | | ........ | ............ | ............ | ............ |
| Nov. 7 | 223 | ρ | Capricorni ...... | E. | 41.6 | 59.5 | 17.3 | 35.5 | 53.6 | 11.3 | ...... | 22 09 35.38 | + 1.50 | + 0.40 | 22 09 34.92 | 20 20 29.59 | 1 49 05.33 | 49 05.87 | ........ | ............ | ............ | ............ |
| | 224 | ψ | Capricorni...... | | 34.2 | 52.8 | 11.8 | 30.8 | 50.0 | 08.6 | 27.8 | 22 26 30.86 | (— 13.23) | + 0.40 | 22 26 30.22 | 20 37 24.64 | 1 49 05.58 | (+ 3.57) | ........ | ............ | 20 37 24.60 | ............ |
| | 225 | ξ | Cygni .......... | | 48.6 | 07.8 | 27.5 | 47.3 | 07.3 | 26.5 | 46.3 | 22 55 47.33 | | — 0.11 | 22 55 47.36 | 21 06 42.01 | 1 49 05.35 | | ........ | ............ | ............ | ............ |
| | 226 | | Moon's 1st limb. | | 03.6 | 22.3 | 41.0 | 59.8 | 18.8 | 37.5 | 56.3 | 23 06 59.90 | | 0.27 | 23 06 59.31 | 21 03 15.90 | ............ | | 1 10.61 | ............ | 21 03 14.68 | a6 28 36.94 |
| | 227 | δ | Capricorni...... | | 09.8 | 27.6 | 45.2 | 03.3 | 21.0 | 38.8 | 56.8 | 23 28 03.21 | | 0.27 | 23 28 02.68 | 21 38 57.11 | 1 49 05.57 | | ........ | ............ | 21 38 57.21 | ............ |
| | 228 | μ | Capricorni...... | | 31.7 | 49.3 | 06.8 | 24.5 | 42.3 | 59.6 | 17.5 | 23 34 24.53 | | 0.27 | 23 34 24.04 | 21 45 18.47 | 1 49 05.57 | | ........ | ............ | 21 45 18.52 | ............ |
| | 229 | α | Gruis .... ...... | | 49.8 | 15.3 | 40.5 | 05.6 | 31.3 | 56.6 | 22.0 | 23 48 05.87 | | — 0.27 | 23 48 04.74 | 21 58 59.34 | 1 49 05.40 | | ........ | ............ | ............ | ............ |
| 8 | 230 | δ | Capricorni...... | W. | 13.2 | 31.3 | 48.6 | 06.8 | 24.6 | 42.3 | 00.3 | 23 28 06.73 | — 1.50 | + 0.27 | 23 28 06.23 | 21 38 57.09 | 1 49 09.14 | 49 09.37 | ........ | 21 38 57.26 | 21 38 57.19 | ............ |
| | 231 | μ | Capricorni...... | | 35.2 | 53.0 | 10.2 | 28.0 | 45.7 | 03.3 | 20.8 | 23 34 28.03 | (— 8.81) | + 0.19 | 23 34 27.55 | 21 45 18.46 | 1 49 09.09 | (+ 3.74) | ........ | 21 45 18.70 | 21 45 18.51 | ... ........ |
| | 232 | α | Gruis .... ...... | | 52.8 | 18.8 | 43.8 | 09.3 | 34.5 | 00.3 | 24.8 | 23 48 09.19 | | ........ | 23 48 08.21 | 21 58 59.34 | 1 49 08.87 | | ........ | ............ | ............ | a6 28 34.05 |
| | 233 | | Moon's 1st limb. | | 59.8 | 17.8 | 36.3 | 54.5 | 12.8 | 31.0 | 48.8 | 0 02 54.43 | | ........ | 0 02 53.92 | 22 00 15.98 | ............ | | 1 07.75 | 22 00 26.29 | 22 00 14.81 | j6 28 34.53 |
| | 234 | σ | Aquarii......... | | 11.3 | 28.8 | 46.3 | 03.5 | 20.7 | 38.5 | 55.8 | 0 12 03.56 | | + 0.11 | 0 12 03.11 | 22 22 53.79 | 1 49 09.32 | | ........ | 22 22 53.69 | 22 22 53.84 | ............ |
| | 235 | ξ | Pegasi.......... | | 27.0 | 44.6 | 01.8 | 19.3 | 36.7 | 53.3 | 11.3 | 0 23 19.14 | | 0.27 | 0 23 18.89 | 22 34 09.76 | 1 49 09.13 | | ........ | ............ | ............ | ............ |
| | 236 | δ | Aquarii .... .... | | 08.8 | 26.8 | 44.3 | 02.2 | 20.6 | 38.0 | 55.8 | 0 36 02.36 | | 0.27 | 0 36 01.86 | 22 46 52.73 | 1 49 09.13 | | ........ | 22 46 52.87 | 22 46 52.81 | ............ |
| | 237 | α | Piscis Australis. | | 43.8 | 03.8 | 23.0 | 43.3 | 03.0 | 22.6 | 42.5 | 0 38 43.14 | | 0.77 | 0 38 42.50 | 22 49 33.39 | 1 49 09.11 | | ........ | ............ | ............ | ............ |
| | 238 | α | Pegasi......... | | 44.3 | 02.3 | 19.8 | 37.6 | 55.4 | 12.8 | 30.3 | 0 46 37.50 | | + 2.06 | 0 46 37.42 | 22 57 28.46 | 1 49 08.96 | | ........ | ............ | ............ | ............ |
| 9 | 239 | σ | Aquarii .... .... | E. | 14.6 | 32.3 | 49.4 | 06.8 | 24.3 | 41.5 | 59.3 | 0 12 06.89 | + 1.50 | ........ | 0 12 06.86 | 22 22 53.78 | 1 49 13.08 | 49 13.35 | ........ | 22 22 53.68 | 22 22 53.83 | ............ |
| | 240 | ξ | Pegasi.......... | | 30.8 | 48 3 | 05.5 | 22.8 | 40.3 | 57.3 | 14.9 | 0 23 22.84 | (— 3.09) | — 0.20 | 0 23 22.87 | 22 34 09.75 | 1 49 13.12 | (+ 4.17) | ........ | ............ | ............ | ............ |
| | 241 | δ | Aquarii .... .... | | 12.3 | 30.3 | 48.2 | 05.8 | 23.8 | 41.5 | 59.6 | 0 36 05.93 | | — 0.47 | 0 36 05.86 | 22 46 52.71 | 1 49 13.15 | | ........ | 22 46 52.76 | 22 46 52.79 | ............ |

*a* Deduced from corresponding observations made at Greenwich Observatory.
*c* Deduced from corresponding observations made at Philadelphia High School Observatory.
*e* 63s.95. = computed time of moon's semi-diam. passing meridian.
*g* 64s.00. = computed time of moon's semi-diam. passing meridian.
*i* No further observations this morning, in consequence of the thickening clouds.

*b* 64s.90. = computed time of moon's semi-diam. passing meridian.
*d* Oct. 16.—Clouds prevent observations being made to-night.
*f* Not satisfactory, because of clouds.
*h* 65s.24. = computed time of moon's semi-diam. passing meridian.
*j* Deduced from corresponding observations made at Radcliffe Observatory

*Meridian transit observations made at mouth of Rio Grande, &c.*—Continued.

| Date. | No. for reference. | Name of object. | Illuminated end of axis. | Seconds of transit over the seven wires. | | | | | | | Concluded transit over the mean of the seven wires. | Error of— | | Corrected transit. | Tabular right ascension of known stars and moon's centre. | Chronometer apparently fast of sider'l time. | Adopted chronometer fast at 0h. sider'l time and (gaining rate.) | Sidereal time of semi-diam. passing meridian of station. | App. R. A. of centre deduced from observations made at— | | Long. west of Greenwich deduced from observations of each night. |
|---|---|---|---|---|---|---|---|---|---|---|---|---|---|---|---|---|---|---|---|---|---|
| | | | | I. | II. | III. | IV. | V. | VI. | VII. | | Collima'n, (azimuth.) | Level. | | | | | | High School Observatory, Phila. | Royal Observatory, Gr'nwich. | |
| 1853. | | | | s. | s. | s. | s. | s. | s. | s. | h. m. s. | " | " | h. m. s. | h. m. s. | h. m. s. | m. s. | m. s. | h. m. s. | h. m s. | h. m. s. |
| Nov. 9 | 242 | α Piscis Australis. | E. | 47.3 | 06.8 | 26.5 | 46.6 | 06.3 | 26.0 | 46.3 | 0 38 46.54 | + 1.50 | — 0.52 | 0 38 46.43 | 22 49 33.37 | 1 49 13.06 | 49 13.35 | ....... | ........... | ........... | ........... |
| | 243 | α Pegasi......... | | 48.5 | 06.2 | 23.6 | 41.3 | 59.0 | 16.8 | 34.4 | 0 46 41.40 | (— 3.09) | 0.68 | 0 46 41.41 | 22 57 28.45 | 1 49 12.96 | (+ 4.17) | ....... | ........... | ........... | a6 28 32.15 |
| | 244 | Moon's 1st limb. | | 54.7 | 12.3 | 30.3 | 48.2 | 06.3 | 23.5 | 41.3 | 0 54 48.09 | | 0.68 | 0 54 48.02 | 22 53 03.22 | ........... | | 1 05.53 | 22 53 13.08 | 22 53 02.20 | 6 28 30.50 |
| | 245 | φ Aquarii........ | | ..... | ..... | ..... | ..... | 15.3 | 32.3 | 49.5 | 0 55 57.87 | | 0.84 | 0 55 57.87 | 23 06 44.69 | 1 49 13.18 | | ....... | 23 06 44.49 | 23 06 44.54 | ........... |
| | 246 | ψ³ Aquarii .... .... | | 42.3 | 59.4 | 16.8 | 34.5 | 51.8 | 09.0 | 26.6 | 1 00 34.34 | | — 1.65 | 1 00 34.23 | 23 11 20.85 | 1 49 13 38 | | ....... | 23 11 21.12 | 23 11 20.97 | ........... |
| 10 | 247 | ξ Pegasi......... | W. | 35.0 | 52.6 | 09.8 | 27.5 | 44.8 | 01.8 | 19.4 | 0 23 27.27 | — 1.50 | + 1.00 | 0 23 27.12 | 22 34 09.73 | 1 49 17.39 | 49 17.72 | ....... | ........... | ........... | ........... |
| | 248 | α Piscis Australis. | | 51.6 | 12.2 | 31.5 | 51.6 | 11.3 | 31.3 | 50.8 | 0 38 51.47 | (— 6.24) | 1.00 | 0 38 51.01 | 22 49 33.36 | 1 49 17.65 | (+ 4.15) | ... .... | ........... | ........... | ........... |
| | 249 | α Pegasi......... | | 53.3 | 10.8 | 28.3 | 46.3 | 03.8 | 21.4 | 38.9 | 0 46 46.11 | | 0.57 | 0 46 46.03 | 22 57 28.43 | 1 49 17.60 | | ....... | ........... | .. ........ | ........... |
| | 250 | φ Aquarii........ | | 10.6 | 28.3 | 45.0 | 02.6 | 19.8 | 36.8 | 53.9 | 0 56 02.43 | | 0.00 | 0 56 02.21 | 23 06 44.68 | 1 49 17.53 | | ....... | 23 06 44.49 | 23 06 44.74 | ........... |
| | 251 | ψ³ Aquarii........ | | 46.5 | 03.8 | 21.4 | 38.5 | 56.3 | 13.3 | 30.8 | 1 00 38.66 | | 0.82 | 1 00 38.41 | 23 11 20.84 | 1 49 17.57 | | ....... | 23 11 21.09 | 23 11 20.97 | ........... |
| | b252 | 27 Piscium........ | | 37.5 | 54.8 | ...... | ..... | 46.3 | 03.3 | ...... | 1 40 29.10 | | 0.82 | 1 40 28.91 | 23 51 11.10 | 1 49 17.81 | | ....... | 23 51 11.29 | 23 51 11.13 | a6 28 26.23 |
| | 253 | Moon's 1st limb. | | 47.9 | 05.8 | 23.2 | 40.7 | 58.3 | 15.6 | 33.3 | 1 43 40.69 | | 1.18 | 1 43 40.47 | 23 42 31.72 | ........... | | 1 03.57 | 23 42 41.18 | 23 42 31.11 | c6 28 31.07 |
| | b254 | 33 Piscium........ | | 17.3 | 34.5 | ...... | 09.0 | ...... | ...... | ...... | 1 47 08.95 | | + 1.65 | 1 47 08.73 | 23 57 50.98 | 1 49 17.75 | | ....... | 23 57 51.04 | 23 57 50.99 | ........... |
| 11 | 255 | 27 Piscium........ | E. | 41.7 | 59.0 | ..... | 32.8 | 50.6 | 07.4 | 24.8 | 1 40 33.34 | + 1.50 | — 0.27 | 1 40 32.94 | 23 51 11.09 | 1 49 21.85 | 49 21.65 | ....... | 23 51 11.28 | 23 51 11.12 | ........... |
| | 256 | 33 Piscium........ | | 21.5 | 38.8 | 55.8 | 13.3 | 30.3 | 47.3 | 04.8 | 1 47 13.11 | (— 16.22) | 0.66 | 1 47 12.59 | 23 57 50.97 | 1 49 21.62 | (+ 4.20) | ... .... | 23 57 51.03 | 23 57 50.98 | ........... |
| | 257 | Andromedæ .... | | 13.6 | 32.9 | 52.3 | 11.7 | 31.3 | 50.6 | 10.0 | 1 50 11.77 | | 0.82 | 1 50 11.77 | 0 00 50.18 | 1 49 21.59 | | ....... | ........... | ........... | ........... |
| | 258 | β Ceti........... | | 43.3 | 01.3 | 19.3 | 37.2 | 55.4 | 13.5 | 31.8 | 2 25 37.40 | | 0.82 | 2 25 36.65 | 0 36 15.03 | 1 49 21.62 | | ....... | ........... | ........... | ........... |
| | 259 | Moon's 1st limb. | | 45.8 | 03.0 | 20.5 | 37.6 | 55.3 | 12.4 | 29.8 | 2 30 37.77 | | 1.27 | 2 30 37.31 | 0 29 47.74 | ........... | | 1 02.56 | 0 29 56.95 | 0 29 47.14 | a6 28 23.32 |
| | 260 | 20 Ceti........... | | 03.3 | 20.5 | 37.4 | 54.8 | 11.8 | 28.6 | 46.2 | 2 34 54.66 | | — 1.65 | 2 34 54.16 | 0 45 32.32 | 1 49 21.84 | | ....... | 0 45 32.36 | 0 45 32.38 | ........... |
| 12 | 261 | δ Piscium...... . | W. | 41.0 | 58.3 | 15.5 | 32.8 | 50.2 | 07.3 | 24.0 | 2 30 32.73 | — 1.50 | — 0.27 | 2 30 32.38 | 0 41 06.05 | 1 49 26.33 | 49 26.13 | ....... | 0 41 06.00 | 0 41 05.96 | ........... |
| | 262 | 20 Ceti........... | | 07.8 | 24.8 | 41.6 | 59.3 | 16.3 | 33.3 | 50.2 | 2 34 59.04 | (— 6.69) | 1.06 | 2 34 58.67 | 0 45 32.31 | 1 49 26.36 | (+ 4.30) | ....... | 0 45 32.37 | 0 45 32.37 | ........... |
| | 263 | G. C. 66 ........ | | 56.6 | 14.2 | 30.9 | 48.3 | 05.4 | 22.8 | 40.3 | 2 44 48.36 | | 3.02 | 2 44 47.92 | 0 55 21.67 | 1 49 26.25 | | ....... | 0 55 21.70 | 0 55 21.70 | ........... |
| | 264 | G. C. 121 ....... | | 07.3 | 24.3 | 41.3 | 58.8 | 15.8 | 32.9 | 50.0 | 3 11 58.63 | | 2.48 | 3 11 58.22 | 1 22 31.85 | 1 49 26.37 | | ....... | 1 22 31.83 | 1 22 31.89 | ........... |
| | 265 | Moon's 1st limb. | | 23.2 | 10.4 | 28.0 | 45.3 | 03.3 | 20.3 | 37.6 | 3 16 45.44 | | 2.11 | 3 16 45.05 | 1 15 57.47 | ........... | | 1 02.26 | ........... | 1 15 56.83 | a6 28 34.55 |
| | 266 | α Eridani......... | | 07.8 | 40.6 | 12.5 | 45.3 | 16.8 | 49.3 | 21.4 | 3 21 44.81 | | 1.66 | 3 21 43.76 | 1 32 17.16 | 1 49 26.60 | | ....... | ........... | ........... | ........... |
| | 267 | o Piscium ........ | | 15.5 | 33.0 | 50.2 | 07.6 | 24.8 | 41.8 | 59.3 | 3 27 07.46 | | — 1.10 | 3 27 07.15 | 1 37 40.93 | 1 49 26 62 | | ....... | 1 37 40.84 | 1 37 41.06 | ........... |
| 13 | 268 | ν Piscium........ | E. | 28.9 | 46.3 | 03.4 | 20.3 | 37.8 | 54.8 | 12.2 | 3 23 20.53 | + 1.50 | — 1.10 | 3 23 20.32 | 1 33 49.77 | 1 49 30.55 | 49 30.25 | ....... | ........... | 1 33 49.80 | ........... |
| | 269 | o Piscium........ | | 19.6 | 37.3 | 54.3 | 11.5 | 29.0 | 46.3 | 03.6 | 3 27 11.66 | (— 6.20) | 2.20 | 3 27 11.49 | 1 37 40 93 | 1 49 30.56 | (+ 3.88) | ....... | 1 37 40.84 | 1 37 41.06 | ....... ... |
| | 270 | Moon's 1st limb. | | 08.3 | 25.8 | 43.6 | 00.8 | 18.8 | 36.4 | 53.9 | 4 03 01.09 | | 3.08 | 4 03 00.87 | 2 02 01.52 | ........... | | 1 02.62 | ........... | 2 02 00.84 | a6 28 35.93 |
| | 271 | ξ² Ceti........... | | 03.2 | 20.3 | 37.3 | 54.8 | 11.8 | 29.3 | 46.6 | 4 09 54.76 | | 3.85 | 4 09 54.48 | 2 20 23.85 | 1 49 30.63 | | ....... | 2 20 23.75 | 2 20 23.80 | ........... |
| | 272 | B. A. C. 845.... | | 42.3 | 59.5 | 16.4 | 33.8 | 51.3 | 08.5 | 25.8 | 4 26 33.94 | | 3.85 | 4 26 33.68 | 2 37 02.98 | 1 49 30.70 | | ... ... | 2 37 03.10 | 2 37 02.95 | ........... |

| | | | | | | | | | | | | | | | | | | | | | |
|---|---|---|---|---|---|---|---|---|---|---|---|---|---|---|---|---|---|---|---|---|---|
| 14 | 273 | ζ² Ceti.......... | W. | 06.3 | 23.8 | 40.9 | 58.3 | 15.6 | 32.8 | 50.0 | 4 09 58.54 | — 1.50 | — 0.82 | 4 09 58.27 | 2 20 23.85 | 1 49 34.42 | 49 33.89 | ........ | 2 20 23.75 | 2 20 23.80 | .......... |
| | 274 | B. A. C. 845..... | | 45.8 | 03.3 | 20.3 | 37.5 | 55.2 | 12.3 | 29.6 | 4 26 37.71 | (— 5.71) | 1.98 | 4 26 37.38 | 2 37 02.98 | 1 49 34.40 | (+ 4.08) | ........ | 2 37 03.10 | 2 37 02.95 | .......... |
| | 275 | G. C. 244........ | | 49.6 | 07.7 | 25.3 | 43.3 | 01.4 | 19.0 | 36.8 | 4 30 43.30 | | 2.25 | 4 30 42.99 | 2 41 08.80 | 1 49 34.19 | | ........ | 2 41 08.75 | 2 41 08.75 | .......... |
| | 276 | G. C. 254........ | | 31.5 | 50.2 | 08.2 | 26.6 | 44.8 | 03.3 | 21.4 | 4 40 26.57 | | 2.88 | 4 40 26.23 | 2 50 51.99 | 1 49 34.24 | | ........ | ........ | 2 50 51.96 | a6 28 33.60 |
| | d277 | Moon's 1st limb. | | 20.3 | 38.3 | 56.3 | 14.3 | 32.5 | 50.2 | 08.3 | 4 50 14.31 | | 2.88 | 4 50 13.96 | 2 48 52.10 | ............ | | 1 03.50 | 2 49 01.40 | 2 48 51.37 | c6 28 30.44 |
| | 278 | Moon's 2d limb. | | 27.6 | 45.5 | 03.4 | 21.8 | 39.4 | 57.3 | 15.3 | 4 52 21.47 | | 2.75 | 4 52 21.11 | 2 48 52.10 | ............ | | 1 03.50 | ............ | ............ | .......... |
| | 279 | G. C. 274........ | | 28.8 | 48.3 | 07.5 | 27.5 | 47.2 | 06.8 | 26.3 | 4 55 27.49 | | 2.54 | 4 55 26.90 | 3 05 52.63 | 1 49 34.27 | | ........ | ............ | ............ | .......... |
| | 280 | τ¹ Ariet s........ | | 27.8 | 46.0 | 04.2 | 22.4 | 40.8 | 58.9 | ...... | 5 02 22.54 | | — 2.06 | 5 02 22.25 | 3 12 47 93 | 1 49 34.32 | | ........ | 3 12 47.99 | 3 12 48.01 | .......... |
| 15 | 281 | G. C. 274........ | E. | 33.3 | 52.8 | 12.5 | 32.3 | 51.8 | 11.6 | 31.0 | 4 55 32.19 | + 1.50 | — 1.92 | 4 55 31.50 | 3 05 52.63 | 1 49 38.87 | 49 38.41 | ........ | ............ | ............ | .......... |
| | 282 | τ¹ Arietis........ | | 32.4 | 50.7 | 08 8 | 26.9 | 45.3 | 03.5 | 22.2 | 5 02 27.11 | (— 11.22) | 1.92 | 5 02 27.01 | 3 12 47.94 | 1 49 39.07 | (+ 4.76) | ........ | 3 12 48.00 | 3 12 48.02 | .......... |
| | 283 | η Tauri.......... | | 31.6 | 50.3 | 08.8 | 27.4 | 46.3 | 04.8 | 23.3 | 5 28 27.50 | | 1.92 | 5 28 27.45 | 3 38 48.33 | 1 49 39.12 | | ........ | 3 38 48.48 | 3 38 48.46 | .......... |
| | 284 | Moon's 2d limb. | | 18.3 | 36.5 | 55.3 | 13.3 | 31.8 | 50.2 | 08.6 | 5 41 13.43 | | 2.80 | 5 41 13.25 | 3 37 09.67 | ............ | | 1 04.67 | ............ | 3 37 08.86 | a6 28 26.41 |
| | 285 | G. C. 344........ | | 48.2 | 06.4 | 24.5 | 43.0 | 01.6 | 19.8 | 38.5 | 5 45 43.14 | | 3 02 | 5 45 42.97 | 3 56 03.88 | 1 49 39.09 | | ........ | ............ | ............ | .......... |
| | 286 | γ Tauri.......... | | 15.5 | 33.3 | 50.4 | 08.3 | 26.3 | 43.8 | 01.6 | 6 01 08.46 | | 3.02 | 6 01 08.20 | 4 11 29.14 | 1 49 39.06 | | ........ | ............ | 4 11 28.95 | .......... |
| | 287 | δ² Tauri.......... | | 26.6 | 44.4 | 02.0 | 19.8 | 37.8 | 55.6 | 13.5 | 6 05 19.94 | | — 2.97 | 6 05 19.71 | 4 15 40.75 | 1 49 38.96 | | ........ | 4 15 40.70 | 4 15 40.69 | .......... |
| e16 | 288 | δ² Tauri.......... | W. | ...... | ...... | ...... | 25.3 | 43.3 | 01.0 | 18.6 | 6 05 25.30 | — 1.50 | + 0.55 | 6 05 25.05 | 4 15 40.77 | 1 49 44.28 | 49 43.41 | ........ | 4 15 40.72 | 4 15 40.71 | .......... |
| | 289 | G. C. 370........ | | ...... | ...... | 00.3 | 18.8 | 37.3 | ...... | 14.3 | 6 07 18.90 | (— 11.00) | + 0.55 | 6 07 18.73 | 4 17 34.33 | 1 49 44.40 | (+ 5.30) | ........ | ............ | ............ | .......... |
| 18 | 290 | α Columbæ........ | E. | 17.0 | 37.8 | 58.3 | 18.8 | 39.5 | 00.3 | 21.2 | 7 24 18.99 | + 1.50 | — 2.20 | 7 24 18.28 | 5 34 22.34 | 1 49 55.94 | 49 54.61 | ........ | ............ | ............ | .......... |
| | 291 | 132 Tauri.......... | | 02.6 | 21.3 | 40.3 | 58.7 | 17.6 | 36.3 | 55.5 | 7 29 58.90 | (— 10.57) | 2.20 | 7 29 58.94 | 5 40 02.79 | 1 49 56.05 | (+ 5.33) | ........ | ............ | 5 40 02.82 | .......... |
| | 292 | 136 Tauri.......... | | 06.8 | 26.0 | 45.3 | 04.3 | 23.8 | 42.8 | 02.6 | 7 34 04.51 | | 2.20 | 7 34 04.43 | 5 44 08.69 | 1 49 55.74 | | ........ | ............ | 5 44 08.69 | .......... |
| | 293 | G. C. 535........ | | 04.2 | 22.4 | 40.8 | 59.3 | 18.3 | 36.3 | 55.3 | 7 55 59.51 | | 2.20 | 7 55 59.42 | 6 06 03.48 | 1 49 55.94 | | ........ | ............ | 6 06 03.36 | .......... |
| | 294 | Moon's 2d limb. | | 38.6 | 56.3 | 15.5 | 34.8 | 54.4 | 13.6 | 33.3 | 8 18 34.94 | | 3.70 | 8 18 34.77 | 6 12 53.80 | ............ | | 1 07.95 | ............ | 6 12 53.44 | a6 28 28.67 |
| | 295 | ε Geminorum...... | | 55.8 | 14.8 | 33.6 | 52.6 | 11.5 | 30.3 | 49.3 | 8 24 52.56 | | 3.80 | 8 24 52.38 | 6 34 56.36 | 1 49 56.02 | | ........ | ............ | 6 34 56.26 | .......... |
| | 296 | α Canis Majoris... | | 45.8 | 04.0 | 21.5 | 39.4 | 57.3 | 15.0 | 32.6 | 8 28 39.37 | | 3.85 | 8 28 38.77 | 6 38 42.71 | 1 49 56.06 | | ........ | ............ | ............ | .......... |
| | 297 | ξ Geminorum...... | | 27.9 | 46.3 | 04.2 | 22.6 | 40.8 | 59.3 | 17.5 | 8 45 22.66 | | — 3.85 | 8 45 22.44 | 6 55 26.22 | 1 49 56.22 | | ........ | ............ | 6 55 26.25 | .......... |
| f21 | 298 | γ Cancri.......... | W. | 05.3 | 24.3 | 42.5 | 01.5 | 19.6 | 37.8 | 56.2 | 10 25 01.03 | — 1.50 | — 3.30 | 10 25 00.63 | 8 34 48.94 | 1 50 11.69 | 50 10.00 | ........ | ............ | 8 34 48.86 | .......... |
| | 299 | Moon's 2d limb.. | | 34.4 | 53.3 | 12.0 | 30.8 | 49.3 | 08.2 | 26.6 | 11 00 30.66 | (— 10.57) | 3.30 | 11 00 30.26 | 8 54 58.53 | ............ | (+ 4.94) | 1 07.00 | ............ | 8 54 58.29 | a6 28 29.45 |
| | 300 | λ Leonis.......... | | 37.8 | 56.6 | 15.3 | 34.3 | 52.8 | 11.5 | 29.8 | 11 13 34.01 | | — 4.67 | 11 13 33.53 | 9 33 21.76 | 1 50 11.77 | | ........ | ............ | ............ | .......... |
| 22 | 301 | λ Leonis.......... | E. | 42.8 | 01.6 | 20.2 | 38.3 | 57.3 | 15.5 | 34.4 | 11 13 38.59 | + 1.50 | — 2.75 | 11 13 38.47 | 9 23 21.80 | 1 50 16.67 | 50 14.80 | ........ | ............ | ............ | .......... |
| | 302 | Moon's 2d limb. | | 34.8 | 53.2 | 11.6 | 29.8 | 48.3 | 06.3 | 24.3 | 11 52 29.76 | (— 10.57) | 2.75 | 11 52 29.56 | 9 47 13.58 | ............ | (+ 4.80) | 1 06.23 | ............ | 9 47 13.17 | a6 28 26.91 |
| | 303 | γ Leonis.......... | | 16.3 | 34.0 | 52.6 | 10.8 | 29.0 | 47.2 | 05.5 | 12 02 10.77 | | — 4.40 | 12 02 10.51 | 10 11 53.58 | 1 50 16.93 | | ........ | ............ | 10 11 53.61 | .......... |

*a* Deduced from corresponding observations made at Greenwich observatory.

*c* Deduced from corresponding observations made at Radcliffe observatory.

*e* Clouds prevent further observations this night.

*b* Clouds.

*d* No. 277—moon's 1st limb perfect.

*f* Clouds prevent more observations this night.

TABLE B.

*Results of observations made at mouth of Rio Grande for equatorial intervals of 46-inch transit, by Troughton & Simms—illumination east.*

| Stars observed. | First wire. | Second wire. | Third wire. | Fifth wire. | Sixth wire. | Seventh wire |
|---|---|---|---|---|---|---|
| | s. | s. | s. | s. | s. | s. |
| α Herculis | 50.96 | 33.97 | 17.08 | 17.08 | 34.17 | 51.35 |
| γ Draconis | 51.07 | 33.92 | 17.11 | 17.11 | 34.14 | 51.38 |
| h² Sagittarii | 50.99 | 33.98 | 16.87 | 17.19 | 34.20 | 51.35 |
| γ Aquilæ | 50.92 | 34.00 | 17.17 | 17.22 | 34.29 | 51.22 |
| b Sagittarii | 51.29 | 34.04 | 17.11 | 17.11 | 34.13 | 51.29 |
| β Capricorni | 51.18 | 34.10 | 17.27 | 17.08 | 34.15 | 51.13 |
| μ Capricorni | 51.08 | 33.92 | 16.82 | 17.11 | 84.02 | 51.13 |
| α Pegasi | 51.23 | 33.90 | 17.00 | 17.24 | 33.96 | 51.38 |
| π Capricorni | 51.20 | 34.19 | 17.05 | 17.15 | 33.96 | 51.15 |
| ξ Cygni | 51.02 | 33.90 | ............... | 17.38 | 34.33 | 51.46 |
| ψ³ Aquarii | 51.14 | 33.93 | 17.06 | 17.06 | 34.08 | 51.14 |
| β Aquilæ | 51.11 | 33.96 | 17.20 | 17.30 | 34.16 | 51.51 |
| δ Aquilæ | 51.19 | 34.16 | 16.98 | 17.13 | 34.01 | 51.34 |
| α Aquilæ | ............... | ............... | 17.22 | ............... | ............... | ........... |
| α² Capricorni | 51.01 | ............... | 17.05 | 17.24 | 34.10 | 51.30 |
| α Cygni | 51.26 | 34.08 | 16.90 | 17.23 | 34.29 | 51.22 |
| 61¹ Cygni | 51.12 | 34.11 | 17.13 | ............... | 34.22 | ........... |
| α Cephei | 51.16 | 34.10 | 17.20 | 17.13 | 34.17 | 51.39 |
| β Cephei | 51.20 | 34.24 | 17.19 | 17.19 | 34.25 | 51.44 |
| t² Aquarii | 51.15 | 34.10 | 17.14 | 17.34 | 34.24 | 51.20 |
| α Piscis Australis | ............... | 33.98 | 16.99 | 17.12 | 34.07 | 51.45 |
| α Persei | ............... | 34.11 | 17.27 | 17.14 | 34.15 | 51.38 |
| δ Capricorni | 51.21 | 34.08 | 17.18 | 17.18 | 33.99 | 51.27 |
| ξ Pegasi | 51.15 | 33.87 | ............... | 17.33 | 34.17 | 51.49 |
| 20 Ceti | 51.17 | 34.13 | 17.19 | 17.34 | 34.13 | 51.42 |
| Mean | =51.13 | 34.03 | 17.09 | 17.19 | 34.14 | 51.32 |

*Equatorial intervals of 46-inch transit, by Troughton & Simms—illumination east.* (*C. N. Thom, computer.*)

| First wire. | Second wire. | Third wire. | Fifth wire. | Sixth wire. | Seventh wire. |
|---|---|---|---|---|---|
| 51.13s.<br>1.7086758 | 34.03s.<br>1.5318619 | 17.09s.<br>1.2327421 | 17.19s.<br>1.2352759 | 34.14s.<br>1.5332635 | 51.32s.<br>1.7102866 |

Equatorial reduction to middle wire ........................................ = —0s.06

Log ........................................ —0s.06 = —2.7781513

TABLE B—Continued.

*Computation of probable error of equatorial interval of each wire from the middle wire of 46-inch transit, by Troughton & Simms—illumination east. (C. N. Thom, computer.)*

| First wire. | | | Second wire. | | | Third wire. | | | Fifth wire. | | | Sixth wire. | | | Seventh wire. | | |
|---|---|---|---|---|---|---|---|---|---|---|---|---|---|---|---|---|---|
| Each result. | Δ(final result — each result.) | $\Delta^2$. | Each result. | Δ(final result — each result.) | $\Delta^2$. | Each result. | Δ(final result — each result.) | $\Delta^2$. | Each result. | Δ(final result — each result.) | $\Delta^2$. | Each result. | Δ(final result — each result.) | $\Delta^2$. | Each result. | Δ(final result — each result.) | $\Delta^2$. |
| *s.* | *s.* | *s.* | *s.* | *s.* | *s.* | *s.* | *s.* | *s.* | *s.* | *s.* | *s.* | *s.* | *s.* | *s.* | *s.* | *s.* | *s.* |
| 50.96 | 0.17 | 0.029 | 33.97 | 0.06 | 0.004 | 17.08 | 0.01 | 0.000 | 17.08 | 0.11 | 0.012 | 34.17 | 0.03 | 0.001 | 51.35 | 0.03 | 0.001 |
| 51.07 | 0.06 | 0.004 | 33.92 | 0.11 | 0.012 | 17.11 | 0.02 | 0.000 | 17.11 | 0.08 | 0.006 | 34.14 | 0.00 | 0.000 | 51.38 | 0.06 | 0.004 |
| 50.99 | 0.14 | 0.020 | 33.98 | 0.05 | 0.002 | 16 87 | 0.22 | 0.048 | 17.19 | 0.00 | 0.000 | 34.20 | 0.06 | 0.004 | 51.35 | 0.03 | 0.001 |
| 50.92 | 0.21 | 0.044 | 34.00 | 0 03 | 0.001 | 17.17 | 0.08 | 0.006 | 17.22 | 0.03 | 0.001 | 34.29 | 0.15 | 0.022 | 51.22 | 0.10 | 0.010 |
| 51.29 | 0.16 | 0.026 | 34.04 | 0.01 | 0.000 | 17.11 | 0.02 | 0.000 | 17.11 | 0.08 | 0.006 | 34.13 | 0.01 | 0.000 | 51.29 | 0.03 | 0.001 |
| 51.18 | 0.05 | 0.002 | 34.10 | 0.07 | 0.005 | 17.27 | 0.18 | 0.032 | 17.08 | 0.11 | 0.012 | 34.15 | 0.01 | 0.000 | 51.13 | 0.19 | 0.036 |
| 51.08 | 0.05 | 0.002 | 33.92 | 0.11 | 0.012 | 16.82 | 0.27 | 0.073 | 17.11 | 0.08 | 0.006 | 34.02 | 0.12 | 0.014 | 51.13 | 0.19 | 0.036 |
| 51.23 | 0.10 | 0.010 | 33.90 | 0.13 | 0.017 | 17.00 | 0.09 | 0.008 | 17.24 | 0.05 | 0.002 | 33.96 | 0.18 | 0.032 | 51.38 | 0.06 | 0.004 |
| 51.20 | 0.07 | 0.005 | 34.19 | 0.16 | 0.026 | 17.05 | 0.04 | 0.001 | 17.15 | 0.04 | 0.001 | 33.96 | 0.18 | 0.032 | 51.15 | 0.17 | 0.029 |
| 51.02 | 0.11 | 0.012 | 33.90 | 0.13 | 0.017 | 17.06 | 0.03 | 0.001 | 17.38 | 0.29 | 0.055 | 34.33 | 0.19 | 0.036 | 51.46 | 0.14 | 0.020 |
| 51.14 | 0.01 | 0.000 | 33.93 | 0.10 | 0.010 | 17.20 | 0.11 | 0.012 | 17.06 | 0.13 | 0.017 | 34.08 | 0.06 | 0.004 | 51.14 | 0.18 | 0.032 |
| 51.11 | 0.02 | 0.000 | 33.96 | 0.07 | 0.005 | 16.98 | 0.11 | 0.012 | 17.30 | 0.11 | 0.012 | 34.16 | 0.02 | 0.000 | 51.51 | 0.19 | 0.036 |
| 51.19 | 0.06 | 0.004 | 34.16 | 0.13 | 0.017 | 17.22 | 0.13 | 0.017 | 17.13 | 0.06 | 0.004 | 34.01 | 0.13 | 0.017 | 51.34 | 0.02 | 0.000 |
| 51.01 | 0.12 | 0.014 | 34.08 | 0.05 | 0.002 | 17.05 | 0.04 | 0.001 | 17.24 | 0.05 | 0.002 | 34.10 | 0.04 | 0 001 | 51.30 | 0.02 | 0.000 |
| 51.26 | 0.13 | 0.017 | 34.11 | 0.08 | 0.006 | 16.90 | 0.19 | 0.036 | 17.23 | 0.04 | 0.001 | 34.29 | 0.15 | 0.022 | 51.22 | 0.10 | 0.010 |
| 51.12 | 0.01 | 0.000 | 34.10 | 0.07 | 0.005 | 17.13 | 0.04 | 0.001 | 17.13 | 0.06 | 0.004 | 34.22 | 0.08 | 0.006 | 51.39 | 0.07 | 0.005 |
| 51.16 | 0.03 | 0.001 | 34.24 | 0.21 | 0.044 | 17.20 | 0.11 | 0.012 | 17.19 | 0.00 | 0.000 | 34.17 | 0.03 | 0.001 | 51.44 | 0.12 | 0.014 |
| 51.20 | 0.07 | 0.005 | 34.10 | 0.07 | 0.005 | 17.19 | 0.10 | 0.010 | 17.34 | 0.15 | 0.022 | 34.25 | 0.11 | 0.012 | 51.20 | 0.12 | 0.014 |
| 51.15 | 0.02 | 0.000 | 33.98 | 0.05 | 0.002 | 17.14 | 0.05 | 0.002 | 17.12 | 0.07 | 0.005 | 34.24 | 0.10 | 0.010 | 51.45 | 0.13 | 0.017 |
| 51.21 | 0.08 | 0.006 | 34.11 | 0.08 | 0.006 | 16.99 | 0.10 | 0.010 | 17.14 | 0.05 | 0.002 | 34.07 | 0.07 | 0.005 | 51.38 | 0.06 | 0.004 |
| 51.15 | 0.02 | 0.000 | 34.08 | 0.05 | 0.002 | 17.27 | 0.18 | 0.032 | 17.18 | 0.09 | 0.008 | 34.15 | 0.01 | 0.000 | 51.27 | 0.05 | 0.002 |
| 51.17 | 0.04 | 0.001 | 33.87 | 0.16 | 0.026 | 17.18 | 0.09 | 0.008 | 17.33 | 0.14 | 0.020 | 33.99 | 0.15 | 0.022 | 51.49 | 0.17 | 0.029 |
| | | | 34.13 | 0.10 | 0.010 | 17.19 | 0.10 | 0.010 | 17.34 | 0.15 | 0.022 | 34.17 | 0.03 | 0.001 | 51.42 | 0.10 | 0.010 |
| | | | | | | | | | | | | 34.13 | 0.01 | 0.000 | | | |
| Eq'l int. = | *s.* 51.13 ± | *s.* 0.005 | Eq'l int. = | *s.* 34.03 ± | *s.* 0.005 | Eq'l int. = | *s.* 17.09 ± | *s.* 0.006 | Eq'l int. = | *s.* 17.19 ± | *s.* 0.005 | Eq'l int. = | *s.* 34.14 ± | *s.* 0.005 | Eq'l int. = | *s.* 51.32 ± | *s.* 0.005 |

TABLE C.

*Collimation error of 46-inch transit, determined from observations made at the mouth of the Rio Grande, October 27, 28, and 29, 1853—illuminated end of axis east. (C. N. Thom, computer.)*

| Date of observation. | Star observed. | Collimation of middle wire, in time. | Date of observation. | Star observed. | Collimation of middle wire, in time. |
|---|---|---|---|---|---|
| 1853. | | *s.* | 1853. | | *s.* |
| October 27 | β Cephei......... | 0 096 | October 28 | β Ur. Min........ | 0.150 |
| 27 | γ Cephei......... | 0.273 | 29 | β Cephei......... | 0.165 |
| 27 | G. C. 177.......... | 0.050 | 29 | G. C. 1967........ | 0.081 |
| 27 | G. C. 210..... ... | 0.158 | 29 | G. C. 907......... | 0.086 |
| 27 | β Ur. Min........ | 0.163 | 29 | G. C. 958......... | 0.357 |
| 28 | β Cephei......... | 0.079 | 29 | γ Cephei......... | 0.125 |
| 28 | G. C. 1967........ | 0.090 | 29 | G. C. 997......... | 0 210 |
| 28 | γ Cephei......... | 0.153 | 29 | G. C. 59.......... | 0.179 |
| 28 | G. C. 997......... | 0.070 | 29 | G. C. 107......... | 0.162 |
| 28 | G. C. 59.......... | 0.134 | 29 | G. C. 177......... | 0.345 |
| 28 | G. C. 107......... | 0.229 | 29 | G. C. 210......... | 0.083 |
| 28 | G. C. 177......... | 0.079 | 29 | β Ur. Min........ | 0.460 |
| 28 | G. C. 210......... | 0.099 | | | |

Sum.............................................................. = 25)4.076
Mean collimation of middle wire (in time).................................. = + 0s.163
Do............do.........(in arc)........................................ = + 2''.44
Collimation of mean of wires (in time)..................................... = + 0s.10
Do............do........(in arc)......................................... = + 1''.50

TABLE C—Continued.

*Computation of probable error of collimation of middle wire of 46-inch transit, by Troughton & Simms—illumination east. (C. N. Thom, computer.)*

| Each result. | Δ final result—each result. | $\Delta^2$ | Each result. | Δ final result—each result. | $\Delta^2$ |
|---|---|---|---|---|---|
| s. | s. | s. | s. | s. | s. |
| 0.096 | 0.067 | 0.004 | 0.150 | 0.013 | 0.000 |
| 0.273 | 0.110 | 0.012 | 0.165 | 0.002 | 0.000 |
| 0.050 | 0.113 | 0.013 | 0.081 | 0.082 | 0.007 |
| 0.158 | 0.005 | 0.000 | 0.086 | 0.077 | 0.006 |
| 0.163 | 0.000 | 0.000 | 0.357 | 0.194 | 0.038 |
| 0.079 | 0.084 | 0.007 | 0.125 | 0.038 | 0.001 |
| 0.090 | 0.073 | 0.005 | 0.210 | 0.047 | 0.002 |
| 0.153 | 0.010 | 0.000 | 0.179 | 0.016 | 0.000 |
| 0.070 | 0.093 | 0.008 | 0.162 | 0.001 | 0.000 |
| 0.134 | 0.029 | 0.001 | 0.345 | 0.182 | 0.033 |
| 0.229 | 0.066 | 0.004 | 0.083 | 0.080 | 0.006 |
| 0.079 | 0.084 | 0.007 | 0.460 | 0.297 | 0.088 |
| 0.099 | 0.064 | 0.003 | | | |

Final result.................................................................. = + 0s.16
Probable error............................................................... = ± 0s.01

TABLE D.

*Determination of the value of one division of the level used with the 46-inch transit, (by Troughton & Simms,) from observations made at the mouth of the Rio Grande, August 19, 1853. Micrometer attached to zenith. Telescope No. 4. Val. of one rev. = 43″.82. (C. N. Thom, computer.)*

| Observation. | North end. | Difference. | South end. | Difference. | Mean. | Micrometer reading. | Difference. | Difference in arc. | Val. of one division. |
|---|---|---|---|---|---|---|---|---|---|
| | | | | | | | | ″ | ″ |
| 1 | 59 | .. | 19 | .. | .... | 16 52.0 | | | |
| | | 44 | .. | 44 | 44.0 | ...... | 1 05.5 | 46.23 | 1.051 |
| | 15 | .. | 63 | .. | .... | 15 46.5 | | | |
| 2 | 51 | .. | 25 | .. | .... | 15 59.3 | | | |
| | | 36 | .. | 35 | 35.5 | ...... | 0 83.7 | 36.68 | 1.033 |
| | 15 | .. | 60 | .. | .... | 16 43.0 | | | |
| 3 | 53 | .. | 21 | .. | .... | 16 36.5 | | | |
| | | 40 | .. | 39 | 39.5 | ...... | 0 98.0 | 42.94 | 1.087 |
| | 13 | .. | 60 | .. | .... | 15 38.5 | | | |
| 4 | 22 | .. | 49 | .. | .... | 12 88.5 | | | |
| | | 29 | .. | 30 | 29.5 | ...... | 0 71.5 | 31.33 | 1.062 |
| | 51 | .. | 19 | .. | .... | 13 60.0 | | | |
| 5 | 51 | .. | 19 | .. | .... | 13 60.0 | | | |
| | | 39 | .. | 38.5 | 38.75 | ...... | 0 97.0 | 42.50 | 1.097 |
| | 12 | .. | 57.5 | .. | .... | 12 63.0 | | | |
| 6 | 12 | .. | 57.5 | .. | .... | 12 63.0 | | | |
| | | 36 | .. | 36.5 | 36.25 | ...... | 0 87.5 | 38.34 | 1.058 |
| | 48 | .. | 21.0 | .. | .... | 13 50.5 | | | |

Sum.................................................................................. = 6).388
Mean value of one division.................................................. = 1″.066

## TABLE E.

*Table of corrections for errors of collimation, level, and azimuth, at astronomical station near mouth of Rio Grande. (C. N. Thom, computer.)*

LATITUDE = 25° 57′.

[NOTE.—In the following tables the decimal fractions are to be multiplied by every *second of arc*, the result being the correction in *time* to be applied to stars having north polar distances corresponding to those in these tables.]

| N. P. D. | Z. dist. | COLLIM'N FOR 1″. | LEVEL FOR 1″. | AZIMUTH FOR 1″. | N. P. D. | Z. dist. | COLLIM'N FOR 1″. | LEVEL FOR 1″. | AZIMUTH FOR 1″. |
|---|---|---|---|---|---|---|---|---|---|
| | | 1 / 15 sin N. P. D. | cos Z. dist. / 15 sin N. P. D. | Sin Z. dist. / 15 sin N. P. D. | | | 1 / 15 sin N. P. D. | cos Z. dist. / 15 sin N. P. D. | sin Z. dist. / 15 sin N. P. D. |
| ° | ° ′ | | | | ° | ° ′ | | | |
| 25 sub.-polo .. | 89 03 | 0.158 | 0.0026 | 0.158 | 34 sub.-polo. | 30 03 | 0.119 | 0.103 | 0.060 |
| 24 | 88 03 | 0.164 | 0.0056 | 0.164 | 35 | 29 03 | 0.116 | 0.102 | 0.056 |
| 23 | 87 03 | 0.170 | 0.0088 | 0.170 | 36 | 28 03 | 0.113 | 0.100 | 0.053 |
| 22 | 86 03 | 0.178 | 0.0109 | 0.177 | 37 | 27 03 | 0.111 | 0.099 | 0.050 |
| 21 | 85 03 | 0.186 | 0.0160 | 0.185 | 38 | 26 03 | 0.108 | 0.097 | 0.047 |
| 20 | 84 03 | 0.195 | 0.0202 | 0.194 | 39 | 25 03 | 0.106 | 0.096 | 0.045 |
| 19 | 83 03 | 0.205 | 0.0248 | 0.203 | 40 | 24 03 | 0.103 | 0.095 | 0.042 |
| 18 | 82 03 | 0.216 | 0.0298 | 0.214 | 41 | 23 03 | 0.101 | 0.093 | 0.040 |
| 17 | 81 03 | 0.228 | 0.0354 | 0.225 | 42 | 22 03 | 0.100 | 0.092 | 0.037 |
| 16 | 80 03 | 0.242 | 0.0418 | 0.238 | 43 | 21 03 | 0.098 | 0.091 | 0.035 |
| 15 | 79 03 | 0.258 | 0.0488 | 0.253 | 44 | 20 03 | 0.096 | 0.090 | 0.034 |
| 14 | 78 03 | 0.278 | 0.0571 | 0.270 | 45 | 19 03 | 0.094 | 0.089 | 0.031 |
| 13 | 77 03 | 0.296 | 0.0664 | 0.289 | 46 | 18 03 | 0.093 | 0.088 | 0.029 |
| 12 | 76 03 | 0.321 | 0.0773 | 0.311 | 47 | 17 03 | 0.091 | 0.087 | 0.027 |
| 11 | 75 03 | 0.351 | 0.0901 | 0.338 | 48 | 16 03 | 0.089 | 0.086 | 0.025 |
| 10 | 74 03 | 0.384 | 0.105 | 0.369 | 49 | 15 03 | 0.088 | 0.085 | 0.023 |
| 9 | 73 03 | 0.426 | 0.124 | 0.408 | 50 | 14 03 | 0.087 | 0.084 | 0.021 |
| 8 | 72 03 | 0.479 | 0.147 | 0.456 | 51 | 13 03 | 0.086 | 0.083 | 0.019 |
| 7 | 71 03 | 0.547 | 0.178 | 0.517 | 52 | 12 03 | 0.085 | 0.083 | 0.018 |
| 6 | 70 03 | 0.638 | 0.217 | 0.599 | 53 | 11 03 | 0.083 | 0.082 | 0.016 |
| 5 | 69 03 | 0.765 | 0.273 | 0.698 | 54 | 10 03 | 0.082 | 0.081 | 0.014 |
| 5 | 59 03 | 0.765 | 0.393 | 0.656 | 55 | 9 03 | 0.081 | 0.080 | 0.013 |
| 6 | 58 03 | 0.638 | 0.337 | 0.541 | 56 | 8 03 | 0.080 | 0.080 | 0.011 |
| 7 | 57 03 | 0.547 | 0.297 | 0.459 | 57 | 7 03 | 0.079 | 0.079 | 0.010 |
| 8 | 56 03 | 0.479 | 0.267 | 0.397 | 58 | 6 03 | 0.078 | 0.078 | 0.008 |
| 9 | 55 03 | 0.426 | 0.244 | 0.349 | 59 | 5 03 | 0.077 | 0.077 | 0.007 |
| 10 | 54 03 | 0.384 | 0.225 | 0.311 | 60 | 4 03 | 0.077 | 0.077 | 0.005 |
| 11 | 53 03 | 0.351 | 0.210 | 0.279 | 61 | 3 03 | 0.076 | 0.076 | 0.004 |
| 12 | 52 03 | 0.321 | 0.197 | 0.253 | 62 | 2 03 | 0.075 | 0.075 | 0.003 |
| 13 | 51 03 | 0.296 | 0.186 | 0.230 | 63 | 1 03 | 0.074 | 0.075 | 0.001 |
| 14 | 50 03 | 0.278 | 0.177 | 0.211 | 64 | 0 03 | 0.074 | 0.074 | 0.000 |
| 15 | 49 03 | 0.258 | 0.169 | 0.194 | 65 | 0 57 | 0.073 | 0.073 | 0.001 |
| 16 | 48 03 | 0.242 | 0.162 | 0.180 | 66 | 1 57 | 0.073 | 0.073 | 0.002 |
| 17 | 47 03 | 0.228 | 0.155 | 0.167 | 67 | 2 57 | 0.072 | 0.072 | 0.004 |
| 18 | 46 03 | 0.216 | 0.150 | 0.155 | 68 | 3 57 | 0.071 | 0.072 | 0.005 |
| 19 | 45 03 | 0.205 | 0.145 | 0.145 | 69 | 4 57 | 0.071 | 0.071 | 0.006 |
| 20 | 44 03 | 0.195 | 0.140 | 0.135 | 70 | 5 57 | 0.071 | 0.070 | 0.007 |
| 21 | 43 03 | 0.186 | 0.136 | 0.127 | 71 | 6 57 | 0.070 | 0.070 | 0.008 |
| 22 | 42 03 | 0.178 | 0.132 | 0.119 | 72 | 7 57 | 0.070 | 0.069 | 0.010 |
| 23 | 41 03 | 0.170 | 0.129 | 0.112 | 73 | 8 57 | 0.069 | 0.069 | 0.111 |
| 24 | 40 03 | 0.164 | 0.125 | 0.105 | 74 | 9 57 | 0.069 | 0.068 | 0.012 |
| 25 | 39 03 | 0.158 | 0.122 | 0.099 | 75 | 10 57 | 0.069 | 0.068 | 0.013 |
| 26 | 38 03 | 0.152 | 0.120 | 0.094 | 76 | 11 57 | 0.068 | 0.067 | 0.014 |
| 27 | 37 03 | 0.147 | 0.117 | 0.088 | 77 | 12 57 | 0.068 | 0.067 | 0.015 |
| 28 | 36 03 | 0.142 | 0.115 | 0.083 | 78 | 13 57 | 0.068 | 0.066 | 0.016 |
| 29 | 35 03 | 0.137 | 0.113 | 0.079 | 79 | 14 57 | 0.068 | 0.066 | 0.017 |
| 30 | 34 03 | 0.133 | 0.110 | 0.073 | 80 | 15 57 | 0.067 | 0.065 | 0.019 |
| 31 | 33 03 | 0.129 | 0.108 | 0.070 | 81 | 16 57 | 0.067 | 0.064 | 0.020 |
| 32 | 32 03 | 0.126 | 0.106 | 0.067 | 82 | 17 57 | 0.067 | 0.064 | 0.021 |
| 33 | 31 03 | 0.122 | 0.105 | 0.063 | 87 | 18 57 | 0.067 | 0.063 | 0.022 |

TABLE E—Continued.

| N. P. D. | Z. dist. | COLLIM'N FOR 1″. | LEVEL FOR 1″. | AZIMUTH FOR 1″. | N. P. D. | Z. dist. | COLLIM'N FOR 1″. | LEVEL FOR 1″. | AZIMUTH FOR 1″. |
|---|---|---|---|---|---|---|---|---|---|
| | | 1 / 15 sin N. P. D. | cos. Z. dist. / 15 sin N. P. D. | sin Z. dist. / 15 sin N. P. D. | | | 1 / 15 sin. N. P. D. | cos Z. dist. / 15 sin N. P. D. | sin Z. dist. / 15 sin N. P. D. |
| | ° ″ | | | | ° | ° ″ | | | |
| 84 sub.-polo.. | 19 57 | 0.067 | 0.063 | 0.023 | 120 sub.-polo | 55 57 | 0.077 | 0.043 | 0.064 |
| 85 | 20 57 | 0.067 | 0.062 | 0.024 | 121 | 56 57 | 0.077 | 0.042 | 0.065 |
| 86 | 21 57 | 0.067 | 0.062 | 0.025 | 122 | 57 57 | 0.078 | 0.042 | 0.067 |
| 87 | 22 57 | 0.067 | 0.061 | 0.026 | 123 | 58 57 | 0.079 | 0.041 | 0.068 |
| 88 | 23 57 | 0.067 | 0.061 | 0.027 | 124 | 59 57 | 0.080 | 0.040 | 0.070 |
| 89 | 24 57 | 0.067 | 0.060 | 0.028 | 125 | 60 57 | 0.081 | 0.039 | 0.071 |
| 90 | 25 57 | 0.067 | 0.060 | 0.029 | 126 | 61 57 | 0.082 | 0.039 | 0.073 |
| 91 | 26 57 | 0.067 | 0.059 | 0.030 | 127 | 62 57 | 0.083 | 0.038 | 0.074 |
| 92 | 27 57 | 0.067 | 0.059 | 0.031 | 128 | 63 57 | 0.084 | 0.037 | 0.076 |
| 93 | 28 57 | 0.067 | 0.058 | 0.032 | 129 | 64 57 | 0.085 | 0.036 | 0.078 |
| 94 | 29 57 | 0.067 | 0.058 | 0.033 | 130 | 65 57 | 0.087 | 0.035 | 0.079 |
| 95 | 30 57 | 0.067 | 0.057 | 0.034 | 131 | 66 57 | 0.088 | 0.034 | 0.081 |
| 96 | 31 57 | 0.067 | 0.057 | 0.035 | 132 | 67 57 | 0.089 | 0.034 | 0.083 |
| 97 | 32 57 | 0.067 | 0.056 | 0.036 | 133 | 68 57 | 0.091 | 0.033 | 0.085 |
| 98 | 33 57 | 0.067 | 0.056 | 0.038 | 134 | 69 57 | 0.092 | 0.032 | 0.087 |
| 99 | 34 57 | 0.067 | 0.055 | 0.039 | 135 | 70 57 | 0.094 | 0.031 | 0.089 |
| 100 | 35 57 | 0.068 | 0.055 | 0.040 | 136 | 71 57 | 0.096 | 0.030 | 0.091 |
| 101 | 36 57 | 0.068 | 0.054 | 0.041 | 137 | 72 57 | 0.097 | 0.029 | 0.093 |
| 102 | 37 57 | 0.068 | 0.054 | 0.042 | 138 | 73 57 | 0.099 | 0.027 | 0.096 |
| 103 | 38 57 | 0.068 | 0.053 | 0.043 | 139 | 74 57 | 0.101 | 0.026 | 0.097 |
| 104 | 39 57 | 0.069 | 0.053 | 0.044 | 140 | 75 57 | 0.103 | 0.025 | 0.101 |
| 105 | 40 57 | 0.069 | 0.052 | 0.045 | 141 | 76 57 | 0.106 | 0.024 | 0.103 |
| 106 | 41 57 | 0.069 | 0.051 | 0.046 | 142 | 77 57 | 0.108 | 0.023 | 0.106 |
| 107 | 42 57 | 0.070 | 0.051 | 0.047 | 143 | 78 57 | 0.111 | 0.021 | 0.109 |
| 108 | 43 57 | 0.070 | 0.050 | 0.049 | 144 | 79 57 | 0.113 | 0.020 | 0.112 |
| 109 | 44 57 | 0.070 | 0.050 | 0.050 | 145 | 80 57 | 0.116 | 0.018 | 0.115 |
| 110 | 45 57 | 0.071 | 0.049 | 0.051 | 146 | 81 57 | 0.119 | 0.017 | 0.118 |
| 111 | 46 57 | 0.071 | 0.049 | 0.052 | 147 | 82 57 | 0.122 | 0.015 | 0.121 |
| 112 | 47 57 | 0.072 | 0.048 | 0.053 | 148 | 83 57 | 0.126 | 0.013 | 0.125 |
| 113 | 48 57 | 0.072 | 0.047 | 0.055 | 149 | 84 57 | 0.130 | 0.011 | 0.129 |
| 114 | 49 57 | 0.073 | 0.047 | 0.056 | 150 | 85 57 | 0.133 | 0.009 | 0.133 |
| 115 | 50 57 | 0.073 | 0.046 | 0.057 | 151 | 86 57 | 0.137 | 0.007 | 0.137 |
| 116 | 51 57 | 0.074 | 0.046 | 0.058 | 152 | 87 57 | 0.142 | 0.005 | 0.142 |
| 117 | 52 57 | 0.074 | 0.045 | 0.060 | 153 | 88 57 | 0.147 | 0.003 | 0.147 |
| 118 | 53 57 | 0.075 | 0.044 | 0.061 | 154 | 89 57 | 0.152 | 0.000 | 0.152 |
| 119 | 54 57 | 0.076 | 0.044 | 0.062 | | | | | |

TABLE F.

*Right ascensions of moon's centre used in computing the longitude of astronomical station near mouth of the Rio Grande, deduced from corresponding moon culminations, observed at Greenwich, Philadelphia High School, and Radcliffe observatories,* 1853. *(C. N. Thom, computer.)*

| Date. | Right ascension of moon's centre. | | Difference observed: — N. A. | Right ascension of moon's centre observed at Philadel. High School observatory. | Date. | Right ascension of moon's centre. | | Difference observed: — N. A. | Right ascension of moon's centre observed at Philadel. High School observatory. |
|---|---|---|---|---|---|---|---|---|---|
| | Greenwich observations. | Nautical Almanac. | | | | Greenwich observations. | Nautical Almanac. | | |
| 1853. | *h. m. s.* | *h. m. s.* | *s.* | *h. m. s.* | 1853. | *h. m. s.* | *h. m. s.* | *s.* | *h. m. s.* |
| August 12 | 15 44 14.00 | 15 44 14.73 | — 0.73 | ............... | Oct. 13 | 23 08 15.62 | 23 08 16.56 | — 0.94 | 22 18 43.58 |
| 13 | 16 45 08 12 | 16 45 08.76 | 0.64 | ............... | 14 | 23 57 27.51 | 23 57 28.53 | 1.02 | ............... |
| 14 | 17 49 14.20 | 17 49 15.01 | 0.81 | ............... | 15 | 0 44 53.86 | 0 44 54.80 | 0.94 | ............... |
| 15 | 18 54 04.71 | 1.8 54 05.69 | 0.98 | ............... | 16 | 1 31 32.27 | 1 31 33.36 | 1.09 | ............... |
| 16 | 20 00 25.36 | 20 00 26.51 | 1.15 | ............... | 17 | 2 18 16.89 | 2 18 17.81 | 0.92 | 2 28 07.46 |
| 17 | 21 03 07.50 | 21 03 08.82 | 1.32 | ............... | 18 | 3 05 53.28 | 3 05 54.03 | 0.75 | 3 15 59.50 |
| 18 | 22 01 55.78 | 22 01 57.03 | 1.25 | ............... | 19 | 3 54 56.38 | 3 54 56.86 | 0.48 | 4 05 23.77 |
| 19 | 22 56 38.39 | 22 56 39.41 | 1.02 | 23 07 34.76 | 20 | 4 45 45.37 | 4 45 45.58 | 0.21 | ............... |
| 20 | 23 47 49.06 | 23 47 50.04 | 0.98 | ............... | 21 | 5 58 19.33 | 5 58 19.40 | — 0.07 | ............... |
| 21 | 0 36 24.88 | 0 36 25.73 | 0.85 | 0 46 19.72 | 22 | 6 32 15.98 | 6 32 15.86 | + 0.12 | ............... |
| 22 | 1 23 29.32 | 1 23 30.03 | 0.71 | ............... | 23 | 7 26 55.45 | 7 26 55.23 | + 0.22 | ............... |
| 23 | 2 10 04.52 | 2 10 05.09 | 0.57 | ............... | Nov. 7 | 21 03 14.68 | 21 03 15.90 | — 1.22 | ............... |
| 24 | 2 57 07.07 | 2 57 07.66 | 0.59 | ............... | 8 | 22 00 14.81 | 22 00 15.98 | 1.17 | *22 00 26.29 |
| Sept. 11 | 18 33 26.68 | 18 33 26.79 | 0.11 | ............... | 9 | 22 53 02.20 | 22 53 03.22 | 1.02 | *22 53 13.08 |
| 12 | 19 37 45.20 | 19 37 45.84 | 0.64 | ............... | 10 | 23 42 31.11 | 23 42 31.72 | 0.61 | *23 42 41.18 |
| 13 | 20 40 03.21 | 20 40 04.07 | 0.86 | 20 52 39.82 | 11 | 0 29 47.14 | 0 29 47.74 | 0.60 | ............... |
| 14 | 21 39 01.98 | 21 39 03.06 | 1.08 | ............... | 12 | 1 15 56.83 | 1 15 57.47 | 0.64 | ............... |
| 15 | 22 34 17.31 | 22 34 18.61 | 1.30 | ............... | 13 | 2 02 00.84 | 2 02 01.52 | 0.68 | ............... |
| 16 | 23 26 09.87 | 23 26 11.40 | 1.53 | 23 36 38.50 | 14 | 2 48 51.37 | 2 48 52.10 | 0.73 | *2 49 01.40 |
| 17 | 0 15 26.56 | 0 15 27.89 | 1.33 | ............... | 15 | 3 37 08.86 | 3 37 09.67 | 0.81 | ............... |
| 18 | 1 03 03.29 | 1 03 04.57 | 1.28 | 1 12 52.18 | 16 | 4 27 17.41 | 4 27 18.31 | 0.90 | ............... |
| 19 | 1 49 57.56 | 1 49 58.79 | 1.23 | ............... | 17 | 5 19 19.95 | 5 19 20.47 | 0.52 | ............... |
| 20 | 2 37 02.74 | 2 37 03.92 | 1.18 | ............... | 18 | 6 12 53.44 | 6 12 53.80 | 0.36 | ............... |
| October 9 | 19 18 51.49 | 19 18 52.07 | 0.58 | ............... | 19 | 7 07 14.64 | 7 07 14.86 | 0.22 | ............... |
| 10 | 20 21 36.47 | 20 21 37.14 | 0.67 | ............... | 20 | 8 01 31.27 | 8 01 31.30 | 0.03 | ............... |
| 11 | 21 20 54.49 | 21 20 55.25 | 0.76 | ............... | 21 | 8 54 58.29 | 8 54 58.53 | 0.24 | ............... |
| 12 | 22 16 20.45 | 22 16 21.30 | — 0.85 | 22 27 27.06 | 22 | 9 47 13.17 | 9 47 13.58 | — 0.41 | ............... |

* Radcliffe observatory.

## TABLE. G.

*Tabulation of results for longitude of astronomical station near mouth of Rio Grande, derived from observations made with 46-inch transit (by Troughton & Simms) and with sidereal chronometer No. 2440, (Parkinson & Frodsham:) By G. C. Gardner and J. H. Clark, under the direction of Major W. H. Emory, Chief Astronomer and Surveyor of United States and Mexican boundary survey.*

| Date of observation. | Moon's limb observed. | Longitude west of Greenwich, deduced from corresponding observations made at— | | | Adopted values of the observations for each night. | Date of observation. | Moon's limb observed. | Longitude west of Greenwich, deduced from corresponding observations made at— | | | Adopted values of the observations for each night. |
|---|---|---|---|---|---|---|---|---|---|---|---|
| | | Greenwich Observatory. | Radcliffe Observatory. | Phila. High School Observatory. | | | | Greenwich Observatory. | Radcliffe Observatory. | Phila. High School Observatory. | |
| 1853. | | 6*h*. 28*m*. | 6*h*. 28*m*. | 6*h*. 28*m*. | | 1853. | | 6*h*. 28*m*. | 6*h*. 28*m*. | 6*h*. 28*m*. | |
| | | *s*. | *s*. | *s*. | *s*. | | | *s*. | *s*. | *s*. | *s*. |
| Aug. 12 | 1st........ | 35.04 | ............ | ............ | 35.04 | Oct. 10 | 1st....... | 40.56 | ............ | ............ | 40.56 |
| 13 | | 40.00 | ............ | ............ | 40.00 | 12 | | 24.11 | ............ | 24.96 | 74.03 |
| 15 | | 35.91 | ............ | ............ | 35.91 | 13 | | 20.87 | ............ | 28.00 | 76.87 |
| 16 | | 39.85 | ............ | ............ | 39.85 | 17 | 2d....... | 25.89 | ............ | 34.37 | 94.63 |
| 17 | | 29.28 | ............ | ............ | 29.28 | 18 | | 20.69 | ............ | 24.09 | 68.87 |
| 18 | 2d........ | 20.69 | ............ | ............ | 20.69 | 19 | | 24.86 | ............ | 27.56 | 79.98 |
| 19 | | 22.33 | ............ | 33.62 | 89.57 | 20 | | 42.03 | ............ | ............ | 42.03 |
| 20 | | 14.71 | ............ | ............ | 14.71 | 21 | | 41.25 | ............ | ............ | 41.25 |
| 21 | | 27.27 | ............ | 35.90 | 99.07 | Nov. 7 | 1st....... | 36.94 | ............ | ............ | 36.94 |
| 22 | | 27.22 | ............ | ............ | 27.22 | 8 | | 34.05 | 34.53 | ............ | 68.58 |
| 23 | | 33.54 | ............ | ............ | 33.54 | 9 | | 32.15 | 30.50 | ............ | 62.65 |
| 24 | | 32.10 | ............ | ............ | 32.10 | 10 | | 26.23 | 31.07 | ............ | 57.30 |
| Sept. 12 | 1st........ | 30.23 | ............ | ............ | 30.23 | 11 | | 23.32 | ............ | ............ | 23.32 |
| 13 | | 30.48 | ............ | 30.60 | 91.68 | 12 | | 34.55 | ............ | ............ | 34.55 |
| 14 | | 37.08 | ............ | ............ | 37.08 | 13 | | 35.93 | ............ | ............ | 35.93 |
| 15 | | 37.19 | ............ | ............ | 37.19 | 14 | 1st & 2d. | 33.60 | 30.44 | ............ | 64.04 |
| 16 | | 30.72 | ............ | 23.86 | 78.44 | 15 | 2d....... | 28.41 | ............ | ............ | 28.41 |
| 17 | 2d........ | 24.60 | ............ | ............ | 24.60 | 18 | | 28.67 | ............ | ............ | 28.67 |
| 18 | | 29.69 | ............ | 36.03 | 101.75 | 21 | | 29.45 | ............ | ............ | 29.45 |
| Oct. 9 | 1st........ | 38.86 | ............ | ............ | 38.86 | 22 | | 26.91 | ............ | ............ | 26.91 |

$$\frac{\text{Sum of "Adopted values of the observations for each night,"}}{\text{Number of observations giving to each its value*..............}} = \frac{1951.78}{64} = 30.48$$

| | | *h. m. s.* |
|---|---|---|
| Longitude of astronomical station near mouth of Rio Grande, west of Greenwich Observatory.................................. | = | 6 28 30.48 |
| Probable error.......... .................................................. | = | ± 0.56 |

NOTE.—Radcliffe Observatory is 5*m*. 02*s*.60 west of Greenwich, (Rad. Observations, vol. XIV, page IX;). High School Observatory, Philadelphia, is 5*h*. 00*m*. 37*s*.56 west of Greenwich Observatory. In reducing the results from the Radcliffe and High School observations to Greenwich Observatory, the above differences of longitudes have been applied.

* In the column, "Adopted values of the observations for each night," the results have been obtained by giving double weight to the High School observations, on account of its relative distance from mouth of Rio Grande, and equal weight to Radcliffe and Greenwich observations.

*Computation of probable error of the final result for longitude of astronomical station near mouth of the Rio Grande.*

1. RESULTS FROM GREENWICH OBSERVATIONS.

(Final longitude = 6*h*. 28*m*. 30*s*.48.)

| Date. | Each result. | Δ (final result — each result.) | Δ² | Date. | Each result. | Δ (final result — each result.) | Δ |
|---|---|---|---|---|---|---|---|
| 1853. | *s.* | *s.* | *s.* | 1853. | *s.* | *s.* | *s.* |
| Aug. 12 | 35.04 | 4.56 | 20.79 | Oct. 10 | 40.56 | 10.08 | 101.61 |
| 13 | 40.00 | 9.52 | 90.63 | 12 | 24.11 | 6.37 | 40.57 |
| 15 | 35.91 | 5.43 | 29.48 | 13 | 20.87 | 9.61 | 92.35 |
| 16 | 39.85 | 9.37 | 87.73 | 17 | 25.89 | 4.59 | 21.07 |
| 17 | 29.28 | 1.20 | 1.44 | 18 | 20.69 | 9.79 | 95.84 |
| 18 | 20.69 | 9.79 | 95.84 | 19 | 24.86 | 5.62 | 31.58 |
| 19 | 22.33 | 8.15 | 66.42 | 20 | 42.03 | 11.55 | 133.40 |
| 20 | 14.71 | 15.77 | 248.69 | 21 | 41.25 | 10.77 | 116.00 |
| 21 | 27.27 | 3.21 | 10.30 | Nov. 7 | 36.94 | 6.46 | 41.73 |
| 22 | 27.22 | 3.26 | 10.63 | 8 | 34.05 | 3.57 | 12.74 |
| 23 | 33.54 | 3.06 | 9.36 | 9 | 32.15 | 1.67 | 2.79 |
| 24 | 32.10 | 1.62 | 2.62 | 10 | 26.23 | 4.25 | 18.06 |
| Sept. 12 | 30.23 | 0.25 | 0.06 | 11 | 23.32 | 7.16 | 51.26 |
| 13 | 30.48 | 0.00 | 0.00 | 12 | 34.55 | 4.07 | 16.56 |
| 14 | 37.08 | 6.60 | 43.56 | 13 | 35.93 | 5.45 | 29.80 |
| 15 | 37.19 | 6.71 | 46.02 | 14 | 33.60 | 3.12 | 9.73 |
| 16 | 30.72 | 0.24 | 0.06 | 15 | 28.41 | 2.07 | 4.28 |
| 17 | 24.60 | 5.88 | 34.57 | 18 | 28.67 | 1.81 | 3.28 |
| 18 | 29.69 | 0.79 | 0.62 | 21 | 29.45 | 1.03 | 1.06 |
| Oct. 9 | 38.86 | 8.38 | 70.22 | 22 | 26.91 | 3.57 | 12.74 |

2. RESULTS FROM PHILADELPAIA HIGH SCHOOL OBSERVATIONS.

(Final longitude = 6*h*. 28*m*. 39*s*.48.)

| Date. | Each result. | Δ (final result — each result.) | Δ² | Date. | Each result. | Δ (final result — each result.) | Δ² |
|---|---|---|---|---|---|---|---|
| 1853. | *s.* | *s.* | *s.* | 1853. | *s.* | *s.* | *s.* |
| Aug. 19 | 33.62 | 3.14 | 9.86 | Oct. 12 | 24.96 | 5.52 | 30.47 |
| 21 | 35.90 | 5.42 | 29.37 | 13 | 28.00 | 2.48 | 6.04 |
| Sept. 13 | 30.60 | 0.12 | 0.01 | 17 | 34.37 | 3.89 | 15.13 |
| 16 | 23.86 | 6.62 | 43.82 | 18 | 24.09 | 6.39 | 40.8 |
| 18 | 36.03 | 5.55 | 30.80 | 19 | 27.56 | 2.92 | 8.53 |

3. RESULTS FROM RADCLIFFE OBSERVATIONS.

(Final longitude = 6*h*. 28*m*. 30*s*.48.)

| Date. | Each result. | Δ (final result — each result.) | Δ² | Date. | Each result. | Δ (final result — each result.) | Δ |
|---|---|---|---|---|---|---|---|
| 1853. | *s.* | *s.* | *s.* | 1853. | *s.* | *s.* | *s.* |
| Nov. 8 | 34.53 | 4.05 | 16.40 | Nov. 10 | 31.07 | 0.59 | 0.35 |
| 9 | 30.50 | 0.02 | 0.00 | 14 | 30.44 | 0.04 | 0.00 |

Final longitude ........................................... = 6*h*. 28*m*. 30*s*.48
Probable error ........................................... = ± 0*s*.56

## TABLE H.

*Tabulation of results for longitude of astronomical station near mouth of Rio Grande, derived from observations made with 46-inch transit, (by Troughton & Simms,) and with sidereal chronometer No. 2440, (by Parkinson & Frodsham) by G. C. Gardner and J. H. Clark, under the direction of Major W. H. Emory, Chief Astronomer and Surveyor of United States and Mexican boundary survey.*

MOON'S FIRST LIMB.

| Date of observation. | Longitude west of Greenwich, deduced from corresponding observations made at— | | | Adopted values of the observations for each night. |
|---|---|---|---|---|
| | Greenwich Observatory. | Radcliffe Observatory. | Philadelphia High School Observatory. | |
| 1853. | *h. m. s.* | *h. m. s.* | *h. m. s.* | *s.* |
| August 12 | 6 28 35.04 | .............. | .............. | 35.04 |
| 13 | 6 28 40.00 | .............. | .............. | 40.00 |
| 15 | 6 28 35.91 | .............. | .............. | 35.91 |
| 16 | 6 28 39.85 | .............. | .............. | 39.85 |
| 17 | 6 28 29.28 | .............. | .............. | 29.28 |
| Sept. 12 | 6 28 30.23 | .............. | .............. | 30.23 |
| 13 | 6 28 30.48 | .............. | 6 28 30.60 | 91.68 |
| 14 | 6 28 37.08 | .............. | .............. | 37.08 |
| 15 | 6 28 37.19 | .............. | .............. | 37.19 |
| 16 | 6 28 30.72 | .............. | 6 28 23.86 | 78.44 |
| October 9 | 6 28 38.86 | .............. | .............. | 38.86 |
| 10 | 6 28 40.56 | .............. | .............. | 40.56 |
| 12 | 6 28 24.11 | .............. | 6 28 24.96 | 74.03 |
| 13 | 6 28 20.87 | .............. | 6 28 28.00 | 76.87 |
| Nov. 7 | 6 28 36.94 | .............. | .............. | 36.94 |
| 8 | 6 28 34.05 | 6 28 34.53 | .............. | 68.58 |
| 9 | 6 28 32.15 | 6 28 30.50 | .............. | 62.65 |
| 10 | 6 28 26.23 | 6 28 31.07 | .............. | 57.30 |
| 11 | 6 28 23.32 | .............. | .............. | 23.32 |
| 12 | 6 28 34 55 | .............. | .............. | 34.55 |
| 13 | 6 28 35.93 | .............. | .............. | 35.93 |
| 14 | 6 28 33.60 | 6 28 30.44 | .............. | 64.04 |

$$\frac{\text{Sum of adopted values of the observations for each night, } 1068.33}{\text{No. of observations giving to each its value* ............ } 34} = 31.42$$

MOON'S SECOND LIMB.

| Date of observation. | Longitude west of Greenwich, deduced from corresponding observations made at— | | | Adopted values of the observations for each night. |
|---|---|---|---|---|
| | Greenwich Observatory. | Radcliffe Observatory. | Philadelphia High School Observatory. | |
| 1853. | *h. m. s.* | *h. m. s.* | *h. m. s.* | *s.* |
| Aug. 18 | 6 28 20.69 | .............. | .............. | 20.69 |
| 19 | 6 28 22.33 | .............. | 6 28 33.62 | 89.57 |
| 20 | 6 28 14.71 | .............. | .............. | 14.71 |
| 21 | 6 28 27.27 | .............. | 6 28 35.90 | 99.07 |
| 22 | 6 28 27.22 | .............. | .............. | 27.22 |
| 23 | 6 28 33.54 | .............. | .............. | 33.54 |
| 24 | 6 28 32.10 | .............. | .............. | 32.10 |
| Sept. 17 | 6 28 24.60 | .............. | .............. | 24.60 |
| 18 | 6 28 29.69 | .............. | 6 28 36.03 | 101.75 |
| Oct. 17 | 6 28 25.89 | .............. | 6 28 34.37 | 94.63 |
| 18 | 6 28 20.69 | .............. | 6 28 24.09 | 68.87 |
| 19 | 6 28 24.86 | .............. | 6 28 27.56 | 79.98 |
| 20 | 6 28 42.03 | .............. | .............. | 42.03 |
| 21 | 6 28 41.25 | .............. | .............. | 41.25 |
| Nov. 14 | 6 28 33.60 | 6 28 30.44 | .............. | 64.04 |
| 15 | 6 28 28.41 | .............. | .............. | 28.41 |
| 18 | 6 28 28.67 | .............. | .............. | 28.67 |
| 21 | 6 28 29.45 | .............. | .............. | 29.45 |
| 22 | 6 28 26.91 | .............. | .............. | 26.91 |

$$\frac{\text{Sum of adopted values of the observations for each night, } 947.49}{\text{No. of observations giving to each its value* ............ } 32} = 29.61$$

| | *h. m. s.* | | *h. m. s.* |
|---|---|---|---|
| Resulting longitudes from observations on moon's 1st limb... | = 6 28 31.42 | Mean longitude........................................ | = 6 28 30.52 |
| Do..............do..............do.......2d limb... | = 6 28 29.61 | | |

Longitude of astronomical station near mouth of Rio Grande, west of Greenwich Observatory.......................... = 6*h*. 28*m*. 30*s*.52

NOTE.—Radcliffe Observatory is 5*m*. 02*s*.60 west of Greenwich, (Rad. Observations, vol. XIV, page IX.) High School Observatory, Philadelphia, is 5*h*. 00*m*. 37*s*.56 west of Greenwich Observatory. In reducing the results from the Radcliffe and High School observations to Greenwich observations, the above differences of longitudes have been applied.

* In the column "Adopted values of the observations for each night," the results have been obtained by giving double weight to the High School observations, on account of its relative distance from the mouth of the Rio Grande, and equal weight to Radcliffe and Greenwich observations.

## TABLE I.

*Tabulation of results for longitude of astronomical station near mouth of Rio Grande, derived from observations made with 46-inch transit, (by Troughton & Simms,) and with sidereal chronometer No. 2440, (by Parkinson & Frodsham:) By G. C. Gardner and J. H. Clark, under the direction of Major W. H. Emory, Chief Astronomer and Surveyor of United States and Mexican boundary survey. (C. N. Thom, computer.)*

| Date of observation. | Moon's limb observed. | Longitude west of Greenwich, deduced from corresponding observations made at— | | | Adopted values of the observations for each night. |
|---|---|---|---|---|---|
| | | Greenwich Observatory. | Radcliffe Observatory. | Phila. High School Observatory. | |
| 1853. | | *h. m. s.* | *h. m. s.* | *h. m. s.* | *s.* |
| Aug. 13 | 1st....... | 6 28 40.00 | 6 28 00.00 | ............ | 40.00 |
| 17 | | 6 28 29.28 | ............ | ............ | 29.28 |
| 18 | 2d.... ... | 6 28 20.69 | ............ | ............ | 20.69 |
| 19 | | ............ | ............ | 6 28 33.62 | 67.24 |
| 21 | | ............ | ............ | 6 28 35.90 | 71.80 |
| 23 | | 6 28 33.54 | ............ | ............ | 33.54 |
| 24 | | 6 28 32.10 | ............ | ............ | 32.10 |
| Sept. 13 | 1st....... | 6 28 30.48 | ............ | 6 28 30.60 | 91.68 |
| 16 | | 6 28 30.72 | ............ | 6 28 23.86 | 78.44 |
| 17 | 2d....... | 6 28 24.60 | ............ | ............ | 24.60 |
| 18 | | 6 28 29.69 | ............ | 6 28 36.03 | 101.75 |
| Oct. 9 | 1st....... | 6 28 38.86 | ............ | ............ | 38.86 |
| 12 | | ............ | ............ | 6 28 24.96 | 49.92 |
| Oct. 13 | 1st....... | ............ | ............ | 6 28 28.00 | 56.00 |
| 17 | 2d....... | ............ | ............ | 6 28 34.37 | 68.74 |
| 18 | | 6 28 20.69 | ............ | 6 28 24.09 | 68.87 |
| 19 | | ............ | ............ | 6 28 27.56 | 55.12 |
| 20 | | 6 28 42.03 | ............ | ............ | 42.03 |
| Nov. 8 | 1st...... | ............ | 6 28 34.53 | ............ | 34.53 |
| 9 | | 6 28 32.15 | 6 28 30.50 | ............ | 62.65 |
| 10 | | 6 28 26.23 | 6 28 31.07 | ............ | 57.30 |
| 11 | | 6 28 23.32 | ............ | ............ | 23.32 |
| 13 | | 6 28 35.93 | ............ | ............ | 35.93 |
| 14 | 1st & 2d. | 6 28 33.60 | 6 28 30.44 | ............ | 64.04 |
| 18 | 2d...... | 6 28 28.67 | ............ | ............ | 28.67 |
| 21 | | 6 28 29.45 | ............ | ............ | 29.45 |

$$\frac{\text{Sum of "Adopted values of the observations for each night,"}}{\text{Number of observations giving to each its value*..........}} = \frac{1306.55}{\quad} = 30.38$$

Longitude of astronomical station near mouth of Rio Grande, west of Greenwich Observatory...................... ............ 6*h.* 28*m.* 30*s*.38

NOTE.—Radcliffe Observatory is 5*m.* 02*s*.60 west of Greenwich, (Rad. Observations, vol. XIV, page IX;) High School Observatory, Philadelphia, is 5*h.* 00*m.* 37*s*.56 west of Greenwich Observatory. In reducing the results from the Radcliffe and High School observations to Greenwich Observatory, the above differences of longitudes have been applied.

* In the column, "Adopted values of the observations for each night," the results have been obtained by giving double weight to the High School observations, on account of its relative distance from the mouth of Rio Grande, and equal weight to Radcliffe and Greenwich observations.

## TABLE K.

*Tabulation of results for longitude of astronomical station near mouth of Rio Grande, derived from observations made with 46-inch transit, (by Troughton & Simms,) and with sidereal chronometer No. 2440, (by Parkinson & Frodsham:) By G. C. Gardner and J. H. Clark, under the direction of Major W. H. Emory, Chief Astronomer and Surveyor of the United States and Mexican boundary survey. (C. N. Thom, computer.)*

MOON'S FIRST LIMB.

| Date of observation. | Longitude west of Greenwich, deduced from corresponding observations made at— | | | Adopted values of the observations for each night. |
|---|---|---|---|---|
| | Greenwich Observatory. | Radcliffe Observatory. | Philadelphia High School Observatory. | |
| 1853. | h. m. s. | h. m. s. | h. m. s. | s. |
| August 13 | 6 28 40.00 | 6 28 00.00 | 6 28 00.00 | 40.00 |
| 17 | 6 28 29.28 | ............ | ............ | 29.28 |
| Sept. 13 | 6 28 30.48 | ............ | 6 28 30.60 | 91.68 |
| 16 | 6 28 30.72 | ............ | 6 28 23.86 | 78.44 |
| October 9 | 6 28 38.86 | ............ | ............ | 38.86 |
| 12 | ............ | ............ | 6 28 24.96 | 49.92 |
| 13 | ............ | ............ | 6 28 28.00 | 56.00 |
| Nov. 8 | ............ | 6 28 34.53 | ............ | 34.53 |
| 9 | 6 28 32.15 | 6 28 30.50 | ............ | 62.65 |
| 10 | 6 28 26.23 | 6 28 31.07 | ............ | 57.30 |
| 11 | 6 28 23.32 | ............ | ............ | 23.32 |
| 13 | 6 28 35.93 | ............ | ............ | 35.93 |
| 14 | 6 28 33.60 | 6 28 30.44 | ............ | 64.04 |

$\frac{\text{Sum of adopted values of the observations for each night,}}{\text{Number of observations giving to each its value* ......}} = \frac{661.95}{22} = 30.09$

MOON'S SECOND LIMB.

| Date of observation. | Longitude west of Greenwich, deduced from corresponding observations made at— | | | Adopted values of the observations for each night. |
|---|---|---|---|---|
| | Greenwich Observatory. | Radcliffe Observatory. | Philadelphia High School Observatory. | |
| 1853. | h. m. s. | h. m. s. | h. m. s. | s. |
| Aug. 18 | 6 28 20.69 | 6 28 00.00 | 6 28 00.00 | 20.69 |
| 19 | ............ | ............ | 6 28 33.62 | 67.24 |
| 21 | ............ | ............ | 6 28 35.90 | 71.80 |
| 23 | 6 28 33.54 | ............ | ............ | 33.54 |
| 24 | 6 28 32.10 | ............ | ............ | 32.10 |
| Sept. 17 | 6 28 24.60 | ............ | ............ | 24.60 |
| 18 | 6 28 29.69 | ............ | 6 28 36.03 | 101.75 |
| Oct. 17 | ............ | ............ | 6 28 34.37 | 68.74 |
| 18 | 6 28 20.69 | ............ | 6 28 24.09 | 68.87 |
| 19 | ............ | ............ | 6 28 27.56 | 55.12 |
| 20 | 6 28 42.03 | ............ | ............ | 42.03 |
| Nov. 14 | 6 28 33.60 | 6 28 30.44 | ............ | 64.04 |
| 18 | 6 28 28.67 | ............ | ............ | 28.67 |
| 21 | 6 28 29.45 | ............ | ............ | 29.45 |

$\frac{\text{Sum of adopted values of the observations for each night,}}{\text{Number of observations giving to each its value* ......}} = \frac{708.64}{23} = 30.81$

| | h. m. s. |
|---|---|
| Mean longitude from observations on moon's 1st limb..... | =6 28 30.09 |
| Do..............do................2d limb..... | =6 28 30.81 |
| Mean longitude from observations on moon's 1st and 2d limbs | =6 28 30.45 |

| | h. m. s. |
|---|---|
| Longitude of astronomical station near the mouth of the Rio Grande west of Greenwich Observatory.............................. | =6 28 30.45 |

NOTE.—Radcliffe Observatory is 5*m.* 02.60*s.* west of Greenwich, (Radcliffe Observations, vol. XIV, page IX.) High School Observatory, Philadelphia, is 5*h.* 00*m.* 37.56*s.* west of Greenwich Observatory. In reducing the results from the Radcliffe and High School observations to Greenwich observations, the above differences of longitudes have been applied.

* In the column "Adopted values of the observations for each night," the results have been obtained by giving double weight to the High School observations on account of its relative distance from the mouth of the Rio Grande, and equal weight to the Radcliffe and Greenwich observations.

TABLE VIII.

*Tabulation of results for the latitude of astronomical station at Frontera, Texas, derived from observations made with the zenith telescope No. 4, on twenty-four pairs of stars: By Major W. H. Emory, Chief Astronomer and Surveyor of United States and Mexican boundary survey.*

| Date. | 1st pair. | 2d pair. | 3d pair. | 4th pair. | 5th pair. | 6th pair. | 7th pair. |
|---|---|---|---|---|---|---|---|
| | B. A. C. 2194 S. 2270 N. | B. A. C. 2444 S. 2341 N. | B. A. C. 2469 S. 2504 N. | B. A. C. 2472 S. 2504 N. | B. A. C. 2605 S. 2691 N. | B. A. C. 2788 S. 2798 N. | B. A. C. 2818 S. 2855 N. |
| | ° ′ ″ | ° ′ ″ | ° ′ ″ | ° ′ ″ | ° ′ ″ | ° ′ ″ | ° ′ ″ |
| 1852, March 23 | ...... | ...... | ...... | 31 48 45.44 | 31 48 39.20 | 31 48 47.48 | 31 48 45.62 |
| 24 | ...... | ...... | 31 48 41.45 | 31 48 51.55 | 31 48 43.67 | 31 48 48.23 | 31 48 43.56 |
| 25 | ...... | 31 48 44.19 | 31 48 40.03 | ...... | 31 48 37.33 | 31 48 49 27 | 31 48 44.01 |
| 26 | ...... | ...... | 31 48 38.80 | 31 48 47.83 | ...... | 31 48 49.01 | 31 48 44.01 |
| 27 | 31 48 42.63 | 31 48 46.35 | 31 48 41.18 | 31 48 50.31 | 31 48 38.79 | 31 48 49.33 | 31 48 44.20 |
| 28 | ...... | ...... | 31 48 43.93 | 31 48 47.86 | 3l 48 38.77 | 31 48 49.76 | 31 48 43.12 |
| 30 | ...... | 31 48 44.44 | ...... | ...... | ...... | 31 48 48.56 | 31 48 45.23 |
| Latitude by a mean of each pair. | 31 48 42.63 | 31 48 44.99 | 31 48 41.08 | 31 48 48.60 | 31 48 45.55 | 31 48 48.81 | 31 48 44.25 |
| Corrections for declination | 0.00 | 0.00 | + 1.20 | 0.00 | + 0.69 | − 3.28 | − 1.00 |
| Corrected latitude | 31 48 42.63 | 31 48 44.99 | 31 48 42.28 | 31 48 48.60 | 31 48 46.24 | 31 48 45.53 | 31 48 43.25 |

TABLE VIII—Continued.

| Date. | 8th pair. | 9th pair. | 10th pair. | 11th pair. | 12th pair. | 13th pair. | 14th pair. |
|---|---|---|---|---|---|---|---|
| | B. A. C. 2952 S. 2912 N. | B. A. C. 3109 S. 3033 N. | B. A. C. 3181 S. 3131 N. | B. A. C. 3201 S. 3252 N. | B. A. C. 3201 S. 3261 N. | B. A. C. 3355 S. 3399 N. | B. A. C. 3409 S. 3427 N. |
| | ° ′ ″ | ° ′ ″ | ° ′ ″ | ° ′ ″ | ° ′ ″ | ° ′ ″ | ° ′ ″ |
| 1852, March 23 | 31 48 50.75 | 31 48 44.97 | 31 48 34.71 | 31 48 45.88 | 31 48 49.25 | 31 48 46.75 | ...... |
| 24 | 31 48 49.85 | ...... | ...... | ...... | ...... | ...... | ...... |
| 25 | 31 48 48.87 | 31 48 42.01 | 31 48 40.26 | 31 48 43.12 | 31 48 42.88 | 31 48 48.25 | 31 48 48.33 |
| 26 | 31 48 48.93 | 31 48 46.18 | 31 48 41.27 | 31 48 46.26 | 31 48 44.41 | 31 48 47.64 | 31 48 48.20 |
| 27 | 31 48 50.09 | 31 48 43.94 | 31 48 42.01 | 31 48 46.81 | 31 48 44.94 | 31 48 50.31 | ...... |
| 28 | 31 48 49.93 | 31 48 44.70 | 31 48 42.64 | ...... | ...... | ...... | ...... |
| 30 | 31 48 48.48 | 31 48 44.45 | 31 48 41.37 | 31 48 46.14 | 31 48 47.21 | 31 48 47.19 | 31 48 49.68 |
| Latitude by a mean of each pair. | 31 48 49.56 | 31 48 44.37 | 31 48 40.38 | 31 48 45.64 | 31 48 45.74 | 31 48 48.03 | 31 48 48.74 |
| Corrections for declination | − 3.11 | + 1.27 | + 1.56 | − 1.86 | − 2.86 | − 3.91 | − 1.21 |
| Corrected latitude | 31 48 46.45 | 31 48 45.64 | 31 48 41.94 | 31 48 43.78 | 31 48 42.88 | 31 48 44.12 | 31 48 47.53 |

TABLE VIII—Continued.

| Date. | 15th pair. | 16th pair. | 17th pair. | 18th pair. | 19th pair. | 20th pair. | 21st pair. | 22d pair. |
|---|---|---|---|---|---|---|---|---|
| | B. A. C. 3671 S. 3584 N. | B. A. C. 3710 S. 3736 N. | B. A. C. 3842 S. 3781 N. | B. A. C. 3915 S. 3952 N. | B. A. C. 3990 S. 3973 N. | B. A. C. 4014 S. 4026 N. | B. A. C. 4014 S. 4028 N. | B. A. C. 4066 S. 4126 N. |
| | ° ′ ″ | ° ′ ″ | ° ′ ″ | ° ′ ″ | ° ′ ″ | ° ′ ″ | ° ′ ″ | ° ′ ″ |
| 1852, March 23 | 31 48 42.88 | ...... | 31 48 45.40 | 31 48 45.28 | 31 48 45.81 | 31 48 45.73 | 31 48 43.36 | ...... |
| 24 | ...... | ...... | ...... | ...... | ...... | ...... | ...... | ...... |
| 25 | 31 48 43.03 | 31 48 39.15 | 31 48 42.27 | 31 48 45.28 | 31 48 45.39 | 31 48 47.69 | 31 48 48.38 | ...... |
| 26 | 31 48 43.78 | 31 48 41.70 | 31 48 43.73 | 31 48 44.49 | 31 48 44.88 | 31 48 45.92 | 31 48 45.82 | ...... |
| 27 | 31 48 44.87 | 31 48 40.77 | 31 48 45.56 | 31 48 46.58 | 31 48 45.30 | 31 48 48.59 | 31 48 48.74 | ...... |
| 28 | ...... | ...... | ...... | ...... | ...... | ...... | ...... | ...... |
| 30 | 31 48 44.58 | 31 48 43.00 | 31 48 42.26 | ...... | 31 48 44.99 | 31 48 47.37 | 31 48 48.07 | 31 48 50.56 |
| Latitude by a mean of each pair | 31 48 43.83 | 31 48 41.15 | 31 48 43.84 | 31 48 45.41 | 31 48 45.27 | 31 48 47.06 | 31 48 46.87 | 31 48 50.56 |
| Corrections for declination | − 0.12 | + 2.69 | − 0.33 | 0.00 | − 1.61 | − 2.22 | − 2.95 | − 1.25 |
| Corrected latitude | 31 48 43.71 | 31 48 43.84 | 31 48 43.51 | 31 48 45.41 | 31 48 43.66 | 31 48 44.84 | 31 48 43.92 | 31 48 49.31 |

TABLE VIII—Continued.

| Date. | 23d pair. | 24th pair. | Results for latitude by a mean of each night, (declin's corrected.) | 1st result. | 2d result. | 3d result. | Final result. |
|---|---|---|---|---|---|---|---|
| | B. A. C. 4141 S. 4188 N. | B. A. C. 4212 S. 4258 N. | | Lat. by a mean of all the pairs, (declin's corrected.) | Lat. by a mean of all the observations, (declinations corrected.) | Lat. by a mean of results for each night, (declinations corrected.) | Mean of 1st, 2d, and 3d results. |
| | ° ′ ″ | ° ′ ″ | ° ′ ″ | ° ′ ″ | ° ′ ″ | ° ′ ″ | ° ′ ′ |
| 1852, March 23 | ............... | ............... | 31 48 43.69 | | | | |
| 24 | ............... | ............... | 31 48 45.47 | | | | |
| 25 | ............... | ............... | 31 48 43.31 | | | | |
| 26 | ............... | ............... | 31 48 44.24 | | | | |
| 27 | ............... | ............... | 31 48 44.78 | | | | |
| 28 | ............... | ............... | 31 48 44.76 | | | | |
| 30 | 31 48 44.50 | 31 48 40.80 | 31 48 44.67 | | | | |
| Latitude by a mean of each pair. | 31 48 44.50 | 31 48 40.80 | | | | | |
| Corrections for declination | + 1.70 | — 1.86 | | | | | |
| Corrected latitude | 31 48 46.20 | 31 48 38.94 | | 31 48 44.60 | 31 48 44.56 | 31 48 44.42 | 31 48 44.53 |

Latitude of astronomical station at Frontera, Texas, = 31° 48′ 44″.53.

TABLE IX.*

*Corrections to be applied to the results for latitude of astronomical station at Frontera, Texas, in order to introduce the elements of the stars as observed at the Washington Observatory, in* 1852 *and* 1853.

| Number of pair. | Names of stars. | DECLINATIONS. B. A. C. | DECLINATIONS. Washington Observatory catalogue. | Difference. | ½ differ'ce, or error for correction. | Number of pair. | Names of stars. | DECLINATIONS. B. A. C. | DECLINATIONS. Washington Observatory catalogue. | Difference. | ½ differ'ce, or error for correction. |
|---|---|---|---|---|---|---|---|---|---|---|---|
| | | ° ′ ″ | ° ′ ″ | | | | | ° ′ ″ | ° ′ ″ | | |
| 1 | 2194 | 25 16 27.2 | ............... | ............ | ............ | 13 | 3355 | 21 52 37.10 | 21 52 32.91 | — 4.19 | |
| | 2270 | 38 15 10.2 | ............... | ............ | ............ | | 3399 | 41 46 05.1 | 41 46 01.47 | — 3.63 | — 3.91 |
| 2 | 2444 | 11 57 33.9 | ............... | ............ | ............ | 14 | 3409 | 30 21 37.5 | 30 21 42.02 | + 4.52 | |
| | 2341 | 51 40 15.9 | ............... | ............ | ............ | | 3427 | 33 22 15.4 | 33 22 08.45 | — 6.95 | — 1.21 |
| 3 | 2469 | 28 13 14.8 | 28 13 13.23 | — 1.57 | | 15 | 3671 | 23 58 20.1 | 23 58 19.01 | — 1.09 | |
| | 2504 | 35 22 41.4 | 35 22 45.38 | + 3.98 | + 1.20 | | 3584 | 39 41 26.0 | 39 41 26.85 | + 0.85 | — 0.12 |
| 4 | 2472 | 28 13 18.2 | ............... | ............ | ............ | 16 | 3710 | 28 45 53.2 | 28 45 52.17 | — 1.03 | |
| | 2504 | 35 22 41.4 | ............... | ............ | ............ | | 3736 | 34 49 57.6 | 34 50 04.01 | + 6.41 | + 2.69 |
| 5 | 2605 | 19 42 13.3 | 19 42 15.82 | + 2.52 | | 17 | 3842 | 23 54 44.6 | 23 54 44.11 | — 0.49 | |
| | 2691 | 43 41 09.0 | 43 41 07.85 | — 1.15 | + 0.69 | | 3781 | 39 40 30.1 | 39 40 29.93 | — 0.17 | — 0.33 |
| 6 | 2788 | 21 13 04.8 | 21 13 00.04 | — 4.76 | | 18 | 3915 | 19 14 07.4 | ............... | ............ | ............ |
| | 2798 | 42 28 59.8 | 42 28 58.00 | — 1.80 | — 3.28 | | 3952 | 44 27 23.9 | ............... | ............ | ............ |
| 7 | 2818 | 25 01 17.5 | 25 01 23.85 | + 6.35 | | 19 | 3990 | 21 03 10.7 | 21 03 08.32 | — 2.38 | |
| | 2855 | 38 31 42.2 | 38 31 33.85 | — 8.35 | — 1.00 | | 3973 | 42 33 18.6 | 42 33 17.75 | — 0.85 | — 1.61 |
| 8 | 2952 | 31 14 16.0 | 31 14 13.21 | — 2 79 | | 20 | 4014 | 16 16 27.6 | 16 16 22.96 | — 4.64 | |
| | 2912 | 32 28 07.5 | 32 28 04.07 | — 3.43 | — 3.11 | | 4026 | 47 18 42.1 | 47 18 42.30 | + 0.20 | — 2.22 |
| 9 | 3109 | 30 15 09.4 | 30 15 13.90 | + 4.50 | | 21 | 4014 | 16 16 27.6 | 16 16 22.96 | — 4.64 | |
| | 3033 | 33 29 02.8 | 33 29 00.84 | — 1.96 | + 1.27 | | 4028 | 47 18 17.6 | 47 18 16.34 | — 1.26 | — 2.95 |
| 10 | 3181 | 19 43 16.7 | 19 43 21.36 | + 4.66 | | 22 | 4066 | 22 17 43.8 | 22 17 41.73 | — 2.07 | |
| | 3131 | 43 49 57.8 | 43 49 56.25 | — 1.55 | + 1.56 | | 4126 | 41 29 46.1 | 41 29 45.67 | — 0.43 | — 1.25 |
| 11 | 3201 | 26 33 36.2 | 26 33 33.46 | — 2.74 | | 23 | 4141 | 23 52 08.2 | 23 52 07.81 | — 0.39 | |
| | 3252 | 37 08 55.7 | 37 08 54.73 | — 0.97 | — 1.86 | | 4188 | 39 51 02.6 | 39 51 06.39 | + 3.79 | + 1.70 |
| 12 | 3201 | 26 33 36.2 | 26 33 33.46 | — 2.74 | | 24 | 4212 | 21 43 43.3 | 21 43 39.31 | — 3.99 | |
| | 3261 | 37 03 39.3 | 37 03 36.32 | — 2.98 | — 2.86 | | 4258 | 41 42 03.4 | 41 42 03.67 | + 0.27 | — 1.86 |

* The reference on page 193 to table IX*a* should be VIII.

TABLE X.

*Result of observations on the prime vertical for latitude: By Lieut. A. W. Whipple, at Presidio de San Elceario.*

| Date. | Star observed. | Result from each observation. | Res'lt from mean of wires. | Date. | Star observed. | Result from each observation. | Res'lt from mean of wires. | Final result. |
|---|---|---|---|---|---|---|---|---|
| 1851. | | ° ′ ″ | ° ′ ″ | 1851. | | ° ′ ″ | ° ′ ″ | |
| Jan. 29 | β Geminorum........ | 31 35 13.80 | | Feb. 3 | 2082 Aurigæ......... | 31 35 12.73 | | Lat. of Presidio de San Elceario.. ° ′ ″ 31 35 12.616 |
| | | 11.28 | 31 35 12.62 | | | 13.67 | 31 35 13.43 | |
| | | 12.72 | | | | 13.90 | | |
| | 1768 Aurigæ....... | 10 54 | 11.32 | | 1768 Aurigæ ........ | 12.49 | | |
| | | 12.09 | | | | 13.55 | 12.99 | |
| | | | | | | 12.93 | | |
| | 2082 Aurigæ....... | 11.87 | | | | | | |
| | | 09.35 | 10.63 | Feb. 4 | 1768 Aurigæ ........ | 11.20 | | |
| | | 10.68 | | | | 10.96 | 10.96 | |
| | | | | | | 10.71 | | |
| Feb. 3 | β Geminorum ........ | 12.56 | | | | | | |
| | | 13.96 | 13.80 | | 2340 Geminorum.... | 17.39 | | |
| | | 14.90 | | | | 14.14 | 15.18 | |
| | | | | | | 13.95 | | |

TABLE XI.

*Tabulation of results for the latitude of astronomical station on the Rio Grande, near the mouth of the cañon, derived from observations made with zenith telescope No. 4, on twenty-one pairs of stars: By Major W. H. Emory, Chief Astronomer and Surveyor of United States and Mexican boundary survey.*

| Date. | 1st pair. | 2d pair. | 3d pair. | 4th pair. | 5th pair. | 6th pair. | 7th pair. |
|---|---|---|---|---|---|---|---|
| | B. A. C. 4594 S. 4627 N. | B. A. C. 4706 S. 4747 N. | B. A. C. 4810 S. 4783 N. | B. A. C. 4873 S. 4841 N. | B. A. C. 5048 S. 4958 N. | B. A. C. 5223 S. 5092 N. | B. A. C. 5234 S. 5287 N. |
| | ° ′ ″ | ° ′ ″ | ° ′ ″ | ° ′ ″ | ° ′ ″ | ° ′ ″ | ° ′ ″ |
| 1852, June 24................ | 31 02 20.04 | 31 02 26.01 | 31 02 27.73 | 31 02 28.16 | 31 02 31.35 | 31 02 23.79 | 31 02 28.00 |
| 25................ | 31 02 30.26 | 31 02 28.49 | 31 02 26.49 | 31 02 27.37 | 31 02 31.26 | 31 02 21.76 | 31 02 24.00 |
| 26................ | .............. | 31 02 22.10 | .............. | 31 02 30.45 | 21 02 23.19 | .............. | .............. |
| Latitude by a mean of each pair. | 31 02 25.12 | 31 02 25.53 | 31 02 27.11 | 31 02 28.66 | 31 02 28.60 | 31 02 22.78 | 31 02 26.00 |
| Corrections for declinations.... | — 2 53 | — 0.37 | 0.00 | + 1.02 | — 3.93 | 0.00 | 0.00 |
| Corrected latitude............ | 31 02 22.59 | 31 02 25.16 | 31 02 27.11 | 31 02 29.68 | 31 02 24.67 | 31 02 22.78 | 31 02 26.00 |

TABLE XI—Continued.

| Date. | 8th pair. | 9th pair. | 10th pair. | 11th pair. | 12th pair. | 13th pair. | 14th pair. |
|---|---|---|---|---|---|---|---|
| | B. A. C. 5541 S. 5473 N. | B. A. C. 5652 S. 5693 N. | B. A. C. 5732 S. 5706 N. | B. A. C. 5828 S. 5895 N. | B. A. C. 5841 S. 5795 N. | B. A. C. 5860 S. 5886 N. | B. A. C. 5962 S. 5927 N. |
| | ° ′ ″ | ° ′ ″ | ° ′ ″ | ° ′ ″ | ° ′ ″ | ° ′ ″ | ° ′ ″ |
| 1852, June 24................ | 31 02 26.95 | 31 02 24.83 | .............. | 31 02 27.53 | .............. | .............. | .............. |
| 25................ | 31 02 29.16 | 31 02 24.44 | 31 02 28.85 | .............. | 31 02 29.28 | 31 02 26.96 | 31 02 27.10 |
| 26................ | .............. | 31 02 26.33 | .............. | .............. | 31 02 27.17 | 31 02 25.62 | 31 02 27.54 |
| Latitude by a mean of each pair. | 31 02 28.05 | 31 02 25.20 | 31 02 28.85 | 31 02 27.53 | 31 02 28.23 | 31 02 26.29 | 31 02 27.32 |
| Corrections for declinations.... | 0.00 | — 1.25 | 0.00 | 0.00 | + 0.32 | + 0.05 | 0.00 |
| Corrected latitude............ | 31 02 28.05 | 31 02 23.95 | 31 02 28.85 | 31 02 27.53 | 31 02 28.55 | 31 02 26.34 | 31 02 27.32 |

TABLE XI—Continued.

| Date. | 15th pair. B. A. C. 5962 S. 5980 N. | 16th pair. B. A. C. 6147 S. 6178 N. | 17th pair. B. A. C. 6241 S. 6349 N. | 18th pair. B. A. C. 6322 S. 6355 N. | 19th pair. B. A. C. 6341 S. 6355 N. | 20th pair. B. A. C. 6453 S. 6390 N. |
|---|---|---|---|---|---|---|
| | ° ′ ″ | ° ′ ″ | ° ′ ″ | ° ′ ″ | ° ′ ″ | ° ′ ″ |
| 1852, June 24................. | 31 02 28.02 | 31 02 27.92 | 31 02 27.99 | ................. | ................. | 31 02 28.98 |
| 25................. | 31 02 27.32 | 31 02 28.91 | ................. | 31 02 23.42 | 31 02 22.59 | 31 02 26.73 |
| 26................. | 31 02 26.70 | 31 02 26.38 | ................. | 31 02 23.98 | 31 02 23.54 | 31 02 26.34 |
| Latitude by a mean of each pair. | 31 02 27.35 | 31 02 27.74 | 31 02 27.99 | 31 02 23.70 | 31 02 23.06 | 31 02 27.35 |
| Corrections for declinations.... | 0.00 | — 1.96 | — 0.82 | + 0.99 | + 1.47 | — 1.75 |
| Corrected latitude............. | 31 02 27.35 | 31 02 25.78 | 31 02 27.17 | 31 02 24.69 | 31 02 24.53 | 31 02 25.60 |

TABLE XI—Continued.

| Date. | 21st pair. B. A. C. 6453 S. 6391 N. | Results for latitude by a mean of each night, (declina's correctd.) | 1st result. Lat. by a mean of all the pairs, (declinations corrected.) | 2d result. Lat. by a mean of all the observations, (declinations corrected.) | 3d result. Lat. by a mean of results for each night, (declinations corrected.) | Final result, (being a mean of 1st, 2d, 3d results.) |
|---|---|---|---|---|---|---|
| | ° ′ ″ | ° ′ ″ | ° ′ ″ | ° ′ ″ | ° ′ ″ | ° ′ ″ |
| 1852, June 24................. | 31 02 27.05 | 31 02 26.06 | | | | |
| 25................. | 31 02 28.71 | 31 02 26.48 | | | | |
| 26................. | 31 02 26.41 | 31 02 25.27 | | | | |
| Latitude by a mean of each pair. | 31 02 27.39 | | | | | |
| Corrections for declinations.... | — 1.75 | | | | | |
| Corrected latitude............. | 31 02 25.64 | | 31 02 26.15 | 31 02 26.02 | 31 02 26.27 | 31 02 26.15 |

Latitude of astronomical station on the Rio Grande, near mouth of the cañon.................... = 31° 02′ 26″.15

TABLE XI*a*.

*Corrections to be applied to the results for latitude of astronomical station on the Rio Grande, near mouth of the cañon, in order to introduce the elements of the stars given in the Twelve-Year Catalogue.*

| Number of pair. | Names of stars. | Declinations. B. A. C. | Declinations. T. Y. C. | Difference. | ½ difference or error for correction. |
|---|---|---|---|---|---|
| | | ° ′ ″ | ° ′ ″ | | |
| 1 | 4594 | 26 27 29.2 | 26 27 24.14 | − 5.06 | − 2.53 |
| | 4627 | 35 31 04.1 | | | |
| 2 | 4706 | 25 48 17.5 | 25 48 16.77 | − 0.73 | − 0.37 |
| | 4747 | 36 12 14.7 | | | |
| 3 | 4810 | 22 55 24.2 | ........ | ........ | ........ |
| | 4783 | 39 04 23.0 | ........ | ........ | ........ |
| 4 | 4873 | 17 36 10.4 | | | |
| | 4841 | 44 17 27.1 | 44 17 29.13 | + 2.03 | + 1.02 |
| 5 | 5048 | 21 07 34.4 | 21 07 27.45 | − 6.95 | |
| | 4958 | 40 59 06.0 | 40 59 05.09 | − 0.91 | − 3.93 |
| 6 | 5223 | 14 34 47.7 | ........ | ........ | ........ |
| | 5092 | 47 35 29.2 | ........ | ........ | ........ |
| 7 | 5234 | 18 36 31.6 | ........ | ........ | ........ |
| | 5287 | 43 34 40.2 | ........ | ........ | ........ |
| 8 | 5541 | 30 49 01.4 | ........ | ........ | ........ |
| | 5473 | 31 14 37.7 | ........ | ........ | ........ |
| 9 | 5652 | 30 13 26.6 | | | |
| | 5693 | 31 57 12.8 | 31 57 10.31 | − 2.49 | − 1.25 |
| 10 | 5732 | 15 10 24.9 | ........ | ........ | ........ |
| | 5706 | 46 47 03.1 | ........ | ........ | ........ |
| 11 | 5828 | 25 01 10.2 | ........ | ........ | ........ |
| | 5895 | 37 05 21.0 | ........ | ........ | ........ |
| 12 | 5841 | 11 01 51.4 | 11 01 52.04 | + 0.64 | + 0.32 |
| | 5795 | 51 02 06.1 | | | |
| 13 | 5860 | 24 39 07.2 | 24 39 07.30 | + 0.10 | + 0.05 |
| | 5886 | 37 17 14.3 | | | |
| 14 | 5962 | 30 52 52.2 | ........ | ........ | ........ |
| | 5927 | 31 16 27.0 | ........ | ........ | ........ |
| 15 | 5962 | 30 52 52.2 | ........ | ........ | ........ |
| | 5980 | 32 35 18.0 | ........ | ........ | ........ |
| 16 | 6147 | 30 32 37.4 | | | |
| | 6178 | 31 22 19.7 | 31 22 15 77 | − 3.93 | − 1.96 |
| 17 | 6241 | 23 12 47.1 | 23 12 45 13 | − 1.97 | |
| | 6349 | 38 46 31.4 | 38 46 31.74 | + 0.34 | − 0.82 |
| 18 | 6322 | 23 30 30.9 | 23 30 30.14 | − 0.76 | |
| | 6355 | 38 38 46.4 | 38 38 49.14 | + 2.74 | + 0.99 |
| 19 | 6341 | 23 29 14.9 | 23 29 15.11 | + 0.21 | |
| | 6355 | 38 38 46.4 | 38 38 49.14 | + 2.74 | + 1.47 |
| 20 | 6453 | 22 27 34.5 | 22 27 30.99 | − 3.51 | − 1.75 |
| | 6390 | 39 30 57.2 | | | |
| 21 | 6453 | 22 27 34.5 | 22 27 30.99 | − 3.51 | − 1.75 |
| | 6391 | 39 27 29.9 | | | |

## TABLE XII.

*Tabulation of results for the latitude of astronomical station opposite Presidio del Norte, derived from observations made with zenith telescope No. 4, on twenty-six pairs of stars: By Major W. H. Emory, Chief Astronomer and Surveyor of the United States and Mexican boundary survey.*

| Date. | 1st pair. | 2d pair. | 3d pair. | 4th pair. | 5th pair. | 6th pair. | 7th pair. |
|---|---|---|---|---|---|---|---|
| | B. A. C. 4993 S. 5072 N. | B. A. C. 5048 S. 5084 N. | B. A. C. 5132 S. 5122 N. | B. A. C. 5132 S. 5130 N. | B. A. C. 5146 S. 5168 N. | B. A. C. 5273 S. 5295 N. | B. A. C. 5426 S. 5460 N. |
| | ° ′ ″ | ° ′ ″ | ° ′ ″ | ° ′ ″ | ° ′ ″ | ° ′ ″ | ° ′ ″ |
| 1852, July 15.......... | 29 34 07.15 | .......... | 29 34 07.16 | 29 34 06.89 | .......... | 29 34 08.32 | 29 34 03.90 |
| 16.......... | 29 34 08.49 | .......... | 29 34 08.30 | 29 34 08.77 | .......... | 29 34 07.42 | 29 34 04.46 |
| 18.......... | .......... | 29 34 11.00 | .......... | .......... | 29 34 09.50 | 29 34 06.71 | 29 34 04.77 |
| 21.......... | .......... | .......... | .......... | .......... | .......... | .......... | 29 34 05.26 |
| 22.......... | .......... | .......... | .......... | .......... | .......... | 29 34 07.53 | .......... |
| Aug. 10.......... | .......... | .......... | .......... | .......... | .......... | .......... | .......... |
| 12.......... | .......... | .......... | .......... | .......... | .......... | .......... | .......... |
| 18.......... | .......... | .......... | .......... | .......... | .......... | .......... | .......... |
| Latitude by a mean of each pair. | 29 34 07.82 | 29 34 11.00 | 29 34 07.73 | 29 34 07.83 | 29 34 09.50 | 29 34 07.49 | 29 34 04.60 |
| Corrections for declinations.... | − 0.96 | − 2.74 | 0.00 | 0.00 | − 1.10 | − 0.60 | 0.00 |
| Corrected latitude.......... | 29 34 06.86 | 29 34 08.26 | 29 34 07.73 | 29 34 07.83 | 29 34 08.40 | 29 34 06.89 | 29 34 04.60 |

## TABLE XII—Continued.

| Date. | 8th pair. | 9th pair. | 10th pair. | 11th pair. | 12th pair. | 13th pair. | 14th pair. |
|---|---|---|---|---|---|---|---|
| | B. A. C. 5527 S. 5546 N. | B. A. C. 5677 S. 5619 N. | B. A. C. 5883 S. 5788 N. | B. A. C. 5900 S. 5929 N. | B. A. C. 6021 S. 5986 N. | B. A. C. 6150 S. 6087 N. | B. A. C. 6241 S. 6235 N. |
| | ° ′ ″ | ° ′ ″ | ° ′ ″ | ° ′ ″ | ° ′ ″ | ° ′ ″ | ° ′ ″ |
| 1852, July 15.......... | .......... | .......... | 29 34 06.86 | .......... | 29 34 08.74 | .......... | .......... |
| 16.......... | 29 34 05.54 | 29 34 04.11 | 29 34 06.50 | 29 34 04.90 | .......... | 29 34 08.21 | 29 34 07.82 |
| 18.......... | 29 34 06.34 | 29 34 03.93 | .......... | 29 34 03.97 | 29 34 09.05 | 29 34 08.17 | 29 34 07.24 |
| 21.......... | 29 34 04.93 | 29 34 04.19 | 29 34 06.42 | 29 34 04.71 | 29 34 09.58 | 29 34 07.50 | 29 34 07.88 |
| 22.......... | 29 34 06.42 | 29 34 03.82 | 29 34 07.31 | 29 34 05.49 | 29 34 08.49 | 29 34 07.74 | 29 34 07.49 |
| Aug. 10.......... | .......... | 29 34 02.55 | .......... | 29 34 03.09 | 29 34 08.69 | 29 34 07.87 | 29 34 05.69 |
| 12.......... | .......... | 29 34 02.71 | 29 34 06.85 | 29 34 04.27 | 29 34 08.76 | 29 34 07.62 | 29 34 06.20 |
| 18.......... | .......... | 29 34 02.50 | 29 34 06.42 | 29 34 03.70 | 29 34 08.00 | 29 34 06.93 | 29 34 07.53 |
| Latitude by a mean of each pair. | 29 34 05.81 | 29 34 03.40 | 29 34 06.73 | 29 34 04.30 | 29 34 08.76 | 29 34 07.72 | 29 34 07.12 |
| Corrections for declinations.... | 0.00 | 0.00 | + 0.23 | + 1.69 | 0.00 | + 0.10 | − 1.08 |
| Corrected latitude.......... | 29 34 05.81 | 29 34 03.40 | 29 34 06.96 | 29 34 05.99 | 29 34 08.76 | 29 34 07.82 | 29 34 06.04 |

TABLE XII—Continued.

| Date. | 15th pair. | 16th pair. | 17th pair. | 18th pair. | 19th pair. | 20th pair. | 21st pair. | 22d pair. |
|---|---|---|---|---|---|---|---|---|
| | B. A. C. 6387 S. 6349 N. | B. A. C. 6387 S. 6355 N. | B. A. C. 6453 S. 6466 N. | B. A. C. 6589 S. 6599 N. | B. A. C. 6648 S. 6740 N. | B. A. C. 6673 S. 6740 N. | B. A. C. 6714 S. 6740 N. | B. A. C. 6794 S. 6817 N. |
| | ° ′ ″ | ° ′ ″ | ° ′ ″ | ° ′ ″ | ° ′ ″ | ° ′ ″ | ° ′ ″ | ° ′ ″ |
| 1852, July 15 | ........ | ........ | ........ | ........ | ........ | ........ | ........ | ........ |
| 16 | 29 34 07.24 | 29 34 07.70 | ........ | 29 34 08 47 | 29 34 07.01 | 29 34 06 48 | 29 34 06.40 | ........ |
| 18 | 29 34 05.59 | 29 34 05.53 | 29 34 09.97 | 29 34 08 60 | 29 34 06 87 | 29 34 07.61 | 29 34 07.53 | 29 34 09.29 |
| 21 | 29 34 07.48 | 29 34 08.16 | 29 34 09.55 | 29 34 08.88 | 29 34 07.92 | ........ | ........ | 29 34 09 63 |
| 22 | 29 34 06.65 | 29 34 07.22 | 29 34 09.79 | 29 34 08.79 | ........ | ........ | ........ | ........ |
| Aug. 10 | 29 34 05.46 | 29 34 06.06 | ........ | 29 34 08.48 | 29 34 05.73 | 29 34 04.90 | 29 34 04.85 | 29 34 09.88 |
| 12 | 29 34 04.40 | 29 34 05.82 | ........ | 29 34 08.60 | 29 34 05.35 | 29 34 05.38 | 29 34 06.49 | 29 34 07.04 |
| 18 | 29 34 05.46 | 29 34 06.36 | ........ | 29 34 09.68 | 29 34 06.49 | 29 34 05.81 | 29 34 06 04 | 29 34 09 29 |
| Latitude by a mean of each pair. | 29 34 06.04 | 29 34 06.69 | 29 34 09.77 | 29 34 08.79 | 29 34 06.56 | 29 34 06.04 | 29 34 06.26 | 29 34 09.02 |
| Corrections for declinations | − 0.01 | + 1.45 | − 1.71 | + 0.39 | + 0.09 | 0.00 | 0.00 | + 0.24 |
| Corrected latitude | 29 34 06.03 | 29 34 08.14 | 29 34 08.06 | 29 34 09.18 | 29 34 06.65 | 29 34 06.04 | 29 34 06.26 | 29 34 09.26 |

TABLE XII—Continued.

| Date. | 23d pair. | 24th pair. | 25th pair. | 26th pair. | Results for latitude by a mean of each night. (declinations corrected.) | 1st result. | 2d result. | 3d result. |
|---|---|---|---|---|---|---|---|---|
| | B. A. C. 6882 S. 6851 N. | B. A. C. 6883 S. 6851 N. | B. A. C. 6973 S. 7029 N. | B. A. C. 6978 S. 7029 N. | | Lat. by a mean of all the pairs, (declinations corrected.) | Lat. by a mean of all the observations, (declinations corrected.) | Lat. by a mean of results for each night, (declinat'ns corrected.) |
| | ° ′ ″ | ° ′ ″ | ° ′ ″ | ° ′ ″ | ° ′ ″ | ° ′ ″ | ° ′ ″ | ° ′ ″ |
| 1852, July 15 | ........ | ........ | ........ | ........ | 29 34 07.19 | | | |
| 16 | ........ | ........ | ........ | ........ | 29 34 07.00 | | | |
| 18 | 29 34 07.60 | 29 34 05.45 | 29 34 10.14 | 29 34 10.54 | 29 34 07.37 | | | |
| 21 | 29 34 07.61 | 29 34 06.07 | 29 34 10.15 | 29 34 09.89 | 29 34 07.62 | | | |
| 22 | ........ | ........ | ........ | ........ | 29 34 07.27 | | | |
| Aug. 10 | 29 34 07.07 | ........ | 29 34 09.79 | 29 34 09.64 | 29 34 06.84 | | | |
| 12 | 29 34 06.75 | ........ | 29 34 08.31 | 29 34 08.90 | 29 34 06.65 | | | |
| 18 | 29 34 07.36 | ........ | ........ | ........ | 29 34 06.76 | | | |
| Latitude by a mean of each pair. | 29 34 07.28 | 29 34 05.76 | 29 34 09.60 | 29 34 09.74 | | | | |
| Corrections for declinations | 0.00 | 0.00 | 0.00 | 0.00 | | | | |
| Corrected latitude | 29 34 07.28 | 29 34 05.76 | 29 34 09.60 | 29 34 09.74 | ........ | 29 34 07.21 | 29 34 07.08 | 29 34 07.09 |

Latitude of astronomical station opposite Presidio del Norte, (mean of 1st, 2d, and 3d results) ........ = 29° 34′ 07″.13

TABLE XII *a*.

*Corrections to be applied to the results for latitude of astronomical station at Presidio del Norte, in order to introduce the elements of the stars, as given in the Twelve-Year Catalogue.*

| Number of pairs. | Names of stars. | DECLINATIONS. B. A. C. | DECLINATIONS. T. Y. C. | Difference. | ½ difference or error for correction. | Number of pairs. | Names of stars. | DECLINATIONS. B. A. C. | DECLINATIONS. T. Y. C. | Difference. | ½ difference or error for correction. |
|---|---|---|---|---|---|---|---|---|---|---|---|
| | | ° ′ ″ | ° ′ ″ | | | | | ° ′ ″ | ° ′ ″ | | |
| 1 | 4993 | 25 40 49.73 | 25 40 47.81 | — 1.92 | — 0.96 | 14 | 6241 | 23 12 57.13 | 23 12 55.32 | — 1.81 | |
| | 5072 | 33 28 09.53 | ............ | ............ | ............ | | 6235 | 36 00 11.14 | 36 00 10.78 | — 0.36 | — 1.08 |
| 2 | 5048 | 21 07 15.76 | 21 07 08.88 | — 6.88 | | 15 | 6387 | 20 24 36.31 | ............ | ............ | ............ |
| | 5084 | 37 54 06.16 | 37 54 07.55 | + 1.39 | — 2.74 | | 6349 | 38 46 44.14 | 38 46 44.11 | — 0.03 | — 0.01 |
| 3 | 5132 | 17 38 30.43 | ............ | ............ | ............ | 16 | 6387 | 20 24 36.31 | ............ | ............ | ............ |
| | 5122 | 41 20 38.50 | ............ | ............ | ............ | | 6355 | 38 39 00.22 | 38 39 03.12 | + 2.90 | + 1.45 |
| 4 | 5132 | 17 38 30.43 | ............ | ............ | ............ | 17 | 6453 | 22 27 49.68 | 22 27 46.25 | — 3.43 | — 1.71 |
| | 5130 | 41 24 29.02 | ............ | ............ | ............ | | 6466 | 36 42 57 25 | ............ | ............ | ............ |
| 5 | 5146 | 18 09 15.41 | 18 09 13.21 | — 2.20 | | 18 | 6589 | 21 08 06.41 | ............ | ............ | ............ |
| | 5168 | 30 50 29.15 | 30 50 29.15 | 0.00 | — 1.10 | | 6599 | 37 52 27.96 | 37 52 28.73 | + 0.77 | + 0.39 |
| 6 | 5273 | 20 45 01.84 | 20 45 00.64 | — 1.20 | — 0.60 | 19 | 6648 | 29 20 12.04 | 29 20 12.21 | + 0.17 | + 0.09 |
| | 5295 | 38 22 50.69 | ............ | ............ | ............ | | 6740 | 29 48 59.30 | ............ | ............ | ............ |
| 7 | 5426 | 19 11 12.58 | ............ | ............ | ............ | 20 | 6673 | 29 09 10.83 | ............ | ............ | ............ |
| | 5460 | 40 04 07.93 | ............ | ............ | ............ | | 6740 | 29 48 59.30 | ............ | ............ | ............ |
| 8 | 5527 | 20 48 31.11 | ............ | ............ | ............ | 21 | 6714 | 29 08 29.66 | ............ | ............ | ............ |
| | 5546 | 38 24 04.27 | ............ | ............ | ............ | | 6740 | 29 48 59.30 | ............ | ............ | ............ |
| 9 | 5677 | 24 54 37.16 | ............ | ............ | ............ | 22 | 6794 | 18 46 35.30 | ............ | ............ | ............ |
| | 5619 | 34 18 58.74 | ............ | ............ | ............ | | 6817 | 40 13 37.25 | 40 13 37.73 | + 0.48 | + 0.24 |
| 10 | 5883 | 23 06 13.03 | 23 06 13.50 | + 0.47 | + 0.23 | 23 | 6882 | 24 23 40.51 | ............ | ............ | ............ |
| | 5788 | 36 07 59.98 | ............ | ............ | ............ | | 6851 | 34 41 36.22 | ............ | ............ | ............ |
| 11 | 5900 | 20 12 40.87 | 20 12 44.25 | + 3.38 | + 1.69 | 24 | 6883 | 24 31 41.36 | ............ | ............ | ............ |
| | 5929 | 38 59 54.13 | ............ | ............ | ............ | | 6851 | 34 41 36.22 | ............ | ............ | ............ |
| 12 | 6021 | 27 48 46.56 | ............ | ............ | ............ | 25 | 6973 | 27 21 53.92 | ............ | ............ | ............ |
| | 5986 | 31 17 13.05 | ............ | ............ | ............ | | 7029 | 31 43 00.37 | ............ | ............ | ............ |
| 13 | 6150 | 28 44 52.29 | 28 44 51.82 | — 0.47 | | 26 | 6978 | 27 19 29.98 | ............ | ............ | ............ |
| | 6087 | 30 12 24.00 | 30 12 24.66 | + 0.66 | + 0.10 | | 7029 | 31 43 00.37 | ............ | ............ | ............ |

TABLE XIII.

*Results for latitude of Eagle Pass, from observations made with sextant, by Lieut. Michler, in* 1852.

| AUGUST 19. | | AUGUST 20. | |
|---|---|---|---|
| Polaris. | ε Sagittarii. | Polaris. | ε Sagittarii. |
| ° ′ ″ | ° ′ ″ | ° ′ ″ | ° ′ ″ |
| 28 48 17.6 | 26 55 57.9 | 28 48 37.9 | 26 55 43.3 |
| 28 48 41.9 | 26 56 14.7 | 28 48 43.5 | 26 55 48.2 |
| 28 48 31.1 | 26 56 05.4 | 28 48 39.8 | 26 55 56.5 |
| 28 48 31.8 | 26 56 06.4 | 28 48 37.1 | 26 56 17 6 |
| 28 48 30.2 | 26 56 03.0 | | 26 56 06.7 |
| 28 48 21.0 | 26 56 10.4 | Sum ............ =4) 158.3 | 26 56 07.2 |
| 28 48 29.9 | 26 56 07.8 | | 26 56 12.6 |
| | 26 56 05.8 | Mean............. = 28 48 39.6 | 26 56 05.1 |
| Sum .... ......... =7) 203.5 | 26 55 59.0 | Corr. for refraction. = 1 32.26 | 26 56 10.4 |
| | 26 55 54.8 | | 26 56 22.7 |
| Mean............. = 28 48 29.07 | 26 56 01.5 | Lat. by Polaris.... = 28 47 07.3 | 26 56 17.8 |
| Corr. for refraction.. = 1 32.00 | 26 56 10.2 | | 26 56 11.0 |
| | | | 26 55 51.9 |
| Lat by Polaris...... = 28 46 57.07 | Sum ............ =12) 672 56.9 | | 26 55.38.0 |
| | | | 26 56 06.0 |
| | Mean............ = 26 56 04.7 | | |
| | Corr. for refraction. = 1 39.17 | | Sum ..... ....... =15) 840 55.0 |
| | Meridian altitude.. = 26 54 25 53 | | Mean............ = 26 56 03.7 |
| | Star's decl'n (S)... = 34 26 57.30 | | Corr. for refraction. = 1 39.18 |
| | 61 21 22.83 | | Meridian altitude.. = 26 54 24.52 |
| | 90 00 00.00 | | Star's decl'n (S)... = 34 26 57.00 |
| | Lat. by 12 obs'ns.. = 28 38 37.17 | | 61 21 21.52 |
| | Lat. by observat'ns on Polaris....... = 28 46 57.07 | | 90 00 00.00 |
| | | | Lat. by ε Sagittarii. = 28 38 38.48 |
| | Sum ............ =2) 85 34.24 | | Lat. by Polaris.... = 28 47 07.34 |
| | Latitude........... = 28 42 47.1 | | Sum ...... =2)57 25 45.82 |
| | | | Latitude.......... = 28 42 52.91 |

TABLE XIII—Continued.

## *Result for latitudes of Eagle Pass*—Continued.

| SEPTEMBER 8. | | SEPTEMBER 9. | |
|---|---|---|---|
| Polaris. | Fomalhaut. | Polaris. | Fomalhaut. |
| ′ ′ ′ | ° ′ ″ | ° ′ ″ | ° ′ ″ |
| 28 47 10.2 | 30 57 58.03 | 28 46 41.3 | 30 58 01.8 |
| 28 46 55.8 | 30 57 52.70 | 28 47 01.1 | 30 57 33.4 |
| 28 46 59.8 | 30 57 48.64 | 28 47 11.7 | 30 57 40.9 |
| 28 46 45.1 | 30 57 41.28 | 28 47 10.3 | 30 57 43.1 |
| 28 46 55.0 | 30 57 41.95 | 28 47 22.5 | 30 57 47.3 |
| 28 47 03.5 | 30 57 51.12 | | 30 57 49.8 |
| 28 47 04.0 | 30 57 54.99 | Sum .... ........ =5) 235 26.9 | 30 57 33.4 |
| | 30 57 58.79 | | 30 57 30.9 |
| Sum .... .......... =7) 328 53.4 | 30 57 42.69 | Mean............ = 47 05.4 | 30 57 28.4 |
| | 30 57 38.82 | Lat. by mean of 5 | 30 57 30.0 |
| Mean............. = 46 59.1 | 30 57 48.35 | obs'ns on Polaris. = 28 47 05.4 | 30 57 19.5 |
| Lat. by mean of 7 ob- | 30 57 57.61 | | 30 57 51.0 |
| servat's on Polaris = 28 46 59.1 | 30 57 41.37 | | 30 57 29.4 |
| | 30 57 44.23 | | 30 57 16.6 |
| | 30 57 40.46 | | 30 57 28.4 |
| | | | 30 57 20.0 |
| | Sum .... ........ =15) 724.03 | | 30 57 23.5 |
| | | | 30 57 39.8 |
| | Meridian altitude.. = 30 57 48.27 | | 30 57 38.9 |
| | Star's decl'n (S)... = 30 24 05.00 | | 30 57 23.9 |
| | | | 30 57 59.4 |
| | 61 21 53.27 | | 30 58 03.7 |
| | 90 00 00.00 | | |
| | | | Sum .... ........ =22) 813.1 |
| | Lat. by Fomalhaut. = 28 38 06.73 | | |
| | Lat. by Polaris.. . = 28 46 59.10 | | Meridian altitude... = 30 57 36.9 |
| | | | Star's decl'n (S.)... = 30 24 05.0 |
| | Sum ...... ...... =2)57 25 05.83 | | |
| | | | 61 21 41.9 |
| | Latitude.......... = 28 42 32.91 | | 90 00 00.0 |
| | | | Lat. by Fomalhaut.. = 28 38 18.1 |
| | | | Lat. by Polaris..... = 28 47 05.4 |
| | | | Latitude........... = 28 42 41.7 |

## *Results for latitude of Eagle Pass, for each date of observation, in* 1852.

| Date | | ° ′ ″ |
|---|---|---|
| Aug. 19 | Latitude by 7 observations on Polaris.......... | = 28 46 57.07 |
| | Latitude by 12 observations on ε Sagittarii.......... | = 28 38 37.17 |
| | Sum.......... | = 2)57 25 34.24 |
| | Latitude.......... | = 28 42 47.12 |
| Aug. 20 | Latitude by 4 observations on Polaris.......... | = 28 47 07.34 |
| | Latitude by 15 observations on ε Sagittarii.......... | = 28 38 38.48 |
| | Sum.......... | = 2)57 25 45.82 |
| | Latitude.......... | 28 42 52.91 |
| Sept. 8 | Latitude by 7 observations on Polaris.......... | = 28 46 59.10 |
| | Latitude by 15 observations on Fomalhaut.......... | = 28 38 06.73 |
| | Sum.......... | = 2)57 25 05.83 |
| | Latitude.......... | = 28 42 32 91 |

TABLE XIII—Continued.

*Results for latitude of Eagle Pass for each date of observation*—Continued.

| | | | ° ′ ″ |
|---|---|---|---|
| Sept. 9 | Latitude by 5 observations on Polaris | = | 28 47 05.40 |
| | Latitude by 22 observations on Fomalhaut | = | 28 38 18.10 |
| | Sum | = | 2)57 25 23.50 |
| | Latitude | = | 28 42 41.75 |

RECAPITULATION.

| | | ° ′ ″ |
|---|---|---|
| Latitude August 19, 1852 | = | 28 42 47.12 |
| Do...August 20 | = | 28 42 52.91 |
| Do...September 8 | = | 28 42 32.91 |
| Do...September 9 | = | 28 42 41.75 |
| Sum | = | 4) 170 54 69 |
| Mean | = | 42 43.67 |

Latitude of Eagle Pass = 28° 42′ 43.″67.

TABLE XIV.

*Tabulation of results for the latitude of astronomical station at Ringgold Barracks, derived from observations made with the zenith telescope No. 4, on thirty-two pairs of stars: By Major W. H. Emory, Chief Astronomer and Surveyor of United States and Mexican boundary survey.*

| Date. | 1st pair. | 2d pair. | 3d pair. | 4th pair. | 5th pair. | 6th pair. | 7th pair. |
|---|---|---|---|---|---|---|---|
| | B. A. C. 4285 N. 4292 S. | B. A. C. 4367 S. 4433 N. | B. A. C. 4468 S. 4479 N. | B. A. C. 4468 S. 4535 N. | B. A. C. 4553 S. 4640 N. | B. A. C. 4566 S. 4640 N. | B. A. C. 4652 N. 4729 S. |
| | ° ′ ″ | ° ′ ″ | ° ′ ″ | ° ′ ″ | ° ′ ″ | ° ′ ″ | ° ′ ″ |
| 1853, June 4 | | 26 22 28.20 | 26 22 27.25 | 26 22 25.66 | | 26 22 28.76 | |
| 6 | 26 22 24.14 | 26 22 31.27 | | | 26 22 29.26 | 26 22 30.35 | |
| 14 | | | | | | | |
| 19 | | 26 22 23.82 | | | 26 22 28.22 | 26 22 29.56 | |
| 24 | | | | | | | 26 22 26.42 |
| 26 | | | | | | | 26 22 26.73 |
| 27 | | | | | | 26 22 28.83 | |
| 28 | | | | | | | 26 22 25.26 |
| 29 | | | | | | | |
| Latitude by a mean of each pair. | 26 22 24.14 | 26 22 27.76 | 26 22 27.25 | 26 22 25.66 | 26 22 28.74 | 26 22 29.37 | 26 22 26.14 |
| Corrections for declinations | 0.00 | — 0 34 | 0.00 | + 0.49 | 0.00 | 0.00 | 0.00 |
| Corrected latitude | 26 22 24.14 | 26 22 27.42 | 26 22 27.25 | 26 22 26.15 | 26 22 28.74 | 26 22 29.37 | 26 22 26.14 |

TABLE XIV—Continued.

| Date. | 8th pair. B. A. C. 4721 S. 4783 N. | 9th pair. G. C. 1147 S. 1163 N. | 10th pair. B. A. C. 4751 S. 4783 N. | 11th pair. B. A. C. 4864 N. 4953 S. | 12th pair. B. A. C. 4864 N. 4993 S. | 13th pair. G. C. 1273 N. 1281 S. | 14th pair. B. A. C. 5252 S. 5473 N. |
|---|---|---|---|---|---|---|---|
| | ° ′ ″ | ° ′ ″ | ° ′ ″ | ° ′ ″ | ° ′ ″ | ° ′ ″ | ° ′ ″ |
| 1853, June 4 | ............ | ............ | ............ | ............ | ............ | ............ | ............ |
| 6 | 26 22 24.90 | ............ | 26 22 28.76 | ............ | ............ | ............ | ............ |
| 14 | ............ | ............ | ............ | ............ | ............ | 26 22 26.74 | ............ |
| 19 | ............ | 26 22 26.95 | ............ | ............ | ............ | 26 22 30.44 | ............ |
| 24 | ............ | 26 22 26.02 | ............ | 26 22 26.24 | 26 22 27.05 | 26 22 27.50 | 26 22 30.48 |
| 26 | ............ | 26 22 26.92 | ............ | 26 22 26.50 | 26 22 28.14 | ............ | ............ |
| 27 | ............ | 26 22 28.42 | ............ | 26 22 27.46 | 26 22 28.52 | 26 22 29.13 | 26 22 30.12 |
| 28 | ............ | 26 22 28.02 | ............ | 26 22 27.10 | 26 22 28.28 | 26 22 29.40 | 26 22 30.34 |
| 29 | ............ | 26 22 27.74 | ............ | 26 22 26.69 | 26 22 27.95 | 26 22 26.38 | 26 22 30.54 |
| Latitude by a mean of each pair. | 26 22 24.90 | 26 22 27.35 | 26 22 28.76 | 26 22 26.80 | 26 22 27.99 | 26 22 28.76 | 26 22 30.37 |
| Corrections for declinations.... | 0.00 | 0.00 | — 3.40 | + 0.10 | — 0.96 | 0.00 | 0.00 |
| Corrected latitude............ | 26 22 24.90 | 26 22 27.35 | 26 22 25.36 | 26 22 26.90 | 26 22 27.03 | 26 22 28.76 | 26 22 30.37 |

TABLE XIV—Continued.

| Date. | 15th pair. G. C. 1341 N. 1417 S. | 16th pair. B. A. C. 5452 S. 5473 N. | 17th pair. G. C. 1352 N. 1417 S. | 18th pair. G. C. 1353 N. 1417 S. | 19th pair. G. C. 1369 N. 1415 S. | 20th pair. B. A. C. 5716 S. 5834 N. | 21st pair. B. A. C. 5716 S. 5895 N. |
|---|---|---|---|---|---|---|---|
| | ° ′ ″ | ° ′ ″ | ° ′ ″ | ° ′ ″ | ° ′ ″ | ° ′ ″ | ° ′ ″ |
| 1853, June 4 | ............ | ............ | ............ | ............ | ............ | ............ | ............ |
| 6 | ............ | ............ | ............ | ............ | ............ | ............ | ............ |
| 14 | 26 22 29.38 | ............ | 26 22 30.94 | 26 22 30.20 | ............ | ............ | ............ |
| 19 | 26 22 30.76 | ............ | 26 22 31.40 | 26 22 30.74 | ............ | 26 22 26.69 | 26 22 25.98 |
| 24 | ............ | 26 22 30.63 | ............ | ............ | 26 22 28.19 | 26 22 27.15 | 26 22 25.07 |
| 26 | ............ | ............ | ............ | ............ | ............ | 26 22 30.27 | 26 22 25.94 |
| 27 | ............ | 26 22 30.98 | ............ | ............ | 26 22 30.02 | 26 22 25.39 | 26 22 24.67 |
| 28 | ............ | 26 22 30.16 | ............ | ............ | 26 22 29.73 | 26 22 24.85 | 26 22 24.46 |
| 29 | ............ | 26 22 31.74 | ............ | ............ | 26 22 29.62 | 26 22 25.38 | 26 22 25.43 |
| Latitude by a mean of each pair. | 26 22 30.07 | 26 22 30.88 | 26 22 31.17 | 26 22 30.47 | 26 22 29.39 | 26 22 26.62 | 26 22 25.26 |
| Corrections for declinations.... | 0.00 | 0.00 | 0.00 | 0.00 | 0.00 | 0.00 | 0.00 |
| Corrected latitude............ | 26 22 30.07 | 26 22 30.88 | 26 22 31.17 | 26 22 30.47 | 26 22 29.39 | 26 22 26.62 | 26 22 25.26 |

TABLE XIV—Continued.

| Date. | 22d pair. B. A. C. 5941 S. 6062 N. | 23d pair. B. A. C. 5941 S. 6068 N. | 24th pair. G. C. 1554 S. 1596 N. | 25th pair. B. A. C. 6428 N. 6460 S. | 26th pair. G. C. 1652 N. 1736 S. | 27th pair. N. 1652 G. C. S. 6663 B. A. C. | 28th pair. B. A. C. 6460 S. 6476 N. | 29th pair. B. A. C. 6495 N. 6528 S. |
|---|---|---|---|---|---|---|---|---|
| | ° ′ ″ | ° ′ ″ | ° ′ ″ | ° ′ ″ | ° ′ ″ | ° ′ ″ | ° ′ ″ | ° ′ ″ |
| 1853, June 4 | ... | ... | ... | ... | ... | ... | ... | ... |
| 6 | ... | ... | ... | ... | ... | ... | ... | ... |
| 14 | ... | ... | 26 22 28.42 | ... | 26 22 28.68 | 26 22 27.66 | ... | ... |
| 19 | ... | ... | 26 22 26.72 | ... | ... | ... | ... | ... |
| 24 | 26 22 26.39 | 26 22 27.43 | 26 22 27.31 | ... | 26 22 28.55 | ... | ... | ... |
| 26 | 26 22 25.99 | 26 22 26.60 | 26 22 26.87 | 26 22 25.78 | ... | ... | 26 22 28.09 | ... |
| 27 | 26 22 28.30 | 26 22 28.26 | 26 22 28 84 | ... | ... | ... | 26 22 29.35 | 26 22 26.56 |
| 28 | 26 22 27.28 | 26 22 27.72 | 26 22 27.37 | 26 22 27.31 | ... | ... | 26 22 28.53 | 26 22 28.35 |
| 29 | 26 22 27.43 | 26 22 28.17 | 26 22 28.36 | 26 22 26.98 | ... | ... | 26 22 30.32 | ... |
| Latitude by a mean of each pair | 26 22 27.08 | 26 22 27.64 | 26 22 27.70 | 26 22 26.69 | 26 22 28.61 | 26 22 27.66 | 26 22 29.07 | 26 22 27.45 |
| Corrections for declinations.... | — 0.86 | — 0.86 | 0.00 | + 1.53 | 0.00 | 0.00 | — 0.60 | — 0.24 |
| Corrected latitude | 26 22 26.22 | 26 22 26.78 | 26 22 27.70 | 26 22 28.22 | 26 22 28.61 | 26 22 27.66 | 26 22 28.47 | 26 22 27.21 |

TABLE XIV—Continued.

| Date. | 30th pair. B. A. C. 6642 S. 6667 N. | 31st pair. B. A. C. 6647 S. 6667 N. | 32d pair. B. A. C. 6745 N. 6772 S. | Results for lat. by a mean of each night, (decl'ns corrected.) | 1st result. Lat. by a mean of all the pairs, (decl'ns corrected.) | 2d result. Lat. by a mean of all the observat'ns, (decl'ns corr'd.) | 3d result. Lat. by a mean of results for each night, (dec. corr'd.) | Final result. Being a mean of 1st, 2d, and 3d results. |
|---|---|---|---|---|---|---|---|---|
| | ° ′ ″ | ° ′ ″ | ° ′ ″ | ° ′ ″ | ° ′ ″ | ° ′ ″ | ° ′ ″ | ° ′ ″ |
| 1853, June 4 | ... | ... | ... | 26 22 27.51 | | | | |
| 6 | ... | ... | ... | 26 22 27.49 | | | | |
| 14 | ... | ... | ... | 26 22 29.29 | | | | |
| 19 | ... | ... | ... | 26 22 28.30 | | | | |
| 24 | ... | ... | ... | 26 22 27.28 | | | | |
| 26 | 26 22 30.49 | 26 22 31.76 | 26 22 26.55 | 26 22 27.35 | | | | |
| 27 | 26 22 28 66 | ... | 26 22 28.41 | 26 22 28.16 | | | | |
| 28 | 26 22 29.22 | ... | 26 22 27.29 | 26 22 27.72 | | | | |
| 29 | 26 22 30.28 | ... | 26 22 27.84 | 26 22 28.09 | | | | |
| Latitude by a mean of each pair | 26 22 29.66 | 26 22 31.76 | 26 22 27.52 | | | | | |
| Corrections for declinations.... | 0.00 | — 2.37 | + 0.22 | | | | | |
| Corrected latitude | 26 22 29.66 | 26 22 29.39 | 26 22 27.74 | ... | 26 22 27.86 | 26 22 27.60 | 26 22 27.91 | 26 22 27.79 |

Latitude of astronomical station at Ringgold Barracks = 26° 22′ 27″.79.

## TABLE XIV *a*.

*Corrections to be applied to the results for latitude of astronomical station at Ringgold Barracks, in order to introduce the elements of the stars, as given in the Twelve-Year Catalogue.*

| Number of pair. | Names of stars. | DECLINATIONS. | | Difference. | ½ difference, or error for correction. |
|---|---|---|---|---|---|
| | | B. A. C. | T. Y. C. | | |
| | | ° ′ ″ | ° ′ ″ | | |
| 1 | 4285 | 40 05 39.5 | ...... | ...... | ...... |
| | 4292 | 12 46 43.5 | ...... | ...... | ...... |
| 2 | 4367 | 11 46 01.7 | ...... | ...... | ...... |
| | 4433 | 40 56 55.0 | 40 56 54.32 | — 0.68 | — 0.34 |
| 3 | 4468 | 11 56 20.9 | ...... | ...... | ...... |
| | 4479 | 37 49 06.2 | ...... | ...... | ...... |
| 4 | 4468 | 14 56 20.9 | ...... | ...... | ...... |
| | 4536 | 37 57 07.1 | 37 57 08.08 | + 0.98 | + 0.49 |
| 5 | 4553 | 23 17 50.3 | ...... | ...... | ...... |
| | 4640 | 29 23 14.1 | ...... | ...... | ...... |
| 6 | 4566 | 23 15 32.2 | ...... | ...... | ...... |
| | 4640 | 29 23 14.1 | ...... | ...... | ...... |
| 7 | 4652 | 32 45 57.9 | ...... | ...... | ...... |
| | 4729 | 19 57 56.3 | ...... | ...... | ...... |
| 8 | 4721 | 13 39 55.5 | ...... | ...... | ...... |
| | 4783 | 39 04 23.0 | ...... | ...... | ...... |
| 9 | 1147 | ...... | 13 41 56.70 | ...... | ...... |
| | 1163 | ...... | 38 57 59 91 | ...... | ...... |
| 10 | 4751 | 13 42 03.5 | 13 41 56.70 | — 6.80 | — 3.40 |
| | 4783 | 39 04 23.0 | ...... | ...... | ...... |
| 11 | 4864 | 27 10 06.4 | ...... | ...... | ...... |
| | 4953 | 25 36 12.5 | 25 36 12.70 | + 0.20 | + 0.10 |
| 12 | 4864 | 27 10 06.4 | ...... | ...... | ...... |
| | 4993 | 25 41 08.8 | 25 41 06.88 | — 1.92 | — 0.96 |
| 13 | 1273 | ...... | 39 31 03.66 | ...... | ...... |
| | 1281 | ...... | ...... | ...... | ...... |
| 14 | 5252 | 21 25 58.6 | ...... | ...... | ...... |
| | 5473 | 31 14 37.7 | ...... | ...... | ...... |
| 15 | 1341 | ...... | 34 14 20.52 | ...... | ...... |
| | 1417 | ...... | 18 41 37.79 | ...... | ...... |
| 16 | 5452 | 21 29 58 5 | ...... | ...... | ...... |
| | 5473 | 31 14 37.7 | ...... | ...... | ...... |
| 17 | 1332 | ...... | 34 09 18.85 | ...... | ...... |
| | 1417 | ...... | 18 41 37.79 | ...... | ...... |
| 18 | 1353 | ...... | 34 03 19.08 | ...... | ...... |
| | 1417 | ...... | 18 41 37.79 | ...... | ...... |
| 19 | 1369 | ...... | 42 12 52.35 | ...... | ...... |
| | 1415 | ...... | 10 26 01.70 | ...... | ...... |
| 20 | 5716 | 15 40 48.9 | ...... | ...... | ...... |
| | 5834 | 36 58 54.5 | ...... | ...... | ...... |
| 21 | 5716 | 15 40 48.9 | ...... | ...... | ...... |
| | 5895 | 37 05 21.0 | ...... | ...... | ...... |
| 22 | 5941 | 12 40 25.9 | 12 40 24.18 | — 1.72 | — 0.86 |
| | 6062 | 40 01 00.3 | ...... | ...... | ...... |
| 23 | 5941 | 12 40 25.9 | 12 40 24.18 | — 1.72 | — 0.86 |
| | 6068 | 40 02 18.3 | ...... | ...... | ...... |
| 24 | 1554 | ...... | 16 45 48.19 | ...... | ...... |
| | 1596 | ...... | 35 59 58.41 | ...... | ...... |
| 25 | 6428 | 48 35 49.0 | 48 35 53 28 | + 4.28 | ...... |
| | 6460 | 4 00 47.1 | 4 00 45 89 | — 1.21 | + 1.53 |
| 26 | 1652 | ...... | 33 11 29.68 | ...... | ...... |
| | 1736 | ...... | 19 30 28.82 | ...... | ...... |
| 27 | 1652 | ...... | 33 11 29.68 | ...... | ...... |
| | 6663 | 19 35 46.5 | ...... | ...... | ...... |
| 28 | 6460 | 4 00 47.1 | 4 00 45.89 | — 1.21 | — 0.60 |
| | 6476 | 48 40 27.0 | ...... | ...... | ...... |
| 29 | 6495 | 39 00 44.9 | ...... | ...... | ...... |
| | 6528 | 13 38 40.7 | 13 38 40.22 | — 0.48 | — 0.24 |
| 30 | 6642 | 16 38 58.4 | ...... | ...... | ...... |
| | 6667 | 36 01 14.5 | ...... | ...... | ...... |
| 31 | 6647 | 16 40 08.0 | 16 40 03.25 | — 4.75 | — 2.37 |
| | 6667 | 36 01 14.5 | | | |
| 32 | 6745 | 42 28 27.6 | ...... | ...... | ...... |
| | 6772 | 10 15 05.1 | 10 15 05.54 | + 0.44 | + 0.22 |

## TABLE XV.

*Tabulation of results for the latitude of astronomical station at the mouth of the Rio Bravo, derived from observations made with zenith telescope No. 4, on twenty pairs of stars: By Major W. H. Emory, Chief Astronomer and Surveyor of the United States and Mexican boundary survey.*

| Date. | 1st pair. G. C. 1390 N. 1399 S. | 2d pair. G. C. 1577 N. 1597 S. | 3d pair. B. A. C. 5460 N. 5532 S. | 4th pair. B. A. C. 5367 S. 5432 N. | 5th pair. B. A. C. 5686 S. 5788 N. | 6th pair. B. A. C. 5716 S. 5788 N. | 7th pair. B. A. C. 5821 S. 5886 N. | 8th pair. B. A. C. 5929 N. 5941 S. |
|---|---|---|---|---|---|---|---|---|
| | ° ′ ″ | ° ′ ″ | ° ′ ″ | ° ′ ″ | ° ′ ″ | ° ′ ″ | ° ′ ″ | ° ′ ″ |
| August 5, 1853 | 25 57 21.82 | 25 57 19.50 | .......... | .......... | 25 57 23.75 | 25 57 21.77 | 25 57 23.67 | .......... |
| 6, 1853 | 25 57 22.14 | 25 57 22.77 | 25 57 22.00 | .......... | 25 57 21 45 | 25 57 20.08 | 25 57 21.95 | 25 57 23.74 |
| 7, 1853 | 25 57 21.86 | 25 57 20.24 | 25 57 21.21 | 25 57 22.86 | 25 57 21.88 | 25 57 20.06 | 25 57 21.38 | 25 57 22.76 |
| 9, 1853 | 25 57 22.72 | 25 57 21.11 | .......... | .......... | .......... | .......... | 25 57 21.71 | 25 57 22.51 |
| 10, 1853 | 25 57 22.28 | 25 57 20.52 | 25 57 22.27 | .......... | 25 57 21.16 | 25 57 18.89 | 25 57 21.18 | 25 57 23.39 |
| 11, 1853 | 25 57 21.83 | 25 57 21.60 | .......... | .......... | .......... | .......... | 25 57 22.53 | 25 57 22.66 |
| 16, 1853 | 25 57 21.50 | 25 57 20.68 | .......... | .......... | 25 57 20.67 | 25 57 18.62 | 25 57 22.91 | 25 57 23.81 |
| 17, 1853 | 25 57 22.90 | 25 57 21.25 | .......... | .......... | .......... | 25 57 20.82 | 25 57 23.73 | 25 57 23.37 |
| 18, 1853 | 22 57 22.56 | 25 57 21.50 | .......... | .......... | .......... | .......... | 25 57 23.38 | 25 57 23.30 |
| Latitude by a mean of each pair | 25 57 22.18 | 25 57 21.02 | 25 57 21.83 | 25 57 22.86 | 25 57 21.78 | 25 57 20.04 | 25 57 22.49 | 25 57 23.19 |

## TABLE XV—Continued.

| Date. | 9th pair. B. A. C. 6087 N. 6106 S. | 10th pair. B. A. C. 6365 N. 6482 S. | 11th pair. B. A. C. 6365 N. 6528 S. | 12th pair. G. C. 1805 N. 1850 S. | 13th pair. G. C. 1805 N. 1852 S. | 14th pair. G. C. 1710 N. 1756 S. | 15th pair. B. A. C. 6744 N. 6777 S. | 16th pair. B.A. C. 6851 N. 6868 S. |
|---|---|---|---|---|---|---|---|---|
| | ° ′ ″ | ° ′ ″ | ° ′ ″ | ° ′ ″ | ° ′ ″ | ° ′ ″ | ° ′ ″ | ° ′ ″ |
| August 5, 1853 | 25 57 23.56 | 25 57 20.52 | 25 57 21.88 | .......... | .......... | 25 57 21.85 | .......... | 25 57 24.32 |
| 6, 1853 | 25 57 21.70 | .......... | .......... | 25 57 23.73 | 25 57 23.45 | 25 57 20.44 | 25 57 23.27 | .......... |
| 7, 1853 | 25 57 22.20 | 25 57 20.05 | 25 57 21.17 | 25 57 22.87 | 25 57 23.07 | 25 57 20.54 | 25 57 21.02 | 25 57 21.12 |
| 9, 1853 | 25 57 21.94 | 25 57 18.98 | 25 57 20.71 | .......... | 25 57 23.09 | 25 57 19.64 | 25 57 20.66 | 25 57 22.97 |
| 10, 1853 | 25 57 22.25 | 25 57 19.29 | 25 57 20.90 | .......... | 25 57 24.24 | 25 57 20.82 | .......... | .......... |
| 11, 1853 | 25 57 22.86 | 25 57 21.15 | 25 57 22.13 | .......... | 25 57 22.47 | 25 57 20.19 | 25 57 20.93 | 25 57 21.52 |
| 16, 1853 | 25 57 22.00 | 25 57 19.40 | 25 57 19.85 | .......... | 25 57 22.22 | 25 57 19.35 | .......... | 25 57 21.97 |
| 17, 1853 | 25 57 22.80 | 25 57 21.56 | 25 57 22.03 | .......... | 25 57 23.83 | 25 57 20.69 | 25 57 21.17 | 25 57 22.63 |
| 18, 1853 | 25 57 21.62 | 25 57 20.92 | 25 57 22.00 | .......... | 25 57 23.71 | 25 57 19.82 | 25 57 21.45 | 25 57 22.70 |
| Latitude by a mean of each pair | 25 57 22.32 | 25 57 20.23 | 25 57 21.33 | 25 57 23.30 | 25 57 23.26 | 25 57 20.37 | 25 57 21.42 | 25 57 22.46 |

## TABLE XV—Continued.

| Date. | 17th pair. B. A. C. 7222 S. 7254 N. | 18th pair. B. A. C. 7383 N. 7641 S. | 19th pair. B. A. C. 7559 N. 7796 S. | 20th pair. B. A. C. 7565 N. 7963 S. | Results for lat. by a mean of each night, (decl'ns corrected.) | 1st result. Lat. by a mean of all the pairs, (dec. corr'd.) | 2d result. Lat. by a mean of all the obs., (dec. corr'd.) | 3d result. Lat. by a mean of results for each night, (dec. corr'd.) | Final result. Being a mean of 1st, 2d, and 3d results. |
|---|---|---|---|---|---|---|---|---|---|
| | ° ′ ″ | ° ′ ″ | ° ′ ″ | ° ′ ″ | ° ′ ″ | ° ′ ″ | ° ′ ″ | ° ′ ″ | ° ′ ″ |
| August 5, 1853 | .......... | .......... | .......... | .......... | 25 57 22.26 | | | | |
| 6, 1853 | 25 57 21.99 | 25 57 23.18 | 25 57 21.54 | 25 57 22.85 | 25 57 22.27 | | | | |
| 7, 1853 | 25 57 21.60 | 25 57 22.02 | 25 57 20.10 | 25 57 22.34 | 25 57 21.52 | | | | |
| 9, 1853 | 25 57 19.76 | 25 57 22.06 | 25 57 21.09 | 25 57 22.71 | 25 57 21.45 | | | | |
| 10, 1853 | 25 57 22.26 | 25 57 22.82 | 25 57 21.63 | 25 57 22.36 | 25 57 21.65 | | | | |
| 11, 1853 | 25 57 21.54 | 25 57 22.60 | 25 57 21.85 | .......... | 25 57 21.85 | | | | |
| 16, 1853 | 25 57 21.18 | .......... | .......... | .......... | 25 57 21.09 | | | | |
| 16, 1853 | 25 57 21.60 | .......... | .......... | .......... | 25 57 22.18 | | | | |
| 18, 1853 | 25 57 21.85 | .......... | .......... | .......... | 25 57 22.07 | | | | |
| Lat. by a m'n of each pair | 25 57 21.47 | 25 57 22.54 | 25 57 21.24 | 25 57 22.56 | | 25 57 21.89 | 25 57 21.78 | 25 57 21.82 | 25 57 21.83 |

Latitude of astronomical station at the mouth of Rio Bravo.......... = 25° 57′ 21″.83

# E.

*Table of latitudes and longitudes of points on and near the boundary between the U. States and Mexico.*

| Station. | Latitude north. | DETERMINED. | | Long. west of Greenwich. | DETERMINED. | | Observer. |
|---|---|---|---|---|---|---|---|
| | | When. | How. | | When | How. | |
| | ° ′ ″ | | | ° ′ ″ | | | |
| Camp Riley, (Major Emory's Astronomical Observatory.) | 32 35 43.53 | 1849 | Zenith telescope... | 117 06 29.7 | 1849 | Moon culminations. | W. H. Emory. |
| "East Base" Station | 32 35 42.33 | 1849 | Triangulation from Camp Riley. | 117 06 29.7 | 1849 | Triangulation from Camp Riley. | Do. |
| "West Base" Station | 32 34 33.10 | 1849 | ....do | 117 09 03.23 | 1849 | ....do | Do. |
| Monument No. 1, marking the initial point of boundary. | 32 31 59.63 | 1849 | ....do | 117 08 29.7 | 1849 | ....do | Do. |
| Monument No. 2, (Station 4) | 32 32 25.2 | 1849 | ....do | 117 03 31.7 | 1849 | ....do | Do. |
| Station No. 1 | 32 33 11.8 | 1849 | ....do | 116 53 05.9 | 1849 | ....do | Do. |
| Station No. 7 | 32 34 02.0 | 1849 | ....do | 116 44 17.6 | 1849 | ....do | Do. |
| Boundary Peak (A.) | 32 36 35.9 | 1849 | ....do | 116 18 14.6 | 1849 | ....do | Do. |
| Camp 118, (San Pasqual) | 33 03 42.0 | 1846 | Sextant | 117 06 42.2 | 1846 | Sextant | Do. |
| Camp 114, (near Warner's Ranch) | 33 16 57.0 | 1846 | ....do | 116 41 56.2 | 1846 | ....do | Do. |
| Camp 112, (Vallecito) | 32 58 15.0 | 1846 | ....do | 116 23 53.2 | 1846 | ....do | Do. |
| Camp 111 (Carrizo Creek) | 32 52 33.0 | 1846 | ....do | 116 00 22.2 | 1846 | ....do | Do. |
| First Wells | 32 40 22.0 | 1846 | ....do | 114 00 28.0 | 1846 | ....do | Do. |
| Station 46, (left bank of Rio Colorado, below junction of Rio Gila.) | 32 43 48 | 1851 | ....do | 114 39 58.2 | 1851 | ....do | Lieut. Whipple, Top. Engineers. |
| New initial point of boundary on Rio Colorado, 20 miles below the mouth of Rio Gila. | 32 29 44.45 | 1855 | Zenith telescope... | 114 48 44.53 | 1855 | Triangulation from mouth of Gila. | Lieut. Michler, Top. Engineers. |
| Monument (pyramid of cast iron) on Sonora line, near the Colorado. | 32 29 01.48 | 1855 | Triangulation from initial point. | 114 46 14.43 | 1855 | Triangulation from initial point. | Lieut. Michler. |
| Quitobaquita | 31 56 26.57 | 1855 | Zenith telescope.... | 112 52 25.73 | 1855 | Moon culminations. | Capt. Jimenez. |
| Junction of Gila and Colorado | 32 43 32.3 | 1849 | Triangulation from observatory. | 114 36 09.9 | 1849 | Triangulation from observatory. | W. H. Emory. |
| Station No. 7, on Rio Gila | 32 43 56.8 | 1852 | Sextant | 114 25 33.7 | 1852 | By survey | Do. |
| Station No. 8, on Rio Gila | 32 44 29.2 | 1852 | ....do | 114 19 35.7 | 1852 | ....do | Do. |
| Camp 105, on Rio Gila, (Emory's Recon.) | 32 43 17 | 1846 | ....do | | | | Do. |
| Station No. 9, on Rio Gila, (Emory's Reconnaissance.) | 32 41 36.3 | 1852 | ....do | 114 17 32.5 | 1852 | By survey | Lieut. Whipple, Top Engineers. |
| Station No. 10, on Rio Gila | 32 40 25.2 | 1852 | ... do | 114 13 20.0 | 1852 | By survey | Do. |
| Station No. 11, on Rio Gila | 32 41 49.3 | 1852 | ....do | 114 00 33 | 1852 | ....do | Do. |
| Station No. 12, on Rio Gila | 32 42 39.7 | 1852 | ....do | 113 58 15 | 1852 | ....do | Do. |
| Camp 103, on an island in the Gila, (Emory's Reconnaissance.) | 32 43 38 | 1846 | ....do | | | | W. H. Emory. |
| Station No. 13, on Rio Gila | 32 46 02.5 | 1852 | ....do | 113 46 59 | 1852 | By survey | Lieut. Whipple. |
| Station No. 14, on Rio Gila | 32 46 44.8 | 1852 | ....do | 113 44 22 | 1852 | ....do | Do. |
| Station No. 15, on Rio Gila | 32 49 40.8 | 1852 | ....do | 113 36 45 | 1852 | ....do | Do. |
| Camp No. 101, on Rio Gila. (Emory's Reconnaissance.) | 32 55 52 | 1846 | ....do | | | | W. H. Emory. |
| Station No. 16, on Rio Gila | 32 55 56.4 | 1852 | ....do | 113 18 54 | 1852 | ....do | Lieut. Whipple |
| Station No. 17, of 1852, on Rio Gila, or station No. 42, of 1851. | 32 58 58.6 | 1851-2 | ....do | 113 11 15 | 1851-2 | ....do | Do. |
| Camp 99, on Rio Gila, (Emory's Reconnaissance.) | 32 59.22.0 | 1846 | ....do | | | | W. H. Emory. |
| Camp 97, between Pimos and Coco Maricopas Villages, (Emory's Reconnaissance.) | 33 09.28.0 | 1846 | ....do | | | | Do. |
| Camp 95, on the Gila, (Emory's Reconnaissance.) | 33 04 21.0 | 1846 | ....do | | | | Do. |
| Camp 93, on Rio Gila, (Emory's Reconnaissance.) | 33 05 40.0 | 1846 | ....do | | | | Do. |
| Camp 91, on the San Pedro, near its mouth, (Emory's Reconnaissance.) | 32 57 43.0 | 1846 | ....do | | | | Do. |
| Camp 89, Disappointment Creek, (Emory's Reconnaissance.) | 33 14 54.0 | 1846 | ....do | | | | Do. |
| Camp 87, on the San Francisco, about two miles from its mouth, (Emory's Reconnaissance.) | 33 14 29.0 | 1846 | ....do | | | | Do. |

## E.—*Table of Latitudes and Longitudes*—Continued.

| Station. | Latitude north. | Determined. When. | Determined. How. | Long. west of Greenwich. | Determined. When. | Determined. How. | Observer. |
|---|---|---|---|---|---|---|---|
| | ° ′ ″ | | | ° ′ ″ | | | |
| Camp 86, on the San Francisco, about two miles from its mouth, (Emory's Reconnaissance.) | 33 12 10.0 | 1846 | Sextant ....... | ............. | ..... | .................. | W. H. Emory. |
| Camp 83, on Rio Gila, (Emory's Reconnaissance.) | 32 53 16.0 | 1846 | ....do....... | ............. | ..... | .................. | Do. |
| Camp 81, on Rio Gila, (Emory's Reconnaissance.) | 32 44 52.0 | 1846 | ....do....... | ............. | ..... | .................. | Do. |
| Camp 80, on Rio Gila, (Emory's Reconnaissance.) | 32 38 13.0 | 1846 | ....do....... | ............. | ..... | .................. | Do. |
| Camp 78, first camp on the Rio Gila, (Emory's Reconnaissance.) | 32 50 08.0 | 1846 | ....do....... | ............. | ..... | .................. | Do. |
| Camp 77, Night Creek, (Emory's Reconnaissance.) | 32 50 54.0 | 1846 | ....do....... | ............. | ..... | .................. | Do. |
| Copper Mines.......................... | 32 47 53.1 | 1851 | ....do....... | 108 04 39.7 | 1851 | Sextant........... | Lieut. Whipple. |
| Camp 75, in the mountains, between the del Norte and Copper Mines, (Emory's Reconnaissance.) | 32 42 11.0 | 1846 | ....do....... | ............. | ..... | .................. | W. H. Emory. |
| Camp 73, first camp after leaving Rio del Norte, (Emory's Reconnaissance.) | 32 55 04.0 | 1846 | ....do....... | ............. | ..... | .................. | Do. |
| Camp 70, east bank of Rio del Norte, (Emory's Reconnaissance.) | 33 20 02.0 | 1846 | ....do....... | ............. | ..... | .................. | Do. |
| Camp 68, west bank of Rio del Norte, (Emory's Reconnaissance.) | 33 41 19.0 | 1846 | ....do....... | ............. | ..... | .................. | Do. |
| Camp 65, west bank of Rio del Norte, about two miles below Lamitar, (Emory's Reconnaissance.) | 34 07 39.0 | 1846 | ....do....... | ............. | ..... | .................. | Do. |
| Camp 62, a little south of and about one mile west of Peralta, (Emory's Reconnaissance.) | 34 48 33.0 | 1846 | ....do....... | ............. | ..... | .................. | Do. |
| Camp at Peralta, near Señora Chavis's private chapel, (Emory's Reconnaissance.) | 34 50 57.0 | 1846 | ....do....... | ............. | ..... | .................. | Do. |
| Albuquerque .......................... | 35 05 51.0 | 1853 | ....do....... | 106 37 52.0 | 1853 | Moon's culminat'n. | Lieut. Whipple. |
| Camp on the Rio del Norte, near the Alameda, (Emory's Reconnaissance.) | 35 11 20.0 | 1846 | ....do....... | ............. | ..... | .................. | W. H. Emory. |
| Camp on the Rio del Norte, about one mile below San Felipe, (Emory's Reconnaissance.) | 35 25 30.0 | 1846 | ....do....... | ............. | ..... | .................. | Do. |
| Camp Santa Fé, (Emory's Reconnaissance.) | 35 41 06.0 | 1846 | ....do....... | ............. | ..... | .................. | Do. |
| Lieutenant Whipple's astronomical station, near Doña Ana. | 32 22 13.4 | 1851 | Transits over prime vertical. | 106 50 11.25 | 1851 | Signal flashes simultaneously obser'd at Frontera. | Lieut. Whipple. |
| Doña Ana (church).................... | 32 23 13.8 | 1851 | Survey............ | 106 48 32.5 | 1851 | Survey............ | Do. |
| Initial point of parallel 32° 22′ in the channel of Rio Bravo. | 32 22 00.0 | 1851 | Triangulation from astronom'l station. | 106 50 56.25 | 1851 | Signal flashes . .... | Do. |
| First monument west of Rio Bravo, on parallel 32° 22′. | 32 22 00.0 | 1851 | ....do....... | ............. | 1851 | Triangulation from astronom'l station. | Do. |
| Station No. 5 (near parallel 32° 22′)...... | 32 22 03.8 | 1851 | .................. | ............. | 1851 | Flashes of gunpowder. | Do. |
| Station No. 8.....do.......do.......... | 32 22 13.4 | 1851 | .................. | ............. | 1851 | ....do............. | Do. |
| Station No. 9.....do.......do.......... | 32 22 20.7 | 1851 | .................. | ............. | 1851 | ....do............. | Do. |
| Station No. 11.....do.......do.......... | 32 22 25.6 | 1851 | .................. | ............. | 1851 | ....do............. | Do. |
| Station No. 12.....do.......do.......... | 32 22 31.1 | 1851 | .................. | 108 04 50 | 1851 | ....do............. | Do. |
| Ojo de Inez.......................... | 32 25 18.5 | 1851 | Sextant........... | ............. | 1851 | Sextant .......... | Do. |
| Sugar Loaf Camp, south of Station No. 18, on parallel 32° 22′. | 32 20 21.8 | 1851 | ....do....... | 109 01 16.3 | 1851 | ....do............. | Do. |
| Camp Reed.......................... | 32 05 09.6 | 1851 | ....do....... | 109 02 17 | 1851 | ....do............. | Do. |
| Dry Camp.......................... | 32 08 33.8 | 1851 | ....do....... | 109 11 45 | 1851 | ....do............. | Do. |
| Camp near Dos Cabazas del Chiricahui... | 32 08 43.7 | 1851 | ....do....... | 109 24 45 | 1851 | ....do............. | Do. |
| General Conde's Camp, Salt Lake, September 6th and 7th. | 32 03 54.0 | 1851 | ....do....... | 109 47 10 | 1851 | ....do............. | Do |

## E.—*Table of Latitudes and Longitudes*—Continued.

| Station. | Latitude north. | DETERMINED. When | DETERMINED. How. | Long. west of Greenwich. | DETERMINED. When | DETERMINED. How. | Observer. |
|---|---|---|---|---|---|---|---|
| | ° ′ ″ | | | ° ′ ″ | | | |
| Camp, Salt Lake Spring, October 14, 1851. | 32 02 38.8 | 1851 | Sextant | | 1851 | Sextant | Lieut. Whipple. |
| Señor Salazar's terminal point of parallel 32° 22′. | 32 22 01.0 | 1851 | | 109 50 56.25 | 1851 | Moon culminations. | Do. |
| Camp near terminal point | 32 22 06.6 | 1851 | Sextant | 109 50 15.75 | 1851 | Sextant | Do. |
| Castro Spring | 32 25 54.6 | 1851 | do. | 109 48 35.2 | 1851 | do. | Do. |
| Pools in valley of Saos, bed of Rio Santo Domingo. | 32 40 05.7 | 1851 | do. | 109 33 20 | 1851 | do. | Do. |
| Quercus Cañon | 31 56 15.0 | 1851 | do. | 110 08 35.0 | 1851 | do. | Do. |
| First station on Rio San Pedro | 31 54 31.2 | 1851 | do. | 110 11 52.0 | 1851 | do. | Do. |
| San Pedro Springs | 31 50 52.0 | 1851 | do. | 110 12 16.5 | 1851 | Moon culminations. | Do. |
| Tucson astronomical station | 32 12 32.0 | 1852 | do. | 110 53 10.0 | 1852 | Sextant | Do. |
| Tucson (church) | 32 12 54.5 | 1852 | Survey | 110 52 55 | 1852 | do. | Do. |
| Station 6 miles north of Tubac | 31 41 58.53 | 1852 | Sextant | 110 57 06 | 1852 | do. | Do. |
| Tubac | | 1852 | Survey | 110 57 50 | 1852 | do. | Do. |
| Station near the mission of Tomocacori | 31 34 47.16 | 1855 | Sextant | 110 56 57.90 | 1855 | do. | Capt. Jimenez. |
| Ojo del Sopori | 31 43 54.89 | 1855 | do. | | | | |
| Bamori | 31 39 40.87 | 1855 | do. | 111 11 04.05 | 1855 | Sextant | Do. |
| Hacienda of Aribaca | 31 35 02.30 | 1855 | do. | 111 14 12.60 | 1855 | do. | Do. |
| Las Boquillas | 31 39 27.15 | 1855 | do. | | 1855 | do. | Do. |
| Near the Sierra de la Arteza | 31 53 06.76 | 1855 | do. | | 1855 | do. | Do. |
| Station upon the road, July 15th | 31 46 58.64 | 1855 | do. | 111 47 03.45 | 1855 | do. | Do. |
| Station upon the road between Cobota and Sierra de la Nariz. | 31 43 37.03 | 1855 | do. | 112 14 02.55 | 1855 | do. | Do. |
| Station upon the road, July 18th | 31 52 24.74 | 1855 | do. | | | | Do. |
| Altar (Sonora) | 30 42 44.26 | 1854 | do. | 111 44 12.0 | 1854 | do. | Do. |
| * Los Nogales | 31 21 00.1 | 1855 | Zenith telescope | 110 51 02.1 | 1855 | Moon culminations. | J. H. Clark. |
| Astron'l station at head of Santa Cruz river | 31 17 56.28 | 1855 | do. | | | | Do. |
| Santa Cruz, (church) | 31 13 22.5 | 1852 | Survey from astronomical station. | 110 30 27.5 | 1855 | Survey | Lat. by Lt. Whipple and long. by the survey of United States boundary commiss'n. |
| Agua Prieta Ravine | 31 18 23.5 | 1852 | Sextant | 109 33 35.0 | 1855 | do. | Do. do. |
| San Bernardino | 31 19 40.35 | 1855 | Zenith telescope | | | | J. H. Clark. |
| San Luis Spring | 31 20 32.88 | 1855 | do. | | | | Do. |
| Agua del Perro | 31 20 57.56 | 1855 | do. | | | | Do. |
| Espia | 31 20 56.43 | 1855 | do. | | | | Do. |
| Carrizalillo | 31 50 55.26 | 1855 | do. | | | | Do. |
| Janos | 30 52 00.0 | 1852 | Sextant | | | | Lieut. Whipple. |
| Corralitos | 30 42 25.0 | 1852 | do. | | | | Do. |
| Fort Fillmore, (astronomical station) | 32 13 34.8 | 1852 | do. | | 1852 | Survey | W. H. Emory. |
| Fort Fillmore, (officers' quarters) | 32 13 38.5 | 1852 | Survey from astronomical station. | 106 42 15.0 | 1852 | do. | Do. |
| Frontera, (Maj. Emory's observatory) | 31 48 44.31 | 1852 | Zenith telescope | 106 33 04.5 | 1851–2 | Moon culminations. | Do. |
| Astronomical station, near initial point of boundary, (parallel 31° 47′.) | 31 04 00.0 | 1854–5 | do. | | | | J. H. Clark. |
| Initial point in river, on parallel 31° 47′ | 31 47 00.0 | 1855 | do. | 106 31 20.8 | 1855 | Triangulation from Frontera. | Do. |
| Monument near initial point, on right bank of river. | 31 47 00.0 | 1855 | do. | 106 31 23.5 | 1855 | do. | Do. |
| El Paso del Norte, (Salazar's observatory) | 31 44 15.7 | | | 106 29 05.4 | 1852 | Signal flashes simultaneously observed at Frontera. | †Long. by W. H. Emory, lat. by Señor Salazar. |
| El Paso del Norte, (cathedral) | 31 44 15.7 | | | 106 29 00.0 | 1852 | do | Do. do. |
| San Elceario, (observatory) | 31 35 12.62 | 1851 | Transits over prime vertical. | 106 16 15.0 | 1852 | Moon culminations. | Lieut. Smith. |
| San Elceario, (cathedral) | 31 35 02.3 | 1851 | do. | 106 16 13.8 | 1852 | do | W. H. Emory. |
| Mouth of Cañon, (Major Emory's observatory.) | 31 02 26.15 | 1852 | Zenith telescope | 105 37 15.0 | 1852 | Flashes of gunpowder simultaneously obs. at San Elceario. | Do. do. |

*Since this point was established, the corresponding observations at Greenwich observatory have been furnished in manuscript by Prof. Airy, Astronomer Royal; and the result deduced therefrom is 7*h.* 23*m.* 35*s.*3, showing a difference of 11*s.*2 from the adopted longitude.

† Moon culminations also observed by Salazar, and resulting longitude found to correspond.

W. H. E.

## E.—*Table of Latitudes and Longitudes*—Continued.

| Station. | Latitude North. | DETERMINED. | | Longitude West of Greenwich. | DETERMINED. | | Observer. |
|---|---|---|---|---|---|---|---|
| | | When. | How. | | When. | How. | |
| | ° ′ ″ | | | ° ′ ″ | | | |
| Near mouth of Cañon, where San Antonio road strikes the Rio Bravo. | 31 02 25.4 | 1852 | Survey from astronomical station. | 105 37 23.7 | 1852 | Survey from astronomical station. | W. H. Emory. |
| Presidio del Norte, (Major Emory's observatory, opposite.) | 29 34 07.13 | 1852 | Zenith telescope... | 104 24 45.3 | 1852 | Moon's culminat'ns. | Do. |
| Presidio del Norte, (cathedral) | 29 33 53.12 | 1852 | do. | 104 26 27.7 | 1852 | Triangulation from observatory. | Salazar. |
| Camp No. 1, (Lieut. Michler's, Station No. 91, survey of Rio Bravo del Norte.) | 29 47 12.9 | 1853 | Sextant | 102 17 21.0 | 1853 | Survey | Lieut. Michler. |
| Camp No. 3, Station No. 130 | 29 48 41.2 | 1853 | do. | 102 04 19.0 | 1853 | do. | Do. |
| Camp No. 4, Station No. 171 | 29 48 36.8 | 1853 | do. | 101 51 52.0 | 1853 | do. | Do. |
| Camp No. 5, Station No. 211 | 29 46 18.3 | 1853 | do. | 101 41 05.0 | 1853 | do. | Do. |
| Camp No. 6, Station No. 294 | 29 45 08.6 | 1853 | do. | 101 26 29.0 | 1853 | do. | Do. |
| Camp No. 7, Station No. 325, opposite mouth of Rio Pecos. | 29 41 45.5 | 1853 | do. | 101 19 35.0 | 1853 | do. | Do. |
| Camp No. 12, above Eagle Pass | 28 43 03.2 | 1853 | do. | 100 30 24.0 | 1853 | do. | Do. |
| Fort Duncan, (observatory) | 28 42 43.67 | 1852 | do. | 100 30 26.7 | 1852 | Moon's culminat'ns. | W. H. Emory's longitude, and Lt. Michler's latitude. |
| Fort Duncan, (flag-staff) | 28 42 16.4 | 1852 | do. | 100 30 19.3 | 1852 | do. | Do. do. |
| Falls of Presidio de Rio Grande | 28 16 11.5 | 1853 | do. | | 1852 | | Lieut. Michler. |
| Fort McIntosh, (astronom'l station, near) | 27 30 22.75 | 1852 | do. | 99 28 47.0 | 1852 | Survey | W. H. Emory. |
| Fort McIntosh | 27 30 08.0 | 1852 | do. | 99 29 07.0 | 1852 | do. | Do. |
| Redmond's Ranch, or Bellville | 26 52 06.8 | 1853 | do. | 99 17 27.0 | 1853 | Sextant | Do. |
| Roma | 26 24 20.8 | 1853 | do. | 98 59 17.0 | 1853 | do. | Do. |
| Ringgold barracks, (observatory) | 26 22 27.8 | 1853 | Zenith telescope... | 98 46 32.85 | 1853 | Moon's culminat'ns. | Do. |
| Ringgold barracks, (flag-staff of garrison.) | 26 22 30.5 | 1853 | do. | 98 46 37.93 | 1853 | do. | Do. |
| Edinburgh | 26 05 53.9 | 1853 | Sextant | 98 13 37.5 | 1853 | Sextant | Do. |
| Reynosa, Mexico, (church steeple) | 26 05 34.1 | 1853 | Survey | 98 14 22.4 | 1853 | Survey | Do. |
| Old Fort Brown | 25 53 16.3 | 1853 | Sextant | 97 26 22.5 | 1853 | do. | Do. |
| Observatory near mouth of Rio Bravo | 25 57 21.82 | 1853 | Zenith telescope... | 97 07 37.5 | 1853 | Moon's culminat'ns. | Do. |
| Northern point at mouth of Rio Bravo | 25 57 18.20 | 1853 | do. | 97 07 22.5 | 1853 | do. | Do. |
| Mouth of Rio Bravo | 25 57 10.0 | | | 97 07 17.0 | 1853 | do. | Do. |
| Camp west of, and near, Fort Inge, Texas. | 29 10 18.4 | 1851 | Sextant | 99 47 12.0 | 1853 | Survey | Do. |
| Camp on Leona river, 15,000 feet north of Fort Inge, Texas. | 29 12 47.1 | 1850 | do. | | | | Lieut. Whipple. |
| Fort Inge, Texas | 29 10 18.4 | 1851 | do. | 99 47 10.0 | 1853 | Survey | W. H. Emory. |
| Near Turkey creek | 29 13 46.0 | 1850 | do. | | | | Lieut. Whipple. |
| Las Moras | 29 18 35.0 | 1850 | do. | | | | Do. |
| Rio San Pedro, (1st crossing) | 29 29 21.6 | 1852 | do. | 100 57 35.0 | 1852 | Survey | Lieut. Michler. |
| Devil's Camp | 29 57 02.0 | 1850 | do. | | | | Lieut. Whipple. |
| Devil's River Valley | 80 03 52.1 | 1850 | do. | | | | Do. |
| Camp XV, where road leaves San Pedro going to El Paso. | 30 10 38.4 | 1851 | do. | | | | W. H. Emory. |
| Camp Steel | 30 23 59.6 | 1850 | do. | 101 11 13.2 | 1850 | Sextant | Lieut. Whipple. |
| Howard's Spring | 30 28 00.5 | 1850 | do. | 101 27 15.0 | 1850 | do. | Do. |
| Camp on Rio Pecos | 30 59 59.5 | 1850 | do. | | | | Do. |
| Camp where road leaves Rio Pecos, going west. | 30 58 48.0 | 1851 | do. | | | | W. H. Emory. |
| Escondido creek | 30 52 23.0 | 1850 | do. | | | | Lieut. Whipple. |
| Camanche Spring | 30 52 59.5 | 1850 | do. | | | | Do. |
| Leon Spring | 30 53 33.1 | 1850 | do. | 103 04 13.0 | 1850 | Survey | Do. |
| Prairie Camp | 30 49 01.7 | 1850 | do. | | | | Do. |
| Limpia Camp | 30 44 51.0 | 1850 | do. | | | | Do. |
| Limpia, (Vallecito) | 30 41 26.0 | 1850 | do. | | | | Do. |
| Alamo Grove | 30 36 30.6 | 1850 | do. | | | | Do. |
| Camp on the Tascite | 30 12 51.0 | 1852 | do. | 104 14 48.0 | 1852 | Sextant | W. H. Emory. |
| Snow Camp | 30 36 28.7 | 1850 | do. | | | | Lieut. Whipple. |
| Dead Man's Hole | 30 40 49.9 | 1850 | do. | 104 22 05.5 | 1850 | Sextant | Do. |
| Well's Camp | 30 53 17 5 | 1850 | do. | | | | Do. |
| Eagle Spring | 30 59 58.5 | 1850 | do. | | | | Do. |
| Dry Camp | 31 03 58.2 | 1850 | do. | | | | Do. |

# CHAPTER IX.

## METEOROLOGY.

---

Sir: The meteorological notes taken during the march from San Antonio to El Paso, during the latter part of 1850, though sufficiently interesting of themselves, do not furnish data for averaging the temperature, &c., and therefore cannot be recorded in the same form as that adopted for the publication of observations taken at a fixed observatory.

The principal and most interesting portion of the observations is the result deduced and embodied in the barometrical profile of the road already prepared.

The record of both wet and dry bulb thermometers was carefully kept. The highest degree noted was on the 23d October, 1850, at 3 P. M., eighty-four degrees; while the lowest was at sunrise of the 6th of December, of the same year, when the mercury fell to 1°.5 Fahrenheit. These results are interesting only so far as noting these two extreme points. From the nature of the marches made, it was impossible to note with any regularity the daily change in any of the instruments.

The chief phenomena noted are those of a local character. The effect of the different ranges of mountains and the long succession of arid plains upon the condition of the atmosphere is shown by the markings of the hygrometer. In passing from the shores of the Gulf to San Pedro, or Devil's river, but little change takes place—the same succession of dews, the usual quantity of rain, and, indeed, all the characteristics of a climate enjoying its proper share of humidity are met with. The clouds of the usual forms, cirrus and nimbus, float about, and nothing as yet gives notice that we are approaching a different country. One single day's march, and this is perceptibly changed. The summit of the valley of the San Pedro reached, the hygrometrical condition of the atmosphere is altered at once, the appearance of the vegetation is different, and the whole face of the country shows the effect of the diminution of moisture so accurately and so immediately pointed out by the hygrometer. We cannot speak with certainty of the effect of the change on any of the instruments except the hygrometer; but that the barometer is seriously affected there can be no doubt, though to what extent can only be told by more perfect unhurried examinations. The observations point out the existence of such a change; they show, too, the line of country at which the change commences; and it only remains to fix the exact amount of correction to be used, to make the barometer as useful in these regions as in those countries bordering on the seacoast, or where the great lack of humidity is not so sensibly felt.

During the march, there was experienced a norther of the most perfect character; this occurred on the 4th and 6th of December, and it was at the latter date that the lowest temperature was noted.

The norther commenced at 4 P. M. of the 4th December, and was preceded by no change by which its approach could be predicted. A calm, pleasant day, with the thermometer ranging from 40° to 70° Fahrenheit, was ended by a sudden rising of the wind from the southwest; this changed to the northeast, and blew heavily from that quarter for more than twenty-four hours; during this time the thermometer fell to 1°.5 Fahrenheit, and snow fell to the depth of one inch and a half.

The cold weather lasted for about three days, and a most delightful calm succeeded the severest norther noted in the record. A few days after this, the regular observations were taken up and continued at San Elceario and Frontera; those results, reduced for one year to the form adopted for publication, will be more interesting than these under discussion can be made.

The appearance of the clouds varies so little that it forms no meteorological feature of sufficient importance to be accurately noted. The changes, as might be expected, are from the forms in which a certain degree of moisture necessarily enters to those in which the appearance is that of a fleecy mass of cotton without shape. These last are so far removed from the earth's surface as to be almost entirely out of the influence of the currents of wind indicated by the weather-vanes. Their formation seems gradual, and the increase in size is apparently due to a decrease in the distance. They came and vanished sometimes from the same spot in the heavens; and for weeks together scarcely one "direction" due to the course of the wind could be noted. In watching them carefully, their volume would seem to be lessened or increased, and yet the parts detached could not be seen to float away, nor was there any approach of additional vapor to be seen by which the size of the cloud could be increased.

The character of the winds, with their force and direction, was carefully noted; in particular their effect on the barometer was the subject of repeated observations. The results of these observations are more accurately noted in another place. And though the effect produced was first noticed on the march, yet subsequent observations at the fixed observatory only served to strengthen and confirm the opinion which was at that time advanced as to the effect of any change from east to west, or *vice versa*, on the barometrical column.

The records of the observations taken at the fixed observatories at San Elceario and Frontera are given fully for one year. These observations were made in the immediate valley of the Rio Grande, and show the changes in the different instruments noted. With regard to the value to be placed on the observations for humidity, it should be observed that the time embraced in the record was one of great freedom from moisture, both at the points observed and at situations on the river far above the observatory. The river during the summer of 1851* was nearly dry in several places in our immediate vicinity, a slight current only marking its progress near Frontera, while its bed served as the best road thence to El Paso.

The chart prepared to accompany this report shows at a glance the most important results deduced from our observations.

The results given in the separate columns of the tabulated forms are deduced from six daily observations, viz: at sunrise, 9 A. M., noon, 3 P. M., sunset, and 8 P. M. During the long days of summer this last hour was changed to 9 P. M., thus making the interval between sunset and the time of the last evening observation more nearly equal in the different seasons.

The columns in which are noted the daily means for thermometer and dew-point observations

* The year 1851 was notoriously a dry year in all the northern States of Mexico, and so far the selection of that year is unfortunate as affording a measure of the average rain, but it happened to be the only year when a single observer was stationary for any length of time at the same place.

W. H. E.

will, of course, present different records from those which would have been shown had the results merely been deduced from the two daily extremes of heat and cold, or the dew-points calculated from those observations only.

In addition to all these observations, the 21st day of each month, as the regular meteorological term-day, was carefully noted by the record of observations for each hour of the twenty-four.

The remainder of the meteorological data serves in a great measure merely for the calculation of the elevation of points on the line of survey or travel. These results will be found embodied in the different profiles of the country over which the line passed.

The observations of 1855, by a careful comparison with others of the same character, taken simultaneously at different places, have enabled me to establish the height of the initial point of the boundary on the Rio Grande in a manner that must be more satisfactory than any yet adopted.

This elevation varies slightly from that of El Paso.

In the computation for elevation I have used the French formula of Delcros, and have employed some other corrections consequent upon the value of horary variation, founded on the observations for that quantity taken at San Elceario. In most instances, however, the points of observation were too remote from the fixed observatory for the horary correction to be of any great value. In these the usual corrections for temperature, &c., only were used.

The effect of the direction and force of the wind on the mercury of the barometer has been referred to above, and I mention it here only to state that my observations on this subject were sufficient to assure me of the great necessity of noticing these values in connexion with the barometer more particularly when observations are being made for altitude. The exact value of the quantity I have not ascertained, but that it exists I am confident; and I trust that future and more prolonged observations will fix the value in a manner sufficiently accurate for its use as a correction in barometrical computations.

All of which is respectfully submitted by your obedient servant,

MARINE T. W. CHANDLER,
*Assistant in charge of Meteorological Department.*

Major William H. Emory, 1*st Cavalry U. S. A.*,
*Commissioner United States and Mexican Boundary Survey.*

Note.—Of the immense mass of materials collected, showing the meteorological character of the country adjacent to the boundary line, I have deemed it proper to produce here only a short abstract from the tables. Those who may desire further information can obtain it by reference to the records filed in the Department of the Interior.

W. H. E.

*Abstract of results from meteorological records.*

| Date. | Station. | Mean height of barometer. | Mean height of thermometer. | Dew point. | Greatest heat. | Least heat. | Rain, inches. |
|---|---|---|---|---|---|---|---|
| 1851. | | | | | | | |
| January | San Elceario | 26.26 | 46.3 | 31 | 67 | 47 | .004 |
| February | ......do | 26.354 | 46.29 | 39.19 | ............ | ............ | 0.795 |
| March | ......do | 26.370 | 57.7 | 47.9 | 81 | 22.5 | 0.015 |
| April | ......do | 26.295 | 67 | 45.2 | 87.5 | 40.5 | 0.092 |
| May | Frontera | 26.146 | 76.4 | 42.0 | 95 | 50.5 | 0.013 |
| June | ......do | 26.173 | 86.8 | 36.6 | 103 | 59 | 0.016 |
| July | ......do | 26.174 | 85.9 | 41.2 | 99 | 71 | 1.537 |
| August | ......do | 26.206 | 84.1 | 42.1 | ............ | ............ | 1.613 |
| September | ......do | 26.254 | 79.13 | 57.89 | 92 | 65 | 1.052 |
| October | ......do | 26.233 | 67.6 | 42.1 | 87 | 47 | 0.013 |
| November | ......do | 26.233 | 50.8 | 36.6 | 73 | 25 | 0.211 |
| December | ......do | 26.317 | 45.5 | 37.7 | 63 | 27 | 1.255 |
| 1854. | | | | | | | |
| December | Near junction of Gila and Colorado | 29.979 | 59.8 | ............ | 72 | 48.5 | ............ |
| 1855. | | | | | | | |
| February | ......do............do | 29.937 | 68 | ............ | 82 | 53 | ............ |

BAROMETRIC HEIGHTS.

| | Feet. |
|---|---|
| Fort Brown | 165.5 |
| Ringgold Barracks | 521.6 |
| Edinburgh | 422.3 |
| Fort McIntosh | 806.4 |
| Eagle Pass or Fort Duncan | 1461.0 |
| San Antonio | 578.7 |
| Castroville | 671.9 |
| Quihi | 855.6 |
| Rio Seco | 936.7 |
| Comanche creek | 923.6 |
| Camp near Fort Inge | 910.8 |
| Camp near Nueces | 931.7 |
| Elm creek | 1093.5 |
| Zoqueté creek | 983.0 |
| San Felipe | 817.9 |
| Painted Caves | 952.4 |
| San Pedro or Devil's river | 1810.0 |
| Second crossing San Pedro | 1843.2 |
| Head of San Pedro | 1680.5 |
| Howard's spring | 2053.5 |
| Live Oak creek | 2083.4 |
| Pecos | 2026.9 |
| Escondido spring | 2806.1 |
| Leon spring | 3098.2 |
| Limpia | 4004.3 |
| Head of Limpia | 4688.4 |
| Eagle spring | 4535.5 |
| Station near Presidio del Norte | 2779.0 |
| Rio Bravo (where road from San Antonio strikes it) | 3484.0 |
| San Elceario | 3607.3 |
| Initial point on Rio Bravo, parallel 31° 47′ N | 3684.3 |
| Frontera | 3796.3 |
| Neides' spring | 4309.8 |
| Cook's spring | 4777.0 |
| Santa Rita del Cobre | 6106.4 |
| Ojo de Vaca | 4988.6 |
| Carrizalillo | 4454.7 |
| Espia | 4027.5 |
| Ojo de Inez or de Gavilan | 5293.4 |
| Ojo del Perro | 4691.7 |
| Alamo Hueco | 4650. |
| Ojo del Picacho | 4694.3 |
| Salt Lake, (parallel 32° 22′ N) | 3994.2 |
| Salt Lake spring, (playa de los Pimos) | 4193.7 |
| Quercus Cañon | 4169.7 |
| Camp on Gila, near Mount Graham | 2976.1 |
| Summit of San Luis mountain | 5818.9 |
| Ojo de San Luis | 5044.0 |
| Guadalupe Cañon | 4447.8 |
| San Bernardino | 3676.8 |
| Agua Prieta | 4017.0 |
| Spring at head of Rio San Pedro, 1st branch east | 4383.8 |
| Rio San Pedro, near parallel 32° 22′ | 3717.6 |
| Summit of pass to and near Santa Cruz | 5469.5 |
| Santa Cruz | 4498.3 |
| Los Nogales | 3835.7 |
| Junction of Gila and Colorado | 275.0 |
| New Initial Point on Colorado | 156.3 |

# MAGNETIC OBSERVATIONS.

*Magnetic observations on the boundary line between the United States and Mexico, made in* 1855, *under the direction of Major W. H. Emory, United States commissioner under the treaty of* 1853; *and general discussion of the magnetic observations made in connexion with the Mexican Boundary Surveys.*

RECOMPUTED BY J. E. HILGARD, UNITED STATES COAST SURVEY.

## I. *Magnetic observations in* 1855.

Observations of declination, dip, and absolute horizontal intensity were made at eight stations, being those at which astronomical observations were made in determining the boundary between the United States and Mexico, under the treaty of 1853. The magnetic observations were intrusted to Mr. Marine T. W. Chandler, who succeeded in obtaining very complete determinations, as the subjoined abstracts show.

The *declination* was obtained by referring the direction of the needle to the astronomical meridian carefully determined for the survey of the line. The needle of a goniometer (by Young) was found to show a fair mean of five good needles of different lengths, and was therefore relied on at subsequent stations. The results are given in the general table below.

Observations of *inclination* were made with a ten-inch dip-circle (by Gambey) of superior construction. Two needles were used at each of the stations; and at three of them, viz: Carrizalillo, Espia, and Los Nogales, the poles were repeatedly reversed, so as to obtain the corrections to be applied when no reversal of poles was made. These corrections are + 12′ for needle No. 1, and — 15′ for No. 2, in the position of the poles called direct, and have been so applied in the following abstract of results:

| Station. | Needle No. 1. | | Needle No. 2. | | Remarks. |
|---|---|---|---|---|---|
| | Dip. | No. of sets. | Dip. | No. of sets. | |
| | ° ′ | | ° ′ | | |
| Initial Point | 58 39 | 3 | 58 19 | 3 | |
| Carrizalillo | 58 31 | 3 | 58 13 | 3 | Poles reversed in each set. |
| Espia | 57 59 | 1 | 57 50 | 2 | " " " " |
| Ojo del Perro | 57 28 | 2 | 57 5 | 2 | |
| San Luis Springs | 57 37 | 1 | 57 21 | 1 | |
| San Bernardino | 57 19 | 4 | 56 58 | 4 | |
| Santa Cruz river | 57 28 | 2 | 57 17 | 2 | |
| Los Nogales | 57 13 | 1 | 57 1 | 1 | Poles reversed in each set. |

The difference of about 16′ between the results by the two needles is too large to admit of the mean being taken. An examination of the pivots having shown some corrosion on a pivot of No. 2, the probability is that the results by No. 1 are to be preferred, especially as the observations with that needle show a greater consistency among themselves. The results by No. 1 are therefore adopted in the general table.

*Observations for horizontal intensity* were made with a unifilar magnetometer by Jones. The deflections were measured on a nine-inch circle, according to Lamont's method, in which the two magnets remain at right angles. In the vibration experiments, the time of 400 vibrations is usually observed, of which six values are obtained in each set, in the usual way. Experiments to determine the moment of inertia of the magnet and its attachments were made repeatedly by vibrating it loaded with a brass ring, marked No. 11, of which the outside diameter is 2.899 inches, the inside diameter 2.462 inches, and the weight 719.90 grains; hence its moment of inertia, $K_{,} = 9.04$, expressed in feet and grains. The magnet used, marked X 7, is of the usual form, being a hollow cylinder of 0.3 inch in diameter, and 3.66 inches in length, and carrying a mirror. Its temperature coefficient was determined at Washington city, in February, 1856, by vibrations at temperature near 30° and 70°, and was ascertained

$$q = 0.0003.$$

The following is an abstract of the observations; to which is to be added, that, in the experiments without the inertia ring, the effect of 90° of torsion was 7′.5; in those with the ring, 15′.

*Abstract of observations for horizontal intensity.*

| Station. | VIBRATIONS. | | | | DEFLECTIONS. | | Date. |
|---|---|---|---|---|---|---|---|
| | Without ring. | | With ring. | | $r = 1.3$ feet. | | |
| | $T$ Time of 1 vibr. | Temperature. | $T_r$ Time of 1 vibr. | Temperature. | $u$ | Temperature. | |
| | s. | ° | s. | ° | ° ′ | ° | |
| Initial Point.......... | 3.795 | 74.5 | 7.946 | 69.5 | 2 29.6 | 61 | 1855. |
| | 3.795 | 59 | 7.935 | 63 | 28.7 | 53.5 | |
| | | | | | 30.0 | 41 | |
| Mean.......... | 3.795 | 67 | 7.941 | 66 | 2 29.4 | 52 | January 4. |
| Carrizalillo.......... | 3.817 | 70 | ........ | ........ | 2 31.2 | 59 | |
| | 3.823 | 71.5 | 7.983 | 76 | 2 31 | 67.5 | |
| | 3.826 | 83 | ........ | ........ | 2 29.9 | 64.5 | |
| Mean.......... | 3.822 | 75 | 7.983 | 76 | 2 30.7 | 64 | March 1. |
| Espia.......... | 3.770 | 63 | 7.910 | 70 | ........ | ........ | March 22. |
| Ojo del Perro.......... | 3.791 | 63 | ........ | ........ | ........ | ........ | April 3. |
| San Luis Springs.......... | 3.751 | 61 | ........ | ........ | 2 30.0 | 64.5 | |
| | 3.757 | 73 | ........ | ........ | 2 30.0 | 66.5 | |
| | | | | | 2 27.0 | 65 | |
| Mean.......... | 3.754 | 67 | ........ | ........ | 2 29.0 | 65 | April 19. |
| San Bernardino.......... | 3.776 | 78.5 | | | | | |
| | 3.778 | 82.5 | | | | | |
| | 3.764 | 81. | | | | | |
| Mean.......... | 3.773 | 81 | ........ | ........ | ........ | ........ | April 28. |
| Santa Cruz River.......... | 3.798 | 72 | | | | | |
| | 3.804 | 74 | | | | | |
| Mean.......... | 3.801 | 73 | ........ | ........ | ........ | ........ | May 14. |
| Los Nogales.......... | 3.805 | 94 | 7.949 | 80 | 2 26.5 | 81.5 | |
| | | | | | 25.2 | 83 | |
| Mean.......... | ........ | ........ | ........ | ........ | 2 25.85 | 82 | June 16. |

From the preceding data we first deduce the moment of inertia, $K$, of the magnet and its attachments, by the equation $K = K_r \frac{T^2}{T_r^2 - T^2}$, where $T_r$ and $T$ are the terms of one vibration with and without the inertia ring, corrected for torsion, and reduced to the temperature of experiments without the ring, and obtain the following values:

| | |
|---|---|
| At Initial Point, | $K = 2.669$ |
| Carrizalillo, | 2.680 |
| Espia, | 2.659 |
| Los Nogales, | 2.668 |
| Mean, | 2.669 |

From the experiments of deflection we next deduce the values of ratio of $m$, the magnetic moment of the magnet, to $X$, the horizontal component of the earth's form, by the expression $\frac{m}{X} = \frac{1}{2} r^3 \sin u$, and obtain at

| | | |
|---|---|---|
| Initial Point, | $\frac{m}{X} = 0.0477$, | temp. 52° |
| Carrizalillo, | 0.0481, | " 64° |
| San Luis, | 0.0476, | " 65° |
| Los Nogales, | 0.0466, | " 82° |

Computing for the same stations the product $m\,X = \frac{\pi^2 K}{T^2}$, where $T$ is corrected for torsion, and reduced to the temperature of the corresponding deflections, and eliminating $X$, we get the following values of $m$.

| Station. | Date. | $m$ | Temperature. | $m$ reduced to 66°. |
|---|---|---|---|---|
| | | | ° | |
| Initial Point | January 4 | 0.2959 | 52 | 0.2947 |
| Carrizalillo | March 1 | 0.2951 | 64 | 0.2949 |
| San Luis | April 19 | 0.2982 | 65 | 0.2981 |
| Los Nogales | June 16 | 0.2915 | 82 | 0.2929 |

Although the difference in these values of $m$ may be in a great measure due to errors of observations, rather than to fluctuations in the magnetism of the magnet, still the best results appear to be obtained by using the above values of $m$ for the respective stations, and assuming a uniform rate of change during the intervals.

Computing, lastly, $m\,X$ for each of the stations, and dividing by $m$ determined in the manner indicated and reduced to the temperature of the vibrations, we obtain the values of $X$ given in the subjoined table, which exhibits collectively the results obtained.

*General table of results.*

| Station. | Latitude. | Longitude. | Declination east. | Dip. | Horizontal intensity. | Total intensity. |
|---|---|---|---|---|---|---|
| | ° ′ | ° ′ | ° ′ | ° ′ | | |
| Initial Point | 31 47 | 106 28 | 11 55 | 58 39 | 6.202 | 11.92 |
| Carrizalillo | 31 51 | 107 56 | 12 2 | 58 31 | 6.125 | 11.73 |
| Espia | 31 21 | 107 56 | 12 5 | 57 59 | 6.242 | 11.77 |
| Ojo del Perro | 31 21 | 108 20 | 11 58 | 57 28 | 6.156 | 11.45 |
| San Luis Springs | 31 20 | 108 48 | 11 45 | 57 37 | 6.265 | 11.70 |
| San Bernardino | 31 20 | 109 14 | 11 45 | 57 19 | 6.252 | 11.58 |
| Santa Cruz River | 31 18 | 110 31 | 12 13 | 57 28 | 6.169 | 11.47 |
| Los Nogales | 31 21 | 110 51 | 11 45 | 57 13 | 6.262 | 11.56 |

II. *Discussion of lines of equal magnetic declination, dip, and horizontal intensity.*

In this discussion, the observations made in previous years in connexion with the Mexican boundary surveys, and published in the fifth volume, new series, of the Memoirs of the Academy, have been combined with those communicated in the present paper. Observations made under the directicn of Professor A. D. Bache, Superintendent of the Coast Survey, at stations Dollar Point, East Base, and Jupiter, near Galveston, Texas, and near San Diego, Monterey, and San Francisco, and affording important co-ordinates for the curvature of the lines, have also been introduced; likewise, an observation of the declination at the Great Salt Lake, by Captain Howard Stansbury, U. S. Topographical Engineers, published in his report of the survey of that region.

The method employed in determining the lines of equal declination and dip was partly graphical and partly analytical, being the same pursued by Professor Bache and Mr. J. E. Hilgard in their discussion of the Coast Survey magnetic observations.—(Coast Survey Report for 1855, Appendix, p. 47.) The stations were projected on a map, and their positions referred to a right line graphically assumed as axis of co-ordinates, the origin being chosen about the mean position of the stations, and the direction so as nearly to divide the positive and negative ordinates equally.

The co-ordinates being read off on any convenient linear scale, conditional equations are formed for each station or group of stations, and the whole scheme is solved by the method of least squares. The conditional equations representing an interpolation by second differences are of the form,

$$V = V_0 + v + x X + y Y + z X Y + p X^2 + q y^2,$$

when $V$ is the observed declination (or dip);

$V_0$, the assumed declination at the origin; $v$, the correction to be applied;

$X$ and $Y$, co-ordinates of position.

$x$, $y$, $z$, $p$, $q$, coefficients to be determined.

The solution of a considerable number of such equations involves a great deal of labor, which the results amply repay, however. The process being well known, there is no occasion to give the steps of the calculations in this place. After determining the coefficients, the co-ordinates of points in the lines sought were computed, the lines projected on the map, and the latitudes and longitudes of points read off and tabulated.

In the absence of any data to determine the secular changes, the results are doubtless liable to an uncertainty from that source. We know, however, that the changes are small, and, for the limited period over which the observations extend, they may be considered as merged in the local errors, and the average date of 1852 as belonging to the resulting lines on the map.

The following tables give a general *résumé* of the observations, and the corresponding values in the computed system; also the residuals, the distribution of which is the best evidence of the successful representation of the general facts involved.

The geographical position of points in the lines of equal declination and dip—isogonic and isoclinal lines—are also given in tables from which they may be readily projected in any map.

*Observations of Declinations.*

| No. | Station. | Latitude. | Longitude. | Date. | Declination east, observed. | Declination east, computed. | Residual, computed — obs. |
|---|---|---|---|---|---|---|---|
| | | ° ′ | ° ′ | | ° ′ | ° ′ | ′ |
| 1 | Dollar Point | 29 26 | 94 53 | 1848 | 8 57 | 9 03 | + 06 |
| 2 | East Base | 29 13 | 94 55 | 1853 | 9 05 | 9 02 | — 03 |
| 3 | Jupiter | 28 55 | 95 20 | 1853 | 9 09 | 9 10 | + 01 |
| 4 | Rio Grande, mouth | 25 57 | 97 07 | 1853 | 9 00 | 8 56 | — 04 |
| 5 | Ringgold Barracks | 26 23 | 98 43 | 1853 | 9 15 | 9 18 | + 03 |
| 6 | Fort McIntosh | 27 30 | 100 05 | 1852 | 10 00 | 9 46 | — 04 |
| 7 | Eagle Pass | 28 42 | 100 30 | 1852 | 10 01 | 10 07 | + 06 |
| 8 | Presidio del Norte | 29 34 | 104 25 | 1852 | 10 16 | 10 53 | + 37 |
| 9 | Mouth of Cañon | 31 02 | 105 37 | 1852 | 12 01 | 11 28 | — 33 |
| 10 | Emory's Initial Point | 31 47 | 106 28 | 1855 | 11 55 | 11 48 | — 07 |
| 11 | Frontera | 31 49 | 106 29 | 1852 | 12 24 | 11 49 | + 25 |
| 12 | Doña Ana | 32 22 | 106 45 | 1851 | 12 07 | 12 02 | — 05 |
| 13 | Carrizalillo | 31 51 | 107 56 | 1855 | 12 02 | 11 58 | — 04 |
| 14 | Espia | 31 21 | 107 56 | 1855 | 12 05 | 11 48 | — 17 |
| 15 | Copper Mines | 32 48 | 108 04 | 1851 | 11 22 | 12 18 | + 56 |
| 16 | Ojo del Perro | 31 21 | 108 20 | 1855 | 11 59 | 11 50 | — 09 |
| 17 | San Luis Springs | 31 20 | 108 48 | 1855 | 11 45 | 11 52 | + 07 |
| 18 | San Bernardino | 31 20 | 109 14 | 1855 | 11 45 | 11 53 | + 08 |
| 19 | Santa Cruz River | 31 18 | 110 31 | 1855 | 11 45 | 11 58 | + 13 |
| 20 | Los Nogales | 31 21 | 110 51 | 1855 | 12 13 | 12 00 | — 13 |
| 21 | San Pedro | 32 59 | 110 40 | 1851 | 12 25 | 12 37 | + 12 |
| 22 | Pimos Villages | 33 07 | 111 44 | 1851 | 12 52 | 12 46 | — 06 |
| 23 | Gila Junction | 32 43 | 114 53 | 1851 | 12 50 | 12 45 | — 05 |
| 24 | San Isabel | 33 09 | 116 38 | 1852 | 12 34 | 12 55 | + 21 |
| 25 | Camp Riley | 32 36 | 117 05 | 1849 | 12 57 | 12 44 | — 13 |
| 26 | San Diego | 32 42 | 117 12 | 1849 | 13 15 | 12 47 | — 28 |
| 27 | San Diego C. S | 32 41 | 117 13 | 1851 | 12 29 | 12 48 | + 19 |
| 28 | Monterey | 36 38 | 121 54 | 1851 | 14 58 | 14 54 | — 04 |
| 29 | San Francisco | 37 48 | 122 27 | 1852 | 15 30 | 15 34 | + 04 |
| 30 | Salt Lake City | 40 46 | 112 08 | 1850 | 15 34 | 15 34 | 00 |

## *Isogonic Lines.*

GEOGRAPHICAL POSITIONS OF POINTS.

| Longit'de. | 9° | 10° | 11° | 12° | 13° | 14° | 15° | Declination east. |
|---|---|---|---|---|---|---|---|---|
| ° | ° ′ | ° ′ | ° ′ | ° ′ | ° ′ | ° ′ | ° ′ | |
| 95 | 28 50 | ...... | ...... | ...... | ...... | ...... | ...... | |
| 96 | 27 28 | ...... | ...... | ...... | ...... | ...... | ...... | |
| 97 | 26 23 | ...... | ...... | ...... | ...... | ...... | ...... | |
| 98 | 25 34 | 30 17 | ...... | ...... | ...... | ...... | ...... | |
| 99 | 24 57 | 29 18 | ...... | ...... | ...... | ...... | ...... | |
| 100 | ...... | 28 32 | ...... | ...... | ...... | ...... | ...... | |
| 101 | ...... | 27 54 | ...... | ...... | ...... | ...... | ...... | |
| 102 | ...... | 27 27 | 31 12 | ...... | ...... | ...... | ...... | |
| 103 | ...... | 27 4 | 30 35 | ...... | ...... | ...... | ...... | |
| 104 | ...... | ...... | 30 7 | ...... | ...... | ...... | ...... | |
| 105 | ...... | ...... | 29 45 | 33 8 | ...... | ...... | ...... | |
| 106 | ...... | ...... | 29 27 | 32 36 | ...... | ...... | ...... | |
| 107 | ...... | ...... | 29 14 | 32 13 | ...... | ...... | ...... | |
| 108 | ...... | ...... | 29 4 | 31 54 | 34 54 | ...... | ...... | |
| 109 | ...... | ...... | ...... | 31 39 | 34 29 | ...... | ...... | |
| 110 | ...... | ...... | ...... | 31 28 | 34 9 | ...... | ...... | Latitude. |
| 111 | ...... | ...... | ...... | 31 20 | 33 54 | ...... | ...... | |
| 112 | ...... | ...... | ...... | 31 14 | 33 43 | ...... | ...... | |
| 113 | ...... | ...... | ...... | 31 10 | 33 33 | 36 2 | ...... | |
| 114 | ...... | ...... | ...... | ...... | 33 24 | 35 47 | ...... | |
| 115 | ...... | ...... | ...... | ...... | 33 17 | 35 35 | 38 3 | |
| 116 | ...... | ...... | ...... | ...... | 33 14 | 35 25 | 37 46 | |
| 117 | ...... | ...... | ...... | ...... | 33 12 | 35 17 | 37 31 | |
| 118 | ...... | ...... | ...... | ...... | ...... | 35 10 | 37 19 | |
| 119 | ...... | ...... | ...... | ...... | ...... | 35 5 | 37 9 | |
| 120 | ...... | ...... | ...... | ...... | ...... | 35 2 | 37 1 | |
| 121 | ...... | ...... | ...... | ...... | ...... | 35 0 | 36 54 | |
| 122 | ...... | ...... | ...... | ...... | ...... | 34 58 | 36 48 | |
| 123 | ...... | ...... | ...... | ...... | ...... | ...... | 36 44 | |
| 124 | ...... | ...... | ...... | ...... | ...... | ...... | 36 41 | |

## *Observations of Dip.*

| No. | Station. | Latitude. | Longitude. | Date. | Dip observed. | Dip computed. | Residual, comp. obs. |
|---|---|---|---|---|---|---|---|
| 1 | Dollar Point | 29° 26′ | 94° 53′ | 1848 | 57° 58′ | 58° 00′ | + 2′ |
| 2 | East Base | 29 13 | 94 55 | 1853 | 57 42 | 57 45 | + 3 |
| 3 | Jupiter | 28 55 | 95 20 | 1853 | 57 12 | 57 07 | — 5 |
| 4 | Rio Grande, mouth | 25 57 | 97 07 | 1853 | 52 23 | 52 14 | — 9 |
| 5 | Ringgold Barracks | 26 23 | 98 43 | 1853 | 52 27 | 52 35 | + 8 |
| 6 | Fort McIntosh | 27 30 | 100 05 | 1852 | 54 07 | 53 58 | — 9 |
| 7 | Fort Duncan | 28 42 | 100 30 | 1852 | 55 31 | 55 35 | + 4 |
| 8 | Presidio del Norte | 29 34 | 104 25 | 1852 | 55 41 | 55 59 | + 18 |
| 9 | Mouth of Cañon | 31 02 | 105 37 | 1852 | 57 38 | 57 45 | + 7 |
| 10 | San Elceario | 31 35 | 106 16 | 1852 | 58 57 | 58 17 | — 30 |
| 11 | Frontera | 31 48 | 106 33 | 1852 | 59 05 | 58 32 | — 33 |
| 12 | Doña Ana | 32 22 | 106 47 | 1851 | 59 06 | 59 08 | + 2 |
| 13 | IX | 22 22 | 107 24 | 1851 | 59 09 | 59 00 | — 9 |
| 14 | Copper Mines | 32 47 | 108 04 | 1851 | 59 17 | 59 23 | + 6 |
| 15 | Emory's Initial Point | 31 47 | 106 28 | 1855 | 58 39 | 58 30 | — 9 |
| 16 | Carrizalillo | 31 51 | 107 56 | 1855 | 58 31 | 58 23 | — 8 |
| 17 | Espia | 31 21 | 107 56 | 1855 | 57 39 | 57 41 | — 18 |
| 18 | Ojo del Perro | 31 21 | 108 20 | 1855 | 57 28 | 57 40 | + 12 |
| 19 | San Luis | 31 20 | 108 48 | 1855 | 57 37 | 57 36 | — 1 |
| 20 | San Bernardino | 31 20 | 109 14 | 1855 | 57 19 | 57 30 | + 11 |
| 21 | Santa Cruz River | 31 18 | 110 31 | 1855 | 57 28 | 57 21 | — 7 |
| 22 | Los Nogales | 31 21 | 110 51 | 1855 | 57 13 | 57 21 | + 8 |
| 23 | Ojo de Inez, or Gavilan | 32 45 | 108 14 | 1851 | 59 18 | 59 22 | + 5 |
| 24 | Station 1 (along the Gila) | 32 50 | 109 34 | 1851 | 59 19 | 59 12 | — 7 |
| 25 | 2 | 32 50 | 109 37 | 1851 | 59 12 | 59 12 | 0 |
| 26 | 3 | 32 53 | 109 44 | 1851 | 59 12 | 59 15 | + 3 |
| 27 | 4 | 32 57 | 109 49 | 1851 | 59 20 | 59 18 | — 2 |
| 28 | 5 | 33 04 | 109 55 | 1851 | 59 27 | 59 25 | — 2 |
| 29 | 6 | 33 06 | 110 00 | 1851 | 59 38 | 59 30 | — 8 |
| 30 | 7 | 33 10 | 110 03 | 1851 | 59 42 | 59 33 | — 9 |
| 31 | 8 | 33 12 | 110 10 | 1851 | 59 37 | 59 35 | — 2 |
| 32 | 9 | 33 13 | 110 19 | 1851 | 59 45 | 59 35 | — 10 |
| 33 | 10 | 33 12 | 110 19 | 1851 | 59 34 | 59 30 | — 4 |
| 34 | 12 | 33 09 | 110 26 | 1851 | 59 37 | 59 28 | — 9 |
| 35 | 13 | 33 09 | 110 28 | 1851 | 58 58 | 59 26 | + 28 |
| 36 | 15 | 33 09 | 110 31 | 1851 | 59 28 | 59 25 | — 3 |
| 37 | 17 | 33 12 | 110 42 | 1851 | 59 23 | 59 28 | + 5 |
| 38 | 19 | 33 05 | 110 35 | 1851 | 59 5 | 59 19 | + 14 |
| 39 | 20 | 32 59 | 110 40 | 1851 | 59 11 | 59 13 | + 2 |
| 40 | 21 | 33 03 | 110 46 | 1851 | 58 59 | 59 16 | + 17 |
| 41 | 22 | 33 05 | 110 50 | 1851 | 59 13 | 59 18 | + 5 |
| 42 | 23 | 33 07 | 110 55 | 1851 | 59 23 | 59 20 | — 3 |
| 43 | 24 | 33 06 | 111 02 | 1851 | 59 20 | 59 18 | — 2 |
| 44 | 26 | 33 04 | 111 11 | 1851 | 59 25 | 59 14 | — 11 |
| 45 | 27 | 33 03 | 111 16 | 1851 | 59 20 | 59 12 | — 8 |
| 46 | 28 | 33 01 | 111 23 | 1851 | 59 16 | 59 10 | — 6 |
| 47 | 29 | 33 04 | 111 34 | 1851 | 59 06 | 59 10 | + 4 |
| 48 | 30 | 33 08 | 111 44 | 1851 | 59 06 | 59 14 | + 8 |
| 49 | 31 | 33 10 | 111 54 | 1851 | 59 28 | 59 16 | — 12 |
| 50 | 32 | 33 09 | 111 57 | 1851 | 59 22 | 59 16 | — 6 |
| 51 | 38 | 33 00 | 112 39 | 1851 | 58 53 | 58 57 | + 4 |
| 52 | 39 | 32 59 | 112 43 | 1851 | 58 49 | 58 56 | + 7 |
| 53 | 40 | 33 02 | 112 55 | 1851 | 59 16 | 58 59 | — 17 |
| 54 | 42 | 32 58 | 113 11 | 1851 | 59 17 | 58 52 | — 25 |
| 55 | 43 | 32 49 | 113 33 | 1851 | 58 43 | 58 39 | — 4 |
| 56 | 44 | 32 44 | 113 50 | 1851 | 58 30 | 58 30 | 0 |
| 57 | 45 | 32 41 | 114 05 | 1851 | 58 25 | 58 26 | + 1 |
| 58 | Gila Junction | 32 43 | 114 33 | 1851 | 58 30 | 58 28 | — 2 |
| 59 | New River | 32 42 | 115 25 | 1849 | 58 19 | 58 20 | + 1 |
| 60 | Santa Isabella | 33 08 | 116 41 | 1849 | 58 48 | 58 44 | — 4 |
| 61 | Santa Maria | 33 02 | 116 51 | 1849 | 58 42 | 58 37 | — 5 |
| 62 | San Diego | 32 42 | 117 08 | 1849 | 57 33 | 58 14 | + 41 |
| 63 | San Diego C. S. | 32 41 | 117 13 | 1851 | 57 38 | 58 12 | + 34 |
| 64 | San Francisco | 37 46 | 122 27 | 1852 | 62 32 | 62 40 | + 8 |
| 65 | Sacramento | 38 34 | 121 17 | 1852 | 64 03 | 63 37 | — 26 |

### *Isoclinal Lines.*

GEOGRAPHICAL POSITIONS OF POINTS.

| Long. | 52° | 53° | 54° | 55° | 56° | 57° | 58° | 59° | 60° | 61° | 62° | 63° | Dip. |
|---|---|---|---|---|---|---|---|---|---|---|---|---|---|
| | ° ′ | ° ′ | ° ′ | ° ′ | ° ′ | ° ′ | ° ′ | ° ′ | ° ′ | ° ′ | ° ′ | ° ′ | |
| 95 | 25 30 | 26 09 | 26 48 | 27 27 | 28 07 | 28 47 | 29 26 | ......... | ......... | ......... | ......... | ......... | |
| 96 | 25 38 | 26 18 | 26 57 | 27 37 | 28 17 | 28 57 | 29 37 | ......... | ......... | ......... | ......... | ......... | |
| 97 | 25 46 | 26 26 | 27 06 | 27 47 | 28 27 | 29 08 | 29 49 | ......... | ......... | ......... | ......... | ......... | |
| 98 | 25 34 | 26 35 | 27 15 | 27 56 | 28 37 | 29 18 | 30 00 | ......... | ......... | ......... | ......... | ......... | |
| 99 | 26 02 | 26 43 | 27 24 | 28 05 | 28 47 | 29 28 | 30 11 | ......... | ......... | ......... | ......... | ......... | |
| 100 | 26 09 | 26 51 | 27 33 | 28 14 | 28 56 | 29 38 | 30 21 | ......... | ......... | ......... | ......... | ......... | |
| 101 | ......... | 26 59 | 27 41 | 28 22 | 29 05 | 29 48 | 30 22 | ......... | ......... | ......... | ......... | ......... | |
| 102 | ......... | ......... | 27 49 | 28 31 | 29 14 | 29 57 | 30 42 | ......... | ......... | ......... | ......... | ......... | |
| 103 | ......... | ......... | ......... | 28 40 | 29 23 | 30 06 | 30 52 | ......... | ......... | ......... | ......... | ......... | |
| 104 | ......... | ......... | ......... | ......... | 29 32 | 30 16 | 31 02 | ......... | ......... | ......... | ......... | ......... | |
| 105 | ......... | ......... | ......... | ......... | 29 40 | 30 24 | 31 11 | 31 59 | 32 49 | ......... | ......... | ......... | |
| 106 | ......... | ......... | ......... | ......... | 29 47 | 30 32 | 31 20 | 32 09 | 32 58 | ......... | ......... | ......... | |
| 107 | ......... | ......... | ......... | ......... | 29 54 | 30 39 | 31 28 | 32 18 | 33 07 | ......... | ......... | ......... | |
| 108 | ......... | ......... | ......... | ......... | 30 00 | 30 46 | 31 36 | 32 27 | 33 16 | ......... | ......... | ......... | |
| 109 | ......... | ......... | ......... | ......... | 29 05 | 30 53 | 31 43 | 32 35 | 33 25 | ......... | ......... | ......... | Latitude |
| 110 | ......... | ......... | ......... | ......... | 30 10 | 30 59 | 31 50 | 32 43 | 33 33 | ......... | ......... | ......... | |
| 111 | ......... | ......... | ......... | ......... | ......... | 31 05 | 31 57 | 32 50 | 33 49 | ......... | ......... | ......... | |
| 112 | ......... | ......... | ......... | ......... | ......... | 31 11 | 32 04 | 32 57 | 33 49 | ......... | ......... | ......... | |
| 113 | ......... | ......... | ......... | ......... | ......... | 31 17 | 32 11 | 33 04 | 33 57 | ......... | ......... | ......... | |
| 114 | ......... | ......... | ......... | ......... | ......... | 31 22 | 32 16 | 33 10 | 34 04 | ......... | ......... | ......... | |
| 115 | ......... | ......... | ......... | ......... | ......... | 31 26 | 32 21 | 33 16 | 34 11 | 35 07 | ......... | ......... | |
| 116 | ......... | ......... | ......... | ......... | ......... | 31 31 | 32 26 | 33 22 | 34 18 | 35 15 | ......... | ......... | |
| 117 | ......... | ......... | ......... | ......... | ......... | 31 35 | 32 31 | 33 28 | 34 24 | 35 22 | 36 19 | ......... | |
| 118 | ......... | ......... | ......... | ......... | ......... | 31 39 | 32 26 | 33 33 | 34 30 | 35 29 | 36 27 | ......... | |
| 119 | ......... | ......... | ......... | ......... | ......... | ......... | ......... | ......... | ......... | 35 36 | 36 35 | 37 35 | |
| 120 | ......... | ......... | ......... | ......... | ......... | ......... | ......... | ......... | ......... | ......... | 36 42 | 37 45 | |
| 121 | ......... | ......... | ......... | ......... | ......... | ......... | ......... | ......... | ......... | ......... | 36 49 | 37 54 | |
| 122 | ......... | ......... | ......... | ......... | ......... | ......... | ......... | ......... | ......... | ......... | ......... | 38 02 | |
| 123 | ......... | ......... | ......... | ......... | ......... | ......... | ......... | ......... | ......... | ......... | ......... | 38 11 | |

*Horizontal intensity.*—Combining the eight stations of 1855 among themselves, we obtain as a mean result, in latitude 31° 27′, longitude 108° 45′, $X = 6.21$, with a probable error of $\pm 0.01$; also an increase of $+ 0.10$ in going south 30′.7 or east 506′, and the direction of the line of equal horizontal intensity N. 87½° E.

It may be observed, that this rate of change in going south is evidently too large, for according to the decrease of dip it would require a southing of 42′ to cause an increase of the horizontal force of $+ 0.10$, if the total force was constant; but as the latter also decreases in going south, the actual rate of change of horizontal force is probably only half of that above obtained. Moreover, when we consider that the same value of X is found on the coast of Mississippi, between New Orleans and Mobile, we see that the small increase in going east should be decrease of similar amount, and that the direction of the line should be about N. 94° E. The distribution of stations is such that these discrepancies in the rate of change are quite within the probable errors of observation and station errors; nor is the value of the mean result affected thereby, which forms a valuable datum in absolute measure, in an almost inaccessible region of the globe.

In order to compare this measure of force with that previously obtained on the northern line by observations with a Fox apparatus, and expressed in the arbitrary scale, we may have recourse to the observations of Captain Lefroy at Toronto, which gives the total force in British units = 13.86 at the time that it is found 1.836 in the arbitrary scale. Applying the same ratio to our mean total intensity, 11.65, we find 1.543, and we have the following comparison:

| Latitude. | Longitude. | Total intensity. |
|---|---|---|
| ° ′ | ° ′ | |
| 31 27 | 108 45 | 1.543 |
| 32 43 | 108 30 | 1.580 |

the latter from three stations in 1851; exhibiting a closer correspondence than might be expected from the circuitous comparison involved.

United States & Mexican Boundary Survey.

W. H. Emory U.S. Commr.

www.ingramcontent.com/pod-product-compliance
Lightning Source LLC
LaVergne TN
LVHW020123110826
845151LV00001B/260

* 9 7 8 1 4 2 5 5 4 0 9 0 6 *